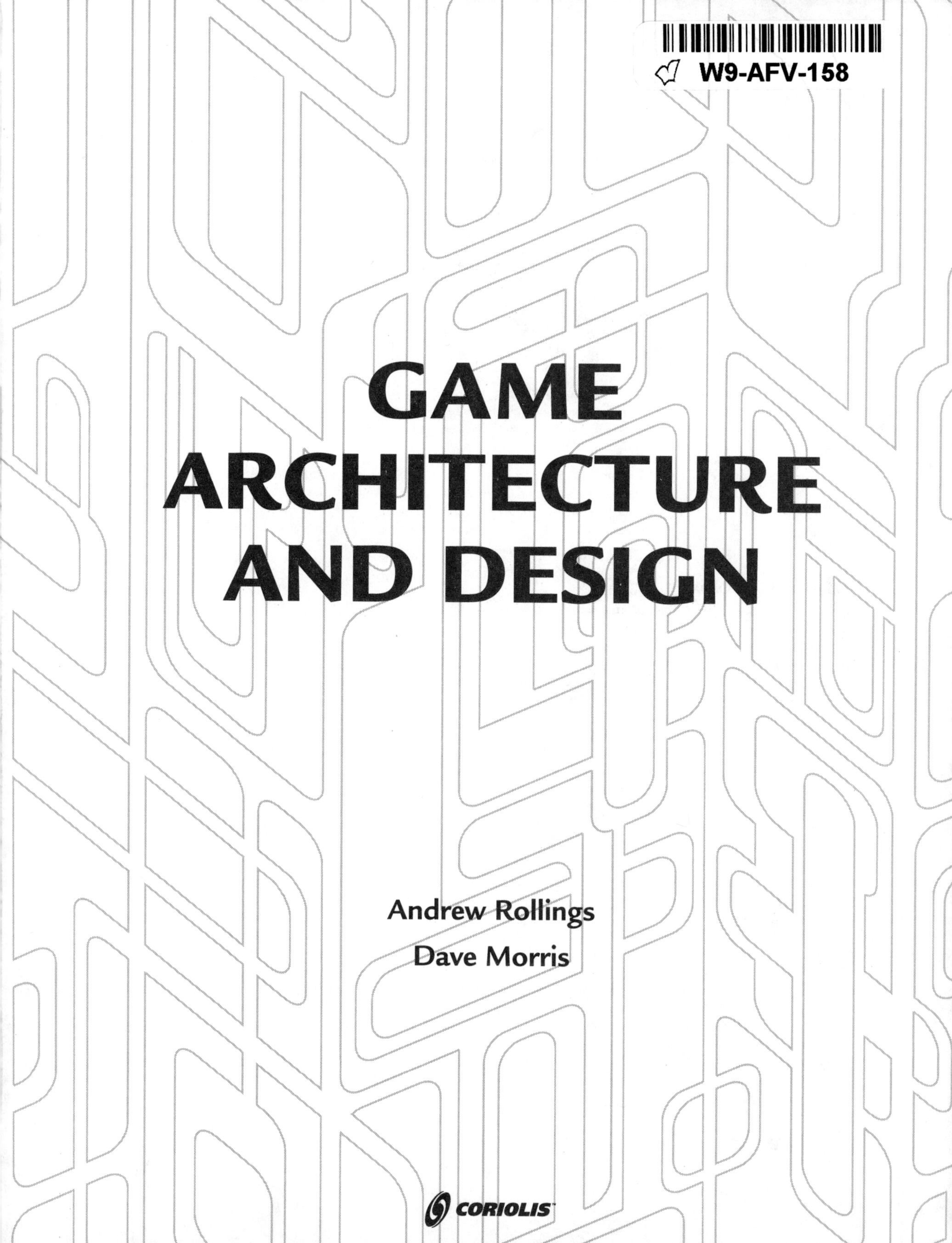

GAME ARCHITECTURE AND DESIGN

Andrew Rollings
Dave Morris

CORIOLIS

President, CEO
Keith Weiskamp

Publisher
Steve Sayre

Acquisitions Editor
Stephanie Wall

Marketing Specialist
Tracy Schofield

Project Editor
Dan Young

Technical Reviewer
Andrew Indovina

Production Coordinator
Wendy Littley

Cover Design
Jesse Dunn

Layout Design
April Nielsen

CD-ROM Developer
Brian J. Roettger

Game Architecture and Design

The Coriolis Group, LLC
14455 North Hayden Road
Suite 220
Scottsdale, Arizona 85260

480/483-0192
FAX 480/483-0193
http://www.coriolis.com

Library of Congress Cataloging-in-Publication Data
Rollings, Andrew, 1972-
Game Architecture and Design / by Andrew Rollings and Dave Morris.
p. cm.
Includes index.
ISBN 1-57610-425-7
1. Object-oriented programming (Computer science) 2. Computer games. I. Morris, Dave, 1957- II. Title.

QA76.64 .R647 2000
794.8'15117-- dc21 99-045764
CIP

Printed in the United States of America

10 9 8 7 6 5 4 3 2 1

14455 North Hayden Road • Suite 220 • Scottsdale, Arizona 85260

Dear Reader:

Coriolis Technology Press was founded to create a very elite group of books: the ones you keep closest to your machine. Sure, everyone would like to have the Library of Congress at arm's reach, but in the real world, you have to choose the books you rely on every day *very* carefully.

To win a place for our books on that coveted shelf beside your PC, we guarantee several important qualities in every book we publish. These qualities are:

- *Technical accuracy*—It's no good if it doesn't work. Every Coriolis Technology Press book is reviewed by technical experts in the topic field, and is sent through several editing and proofreading passes in order to create the piece of work you now hold in your hands.
- *Innovative editorial design*—We've put years of research and refinement into the ways we present information in our books. Our books' editorial approach is uniquely designed to reflect the way people learn new technologies and search for solutions to technology problems.
- *Practical focus*—We put only pertinent information into our books and avoid any fluff. Every fact included between these two covers must serve the mission of the book as a whole.
- *Accessibility*—The information in a book is worthless unless you can find it quickly when you need it. We put a lot of effort into our indexes, and heavily cross-reference our chapters, to make it easy for you to move right to the information you need.

Here at The Coriolis Group we have been publishing and packaging books, technical journals, and training materials since 1989. We're programmers and authors ourselves, and we take an ongoing active role in defining what we publish and how we publish it. We have put a lot of thought into our books; please write to us at **ctp@coriolis.com** and let us know what you think. We hope that you're happy with the book in your hands, and that in the future, when you reach for software development and networking information, you'll turn to one of our books first.

Keith Weiskamp
President and CEO

Jeff Duntemann
VP and Editorial Director

Look For This Other Book From The Coriolis Group:

This book is dedicated to the memory of Ram De Silva,
respected colleague and beloved friend.

❧

About The Authors

Andrew Rollings holds a B.S. (Hons) in Physics from Imperial College, London, and Bristol University and has worked as a technical consultant spanning the games industry and the financial industry since 1995. With Dave, he operates a consultancy covering all aspects of game design from concept to full-technical planning. He can be reached at **andrew_rollings@hotmail.com**.

Dave Morris holds an M.A. (Hons) in Physics from Oxford University and has worked as a best-selling author and game designer for 15 years, thereby straddling Snow's "Two Cultures" without even trying. Among his consultancy positions, he is creative advisor to a multi-million dollar Web company. He can be reached at **david.j.morris@dial.pipex.com**.

Acknowledgments

A work of this kind, drawing on our combined experiences over many years in the computer games industry, owes a debt of gratitude to all the people we have worked with. The impossibility of acknowledging everyone in person does not mean that we fail to value every contribution, suggestion or conversation that has helped us to refine these ideas. So, let us start by thanking all who have been our colleagues on any development project, great or small.

It is possible to single out a few individuals among the many. Ian Turnbull, former development director at Eidos Interactive, contributed enormously both with his friendship and with his wise counsel regarding the economic realities of the industry. Without his guidance, this book would be merely a theoretical work. It is Ian's down-to-earth clear-headedness that reminded us to make it more than that: a practical handbook for developers.

We would also like to thank Steve Foster of Insight Change Management, who has been extraordinarily patient over the course of many speculative discussions, often stretching long into the night, concerning the future directions and methodology of game development. His contribution has been much more than merely academic, however. When problem projects have weighed us down, it has been Steve's cheerful encouragement that has given us the resolve to keep going.

Our very first game design was with Nick Henfrey, a friend of many years' standing. His input, as both a game designer and IT manager, has enriched this book beyond measure. Moreover, he remains to this day the unbeaten demon king of *Warcraft 2*!

Sam Kerbeck, that rare combination of gentleman and genius, assisted us enormously with technical advice, and we are indebted to him for ably clarifying many of the more abstruse issues of architecture and coding.

Special thanks are due to Tim Harford, who pitched in selflessly with a number of challenging tutorials that firmed up our grasp of game theory. Additionally, Tim could always be relied on to remind us of an important truth that can sometimes get overlooked in the midst of a long project: we love games, and *that's* the reason we're in this industry.

The fact that you are holding this book at all is due to the sterling efforts of the folk at The Coriolis Group, in particular Dan Young, project editor, Stephanie Wall, acquisitions editor, and Paula Kmetz, managing editor. We have worked with many book publishers on both sides of the Atlantic, so we can state with certainty that the courtesy, diligence, and professionalism to be found at The Coriolis Group are unsurpassed.

Andrew would also like to thank Stephanie Park, for all of her encouragement.

Lastly, there are the very personal thanks we owe to our families: Roz Morris, Joan and Victor Morris, and Lilian and Steve Rollings, without whom *nothing* would be possible or worthwhile.

Contents At A Glance

Table Of Contents

Part IV Appendixes

Introduction

The philosophy behind this book is simple, stark and absolutely true. If you are failing to plan, then you are planning to fail.

Of course, games are unique. Game development constantly throws up unexpected issues. Coping with accelerating technology is like holding onto the tiger's tail. Worse, sometimes the client revises their requirements halfway through.

But these are not reasons to forego planning. A good design provides a goal to aim for that will guide you when changes are unavoidable. Frequently, the design anticipates at least the domain of future changes. A full-project plan establishes a framework for change. Planning does not end where development begins. Rather, you sustain the plan through any changes that need to be made so that, although the target may shift, you never lose sight of where you're going.

So, yes, games are unique. For that reason, they require a unique kind of planning. That is the methodology that we have set out in this book. To illustrate these points, we make copious use of case studies. These are based on common circumstances in the industry, but are fictional—any similarity to real company or product names is unintentional, except where explicitly stated otherwise. In addition, we have referenced several trademarked games and replicated trademarked images (such as *Pac-Man*, owned by Namco) to enhance the instructional and visual delivery of game concepts specific to this book.

Who should read this book? The short answer is, everyone who is or intends to be involved in computer game development. All members of a team can benefit from understanding each other's area of responsibility. However, each section addresses issues specific to one part of the development team. We recommend that you begin by reading the section of primary relevance to your own expertise.

Part I: Game Design

The book treats pure game design separately from architecture and formal planning. The game design constitutes a feature-based description of the end product that can be used as a shared creative vision by the whole team. As development progresses and change becomes obligatory, it is the designer's task to evolve the game design also so that the intent of the project remains clear.

We reject the assertion that gameplay is entirely unpredictable and thus cannot be designed. In this section, well-understood techniques from game theory, mathematics, and creative writing are applied to the design process in order to elaborate a development model based on successive iterations of the product.

It is clear that many games contain a spark of gameplay brilliance that could have been nurtured into a flame if the designers better understood the basic issues of gameplay. Part I shows you how to achieve this in your own designs.

Part II: Team Building And Management

The book advocates formal process because we have found it to work. Many developers are wary of formal process because they fear it will lead to bureaucracy and over-management. In fact, the reverse is true.

Consider an analogy. In the martial arts, much emphasis during training is placed on constant repetition of predefined sequences of movement, called *kata*. The student may wonder how a formal routine of countering blows to the head, chest, and abdomen can possibly be of use in the infinite combinations of moves that can occur in real-life. And then, one day, somebody takes a swing at you and your arm comes up to block. You didn't even need to think about it.

Similarly, we espouse the application of formal process precisely *because* it lessens the need for management. Instead the emphasis is on honing everyone's skills as part of a team, with the developers themselves taking responsibility through self-management. Thus, Part II details simple, common-sense procedures that are easy to adopt and will soon become second nature. The payoff will be seen in increased efficiency, reliability, and team morale.

Part III: Game Architecture

The architectural plan of the project is the point of contact that draws together the conceptual, artistic or gameplay factors with the technical requirements. Envisage the design as an ideal view of what the game should be. The architecture maps out how to converge reality with that ideal view.

A perfect architecture should aim to achieve all of the following:

Modularity

Separating the project into completely encapsulated modules allows each to be independently tested, modified or replaced without impacting the rest of the system.

Reusability

Reinventing the wheel every time makes no sense. Modules should be designed to be extensible and portable so that they can be plugged into other projects.

Robustness

A high degree of reliability is best attained by building architecture free of module interdependencies. The final goal is a meta-architecture capable of building games that are always able to function in unexpected circumstances—in short, that are crash-proof. Though such a goal is considerably beyond the scope of this book, the subject is treated in an introductory manner by means of object-oriented design patterns.

Trackability

The project plan is derived directly from the architecture, yielding a schedule that allows realistic measurement of progress.

Projects fail because of poorly thought-out architecture that fails to assist in creating the intended game or, worse, constrain development in an unsuitable format. We show how design shades into architecture, which shades into the technical design and documentation, which in turn shades into code—as a continuous cohesive process always directed towards the (evolving) vision described in the game design.

Part IV: Appendixes

Here we use real-life projects as case studies to illustrate the techniques of the book. We show how to begin with a feature-based description of the desired end product—the vision document that we call the *gameplay design*. When this is mapped to a logical abstraction of the game environment then you have the *software plan*, which describes discrete modules of the game and how they will interface. Finally, the details of implementation are added to create the *technical design* of the project. Then the coding starts.

Summing Up

Game developers are the most enthusiastic, creative and motivated workers in the software industry. But they have been ill served by the development models in place today. Too often, the development teams are left baling water when it would make more sense to fix the leak instead.

Many development houses have finally seen the need for change, but few know what changes are needed. In this book we set out a new development model for game software. Beginning with the core concept, the book covers all you need to know to organize a team, plan your project, and commence development with confidence.

Rest assured, these are not abstract theories. We have applied our methodology in practice with great success. This development model is one that works. Our aim is to tell you how to fix that leak so that you can get on with the important business of creating games. Good luck!

PART I

GAME DESIGN

Chapter 1
First Concept

Key Topics:

- *Types of games*
- *Storylines*
- *Originality*
- *Feasibility*

This chapter focuses on how to assemble the basic gameplay treatment, which is really just a document of no more than five or six pages. It is a proto-manifesto to communicate your concept for the game, and, most of all, your feeling of what the game would be like to play.

Eventually, the treatment will grow into a full specification for the game, but writing this initial treatment will help you solidify your thoughts about the game. Even better, it gives you an idea you can use to sell the game to others—the publishers, programmers, and artists who will be developing the game.

To begin, you'll learn ways to find and shape your concepts, view the treatment for a specific game, and examine why the game took its final form.

The Shock Of The New

The designer's job is to create something new. Everybody thinks their job is difficult, but this one truly is. The poet from the Book of Ecclesiastes says, "Under the sun there is no new thing." If the statement is true, isn't it the kiss of death to creativity? Why bother to try to create anything if it isn't going to be original?

The question of originality in games is a troublesome one. Maybe you've heard that there are only seven original ideas in the world; everything else is just a reworking of those? So, in theory as in Ecclesiastes, there are no original ideas.

Of course, it's not all bad news. Occasionally there is the opportunity to rework one of the old ideas in completely new ways, and we are lucky to live in an age that is rife with these opportunities. The advent of computers has allowed us to formulate, calculate, and express our ideas in new ways. And the field of computer gaming has provided us with a new means of recreation, taking all the old ideas and obsessions that have occupied mankind since long before Ecclesiastes and giving them a new spin.

Artists of every generation have drawn on the ideas and works that have come before them. Your own creativity is a result of the sources that you borrow from, the unique mix of ideas that synthesize in your own work.

And there's something else that's encouraging to the creative artist. Ideas aren't like seams of ore; you don't deplete them and then they're gone. Rather, they're like living things. Ideas that are overused can become inactive for a while. They regenerate.

So, when you're searching around for a first concept, take the path less traveled. Start by looking for inspiration where others haven't been for a while. Bad game concepts are never more than plagiarism: "I'm going to do *Command & Conquer* but with more vehicles." Good game concepts bring something fresh: "It's a Frankenstein strategy game where you plunder graves and battlegrounds for spare parts."

Of course, some ideas may be just too plain wacky to work, which doesn't necessarily mean that they are bad ideas. Maybe their time has not yet come, either because the technology isn't there (*Wolfenstein* came first, but *Doom* did all the business) or because the market has not yet been created. Would we have been ready for *Pac-Man* two years earlier?

Having The Idea

The oldest profession is not what you think. It's the shaman. The visionary. The dreamer.

How many industries can claim to deal in daydreams?

Dreams are where every game begins. Before the code, before the software plan, before the concept artwork, even before the first document, the game starts life as a spark in the designer's imagination, and the idea is the single most persistent entity in the game development cycle. It can evolve and develop as the game progresses, but it was there from the start. It is the seed from which the game grows.

Just as programmers are often warned not to rush into coding (as will be seen later in the book), designers must guard against rushing to get their ideas down on paper. When that daydream comes, give it time. Resist the urge to go straight to the word processor. I firmly believe ideas have a gestation period, the time your subconscious takes to mull over the concept and hand it up to you in its raw form. Writing anything down too soon warps the process, because it allows your critical and analytical faculties to come into play, which can kill the idea before it's been fully formed. When you start to hear quotes from the treatment document in your head, and when you're scribbling pictures to show what the game screens will be like—*then* it's time to start.

So indulge your subconscious mind, and kindle your creative spark. Allow yourself to daydream, but, when you have finished daydreaming, get ready for some serious effort. Edison said that genius is 1 percent inspiration and 99 percent perspiration. Well, enjoy this 1 percent; everything after is pure hard work.

We'll deal successively with the four phases of the creative process:

- *Inspiration*—Where to get ideas
- *Synthesis*—Combining ideas
- *Resonance*—Creating synergy from ideas
- *Convergence*—Finishing the concept

Inspiration

Early directors were electrified with the possibilities of their new medium of film. Casting about for ideas to put up on the screen, they drew their inspiration from anywhere and everywhere. German Expressionism, a creative lineage that can be traced right down to Tim Burton today, mixed elements of fairy tales, theater, and Freudian psychology. Kung Fu movies are reminiscent of Chinese opera without singing. *Star Wars* is music hall drama by way of Saturday morning serials.

While directors are happy to swipe ideas from everywhere, games designers have not been quite so adventurous. Except for a few notable exceptions, their inspiration comes always from the same safe sources. Only so many shoot-'em-ups can be inspired by *Aliens* and still seem even remotely fresh. Computer Role Playing Games (CRPGs) based on the 1970's game mechanics of *Dungeons & Dragons* are dated. Tabletop role-playing has progressed so far since then. It's time to look to new pastures for fresh ideas.

Nearly every game released today seems to be related to the others in the market. Looking at a single genre, like the realtime strategy game, you don't so much see a rich tapestry of diversity as the same game repeated in slightly different forms. A herd mentality dictates that only "safe" games are released. (For safe, read *unoriginal*: "It's like *Command & Conquer*, only with ants!")

Think of it. Creative motherlodes are waiting to be mined. So start with a brainstorming session in which anything goes. Leaf through an encyclopedia. Go to a museum. Browse obscure sites on the Web. Watch a movie with subtitles. Sit in on a random lecture at your local university. Do anything to get rid of the stale thinking.

Originality can present itself in many aspects of a game: the gameplay, the story, the setting, the characters, the interface, or in the technology. If you can bring a freshness to most of these, you can make a great game. If you manage to make *all* of them new and exciting, you've probably just spawned a new genre!

Stephen King says that the spark of originality comes when you put familiar things together in an unexpected way. A vampire game? Don't put your vampire in a cyberpunk city (that's old) or in a Transylvanian castle (that's ancient). How about a pirate setting? No bats, maybe, but the vampire can transform into a shark instead, as well as rolling banks of sea fog. By night, they have to return to rotting hulks, rather than coffins, on the seabed. Or, for something more exotic, use the style and tropes of Indonesian shadow puppet theater, a whole mythology that is ripe for the taking.

Make sure, though, that the idea has some public resonance. For example, *Grim Fandango* used the Mexican "El Día de los Muertos" or "The Day of the Dead" as its theme, and it worked effectively because its mythology is known worldwide.

Synthesis

Of course, it isn't enough to have an idea, or even to have lots of ideas and compile them. You have to make them work. Otherwise, your game may trundle out of the metaphoric hangar and taxi down the runway, but it's never going to get airborne.

An old saying claims that new concepts are produced by chimeras flying in a void. (In ancient myth, a chimera was a monster that had body parts from a dozen different animals.) Think of that as the raw ideas you're throwing into your game. To ensure that the hybrid isn't stillborn—and, more importantly, that it produces something new—you need to pick the right mix of parts.

Let's go back to vampires for a moment. Say you're fixated on the idea of a vampire game, and for other reasons (possibly commercial), you want an outer-space setting (a starship, for example).

One possible scenario for such a game would be to have the starship visit a backward, superstitious planet and take delivery of a stack of wooden boxes. Later, with the starship underway, a box opens and a cloaked figure emerges. Why *wouldn't* you do that? Because it's boring! Why bother to transplant my vampires into space if I'm just going to rehash the old clichés? Instead, I need to think about how I'm going to synthesize a game out of the two concepts.

Vampires sleep in coffins, but that doesn't have to literally mean a wooden box. What if the crew of my starship goes into a "cold sleep" when they don't have duties to perform? The vampire could then be one of the crew, drawing frozen blood samples from his slumbering shipmates whenever he can. As an adventure game, it's not entirely original (shades of *Alien*), but it isn't exactly a cliché either.

Everyone also knows that vampires come out only at night. Does that mean a certain distance from a nearby star, or will I say that it is always night in space? How about in hyperspace? Does that count as night or day? If this is a strategy game, the vampires maybe can't stay close to bright stars for too long, which immediately gives me some thoughts on how to develop the game balance. In the context of an adventure game, the same idea might lead me to say that the vampires can't enter the engineering bay (too much UV from the warp core), and that this fact would function as a potential clue to the vampire's identity.

Look at the ideas in the mix. Ask yourself what each idea can contribute to the others so that the emergent game makes full use of all of them.

Resonance

In an outstanding episode of his *Sandman* comic book series, Neil Gaiman has his heroine visit Paris at the time of the French Revolution in search of the severed head of Orpheus, the legendary Greek hero. Decapitation gives Gaiman his plot link. One memorable scene in the story takes place in a room piled high with heads. Most of the heads have come from the guillotines; only Orpheus' can speak.

The concept is disturbing in itself, but what gives this story its power is the resonance between the elements Gaiman has chosen. The *Sandman* comic often features the dream world: Paris during the Reign of Terror is a place out of nightmare. The story takes place when the executions are out of control, a hysterical bloodbath. Civilization is being destroyed by insane violence, and a flashback reminds us of Orpheus' fate. (He was torn apart by madwomen.) The story's title is *Thermidor*, the revolutionary Convention's new name for the month of July. The Convention's aim was to expunge classical traditions and make the world anew. But, as Gaiman shows, it is never as easy as that.

Resonance is a way of making the whole greater than the sum of the parts. This is the definition of synergy, and it is an effective means of making the story and the subject matter significant to the game players. It applies to game design as much as to any other creative work. Adventure games, built around a clear story line, will benefit most.

Begin by deciding your theme. In *Warcraft Adventures*, for example, the hero was to be a young orc brought up after the victory of the human and elfish alliance. Cut off from their homeland, the orcs are a subjugated race confined to reservations. The hero's quest is to regain face and win back the honor lost in defeat. In the circumstances and even the tribal costume of the orcs, the game's designers appear to be evoking comparison with American Indians. You may question the social commentary, but the resonance is undeniably effective.

You will also find that people create their own resonance if the game is powerful enough. Take a look at the *Half Life Alternative Background Story* Web site: **http://halflife.gamehut.com**. This site is where people have contributed to creating a rich tapestry of fictional stories, filling in details on the background of the world(s) that *Half Life* is based in and around.

Convergence

Up to this point, I've been encouraging you to ignore your critical and analytical instincts. You simply can't give birth to new ideas while worrying about whether or not they're any good.

But now we're passing out of the artistic stage and into the *craft* of games design. Craftsmanship demands a critical sense. You have to be able to judge if your ideas are going to work together to make a good game. Good critical judgment can come only from experience. Look at every game that's remotely like your new concept. Do those games work? If not, why not?

Obviously, it's far better to anticipate flaws so you can correct them now. Once the whole programming and art team is assembled, changes in design are expensive and paid for by the hour. An accurate critical sense can save thousands of dollars further down the line.

Shaping The Idea

According to the common model of drama, there are five elements: style, plot, character, setting, and theme. These same elements have been combined over the last 20 centuries to theater, opera, novels, films, and television. And today, they still work.

Dramatic Effect

It might seem strange to claim that computer games can be thought of as a dramatic form. Doesn't interactivity mean that you can't simply apply the traditional analysis? The player is in control of the game, after all. But I would say that an interactive game is really no different from a work of more "classical" art. For example, if you read the epic poem, *The Iliad*, you construct your own unique narrative, which certainly differs from what Homer had in mind. Even puzzle games like *Tetris* in one sense tell a story, and are thus "dramatic" to an extent.

All good computer games must entertain, and most gain a great deal of their entertainment value from drama. The fact that the player has a greater control of the drama than in any other genre of art is a difference in degree, not form. The underlying rules of drama therefore still apply, because they are aesthetic rules dictated by the human mind. So it's instructive to look at the dramatic elements of a game, which we will do in the following few sections.

Style

How do you define a genre? Is the first-person shoot-'em-up a genre all its own? Did *Dune 2* really spawn a new genre when it gave rise to all those realtime strategy games?

No; a genre is much broader than that. In literature, "fantasy" is a genre; Tolkien rip-offs—ubiquitous though they are—are just a variant in style. It's similar with games. The genres are identifiable by the goal of the designer, whether that was to frighten you, engage your intellect, or delight you with the beauty of phantasmagoric scenes. I'm doubtful that taxonomy is of much value in these cases, but we could say the broad genres are:

- *Action*—Lots of frantic button pushing
- *Adventure*—The story matters

- *Strategy*—Nontrivial choices
- *Simulation*—Optimization exercises
- *Puzzle*—Hard analytic thinking
- *Toys*—Software you just have fun with
- *Educational*—Learning by doing

Obviously, this is not an exhaustive list and some of the list members can be combined with others (for example, *Alone in the Dark* is primarily an adventure game that combines elements of action and puzzle games). Games, like films, can and do straddle multiple genres.

The equivalent of what Aristotle termed *style* is the way the game is executed. At heart, both *Duke Nukem* and *Tomb Raider* are action-adventure games, but their styles make us perceive them as different genres. And role playing games (RPGs), I would argue, aren't a genre at all: they are all fundamentally *Dungeons & Dragons* clones, adding an element of simulation (existence in a fantasy world) to an action-adventure format. (Admittedly, all games attempt to create the impression of immersion in the game's imaginary universe. But only RPGs go so far as to simulate how many cockatrice eggs you can get for a groat.)

Plot

The worst kinds of game are those (usually adventure games) in which it's obvious that the designer thought he was writing a film or a novel. It's the frustrated-author syndrome, and you know you're bearing the brunt of it when your choices in the game have shrunk to one linear path, or when you find yourself scrolling through the never-ending character conversation waiting to get to the action. These designers are entertaining nobody but themselves.

I used to write choose-your-own adventure gamebooks, an early low-tech form of adventure game. But I have also written novels, which is probably why I don't feel the need to impose an absolute authorial stance on my game designs. When writing a gamebook, I aim for a minimum of three main routes through the narrative, with smaller branches along each main route, and several ways to solve each problem encountered along the way. Compare that with a modern computer adventure like *Grim Fandango*. It has one route through the story, and only one correct solution to every problem. You may enjoy it for the artwork, music, even the story (all of which are breathtaking), but this in effect is just a film that you're having to solve puzzles to view. Every time you solve a puzzle, you are rewarded by being shown a little bit more of the movie.

Interactive fiction is possible, but the end result is not a game as such, and this is the wrong kind of interactivity to include anyway. (There will be more on this in Chapter 3.)

There is plot in any game, but for the most part it is created by the player himself. It is the player, not the game's designer, who is the author of the game's events. The game is a tool for allowing the players to create stories.

You can see this in any game. Ask an *Age of Empires* enthusiast to describe some of his games. Most likely, he'll start telling you about the two priests he sent in to convert a key enemy tower while his archers created a diversion. Or how his scout led a lion right into the enemy camp. These are stories. Sharing them with each other is not so different from Neolithic hunters describing the day's adventures around a campfire, or Homer recounting the Trojan Wars.

Of course, there is often a *backstory*—the scene and setting that is particularly important in adventure games. The designer must bear in mind that the players are impatient to begin playing. They haven't paid $45 to sit through interminable Full Motion Videos (FMVs). They want to get their hands on the game. A good designer makes his ego transparent in the game.

Also, it's important to square the need for scene setting with the player's unfamiliarity with your game world at the start. Notice how the best games minimize how much the player has to wade through. In *Half Life*, it's your first day at work, which neatly explains away why you know so little. *Ecstatica* makes its set-up with startling simplicity: a fairy-tale village, the bridge collapses behind you, and the game begins. Resort to cliché if you have to; just get the story started. As long as the gameplay is original, no one will fault you for skimming through the set-up. Look at *Warcraft*!

Character

Publishers and designers have different reasons for favoring games with identifiable characters. From the publisher's perspective, a character is a merchandisable commodity. Once you have a Lara Croft, the fact that she originated in a game is irrelevant. She belongs to the marketing department, who can leverage her everywhere.

The designer's motives are different. A character enhances the story (that the player is creating), and this applies to the player's own characters as well as the ones you write into the game.

You think *SimCity* doesn't feature a character? Wrong. The character is the *player*, who is a god albeit of a very restricted world. You think that a god could be any character, that the designer doesn't have any say in it? Wrong, again. The choices that the game presents to the player define the kinds of character that the player can be. The god of *Populous* is not a kindly old guy with a beard!

Setting

Think of the leafy glades of *Warcraft*, the barren war-ravaged landscapes of *Command & Conquer*, the dark gothic catacombs of *Dungeon Keeper*. Who lives there? What are they like? If your players are asking themselves these questions, then you've got them hooked.

How about puzzle games like *Tetris*? Do they have a setting? Of course they do. It is a formalized universe governed by a few logical rules: the landscape of the reasoning mind.

Theme

The theme of a dramatic work is the philosophical idea that the author is trying to express. You can think of it as the "defining question" of the work. Can love triumph? Is murder ever justified? Are dreams real?

I've already said that the true author of a game narrative is (or should be) the player. Level design can steer the player towards the favored themes of the designer, but it's like leading the proverbial horse to water. You can't make the player think your way.

If a game is to have themes, they should come as a mix-'n'-match bag that leaves the player with freedom of choice. This doesn't apply only to adventure games. *Starcraft*'s different species and the levels of each species' campaign tend to slant towards a theme. By one Freudian reading, the Terrans are the ego, the Protoss are the superego, and the Zerg are the id. It doesn't matter if you see the theme. It doesn't even matter if the designers thought of it themselves. But it shapes the way you think about the species you've chosen, and so it shapes the way you feel about the game.

The Treatment

So, your game has wheels, but can you drive it around the block? The only answer is to put it to the test, and the first test of your concept comes now, when it's time to put it all down on paper. When you start to do this, you'll see the previous gaps in your thinking. Maybe you hadn't considered the multiplayer issue, or how complex the interface is going to get. Writing it down exposes these points, and it can come as a short, sharp shock after the heady indulgence of your flight of fancy. After you've written the treatment, you'll know if this game has potential, or whether you should give up on it right now!

When you're writing the first treatment, you can cut loose and put in all those great ideas you've had. At this stage, you don't need to worry about technical constraints. In fact, you should deliberately avoid thinking about them. The devil is in the details, and this is supposed to be a vision statement for the game. Remember the saying: "Programmers can't see the forest through the trees; designers can't see the trees through the forest." And this is exactly how it should be.

What points should the treatment cover? I don't believe a checklist is useful creatively. It would be nice if creativity were a straightforward process that could be learned, but (in spite of all those "How to write a bestseller" books) I have to tell you it just isn't so. Again, the best advice is to let your instincts steer you. The points you find yourself covering in the treatment are the ones that make your concept special; their details may get pushed into the background for the time being, but it doesn't matter. They can wait until you do the full spec.

So, have you written your treatment? Hardly like working at all, was it? I hope you enjoyed that part, because it won't get that breezy again until you're playtesting the beta version.

Taking Stock

You'll recall I previously said that I didn't like checklists as part of the *creative* phase. But now it's time to get *critical*, and there are some points you'll need to consider:

- Analysis
- Evaluation
- Justification

Analysis

Now turn another eye on your beloved concept, an eye of cold, objective criticism. Deconstruct it; pick it apart. Think about what's in there—the ancestors of your chimera—and what motivated you to put them there. Here are some pointers to get started:

- What is the game genre(s)?
- Which existing games most closely resemble your concept?
- In what way are you proposing to do things the same as in those games?
- In what ways are you going to do things differently?

Evaluation

Ask yourself if your game is different enough. Particularly if it's an entry into an already crowded genre (such as realtime strategy), it will need a good strong list of unique selling points (USP list). But just because a feature is original and unique is not sufficient reason to include it. Take another look at the USP list.

Decide:

- Will this feature be fun? (This is *always* Rule #1.)
- Will this feature lead to good gameplay?
- Why hasn't anybody used this feature before? (Is it *really* that you were first to think of it?)
- Is it realistic to expect the team to be able to implement this feature?
- Will the feature be workable? (A player can handle only so much with three mouse buttons.)

(These factors begin to touch upon the concept of feasibility, which I'll discuss in a moment, but, for now, let's just concentrate on the issues involving gameplay.)

Justification

After working up the treatment, you will typically present your concept to both the client (publisher) and the development team. Both must buy into it if the project is to succeed.

If you thought you'd critiqued your own brainchild thoroughly, just wait until you hear the comments from your team. You must be ready to explain and defend your ideas. It's essentially akin to the modern scientific method: advance a theory and see if anyone can demolish it.

Try not to get touchy. Creative people very rarely enjoy negative criticism, but, if you can't marshal arguments in support of the creative decisions you've made, how do you expect your team to get behind it? Even more importantly, you need to understand that the development process has now begun. Simply gathering the team and discussing the treatment has already set up a "thought testbed" that is the first stage in proving (or junking) your idea.

Getting It Down

As an example, Case Study 1.1 is the treatment of a game that has not (to date) been developed. I leave it to you to decide whether it would pass the evaluation and criticism stages needed to get a green light.

Feasibility

I've assumed thus far that you're designing your game in an ivory tower. You can think up a concept, play around with it, work it up into a treatment, and never stop to consider the practical limits on development. If only it were that simple!

I like to have a portfolio of ideas to draw on. I have about a dozen game concepts that I've taken to the first treatment stage that we've been looking at. It's handy to have a file filled with ready-made ideas sometimes (and not least when you're looking for a job). But the odds are that most of these ideas will never find their niche. And, even if they all do, other factors will change them. The full design specifications will be very different from those first treatments. The factors that will enforce those changes are covered in the following sections.

Commercial

A game is released that uses many of the things that you thought made your game unique. If you forge ahead, it's going to look like you're copying the other game. Find a way to change direction: add humor, or change the game to make it more simple or complex. Anything to move off the other guy's patch and plant your own flag.

Technological

Your R&D group can't deliver that 3D engine or the character Artificial Intelligence (AI) on which your game depends. Plan for this in advance. Your design should have alternatives. If it's impossible to develop a game without technology that exists from the start, that game should never be given the green light.

Case Study 1.1 Grimm—It Ain't No Fairytale!

Abstract

Grimm is set in a fantasy world that is derived from the most ancient folk-tales. Players are clans and will sometimes struggle as rivals, but often must ally to counter threats to the whole realm.

How *Grimm* differs from standard CRPGs is that quests and interactions are oriented to the community rather than single individuals. In this sense, the game is like a cross between *Might & Magic* and *SimCity* or *Warcraft.* You can use your most powerful characters, the Heroes, as a standard adventuring team if you like, but that leaves your clan vulnerable while they're away. Offense and defense must be balanced, and, as your clan gains wealth and power, your Heroes will become stronger and more skillful.

Clans

Each clan comprises:

- Four Heroes: the Lord, the Lady, the Priest, and the Wizard.
- Up to 12 Elders: initially with undefined powers.
- Up to 24 Clansmen: the generic "citizens" of the clan.

Heroes

The *Heroes* are the most powerful characters, each representing an archetypal power:

- The *Lord's* power is *battle*, and his clan responsibility is *military fortifications.*
- The *Lady's* power is *wisdom*, and her clan responsibilities are *agriculture* and *trade.*
- The *Priest's* power is *spirituality*, and his clan responsibilities are *health* and *protection from evil.*
- The *Wizard's* power is *secret knowledge*, and his responsibility is *magical research.*

Elders

The Elders start out with no special responsibility. By assigning an Elder as lieutenant to one of the four Heroes, you cause him to "borrow" some of his master's power. An Elder assigned to the Lord becomes a Knight; if assigned to the Priest, he becomes an Acolyte; if the Lady, a Minister. Once an Elder has one of these titles, he becomes a lower-level equivalent of the Hero he serves with approximately one-third of their power.

The Wizard's lieutenants are special. Each gets a special title. Instead of being one-third as powerful as the Hero as in other cases, the Wizard's lieutenants are as powerful as their master but only in one area of magic. The Illusionist can conjure mirages; the Summoner can create temporary servants; and the Elementalist can hurl bolts of fire and cause wind and rain.

Building Up The Clan

The player does not directly control the ordinary Clansmen. Rather, their AI just responds to the power structure of the ruling council (Heroes plus Elders). The Clansmen's activities will reflect the priorities you've set in the council. For instance, if you assign six Elders to the Lady, then half the Clansmen will concern themselves with trade and harvesting.

The clanhouse is a walled enclosure (like a Motte & Bailey castle) that constitutes the player's "city." Clansmen do not leave the vicinity of the clanhouse under any circumstances.

Maintaining The Clan

Each Hero's area of responsibility is magically tied to him/her, the way the land was supposedly tied to the High King in Celtic times. This means that, when the Lord is absent from the clan, the walls will no longer be maintained and will gradually crumble, the Clansmen assigned to sentry duty will become less alert and capable, etc.

Quests

Quests must be undertaken by a group of no more than three characters. These could be three Heroes, but note the drawback mentioned above (your clan will decline in their absence). More often, you'll send one Hero with the power most suited to the quest and a couple of Elders with different powers to back him up. Therefore, the first phase of any quest is usually to find out what's in store, so you can pick your adventuring team to meet the likely challenges.

Examples Of Quests

The gods demand that a player clears and blesses a path through the Forest of Thorns. The player knows that the Priest will be needed for the blessing. The Lady would be useful for scouting a path, but he cannot spare her so he sends a Minister in her place. The third member of the team is a Knight to deal with bandits that are rumored to live in the forest.

Following on from the previous quest, when the path is blessed, a mysterious stranger comes through the forest and bestows a broken sword on the clan. He departs without saying anything, but the Priest learns from prayer that the stranger was the Herald of the Sea Goddess. Presumably, if the clan can locate the other half of the sword, they can forge it into a useful magic weapon. But what if that other part resides with another clan that won't give it up?

A marauding band of skeletal warriors appear at the edge of the map, attacking any passers-by. Trade suffers, and Clansmen are reluctant to go out to the fields. If nothing is done, the skeletons start to build a tower. Players must act to stop them before a necromancer moves in and starts calling new soldiers from out of the graveyards.

The Trickster God steals the sun, causing continual darkness to descend on the world. The crops and cattle are dying as eternal winter sets in. Someone must find where the sun has been hidden and restore it to its rightful place in the sky.

Economy

Wealth (in the form of gold) is gained by prospecting and trade. Gold is used for a one-off payment to build and repair structures, as in most strategy games. It can also be gained in the form of ransoms, as gifts from the King, or by selling magic items to passing Non Player Character (NPC) merchants.

Buildings

Each Hero has his or her principal domain: the Lord has the Barracks, the Lady the Hall, the Priest the Church, and the Wizard the Tower. These structures broadcast a continual supply of power to the Hero. Upgrading the structure (with gold) increases its "power supply."

Other structures also provide special functions (for example, the watchtower from which balloons can be sent aloft to spy out the land). Some of these peripheral structures are specials that you can build only once you've got a certain item (such as an ancient codex allowing a clan to build a Naphtha Turret).

Birth And Death

New clansmen are born after one is killed or promoted, and this period of time depends on the power of the Lady. If an Elder is killed, a clansman can be promoted by the Heroes.

If a Hero is killed, he awakens in the Afterlife and must journey back to the temporal plane. In his absence, the clanhouse declines in the area he's responsible for, so the death of a Hero is a serious business and you must try to get him back from the Afterlife as quickly as possible.

A journey through the Afterlife is always fraught with peril, but it is an opportunity for the character to gain experience. Also, you may meet up with slain Heroes from other clans, and forming an alliance may be the best policy.

A Typical Game

A campaign starts with just the four Heroes, four Elders, and four Clansmen. The way in which you assign the Elders will decide the activities of the Clansmen. One Elder to each Hero leads to a well-balanced development of the clanhouse, but some levels may require you to specialize. (For instance, a clanhouse set on haunted plains might make early concentration on religious affairs a priority.)

According to your policy decisions and any gold or items found, the clanhouse will grow and upgrade. Typically, to upgrade a building requires only time and manpower. Upgrades at a building (for example, the plow to increase farm productivity) then become available but cost gold to perform. And special quest items are needed to construct special buildings.

New Elders are usually encountered on quests, or may arrive as rewards between levels. ("The High King is pleased and sends you his cousin to serve as Elder.") More Clansmen gather to serve you as your Clanhouse's renown and experience spread.

It's envisaged that the view would be 3D or isometric, as in *Diablo*. Control during a level is via the usual interface for realtime strategy games. Between levels, you would have a strategic interface that allows you to reassign Elders, send campaign messages, etc.

Network Gaming

Played on a local network, the game can be run as a regular multiplayer RPG, or one player can use the built-in editor to become Games Master and design the Quest Challenge. Using a set number of points, he must "buy" adversaries, hide clues, ward quest objectives, etc. The players then attempt to complete the quest, the winner earning points to spend on designing his own Quest Challenge.

The One King

The land is ruled by an NPC King who is sufficiently powerful to be a tough adversary for all the players' clans combined. The King will set tasks for clans (usually a contest like "Bring me the antlers of the questing beast") and success earns royal favor that the player can use later. Favor can also be gained just by Heroes spending time at court, but (as noted above) this entails a penalty in the form of clanhouse deterioration.

Online Gaming

The problem with "Multiuser Dungeons" (MUDs) is that they usually turn into an ego trip for power-gamers. Players who have been in the game a while get so powerful that newcomers are put off: they just have no way of matching the old hands in power.

Grimm gets around this by making a clan's power mainly a matter of versatility rather than brute strength. You might collect a hundred magic items, all with different powers, but each character can take only two items on an adventure. So the long-term player will usually have more items to choose from, but he's not impossibly more powerful than the newcomer.

In addition, the One King imposes laws that all must obey. For example:

- No one may attack allies without giving one minutes' notice of breaking off the alliance.
- A group that includes a Priest may not kill an enemy who has surrendered.
- No hostilities are allowed within the Royal Parks.
- A Lady on her own must never be attacked.

These laws provide a regulatory structure that ensures the game never degenerates into a free-for-all. Players can still plot, scheme, and cheat one another, but the need to observe certain rules of engagement enhances the fun.

Developmental

Gameplay emerges from rules. The most experienced designers have a feel for how their game will play, but this isn't an exact science. Development must begin with a prototype that proceeds through successive iterations towards the finished game. Each stage of the iteration will reveal features that ought to work but don't, and other features that nobody expected at all. Know what you want to examine at each iteration, but don't presuppose the results or you're heading for disaster.

If your concept has made it this far and you're not ready to abandon yet, then well done! It could be that you're on to a winner. It might even be (Ecclesiastes notwithstanding) that you really have devised something new under the sun!

Chapter 2 will tell you how to start turning this winning design into a fully fledged game.

Chapter 2
Core Design

Key Topics:

- ***Working up the concept***
- ***Adding gameplay***
- ***Developing the game spec***
- ***Prototyping***

In this chapter, we're going to show how to turn a raw idea into a first-pass working document. By now, you have your game concept—which means that you already know the environment in which the player will be making choices, whether that be a starship, a dream world, or the British empire. You will even have a good idea what those choices will involve—searching for dilithium, hiding from pursuers, or sending armies off to war. Now it's time to pin down the details. What are the spells, weapons, units, or tactics that will feature in the game?

Throughout this chapter, I will be using as an example one of my own designs, *Warrior Kings*, a medieval realtime strategy game that I wrote and planned for development by a team based Eidos Interactive.

What Is A Game?

If we want to start putting in some gameplay, the question "what is a game?" can serve as a good starting point.

But, first, let's consider what a game is *not*:

- A bunch of cool features
- A lot of fancy graphics
- A series of challenging puzzles
- An intriguing setting and story

Cool Features

Cool features are just fine; in fact, they are a necessity. However, cool features do not, of themselves, make the game. You know those brainstorming sessions with your developers that end with everybody saying, "Wouldn't it be great if you could give a whole bunch of swordsmen an order and every swordsman would do something a tiny bit different?"

Even if all those great little ideas didn't take forever to implement, there's a point at which cramming in extra features just starts to damage the elegance of the gameplay. This tendency to add unnecessary features, commonly known as "gold plating," is the result of someone who, at some point, thought the features were cool. They may well be, but just know when to draw the line.

Fancy Graphics

Games need fancy graphics, just as a blockbuster movie needs special effects—but neither contributes to the story. I would certainly never turn down any fancy graphics that the technology can provide, but the game has to be able to work without them. In fact, in today's market, not having fancy graphics is effectively commercial suicide. This can be really unfair, because many of the products with fancy graphics have no real gameplay behind them. If you put more effort into gameplay than the graphics, it is likely that the other games will still sell more units than yours simply because they look nicer, even if the underlying game is inferior.

The following quote from an industry master summarizes this quandary quite nicely.

"We need graphics. We need a good interface, we need visual clarity for our information to come across, and we need graphics to do this. But when a designer is asked how his game is really going to make a difference, I hope he has an answer that talks about gameplay, fun and creativity—as opposed to an answer that simply focuses on how good it looks."

—Sid Meier, quoted in Edge *magazine, September 1997*

Puzzles

All games have puzzles. From determining where to build your castle extension to figuring out how to kill a wave of tricky aliens, games can universally be described as sets of linked puzzles.

You may or may not like puzzles. Personally, I find logic puzzles tedious. Heuristic puzzles can be diverting, granted, but often that's just the problem: they divert attention from an interesting story or game. On the other hand, some people like them, although a "pure" puzzle game does not exist in the wild, as they are usually merged with another genre to boost the interest level. (A good example of this would be *Tetris*.)

Either way, puzzles are not gameplay in themselves. Puzzles are specific problems. Game design is about creating a system that will spawn generic problems.

Setting And Story

Again, who could bring themselves to drown this kitten? A good setting encourages *immersion*—what Coleridge called "the willing suspension of disbelief." And a good story draws the player in and impels him through the action. But, again, it will all add up to nothing if the gameplay isn't there.

Note

Silver, the role-playing game, was initially released to great reviews in the press, and hailed as the greatest thing to happen to role-playing games on the PC—until you actually sat down and played it, when it became abundantly clear that it was yet another linear puzzler, with very little gameplay and a simplistic storyline behind the slick exterior.

Another thing to avoid is using your game as a vehicle to tell a story, another symptom of Frustrated Author Syndrome, and a very bad motive for wanting to be a game designer. Case Study 2.1 provides an example of a story versus gameplay.

Games Aren't Everything

None of the factors we just looked at are sufficient—in and of themselves—for gameplay. All they can do is enhance a game or, in the case of puzzles especially, dovetail into the kind of choices that define a game.

But I've got a confession: I don't like the term *computer game*, anyway. What's so special about games? Consider your idea in a new light. Does it *have* to be game? It's like I said in the last chapter. Rule Number One isn't "Make sure it's a game." It's "Make sure it's *fun*!"

Many products are ruined by trying to force the elements of gameplay (or, worse, pseudo-gameplay). Designers so often think they have to do this, it's become a kind of dogma. They're called *games*, aren't they? So surely they have to have gameplay in there, whether it enhances the product or not? Kids' software is the most glaring example of this. Look at the way children's products are forever exhorting them with pseudo-gameplay like "See how many blossoms you can collect while steering Roger Raccoon's boat across the river and avoiding the rapids." This is not a task I would set for a dog, much less a child.

Games are something that computers can do very well. It is not the only thing—interactivity is what computers are good at, and although games are interactive, so are many other things—and that includes many things that nobody has used the computer to do yet.

A question that continually vexes people in the entertainment software industry is why games don't really seem able to break into the hypothetical mass market. Of the various reasons given, the most common grumble is that it's still not easy enough for the average

Case Study 2.1 Story Vs. Gameplay

Baldur's Gate is an adventure game with quite a linear structure. Going the wrong way too early will certainly get you killed; therefore, much of the playing experience involves finding this out the hard way and then starting again with a saved game. Sometimes you meet people who have been sent to kill you or have other nefarious goals. You are given various dialogue responses, allowing you either to admit who you are or to lie. But it rarely makes any difference. Whatever you say, you will usually get the encounter the designers intended.

Although there is a lot of story here, there's little gameplay. The experience is much more like reading a slightly interactive novel than playing a game. The question is how would this story stand up as a novel? Or a film? Both of these other mediums are ideal for storytelling. On the other hand, computers are good for interactivity.

If we end up creating an inferior version of something that can be done better in another form, maybe we're not making best use of the computer's strengths.

person to install and run a game. "When you can put the disk in the machine and just start playing," they say, "that's a game for the mass market."

But setting up an old-style board game is a lot more effort than installing a computer game. You have to lay out the map or board, place all the counters, and sort the cards. And there are no tutorial levels with board games. Before you can start playing, you have to load the rules into memory the old-fashioned way—reading them! The ugly facts are that games have only quite limited appeal. I like games, and I guess from the fact that you're reading this you probably do too. But there's nothing sacred about gameplay, as shown in Case Study 2.2.

Although we began with the question "What is a game?" maybe it's better to ask: "Does this *need* to be a game?" That's why I prefer the term *entertainment software*, as it reminds you of what you're trying to do, which is to entertain. If you have it in you to invent an entirely new genre in entertainment software, do it. Don't let games get in your way!

Games Mean Gameplay

Assuming that your idea is not actually the stepping-off point for some entirely new genre—that it will, in fact, work better as a game than as anything else—what will now be uppermost in your mind is to make it a *good* game.

A good game is one that you can win by doing the unexpected and making it work. This is almost a definition of gameplay. We'll be looking at others, and examining them in detail, in the next chapter. However, it will do as our working definition for now. Phrased another way, gameplay encourages the player to employ strategy. This does not mean that all games are strategy games (in the sense of belonging to the strategy genre); it just means that all well-designed games, from *Tetris* to *Quake*, require the development of strategies to play them effectively.

Case Study 2.2 A Missed Opportunity?

Grim Fandango is an extremely impressive product of the quality we would expect from LucasArts. The visuals are gorgeous, the music and vocal talent are faultless, the setting is genuinely and breathtakingly original, and the dialogue and storyline are better than most movies. You think I'm going to say the puzzles are bad? Not a bit of it. The puzzles are fun and fit perfectly with the overall style. And, what's more, the interface is unobtrusive and helps ensure that solving the puzzles doesn't break the flow of the story.

But here's a question. Why did the designer insist on *Grim Fandango* being an adventure game? If your main enjoyment comes from solving puzzles, you'll happily work your way through it and maybe you'll appreciate having a funny and dramatic story line to carry you through. But what about all the people who could have enjoyed the story but not the game? For every hard-core gamer, there are many more PC owners who would rather not have a story continually interrupted by having to solve puzzles before you can find out what happens next.

As I said, *Grim Fandango* is of very high quality. Easily good enough that you could simply sit through a rolling demo of the entire game, with every puzzle solved for you, and enjoy it perfectly well as an animated movie. My point is that it could have been sold both as an interactive adventure *and* as a sit-back-and-watch kind of story. And it could have had an option to let you think about the puzzles, but with the addition of an "I give up!" key that would have the hero solve the ones that stumped you. It could even have had a "Gimme a clue!" key so the hero could help you out.

With hardly any extra development effort, *Grim Fandango* could have been a product that empowered the consumer with free choice in how to use it. It didn't have to be only a game.

This brings us back to the question at the start of this chapter. What is a game? If you look at all existing games, you can see that the aim is to achieve one or more of these goals:

- Collect something (point-scoring games, and so on)
- Gain territory (the classic wargame from *Go* onwards)
- Get somewhere first (a race, either literally or figuratively—for example, an arms race)
- Discovery (exploration or deduction—very rarely an end in itself)
- Eliminate other players

Racing and conquest-type games both involve visible objectives. You can immediately see at any point how well you're doing. Collection games often don't involve visible objectives, which is why the designer often finds some way to give in-game rewards for the points scored, as the following examples reveal:

- In most role-playing games (RPGs), you earn experience points to spend on improving your character's skills, attributes, and spells.
- In strategy games, you gather resources to spend on new units and upgrades.
- In adventure games, you collect items to use in later puzzles.

Remember that I did say few games involve just one type of objective. *Age of Empires*, for example, has some elements of a race: you want to be the first to snatch the scarcer resources, and you can even play the game as a race to build a 'Wonder Of The World.' *Age of Empires* also has two levels of collection: the obvious one involving the resources, and an abstract victory-points system tacked on behind the scenes. And of course there's the further objective (the primary one in most scenarios) of wiping out the other players.

When you are designing multiple objectives into your game, make sure that they interact as shown in Case Study 2.3. Otherwise, you are really designing two or more games in parallel, and the parts will not combine to become a whole.

We're saving a detailed analysis of the specifics of gameplay for the next chapter. For now, just aim for clarity. You are about to start documenting your vision of the game. Ask yourself the following questions:

- What are the aims of the game?
- How will players achieve those aims?
- What will the game be like to play?
- What are the rules that will create that gameplay?

Creating The Game Spec

In the last chapter, we talked about preparing treatments. Every treatment can be different. The treatment is an outline concept, and at most a sketch of the game design. Consequently, it can afford to focus on the game's unique features and gloss over—or even completely ignore—the details.

Not so for the game specification. Why are you writing it, after all? It isn't to sell the game; you have the treatment to do that. Instead, your purpose now is to describe how the game will work and to communicate how you see that end result being accomplished. Because of this, you must address certain points in every game spec you write. We'll run through an inventory of these points, with the five most-important ones being:

Case Study 2.3 Integrating Game Objectives

A few years ago, I was asked to suggest ways to improve the gameplay of a Japanese PlayStation title called *Nessa no Hoshi*. The original game involved exploration of an alien desert environment, interspersed with *Street Fighter*-like battle sequences.

The problem was that there were two quite distinct games there. In exploration mode, the player was finding things like hints, maps, and keys that enabled further exploration. In battle mode, the rewards were things that helped in later battles: weapons and recovery items.

I recommended integrating the two modes of play. Thus, the rewards earned in exploration mode would often be useful in battle mode, and vice versa.

- Features
- Gameplay
- Interface
- Rules
- Level design

While preparing the game spec, be sure to document your reasoning. (*Documentation* might be rather a grand word for it at this stage, actually. I'm really thinking of those diagrams and calculations that end up scrawled on the backs of envelopes.) This will form the basis of the designer's notes, which we'll discuss in Chapter 4.

Features

Features are what make your game different from any other game, and this is one reason why features are a good place to start. Another is that a feature-based description of the game will endure throughout the development process, whereas it is very likely that most of the rules you write in an attempt to create those features will have to change further down the line.

This is because features are *emergent* from rules. Although the concept of emergence is something else that we'll cover in detail in the next chapter, emergent factors are those that arise from the interaction between several rules. Emergence, we might say, is that which makes the whole greater than the sum of the parts. Case Study 2.4 provides an instance of emergence (as shown in Figure 2.1).

Types Of Features

Broadly, there are three categories of features. The first two are valuable, while the third takes development time but adds little (if anything) to the game itself:

- Some features are vital to make the game work properly. In *Warrior Kings*, troops can be placed in formations, and the gameplay comes from knowing when to group units in formation and when not to (and which formations to use if you do). Without formations, you would have lost a whole dimension of choice. These are *integral* features.
- Some features enhance your enjoyment of the game but have no effect on the way the game is played. These features convey the look and feel of the game, and help draw you

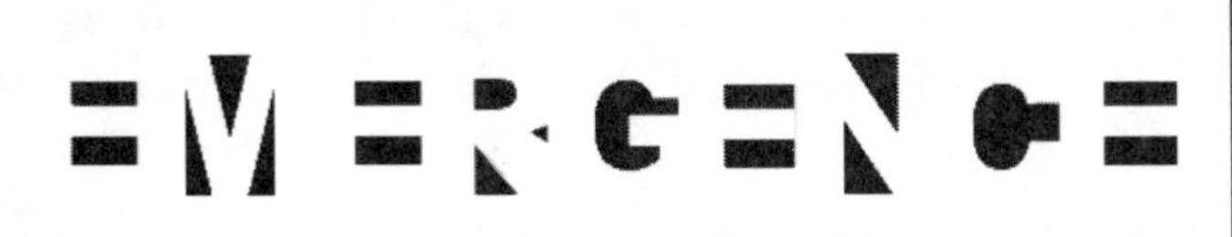

Figure 2.1
Emergence.

Case Study 2.4 An Instance Of Emergence

In *Populous: The Beginning,* when enemy warriors run up to one of your preacher characters, they will stop at a short distance as the preacher starts chanting. For a while, they sit listening. If the process is not interrupted, they will then convert to the preacher's side.

That's one rule. Another is that if enemy warriors have started fighting, a preacher cannot convert them.

What this means in practice is that you can leave your preachers in a perimeter defense around your settlement. The first wave of enemy warriors will be converted. This is automatic, and the player is free to get on with other things. But now consider the second wave of enemy warriors. They come running up, and the first thing they encounter is not the preacher's conversion radius but the attack radius of the last lot of warriors to be converted. A fight breaks out between the groups of warriors, and the preachers cannot intervene to convert the second wave.

The feature that emerges is that you cannot leave your defenses unmanaged. From time to time, you need to scroll around your settlement and move newly converted warriors behind the preachers.

I have no idea whether this was what the designer intended or not. Very possibly it was. However, it is a good example of emergence because it is not immediately obvious that those two rules would give rise to this feature.

into the story. An example would be a game like *StarCraft* that customizes the interface to reflect the species you are playing. These types of feature are called *chrome*.

- Some features are gameplay substitutes. They don't enhance the game in any way, merely giving you another exactly equivalent choice—which is no choice at all. An example would be a computer role-playing game (CRPG) that lists different costs for a slice of cheese, a turnip, and a loaf of bread, even though all have the same food value. If a game designer keeps trying to include features like that, it means he isn't seeing enough of the outside world.

Gameplay

The treatment described the features. Your aim in writing the spec is to describe how those features will create gameplay.

We already discussed gameplay briefly, and we will revisit it later in the book, so I won't spend too long on it here. Your description of anticipated gameplay in the game spec serves three purposes:

- It explains to the developers how the game is supposed to work.
- It provides a vision statement that can be referred to during development.
- It helps you focus on which features are integral and which are merely chrome.

Let's look at an example from the *Warrior Kings* design. I wanted to include some kind of supply rules. As a long-time wargamer, it has always irked me that supply lines aren't an issue in games like *Age of Empires* or *Warcraft II*. You can draw on your resource stocks, anywhere and instantly. This seems a bit of a cheat. It means that players get no reward for using strategies that are valid in the real world, like consolidating their territory or using *chevauchée*, the tactic of ravaging your own crops and farms to prevent an invading army from foraging any food. This certainly doesn't help to foster that willing suspension of disbelief. More significantly, if there aren't any supply rules, there won't be any sieges, which is a bit of a drawback in a medieval game!

But I needed to think about what I really wanted from my supply rules. If I tried to model everything from real-world warfare, the player would get bogged down in logistical details that would be no fun at all. Who wants to have their army grind to a halt or (worse) start dying of .Darvation because you didn't have time to attend to your supply lines?

An early intention was to delegate logistics to an AI assistant. My philosophy is that any no-brainer elements of the game—any choice that the player will always make, that is—can and should be left to the AI. (The corollary, of course, is that these are the things that it's easiest to program the AI for.)

But supply lines aren't that simple. Without going into a detailed analysis, it's clear that the routes you secure for supplying your army are not obvious. You may send an army by land to destroy opposing forces, but you may arrange to supply it from the sea, for example.

I eventually reasoned that it wasn't necessary to model every aspect of supply. I just needed something that the player could handle quickly. Obviously, in reality, a medieval army commander couldn't ignore supply lines, but, to create good gameplay, I needed a set of rules whereby it was the player's *choice* whether to ignore supply matters.

The answer was not to punish a player for failing to supply his troops, but to reward him as long as he succeeds in supplying them. I put in a supply wagon unit that could be supported by semiautonomous quartermasters. Once the player had assigned supply wagons to his army, he didn't have to keep issuing them with orders; they would follow the army around until out of supplies or reassigned. And the answer to the punishment/reward thing? Simple: instead of dying when they run out of food, but they will automatically recover lost hit points as long as they are supplied with food.

So, not only does this mean that there are supply lines in *Warrior Kings*, it also means there is a gameplay choice to be made. If a player thinks he can push through and defeat his opponent in the first attack, he might not bother with supply wagons. But, if he thinks victory will take longer, he will want his units to be able to heal up in the field, and so he'll need to secure his supply lines. The opponent now has the option to counterattack directly or to harass the invader's supply wagons, hoping to win by attrition because his own supply lines are much shorter. And, indeed, he can use *chevauchée*, burning out his own farms, and then sitting it out behind his castle walls in the classic medieval style.

Interface

Always remember what the interface is for. Artists, in particular, often forget this. They think the interface is there to look pretty. Of course, it's nice if it is pretty, but the reason it is there is *to help the player play the game.*

"I find the interface is one of the hardest aspects of game design. It should be intuitive and icons should be kept to a minimum. I have never got an interface right (the) first time. It's one of those things that should be tested and tested until everyone is happy with it."

—Peter Molyneux, quoted in Develop *magazine, May 1998*

Good interface design involves answering the question, "How do I make sure the player isn't having to work against the system?" And really good interface design is both an art and a craft, for it tries to address the question, "How do I make the player forget there are any restrictions on his control of the game?" Case Study 2.5 is an example of an elegant interface.

Rules

The feature-based description tells everyone the game that you are aiming for. At this stage, though, you can only make a guess at the rules that will actually create that game for you. This is why we stress time and again throughout this book that game development must be iterative. You will be continually adding rules, very often only to find that the rule that you've added interacts in some unexpected way with those already in place. So, a little qualitative reasoning at this stage will pay off later.

Case Study 2.5 An Elegant Interface

Dungeon Keeper (Bullfrog) is a complicated sim/strategy game with a lot happening at once. The player manages a dungeon full of monsters, all of which are wandering around in realtime. Because each monster has his own agenda (sleep, eat, study, train, collect his pay, and squabble with other monsters), the game could very easily have become overwhelming.

What rescues the game is a very powerful and user-friendly interface. The player designates tasks (tunnel here, build this type of room) and merely grabs and drops the creatures he wants to do them. A judicious slap now and again serves to chivvy the little devils on! Moreover, although there are many different monster types, a sidebar allows you to see what all of them are up to at any time. You can use the sidebar to select an individual monster, and it's also easy using the sidebar to grab any number when you need them in a hurry.

Although it is reported that Peter Molyneux, the designer, did not like the user interface (as he believed it was still too complex), it has to be said that it was a very efficient tool for handling a large number of simultaneous complex tasks. If Molyneux is correct, then possibly it is true that the game itself is too complex.

Trying to guess at emergent behavior is in principle very complex. However, in reality, it's often quite simple. If characters can become stronger by killing other characters (a feature of many CRPGs, but I'm thinking specifically of *Ultima Online*), then you will get player-killers.

Now, suppose you realize you're not getting the feature you want. You were aiming for the kind of world described in *Lord of the Rings*, but instead you've got people waiting to kill new players for the experience points. You need to understand why this behavior is being fostered by your game world. Adding extremely powerful AI-operated police, for example, is not really the most sensible solution. A shortage of police in the real world is not the primary factor in the murder-rate equation.

Instead, you might reason that altruism exists in real life because society creates a situation that does not reduce to a zero-sum game. In other words, all players can gain from cooperation. So you might look for rules that will create that kind of payoff. The most obvious real-world equivalent is that new players could go around in groups, which directly reflects the synergy of numbers. A single first-level character is an hors d'oeuvre for the player-killer, but 20 are a posse. However, players of CRPGs don't really want to join large groups. Because their paradigm is the solitary hero (Conan, Indiana Jones, and James Bond), you need some rule that gives individuals a benefit for committing to a group rather than being an outlaw. One way is to give player-characters more personal power the more allies they have, which is not unreasonable in a fantasy world in which each individual has a personal link to his deity and temple, say. And this is in fact the kind of solution being proposed by the designers of *Asheron's Call*, Microsoft's online CRPG. Case Study 2.6 is an example of rules serving a game's features.

Level Design

Level design affects the game; it is not just tagged on afterwards. Level design contributes greatly to the style, background, and story line of the game. Still more importantly, the way the levels are constructed can either enhance the inherent gameplay or detract from it. Although the lead designer is rarely the person who oversees the day-to-day design of the levels, he needs to address level-design issues in the game spec itself.

What level design shouldn't do is cover deficiencies in the gameplay. As we'll see in the next chapter, good gameplay consists of choices that are never trivial. Choices should never just be a question of recognizing that X is always better than Y, and so therefore you should always do X. A level that says, "You can't build bridges; find another way," begs the question, "Why are bridges in the game at all, then?" Case Study 2.7 is an example of level design.

Understanding The Game

The ways in which levels can complement the core game design should be described in your game spec. Remember that the spec will be used by the level designers, who may not yet have an accurate picture of how you expect the game to play. Describe how you envisage a

Case Study 2.6 The Rules Must Serve The Features

In *Warrior Kings*, I wanted to make formations useful in a couple of ways. First, they were a visible depiction of the AI behavior protocols, or standing orders, of those troops. But that was merely a handy way to make sure the game helped the player—an extension of the interface rather than a feature of the gameplay, in the same way that archery units in games like *Warcraft* and *Age of Empires* will open fire on the enemy without having to be told, because there is never a case when you wouldn't want them to.

But I also felt that units grouped in formation should be more robust than units on their own. They would be slower and less maneuverable in formation, so this was the main trade-off.

My first-pass solution was to share damage through a formation. This meant that, when one member of the formation was hit, part of that damage (a proportion depending on the formation type) would be split between all other units in the formation. This probably would have worked in a turn-based game, but I didn't even need to reach the testbed stage to see that it wasn't ideal in realtime, where the underlying game mechanics are a lot less visible. It would simply look odd.

So, my next idea (the one I'm using at the time of writing) is that the size and type of the formation increases the toughness of all of its members. When they take damage, a certain amount can just be ignored. This makes formations even more robust than I'd originally intended: a 20-strong battalion of pikemen in orb formation is a match for a 100 barbarians. I'll need to work on that, slowing the formation movement rates, maybe, or increasing the time taken to form up. But it is working now because the player can straightaway see the size and type of his formation, so it's easy to get an intuitive grasp of how good that is, and having units shrug off damage rather than share it around is credible in the context of the game.

typical level so that they don't jump to the wrong conclusions. In particular, point out the ways in which your game differs from a real-life equivalent. Otherwise, you may find the level designers creating levels that *ought* to work, not levels that actually do.

For example, suppose you had just been given the original game spec for *Age of Empires* and you were asked to design a level on paper. Never having seen the game, you might start with two cities on either side of a mountain range. A narrow pass is the only way between the two civilizations. "That pass will be strategically important," you might think. But no; there are no lines of supply in *Age of Empires*. Conquest therefore more closely resembles infection than invasion. That is, if I can get just one villager through that pass into enemy territory, I can build a suite of army buildings on his side of the mountains. I don't need to guard the pass because my supplies can be accessed by any of my villagers anywhere on the map.

This is not to say that *Age of Empires* is not an interesting game, merely that the kinds of scenario that would be interesting in real-world warfare won't necessarily be the same in a world that plays by different rules. Make sure your level designers understand those rules and their likely repercussions, by explicitly discussing them in the game spec.

Case Study 2.7 Interesting Level Design

The game being developed is *Arena*, a first-person action game with fantasy role-playing elements. Oliver, the chief level designer, is discussing his ideas with the game's lead designer, Stelios.

"The fireball spell is turning out to be quite powerful," says Oliver. "In playtesting we've been using them a lot."

Stelios frowns. "That's worrying. Maybe we should put in lots of fire-resistant creatures. No, scratch that—it'd just be a force-to-fit. I should make fire spells take longer to recharge, maybe, or have some other drawback like blowback, so that there's a game choice there..."

Oliver has seen that daydreaming look in Stelios' eyes before. Anxious to get the discussion back to specifics, he presses on: "Well, I have to get next week's level done. We thought we'd make it that the player just can't use the fireball spell on this level; it isn't available. Like all those levels in Dungeon Keeper where you can't build some types of room."

This has the desired effect of breaking Stelios' reverie, at least. "That's no good! The fireball spell is supposed to be an integral part of the game. If my game is designed properly, it can hardly be improved by cutting something out!"

"Okay, then," Oliver says quickly, having learned to be diplomatic when discussing gameplay issues, "would it be interesting if this level only had limited oxygen? The player could still use the fireball spells, but he'd be using up the oxygen every time he did."

"But there's already a lifebreath spell, which the player could use even though he's not underwater." Stelios starts to get that thoughtful look again. "Actually, that's something we could leave the player to figure out for himself, isn't it? And if you make some of the foes on this level completely flameproof, but they need oxygen to breathe too..."

"...Then the player could put on lifebreath and use fireballs to suffocate them," agrees Oliver. "Fiendish! This could be an interesting level after all."

Nonlinear Level Design

It's my belief that the best level design is not linear and instead allows for interactivity. Linear level design requires that the player must tackle problem A, then problem B, and so on. The way to solve each problem might still be interesting, but the linear structure precludes the possibility of strategic thinking, whereby the order in which you tackle the problems is an interesting gameplay element in its own right.

A good game should allow for tactics (short-term decisions, like which gun to use) and strategy (long-term decisions, like what path to take for victory). Following the thesis that level design should provide an opportunity to showcase the game's merits and not close off valid choices, a nonlinear approach is the best way to achieve this.

However, designing interesting nonlinear levels isn't easy. It requires a good underlying game system, and it requires the designer to "let go." He has to trust that the game itself is more interesting than the puzzles he might devise using it. This is an act of faith that is only justified if the design contains good gameplay, which is something we shall be looking at in the next chapter.

Example Game Spec

To round off this chapter, we're going to look at the bare bones of the *Warrior Kings* game spec.

Obviously, there isn't space to put everything here. The complete design would half fill this book! But it's useful to consider this as a checklist of the things you will need to cover. Case Study 2.8 is an example of game spec.

The Value Of Prototypes...

Along with the game spec, I recommend producing any kind of prototypes that you can use as proof of concept. For *Warrior Kings*, I sketched out a simple board game to test the campaign structure that will link a sequence of levels.

Board-game prototypes are fine for something like that. I specifically wanted to keep the campaign system simple, in fact, because it isn't the main point of the game. I didn't want players having to deal with continually moving resources and armies around their provinces, when the game they bought was supposed to be a realtime wargame. So a board-game version was a good way to make sure the campaign system didn't grow out of control.

Board-game prototypes of the game itself are getting harder. Realtime, 3D, and artificial life are all hard to model with paper and pencil. Increasingly, however, there are powerful commercial software development kits (SDKs) that you can use to mock-up your game and even take it into full development. Among several good products, I will mention *NemoDev* from Virtools (**www.nemosoftware.com**), which I find useful for putting together my own prototype designs.

...And The Necessity Of Documents

However, I believe that prototypes are only adjuncts to the game spec document; they cannot replace it.

Documentation explains what you are trying to achieve and how you might get there, whereas a software prototype merely demonstrates the end result. The code architecture may be very different from what the designer imagines when writing the game spec (if, indeed, he thinks about it at all). And, while game rules and features are the province of the designer, the implementation of those rules and features is best left to your software planner.

Case Study 2.8 Game Spec

Summarized template for creating a game spec.

Overview

Warrior Kings is a realtime strategy game set in the Middle Ages. It is not overly historical: this is "fun medieval" not "real medieval." Players build cities and must manage an agricultural and geographically widespread economy while waging war on each other.

Games are expected to take longer than *Age of Empires*, say, because of the need to build up an army of multiple troop types and keep it supplied in the field in order to win total victory.

Players

The game will support both solo and multiplay. Up to six players can compete in freeform games as well as in scenarios with specific objectives, such as maximizing piety (religious merit), being first to build a Star Chamber, etc. Any player may be human or computer.

If time allows, there may be other races with different mixes of units. But such differences will be quite minimal, with only one or two units being unique to each race, i.e., like *Warcraft 2* rather than *StarCraft*.

The first *WK* release will definitely feature a European medieval race. Other possible races are Saracens, Byzantines, and Mongols.

Look And Feel

The main screen will be a full 3D view of a medieval landscape dotted with trees, rivers, farms, etc. Levels will be much larger than the view on the main screen. The camera can be tilted and rotated without restriction, as well as scrolled anywhere on the landscape. Some kind of "fog of war" effect will prevent a player seeing what's going on in any place where he doesn't have characters.

Art style is based principally on late-medieval sources such as Brueghel. Characters will be polygon-based, not sprites: tiny industrious figures tilling the soil, hacking back forests, erecting great cathedrals. Buildings will be based on those of the 14th and 15th centuries.

Films to look at are *The Hunchback Of Notre Dame, The Adventures Of Baron Munchausen*, and *The Seventh Seal*.

Musical sources: *Carmina Burana*, "Siegfried's Funeral March," Gregorian chant, Tudor lute music.

Books: *Strange Landscape, A World Lit Only By Fire*, The Paston Letters.

Interface

Commands are issued via mouse-selected icons. Selecting a unit and then right-clicking on something will "intuit" the command. For example, selecting a military unit and right-clicking on an enemy unit is interpreted as Attack. There will also be keyboard shortcuts.

A side-of-screen interface layout is used as in *Command & Conquer*. This shows statistics for the selected unit(s), available command icons, and a circular minimap of the entire level.

The area in view on the main screen is highlighted on the minimap as a trapezoidal window. Rotating the main view causes this window to rotate, but does not rotate the minimap itself. (This is to avoid disorientating the player.)

Start Up

Most levels begin with several manor houses scattered across the landscape, each with one or more farms. Each player controls several manors. At the start of the game, peasants are already working the farms; they can be reassigned or left at those tasks.

Each player also has at least one palace where his resources are located. Resources must be brought to a palace before they get added to a player's stocks.

The first game choices involve spawning more peasants or townsmen, assigning them to different tasks, collecting resources, building new structures, and exploring the landscape.

Objectives

The object of the game varies according to the scenario. It will be some combination of the following:

- Destroy all enemy characters
- Destroy or capture enemy buildings
- Maximize your own resources
- Steal or damage enemy resources
- Achieve a custom objective (in special scenarios)

Entities

Entities in the game are structures, characters, world objects, and other units.

Characters are civilian or military.

Military units are pikeman, archer, knight, etc.

Features

Features are resources, supply lines, battalions, acts of God, and so on.

Many (not all) key military units can be grouped into battalions. Battalions can be placed in formation, which defines behavior protocols and gives some formation-specific combat advantages, usually at a cost in speed or maneuverability, and so on.

Rules

The five formation types are column, orb, line, scattered, and wedge.

Units that can be grouped into formation are pikemen, archers, knights, lancers, mercenaries, and sergeants.

Allowed formations for pikemen are column, orb, line, and scattered. Allowed formations for archers are... and so on.

Units in scattered formation retreat if taking proportionately more damage than they are inflicting on their target. (This is intended to lead to skirmishing, so the calculation must be done a little ahead of time, to give the unit time to turn and move away. This will require tweaking.)

Gameplay

Placing units in formation assigns them a standard "behavior protocol," which the formation layout allows the player to see at a glance when viewing his army. Units in scattered formation will retreat if seriously threatened (although missile troops will occasionally stop, turn, and loose a volley at their pursuers). Units in wedge will always attack with persistence if an enemy comes within charge range, and so on. (See Features and Rules.)

It's anticipated that the use of formations will allow players to set up reasonably reliable battle plans, preventing the usual problem in realtime wargames where your mix of units arrive at the wrong time because you didn't click the mouse button fast enough. *Warrior Kings* is designed to appeal to the adult market (15 years up), and hand-eye coordination should not be too decisive a factor. Strategic thinking is what counts.

Military units in the field cannot recover hit points unless supplied with food. (See §8 Features.) This encourages players to consolidate before expanding to protect their lines of supply. Conversely, the player who succeeds with a daring raid on enemy supply lines may be able to win in spite of poor odds. The terrain on any given level will determine how easy this may be, with mountain passes being of key strategic importance.

Level Design

Levels with plenty of level, open ground will favor the use of units in formation. Levels where the terrain contains many hills, chasms, and stretches of difficult ground will militate against massed formations, instead encouraging the use of more-mobile and/or -versatile units in small groups.

Most levels will not be exclusively one type of terrain. However, levels must be predominantly level or gently rolling terrain with infrequent cliffs if the feature of troop formations is to be worthwhile. (In the extremely bumpy terrain of *Populous 3*, formations would not be worth including because they would never be used.)

Cavalry tend to be faster than infantry but are more seriously affected by difficult terrain such as marshes, heavy snow, broken heathland, etc. A level with swathes of such terrain will force the player to think about how to use his cavalry.

Technical Requirements

Only a PC version is planned. Minimum spec will be Pentium 200, with a graphics card... and so on.

Marketing

The client's Marketing Department have sales figures and projections for this genre. It's expected that the appeal of *WK* will be akin to the thoughtful strategic gameplay of *Alpha Centauri* or *Settlers* rather than the furiously fast action of *StarCraft*. The game's unique selling points (USPs) are... and so on.

This summary of the game spec for *Warrior Kings* should give you a template to follow as you design your latest blockbuster.

Chapter 3
Gameplay

Key Topics:

- *Gameplay means interesting choices*
- *The use of strategies*
- *Different kinds of interactivity*

Now, let's take a closer look at some of the things we mentioned in the last chapter. In particular, we'll be examining gameplay—what it means, how to achieve it, and how to enhance it.

What's so special about gameplay? Absolutely nothing. We already said that a software product doesn't have to be a game to be entertaining. Famously, *SimCity* has been described by its creator as more of a toy than a game. And the foremost aim of simulation war games is to re-create the reality on which they're modeled. If you have a pure Conquistador simulation, it may not be a good well-balanced game at all (it may not be possible for the Aztec player to win), but it could still be fun to play.

Only precedent makes us demand gameplay in entertainment software. No one demands the same thing of a movie or a book. Plenty of things are enjoyable that aren't games. Who's going to say, "Hey, that Hamlet is a great drama but where's the gameplay?"

Rule Number One is still that your product should be fun (which is where the entertainment part comes in). To be a "good" software product implies that it will also be interactive. That's what will make it deliver something that you could not deliver in any other medium. But gameplay? That's a matter of choice.

Later in this chapter, we'll discuss some other kinds of entertainment software that are interactive (certainly) and fun (hopefully) but aren't necessarily games at all. I'll start with an examination of gameplay not because it's sacred but because—if you're trying to design a game—an understanding of gameplay is essential.

What Is Gameplay?

Imagine you are playing a role-playing game, and that your group of adventurers comprises the usual mix of knight, priest, dwarf, and thief. (Okay, it's boring already, but we're looking at gameplay here, not originality.) During an encounter, you typically want your fighters—that's the dwarf and the knight—at the front of the group while your thief snipes from one side with arrows or throwing knives. Your priest, who is vulnerable, stays at the back to cast spells.

Now, suppose the priest has two kinds of spells, each of which costs the same number of magic points. One spell injures the enemy (we'll call these "E-Bolts"), and the other heals injuries to your own group ("Band-aids"). Which should he cast during a fight?

First off, suppose the E-Bolts do as much damage as a sword blow and that the Band-aids heal the same amount. When facing opponents who are equally matched with your own fighters, E-Bolts and Band-aids are equally useful. Against a single foe that uses several weapons (an insect creature with a sword in each of six hands, for example), You are obviously better off using E-Bolts. When facing a horde of opponents with individually weak attacks, such as a pack of rats, you are probably going to use Band-aids. The point is that, in each case, you can quite easily decide which spell is better.

However, suppose instead that Band-aids still affect only a single target, but E-Bolts are area-effect spells that damage all the enemies in a given radius. Suppose, also, that E-Bolts don't do quite as much damage as before, but the target's armor no longer makes a difference. Now which is the best to use?

There's no easy answer, as this depends on lots of things—which is what makes it an interesting choice. And that's what gameplay is all about.

Implementing Gameplay

Sid Meier said, "A game is a series of interesting choices." To be worthwhile, gameplay choices must be nontrivial. Each strategy that the player considers must have an upside and a downside. If there is only an upside, the AI should take care of it automatically. If there's only a downside, no one will ever use that strategy. So why bother including it in the game?

A decision has gameplay value if it has an upside and a downside *and* the overall payoff depends on other factors. Usually, this will be something along the lines of "What if the other player uses neutron torpedoes?" or "What if I'm too close to the sun when the warp drive kicks in?" So you choose the option that seems best in the circumstances. It might be that you can see a better tactic but you simply don't have the manual dexterity to pull it off. That's still a game choice, albeit one that is likely to have hardened strategy gamers grinding their teeth.

It's also important to note that the game must be a *series* of interesting choices, with each decision affecting the next. The value of using the nail gun as opposed to the mining laser depends on whether your previous decision was to run to the center of the room or skulk in the corner, which depends on whether you set the cargo bay doors to blow or not, and so on. Hence, a game allows strategy. Indeed, a well-designed game cannot be won without strategy, and strategy manifests itself as a series of interesting choices. We've come full circle.

All this requires the game to display complexity. This doesn't mean, however, that the rules themselves must be complex. In the last chapter, we looked at the concept of emergence—complexity arising from simple rules. A neat example of emergence that I like is the termite's nest. Termites build towers of dried mud with cooling vanes inside that keep the nest at the precise temperature needed to incubate the eggs. But no termite has a blueprint of this wonderful structure in its head; it has only a few simple rules to follow about where to put each bit of mud.

Emergence results from rules (behaviors) interacting with other rules or the environment. Resist the temptation to design too many rules, as the best games follow the less-is-more principle. In the rest of this chapter, we'll discuss how very often the simplest rule sets are the ones that lead to the most-interesting gameplay.

The Dominant Strategy Problem

How often have you flicked through gaming magazines and seen articles promising "10 killer tactics" or claiming to disclose the ultimate character, weapon, or maneuver in your favorite game?

If those articles are on the level (as they too often are), what they are doing is taking advantage of flaws in the game design. A game shouldn't contain an option that is never worth using. So it certainly shouldn't have a best maneuver, or character, or weapon; otherwise, what is the point of the other maneuvers, characters, and weapons?

To borrow some terminology from game theory, an option that is never worth using under any circumstances is a *dominated* strategy. An option that is so good it's never worth doing anything else is a *dominant* strategy.

Dominance means that some of the options you designed into your game—and maybe even all but one of the options—are useless. If they're useless, it means that players will pretty quickly drop them and won't use them ever again. Not only is that bad game design, it is a waste of development time as well. The only people happy to see dominance in a game are the magazine columnists, because it makes thinking of strategy tips a lot easier.

Summing up, then, a dominated option is worthless, and you waste your time putting it in a game. A dominant option is still worse. It means that *all* the other options are worthless.

Near Dominance

Spend some time looking for dominance to see if you have options that will rarely be used. It's worth taking some time to look for *near dominance* as well. A near-dominated option is one that is useful in only very narrow circumstances. Conversely, a near-dominant option is one that players will use most of the time.

Let's consider an example of a near-dominated option: you put a special weapon in your game, a stun gun that is worth using against only one foe, the raptors. Since the stun gun has no effect on other foes, you won't see it used except on the raptor level. This is obvious, but still it's valuable information. It means you can ask yourself these questions:

1. Did we want the stun gun to be a more common feature?
   - Should we think of other applications?
   - Is the one-off use a positive feature? What should we do to make the most of that?
2. If the stun gun is going to be used only once during the game, how much development time is it worth spending on it?
   - Should we spend a lot of effort on this feature?
   - Is it worth putting in some special effects just for the raptor encounter?
3. What's the best way of building the stun gun into the interface, as compared with weapons that are more commonly used?

A game with lasting appeal must remain interesting even when players know the tricks. Near dominance isn't as disastrous as dominance: a careless player could overlook the near-dominated option, and opponents can exploit that. But near dominance does show which options will get used most, and logically those are the ones on which you'll want to lavish the best graphics.

Avoiding Trivial Choices

Good gameplay is achieved when the player faces problems that have nontrivial solutions. But how do you avoid designing in trivial choices?

For this example, I'll be talking about units in a war game, but they could just as easily be different maneuvers, weapons, spells, or whatever, as the principle is the same. Say that the three units are warriors, barbarians, and archers. Figure 3.1 shows one possible way that the combat relationships among them might work.

This is a transitive relationship. Warriors are best, then barbarians, then archers. Now consider the intransitive version in Figure 3.2.

Warriors still beat barbarians, and barbarians beat archers, but now archers can beat warriors. It's a little bit more interesting. In fact, it ought to remind you of something familiar. That's right, it's Paper-Scissors-Stone. The example in this case comes from Dave and Barry

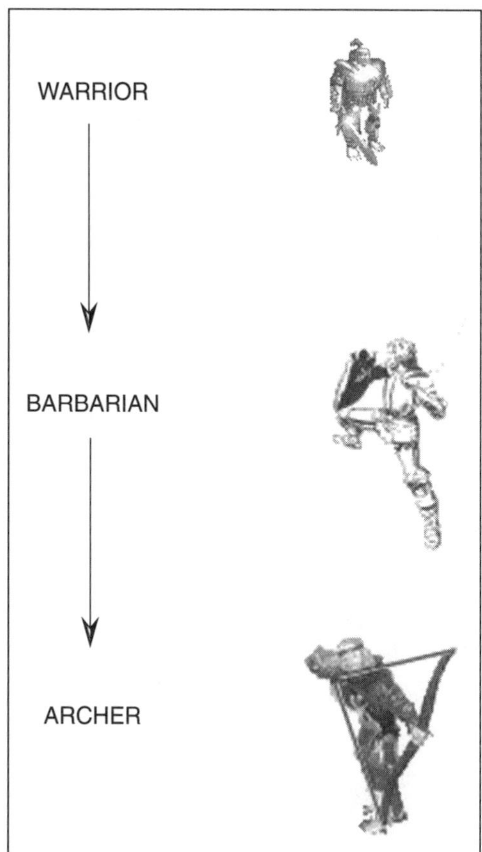

Figure 3.1
Transitive combat relationship.

Murray's 1984 game *The Ancient Art of War*. The warriors were stronger at close quarters than barbarians, but they were slow; the barbarians, on the other hand, were fast enough to reach the archers shooting at them without taking much damage from their arrows.

There's more to be learned from Stone-Paper-Scissors, and we'll analyze it rigorously in Chapter 5. For now, though, it's worth emphasizing that a nontransitive relation like Stone-Paper-Scissors is only the *minimum* condition to get interesting choices. It ensures a dynamic equilibrium, which keeps the game from stagnating, but it's really just first base.

To illustrate this, suppose you're putting a Stone-Paper-Scissors kind of setup into your game and you decide to hard wire it. That is, A beats B, B beats C, C beats A (in each case according to some look-up table that applies in all circumstances). If you did it that way, you would need to decide the values for the look-up table: how *much* better is each unit than the next one round the chain?

Figure 3.3 shows one option, in which a single warrior can beat any number of barbarians.

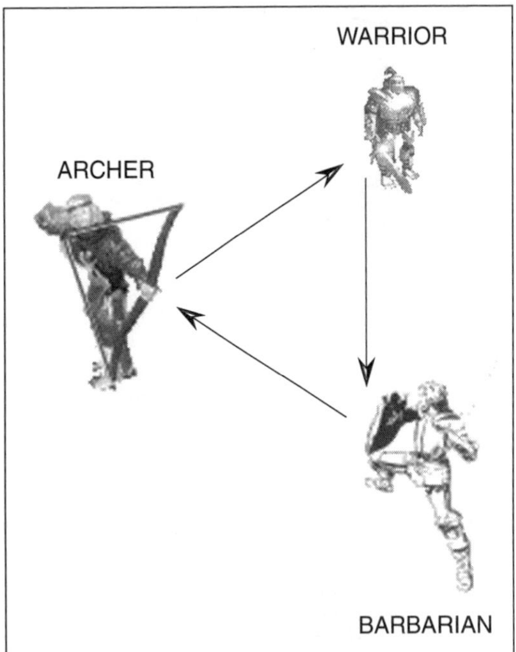

Figure 3.2
Intransitive combat relationship.

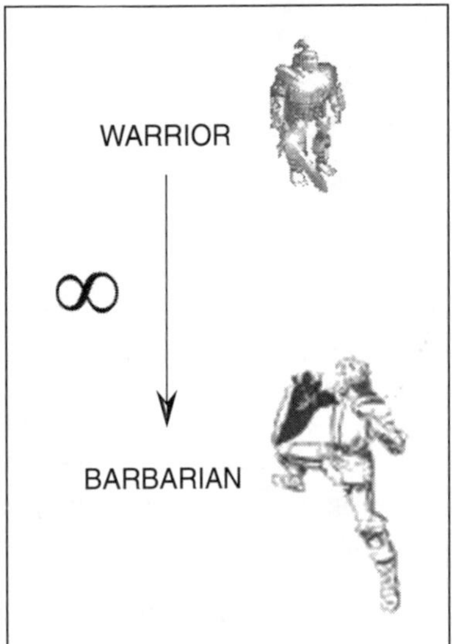

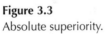

Figure 3.3
Absolute superiority.

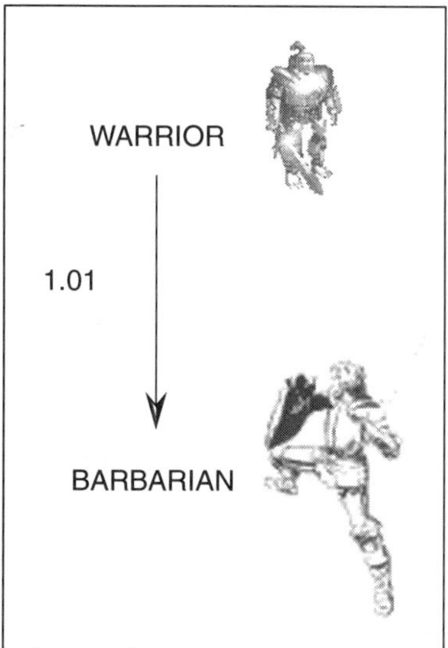

Figure 3.4
Marginal superiority

And Figure 3.4 shows the opposite extreme. Now, the warrior is just a tiny bit better than the barbarian, so 99 warriors are an even match for 100 barbarians.

Which of these is better? Don't waste time thinking about it; it's a trick question! *Neither* of them leads to interesting gameplay. In the first case (assuming all units have the same cost), armies will have to consist of an equal mix of A, B, and C units; all other combinations will lose. In the second case, a player loses very little by fielding the wrong unit, and the unit interaction becomes virtually redundant.

So, you can't hard wire in a single rule and hope for interesting gameplay. It just won't happen. What's needed is a dynamic relationship among different strategies, so that, in some cases, A is much better than B, and, in other cases, there's little to choose between them. And, sometimes, maybe the worm can turn, and B can beat A.

Stone-Paper-Scissors is a first step in avoiding trivial gameplay. It means there isn't a single optimum strategy that wins every time. However, there *should* be an optimum strategy for each situation, "situations" in a good game being complex because they include not only terrain, altitude, weather, time, the obvious things, but also whatever your opponents are doing. Case Study 3.1 provides an example of gameplay.

Ensuring Interesting Choices

Elite was one of the seminal games of the early '80s. The goal of the game was to accumulate wealth in the form of credits by trading among planets. When a player had earned 1,000 credits, he could trade in his pulse laser and get a beam laser and 400 credits in exchange.

Case Study 3.1 Environment Plus Rules Equals Gameplay

At the Battle of Hastings in 1066 AD, King Harold of England had the dual problems of an exhausted army (having just force-marched the length of the country after another battle) and an enemy with a better mix of troops. Duke William of Normandy had more and better archers, as well as cavalry in the form of his Norman knights. Harold, by contrast, was obliged to rely on infantry. The mainstay of his army, his housecarls with their massive axes, were formidable fighters but lacked the mobility for an offensive battle.

Knowing this, Harold drew up his troops on Senlac Hill, near Hastings, and awaited the Norman onslaught.

Under normal conditions, the Norman archers could have skirmished against the unsupported infantry and won eventual victory. Their volleys would pick off targets and, whenever the lumbering infantry in their heavy mail hauberks came too close, the archers could always run away.

That was the classic theory of medieval warfare. On this occasion, Harold had found a way to refute the theory. Shooting uphill, the archers' volleys proved less effective. Harold's men were able to stand their ground, their kite shields interlocked to form a defensive wall around them. Even so, initially some of the arrows found their mark. Now and then one of the English soldiers would fall. The housecarls yearned to charge down the hill, but Harold knew that the enemy archers would counter that by retreating, and then would have the advantage. He ordered his men to stand and, as the day wore on, the Norman archers grew tired. Their arrows carried less force. They fell harmlessly among the housecarls, like twigs.

Harold was wise in warfare, but Duke William also had some tricks. Ordinarily, the Duke would not have ordered his cavalry against the English shield wall. Horses will not charge onto a solid line of infantry (that is, assuming that the infantrymen know this and have the courage to stand firm). Harold's army did not lack for courage, William knew; they had the opposite problem. He sent his knights in wave after wave against the English line. Each time, the knights would wheel around at the last moment, or take a few lance thrusts against the shields of the English footmen, and then ride off.

The English housecarls had suffered arrows raining down on them all day, had little patience for a long wait, and liked much better to be in the thick of battle. Now they had to watch Norman knights turn their backs and flee. Many broke from the line and charged.

Off the hill, the conventional theory of combined arms prevailed. Archers could inflict injury on infantry who lacked the mobility to close with them. If the infantry charged in an effort to catch the archers, enemy knights could ride in amongst them and wreak havoc.

If things had been different, could Harold have won? No one knows, but the point is that he understood that there are ways to change the balance between different troop types. A good commander isn't the one with the best army; he is the one who knows best how to use it.

The 400 credits kept the player in a good position to trade, and the beam laser was far superior to the pulse laser. Therefore, the player would regard the decision to upgrade as a no-brainer. The curious part of the choice was that you had to have 1,000 credits before you could spend 600 on a beam laser. Had the beam laser been available as soon as you had 600 credits, an interesting choice would have been created: whether to upgrade right now (but have no credits left to trade with), or carry on trading armed with a substandard weapon.

In the context of a great game, it was a small-enough flaw, but it remains highly illustrative because a difficult choice had been taken out of the hands of the player.

Here are the kinds of choices a game can involve:

- An option that should sometimes be taken, and sometimes not, depending on other factors
- An option whose timing is critical and depends on the context
- An option that makes little difference whether you take it or not
- An option that is always worth taking
- An option that is never worth taking at any point in the game

The first two are evidently the most interesting in a gameplay sense. The third kind (choices that don't make much difference) are perfectly valid, but they're chrome and should be recognized as such. These should be the first options to be cut as the deadline draws closer. Options always worth taking should be handled by the AI, and options that are never worth taking will be fun only once (if that) and thus you shouldn't waste your developers' time on them.

A Toolbox Of Interesting Choices

Interesting choices are those that require good judgment on the part of the player, which means that the correct choice must vary with the circumstances. So, your aim as a designer is to ensure that those circumstances will never stagnate to the point that there is only one right way to win.

There is no method for finding the best and most-intriguing choices. That's where the creative process comes in! Even so, you can follow a number of tips to ensure that the gameplay choices aren't trivial.

Strategic Choices

Strategic choices are those that affect the course of the game over the medium or long term, which is distinct from tactical choices (which apply *right now*). Strategic choices will have a knock-on effect on the player's range of tactical choices later, so they are a prime means of enabling good gameplay.

StarCraft is a typically well-designed game from Blizzard. One of the choices in the game is whether you should first upgrade the range of your Marines' rifles, or upgrade the damage the rifles do, or research the StimPack that will allow the Marines to fire faster. This decision requires some thought: if you are expecting heavily armored foes, such as a Protoss Zealot, you will probably want the extra damage, but lots of fast-moving opponents like Zerglings call for different tactics. Other factors that will influence your choice are how many Marines you have, what the surrounding terrain is like, whether you have bunkers built, and whether you anticipate an offensive or defensive campaign.

Note

Warzone 2100 includes a beautiful example of strategic decision making. The player needs to build manufacturing plants to spawn his war machines. Optionally, he can build these manufacturing plants in the current level—in which case they deliver units quickly but only for use in that level—or he can build them back at his main base, which means that new units arrive more slowly but the plant can be used to provide units in later levels, too.

Sometimes one option will be called for; sometimes another will be. A player who selects options according to a set plan will not do as well as one who adapts to circumstances. The lesson is that, to create good gameplay, different choices should lead to different kinds of payoff. In this way, you reduce the risk that choices will be trivial, and increase the scope for good judgment.

Supporting Investments

Often a game has—in addition to a primary objective—secondary aims that have to be attended to before you can reach the final goal. For example, the primary goal might be to destroy the enemy, but to do that you might need to build farms to produce food to spawn peasants to trade to make money to recruit soldiers, and so on.

Some expenditure directly achieves your eventual goal. In a war game, an example might be buying a mercenary. Other types of expenditures indirectly work towards your goal, and these are called *supporting investments*.

Primary supporting investments operate at one remove. For instance, improving weapons technology to make your mercenaries tougher, or building an extra barracks to house these mercenaries.

Other supporting investments work more indirectly, for instance, building a smithy so that weapons can be upgraded, or researching construction techniques so that barracks can be built more quickly.

Note that researching construction techniques helps at both the second and third remove: it helps you build barracks to attract mercenaries, and it helps you build smithies to research technology to improve mercenaries. This kind of complexity is excellent, because it makes the decision to research less simple and more interesting.

By including decisions that operate at different levels, you create the need for players to think strategically. The payoff for choosing different investments will alter according to what other players do.

Versatility

A useful rule of thumb for anticipating gameplay is to ask what is the best and worst thing about each possible choice the player can make. For instance:

- This maneuver does the most damage, but it's the slowest.
- This maneuver is the fastest, but it leaves me defenseless.
- This maneuver gives the best defense, but it does little damage.

And then there's a unique kind of choice:

- This maneuver is never the best or the worst, but it's the most versatile.

So, a useful question to ask yourself when designing a weapon or strategy for your game is "When, if ever, is this the best option for the player?" Most choices that you put into the game should be the best in some way. And one of these can be the choice that works only moderately well, but in many different ways: the jack-of-all-trades option.

The more unpredictable the game environment is, the bigger the payoff for the versatility of choice. Beginners in particular will benefit from versatile options, as it means there's something they can do while working their way up the learning curve. But versatile options are handy for expert players, too. Against an expert opponent, we must expect the unexpected, and choosing the versatile maneuver or unit may buy time to put together a more considered response.

One obvious kind of versatility in a war game is speed. The fast-moving character or unit can quickly go where it's needed. So, normally, you won't want the fastest units to also be the best in other ways.

Also, the value of a fast-moving unit depends on the game environment. On the battlefields of the fourteenth century, a knight was deemed to be worth 100 foot soldiers. That wasn't because knights were as tough as a 100 men were but rather, in a terrain of hedgerows, ditches, ploughed fields, and heathland, the knight had more chance of being in the right place at the right time.

An option can be made versatile in many other ways. If a beam weapon can be used to mine asteroids as well as to destroy incoming nuclear missiles, then that versatility can make up for a disadvantage elsewhere. Of course, if there is no compensating disadvantage, there's no interesting choice. Be careful not to make the versatile choice dominant over all others. Also, be aware that the versatility of a choice may not be obvious even to you as designer. In the last chapter, we saw how the designer of the fantasy game *Arena* hadn't originally anticipated the way players might use the fireball spells. Case Study 3.2 provides an example of unexpected versatility.

Case Study 3.2 Unexpected Versatility

In 1997, I was working with Jamie Thomson on *Abraxas*, an online CRPG (Computer Role Playing Game) for a major U.K. developer. One of the things we wanted was for the game world to have its own laws for the players to discover and exploit. As Jamie put it, "We might suddenly find that a player in Ohio has invented the *Abraxas* equivalent of the steam engine."

One of the factors we were considering was combustion. The temperature scale ranged from -30 (equivalent to absolute zero) up to +1,000, with 0 being comfortable room temperature. Materials had an ignition temperature, a burning temperature (within the flame), and a radiative temperature (adjacent to the flame). So, oil would ignite at +6, the temperature of its flame was +4, and the flame modified the ambient temperature by +1. (The range of that effect depended on the size of the flame.)

In one playtesting session, players were transporting barrels of phlogiston, a magical substance that burns with a cold flame. They got caught in a blizzard and the temperature dropped to -8, which was definitely life threatening. Now, the properties of phlogiston were that it ignited at +5, burned at -5 and had a radiative temperature of -1. How could they use it to save themselves? A phlogiston fire couldn't warm them because it would merely reduce the ambient temperature by 1, taking it down to -9.

Then somebody realized that the temperature within the flame was constant irrespective of the environment, and, because phlogiston burned at a negative temperature, it wouldn't ignite them or their belongings. So they started a fire and survived the night by sitting inside the flames at a cold but tolerable -5. They had found a versatile solution that we had never expected.

You can measure versatility by looking at the *switching costs* in the game. This is how much it costs a player to change his mind about the strategy he's using. An example in an espionage game might be if we recruit a spy and later realize we need an assassin instead. The switching cost is however much we wasted on the wrong character, assuming for the sake of argument that the spy is not usable elsewhere. So, say that both cost $1 up front. When deciding which to buy, at first I'd think, "If I buy the spy and I need the assassin, I'll end up paying $2. If I choose right, it costs me just the $1. On the other hand, suppose I buy both now: I only need one, so I'll have definitely wasted $1."

Suppose there is another character, the ninja, who can function as either spy or assassin. How much should the ninja cost? It depends on how unpredictable the game is. In this example, if the game were completely predictable, the player would know in advance which character to recruit, and so versatility is of no value: the ninja should cost $1 just like the others. In a completely unpredictable environment, the average cost would be $1.50 ($1 if we choose right, $2 if we choose wrong), which is what a good gambler would pay you for the ninja. Because the truth will lie between those extremes, the versatile unit should cost more than $1 but less than $2.

Versatility is more prized in an uncertain environment. No game is completely predictable, because you can never know what the other player(s) will do. Even in a relatively predictable game, some levels are more uncertain than others. All of which makes the choice between specialization or versatility an interesting one because it all depends on the circumstances.

Compensating Factors

Say we design an aerial unit that can cross any terrain in the game. It's the best at getting places because no other unit can cross all terrain types: ships can't go on land, mountaineers can't cross oceans, camel riders are slowed by forests, and so on. But this aerial unit can go anywhere. How can we balance that?

- We could make it slow.
- We could make it weak (for example, easily destroyed).
- We could give it low surveillance range (rather unlikely).
- We could make it expensive to buy.

The last of those isn't so good, though, because it doesn't oblige the player to use the unit in an interesting way. He either buys the unit or he doesn't, and once he's made that choice he's committed. The choice whether to buy might be strategically interesting, but it won't lead to clever tactics.

These are all compensating factors. They ensure that any game choice has something in its favor and something weighing against it.

Compensating factors work only when it is clear to the player what they are. Maybe you decide that the powerful unit is worth having despite the fact that it's so expensive. (You intend to make a big push and grab the oil fields.) Maybe you'll fail, but the choice is yours, and it is an informed choice. Case Study 3.3 provides an example of balancing compensating factors.

From a gameplay perspective, compensating factors are worthless if the player finds out about them only *after* making the decision that they apply to—for instance, if we had to choose a commando squad before seeing the mission it were to undertake. Maybe the arctic survival expert's many strengths are counterbalanced by not having the disguise and fast-talk skills of the CIA man. So what if the mission I've picked them both for is a hike through tropical jungle to blow up a bridge?

There are exceptions. *Magic & Mayhem* is a game in which you must pick your spells without knowing which ones your opponent has to choose from, and you are then stuck with only those spells in the duel. But *Magic & Mayhem* makes up for this with other features, and it, in any case, is almost a role-playing game (so gameplay is rarely the most important factor).

Impermanence

All decisions that pay off lead to some kind of advantage. Some advantages are long lasting: I grabbed the crate, and I got the bonus. Others are impermanent: I built my base near the tiberium, sure, but you can still grab it off me.

Case Study 3.3 Balancing Compensating Factors

Shapeshifter is a proposed action-adventure game that allows the player to take the form of various creatures. Each creature has unique abilities. To ensure a degree of strategic choice, the designer, Martin, builds in a cost in magic points each time the player changes shape.

Martin is describing one of the creatures at a development team meeting. "The werewolf is by far the strongest character in the game when the moon is full, and invulnerable to anything but silver bullets, but he's only as tough as a normal man at other times."

One of the level designers, Sandra, is skeptical. "If we have a full-moon level, which I assume we are, then any player who has the points to transform into a werewolf will always do it. And on other levels you can see how long until there's a full moon, so you can save up your points. It's a no-brainer. Is that good gameplay?"

"It's not quite that simple," says Martin. "First of all, didn't we say we can have weather effects? If the moon goes behind a cloud, or if another player casts a fog spell, that weakens the moonlight, and the werewolf isn't so useful."

Sandra isn't entirely convinced. "Well, the weather effects are random, so that makes changing to wolf form just a gamble rather than a game decision. I can see the point if other players can raise a fog, though."

"What about the silver bullets?" points out Kay, the software planner. "Either another player will have one—in which case the werewolf is dead—or not, in which case the werewolf wins hands down."

Martin considers this. "Obviously we don't want it all decided from the start of the level. So there will have to be a silver bullet somewhere on the full-moon level, and finding it has to be difficult."

"It still comes down to another gamble," points out Sandra. "Do I spend a lot of points changing to a werewolf, or go looking for the silver bullet and hope I find it before the werewolf player finds me? It's just luck. I'm not sure these are interesting choices."

"You know what?" said Kay. "It's this simple. The silver bullet is going to be very effective against the werewolf, which means it needs to be less useful in other ways. It might be that it does less damage to other characters, or it might be more expensive. But simply making it rare or hard to find is a bad way to balance it, because that takes the choice whether to use it out of the players' hands."

Impermanence gives the designer another way to confront the player with difficult choices. Would I rather have good armor for the rest of the game, or be completely invulnerable for 30 seconds? Of course, it depends on the circumstances.

Advantages (and disadvantages) can be impermanent in a number of ways:

- They can be destroyed by chance or by enemy action.
- They can be stolen or converted.

- They can apply to something that you don't always have (your heavy cavalry, your jet bike, your wand of flame).
- They can have a certain number of uses (six bullets in a magazine).
- They can last for a certain time (the spell wears off at midnight).

Impermanence is of course another kind of compensating factor. (See above.) But it is one that occurs so often in games, and has such special consequences, that it is worth considering as a separate category of choice.

Shadow Costs

In every game, players are continually being presented with costs and trade-offs. A cost doesn't have to mean money or victory points; it can be simply the things I had to succeed at before I could get to the options I'm facing next. What is the real cost of a game choice, in terms of time, effort, attention, and alternative resources required to get there? In *Warrior Kings*, I can hire mercenaries for gold. But the cost of a mercenary isn't only the gold I spend to hire him. I first had to build shops and townsmen to trade in them, and a tavern to attract the mercenaries to my town in the first place. So, I need to consider everything I had to go through to hire that mercenary. This is the shadow cost.

Note that shadow costs are related to supporting investments. Tracing a flowchart for all supporting investments will show you the kinds of strategic choices the player has to make. Summing all the factors along one particular branch of that flowchart tells you the shadow cost required to reach each node of it. Case Study 3.4 is an example of shadow costs in *Age of Empires*.

Synergies

Synergies are the interaction between different elements of the player's strategic arsenal. They take four forms, as evidenced in Table 3.1.

Table 3.1 Synergies.

Good Fit = Positive Feedback	Economies of Scale: The more units of one type you have, the better each unit is. If your magicians draw strength from each other, then the value of a new magician is greater if you already have many others. Economies of Scope: Of obvious use representing the advantage of a combined arms (for example, infantry units should be supported by tanks). Also covers the use of complementary gadgets (such as mining lasers with mineral scoops, or a gladiator fighting with a net and trident).
Poor Fit = Negative Feedback	Diseconomies of Scale: The first unit is the most useful—after a while, it's not worth getting many more. Some investments are designed to be increasingly costly—although this sometimes disguises a drop in the real shadow cost. Diseconomies of Scope: Mixed troops must move at the pace of the slowest, and must be given different orders. Sometimes a focused approach is better than hedging your bets and being able to do nothing well.

Case Study 3.4 Shadow Costs In Age Of Empires

The primary resources of *Age of Empires* are wood and food. Food is pretty much an inexhaustible resource within the confines of the game, but wood—although easy to harvest—is finite.

Consider a charioteer. The apparent costs of the charioteer are 60 wood, 40 food, and 40 seconds to spawn. This unit's shadow cost, however, changes greatly over the course of the game. Early on, when the player's economy is underdeveloped, both food and wood are expensive. The 40 seconds' spawning time is not so important, though. Later in the game, wood and food are plentiful, and your main concern is how quickly you can pump out new units. In the end game, if there is no convenient supply of wood left, each charioteer you spawn is priceless.

The shadow cost of the charioteer involves other factors too, of course (like the stables you had to build, and the upgrades you've spent to make him a useful unit). But it is the influence of the fluctuating availability of resources that has the most dramatic impact throughout the game.

A shadow cost is the underlying cost to the player of a decision. You can use the variability of shadow costs to add subtlety to your game. Vary the environment and you vary the shadow costs. This is both a challenge for the level designer and an opportunity to give the gameplay more depth that expert players will appreciate.

All four of these synergies should be in play at once because, when they interact, they make decisions of timing more critical. When carefully chosen, they also add verisimilitude and make the game more immersive.

Altering the balance between different synergies critically affects the gameplay. A game with many economies of scale and scope is a game that gives positive feedback and encourages the player who is already winning. Chess is a game of positive feedback; it's very carefully balanced, but even a small mistake is magnified throughout the game. Games like this tend to tip suddenly as a small advantage becomes crushing. Positive feedback in a game with chance elements also encourages gambling: having 20 units is much better than having 10, so, if you're offered a double- or nothing gamble, you'll most likely take it. Monopoly displays this kind of gameplay.

On the other hand, if there's an emphasis on diseconomies, you have negative feedback. Here, advantages are increasingly hard won, and those who are losing will rarely fall far behind. These create a "catch-up" factor. Such a game will tend to last a long time. It's a good simulation of certain types of warfare, such as a land war in Asia or trench warfare. How much fun it is will depend on what else you have put in to keep the player's interest.

A Final Word About Gameplay

As we said in the last chapter, by way of introduction to this whole topic, that a good game is one you win by doing something your opponent did not expect and making it work. This is not simply a case of allowing for interesting choices. As the designer, you also need to make sure those choices will interact. It's not so satisfying to win a game just by out-optimizing the other player on resource production, or whatever. I want his choices to have made a difference to mine. If the aim is just to complete the level with more points than another player scored when he tried it, then your choices and your opponent's choices aren't interacting at all. What you have then is a competition rather than a game.

But worst of all is a game in which you simply have to know the right thing to do, and choices don't enter the picture at all. Then it isn't even a competition, it's a foregone conclusion.

I have to stress again that all this applies only to gameplay, and gameplay isn't everything. Many software entertainment products aren't games at all. There's no harm in that. *Grim Fandango* is a mystery story requiring you to solve puzzles; it is no more a game than a book of riddles is a game, but nobody cares because it's fun.

Interactivity

So much for gameplay; now for interactivity. Interactivity isn't gameplay. It's much more important.

Think about it. You might be playing *Myst*, or you might be playing *Creatures*. What you are doing hardly involves gameplay at all. *Myst* and *Creatures*, like many other entertainment software products, aren't truly games at all. You don't mind—you probably don't even notice—because you are having fun. But, if these products weren't interactive, you would certainly notice. Then you might start wondering if your time wouldn't be better spent reading a book, watching TV, or throwing a ball around in the yard. A noninteractive computer game wouldn't win out against other fun activities.

Interactivity is what computers do best. Thus, interactivity, much more than gameplay, is the heart and soul of entertainment software.

Kinds Of Interactivity

Players can interact with a game or narrative in many different ways. Even so, computer game designers have pretty much restricted themselves to interaction with the *facts*. Their concern is whether I open the first door and get the tiger, or the second door and get the lady.

Maybe this is because designers, like Mr. Gradgrind in Dickens' *Hard Times*, believe that "facts alone are wanted in life." But, in focusing on only the details of action and plot, they are blinding themselves to other possibilities.

Consider the ways that I as a player could potentially interact with a computer game:

- Affecting the game world itself, either by changing the front-end settings or (in simulations and god games) as part of the game itself
- Directly controlling the actions of a character or group of characters
- Influencing a character's actions at one remove (for example, by giving him clues or weapons, like Zeus aiding a favored hero)
- Influencing a character at two removes (for example, by leading him somewhere or pointing something out for him to look at, like a muse providing inspiration)
- Deciding who to follow, rather than what happens—an invisible observer flitting between narrative strands
- Selecting what is interesting to me personally, and making the game give more time to those elements, like any child will, when told a story at bedtime

Now, how many of those kinds of interactivity do you commonly see implemented? The first, certainly, but only insofar as I can make the game easier or harder, or change the speed. Why shouldn't I also be able to say to a computer opponent in *StarCraft*, as I can to a human player, "Hey, let's build up a big army before we start fighting!" or, "Don't attack me because I just want to have fun building a city," in *Age of Empires*?

The second kind of interactivity in that list—direct control of one or more characters—accounts for pretty much everything else. You find almost no games with the other kinds listed, and even the direct-control option is used in a very restricted way. I don't know of any recent games, now that we're in the era of realtime, that allow you to switch control between two characters who are not on the same side. Why not? What inviolable rule says you can play only one side in a game?

This is a failure of imagination. Computers give us the means to create new kinds of games and other toys and entertainment genres that aren't games at all. And, yet, most computer games still remain mutant versions of other media, such as films, novels, and board games. And, since those media have not made much use of interactivity, there has been no prior example to guide the game designers of today. Case Study 3.5 is an example of a different type of interactivity.

New kinds of interactivity promise a world of possibilities that we have hardly begun to explore. To fully realize those possibilities, though, we have to be prepared to let go some of the control that we have come to expect, both as designers and as players.

"Why?" Vs. "What?"

Interactivity doesn't have to be about what happens. It's natural for programmers who are also designers to emphasize the logical details: that's the way they see the world. But it is often more interesting to think about *why* something happens, or how it caused other things to happen.

Case Study 3.5 A Different Kind Of Interactivity

A couple of years back, I was discussing various design proposals with the managing director of a large development house. One of the ideas I was most keen to pitch was *Dalek City*, a tie-in to *Dr. Who*, a BBC science-fiction series of the 1960s. Figure 3.5 is a good visual for a Dalek.

"It's set on Skaro, the Dalek planet," I began. "The Daleks have been mutated by nuclear war and can only move about in mechanized travel machines. At the start of the game, they pick up power by induction, so they can't leave the city."

"Yep, got it," said the managing director. "So you have to get upgrades to let them travel outside the city."

"Well, it's certainly possible for the Daleks to get those upgrades. But you see, you don't play the Daleks in this game."

"What, then?" He was getting impatient. Concepts that take more than 20 seconds to explain are hostile territory to company managing directors.

"There are all kinds of threats to the Daleks. Various mutants live in the jungle around the city. Natural disasters like meteor showers can occur. There's another race, the Thals, who are their ancient enemies..."

Figure 3.5
A Dalek.

"You play the Thals, then."

"Not really. That's the point. You don't play anybody. You can step in and help the Thals if you want. Or you could spawn lots of mutant monsters to overrun the Dalek City."

The managing director evidently thought here was something familiar. "That must cost you resources?"

"No, your resources are unrestricted, up to whatever the game engine can handle. You could just send in so many monsters, raiders, and natural disasters that the Daleks would be wiped out right at the start. The point is, say you do that a few times. Then you try something different: sending in just one monster to begin with. The Daleks kill it and take it to their labs. They start researching it. Pretty soon they don't have any trouble dealing with that kind of monster, and what they've learned will help them in other ways, too."

"I see. It's one of these artificial-life things," the managing director said. (It was more of a growl, really.)

"Kind of. The Daleks are prime candidates for artificial life because their psychology is so simple. They're paranoid, inquisitive, power hungry, and they hate everything. And their society is like a type of insect hive."

The managing director wasn't even growling now, just giving me a worried frown.

I decided to press on. "The aim of the game, you see, is whatever you want it to be. You can just observe the Daleks going about their duties, like your own little formicarium. Or you can trash their city and watch the little buggers get stomped. Or you can test them with various threats and see how they learn and develop. It's the cruel-to-be-kind method—eventually you might find you've nurtured them to the point where they can take anything you throw at them. Played that way, the ultimate aim of the game is to make the Daleks into an opponent you can't beat."

The managing director said nothing for a long while. I almost thought he might be chewing it over. But then he shook his head. "Players don't like games without a clearly defined objective."

Inwardly, I sighed. Drawing another sheaf of papers out of my file, I said, "Okay. Well, in that case, I've got this really good story line for a first-person shooter...."

> *"If you are a process-intensive designer... then the characters in your universe can have free will within the confines of your laws of physics. To accomplish this, however, you must abandon the self-indulgence of direct control and instead rely on indirect control. That is, instead of specifying the data of the plotline, you must specify the processes of the dramatic conflict. Instead of defining who does what to whom, you must define how people can do various things to each other."*
>
> *—Chris Crawford, writing in* Interactive Entertainment Design, *April 1995*

Games guru Chris Crawford talks about process (the laws of the game world) as opposed to data (the details of what happens in the game world). It is the blinkered data-intensive approach of most designers that has mired entertainment software in the simplest forms of interactivity. To illustrate this, think back to some of the early discussions of interactivity using digital TV. Many people proposed a system (which they seemed to regard as a new kind of narrative) in which the viewer could decide what the characters did. Essentially, they were talking about that unlamented genre, the interactive movie.

Now, I ask you, would that work? Imagine an interactive *ER*. You get to choose. Does George Clooney's character obey the hospital's rules, does he give the experimental drugs to the sick kid, or does he just go outside and play basketball? Is that a rewarding way to experience interactive drama?

No, and I'll tell you why it isn't. It assumes that the point of all drama is simply to find out what happens next. In fact, if it's good drama, there ought to be a lot more to it than that. As we saw in Chapter 1, Aristotle listed five elements of drama: plot, style, setting, theme, and characterization. It's the last two that aren't well served by the data-intensive designer. Going back to the hypothetical example, is it the point of the player's choice to guess what George Clooney's character would really do? Then the interactivity reduces merely to an empathy test. Is it to make him do things he wouldn't normally? Then the interactivity is just a nerdy way to test the story line to destruction. In neither case is characterization explored in any detail, and the only theme we apt to uncover is the theme that it's kind of weird when people behave inconsistently.

Now consider a different way we could have played our interactive *ER*. This time we don't get to choose what the characters do or say. Now all we can do is choose which character to follow around the hospital. Doug Ross quarrels with Peter Benton over a diagnosis, and both storm off. We follow Ross, who gives his version of events to a third character. Later, we switch back to Benton, who by now has spoken to various other characters and is pursuing another agenda. It is only later, if ever, that we may stumble upon the resolution or aftermath of the quarrel that we witnessed at the start.

We can't guarantee that this would be fun. (If we could, we'd be writing interactive soap operas instead of designing games.) But we can tell you that it would allow scope for interactive enjoyment of *all* the elements of drama, not only the hard facts of the plot. The protagonists would behave true to character, various themes might be revealed (whether the authors intended them or not), and it would remain an immersive experience.

No doubt there are other ways to play with interactivity. Peter Molyneux has done it before, with *Populous* and *Dungeon Keeper*, and looks set to do it again with *Black & White*. If only more game designers would follow his trailblazing example!

Chapter 4
Detailed Design

Key Topics:

- *The importance of the detailed design document*
- *Interfacing with software planning*
- *Preparing for change*
- *Who needs what*

To this point, everything done on the game design has been the "ivory tower" phase of the project, by which I mean that the designer should have been the only individual working on it full time.

At the end of this phase, you should have completed two documents: the gameplay specification and the designer's notes. The gameplay spec is a "vision statement" that describes the final product and serves as the point that everybody will aim towards. When the code and the gameplay spec converge, the product will be ready to ship. The designer's notes are to be read in parallel with the gameplay spec. These notes explain your reasoning and allow others to challenge your assumptions, as well as your conclusions.

The Designer's Role

"But hang on," you're no doubt saying. Surely a designer shouldn't be a one-man band. Shouldn't he listen to other team members' suggestions about the game? Isn't it better that the game design be a democratic process?

In regard to the last point, I'm of the opinion that the only worthwhile thing ever designed by a committee is the American Constitution. But certainly the designer should solicit and accept input from others. No one can think of everything, and a brainstorming session might yield more ideas in two hours than one person would have in a lifetime.

So, by all means talk about the game to the developers who will be working on it. Your marketing team has a role to play as well, so be certain to talk to them and find out whether the game looks likely to fit the commercial requirements that are expected in two years' time. Most importantly, get your client's views based on the game treatment and concept artwork.

What I meant by the designer working solo up to this point is that it should have been no one else's *full-time* role. With this distinction in mind, it's useful to look at the broad timeline of an existing project, as in Case Study 4.1.

Figures 4.1 and 4.2 show that in developing a game, the total time from concept to gold disk matters less than the costs-to-output ratio. Looking at the example of how *Corpus* was planned, you can see how the costs were kept down. For the first 6 months, only a handful of people were needed on the project. The bulk of the team got involved for only 12 months.

Figure 4.1 shows the current situation. The entire team is put together from day one. The design is worked on by a game designer, and when complete, is handed over to the development team. The release preparations usually involve the designer making last-minute tweaks to the gameplay assisted by some of the team members. With this setup, there is some wastage of time and money as employees are idle on the project for some of the time.

Figure 4.2 shows the ideal situation. The design is worked on by a game designer and a software planner, and when complete is handed over to a development team put together for

Figure 4.1
Inefficient process.

Figure 4.2
Efficient process.

Case Study 4.1 A Development Timeline

Case Study 4.1 shows a development timeline for *Corpus*, a realtime strategy game.

Inspiration
Duration: One month

Process: The initial idea and feasibility discussion, leading to the treatment document.

People: Lead designer with occasional input from architecture and technology groups.

Outcome: The client (publisher) decides whether to green light the project.

Conceptualization
Duration: Three months

Process: Writing the detailed design.

People: Lead designer for months two through four.

Outcome: Two documents, the gameplay spec and the designer's notes.

Blueprint
Duration: Two months

Process: Planning the tier mini-specs, a series of short documents detailing the stages of the development. Each document represents a first "best guess" at the solution to that tier, and a summary of what the tier is intended to achieve.

People: Lead designer and one software planner.

Outcome: Several (for example, six) mini-spec documents.

Technical Architecture
Duration: Two months

Process: Based on the tier mini-specs, the architecture group now prepares a technical design that details the tools and technology components that will be needed. The lead designer explains the concept in the round, then hands over ownership to the project leader. The *Corpus* project leader, a member of the architecture group, will take the project through to conclusion.

People: Project leader, lead architect, and a software planner.

Outcome: Master technical spec and additional tier mini-specs dealing with technical as opposed to gameplay issues. These and the game specs now constitute the project plan. Tier mini-specs are now mapped to milestones (in this case, at quarterly intervals) that form part of the contract with the client.

Tool Building
Duration: Four months

Process: Constructing the components and tool set required for the game. The aim is to achieve a degree of completion in any aspect of the game architecture that is well understood and is not likely to need revising due to interdependencies.

People: Project leader and four members of the tools and technology group.

Outcome: Tools and also game components that will be functionally complete if not feature-complete. In *Corpus*, these comprised a 3D graphics engine, level builder, and a game set editor for unit and building creation.

Assembly
Duration: Twelve months

Process: A project leader and one tools programmer now take charge of a team (for example, four programmers and four artists) to assemble the game according to a phase-based system on a six-week turnaround. The project leader finesses the gameplay to conclusion. The tools programmer supports the tools and can refer back to the tools and technology group when necessary. (In theory, the lead designer is consulted at the test-and-review stage at the end of each tier, and doesn't need to be involved on a day-to-day basis. He or she is free to get on with the design of the next game.)

People: Project leader for 12 months; a tools programmer for 9 months; four programmers for 12 months; four artists for the last 8 to 9 months.

Outcome: The game and completed tools that are sufficient for a nonprogrammer to design further levels.

Levels
Duration: Four months

Process: Game levels are built under the direction of the project leader. (In practice, the project leader will be succumbing to battle fatigue by now, so it's vital that the lead level designer is a capable and creative individual who can shoulder some of the burden. In effect, the project leader should be able to share ownership with the lead level designer during level building.

People: Project leader and three level designers.

Outcome: The finished game with all levels and in-game tutorials in place. The manual text and artwork are also now finalized.

Review
Duration: Three months (at least partially in parallel with Levels stage)

Process: Occurs mostly in parallel with the level building. This may be outsourced, although, typically (as was the case with *Corpus*), the publisher has an in-house Quality Assurance department.

People: Four testers.

Outcome: Bugs are found and fixed. If fundamental problems are identified in gameplay (although there shouldn't *be* any at this late stage), the game can be returned to the developers for tweaking, but this stage should really culminate in the gold master.

the specific project under the supervision of the designer and the software planner. The release preparations involve the designer and the software planner tweaking the software. The amount of people working simultaneously on the project is kept to a sensible minimum.

However, the culture of the games industry has rarely allowed that kind of model to work in the past. Historically, the industry evolved from small groups of enthusiasts who pooled their talents. Nowadays, it's a brave and well-funded development house that can afford to have an entire team of maybe a dozen people assigned to a project right from the start. Who knows? They might get better games that way. The point, however, is moot, as rarely would a game produced in that manner manage to keep its funding long enough to see the light of day.

To contrast with the software factory (see Chapter 11) approach, I call the old style of development the Twelve Musketeers Model: "all for one, one for all" (whatever the monthly burn). Is there any precedent for the switch-over between these two models? Again, we might consider the film industry. In the pioneer days, small groups took a camera out into the Hollywood hills (in those days not a suburban sprawl) and threw a movie together a scene at a time. The script—when there was one—might be provided by either a joint effort or by whichever technician or actor had the best idea of how to write.

This way of doing things didn't even last as long as the aging gunslingers who were often hired to act in those movies. The film industry had to get serious. The route to making money meant making bigger pictures, which meant larger teams. Pretty soon the old gung ho system was not sustainable. Efficiency required better planning, and today we have a much more streamlined process. A writer slogs alone over his word processor to produce the first drafts of the script. Then the director and cinematographer might produce a storyboard and shooting script. Preproduction work (casting, location scouting, etc.) involves only a small team, and only then do the entire crew of a hundred or more sign on. In postproduction, the project again contracts in scale, with the director and editor, the foley artists, the music, and special effects.

It is an object lesson in critical-path analysis that the games industry would do well to learn.

Design Documentation

To reiterate, you should now have the gameplay spec and the designer's notes. The following sections cover these in more detail.

The Gameplay Spec

The gameplay spec is a highly detailed description of the game that, if studied and comprehensively understood, allows the reader to visualize the finished product in its entirety. At the outset, you can consider the gameplay spec to be the very first prototype of the game itself, or you can think of it as a document from the future that describes the game you will have created in one year's time. The gameplay spec is a dynamic and evolving document, as changes will be incorporated throughout development.

Now, take that gameplay spec you've slaved over. Put it in front of your programmers and tell them it's complete. Know what they'll say? "How can it be complete? You haven't got psionics/barbarians/incendiary pigs in there yet."

The confusion arises because people misunderstand what is meant by the word *complete*. In games development, it doesn't mean that a document or code module will not change. It means that it is in a functioning state: it works, even if not perfectly. If the author of that document or code fell under a train, you wouldn't have to throw away his work. Since it is complete, others can use and modify it if needed.

So, *complete* does not mean *finished*. Completion is an ongoing process, and, at each stage of completion, the game could (in theory) be shipped. It might not be in a state to sell even a dozen copies, but it *could* be shipped. When the game is finished, it has all the features that you could possibly think of and everything works perfectly, not only in terms of the code itself, but the gameplay, interface, and everything else.

The French symbolist poet Paul Valéry said that "Work is never finished, only abandoned." If he had been a game designer, this is what he *would* have said: "No game is ever finished, only abandoned." Accept that. Your target is to get your game through as many stages of completion as you can before shipping it.

The Designer's Notes

The designer's notes are really just a matter of documenting whatever was going on in the back of your head while you were dreaming up that spec. Include even the doodles on the backs of envelopes that you did at 2:00 A.M. if you like, just label and explain them.

The designer's notes are useful for two reasons. First, there's the value of all documentation: if you walk off a cliff while daydreaming about your next game, the project won't grind to a halt. Second, there is also a benefit that is analogous to the comments in programming code. One sentence in the gameplay spec (say, a single decision about the relative firepower of two tank units, or the reward for collecting squash melons) might be the result of many hours' cogitation. You'll remember the *what* long after you've forgotten the *why*. Case Study 4.2 gives an example of the need to document the spec.

Using The Design Documents

You must consider two facts:

- The gameplay spec needs to be available to your programmers.
- The programmers will not read the gameplay spec.

They really won't. You can tell them it's vitally important. You can plead with them. You can even offer royalties. But your programmers will *not* read that spec.

Case Study 4.2 The Need For Documenting The Spec

The game under development is *Metropolis*, a resource-management sim. John, the designer, has written a rule that resources are localized in the world. Those quantities of iron and gold displayed at the top of the screen actually exist in the player's Civic Center. The Civic Center building itself has limited capacity of 1,000 units of gold and 1,000 units of iron. Once the Civic Center is full, the player can create more storage space by building storage silos, each of which holds 250 gold and 250 iron units.

Two months later, Ian, one of the programmers, comes to write the code that deals with the resource handling. He questions why the storage structures would have separate capacities for the two resources. "Why not just say the Civic Center can hold 2,000 resource units of either type? Likewise the Storage Silo holds 500 units."

John never prepared a designer's notes document, and cannot think of a reason why Ian's suggestion should not be implemented. The change is approved.

Another two months later, in testing, Steve, a level designer, detects a problem. He has reached full storage capacity and needs to build a new storage silo, which will cost 100 units of iron. But his resource stocks at the Civic Center consist of 1,960 units of gold and 40 of iron, which is not enough iron to pay for the new silo. He calls the others over to show them.

"We could change it so that workers carrying resources can directly use them for tasks," suggests Steve. "That way, as long as the workers you set to build the storage silo are actually carrying the extra 60 iron, they can still do it. It wouldn't need to go through the player's resource stocks."

"I don't like that," counters Ian. "It means changing the way resources are deducted when you spend them. It's too extreme of a change to incorporate at this stage. Of course, you could simply get your workers to first do some other task that requires gold, thus clearing 60 units of space in the Civic Center, and then you'd have room for the 100 iron."

"That breaks Rule Number One," protests John, quoting one of many Rules Number One. "Your opponent should be the other players, not the game system itself. It would mean stopping all workers from delivering gold until the iron stocks were high enough to…" He slaps his forehead. "Doh!"

"What is it?" say Ian and Steve in unison.

"I already thought all this through, months ago! That was why the original spec called for separate gold and iron storage capacities. But I'd forgotten the reason for it."

You may have heard the saying that programmers can't see the wood for the trees, while designers can't see the trees for the wood. It's true, except that programmers sometimes can't even see the trees for the *leaves* on the trees. This is what makes them good at programming, the ability to break things down to quantum levels of each tiny individual step in a process. It's also why they can't or won't take a long document like the gameplay spec and read and absorb it to the point where they've built a model of the whole finished product in their heads.

Indeed, why should they? That's the job of the design and architecture groups. The programmers on the team are there to see to the fine detail.

But they do need the design documentation readily available for several reasons. First, carrying out tasks without knowing the goal is demoralizing and counterproductive. Second, when some aspect of a task is open to question, it's more efficient to refer to the spec than it is to tie up a designer to answer it. Third, although it is financially expedient to have only a single person or small group write the spec, it's beneficial to involve everybody's best ideas in evolving it to perfection. Last, a shared vision of the project contributes to group cohesion and morale.

It's a dilemma. Obviously, the design must be made accessible to the programmers in some other way. You could permanently assign a member of the design group to sit guru-like atop a mountain of 3D Studio MAX boxes and answer questions whenever they arose. Because it's unlikely that this would prove to be cost effective, another solution that is almost as good is to have the design documentation on an intranet Web site.

Figure 4.3 shows how the site might be organized. In this case, it is organized as a small document labeled "Contents Schema" that maps down onto a larger document, "The Gameplay Spec", which in turn maps to another large document beside it, "Designer's Notes" as well as to numerous small single pages, labeled "Work in Progress".

The Contents Schema is merely a top-level breakdown of the design documentation into numbered sections, which can be referred to when making changes. An appropriate level of detail might be as follows:

- 7.3 *Army units (object class)*—Army units are characterized by shared behavior protocols. Non-army units recognize army units and will respond accordingly.
- 7.3.1 *Troops*—Troops are human army units that also inherit from the Human object class.

Types of troops are as follows:

- 7.3.1.1 Foot Soldier
- 7.3.1.2 Archer
- 7.3.1.3 Scout
- 7.3.1.4 Rider

Additionally, comments may be tagged to each entry to provide more detail. So, attached to "Rider" in the example above might be the comment: "Beats an Archer in a one-on-one fight starting at bowshot range but is beaten by a Foot Soldier."

The Contents Schema leads a browser to relevant sections of the full gameplay spec, which also maps across to the designer's notes. Of course, hypertext links also cut across between related sections of the spec, so the viewer is free to explore and learn about the design via a concept path that he decides.

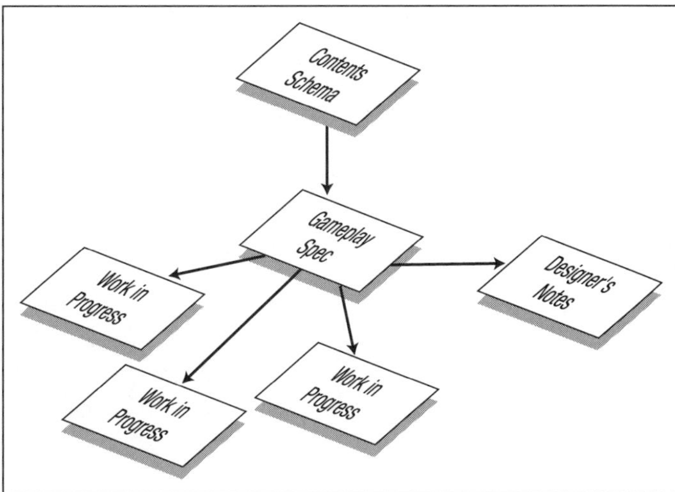

Figure 4.3
The Design intranet site.

As Figure 4.3 shows, you can also map sections of the spec to work in progress. Thus, after a while there would be a page showing the latest animations for a Rider character, a brief description of the character's function in the game, current values of armor, movement speed, and attack damage. Another page might show a mockup of the user interface.

In this form, the programming and art team will be encouraged to explore the game design and participate by suggesting changes and new features. Just be careful that they don't get more interested in perfecting the intranet site than in building the game itself!

Fitting Design To Development

So you have your gameplay spec and your designer's notes nicely presented on an intranet site. By this stage, I would expect there to have been at least one meeting in which you presented the idea and sold it to the team. You'll have had conceptual artwork drawn up and discussed music and sound effects, which you will have also linked in the intranet site. Everyone who'll be working on the game understands the look and feel to aim for. So now it's time for the team to get their heads down and start coding, right? Not yet.

All you have so far are the broad brushstrokes of the concept. Returning to our analogy before, you might liken it to the first draft of a movie's screenplay, which isn't much like a shooting script. It lacks camera directions, storyboards, lighting instructions, and set details. It isn't a plan yet; it's simply a goal.

Current thinking is that games are best built according to an iterative process. Development is sufficiently hazy and risks are sufficiently high that some version of spiral development is ideal, because it allows regular assessment of all the things you didn't anticipate. As well, it lets you closely control the development so that those neat extra "chrome" features that could bust your budget are identifiable and can be dropped if things get tight later on.

Spiral development is consistent with the software-factory model described in Chapter 11. However, it is not the only process that is consistent with that model (the waterfall concept is another). I'll explain why I favor it over the alternatives.

Tiers And Testbeds

Much of gameplay is emergent, in that you don't know quite how all those rules will work in practice until you try them out. This in itself is reason enough to rule out models such as the pure waterfall, wherein each part of the process is finished and coded in stone before the next phase begins. The waterfall model is so called because each phase flows into the other in a strict order, much like a cascading waterfall.

More useful (and quite common in the games industry) is the evolutionary prototype or testbed model, which maintains that the very first priority—within weeks of getting the go-ahead—should be to have a functioning testbed version of the game. The early graphics can be crude dots on a blank field, but you'll get the feeling from talking to exponents of this model that placeholder graphics are almost a point of pride, and the cruder the better!

The idea of the testbed is that you can more or less design your game as you go along. While undoubtedly, a creative designer can eventually produce an excellent game by this model, it does have shortcomings. Development cannot easily be fitted to a schedule. You know only that "one day" you'll have a finished game. Also, the process cannot accommodate critical-path analysis. There is no formal procedure for completing tasks in parallel, and the whole team must wait while changes are implemented. It is only in hindsight that you can see if the order in which tasks were completed was optimal. I'm not much impressed by the argument that an experienced team gets a feel for which tasks to tackle first, and it would impress me less still if I were funding the project.

The idea of developing the game through stages of a successive prototype is a solid solution. These stages are what I have been calling the "tiers" of the build. In each tier, new components of the game can be added, tweaked, and tested. Existing components from an earlier tier can be refined or expanded. The tier model also has the virtue of allowing the team to focus on close horizons. Every six weeks a new iteration is completed, and the game grows in front of your eyes.

A pure evolutionary model falls down, with its eagerness to rush into coding, in the architecture linking the game components. You can lift out and refine the strategic AI, say, but what can you do if you realize, six months down the line, that an early assumption has saddled you with flawed architecture? Unless your client is very understanding, it's too late for a complete rebuild.

So, I recommend holding back on the coding just a little while longer. Produce a testbed to assess your initial ideas by all means, but use off-the-shelf tools to assemble the testbed and plan to junk it when it's served its purpose.

To undertake an iterative development, you first need to take the gameplay spec and turn it into a group of mini-specs. Each mini-spec deals with one tier or phase—a single iteration of the build—so it is like the testbed approach except that your first testbed is purely imaginary. You're saying that you can start with just getting a wireframe environment. Then you'll have a first-person viewpoint to move around anywhere in the environment (x, y, and z) using a developer interface. Then you can include collisions with walls and objects, and then a physics system to govern the dynamics of objects in the game world. Then you'll add weapons and opponents. Here's a good place to splice in the network code so you can playtest head-to-head battles, although note that the skeleton of the network code will probably have been in place from the first iteration. Then you could sort out the opponent AI, then the game editor, and finally the levels themselves.

Each tier mini-spec should outline the following items:

- *The goals*—A designer's wish list of features for that phase
- *The philosophy*—What the phase is intended to test
- *The expected results*—What the phase should have achieved after testing and tweaking
- *The alternatives*—Other best guesses if ideas or concepts must change

Suppose you hand your sheaf of mini-specs to your software planner and lead architect. The first thing they're going to say is that you've addressed only gameplay issues, that there are components needed for the build that aren't written yet. That's good in itself; the tools and components groups can get on with writing those now that they know how they're to be used.

Additionally, other tiers need to be added in-between the ones you've identified: the tiers needed to test technical rather than gameplay issues. This is good, too, as it helps you explain to your programmers that those initial tier documents merely show the ideal way that you as a designer would like to approach the build. As the technical tiers are incorporated, your project moves obviously towards being a team effort.

If you think of building a game like building a bridge, the tier documents tell you where the supports will go. It's an advantage to map out the whole succession of tiers before the team starts coding because it will then be possible to plan an architecture for the game, as shown in Case Study 4.3.

Case Study 4.3 Planning The Mini-Specs To Fit The Architecture

Warbots is a realtime strategy game. The designer, Peter, has outlined an early tier whose aim is to get the 'bots moving around on the landscape and fighting each other. "Basically, I want to be able to click on one of my 'bots, sic him on an enemy 'bot, and he goes over to trash it," explains Peter. "We'll deal with the close-combat rules, damage, and so forth in the next tier."

"Okay," says Nick, the lead programmer. "We have the route finding in place already. We don't have the fog of war yet—it's a later tier—but I assume you want that allowed for. So the 'bot will ask himself if he's in attack range of his target. If he's not, he asks if he knows where the target is. If so, he accesses the route-finding module and moves towards his target."

"That's fine," agrees Peter. "Also, if he doesn't know where his target is, I'd like a question mark or something over his head. Just as a mnemonic for now—it won't go in the finished game."

One of the level designers, Charles, chips in: "Presumably that's because 'bots who can't locate their target will have some other behavior we haven't decided yet?"

"In principle. In fact, the weaker 'bots maybe will run in circles, or head to the target's last-seen position, while the smarter 'bots will have some kind of search routine. Isn't that so?" Peter smiles at the AI programmer, Victoria.

"If there's time, they can be as smart as you like," says Victoria. "But let's rewind to that bit about the 'bot asking if his target is visible. Can 'bots talk to each other?"

"You mean if a different 'bot on the same side can see the target? Sure. The player can see everything that's not in the fog of war. He'll expect his 'bots to be able to as well."

"Okay," Victoria says. "Let me suggest a couple of ways to do this. We could make it that the hunting 'bot accesses his target's coordinates and compares them with the field of all coordinates on the landscape that lie within sight range of friendly units. That's one way. The alternative is that a player's side has an AI assistant that is continually updating a list of visible enemy units. Then your 'bot checks if his target is on that list."

"I don't see the difference," says Peter.

"It makes no difference in this tier. But the visibility question crops up in several tiers, and I'm saying we should address it now."

Nick has been glancing at the mini-spec for the tier dealing with visibility and fog-of-war issues. "You're going to want the fog of war to be obvious in some way? So the areas your units can't see are veiled or grayed-out?" Peter nods. "And obviously enemy units in visibility range will be shown on the player's screen while other enemy units won't," continues Nick. "So that means we'll be creating a data field of all coordinates in sight range and another data field, probably spawned from that, of all enemy units that can be seen."

"Apart from cloaked units," Charles says.

With a wry smile, Nick jots a few notes on the fog-of-war mini-spec. "Cloaked units remind me you'll certainly want to put sensor units in also. So we'll most likely have two visibility fields—for sensor and nonsensor units."

"I don't see where this is leading," protests Peter.

"It won't affect your tier," Victoria assures him. "But the way the design is planned implies an architecture. I now know there'll be a group of visibility data fields and I know how they'll work, so for now I can just put a routine in the AI that tells the 'bot to access those fields. The default, in the absence of any kind of filtering being written for those fields, will be that the 'bot knows where his target is at all times. So the prototype for now will let 'bots hunt each other all over the map, but, when we put in the visibility code, they'll only be able to find opponents they ought to know about."

Why Use Documents At All?

One criticism is frequently leveled at this process. Namely, why the emphasis on preparing and presenting a complete game design document at all? Couldn't the game just as easily be designed on a testbed, and presented to the teams in that form?

It seems strange to have to defend the written word, even on the verge of the 21st century. Certainly, written documentation is not sufficient on its own to communicate the designer's vision of the game. Hence, the emphasis on concept art, inspirational music, references, diagrams, and anything else that you can use to get the concept across. But a written version of the game design *is* vital, and here's why.

In board games and face-to-face role-playing games, the game mechanics are transparent. You can see exactly why you get every result. Light infantry forced off the hill? You shouldn't have left them without support from your cavalry. Riots in the northern provinces? Hand out bigger grain subsidies next autumn.

You don't get that with computer games, because the game mechanics are hidden behind the screen or, more accurately, in the computer chassis standing under the desk. This is fine from the player's perspective (he can fight the Battle of Waterloo in a few hours instead of three weekends), but it's useless if you are trying to use a testbed to explain the workings of the game to your team. And this is why you should use every means possible to make the design document attractive, welcoming and user-friendly, but you must always make sure to keep it at the center of the development process.

Chapter 5
Game Balance

Key Topics:

- ***Player balance and game balance***
- ***Component balance and attribute balance***
- ***Symmetry pros and cons***
- ***The Save Game problem***
- ***Stone-Paper-Scissors and variants***
- ***Scalability of design***
- ***Avoiding overcomplication***

Have you ever admired the elegance of a fine automobile? It happens I'm thinking of a classic like the Rolls Royce Silver Ghost, but it could be any automobile, old or new, or, indeed, any well-made machine. There is a beauty in the perfect marriage of design and function.

So it is with games. To achieve this aesthetic purity, the design must be balanced. A game without balance is untidy and ugly, which is reflected in the experience of playing it. An unbalanced game is less satisfying. Worse, from the developer's viewpoint, it means there has been wasted effort. If the parts of the game are not in balance, there is a risk that some of them will be used rarely, if at all, in which case the time spent developing them has gone to waste.

There are three broad types of game balance, all quite distinct from each other:

- **Player/player** balance is the art of making the game fair so that each player gets no other special advantage but his skill. There can be luck in the game, but it must apply evenly to all players.
- **Player/gameplay** balance involves ensuring that the player's learning curve is matched by rewards that keep him playing. The player should not find that his hardest opponent is the gameplay itself.
- **Gameplay/gameplay** balance means that features within the game must be balanced against each other. If the Tabu Sword does twice the damage of other weapons, it must cost more to buy or be otherwise balanced by compensating factors.

We will consider each kind of balance in turn, seeing how they relate to different game genres.

Player/Player Balance

What do you think: Can Sarah Bryant beat Lion every time? And, if that's so, does it mean *Virtua Fighter* isn't a balanced game?

You can see why the designers of *Virtua Fighter* didn't give all of their characters the exact same moves. That would be kind of dull, wouldn't it? Half the fun is seeing how different martial arts styles compete. In real life, I heard it said that Gracie jujitsu beats all other styles in a one-on-one bout. Maybe that's so. Does it mean that an authentic beat-'em-up that included a Gracie fighter would be unbalanced? Obviously it does, if there is only one Gracie character in the game, and if he *always* beats the other characters, and if the players are exactly equal in their skill and reflexes. Victory then will invariably go to the first player to select a character.

Except that's a lot of "ifs." Suppose I told you I'd been playing a new beat-'em-up and I knew a character who won every time. Would you just accept it, shrug, and say it wasn't worth playing? I don't think so! Rather, wouldn't you lead the way to the arcade and invite me to prove it?

So what if Sarah can whip Lion every time? That's a challenge. It only becomes a game imbalance if a complete novice playing Sarah can beat an expert playing Lion. Even then, the game itself isn't critically unbalanced as long as it's possible for both players to choose from a range of characters. Maybe Sarah isn't so hot versus Jacky. And how does she fare when she has to fight her own clone?

In most games, the designer's aim is to arrange things so that victory is won by skill and judgment. I don't mean that there mustn't be an element of luck. Most strategies entail a gamble, and judging when a risk is worth taking is part of the fun. However, a balanced design should avoid random elements that favor one player, or whose effects are so magnified as the game progresses that victory comes mainly as a result of luck. The most glaring instance of such imbalance is when a player gets a lucky advantage right from the start, perhaps, by starting with his city close to a gold mine, or by entering the game right outside the door of the laser arsenal. How is this kind of undue advantage best avoided?

Obviously, the simplest way to ensure perfect balance is by exact symmetry, which means that players have exactly the same weapons or maneuvers, hit points, or whatever. It also means that the level would have to be symmetrical so that neither player benefited from a better position to begin with. As we saw in the *Virtua Fighter* example, the problem with symmetry is that it may be the fairest solution, but it's rarely the most interesting.

Symmetry

There's a classic Chinese martial arts movie based on the legends of the Water Margin. At one point, two of the heroes square off for a duel. They stand watching each other across the town square, poised in kung fu stance. Hours pass. Days pass. Then a breeze stirs up the dust, and a speck goes in one hero's eye. He blinks, frowns, and suddenly relaxes with a sigh. He bows to the other hero. Such is the mastery of the martial arts these heroes possess that they know the result of the duel without having to fight. Their skill was equal. And so a tiny asymmetry—the loss of concentration due to a speck of dust—was enough to decide the outcome.

Imagine that was a beat-'em-up. You lost because of the wind? Because of a speck of dust in your eye? You'd take that game back to the shop.

No game should ever be decided by factors outside a player's control. This has a simple logical consequence: the game has to be symmetrical at the level of significant game factors. Asymmetries, which are often necessary for reasons of realism or aesthetics, should be confined to the minor factors that cannot individually sway the outcome of the game.

Symmetry In Level Design

Symmetric levels work fine in abstract games. The initial setup in chess is symmetrical, for instance. But if, instead of chess, we were playing a more realistic game that involved knights, castles, and bishops going to war in a medieval setting, we would probably find a symmetric level unappealing. It wouldn't look like a real map. We'd therefore find it hard to suspend our disbelief.

There's another, subtler problem, too. A symmetric level is an obvious way to equalize the odds. In fact, it's too obvious. As solutions go, it's almost an insult to the player's intelligence.

Better is a level that is functionally symmetric but which is not obviously so at first glance. So perhaps each player starts with some impassable geographic barrier protecting one flank of his territory, only in one case it's a mountain range, in another an inland sea, and in another a lava-filled canyon. The ordinary knights and foot soldiers with which the players begin the game have no way of crossing such obstacles. Later in the game, more-advanced units might be available, meaning that those barriers are no longer impassable. That isn't a problem. If I know your defense relies on the inland sea, I have the option of concentrating on building a navy to launch an attack from the sea. Anticipating that, you might build a defensive navy, or you could aim to recruit mountaineers to storm my own fortress first. As long as special units like mountaineers and ships are balanced in cost, the game is still a fair one. And there is also the possibility of bluff, which is so vital in any game of mixed strategies. Seeing a few of my ships out at sea may distract you from the conventional siege army that I'm sending in from the other direction.

What about an asymmetric level where players get to choose their start positions? Insofar as both players have the same choice to begin with, it seems fair. But it's still possible that one player could choose a disastrous position and discover that he has no hope of victory only after playing for some time. That's not a well-balanced level, and passing the decision on to the player doesn't do anything to justify the imbalance. It's like the speck of dust in the kung fu duel. Balance requires that there is no starting position that confers an overwhelming advantage. Giving the player the choice whether to stand upwind or downwind is no good if you then just say, "Oh, you chose downwind, that means you lose!"

The most general solution is to avoid making the initial setup critically important. If there are plenty of gold mines on the map, having just one of them near to your base camp won't be such an overwhelming advantage. This begins to touch on the issue of attribute balance, which we shall be looking at shortly.

Symmetry In Game Design

Symmetry in design means that the choices available to all players are functionally the same. This is the easy way to make sure the game is fair. The *hard* way is to give each player different choices but to try to balance those choices so that every player has the same chance of success.

Warcraft 2 has both orcish and human players, and the units available to each species are broadly the same. For example, the orcs have dragons while the humans have gryphons, but functionally they are not much different, both being tough flying creatures with the ability to bombard units on the ground. Another example are the ogre mages on the orc side who can use berserker rages and explosive runes, corresponding to paladins on the human side who can heal injured comrades and exorcise the undead.

If you look closely at the design of *Warcraft 2*, you see a basically symmetrical picture with a few differences to lend flavor to the two races. Even these very slight differences can prove significant. Consider a level consisting of many mountain passes. The orc player's explosive runes can be used to booby-trap the passes, giving a huge advantage in that specific environment.

How much more difficult, then, to balance the design when each player has fundamentally different units. Yet this is what Blizzard attempted with *StarCraft*—and not only attempted, but largely succeeded. There was no real choice, I suppose. In a medieval fantasy context, it was reasonable to posit similar styles of magic and warfare for the two races, but players would hardly have accepted that different interstellar species would evolve even remotely similar unit types. The amount of playtesting Blizzard undertook to get *StarCraft* balanced must have been astronomical! It makes no real sense to launch yourself on such an uncertain course of development: you have no idea when (if at all) you will end up with a balanced game. The gamble paid off for Blizzard, however. Whatever the cost in added development time, *StarCraft* is a very finely tuned product, and its superior gameplay has been rewarded by hitting the top strategy game slot for 1998.

The common sense approach suggests that a just-broken symmetry is far easier to balance than a complete asymmetry. In many cases, I think that just-broken symmetries have more aesthetic appeal, also. The inimitable Richard Feynman has something interesting to say about this (as he does about most things):

"There is a gate in Japan, a gate in Neiko, which is sometimes called by the Japanese the most beautiful gate in all Japan; it was built in a time when there was a great influence from Chinese art. This gate is very elaborate, with lots of gables and beautiful carving and lots of dragon heads and princes carved into the pillars, and so on. But when one looks closely he sees that in the elaborate and complex design along one of the pillars, one of the small design elements is carved upside down; otherwise the thing is completely symmetrical. If one asks why this is, the story is that it was carved upside down so that the gods will not be jealous of the perfection of man."

—The Feynman Lectures on Physics, Volume One

Also, remember that it's only *games* that ought to be fair. A pure simulation may have the primary aim of authentically re-creating a historical situation, in which case the question of balance between players may be only secondary. I mentioned in Chapter 3 the example of a Conquest of Mexico sim. Played as the Conquistadors and their native allies on the one side versus only the Aztecs on the other, this would be a very unfair game indeed. Played as all the Mesoamerican states on one side versus only the Conquistadors would be unfair *and* unhistorical. There are ways to make a balanced game out of it (by involving many players, for example, or by requiring either of the two main sides to actively forge and maintain alliances with computer-player nations), but, in any true simulation of those events, the Aztecs are doomed. You can make a game fair, but reality rarely is.

Player/Gameplay Balance

Recently a game was released—I think it's better not to name names—that I and many other games designers had been looking forward to for almost two years. The early reports made it sound so innovative and intriguing, but, when it finally hit the market, it was almost universally panned. Even the reviews that praised it for originality gave it a low score. Typical comments went along these lines: "Needless layers of complexity," "makes you perform every last chore yourself," "tasks are out of all proportion to onscreen rewards," and "tiresome and frustrating."

What went wrong is one of the most common design pitfalls: the developers were so busy dreaming up a nifty idea and festooning it with bells and whistles that they forgot somebody would actually have to play the darn thing.

Player/gameplay balance means remembering that this business is all about interactivity. Sure, you want a game that's fair to all players and where all the components and features are worthwhile, but you also have to think about the player's relationship with the game. If you had to retune your TV every time you turned it on, you'd never bother to flop on the couch and channel surf. Likewise, if you have to struggle with a game in order to extract the slightest reward, it's not likely to hold your attention for very long as shown in Case Study 5.1.

Player/gameplay balance entails balancing challenges against the player's improvement curve. This is easy to do in a trivial way in CRPGs (Computer Role Playing Games), for example, where the player doesn't have to get better at playing the game because the character is getting tougher. So challenges can be tailored exactly to fit the character's experience level. But this makes for kind of a poor game: character improvement in a CRPG should be about widening your options, not just making you and your opponents tougher and tougher.

This aspect of game balance can be reduced to three simple rules:

- Reward the player.
- Let the machine do the work.
- Make a game that you can play *with*, not *against*.

Reward The Player

The big reward is to win the game, but, when you first load up and start playing, that's a pretty distant goal. Before any big victories can be won, you have to learn how to play. You'll make mistakes, and mistakes are discouraging. So, every time you learn something new and apply it properly, you need a little reward to offset the discouragement. This seems very obvious—it *is* very obvious—and yet it's often overlooked.

Take the case of a beat-'em-up like *Virtua Fighter*. It takes a while to learn the trickier combinations, and even longer to apply them properly. The results have to reward the player's effort and patience. The reward comes when you see Sarah flip over her opponent's head and give him an unexpected elbow strike to the kidneys. Both the effect on your opponent (the gameplay payoff) and the graphics associated with that combo (the eye candy) have to be worthwhile.

Rewards should widen the gaming experience, not merely fit to points on a learning curve. "I wanted to learn how to do the flying scissors kick, and I did, and it's cool," isn't half so good as, "Now that I can do the flying scissors kick, I can see a whole new use for the reverse punch also."

Let The Machine Do The Work

This is mainly a question of the interface, which is the player's channel of communication with the game and, as such, has no business doing anything except showing the player what is going on in the game world and helping him to make changes to that world.

Also, remember that the player is sitting with a computer in front of him and that a computer is a tool specifically designed to deal with a wide range of tedious tasks. If those tasks aren't going to be fun, don't make the player do them. If you look back over the games of the

Case Study 5.1 Is This Supposed To Be Fun?

Early CRPGs, for some arcane reason, used to begin with the player having to randomly generate scores in attributes such as strength, dexterity, and intelligence. Well, those were the early days, and we didn't know any better. Except that it still goes on. Look at this quotation from a recent RPG:

"By using the plus and minus keys next to each trait on the menu, you can take points away from some traits and add them to others to get the balance you want. If you really don't like the hand you've been dealt, you can click REROLL to get a different set of values for the various traits."

—The *Baldur's Gate* Official Strategy Guide

"If you really don't like the hand you've been dealt..." Or, to put it another way: "If you *have* to be a pain and can't just go along with what you got first time..." But, each time I "reroll," I get a new set of random attributes, which may be higher overall than the first set. Assuming the attribute values make any difference at all to the game, I'm going to want them as high as possible, aren't I? If I'm patient enough, maybe I should keep "rerolling" until every attribute comes up with a value of 18. (The range is from 3 to 18, for another batty reason we don't need to go into here.)

And why don't I keep "rerolling" for hours, until I have the perfect character? Because I bought this product to play a role-playing adventure, not to watch strings of numbers changing. This has been set up merely as an endurance test. When I finally get bored and frustrated enough, I'll accept my attribute scores and get on with the game.

As an example of player/gameplay balance, it's not *quite* in the Stone Age.

last 15 years, you'll find plenty of glaring examples of designers who have gotten confused over the boundary between a chore and a game feature. For years, CRPGs used to be boxed with little bits of graph paper so you could draw a map as you explored each dungeon! It's like we saw in Chapter 3: if a game option is a no-brainer, there's no excuse for not having the AI take care of it. Don't bother the player.

Make A Game You Play *With*, Not *Against*

I've lost count of the number of games that go to great lengths to set up a vivid world, atmospheric locations, and a powerful, intriguing story line—and then go and spoil it all by insisting I can progress only by trial and error.

You know the kind of thing. I'm approaching the crossbowman guarding the exit. I think maybe the transparency potion I bought will mean that he can't see me, but no. He draws, shoots, and it's (sigh) back to the last save. So now I know the potion doesn't work. Maybe if I try running up to him? No, he's too quick on the draw. Back to the last save. Now I try dropping the bottle with the potion. The guard hears it, comes looking—and shoots me. Now I'm stumped. Just at random, I try drinking the potion and then dropping the empty bottle. He's coming this way. This isn't going to work, surely? But it does. He walks past, not seeing me. It's only now I realize that the transparency potion works only when I'm stationary. He goes past, still looking around for whoever dropped the bottle, and I sneak behind his back to the exit.

Is that good design? No, it's lazy design. I should have succeeded by skill and judgment, not because I goofed up enough times that the correct solution was the only one left. Case Study 5.2 provides an example of the save game problem.

Now, I always thought the Save feature was so you could grab some time to live your real life in-between games. Turning it into part of the game just so the player has to put up with episodes like the one in Case Study 5.2 seems mere perversity. I'm not much into dungeon bashes anyway, and I never played *Deathtrap Dungeon*, so I don't know if that trap made it into the finished game when it was released a few years later. But I can tell you it would never even be considered in one of my designs.

Some people think Save Points are the answer, but that assumes that Saves themselves are the problem. They're not. The problem lies in games that are designed around the *need* to save—games that are too arbitrary, or where the learning curve makes it hard for you to progress by dint of skill. (Games that lack player/gameplay balance, in other words.)

Levels constructed around the need to save can destroy the value of a good game design. A case in point is *Myth: The Fallen Lords*. Small squads could be deployed in different formations, creating an interesting hybrid of wargame and RPG that might have been rewarding to play. One would hope that thoughtful analysis would lead the player to a good choice of formation, perhaps in some cases keeping a few characters in reserve to permit flexibility. Instead, too often the levels were pitched to such a degree of difficulty that you could survive only if you had chosen the single best formation. Flexibility in the form of a reserve was a luxury you couldn't afford: the foes would ferociously wipe out your nonoptimal deployment before you had time to change your orders. The only answer was to save frequently and, then, with the benefit of hindsight, engage the foe next time with all your troops placed in the perfect position. Those levels were a shame, too, because the basic game design of *Myth* looked so good.

What is the answer to the Save Game problem? It is better player/gameplay balance, along with level design that has faith in the game design to deliver the goods.

"Experienced gamers have come to regard the save-die-reload cycle as a normal component of the total gaming experience. I want to slap all those people in the face and cry, 'Wake up!'... Any game that requires reloading as a normal part of the player's progress through the system is fundamentally flawed. On the very first playing, even a below-average player should be able to successfully traverse the game sequence. As the player grows more skilled, he may become faster or experience other challenges, but he should never have to start over after dying."

—Chris Crawford, writing in Interactive Entertainment Design, Vol. 8, No. 3 (February 1995)

Case Study 5.2 The Save Game Problem

A few years ago I was working as a consultant at Eidos Interactive and one day happened to be chatting with one of the designers on *Deathtrap Dungeon*.

"I've got a great trap!" he told me gleefully. "The player steps on this platform, it descends into a chamber he thinks is full of treasure, then a ring of flamethrowers go off and he's toasted."

"What if I jump off the platform before it gets to the bottom?"

I meant it as a solution, but he saw it as a loophole. "Yeah, we'll have to make it a teleporter instead. You get flamed as soon as you materialize."

"But, I mean, what is the solution?"

"There isn't one!" He was astonished at me. "I'm saying it's just a killer trap. It'll be *fun*."

"So, there's no clue before you teleport that this might not be a good idea? Charred remains on the teleporter pad or something?"

"Nah, of course not. That's what the Save feature is for."

Gameplay/Gameplay Balance

I remember when *Warcraft 2* came out. The original *Warcraft* had really only featured three essential combat units: the Knight, the Archer, and the Catapult. Those units comprised most of your army. Okay, there were also wizards who could summon demons, but you had to disallow them if you wanted a balanced game. Without the demons, then, *Warcraft* was a very well-balanced game that led players to constantly evolve new strategies.

Warcraft 2 had more than half a dozen essential units and several others (like Sappers) that had very specialized uses but on some levels were invaluable. After looking at the game for a few hours, I got talking to Steve Jackson, now of Lionhead Studios. It turned out he was another *Warcraft* enthusiast. "There are only two ways they could have got the units so well balanced," Steve reckoned. "Either they struck lucky first time, or they must have continually tweaked them for hundreds of hours of playtesting. Either way, it seems incredible."

I haven't spoken to anyone who worked on *Warcraft 2*, but I'd be willing to bet it was the latter. Nobody gets *that* lucky. The game was almost perfectly balanced. In practical terms, that means that you never felt there was a unit you could do without. Nor was there any unit that you felt cost too much, so that you tried to avoid having to use it.

One way the designers of *Warcraft 2* made sure of that was to build in a strong Stone-Paper-Scissors (SPS) relationship between the key units. There'll be more on this later in the chapter, but for now we need only note that this automatically tends to create a game balance. This is because, with strong SPS (i.e., a single unit of one type beats any number of the next type), you have to play using all the unit types: none is dispensable.

What challenges do we face when balancing aspects of gameplay? Broadly, we must consider three things:

- We want there to be a variety of interesting choices rather than a single choice that always dominates.
- This isn't easy to establish because the optimum choices depend on the choices other players make.
- It's not easy to see how frequently different choices will be worth making, yet we need to know that to balance the game.

Sounds like a Catch-22? Not quite, because there are some simple concepts we can use to get a first guess at the value of different choices, even within a dynamic game. These concepts were developed specifically to analyze this kind of problem, and since WWII they have been used extensively to examine problems ranging from nuclear deterrence to the pricing policy of console manufacturers.

The concepts I'm talking about form part of the analytic arsenal of game theory, and we'll be using some of them in the remainder of this chapter.

Component And Attribute Balance

Balancing the elements within a game takes place on two levels. First, there is component balance. This establishes the value of each game choice. For balance to exist, each choice must not be reducible to a simple value relative to some other choice, or, if it can be so reduced, other factors must even it out.

Let's look at an example. In *StarCraft*, Mutalisks are flying units that can move over any terrain and have powerful ranged attacks, but cannot fight other flying units. Wraiths are fast aerial units that can turn invisible but aren't nearly as tough as Mutalisks, although they can attack other flyers. Observers are light aircraft that can see invisible units but are no use in a fight. There is no way you could devise an expression that set the value of each of those units relative to the others because they do such different things.

Alternatively, consider a pirate game in which the ships you can select from are brigantines, galleons, and dreadnoughts. The dreadnoughts are the toughest, next come the galleons, and last, the brigantines. All these units have identical functions in the game. There is nothing a brigantine can do that a galleon or dreadnought can't do better. If the galleon is twice as tough as the brigantine, game balance requires at the first level of approximation that the brigantine should cost half as much to spawn. Actually, when balancing costs, you need to be quite careful that you are looking at all the relevant factors. What I mean by "twice as good" is a unit that is twice as effective as another in *all* functions of both units—in this example, twice as powerful in both offense (damage dealt out per unit time) and defense (hit points).

But I said there were two levels to consider when balancing game choices. The attribute level involves not the relative values of different choices, but the *way* the choices interact. Suppose that Brigantines are the fastest ships in the game and Dreadnoughts are the slowest. From a gameplay standpoint, it's getting more interesting, but what we are concerned with now is not gameplay but game balance. Where component balance dealt with comparison of the three ship types, attribute balance (in this example) is a question of assessing how important speed will be as opposed to combat ability. If the game levels are small, have fixed goals (such as buried treasure), or operate without a time limit, then combat ability far outweighs speed. If the goals are merchant ships that lack firepower—and if there is no direct imperative for players to attack each other—then speed becomes far more important.

You can envision this as a number of sets, with each set establishing the relative value of the Brigantine, Galleon, and Dreadnought with respect to one factor: speed, firepower, upgradability, range, and so on. Attribute balance is then a question of weighting each factor relative to the others. For example, range may turn out to have no value if the levels are small. This allows you to construct an average set combining the effects of all factors. Component balance then requires you to adjust the ships' interactions and/or cost to ensure that they all have a useful role in the game.

As a mnemonic, component choices are the ones that are usually embodied by artifacts in the game: "Hmm, the Vorpal Blade and the Black Javelin are both useful weapons, but I think I need the Wand of Ill Omen to deal with this troll." Attribute choices are more abstract and have to do with how you use the artifacts: "Maybe I'd better not tackle that troll at all; I can get by using stealth." Case Study 5.3 provides an example of component and attribute balancing.

Not surprisingly, attribute balance is a lot harder to get right than component balance, which is really just a question of assessing the relative value of different strategies. Remember that strategy in this context is not restricted to strategy-type wargames, even though such games provide a convenient example of these concepts. Strategy simply means the way the player uses the available game choices—the sequence of moves in a beat-'em-up, the mix of units in a wargame, and so forth.

This gives us the key to game balance. If we can form an approximate picture of the better strategies—that is, the relative frequency that different choices will most probably be used, even only to the level of a ballpark figure—then we can start to tweak the costs and compensating factors to reflect that frequency.

Intransitive Game Mechanics Guarantees Balance

Consider a martial arts beat-'em-up game with three main attacks: forward kick, leg sweep, and stomp. If I choose a leg sweep and you choose a forward kick (Figure 5.1), I dodge your kick and take your legs out from under you: a win to me. If I choose a stomp and you choose a forward kick, your kick catches me as I jump up, and now you win (Figure 5.2). But a stomp beats a leg sweep (Figure 5.3).

Case Study 5.3 Component And Attribute Balance In Dungeon Keeper

Bullfrog's *Dungeon Keeper* is a simulation in which you construct an underground magical lair while fending off occasional attacks by heroes.

Component balance exists in three forms: between different room types, between different spells, and between different creatures. You need to decide which room types to build first and how big you can afford to make them. During a fight, you need to pick the best spells to use. Creatures arrive at random, and you don't have much control over which ones you get, but you do need to decide which are worth spending treasure on to improve their skills.

Attribute balance occurs in several forms. The most obvious is the relative placement of dungeon rooms. Creatures must not have to go far to get food or pay, because you to minimize the time they aren't training. Another form involves which creatures are the best to deploy against different intruders. Faced with fast-moving intruders such as fairies, you need to hit them quick and hard. Slower enemies like wizards allow you to skirmish, continually pulling back creatures for rest and recovery. Deep in your dungeon, too, your aim will often be to capture and convert intruders instead of killing them.

There is another level of attribute balance in this game that is not widely seen: the balance between two subgames. *Dungeon Keeper* can be played either with an isometric third-person viewpoint or by possessing one of your creatures to get a first-person view. Obviously, the former is better for organizing your dungeon. To encourage you to use the first-person view, the game gives an advantage to your side in any fight where you possess a creature and personally get into the scrum. Also, there are some levels where the only way to win is to go to the first-person view.

But was it necessary to achieve that last level of attribute balance? There's a question. Suppose you didn't care for the first-person viewpoint, and you just wanted to play the dungeon sim? Too bad. If you don't get through those first-person levels, you won't be able to complete the game. So there is no doubt the two subgames were balanced, in the sense that you couldn't dispense with either. But whether this particular aspect of balance enhanced gameplay, interactivity, and player choice is another question.

I said earlier that we'd get back to Stone-Paper-Scissors.

First off, notice that the beat-'em-up example really is exactly equivalent to Stone-Paper-Scissors. The example we looked at in Chapter 3, based on *The Ancient Art of War*, was actually a bit more complex than pure SPS. The reason for that was that you could play a mix of unit types, and, after winning a battle, you would have some units left, which would stand you in good stead in the next battle. Whereas in the case of the beat-'em-up, you can play only one maneuver at a time, and, in each comparison of maneuvers, there is one winner and one loser. So, in effect, each exchange of attacks is a new subgame within the overall bout.

So, we're playing this hypothetical beat-'em-up. What's the best strategy? It's an extremely simple game, so it ought to be possible to see a good strategy pretty quickly (if there is one).

Figure 5.1
Leg sweep beats forward kick.

Figure 5.2
Forward kick beats stomp.

Figure 5.3
Stomp beats leg sweep.

Well, I could randomly pick my maneuver each time. This is at least as good as any other strategy if I have no way of knowing what you are going to do. However, if I'm playing against a very dumb computer opponent who picks randomly, I can equal its score by playing a leg sweep every time. That way, we each win, draw, and lose one-third of the time.

Of course, you would soon spot an opponent who *always* chose the leg sweep. You'd then start to use mainly stomps, and your opponent would then start using forward kicks, and so on.

A useful way to represent this game is by means of an interaction matrix like the one shown in Table 5.1.

What this shows is your payoff for playing a maneuver (shown in the rows) matched against the maneuver used by your opponent (shown in the columns). A win is awarded a positive value, a defeat a negative value, and a draw by zero. This is because the game as described is *zero-sum*. In other words, whatever one-player gains, the other player loses. As we'll see

Table 5.1 Payoffs in a Stone-Paper-Scissors-type game.

	Leg Sweep	Forward Kick	Stomp
Leg Sweep	0	+1	-1
Forward Kick	-1	0	+1
Stomp	+1	-1	0

shortly, even when these payoff matrices are only a very abstract model of a game, they can be very useful in balancing different elements of the design.

The intransitive relationship typified by Stone-Paper-Scissors occurs in even the most unlikely games. Nail gun beats shambler, shambler beats rocket launcher, rocket launcher beats zombie, zombie beats nail gun. Or elephants beat chariots beat priests beat elephants. Why is this such a commonly used game mechanic? To answer that, remember the discussion in Chapter 3 about avoiding dominant strategies. A good game design eschews "best" weapons or strategies so as to keep the player's choices interesting. A Stone-Paper-Scissors mechanic simply happens to be a very easy way to make sure no one option beats all others. A great arena for *Quake* has no perfect vantage point, so, to be top dog, a soldier must stay on the move.

But that isn't the whole story. Figure 5.4 shows one of the possible evolving patterns of an SPS-based game. Each point of the triangle represents one of the options, and the line shows how a given player's choices will tend to drift over time, with the proximity to each point indicating the likelihood of picking that option. To start off, suppose our player's favored strategy is always to pick the stone. The other player responds by picking paper. The response is to pick scissors. Quite swiftly, the player is forced towards the middle of the diagram, representing a strategy where all options are equally favored. There is no way to beat that particular strategy in Stone-Paper-Scissors. Unfortunately, there's no way you can win using it, either! Just like in the first law of thermodynamics, you can only break even.

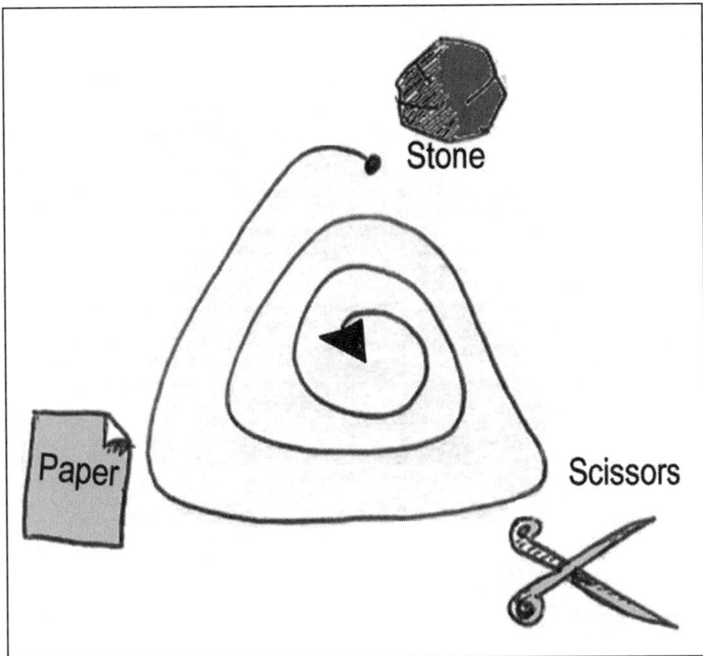

Figure 5.4
Evolution of mixed strategies in Paper-Scissors-Stone.

What if the costs of using each option weren't the same? In the simple beat-'em-up we were looking at before, maybe a stomp costs the most energy and a leg sweep costs the least. Obviously, now we'll see a different mixed strategy. We might expect to see the stomp being used less often than the other moves. But wait: if the stomp is used less often, that would make the forward kick less useful too. It's not intuitive exactly what the optimum choices would be. We have to do some math.

Suppose that a stomp costs 3 Ki, a forward kick costs 2 Ki, and a leg sweep costs 1 Ki. And we need to know how much Ki you knock off your opponent if you win an exchange of moves. Say that's 5 Ki. We can now rewrite the payoff matrix with these costs factored in as shown in Table 5.2.

This is the net payoff, remember. So, for instance, if I choose leg sweep and you choose stomp, the difference in Ki cost to make those moves is +2 in my favor, but I lose -5 because your stomp beats my leg sweep, so the net payoff to me is -3.

Now, let's call the net payoff for using each move L, F, and S, and the frequency that each move is used is l, f, and s. That means the net payoff for using a leg sweep is:

$(0 \times l) + (6 \times f) + (-3 \times s)$.

Thus:

$L = 6f - 3s$,

$F = 6s - 6l$, and

$S = 3l - 6f$.

Now, I also know that each of the three payoffs must be zero. Why? Well, we are looking for an optimum strategy. This is a zero-sum game, meaning that whatever you gain, I lose. We can't both make a net gain. Hence, if there is an optimum strategy that we both follow, it must give us the same total payoff, which must therefore be zero:

$L + F + S = 0$.

And how do we know that the three components of the payoff, L, F, and S, are equal? Because the mixed strategy we are looking for is the equilibrium that both players settle down to using after some time, as we saw in Figure 5.4 For it to be an equilibrium, we couldn't have the payoff for leg sweep being greater than for stomp, for example, because

Table 5.2 Rewritten payoff matrix.

	Leg Sweep	Forward Kick	Stomp
Leg sweep	0	+6	-3
Forward kick	-6	0	+6
Stomp	+3	-6	0

then we'd start using leg sweep more. So, when we finally get to the optimum mixed strategy that we both will stick with,

L = F = S = 0.

It's very easy to solve the equations now and show that the ratio

l:f:s = 2:1:2,

which is a very interesting result. It says that leg sweep and stomp are each used 40 percent of the time and forward kick is used 20 percent. Probably that isn't what you'd have guessed without doing the math. It neatly illustrates something you'll see quite often with these Stone-Paper-Scissors games: if one option is expensive, it's often the other options that are most affected.

This is all very well and good, but there is a caveat. Basing your game around Stone-Paper-Scissors guarantees balance because there cannot be a dominant choice. In such a game, players must avoid predictability because predictability is a weakness that a clever opponent will exploit. However, a game in which you must avoid predictable choices is barely one step ahead of a game with a single best choice. This is why intransitive relationships like Stone-Paper-Scissors are only the first step towards creating rich gameplay. To balance those choices so that they are interesting implies that you will want to design in other factors that influence how the choices interact—be they weapons, maneuvers, units, or whatever. We saw one example of that in Chapter 3: at Hastings, King Harold placed his troops on a ridge so that the normal interaction (archers beat axemen) was changed to archers equal axemen.

In the case of our beat-'em-up, one route to interesting gameplay is by including combination maneuvers. You can then put together a sequence that you hope will prove to have a greater payoff than the individual maneuvers taken on their own. Conversely, skill and judgment give you the chance to anticipate what the other player is leading up to. It helps even more if certain sequences can build up to more than one "grand slam." For instance, a stomp, two forward kicks, and a leg sweep might culminate in a scissors pin; while a stomp, two forward kicks, and another stomp might add up to a knockout. If I play a stomp followed by two forward kicks, you know I can summarily end the bout by playing a stomp. You don't want that, so you think about countering with a forward kick. But you know I know that's what you're thinking, so maybe I'll go for the leg sweep and merely pin you instead. And don't take too long to mull it over; time is also a gameplay factor! Case Study 5.4 provides an example of Stone-Paper-Scissors.

Combinatorial Explosions

In an intransitive game, how many attributes should you include that are capable of changing the basic SPS relation? It's a question of game balance. Too few, and the use of those factors to create a strategy becomes trivial. For instance, if the relationship is archers beat warriors beat barbarians beat archers—and the *only* thing I can do in the whole game to change that relationship is put my warriors on a hilltop, as King Harold did at Hastings—

Case Study 5.4 Attribute Balance Using SPS

Peter, the lead designer of *Warbots*, is discussing some gameplay ideas with Charles, the project manager. Charles had requested a circular unit relationship, similar to *Warcraft 2*, and Peter is sketching out some possibilities.

"Say we have three main combat units," he suggests. "The Drillerbots are fast. Frighteningly fast. They can do lots of little attacks in quick succession that take the slower Hammerbots apart. They make this horrible sound as they do it, too...Nyeeowmm."

"I know, like my root canal work!" laughs Charles. "Ouch."

"Then you've got the Juggerbots. They're slow too, even slower than the Hammerbots, but they're massively armored. The Drillerbot can't even scratch them—sparks everywhere, but no damage. Meanwhile, the Juggerbot is pulling the Drillerbot apart like a crab taking a leisurely snack."

"And the Hammerbots? They can get through the Juggerbots' armor?"

"Crack 'em like nuts," grins Peter. "Only it's not so one-sided as those other matches. The Hammerbot wins, but it's a brutal slugfest with scrap metal flying everywhere."

"Good," says Charles. "So there's no best unit. Have you thought about what the player can do to change the odds?"

"I'm going to talk to Nick about that. He's still working on the physics system, which will affect a lot of things besides combat. It could be that the Drillerbots use laser drills, and they might get less effective as they move away from the player's power pylons, or maybe they weaken over time and then have to recharge."

Charles nods. "As long as it's an automatic recharge, like the units that use energy in *StarCraft*. We don't want players having to fiddle about sending energy to 'bots from their resource stocks."

"Agreed. Also, we could dispense with the mining 'bots. Drillerbots can mine as well as fight, so they have a versatility advantage."

Charles thinks about it. "No, keep the mining 'bots, but make them cheaper and have the Drillerbots better at blasting the ore but not collecting it. It'll give the player some interesting choices. And what about Hammerbots versus Juggerbots?"

"Underwater—under liquid methane, I should say—the Hammerbot's attacks will probably pack less punch. The Juggerbot fights with these kind of vice-grip pincers, which won't be affected so much."

"It all sounds fine," says Charles. As a longtime *Warcraft* fan, he is quite satisfied. "So much for combat. What about other factors—visibility range, say. Can you get that to fit a cyclical pattern, too?"

This takes Peter by surprise. "Of course not..." he starts to say. Then, after a moment's thought, "Hey, maybe we could, at that! Suppose A has the longest radar range but the shortest sight range. B has the longest sight range, just a bit under A's radar range, but has no radar itself.

C has a medium sight range and again no radar, but also is invisible to radar." He writes on a pad, plugging in some numbers. "Yes. A spots B before being spotted itself. Same with B to C and C to A. Hey, that's nifty! I never would have thought you could get an intransitive relationship with visibility ranges."

"See, I'm too dumb to know what's not possible!" laughs Charles. "But enough of this algebra stuff. Which units are we talking about here, A and B and C?"

Peter smiles as another realization dawns on him. "This has a big impact on gameplay. Say we have the Jugger spot the Driller, and so on, so that each 'bot can see the 'bot he's best equipped to take out. That'll make for a fast-moving aggressive game—the predator can always see his prey before he is seen himself. But, if we try it the other way around, so the Hammer sees that Driller coming, the Driller can avoid the Jugger, and so on... then you have a slower, more considered kind of cat-and-mouse game."

"Where the cats are made of titanium steel and the mice weigh eight tons apiece, sure." Sensing they could be one up on his favorite strategy game, Charles looks a little bit like a cat with cream himself right now. "Anyway, which way is better?"

"*Better*?" Peter looks up from his notepad. He couldn't look more astonished if Charles had just asked him to calculate the value of the truth-beauty equation. "I can't say which is better. It depends on the kind of game you want. We could even arrange it so that it sometimes works one way and sometimes the other. Making it vary depending on weather or the day/night cycle is one option. More interesting is if radar is messed up when there are lots of scrap robot chassises lying about, when metal buildings are nearby, that kind of thing."

"I see," says Charles. "So 'bots might see their targets, pounce, there's lots of vicious infighting, but the more the bodies pile up the more difficult it gets to spot your victims..."

"And the easier to spot the 'bots to avoid. Yes. But even that's only part of it. We also have to settle on the attribute balance between visibility range and combat ability. Because, if the cost of building new 'bots is very high, winning every combat becomes critically important. If they're cheap, it doesn't matter so much. And then there's the question of not just whether a 'bot sees another, but the ability of each 'bot to close the gap or to get away."

Charles nods. "Okay, you're right. I was hoping for an easy answer for once, but there's only so far you can get with hand-waving and whiteboards, isn't there?"

"I'll get Nick to knock up a testbed. You'll be amazed what a couple days of tweaking can achieve."

that's not exactly an intriguing game. On the other hand, too many modifying factors and you have a game in which skilled play becomes almost impossible. I'll give a rule of thumb. If you have N factors that could modify your core game mechanic, and each factor is Boolean (in any situation it either holds or it doesn't) then you have 2^N possible combinations. The complexity soon blows up out of control, so you should err on the side of caution.

"In Populous: The Beginning, almost the first decision was whether the game should have lots of character types or only a half-dozen or so. We noticed straight away that it would be easier to understand the game experience with a few, very versatile units rather than many specific ones. Hence we opted to keep it simple to learn yet difficult to master."

—Richard Leinfellner, Executive in Charge of Production at Bullfrog

Design Scalability

A related problem arises when balancing many components. As we shall shortly see, it is possible to construct extensions of the Stone-Paper-Scissors dynamic using five or seven components—and, indeed, any odd number. If strategies can draw as well as winning or losing, there are infinite possibilities. So, where should you draw the line?

Intransitive component relationships are very inflexible to alterations in the design. You cannot construct a five-way dynamic and still expect it to work if you remove one of the components. If you want to try it, skip ahead to Table 5.3 and delete one of the units: you immediately create a dominated strategy, rendering one of the other units redundant. Suppose you're nine months through development, and work is slipping behind schedule. The project lead asks you to take out one of the five characters because there isn't time to do all the animations for him. However, this causes your elegantly balanced design to fall like a house of cards.

On the other hand, it's relatively easy to *add* extra components later in development. The extra component doesn't have to be symmetrical with all the others. It might be useful in only a few cases, or it could be a component that is vital to the game but that is only needed occasionally or in small numbers, like a Lay-the-Dead spell or a scout character.

The lesson is clear. If you're going to scale your design, plan to scale up, not down.

Other Intransitive Relationships

Before examining the limits of a game-theoretical analysis, I'm going to digress. Generally speaking, nontransitive relationships like Stone-Paper-Scissors are so useful in games that it is worth taking a look at some other examples.

How about with more than three options? Is it still possible to construct a SPS-like relationship? Fortunately, yes. (Otherwise, this analysis would be very limited indeed!) Figure 5.5 shows another variation using five units.

Here, samurai beat shungenja and ashigaru. Shugenja beat ashigaru and archers. Ashigaru beat archers and ninja. Archers beat ninja and samurai. And ninja beat samurai and shugenja. No one character type provides a dominant choice, as we can see by drawing the payoff matrix (Table 5.3).

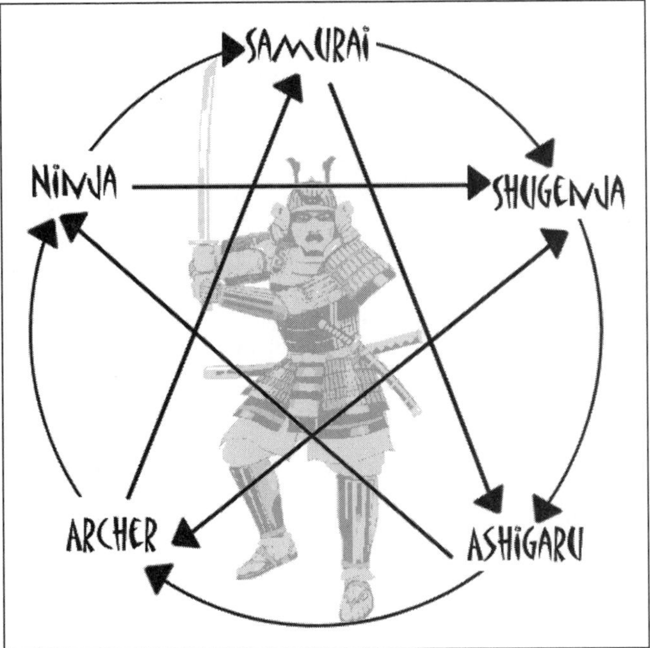

Figure 5.5
Five-way intransitive relationship.

Table 5.3 Payoffs in a five-way intransitive relationship.

	Samurai	Shugenja	Ashigaru	Archer	Ninja
Samurai	0	+1	+1	-1	-1
Shugenja	-1	0	+1	+1	-1
Ashigaru	-1	-1	0	+1	+1
Archer	+1	-1	-1	0	+1
Ninja	+1	+1	-1	-1	0

Similarly, you can construct a seven-way relationship along the same principles. (That, as they say, can be an exercise for the reader.) But Figure 5.6 depicts a less regular relationship.

This is a variant on the original example taken from *The Ancient Art of War*. Archers beat warriors beat barbarians beat archers, as before. Only now there is a new character, the sorcerer, who is beaten by the warrior, beats the barbarian (they're the superstitious ones, I guess) and is an even match for the archer. The payoff matrix again shows that none of the characters is invariably best (Table 5.4).

Against a randomly selected opponent, the barbarian doesn't win as often as any of the others. Does this mean players won't use the barbarian as much? Well, no, because, as soon as I see you aren't using the barbarian, I will start to play more archers, and your only counter is to start using the barbarian again. Case Study 5.5 on page 96 provides an example of using theory analysis.

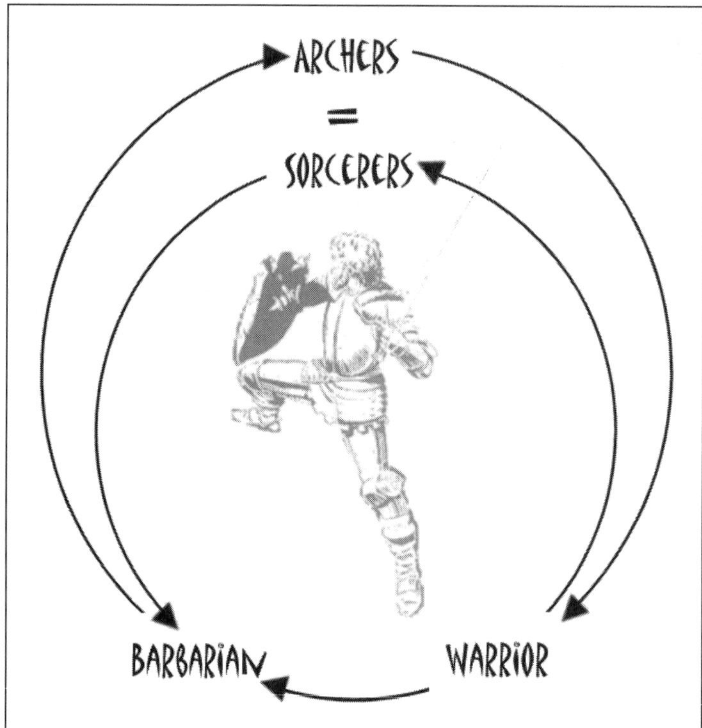

Figure 5.6
A four-way variant on SPS.

Table 5.4 Payoffs in the four-way SPS variant.

	Archer	Warrior	Barbarian	Sorcerer
Archer	0	+1	-1	0
Warrior	-1	0	+1	+1
Barbarian	+1	-1	0	-1
Sorcerer	0	-1	+1	0

Unlike Stone-Paper-Scissors or the more complicated five-option variant just discussed, this has the benefit of asymmetry. The asymmetry makes it more aesthetically appealing, because the player doesn't merely have to learn a cyclical pattern of win/lose relationships. The archer and the sorcerer, although they draw with each other, are interestingly different. Or are they? Let's do a little math.

We would like to know how often these characters might be used in the game. That's the purpose of these payoff matrices, after all: to give some idea of the value of different choices so we can balance them. In this case, let's call the probability of using these characters a, w, b, and s, and the net payoff for using a particular character is A, W, B, and S. We can extract six equations: one from the fact that all of the probabilities will sum to unity (you have to choose one of the units), four directly from the payoff matrix, and the last from the net payoff rule.

Thus, we have

1. $a + w + b + s = 1$,
2. $A = w - b$,
3. $W = b + s - a$,
4. $B = a - w - s$,
5. $S = b - w$, and
6. $A + W + B + S = 0$.

You might wonder about the last assertion. Why does the net payoff have to be zero? Well, this is a zero-sum game. We are looking for an optimum mixed strategy. If it were possible for me to find a mixed strategy with better than zero payoff, you could use it too—and, logically, we couldn't both get a positive payoff.

Anyway, adding the payoff equations (equations 2, 3, 4, and 5) gives

$(w - b) + (b + s - a) + (a - w - s) + (b - w) = 0.$

Everything cancels out to leave

$(b - w) = 0,$

which tells us that

$b = w.$

The warrior and the barbarian must be used equally often. This means the payoff for playing the archer or sorcerer is 0, and the net payoff equation (6) is now

$W + B = 0.$

We can go further than that. If we're getting a payoff only from warriors and barbarians, we know that the payoff W can't be positive and the payoff B negative. If they were, it couldn't be an equilibrium. Obviously, I'd play warriors more often and barbarians less often to increase the net payoff. That would violate our finding that $w = b$. The only way to make it an equilibrium, then, is if

$W = B = 0.$

And this gives

$(a - s) = w = b.$

This is an equation to which there is a range of solutions, bounded by the cases of

$(a, w, b, s) = (1/2, 0, 0, 1/2)$, and $(a, w, b, s) = (1/3, 1/3, 1/3, 0)$.

This tells me that, although not a dominant choice, the archer is the most certain to be used because there is no possible strategy that can afford to dispense with it. More importantly, though, I can now see that this relationship on its own doesn't guarantee the dynamic gameplay of Stone-Paper-Scissors that we saw in Figure 5.4. I could play using only archers and sorcerers, and that would be a stable strategy. On average, you'd gain nothing by fielding a few barbarians against me, for example (although neither would you lose). Certainly, I don't want it to be possible for players not to bother with two of the character types in my game! Accordingly, to balance things out, I have to make sure there are more special situations that favor the other characters. Thus, the sorcerers could be a little bit more powerful at certain times, or (more probably) have some noncombat functions; the barbarians could get extra scouting abilities or recover from injury faster; warriors could be the only character type able to use magic swords; and so on.

How about other four-way relationships? Figure 5.7 shows the classic combined arms diagram for troops in the BG era—where BG stands for "before gunpowder." In fact, this was the core game dynamic of my *Warrior Kings* design.

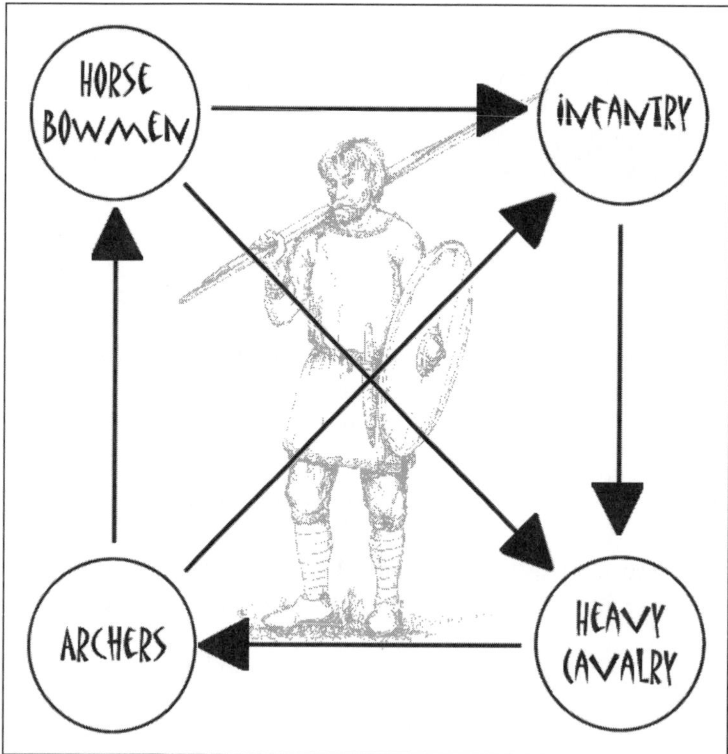

Figure 5.7
Combined arms in ancient and medieval armies.

The principle is one we have touched on earlier. Archers can skirmish against infantry, whose heavy armor prevents them from getting up close and personal. Heavy cavalry, though, are fast enough to ride the archers down. Horse bowmen can pull that skirmishing trick on both infantry and heavy cavalry, being faster than both, but they cannot prevail against archers, because it is impossible to employ the most powerful bows from the saddle. Infantry in regular order can stand firm against a cavalry charge and can present a denser and more effective killing front (which means they win in a melee).

That's all fine and dandy but, as I've drawn it above, it's not a useful interaction system to use in a game. In fact, it would be a disaster. Try constructing the payoff matrix, and you'll soon see that infantry is a dominated choice. It seems, doesn't it, that there's never a case where you'd be fielding horse bowmen and find yourself wishing you had infantry instead? Did all those medieval generals get it wrong? Should they have dropped infantry altogether? More to the point, did I goof up putting it into *Warrior Kings*?

It's a trick question, as I'm sure you've guessed. Infantry is useful because that combined arms diagram is a simplification. It tells us who beats whom, but it doesn't say *how*. Taking another look at the analysis of what's actually happening reveals that infantry is the only troop type that can actually hold territory. The others can win against each other, but they have to advance or give ground to do so. So, returning to the "best at" rule of thumb I mentioned in Chapter 3, we can say that infantry is balanced against the other troop types because it is best at holding territory. The importance that the game levels give to holding territory then determines how often infantry will be used.

You want proof? Look at *Age of Empires*. There, resources once collected are nonlocalized. A single villager can sneak in, build a base, and then you can "teleport" your army right onto the enemy's doorstep. Supply lines have no meaning. Consolidation of territory is therefore much less significant than in real-world warfare. And, in consequence, even when the designers halved the population-slot cost of infantry (in the expansion pack, *Rise of Rome*), they still couldn't succeed in making them an attractive option. This doesn't particularly harm *Age of Empires*, which remains a good fun game; it just means that the infantry units might just as well not be there.

A Game Balance Checklist

Balance in a game takes several forms.

Balance between players ensures the game is fair. Any unfairness is obvious when the game is played between opponents of equivalent skill, making this aspect of balance increasingly important as multiplay between human players becomes increasingly the norm. The only method of making the game absolutely fair is by exact symmetry in the choices available to all players. However, there may be other reasons for avoiding exact symmetry (because it is unrealistic or unaesthetic, for example). A just-broken symmetry can solve this as long as any asymmetries are not likely to magnify in effect throughout the game. Alternatively, you can provide the players with completely different choices so that each player will use radically different strategies. Absolute balance is then all but impossible. If you opt for prominent asymmetry, be sure the key differences are peripheral and do not interact to magnify any imbalance that may exist. It is possible to get away with extreme asymmetry if any unfairness arising from the asymmetry does not become glaringly obvious within the playable lifetime of the game.

The golden rule of player/player balance: A player should never be put in an unwinnable situation through no fault of their own.

Balance between the player and the game mechanics ensures that the player never becomes frustrated by an inability to progress. The interface should not present an unnecessary obstacle to whatever the player is trying to achieve. Remember that small rewards are needed to guide the player along the game's learning curve. These rewards can be cosmetic (a fancy graphic, a cut scene) or integral (experience points, further plot developments, a new weapon). In either case, the best rewards are the ones that widen the player's options because this enriches the gaming experience. Having the player's avatar go up a level and get more hit points is meaningless if you only make all the computer-player opponents tougher as well; rather, you need to astonish and delight the player with new abilities and new kinds of opponent.

The golden rule of player/gameplay balance: The game should be fun to learn as well as to play, and it should be *more* fun the more you master it.

Balance between different elements of the game system operates on two interdependent levels: components (the entities or choices within the game) and attributes (the interaction between components). The purpose of gameplay/gameplay balance is to make sure that no element of the game is redundant. You can get a useful guesstimate of the relative value of different game components by drawing up a Q-factor list for each component. The Q-factor need be no more than an arbitrary rating from one to ten against each attribute. In a strategy game, for example, I might begin by listing each unit's scores with respect to firepower, hit points, mobility, cost, vision range, armor, etc. The easiest way to ensure that no component is dominated (and therefore dispensable) is to recall the advice of Chapter 3, and make each component the best in at least one attribute. Relationships following the pattern of Paper-Scissors-Stone ensure that each component is dynamically rather than statically best. Such patterns oblige the player to continually alter his strategy and thus help create an exciting game.

It is not necessary to make every component equally useful to the player, nor is it likely that such a goal could be achieved in any but the simplest or most abstract of games. However, the cost, availability, or ease of use of each component should reflect its value to the player. This is best refined by continual playtesting throughout the development cycle.

The golden rule of gameplay/gameplay balance: All options in the game must be worth using sometimes, and the net cost of using each option must be commensurate with the payoff you get for using it.

Case Study 5.5 Using Game-Theory Analysis To Achieve Balance

Bloody Century is an operational-level wargame set in an alternate history where WWII dragged on into the 1950s. The designer, Gary, explains his concept to the development leads: "Basically, it's nice and simple with just five units—tanks, infantry, motorized infantry, artillery, and tank killers. Tanks beat everything except killers. Killers beat nothing except tanks. Infantry, motorized infantry, and artillery compete in a standard Stone-Paper-Scissors form."

Gary goes to the whiteboard and draws the payoff matrix he has in mind. "Bear in mind that this is just a first-pass analysis," he cautions the team. "Unlike in Stone-Paper-Scissors, units in a strategy game aren't used up every time they fight. So, if my tank destroys your infantry, I win a +1 payoff *and I keep my tank*. How damaged it may be, of course, is another matter. Here I'm assuming a victory costs about 50 percent of a unit's hit points."

Table 5.5 Payoff matrix for *Bloody Century*.

	Tank	Infantry	Motorized infantry	Artillery	Tank Killer
Tank	0	+1	+1	+1	-1
Infantry	-1	0	+1	-1	+1
Motorized Infantry	-1	-1	0	+1	+1
Artillery	-1	+1	-1	0	+1
Tank Killer	+1	-1	-1	-1	0

Everyone studies this (Table 5.5) with furrowed brows, and some coffee is drunk. At last, the lead level designer, Sarah, ventures a comment. "It doesn't look very well balanced. Tanks beat almost everything, and killers beat almost nothing!"

"Yes," concedes Gary, "but because tanks are effective they'll be used frequently. Because they're used frequently, that makes tank killers very useful too."

"It sounds like a circular argument to me," decides the company president. "What I want to know is, what's the game going to be like to play? Will we see lots of tanks, or killers, or what?"

Sarah has a further point. "And what about the typical mix of units in the game? Are you saying tanks and killers will be used twice as often, or 10 times as often, or what? I'd think players will expect the other units to get a look-in."

"Okay." Gary wipes out the first matrix and starts to draw a new one. "It turns out that what I've described is one SPS game within another SPS game. It's clearer if I write it out like this." (See Table 5.6.)

Table 5.6 Reduced payoff matrix for *Bloody Century*.

	Tank	Other	Tank Killer
Tank	0	+1	-1
Other	-1	0 (on average)	+1
Tank Killer	+1	-1	0

"So what does *this* tell us?" the company president wants to know (presumably unaware that everyone else puts him on a par with Dilbert's boss).

"The way I've assigned the payoffs assumes all units cost the same to build," explains Gary. "On that basis, the tanks and the tank killers will be used equally, with the same frequency as all the other three unit types lumped together." He draws a table (see Table 5.7) to illustrate.

Table 5.7 Unit usage frequency.

Unit Type	Tank	Infantry	Motorized Infantry	Artillery	Tank Killer
Frequency of Use	1/3	1/9	1/9	1/9	1/3

"I don't think much of that!" says Sarah. "You're going to see three times as many tanks as infantry units. It just doesn't feel right."

"Ah, but you can change that by changing the costs," insists Gary. "These are the frequencies you'd see if all units cost the same."

Even the company president has cottoned on by now. "So what happens if the tanks cost twice as much?"

"Well, it's fairly simple, but I won't go into it all now because it involves a bit of math, and it's easier to do on a spreadsheet. Basically, we'd start by drawing a new payoff matrix matching X dollars' worth of tank versus X dollars' worth of infantry, X dollars' worth of motorized infantry and so on."

"For instance?"

"Okay, say a tank costs $3,000, and an infantry unit costs $1,500. So, the matrix would now pit one tank against two infantry. I said that one tank beats one infantry but loses 50 percent of its hit points in the process. That means that the tank will destroy one of the two infantry before it's destroyed, so the two infantry win with a net payoff of $1,500."

"I thought tanks beat infantry," says the company president.

"Not any more. On a hit-points-for-dollars basis, they're now better. You see, I lost one tank worth $3,000, and you lost one infantry unit worth $1,500, so the net worth is $1,500 in your favor."

"Isn't there a risk that, with the new matrix, with the costs factored in, you could get dominated strategies?" wonders Sam, the lead programmer.

"Yes, you've got to check for that. There are bounds to the costs. If you go outside those bounds you get dominance, and then the game can break down. It might *never* be worth using artillery, say, and that might mean it's never worth playing motorized infantry, and so on. But all these things are easy to see when you draw the matrix."

Sarah, at least, is on the road to Damascus by now. "It's excellent. This means I can get some idea how changes in shadow costs on different levels will affect how units are used. That'll be very handy."

Chapter 6

Look And Feel

Key Topics:

- ***Creating immersion***
- ***Ambience***
- ***Interface issues***
- ***Raising player expectations (suspense, foreshadowing)***
- ***A toolbox of storytelling techniques***

In a sense, we now come back to the beginning: Nine out of 10 game concepts *start* with nothing but the look and feel. Take a hypothetical designer. Before he knew he was going to do a horror CRPG, before he decided on the title *Sepulcher*, before he thought of the spells with their side effects and recharge locations, before he devised the combat system that allows queuing of maneuvers—before all that, he probably just had an image of a snowbound Gothic ruin and men in top hats and ankle-length greatcoats approaching the iron-studded front door with pistols in their hands.

Your game began life as merely a twinkle in your eye, but, while writing the design, you had to put daydreams aside and focus on the needs of cold logic. With the design documents prepared and the schedule tacked up on the wall, you might easily have forgotten that you're developing a creative product and not a utility for a bank. Now, you must return to that original wellspring of creativity in order to consider the question of look and feel. It's time to get artistic.

In this chapter, we'll look at the various ways you can create a sense of alternate reality so as to promote *immersion*: the player's sense of actually being in the game's world. Immersion is primarily achieved through three means: ambience, interface, and storytelling.

Ambience

Ambience is everything that contributes to the innate look and feel of the game. I've recently been looking at some screenshots of the *Tekken* demo on the next-generation PlayStation. As well as the two combatants, there's a darkly atmospheric back street and a couple of dozen hooting, jeering, fully rendered spectators gathered in a deserted parking lot to watch these two guys beat up each other.

I'm sure that, having gotten this far through the design section of the book, you don't expect me to start drooling over GFLOPS and trilinear filtering. Instead, I'm going to take the technology for granted. (As good as it is, it's going to get much better still.) In the same way that technology like the SteadiCam and rotoscope have transformed movies, it isn't *how* it's done that matters, it's what *can* be done.

Think about those old-time beat-'em-ups. Two fighters in a sparse setting (which was often no more than a bare stage in the middle of a deserted temple square). Now, you can have a realistic-looking crowd of spectators in an almost photographically real setting, and that obviously creates more of a story right away. Why am I here to fight this guy? If I win, who do I fight next—that giant in bike leathers who's glaring at me from the sidelines? The sneering psycho with the knife? If I lose, how will the crowd react? Will I have to fight them all? And, if I run, how can I find my way out of this rat's maze of back streets?

Okay, *Macbeth* it isn't, but suddenly there's far more depth, richness, and drama than the beat-'em-up genre ever promised before. All because of a few thousand extra polygons, I can now include all kinds of ambient features that create a sense of location and involvement. I can hint at a backstory that goes beyond just beating another guy to score some points. It doesn't matter that none of the things I mentioned may actually occur in the game. As far as the game logic is concerned, it could still be the same beat-'em-up as before. But now it has atmosphere.

More than that, the fact that you can put something extra in means that the decision to leave it out can have added significance, too. Imagine a string of bouts in the parking lot with dozens of street scum looking on. Then the action switches to a dank warehouse. In a makeshift ring marked out by packing crates, I take on my next few opponents by the light of a single, bare lightbulb. A few spectators in fancy suits stand in the background, their faces cut across by indelible shadow. One of them is smoking: I glimpse the light of his cigarette. But, unlike the street scum, these guys watch in silence. The location changes again, and now it's an empty locker-room with just me and my opponent and no one to see us fight. We've come full circle, but now the sparse location and lack of spectators tells a story.

That's what ambience is about: telling a story. Not with intro FMVs and cut-scenes. (That's cheating—and expensive, too.) The story should unfold as part of the game itself, and ambience is all about imbuing each separate element with the backstory so as to create a unity in the final game.

We can broadly categorize the contributing factors to ambience as sound, vision, and touch.

Sound

The excellent thing about sound in games is that you hardly notice it, which means it can work on your subconscious and draw you into the game world without you even being aware of it. Think of the wistful guitar theme in *Diablo*, the stirring call-to-arms of *Warcraft*, the almost ethnic rhythms of *Age of Empires* and *Populous: The Beginning*. While you're engrossed in the gameplay, the music adds much to the sense of atmosphere. And not only the music, but other sound effects, too. Case Study 6.1 identifies several brilliant sound effects.

Sound doesn't have to be only atmospheric, of course. The best elements of a game are those that enhance ambience as well as gameplay. Thus, the priestly chants and war cries of *Populous: The Beginning* don't add only to look and feel, they are also important cues that tell the player what is happening. And, in Looking Glass Studio's excellent *Thief*, both atmosphere and gameplay are enhanced by the guards' muttered comments of "Come out, taffer" (indicating they're looking for you) and "It was just a rat..." (indicating that you're safe...for the time being).

Vision

When I began work on *Warrior Kings*, my first priority was to get the design documents written so the team could press on with the first tier. For once, look and feel hadn't been uppermost in my mind, because I started the project knowing that Eidos (the publisher) wanted something medieval. I had already written an unpublished design, *Dominion*, that I knew I could cannibalize for the sort of gameplay features Eidos needed. So, in the parlance of Chapter 1, I to some extent skipped the inspiration phase and went straight on to the synthesis.

Three months down the line, the team had completed the first tier to test the resource management. You could spawn peasants and townsmen and get them foraging, farming, and shopping. You could also place a few key buildings. (They sprouted instantly, though, as the stages of construction would be slotted in later.) Finally, there was a placeholder interface and blank slots to show where the mini-map and unit status boxes would go.

The team worked hard, and the tier was completed a few days early. I was impressed. A senior executive came round and looked at it. Afterwards, in his office, he told me, "The

Case Study 6.1 Sounds Effects At Their Best

Bullfrog's *Dungeon Keeper* has a particularly effective range of sound effects: the dank dripping sound evoking the sense of vast subterranean space; the echoing chip of pickaxes on veins of gold; the burst of crumbling rocks as your imps carve out new tunnels; the distinctive sounds of the different rooms; the constant mutterings, chants, and eerie little chuckles that quite brilliantly contribute to the ambience of a living, magical, sinister place deep below the earth.

king's palace is rubbish. This game is supposed to be set in the Middle Ages, but that palace looks like a Disney World attraction. You're supposed to see to these things."

My first reaction was naturally that this executive was an idiot. Couldn't he see past the placeholder graphics to the fact that we had gotten some working gameplay? Didn't he understand the point of the iterative development process?

But, when I cooled down, I got to thinking he had a point. Because I'd been concentrating so much on designing the gameplay and the development process, I had kind of overlooked the style. I was thinking that it could come later, but Eidos had several artists already assigned to the *Warrior Kings* project, and, in fact, it was up to me as designer of the game to give them some direction.

One of the members of the *Warrior Kings* team was Martin McKenna, a very talented artist from outside the games industry who had a strong track record with fantasy book covers and role-playing games. He and I discussed various ways to give the game a unique flavor. The Middle Ages is such a common setting that we didn't want to rehash something that had been done a hundred times before.

In search of something different, we looked at Eastern European buildings. Martin started talking about crooked steeples and ivy-covered castles in Grimms' fairy tales. I was thinking of *The Cabinet of Dr. Caligari* and photographs of the Kremlin under a crystal-clear night sky. We remembered the fine, dark look of Jim Henson's *Storyteller* TV series with John Hurt, and the narrow, crabbed buildings of comic book geniuses like Steve Ditko and Berni Wrightson.

Martin started producing concept sketches and feeding them to the 3D artists. Suddenly *Warrior Kings* started to look like no other game we'd seen. Coupled with Julia Hunt's Brueghel-like 3D characters, it was becoming the Middle Ages seen through a filter of folklore and dream. You could imagine the superstitious dread of those little scurrying characters as they hurried home with their bundles of wood, the bustle and squalor of the medieval streets, and the awesome spectacle of a battalion of knights drawn up for battle on the fields beside their impregnable castle.

This example shows the great value of conceptual artwork in creating ambience. Concept artists do not necessarily have to be computer artists. It may be better if they're not, as computer art tends to force a finished look, while artistic ideas are often best developed in a sketchy half-formed way that fosters creativity. The ideal concept artist is, like the game designer, more concerned with broad strokes and capturing a general style than in finishing the fine details.

Figure 6.1 shows the kind of artwork I am talking about. Using such pictures in early documentation helps convey a shared vision to the whole team.

Figure 6.1
One of Russ Nicholson's concept sketches for *Bloody Century.*

Attention To Detail

Games achieve cohesion by adhering to a unified look and feel. I decided, for example, that the FMV for *Gaze* (Case Study 6.5) should eschew the use of the color red. The result is a look made of metallic blues and dusty bronze and gold, implying a world from which the life has been bled. The lead character is then introduced at the end of the FMV as he slots a carnation into his lapel—a scene made all the more striking because it is the first splash of red used in the game.

Remain true to your style. When there is an element of the art that doesn't fit with the rest of the style, the effect is jarring as shown in Case Study 6.2. Concept artwork assists by showing every member of the art team what you are striving for.

Touch

"Okay," you must now be saying to yourself, "sound and vision are obvious enough, but what has touch got to do with computer games?"

Well, I admit I'm cheating a little bit. By *touch*, I don't literally mean the physical sense of touch, I mean the impression of physicality conveyed by the game's look and feel—the *handling* of the game, so to speak.

Case Study 6.2 A Discordant Note

When I first saw the promotional FMV for *War of the Worlds*, I was very impressed. The weird look of the aliens in their council chamber on Mars banished all thoughts of *Mars Attacks!* These insidious tentacled creatures looked like they had been plotting the invasion of Earth since primordial times. And the Martian war machines were exactly what H.G. Wells must have intended: massive Edwardian industrial tech, with valves and pistons and brass finishing. They picked their way through the ruins of London with the dispassion of insects.

But then one bit of artwork went and spoiled it. In a sequence on the bank of the Thames, clumping along the embankment came—surely not?—a gun-toting bipedal robot like something straight out of *RoboCop*. It couldn't have been more intrusive if the lid had popped open and Bugs Bunny had looked out. It was a damned shame, because they had a beautiful look and feel going, and that robot blew it away in a second.

This is important. In the early days of animation, cartoonists had a hard time getting their characters to feel right: The animated characters didn't seem to move with weight, momentum, and force. It was early pioneers like Walt Disney who found the techniques of accurately portraying these physical attributes in a medium relying on sound and vision.

So, it is kind of a cheat, because you have only sound and graphics with which to get the feel across, but that physical sense is a big part of games. Contrast the comic book acrobatics of *Virtua Fighter* with the solidly realistic physics of Bandai's *Ichigeki*. Or the rolling, bouncing vehicles of *Big Red Racing* with the authentic road handling found in *Metropolis Street Racer*.

At the Develop conference in London in 1996, theater director Graham Bruce (**www.trickster.demon.co.uk**) gave one of the most interesting talks. He was discussing how he coached actors for motion capture so as to help them create a sense of the physical environment of the game world, using the specific example of *Actua Soccer*. It was a lesson I took very much to heart, and since then I have always made sure to convey a feeling of the game environment in my design documents. But I don't believe any theater director has been invited to talk at Develop since, which is a pity. Technology alone can take you only so far.

Interface

The ideal interface is transparent: You would prefer simply to think something in order to make it happen. *Black & White*, a PC game in development at Lionhead, is one approach to this. The player casts a defensive spell with a sweeping movement of the mouse, drawing a circle of flame around him. To throw a fireball, he jabs the cursor towards his target. The designers are hoping that the various mouse gestures will become second nature, so that you can make things happen in the game world almost without thinking.

But, when I say the ideal option is the transparent interface, let me add a qualifier. Transparent doesn't have to mean invisible. In a racing game, you wouldn't want an interface that let you drive your car intuitively, because that's not how cars are controlled in real life. The transparent interface in that context wouldn't be one like *Black & White*, but one that felt as close as possible to the experience of actually driving a car.

You can keep the interface transparent by making it enhance the look and feel. Case Study 6.3 provides an example of meshing the interface with look and feel. This is the "hide in plain view" approach. *StarCraft* does this. There is no getting around the unit status boxes and command icons in such a complex wargame, so the designers made a virtue of necessity: Each species has its own custom interface that adds texture to the playing experience.

Sometimes you can't hide the interface, and you can't make it enhance ambience either. It's quite hard to make inventories and automaps atmospheric when you're trying to do an Arthurian role-playing game, for instance. Then at least be sure to minimize the degree to which those aspects of the interface intrude. The "save game" feature is usually an intrusive element of any interface, as it destroys the illusion of reality. The designers of Appeal's

Case Study 6.3 Meshing The Interface With Look And Feel

In 1996, I wrote a strategy game called *2020: Knife Edge* for Domark. Units could be controlled on two levels: imperatives (direct commands like "go here", "attack this building," and so on) and protocols (general commands like "act defensively," "act aggressively," and so on). It was a game of near-future warfare (set in 2020, naturally), and so a high-tech interface was appropriate. You would click on a unit and issue commands from a head-up display just as if you were in the Pentagon War Room. The project lead, Lee Briggs, described the interface style we were striving for as "a civilian implementation of a military interface, like you see in *Star Trek: The Next Generation*."

Later, I came to write *Warrior Kings*. In most strategy games, units like towers and archers are really useful because you don't have to tell them what to do. Ideally, you'd like to set standing orders for all your units, and to have some flexibility into the bargain (that is, maybe you don't *always* want archers to skirmish). My goal was for the player to be able to set behaviors for his units so that the game had a strategic and a tactical level, like *2020: Knife Edge*. Players could set large-scale plans using the protocols and fine-tune them in battle by grabbing individual units and issuing imperatives.

But the high-tech style of *2020: Knife Edge* would not have suited *Warrior Kings* at all. Clicking on a unit and setting its standing order AI didn't really mesh with the medieval setting. Like placing "way points" for patrolling units, it's a mechanism that tends to jar you out of the game world. The solution I found was to link the behavioral protocols to different formations so that the player tells the battalion to draw up in line, column, wedge, or whatever, and this sets the AI for the battalion. Also, this interface became easier to use, because—instead of having to click on a unit to check its standing orders—you could see at a glance from the formation.

Don't think I'm blowing my own trumpet. Yes, it was a good idea. But I should have had that idea a year earlier when I was designing *2020: Knife Edge*!

Outcast, however, found a way to incorporate it into the game world: You save the game by activating a magical crystal that stores an instant in time. (And, since it produces plenty of light and noise as it does, you have to choose carefully where to use it.) Case Study 6.4 provides examples of keeping the interface out of the players' way.

Figure 6.2
Testbed—The minimap is intrusive.

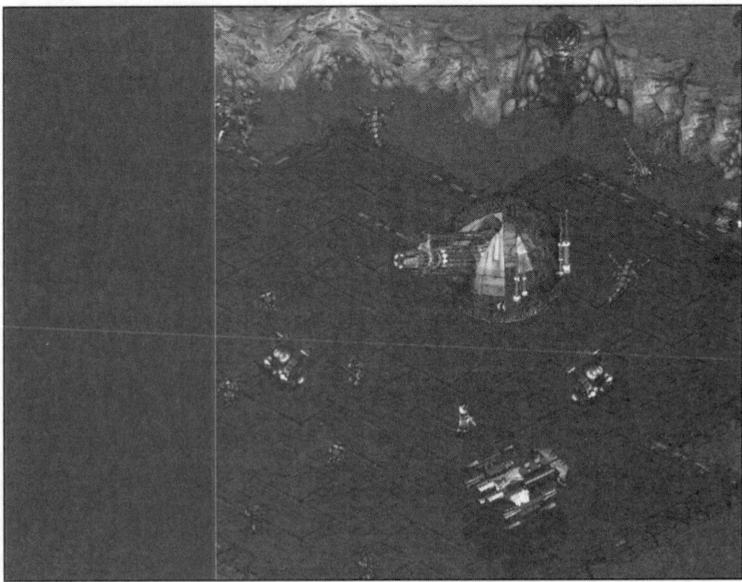

Figure 6.3
Finished game—The interface frames the view.

Case Study 6.4 Sometimes Less Is Less

If you can't make the interface transparent, at least keep it out of the player's way. An early testbed of *Warrior Kings* had a mini-map that appeared in the top left-hand corner of the screen, as in Figure 6.2 (mockups courtesy of the *StarCraft* map editor). I took one look at this arrangement and commented that we'd have to put the command icons and selected unit data below this to make a continuous bar filling the side of the screen, as in Figure 6.3. (I make no claims for originality; of course, it is the standard interface in most realtime strategy games.)

One of the team had an objection. "We don't need the command icons there all the time. Once a player has learned the game, he might want to play with just intuitive right-clicks. For special actions, I'd prefer to just use the keyboard."

"What advantage do we get by hiding the command icon window?" I asked him.

"The screen's less cluttered. The only thing you need to look at apart from the main view is the minimap."

"In fact, that makes it *more* cluttered," I explained. "When you put the interface down the whole side of the screen, it becomes a frame. A frame doesn't obtrude on the main view. But, as soon as you take away the lower part of the frame, the player will see that minimap quite differently. Now it's an obstacle getting in the way of whatever's behind it."

Another approach to interface design is to make the game controls intuitive so that they second-guess what you want. For instance, in *Age of Empires*, a right-click is interpreted dependent upon what you're clicking on. If you click on an enemy unit, the command is interpreted as "attack"; if on an empty location, it's interpreted as "move," and so on.

A third option is to second-guess what the player wants or will do according to what he's done so far. The game version of *Blade Runner* infers which of three women the hero is attracted to by the amount of time he spends with them. This is nice because it's very subtle: The player is not even conscious of making a choice.

Storytelling

According to legend (which is to say, allegedly), two factions were involved in the design of *Doom*. One faction thought that a strong setting and backstory would enhance the players' appreciation of the game. The other took the contrary view: "Story? We don' need no steenkin' story!"

Since the release of *Half-Life*, I think that nobody now needs convincing about the value of story. Sure, in the bad old sense of a story that the game designer had set out to tell you, storytelling in games was worse than redundant; it was an intruder from another medium. Computer games are meant to be interactive. That's the whole point. They shouldn't aim to turn the player into a passive spectator. The designer who wants to do that should write a novel instead.

But *Half-Life* didn't just tell you a story; it helped you create a story. This is more than simply a worthwhile way to bring storytelling into entertainment software: It is the philosopher's stone that turns dross into gold. You see, look and feel is about creating atmosphere so that the player is able to suspend his disbelief, but that is all wasted effort unless you can make the reader *want* to suspend disbelief.

If stories did not matter, boxers would never pretend to hate each other before a fight. Politics would be decided on the issues and not the personalities. *Star Wars* would consist of nothing but fast vehicle chases and swordfights. Yet, we need to know who Luke Skywalker is, and why he's in this spaceship, and who is chasing him through an asteroid belt, before it really matters to us. All the special effects in the world are just wallpaper until you have a story.

A Toolbox Of Storytelling Techniques

Erica Wagner, literary editor of *The Times*, has this to say about the future of entertainment software:

"Sony has already trademarked something they call `emotion synthesis.' Its aim is to involve you in games the way you become involved in films.... That's what I want. I love to read, to listen to stories and go to the movies because I want to be swept out of myself and into another place. Just now—despite astounding 3D graphics and flawless violence synthesis—I can't find that place inside my PC screen."

—Article in The Times "Interface" supplement, June 9, 1999

Ms. Wagner is making a very good point about the direction entertainment software needs to go, but you don't need any special technology to tap into the immersive power of storytelling. Movie makers have been doing it for 80 years. Storytellers knew all the tricks for creating emotional involvement long before Shakespeare's day.

Yet not many game designers seem to have the slightest idea about storytelling—so let me run through some of the key ideas here. Incidentally, before—when explaining game theory—I said that it applied generally to all genres of game even though most of the examples I used were from strategy games. Similarly, the clearest examples of storytelling come from adventure games and CRPGs, but the same techniques can be used in other genres also.

Obstacles

A little old man runs into the inn where the hero is staying and says to him, "There's a vampire up at the castle. You have to kill it."

Very poor. Try this instead: A fearful old man enters the inn and avoids the hero. When the hero asks what has frightened him, the old man gives no reply. Then he goes to a character sitting by the fire and begs him for something, but is refused. "You pawned it, you only get it back when you pay," he is told. If the hero pays on the old man's behalf, he sees what the item is: a crucifix. "You should buy one yourself if you're going to stay in these parts," remarks the pawnbroker.

Neither version is great literature, but the second is far superior. Why? Because it involves an obstacle. Instead of being told the setup, the hero/player has to find it out for himself. This distracts the critical faculty of the mind, which is thereby tricked into a level of acceptance it would not allow if baldly presented with an obviously artificial plot device as in the first version.

Foreshadowing

A story depicts the intrusion of a new world that threatens or transforms the old. In *Age of Empires*, a small settlement is attacked by raiders and, in defending itself, grows to become a major civilization. Or take a movie such as *Total Recall*—the hero starts by thinking he's a construction worker, learns he's a deep-cover spy, gets drawn into a series of adventures, and ends by asserting a new identity and bringing about the rebirth of the planet Mars.

Foreshadowing occurs in the early stages of the story when the new world has yet to intrude on the status quo. It is a way of preparing us for the story by giving a foretaste of what is to come. In *Age of Empires*, this would be a small raid by a few enemy clubmen who are easily fought off. In *Total Recall*, the foreshadowing is quite explicit: The hero dreams of Mars and then is told by the director of Recall, Inc., that he will "be a spy, go to Mars, get the girl, and save the world." (Pretty cool. Only the most assured artists have the confidence to explain all their tricks first and *still* amaze you!)

Use foreshadowing in an introductory sequence to show what is to come. In *Grim Fandango*, we first meet Manny Calavera as he's about to send his latest client, one of the recently departed, on a long dangerous walk through the Petrified Forest of the afterlife. This works as a neat bit of indirect exposition, as the author didn't have to say, "Look, this is Manny. He sends souls to their final resting place and the worst route a soul can take is through the Forest." And it also works as foreshadowing because, before the story is out, Manny is going to have to take that walk himself.

Personalization

The novice author thinks that saving the world is the ultimate goal. Hey, they don't come any bigger than that, right?

Well, how about rescuing your little niece who's gone missing in Central Park at sunset? I reckon that more than measures up. The reason is that saving the world is a sterile goal. Even the worst author recognizes that, and, to solve the problem they usually add, "The world's in danger and *only you* can save it."

What are they trying to do there? They're trying to make the threat personal. Because, when it's personal, the reader or filmgoer or player will care about it.

Look at *Star Wars*. (You can learn a lot about storytelling from *Star Wars*.) Nobody tells Luke Skywalker that he's going to have to save the world. In fact, he's going to have to do that and a whole lot more, but what kicks it off is a plea for help from a beautiful princess. Princess Leia personifies the incomprehensible goals of struggle against a galactic empire. Luke gets drawn in, and we go with him.

The most obvious personal challenge in computer games is the "What in Sam Hill is going on here?" effect, used particularly well in *Half-Life*. *Outcast* uses it even more cleverly to distract us from the fact that they are handing us a save-the-world story—paradoxically made more credible by being told promptly after the intro that we actually have two worlds to save. Nonetheless, when the going gets tough, it is the welfare of the fragrant Dr. Marion Wolfe that really motivates our hero to get going.

Don't make the mistake of locating your personal challenge to the player within the backstory. I don't want to watch an opening FMV that tells me my family has been kidnapped and then throws me into the game to sort it out, because my identification with the lead character begins only when the FMV ends. *Dark Earth* involved a complex plot of betrayal, mystery, and danger, but it made sure that these plot elements were uncovered during the game. By the time I had begun to figure out the intrigue, I'd already been playing for an hour, and, then, just to make sure I took the threat to the world seriously, the game embodied it in a very personal way by having my character get infected with a slow-acting poison. Never mind "You have two hours to save the world"; how about "You have two hours to stop yourself from becoming a monster?"

Resonance

The film director Brian De Palma gave a vivid description of resonance. He likened different elements of the story to charged rods. When they get close enough...*CRACK!*...you get a spark that illuminates the narrative. Too far apart and the discharge cannot happen; too close and you get a closed circuit with no sparks.

One of the best uses of resonance in entertainment software is LucasArts' *Grim Fandango*. The 1930s influence of the setting allows a pseudo-Art Deco motif in the office block where the hero works, which is the headquarters of the Department of Death. Traditional Art Deco was influenced by Egyptian art, making it an excellent metaphor for the afterlife, which is the setting of the game. In *Grim Fandango*, that Art Deco style comes with a spin, though, in that the decorative images used are not Egyptian but Aztec—which pulls us back to the origins of the Day of the Dead festival in pre-Columbian myth. The 1930s trope also works well with the *noir*ish private-eye slant and the slightly shabby elegance familiar to anyone who has ever visited Mexico City. The game begins in the city of El Marrow, which looks like a sleepy town that time has passed by. Indeed, this impression is accentuated by styling the world of the living, which the hero briefly visits, on Richard Hamilton's brashly colorful Pop Art paintings of the 1950s. (Life is to afterlife as Mexico is to the USA? That's resonance.)

Case Study 6.5 presents the kind of look-and-feel document I might circulate to the art team at the outset of a project. Resonances are already suggested at this stage. Rather than point them out, I leave it to you to identify them. (No prizes because they are quite blatant!)

Resonance can be used with varying degrees of subtlety. The least overt involves repeated images that defy instant critical analysis and so work on a very deep level. Examples of this kind of resonance—which we may call *motifs*—are hats in *Miller's Crossing*, water and the lack of it in *Chinatown*, and the use of discordant sounds and background noise in *Touch of Evil*.

(Why all the examples from cinema and nothing from games? I'm coming to that....)

More obvious are symbols that visually express the subtext. Hitchcock's thrillers often symbolize inevitability or danger by shadows that seem to form a web or the bars of a cage. Orson Welles' *Touch of Evil* is set on the border between the USA and Mexico, and the story concerns a moral border: the gray area between the two lead characters, played by Welles and Charlton Heston. I categorize these as more-overt forms of resonant effects because they operate at the mind's liminal threshold.

Least subtle of all is resonance to another story, movie, or game. Charitable critics refer to this as intertextuality or *hommage* (presumably on the theory that saying it in French makes it more respectable). This kind of reference occurs very, very often in games, particularly in the introductory FMVs, whose authors seem to want to copy not only the style of movie directors like Sonnenfeld, Raimi, or Tarantino, but the specific scenes used in the movies, too. The other name for this kind of "resonance" is *plagiarism*, and it is a sure symptom of unoriginality. Advertisers plagiarize all the time, but that's no excuse for anyone else. We're game developers, artists in an exciting new medium; we ought to show a little more creativity. One sign that entertainment software is maturing as an art form will be when we start to see designers employing more-subtle forms of resonance.

Resistance

Storytellers know that people are perverse. When we're being told a story, there's a little bit of us that is kicking against it, continually whispering, "It isn't true!"

Let me show you. Imagine the start of a movie. Bruce Willis is sitting in a dingy strip-club treating yesterday's hangover with a large scotch. Two guys in regulation black suits and shades walk in. "There's a terrorist who's sworn to kill the President. We need you back."

What does Bruce do? Jump to his feet and go straight to work? No. Instead he snarls, "I'm retired," knocks back his whisky, and turns to look at the girls. If he'd agreed at once it would only allow our subconscious imp of the perverse to grumble how unrealistic that was, how he was just doing it for the sake of the story. By showing resistance, however, he makes us start to think, "Come on, man! Agree! There's no movie if you don't." The storyteller suckers us into rooting for his story even before the main character does. There's no better way to enable Coleridge's "willing suspension of disbelief."

Case Study 6.5 An Example Of A Look-And-Feel Document

Gaze is an adventure game set in an alternate reality. The world of *Gaze* is a single vast city that is technologically advanced (electric cars, computers, surveillance satellites) but socially conservative.

Introduction

Our first view is a gray, unchanging surface that is moving like a featureless landscape below us. Then, catching sight of an observation port, we are able to take in the shape and size of what we're looking at. We realize the gray material is the skin of a dirigible, which moves slowly away like a weightless ocean liner to reveal....

A retro-futuristic city. This is the city of the future as imagined in the 1950s: vast office blocks, streets like canyons, gleaming skyscrapers of concrete and glass catching the sun. It's bright, clinical, and overwhelming.

Our viewpoint descends through wisps of cloud around the highest buildings. Recall the architecture of the Third Reich, Fritz Lang's *Metropolis*, the Empire State Building, *The Hudsucker Proxy*. The quality of the light is hazy; the daylight turned bronze close to street level by the fine dust of those swept-clean city streets. Sleek cars like huge cryo-capsules whoosh down tarmac avenues on silent tires. Looking along the block, the avenue goes on and on until lost in the distance, unchanging like a reflection in a pair of blue mirrors.

The crowds on the streets are uniformly dressed: the men in dark suits, the women in gray or white dresses. This is not a world like ours with a dozen different fashions and colors. And that means that the occasional splash of color on a hoarding or in a window display is all the more striking.

And it's quiet. The cars are electric and make very little noise. The people hurry to work without a word. In our opening shot from high above the street, the first sound you hear is just the lawnmower hum of the dirigible's rotors.

What feature of all this is startling? We see it as the camera spirals down, taking a leisurely view of the streets and the people and then turning towards the center of the city as it reaches ground level. We're now looking into the burnished bronze glare of the sun. What we didn't see before was a massive statue that towers above the buildings, matching the highest skyscraper. At first, it might evoke a resonance with the Statue of Liberty, but then we'll see the spiked crown, the balance, and the blindfold. This is not Liberty. It's Justice.

Main playing screen

Gaze is an adventure game, and the main screen is a third-person view like in *Tomb Raider* or *Dark Earth*.

Something we must decide: Does the view ever cut, or is it a continuous tracking shot throughout? *Grim Fandango* and *Dark Earth* use the cut and all shots are static, allowing pre-rendered backdrops. This favors adventure games with strong storylines, because you can use the cut to create suspense: a sudden high angle with the hero far below, a shot from behind as a door opens, etc.

In such games as *Tomb Raider* and *Die by the Sword*, the story matters less. Action is more important (they're almost the descendants of platform games, in a way), and so a smooth tracking shot is sustained throughout. Where every action counts, the player doesn't want to keep switching views.

The graphics engine will determine if the number of characters on screen would be an issue. It would be nice to be able to at least hint at the heaving mass of humanity filling the streets during the rush hour, so as to make more of the utterly deserted streets during the rest of the day. Obviously, the first-person viewpoint always has the advantage that it's one less character on screen. In any case, *Gaze* is a game of suspense and nail-biting tension rather than in-your-face bloodbath action, so, in fight sequences, I'd expect only a few opponents to be on the screen at any one time.

My thinking on this has been that we'd probably go for a continuous tracking shot most of the time, with very occasional cuts or pre-scripted camera movements at key dramatic moments. But that presumably means the scenery can't be as lavishly detailed. We need to decide this.

Overview screen

My original impression had been that, in-between encounter areas, we'd switch to a 2D map of the city on which you'd click to go to a new location. It'd be a nicely drawn map, drawn with false perspective and all that, but it'd still just be a 2D map.

The problem with that is that it's not immersive. It would be far better to have a seamless way of moving between the two views. The ideal would be to pull back from the hero in the close-up main view, and keep moving up and away until you had a high-angle shot of the city with the hero now a tiny figure down on the streets. Not quite as ideal, but almost as good, would be to start pulling out and then cut to the high-angle shot.

Interface

Obviously, we'll want to keep the screen as uncluttered as possible. I'd like to avoid having a status bar. Instead we'll show injuries on the hero himself (a torn shirt, scratches, bruises, and so on) and by the way he's moving (bad injuries cause a limp, he hunches down nursing his arm, and so on).

Movement control and combat is like in *Tomb Raider* (which has the virtue of being familiar to more players than any other game interface!).

Selecting items from your inventory takes you to an extreme close-up of the hero pulling items from inside his jacket, while the full range of items in the inventory is shown across the bottom of the screen. (This view will be more immersive than switching to just a clinical scroll-through item list.) You pick items using either arrow keys to get him to pull out one item after another (use the Return key to select an item) or with function keys tagged to the full inventory of items shown at the bottom of the screen. You can reorganize items in the inventory so you'll have at hand those items you'll need in a hurry.

We need to decide how to handle items that are dropped. We could say you can deposit items only at a chest, say. Otherwise, it's possible to get a very cluttered screen with far too many objects on it. Another way is to have a generic "dropped object" graphic and you discover what the object(s) is/are only when you pick up that graphic. Let's discuss this one.

Characters

For character style, think of those chunkily drawn private eyes in big suits that you get in comic strips from the 1950s. Bob Kane, creator of Batman, seems to have been the main influence on that style.

What I'm envisaging is that most people in La Vista (the city) seem heavy set and move a little stiffly. Their chiseled features evoke a robotic impression. (Don't make too much of all this, though; be subtle. Just because they're conformists doesn't mean they have to stumble around like sleepwalkers!)

But our hero, Bracken, is a free spirit, not a cog in the machine, and the graceful way he moves tells us that. The same is true of Gaze, the mysterious woman for whom the hero is searching and who seems to hold the key to changing this stagnated world. When we get onto motion capture, the actors should be thinking of Bracken as a hawk: proud, swift, capable of both fierce concentration and ferocious activity. Gaze is a tropical fish: fragile, languid, ethereally beautiful. The incidental characters share a kind of '50s uniformity so, to mark a contrast with that, imagine the protagonists cast as silent-movie era stars: Rudolph Valentino for Bracken, Louise Brooks for Gaze.

You can use the same trick even better in computer games than in movies or books because, in an adventure game or an RPG, the player's identification with the hero is much stronger. In *Grim Fandango*, Manny learns about an evil conspiracy and is asked to join the struggle. But he refuses: "I'm not looking to join any military organization. I just want my job back so I can work off my time and get out of this dump." The player knows he's going to get drawn into the struggle anyway, but Manny's resistance to the idea makes it all the more credible.

So, despite what the Borg may say, resistance is *not* futile. It makes a far stronger story.

Plot Points

Every storyteller knows the importance of confounding expectations. Being told you're going with Gandalf on a quest to Mount Doom would be boring if that's exactly what happens, no more and no less. But, in *The Lord of the Rings*, that isn't all that happens. Gandalf gets killed by the Balrog when the journey has hardly begun. Nobody was expecting that—not the characters, nor the reader. This is what is called a *plot point*.

Plot points pivot the story around in a new and surprising direction, as shown in Case Study 6.6. This quickens interest in the story and expands its scope.

Adventure games benefit most from plot points, but you can also use them very effectively in designing specific levels for racing, platform, action, and strategy games.

Begin by roughly dividing the expected playing time by four. The first major plot point should come about a quarter of the way into the game. (In movies and plays, this constitutes

Case Study 6.6 An Unexpected Development

Dungeon Master (not to be confused with Bullfrog's *Dungeon Keeper*) was a seminal CRPG of the 1980s. The setup was that a powerful sorcerer, the White Lord, set the heroes on a quest to retrieve his staff from the underworld and return it to him so that he could use it to destroy the Dark Lord.

As the quest went on, there were little clues that the White Lord might not be the happy-clappy sort of fellow that he made himself out to be. And, lo and behold, if you did take that staff back to him, he suddenly decided that you'd been tainted with evil and started trying to kill you.

The plot had suddenly been completely changed. Previously the player had had a nice, clear goal: get the staff and everything will be okay. Only that turned out to be 100 percent wrong. Now you had to figure out a new goal all by yourself.

Fortunately, by this time in the game you would have found that you understood every spell you could get from combining runes—except for one. And, if you'd figured out the principles behind the magic system, you might start to have an inkling what that mystery spell was for. So, the designer of *Dungeon Master* not only slipped in a neat bit of storytelling, but succeeded in meshing it perfectly with the gameplay.

the end of the first act.) This plot point should deepen the mystery or throw new challenges at the player. The second major plot point comes three-quarters of the way through the game. This time it should clear up mysteries (but not completely), so that the action is freed up to shift to a quicker pace.

Aristotle said that the most effective plot points involved reversals. My own view is that a reversal is often best at the first plot point, but some sort of discovery is ideal at the second. To take an example based on a strategy game, the player might discover that the direct assault he was planning is impossible because of the cliffs in front of his foe's stronghold. That's the first plot point. The second comes when he realizes a smaller commando-type force can be sent in through the mines under the stronghold.

Suspense

I'm going to return to one of my favorite bugbears, the "save game" feature, to show how it encourages lazy storytelling. Imagine an adventure game with an unbeatable opponent. The hero won't have a hope if he fights him one on one. He'll have to run away, lead the bad guy back to a trap he passed earlier, and sucker him into it.

How would the designer show that this particular foe was unbeatable? Nine times out of 10, he wouldn't even try. He'd just say to himself, "The player will probably try to fight the bad guy a couple of times. When he realizes that he's just getting killed straight away each time, he'll soon go back to the last save and try to think of something else."

That's poor, because there are many very effective techniques for building suspense so that the player begins to expect trouble ahead. Foreshadow by having the corridor littered with old skeletons, the baddie's earlier victims. Better, make it a hallway filled with fossilized heroes. Then every step will have the player wondering where the Gorgon is lurking. Use occasional momentary releases in the build-up of tension so that you can crank the suspense up a notch. So, in this case, you might have a sound startle the hero and then a rat scurries out from a pile of rocks. The hero sighs, but the player now sees a shadow with snakes for hair rising up behind him....

You can also demonstrate the danger to the hero. Show another character, perhaps a companion of the hero, being ripped apart or turned to stone. And you can tantalize with false hope: Perhaps the hero shoots, causing a cave-in that seems to bury the Gorgon, but, when the dust clears, she is unscathed. And create a race against time: Cracks are spreading across the roof of the cavern, and the hero has to lure the Gorgon back to the trap and return before the way ahead is blocked for good.

The reason why suspense should be used more in games is because any death of the lead character destroys the illusion. Suspense allows you to create fear and expectation in the player without recourse to the "save game" feature.

Theme

We already saw in Chapter 1 that theme is the inherent question posed by a story. Is freedom more important than life? What makes us who we are? How powerful is love? For the record, the films I'm thinking of are *The Matrix*, *L'Enfant Sauvage*, and *The Last Temptation of Christ*, although you could no doubt think of dozens of other movies with those same themes.

First off, your game shouldn't *answer* the question. Even a book or movie should only pose the question and then explore the specifics of one case. A story is not a manifesto. In an interactive medium like computer games, forcing an answer to the theme on your player is doubly bad. The story is created when the game is played. You cannot know the exact experience the player will get, nor what he or she will conclude about your chosen theme.

Reflect the theme in incidental details to add texture to the story. Shakespeare wasn't afraid to do this overtly in *Hamlet*, staging a play within the play to highlight the hero's moral dilemma. On a minor but very effective level, in *Age of Empires* it is poignant to see a lion killing a villager while your armies battle to the death on a grand scale. More significantly, *Blade Runner* uses a recurring motif of eyes (the windows to the self) to subliminally remind us of its theme: "What is the soul of Man?"

Resolution

The resolution of a story should be:

- *Hard won*—No reward is satisfying if it's attained too easily. (This is not often a failing of computer games!)

- *Not obvious*—You don't want the ending the player has seen coming for the last 10 hours. All the same, in hindsight it must make perfect sense.
- *Satisfying*—Usually this means morally satisfying (the hero wins), but the best authors can make it work as long as it's aesthetically satisfying (e.g., tragedy).
- *Consistent*—The ending must be in keeping with what has gone before in style, theme, and plot development.
- *Achieve closure*—The resolution must do just that: resolve the problem of the story. (The king is dead, long live the king.)

Case Study 6.7 provides an example of an unsatisfying conclusion.

In the film *The Warriors* (incidentally based on Xenophon's account of the Greeks in Persia), the heroes get stranded on the wrong side of town during a gang war. The story involves their journey back home to Coney Island. They arrive home at daybreak, and it seems the nightmare is over. But it isn't easy to wake up. In a mirror of the foreshadowing technique, a threat from the chaos of the story still lingers even when they think they are safe. Use this in your games. Everything has been building to the fight with the end-of-level boss, so there are no surprises to be had there. Put in another challenge after that—something more personal like a test of trust, or a last simple hand-to-hand fight when all the hero's weapons are used up. The sense of catharsis for the player will be far greater.

Sometimes the hero can't make it back. He can create a new order out of the chaos, but he has to sacrifice himself to do so. This is what happens to John Wayne's character in

Case Study 6.7 An Unsatisfying Conclusion

There were many ways that *Might & Magic 2* broke new ground, but the elegant resolution wasn't one of them. Through most of the game, the player had taken a party of adventurers to different cities and ruined castles; explored elemental realms of fire, water, and so on; and fought a sufficiency of orcs, vampires, and other monsters in various locations, usually underground.

The game took the form of several mini-quests building to an impressive climax. The player knew the date, so it was soon possible to feel the icy breath of fate. After many exciting adventures, the player approached the final labyrinth. There was a long struggle against a succession of powerful monsters that guarded the way to the inner mystery.

And what happened then? Our sorcerers and knights were confronted with a control panel and were told that the computer that steered the planet was malfunctioning. To avert collision with an asteroid, you had to solve a coded message. A clock started. You had 15 minutes. And the coded message? It turned out to read: "Fourscore and seven years ago, our fathers..."

That was it. You solved it, the asteroid missed, the computer thanked you, and you could go home. Imagine. Why didn't Tolkien think of that one? I bet he'd have kicked himself if he'd known!

The Searchers: There is no place for him any more in the homestead; he has to walk away back into myth. Computer games don't often make use of self-sacrifice, but it is the strongest kind of resolution. Remember that the cost of saving the world cannot come cheaply.

Change

You probably know the Chinese curse: "May you live in interesting times." Well, all stories are set at interesting times. We don't get to hear about the time Sir Gawain went shopping for a loaf of bread. Instead, we hear about when he had to marry a hideous crone or when he had a year and a day before the Green Knight would hack off his head.

The interest value of a story lies in the fact that something has happened to cause an upheaval in the status quo. The period of the story is a time of change, even outright chaos, when the normal rules are suspended. Anything might happen. In a light-hearted story, the aim may be only to restore things to the way they were. But, even if the story ends with the return of the old order, there must necessarily be the change that T. S. Eliot described: "The end of all our exploring / Will be to arrive where we started / And know the place for the first time."

The inner change in the hero is in fact the point of the story. It is what all stories are about: A protagonist, dormant and waiting (if often unwilling) to change, is catalyzed by events that challenge him to grow or (in the case of tragedy) to fail in the attempt. The quest in *The Lord of the Rings* is not just a long physical trek to Mount Doom to destroy the ring; it is the moral journey of Frodo from innocence to self-knowledge. He starts the story as good because he doesn't know what evil is—an easy choice. By the end, he knows that evil is seductive, but he resists it all the same. He has grown up, and so the story achieves a satisfying closure.

The Sum Of The Parts

You can use many techniques for creating atmosphere, engaging the player's emotions, and unfolding the action of the game in an effective and exciting way. Game designers too often have sought inspiration from too narrow a range of sources, leading to diminishing returns as the same products are endlessly reiterated in slightly different forms. Examining other narrative media, particularly cinema, gives us suggestions for how to enhance our games.

Ultimately, however, entertainment software is a unique medium like no other. Computers give us the means now to create toys, mysteries, puzzles, and stories, either individually or all wrapped up in one package. The authors of the past can point the way, but it is up to us to create a new entertainment medium worthy of our audience.

Chapter 7
Wrapping Up

Key Topics:

- ***Talking to the experts***
- ***Concept and execution***
- ***Coping with change***
- ***Making teams work***
- ***Technology pros and cons***
- ***What makes a great game?***
- ***The future***

By way of summarizing this section, I asked a number of the game industry's luminaries to give their own take on design and development. Before going on to their comments, however, I should add a caveat.

Some years ago, while studying karate, I heard the true story of an Englishman who had gone to train in Japan. His teachers were at pains to correct any romanticized Western notions he may have had concerning the Oriental martial arts. "There is no magic about the martial arts," they told him. "Results are obtained by skill and strength; these will only come through constant practice."

Sometime later, the Englishman was staying at a rural Japanese inn with several of his teachers and a very elderly Chinese priest from the Shaolin Temple. The inn comprised a huge wooden hall with a central pillar supporting the roof. During the conversation, to demonstrate a point about the focusing of *ki* (energy), the Shaolin priest got up and swept his hand against the stout wooden pillar. He had seemed to use no effort at all, and yet the roof of the inn boomed, the reverberations lasting several seconds.

After the old priest had gone to bed, the Englishman had a question for his teachers: "I thought you said there wasn't anything mystical about the martial arts. How about what we just saw?"

The Japanese teachers smiled. "There's nothing mystical about the way ordinary folk do the martial arts, that's right," said the senior sensei. "But that old man is from Shaolin!"

The moral of the story is to remind you that the people we're going to hear from in this chapter are some of the major developers working in entertainment software. It's instructive to hear the way they went about creating their great successes, but don't assume you can just leap in, do it the same way, and get a success overnight.

Metaphorically speaking, these guys are from Shaolin.

The Professionals

The "software factory" model that this book advocates does not accommodate extensive changes in design during development. We assume that you will be starting with a detailed design and attempting to keep changes to a minimum, because this is the most cost-efficient development process. If you can stick only 50 percent to a plan, you're still a long way ahead of the guy who makes it all up as he goes along. Moreover, a detailed design is the only way to make sure a large team remains focused on the same goal.

To allow for the unexpected, we suggest using a developer testbed as part of the design process. However, we do not advocate turning the testbed into the actual game by means of an evolutionary process. Instead, we advise using the testbed to create a game design and technical architecture for the project before proceeding by means of iterations (what is called *spiral development*) to the finished game.

So, it is interesting and instructive to see how some of the classic games of the past were produced. Consequently, we created a questionnaire and gave it to a number of industry luminaries.

The individuals we spoke to were:

- Ian Bell, co-creator of *Elite*.
- Mike Diskett, co-founder of Mucky Foot.
- Peter Molyneux, co-creator of *Populous*, *Dungeon Keeper*, and many others; now co-founder of Lionhead.
- Glenn Corpes, co-creator of *Populous*; now co-founder of Lost Toys.
- Brian Reynolds of Firaxis, designer of *Alpha Centauri*.
- Chris Crawford, creator of *Balance of Power* and many other classics of the 1980s.
- Dave Perry of Shiny Entertainment, famous especially as the creator of *Earthworm Jim* and *MDK*.
- Bill Roper, design guru at Blizzard.

The Game Concept

In Part I, we've worked from the premise that games begin with a raw concept. I said in Chapter 2 that you should aim to begin with a description of the game that is features based. The specific rules may change, but those features are the game you want to end up with.

Consequently, it's interesting to learn how some games that are now acknowledged as classics were expected by their creators to turn out.

Which game are you most pleased with? What made you think it would be a commercial success?

Peter Molyneux: That's a tough one. I'm not completely happy with any game. They all have faults—except *Black & White*, the latest game I'm working on. If I had to pick one it would be *Populous*, the first game I ever did.

At the time, I thought *Populous* would be viewed as quirky and weird. I didn't imagine it would go on to sell 3.5 million copies. The first glimmer I had that this game was going to be special was when I met a journalist who had played it and was so enthusiastic that I thought he must be mad.

Glenn Corpes: *Populous*. At first we had no idea it would be so successful, but, when we were able to play the multiplayer game, it was very obvious that other people would like it—provided that Peter could code a convincing computer opponent.

Mike Diskett: My current game, *Urban Chaos*, which I'm just finishing work on. It's a platforming, action, fighting, driving adventure set in a real city environment with the player taking the part of a cop in the city.

Being a commercial success isn't really something that can be planned for or designed for. Primarily, I design the game that I want to play and want to work on, and hope that it catches the imagination of the public.

Bill Roper: I am in somewhat of a fortunate position in that I am incredibly proud of every game Blizzard [has] published. If I had to choose one that particularly exceeded the expectations of the development team and ourselves, it would be *Starcraft: Brood War*. Although it is an expansion set in name, it has been compared to complete sequels in regards to the amount of new content and gameplay. Through the course of the project, the goal of the team became "We need to outdo *Starcraft* in every way," and I feel that this was, for the great part, accomplished.

Chris Crawford: *Siboot* ("Trust & Betrayal"). As for commercial success—it wasn't. But it was such a *glorious* failure!

Dave Perry: *Earthworm Jim* was probably our most challenging and most fun game to develop. I had just started Shiny, and so I was sleeping on the floor to get the game done. When I was not programming, I was learning to pay payroll or dealing with insurance and building maintenance. It was nuts, but very rewarding.

We took it to the E3 show in Atlanta, and the response was amazing—just what we needed to understand that the hard work was worthwhile. It was also funny, and I think that *Jim* taught us that games really are just a mix of entertainment, and humor is one of the strongest kinds.

Will Wright: I'd have to say *The Sims* at this point, but the game isn't finished yet so it probably doesn't count. Otherwise, I guess I'd pick *SimCity 2000*. I think we got the tuning just right on that one, and it paid off in long shelflife.

Ian Bell: *Elite*. It was an obvious genre that no one else had done.

Planning For Change

I said in Chapter 5 that it makes more sense planning to scale up rather than down. However, because development schedules are frequently underestimated, it seems likely that it must be more common to have to drop features that there wasn't enough time to code for.

With this in mind, the questionnaire asked next about ideas that had been hoped for at the start but that didn't make it into the finished game.

What was the initial concept like compared to how the game turned out in the end?

Ian Bell: Less well rounded.

Mike Diskett: Very different. I'm very much a believer in having a very brief initial design concept, a single-paragraph synopsis. Then let the game evolve during the development. It's quite inefficient and involves throwing lots of work away—going down the wrong path and backtracking—but I think it provides the best gameplay.

Will Wright: One of the features that we started with on *SimCity 2000* was a dynamic hydrological model. This allowed the player to create streams that would run down a watershed along a realistic path and accurately respond to later changes in terrain (pooling, flooding, etc). There is something intrinsically interesting about playing with water and the way it tends to flow. We ended up with the first half of this feature (placing streams and watching them run down hills) in our terrain editor, but the ongoing dynamics proved too costly (in CPU time) to include in the final design.

As far as pure simulations go, I'd have to say I've always been the most proud of the model we built for *SimEarth*. As crude as it was, I still have yet to see any other attempts (on any computer system) to integrate all the aspects of global dynamics that we were modeling: axial tilt, core cooling, magma convections, continental drift, atmospheric formation, global climate, biome distribution, evolution and diversification of life, and the effects of global civilization.

Glenn Corpes: With *Populous*, there was no initial concept. There was look and feel but no game. The "fractally" generated levels were there from day one; the basic grass slopes and water were there from day two; the unique ability to model the landscape with the mouse was there from day three; but the *gameplay* part of the game was thrashed out later, partly inspired by this landscape demo and partly by the genius of Peter Molyneux and the rest of the team talking about it in the pub.

Peter Molyneux: *Populous* started out as a realtime wargame and ended up being called a "God Game" by the Press. The best games are the ones that evolve around a coordinated development strategy.

Bill Roper: The first concept for *Brood War* was to create a "traditional" expansion set—add a new unit or two, some new multiplayer maps, and a new campaign. Also, we wanted to do it in three to five months after *StarCraft* shipped. As we got about two months into the project, it was obvious that we were not going to be happy with just creating what people had come to expect from an expansion set, and we set our goals much higher. This meant not only going back to our developer and restructuring our deal to fall more in line with our new desires, but it also meant adding additional internal resources that we had not originally intended on putting onto the project. We ended up taking a little over eight months to finish *Brood War*, but in the end we released a game that met our goals and we believe benefited and excited the people who play our games.

Chris Crawford: [*Siboot* turned out] radically different. The original concept had the player and a little creature called a siboot marooned together after a crash. Their only means of communicating was through an interspecies iconic language [IIL] that used symbols rather like an extended version of airport sign symbols. The IIL was about the only part of the design that made it through to the final product. I called it "eeyal".

Dave Perry: *Earthworm Jim* was made as we went along. There was no original design document, just a bunch of passionate guys that knew what they were doing. That meant that we could develop the game in the direction of things that were working. I loved it that way, because it meant we could add anything at any time. Nowadays, teams shudder when they think that might happen. They call it "feature creep."

Was there anything that you had hoped to include but that didn't make it into the game?

Ian Bell: Dramatic reward sequences were omitted owing to lack of memory.

Mike Diskett: Being able to go inside every building—a feature we removed because the player would be distracted by interiors that had no relevance, but would feel the need to explore them just in case. Also, shortcuts through sewers used up too much memory on the PlayStation and Jellymatter, a physics system for objects that deform, squash, or bounce. This would only work with floating point numbers, which are too slow on PlayStation.

Glenn Corpes: A lot of the ideas from *Populous 2* were ideas that never made it into *Populous*—stuff like the extension of the mana system and more landscape-modifying effects like the whirlpools and the tornadoes. I also wanted to see a higher-definition landscape with more-varied curves, but this didn't happen until *Populous 3*. I'd also like to have seen a more flexible and intelligent automatic town building around any stretch of flat land. This would have resulted in nicer-looking towns but may well have done nothing for gameplay.

Dave Perry: We wanted to have more and more and more subgames, but we just ran out of space in the cartridge. That meant that the "cow sponge" bath level never saw the light of day.

How did the game change as it progressed?

Ian Bell: It became more general, with the player being able to take more roles.

Mike Diskett: The main character being a cop was just a bit of background info initially, but has evolved into being a major part of the gameplay.

Glenn Corpes: In the early stages, *Populous* was very hectic with huge waves of people pouring into many fights. This caused a lot of problems (not least speed and memory) as it was very difficult to actually finish a two-player game without a couple of hours of intensive clicking. It had to be changed into something where the player felt able to gain control of a level.

Peter Molyneux: *Dungeon Keeper*'s original concept was, "You play the bad guy." This was, I thought, one of the best ideas I'd had. In hindsight, the way the idea was implemented caused it to be not such a compelling game as it should have been. A lot of this was the fault of the interface. For many of my games, the area I am least happy with is the interface. That's why, on our latest game, *Black & White*, I had an objective to be innovative with the interface design.

Bill Roper: Although our original specification [for *Brood War*] called for two new units for each species, what those units actually were changed drastically. As opposed to taking our first idea and just making units that seemed cool, we stopped and looked at the data we had coming in from our players in regards to balance issues. Although we strove to make *StarCraft* an incredibly well-balanced game when it came out, we were still eager and open to perfecting it if at all possible. We saw *Brood War* as a chance to do so by adding units that would balance out not only the early, mid- and end game, but also that would redesign our air-combat paradigm.

Also, the scope of what we wanted to accomplish with the single-player campaign shifted towards telling a much more involved story with in-game cut scenes and hundreds of scripted events. This meant that we would need to do some serious work on the map editor as well, which was not in our original idea. The team was dedicated to coming out with an expansion that would not just enhance the original, but would supplant it in every way. Every decision we made that changed the game—whether in graphics, mechanics, balance, technology, sound, music, or story—was made with that goal in mind.

Dave Perry: [*Earthworm Jim*] Every day it changed, in erratic directions, but always towards a common goal. By using a character that had no limits—he could go to *any* planet, pick up anything, etc.—it means you have complete freedom. The problem that many designers face today is that they are making "reality." Reality is pretty dull.

Chris Crawford: Oy, did it change! This game was a radical departure from anything that had come before. I found myself reworking the design every time I ran into a brick wall—which was often. I went from two-person journey to multiperson interaction, because I wanted a more-varied set of interactions available to the player. The basic conflict underwent many changes: First it was man versus nature; then it was man versus man versus nature. I finally settled on man versus man.

For that, I needed a clean basis of conflict. My theoretical work at the time led me to believe that circular, nontransitive combat relationships offered the most-interesting possibilities, so I developed a conflict system based on such relationships. I'm quite proud of that system, and I'm sad to note how little the rest of the industry has picked up on the enormous potential of such relationships. True, they require some artificiality—I can't think of many circular nontransitive relationships in the real world—but artificiality has never held back game designers in the past. I suspect that most designers just don't understand the concept.

There were lots more changes, but I'll stop on this point.

Brian Reynolds: The important thing is always to get something running that you can actually play, even if it doesn't play the whole game. That way you can actually try the game out and see what the strong points and weak points are. Then you can revise your prototype to enhance some of the good and eliminate some of the bad, then play, revise, play, revise, etc. If you don't play your own game, you won't be able to make it fun for anyone else.

What specifically influenced or caused each change?

Ian Bell: Pieces falling into place.

Mike Diskett: Some changes are through necessity—the work involved is just too much for the benefit to the game. Other times, the changes are a result of a very gradual evolution, small steps leading to a large unexpected overall change.

Glenn Corpes: The first effects in *Populous* were earthquake, volcano, and flood. Early games consisted of one player building flat land as quickly as possible while saving for flood while the other bombarded him with earthquakes and volcanoes. Other effects were inspired by the need to speed up the end game. For example, the knight was designed to allow the leading player to invest people and mana in a character that could mop up large areas of enemies with little help from the player.

Brian Reynolds: As I'm playing my game, I jot down the things that irritate me, and the things I like or want to enhance. Then as soon as I'm done playing I go to work on making the changes.

Dave Perry: We used a system where each person on the team would have to submit ideas as drawings, even if they had no drawing ability. It made the meetings funny as we looked at the programmers' "poohey" drawings, but, also, it put us in the right creative frame of mind. We had many, many, many more ideas than we could ever use in the game.

What would you change now with the benefit of hindsight?

Ian Bell: Some coding stratagems were inefficient, but, gameplaywise, it was about right.

Glenn Corpes: We had to limit the number of characters and buildings in the game because we just couldn't move or draw them fast enough. A few years later, *Populous 2* was able to draw more sprites and move more characters on the same primitive machines as *Populous*, all thanks to us getting better at programming. I'd love to have seen an unlimited, more "alive" version of *Populous 1* rather than the fussier, more confusing, and over-featured *Populous 2*. So, with hindsight, I'd say that we slightly missed the point of what made *Populous 1* so good when we did the sequel. (Didn't miss it by quite as far as those doing the third did, though.)

Chris Crawford: I'd give the characters more-complex interactions. The current design doesn't give them much maneuvering room: They can just talk, deal, and betray. I'd build in another modality of spoken interaction.

Will Wright: I had a game I was working on before *SimCity* (and after my first game). It was called *Probot*. It was on the Commodore 64 and was about 90 percent finished when I put it away and started in earnest on *SimCity*. I always wondered how it might have done in the market.

Dave Perry: I would have arranged for a bigger cartridge!

The Technology

Innovative concepts frequently demand innovative technology. However, the commercial reality of development, particularly for small companies, usually prohibits extensive R&D. In a perfect world, you would not commence development on a leading-edge game without at least a proof-of-concept for the technology required. In fact, fully tried-and-tested technology would be the ideal.

Elsewhere in this book, we have given our development doctrine on this point as: A game should not be given the green light unless the technology required to develop it already exists. (That can include fall-back technology, however.) R&D should be just that: It should not draw from the development budget.

How did the technology surprise you? Looking at the positive aspects first of all, how did it help you in ways you hadn't expected?

Ian Bell: What most surprised me was how the versions that had to make do with a character-based display rather than a true bitmap display were in many ways superior in terms of plotting speed, there being less RAM to clear.

Glenn Corpes: *Populous* was the game it was because of the landscape modification. (I would say that; it was my idea.) It turned out that this was a very therapeutic, fun way to spend your time while waiting for more people to breed and the mana to build up. This was all a lucky byproduct of the limited technology.

Chris Crawford: I was stunned at how fast my inverse parser ran. That's another nifty-keen technology that went unheeded. I had feared that it would gum up, but even the most-complex parsings ran faster than the display.

Dave Perry: We pushed the Sega Genesis to its limits. Every trick over years of development were all in that one title.

Brian Reynolds: Even though we've come to expect a dramatic increase in processor speed and equally dramatic increases in memory and hard drive space every couple years, it still surprises me how much more powerful the machines get during the development of a single game. For me, more memory and faster processors always means better AI.

But, in all the years I've been doing this, I think the biggest outright surprise has been the way in which the coming of Windows has revolutionized the industry, in a positive way. It made game development much easier from a technical point of view, and, at the same time, allowed us to reach a lot more potential players. Anyone who remembers the "config.sys hell" of DOS days has an idea what I'm talking about.

What about the negative aspects of technology? How did it inhibit you? What difficulties did it present?

Glenn Corpes: I felt very limited by the single slope steepness and having only eight possible altitude levels of the landscape. At the time, they seemed like the biggest problems in the system, but, with hindsight, these limitations were probably largely responsible for the success of the game.

Peter Molyneux: Technology is both the boon of development and the bane. It moves so fast that, when you first design a game, you think the design is going to be capable of X only to find within a year you could have done X times 2. The temptation is then to redesign around the new technology, and this is why a lot of projects slip.

Ian Bell: The primary difficulties were lack of code space and RAM space.

Brian Reynolds: Increasing technology levels also increases customer demands. As we progressed from floppy disks to CD-ROMs, and soon most likely from CD-ROMs to DVD, the amount of "disk space" available for a game increases, but so do the demands to fill up that space with quality gameplay. It has become more and more expensive to make a top-quality game.

Dave Perry: The game could have used more voice samples, but they take up tons of cartridge memory, so we were limited to *Groovy*'s and *Whoa Nellie*'s.

Development

One of the messages of this book is that games programming was once a back-bedroom industry. Development teams might comprise two people—or fewer! Rather as with other entertainment genres (such as cinema and music), this is rarely now the case.

We have argued herein that formal process is an efficient method for medium to large teams (10 people or more). The software factory model is the template for one such formal process. Its key strengths are the ability to plan, predict, and track—vital when the cost of developing a blockbuster game is getting so high.

How far did you stick with your original schedule?

Peter Molyneux: Anybody who says they can predict the actual release date of an original concept is either a genius or a fool. I am betting they are a fool. Even if you have a script that details every single point of the game and every hour of someone's time, it's still impossible to predict. The best thing you can do is have objectives to make the game playable as soon as possible, thereby taking out the "it looks beautiful, but what's the game" syndrome that often takes the most time.

Glenn Corpes: We didn't have a schedule. The game took seven months from start to finish. Bullfrog may not have survived if it had taken over a year.

Chris Crawford: I held pretty close to the schedule. I can't remember the exact dates, but I know I wrapped it just in time for Christmas. I now suspect that the game would have been better if I had slipped the schedule by three months, but I've always taken pride in coming close to my deadlines.

Brian Reynolds: For whatever reason, I've tended to have better luck with schedules than most. My first five products were all delivered within two weeks of the planned date. But, my most recent game, *Alpha Centauri*, ran significantly (several months) late.

Dave Perry: We used to make games on time, but, now, as we keep trying to push technology, we guess time very badly indeed. I have learned a lot over the last couple of years, and I have a real respect now for the right balance of technology and innovation in a new game.

Ian Bell: There was no schedule.

How effective was your progress tracking? Did you know exactly where you were in your project to the nearest percentile? If not, what would you do differently to get more accurate tracking next time?

Glenn Corpes: If you'd have asked me about this at the time, I'd have asked you to repeat it in English. I suppose that 10 years later I should have a better answer.

Chris Crawford: All that went on informally inside my head. This was a wild-blue-sky project, requiring not just one but several technologies that had never been invented before, and a fundamental structure that had never been tried before. Nevertheless, I readjusted the internal schedule with the passage of time to ensure that I'd meet the final deadline.

Peter Molyneux: The way we track our progress is to have weekly meetings where everyone states what they've done in the last week and their objectives for the next week, following a development strategy. This has to be centered around at least one person in the team who has a very clear picture of the final game.

Dave Perry: We tend to get more accurate towards the end of the game. Our games cruise along, getting enhanced all the way, trying new ideas. Then, when the light appears at the end of the tunnel, it pops out in no time.

Ian Bell: Progress is made, not tracked.

Would you describe the game development as like the voyage of a ship from port to port, or perhaps an organic process like the growth of a tree? Or can you discuss some other analogy that you feel illustrates it better?

Chris Crawford: Well, not speaking for myself, I can note that there are some designs for which a third analogy works better: The Humongous Heap. The designer just keeps shoveling features onto the pile until it's so big that it bulldozes its way through publishers, distributors, and retailers who figure that a pile that big has to have a pony inside it somewhere.

For me, the process is more like a Napoleonic battle: First comes the grand speech to the troops, full of phrases like "For glory!" and "Vive La France!" Then comes the brutal slugfest in which I hurl my talents at the problem with utter disregard for anything other than victory. If I'm lucky, I breach the enemy defenses and plant my flag on the hilltop. If not, it's a long and painful retreat. I've experienced both.

Glenn Corpes: For many years, I was sure it was the tree method. New genres seemed to be ripe for the picking after a year or so of messing about. These days, it's closer to the voyage, but not too close. Lost Toys' philosophy is to carefully pick where we are going (nowhere too crowded with competition, hopefully) and head rapidly in the general direction with quick, interactive prototypes.

Mike Diskett: Development is like a mountaineer climbing up a cloud-topped mountain without sight of the summit, occasionally slipping down, changing tack round the mountain, but—when the summit is within sight—he knows exactly where he is heading.

Bill Roper: We at Blizzard have always viewed game development as very organic, but much more like some form of controlled chaos. As developers, we have to be willing to constantly be open to changing the game for the better during the design and development process. We have made changes to our games days before we shipped to ensure better gameplay, better balance and—most importantly—that the game is fun. In this constant evolution of the game, ideas come from all areas and not just some single designer who sits upon high sending down changes on stone tablets for the masses to integrate. We do maintain some structure over the process, but we have always been a very "seat of-the-pants" company when it comes to the creation of our games.

Dave Perry: It's like a nightmare. You go to sleep expecting it to be a nice straightforward sleep, but then the nightmare begins—major stress. Finally, when it's all over, you wake up and need major caffeine to get your body going again. The difference is that game development lasts for 18 months!

No, it's kind of organic really: A game grows until it looks like someone would want it, and then you package it up and let them pluck it off the shelf.

Brian Reynolds: Much more the latter: New ideas accreting on top of old ideas, and you can't tell for sure from the early and middle stages what the end result will be.

Ian Bell: It's like the evolution of an ecosystem.

What do you think of the application of formal process? For example, component-based design, planning for reuse, change control, formal code reviews, and so forth?

Ian Bell: Probably a good idea.

Chris Crawford: Absolutely necessary for projects with more than one worker or a budget in excess of, say, $100,000. We must realize, though, that this stuff does to creativity what a foot of water does to a cross-country hiker.

Glenn Corpes: Treating the programming portion of the game development process very seriously is a good thing. Standards, modularity, and an interest in technology like source control should be expected of any good programmer. I don't see any problem with mixing disciplined programming practice with a less formal game design process.

Mike Diskett: I hate the software engineering creeping into game design. Formal processes can only work if you know from the start exactly what the game is, what the final thing will be, but, if you want to explore different avenues and keep the freedom to branch the game down a different route mid-development, then these formal methods just get in the way.

Dave Perry: It will be important in the future, but programmers in small teams have had *so* much sloppy freedom, it will be a challenge to lay down "corporate" procedures that they will graciously accept.

Brian Reynolds: Ugh.

The Team

The first question on this topic concerned the entire team working on the project—not just the artists and coders, but management and marketing, too.

How did you ensure the team meshed?

Ian Bell: By having a very small team.

Chris Crawford: That was the easiest part of the project: There was no team! I did it all by myself. It's always best to concentrate on your strengths and avoid your weaknesses. I know some good designers who couldn't manage their way out of a paper bag—I'm one of them—but I'm hard put to identify any good designer who's also a good manager.

Brian Reynolds: We had the good fortune to found a company with a handpicked team of veterans who already knew they liked working together. As we've grown, we've done our best to perpetuate that environment.

Glenn Corpes: That wasn't my job at the time. The team meshed because it was small and everyone cared. In my opinion, this is the key to game development—which is why we formed Lost Toys rather than stay at Bullfrog, which has 160+ employees.

Peter Molyneux: If there is one secret to a successful game, it is finding a team that gets on together. If everyone you're working with believes in the project, and, if they know you and trust you when you say it will be a major success and they will get rewards, then development of a game can be the most wonderful experience. At the moment, on *Black & White*, every day there is another amazing thing happening in the game, and people are incredibly excited to work on it.

Dave Perry: The team got on great. Just the music choices were a problem. We had music wars. Then, when the insults flew, I once had to make two guys hug in my office.

Note

If a team doesn't need to change, it's possible to operate on a gung-ho team ethic. Small teams frequently operate best this way. However, if new team members need to be integrated, formal process is one way of ensuring the integration goes smoothly.

Did you need to add any new roles as the development progressed?

Glenn Corpes: This was years back, so 95 percent of the programming and art was by myself and Peter Molyneux. There were other programmers, artists, and testers at different times.

Dave Perry: We had so much animation in the game that we needed to hire in people that did digital ink and paint. That means that our animators would just draw the pencil lines, then an intern would clean the lines up, then another would color in the frame. This had to be done to *thousands* of images—way more work than we ever expected.

Chris Crawford: No.

Ian Bell: No.

Costs And Timelines

Computer games have notoriously been plagued by expanding deadlines and escalating costs. It is not uncommon to hear of products shipping up to a year or more late, and there are many instances of games that turned out to be great successes but that had so tried the patience of the publisher that they had been on the verge of cancellation prior to release.

"The game is ready when it's ready," is an outrageous luxury that few small developers can any longer afford. Try sitting in front of your investors and telling them that you want $1 million, but that you can't show them a business plan because game development isn't a predictable industry. You will get short shrift!

The methodology of this book is to undertake development in iterations, or "tiers." Within each tier, you first plan what you want the tier to achieve. Then you build it, then test, and finally review how much of the plan was achieved and what changes need to be accommodated in the next tier. Each tier of the build adds or refines features within a modular structure that allows elements of the code to be independently checked. The final aim of this process is to achieve "completion"—which we defined not as the game being incapable of improvement, but as an ongoing process, at any stage of which it is possible to draw a line under further development and still have a shippable product.

What do you consider to be the typical development timeframe for a AAA title?

Glenn Corpes: Two or three years, which is one or two too many.

Mike Diskett: Two years for an original title.

Brian Reynolds: These days it seems to be about one-and-a-half to two years for us, and I think that's on par with the rest of the industry.

Dave Perry: It is now 18 months—expect that to be 24 soon.

Peter Molyneux: A minimum of two years, more probably three years from concept to box on shelf.

Bill Roper: As computers, video cards, sound cards and speaker systems get more powerful and less expensive, the expectations increase as to what a top-quality game is going to deliver. Add into this the increase in bandwidth and better and better connectivity to the Internet (at least in the U.S.), and gamers expect a fantastic single-player experience as well as an exciting and smooth multiplayer setting in which to game for months, not weeks. This increase in expected performance and content means that team sizes have greatly increased and producing a AAA title is becoming as big of a risk as coming out with a top film.

What this all boils down to is that the accepted design cycle for a game of these proportions is about two years. This is very challenging for developers as it is becoming harder and harder to predict where technology will be that far out, and I think that we are seeing some of the fallout from the rapid growth of that technology, as games that have been in development for one to two years are either cancelled or delayed even longer so that the development team can try and get it caught up with the new standard.

Gameplay

Faced with the opportunity to question developers of this caliber, I obviously felt it was important to try to find out where that vital spark of creativity came from. Although the same caveat applies as before (you may not reproduce the same success just by reproducing the methods), it's interesting to delve into these special qualities of gameplay and look and feel.

What features do you particularly dislike in games and would not accept in one of your own?

Dave Perry: I hate games that take a manual read just to play around with. I want to sit down and play, then, when I get stuck, reach for the manual. I guess I am too impatient.

Glenn Corpes: Too much emphasis on storyline or FMV. Games are supposed to be interactive, so storyline and FMV can only detract from this even if they are top quality. I'd love to live in a world where everyone felt this way, and we could just ditch both.

Brian Reynolds: Interfaces that don't allow full keyboard control of the game. Mouse interfaces are essential for learning games, but being forced to use the mouse repeatedly after I've learned a game just makes my hand hurt.

Will Wright: I really don't like overuse of full-motion video. On the other hand, I try not to be too dogmatic about anything. If I have strong preconceived biases about certain features, then I'll be less likely to approach the design task with an open mind.

Chris Crawford: The deliberate pandering to the least noble elements of the human spirit.

Ian Bell: Gratuitous violence. Poor control design. Juvenile plot lines.

What (if any) were the biggest groundbreakers in the industry?

Glenn Corpes: *Tetris* was an incredible game: Every programmer in the world was kicking themselves for not having the idea and coding it themselves in an afternoon.

Also *Dungeon Master*, the first role player for non-dice juggling perverts. And *Ultima Underworld*, for doing it again in a "realistic" world. And all id games for staying ahead of the technology curve and having the nerve to keep the gameplay at its most basic.

Will Wright: *FS-1 Flight Simulator:* This was the first computer game I ever bought. I was totally amazed that there was a little toy world here that I could fly around in. This was the first PC flight sim (by Bruce Artwick). It had wireframe graphics and was quite primitive by today's standards. But, still, it was a self-contained universe with its own rules of physics that I could play in.

Pinball Construction Set (Bill Budge): This was the first game I played where the object of the game was to construct something. I really enjoyed the interface (drag and drop) and the open-ended nature of this. *PCS* was quite influential in the original design of *SimCity*.

M.U.L.E. was the game that proved that economics (and multiplayer gaming) could be fun. Also, it was a brilliant example of how you could design a game that included both competition and cooperation (in a great balance).

It's really too bad that most people can't experience these games any more.

Peter Molyneux: A product in the recent past that I consider is groundbreaking in the industry is *Quake/Doom*. Its simplicity, compulsiveness, and sheer adrenaline rush is a perfect reflection of what games should be.

Dave Perry: *Donkey Kong Country*, *Command and Conquer*, and *Street Fighter*.

Ian Bell: *Colossal Cave*, *Elite*, and *Tetris*.

What do you think of sequels?

Ian Bell: Easy.

Glenn Corpes: A good thing if there is a good reason to do one, a bad thing in 9 cases out of 10 though—including a few I've been involved with.

Mike Diskett: Sequels are great from a development point of view. You know exactly what the game is—what the work involved is. The public knows exactly what they are getting, but to go beyond version two of a game without taking a totally new direction means dragging the game out further than it should sensibly be stretched.

Dave Perry: They are great if the first game was awesome. I hate, hate, *hate* lamer sequels to lame games.

Chris Crawford: I did one and was none too pleased with it. Sequels should be separated by at least five years. Otherwise, they're just marketing exploitation of the customer base. I'm thinking about designing a new *Balance of Power*. Seeing that it's been 10 years since the last one, I think the time might be right.

Bill Roper: Sequels can be good and bad. Without sequels, we would never have seen *Aliens*. But, then again, we never would have seen *Highlander 2*, either. Basically, a sequel is going to give you what you put into it. If you just want to ride on the laurels of a brand that you have developed, you can do that. At Blizzard, we fall in love with the universes we build, and sequels give us a chance to more fully explore and develop those worlds. We also strive to do more than just give players more of the same in a sequel in that we try to build upon the successful parts of the predecessor while finding ways to improve what we or our fans didn't like.

I think a great example of this was the leaps that occurred between *Warcraft: Orcs and Humans*, *Warcraft II: Tides of Darkness*, and *StarCraft* (the spiritual sequel). If you look at each of these games, you can see where basic gaming tenets were preserved, while the interface, gameplay, graphics, connectivity, and so much more evolved. If developers can use the original as a foundation and then build a greater game upon that experience, then they are creating what I envision a sequel to be.

Would you compromise your next design to get a favorable publishing deal up front?

Chris Crawford: Certainly not. I've spent the last eight years as a starving artist; why should I want to break such a clean streak?

Mike Diskett: If you need money up front from a publisher to create a game, then the design is always a compromise between marketing's perception of what will sell and the developer's individual dream.

Glenn Corpes: It's not a case of compromise. If you think you have a really cool game idea but publishers "don't get it," there is a strong possibility that you don't have a good game design and are just being overly idealistic. Making sure that it's a game that a publisher will want to publish (which equates to a game people want to play) is part of the design process.

Dave Perry: Shiny is lucky. We get to try different ideas. Our games are made for people like ourselves. You won't ever see us making Barbie games. See our *Stunt Helicopter* game (**www.stuntcopter.com**) or our *Baby Angel* game (**www.messiah.com**), or our multiplayer creature game (**www.sacrifice.net**).

Peter Molyneux: Quite often, marketers and publishers have specific objectives for the products that they sign. I think developers—including Lionhead—should be reasonably flexible, so long as publishers can back up their desires with deal points.

Brian Reynolds: If I know what product I want to do, I'm sometimes willing to agree in advance on a title and genre, but, beyond that, we've always reserved creative control of the game and gameplay for ourselves.

Ian Bell: It would depend on personal financial circumstances.

The Future

At the launch party for a (non-games) Internet company recently, one of the investors asked me, "Why don't you guys do more games like *Myst*? I really liked that one. But all the others—*Doom*, *Quake*, *Tomb Raider*—they just leave me cold."

Of course, that's only one view. It would be easy to ignore if the person in question hadn't been a venture capitalist with tens of millions of dollars at his disposal, and if there wasn't strong commercial evidence that games are an extremely niche market.

The question boils down to "How much interactivity do people want?" It's unlikely we'll ever see the computer-age version of the Victorian family round the piano: Put the kids to bed, plug in the PlayStation, and get gaming. If people wanted that kind of thing, they would roleplay, they'd join drama groups, they'd play board games, and there'd be a murder-mystery dinner party every weekend.

Of course, there will always be a solid core of gamers. Many developers disdain the mass market: "Let them watch TV." But the interactivity that computers make possible suggests that there could be products with appeal to both the game-head market and the mass market. These are games that could be played in different ways according to what the user wants. In short, interactivity should not be about forcing the player to make choices; it should be about giving the player control of his choices.

We will examine the issue of where games should go from here in Chapter 8. First, let's see what the games gurus think.

Can games in their current form attract non-gamers, or must games adapt to them?

Peter Molyneux: The future of the games industry has not even begun to be tapped. There have been products like *Tomb Raider* and sports games that have shown the potential of designing games for the mass market as well as the die-hard gamer. This doesn't mean "dumbing down" games, but making them much more accessible. When this truly starts to happen, then games will be huge.

Glenn Corpes: I think games are slowly seeping into mainstream culture. It can't be stopped; it probably can't be accelerated. Aiming games at the mainstream is a non-starter unless you want to work on a sports title.

Mike Diskett: Games are too ugly looking, overcomplicated, and require too much work from the player to be truly mass market. Mass-market games either have to be incredibly simple so as to be immediately comprehended, or complicated with depth and subtleties beyond the capabilities of current hardware.

Will Wright: I'm thinking that they're going to meet in the middle somewhere. Imagine some guy walks into a Wal-Mart and buys *Deer Hunter* one day, because his friend told him to check it out. He brings it home, tries it out, and enjoys it. It was simple and easy. Now he'll probably feel more confident buying a somewhat more advanced game the next time. Now, if he goes back to the store and buys *Falcon 4.0*, he'll probably be getting more than he bargained for. But, of course, there will always be a market for things like *Falcon* for the hardcore gamers.

So I would imagine that, as the mass-market consumers become more computer literate, our industry will evolve the other way. Instead of mostly hard-core games out there (with a few *Deer Hunters* sprinkled in), we'll end up with a bell curve that peaks in the intermediate-level games and tapers down at both the beginner and hard-core ends of the market.

Ian Bell: Games will have to adapt to attract non-gamers.

Brian Reynolds: I think the question is a false dilemma, so I guess my answers are "not usually" and "not really." There is a very significant core market of gamers, and one can make a perfectly decent living writing games for them. It's not essential to bang your head repeatedly against the "mass-market" wall. At Firaxis, we tend to eschew "market research," and instead concentrate on writing games we want to play. We assume that, if we write something we like to play, there are enough people like us out there who will want to buy them.

Bill Roper: The answer is "little bit of both." We at Blizzard have always made games that will be appealing to the core game player without alienating anyone who sits down and wants to see what this whole "computer gaming thing" is all about. We cannot afford to be strict purists who only make games for the hard-core gamer. There is an audience for computer-based entertainment that is growing at an alarming rate, and they need content. At the same time, however, we do not need to compromise our games so that they are unsophisticated and unchallenging.

Making games that are simple to learn but difficult to master is a lofty task that we have set for ourselves, but, if you can get it right, you start seeing not only the lifelong gamer enjoying the experience, but also someone who has never played a game before. What it all really boils down to is three simple letters: F U N. If the game is accessible and fun to play, you will find that your audience will continue to expand with the number of people who have computers who want to have something entertaining to do with their technological marvel.

Dave Perry: Games need to adapt to non-gamers. It's like the way games on the PC used to ask for IRQ numbers and DMA settings. You just have to make it really simple; then you give people a chance to feel good.

Chris Crawford: Games will never break out of their rut. Lord knows I tried to help the industry break out of its rut, but I failed completely, and the industry is so solidly set in its ways that I wouldn't even make the attempt now.

A decade from now, there will be interactive entertainment based on storytelling, but I think it will be independent of games. Think in terms of bookstores versus comic-book stores.

What is your one favorite thing that appeals to you from any one game of your choice?

Glenn Corpes: Rocket jumps in *Quake*.

Mike Diskett: The fear installed in the player in *Dungeon Master* when deep in the dungeon your last torch runs out, and you're left alone in the dark with just the sounds of monsters moving around you for company.

Ian Bell: The ability to play with élan. By this I mean a game that may be played with unnecessary flamboyance—with consummate style as opposed to mere efficiency. *Chuckie Egg* was such a game.

Dave Perry: Multiball in *Pinball*. With about five balls going, you walk away sweating.

Chapter 8
The Future Of Game Design

Key Topics:

- ***Benefits of design***
- ***Checklist of good design elements***
- ***Where games are now***
- ***Where games are going next***

In this chapter, we will review basic gameplay essentials and then take a speculative look at how game concepts and design may evolve in the future. First, though, we'll debunk some of the myths surrounding formal design and its effect on the creative process.

The Necessity Of Design

I'm going to start with a quotation that you might think has a familiar ring: "In these companies there is a designer who directs by word alone and who seldom or never dirties his hands writing code. Designers say to the other team members, 'Program this feature in such-and-such a way,' and yet they do no real work themselves."

Does that sound like something you've heard before? Some dyed-in-the-wool developers still think a formal design isn't necessary, and in a moment we'll review the arguments they usually give to support that view. However, first I have a confession. The quotation above didn't quite read like that in the original. Instead of "designers," it referred to "architects," and, for "writing code," substitute "cutting stone."

The statement is from the thirteenth century, and it bemoans the passing of the "good old days" (the twelfth century) when stonemasons could just fling up a new cathedral without having to bother with architects' plans. But back then, as now, there was good reason to abandon the old trial-and-error process. Building a cathedral was a decades-long project that involved a team of several hundred men. Also, cathedrals that were built according to intuitive, unplanned, "see how it goes" methods were proving unreliable; that is, sometimes they fell down. Unlike software, when cathedrals fell down they killed people.

I guess the quote shows that people have always lamented the need for change, because change normally goes in the direction of making things more formalized, logical, and safe. The pioneers don't care for the sound of that, be they cathedral builders, movie makers, soldiers, or astronauts. Or even game developers.

Don't Be Afraid To Plan

When I first began working in the computer games industry back in 1995, there still was a very reactionary opposition to detailed design and the formal development process. Generally, my experience was that artists were willing to embrace the need for change but that programmers tended to be quite fearful of it. A couple of objections the programmers would raise were, "We don't want designs handed down from on high," and, "You can design a business application, sure—but every game is a brand new project."

Fear perhaps is too strong a word. These were intelligent, talented, experienced people, and naturally they were wary of changing the way they did things. As Case Study 8.1 reveals, they resisted the concept of detailed design mainly because game development had historically been a hit-and-miss affair. The idea of writing the design in stone and sticking to it throughout an 18-month project seemed absurd. And there's a good reason for that: It is absurd. As we discussed in Chapter 4, the gameplay spec is an evolving document. It is not a Holy Writ; instead it is a combination of a vision statement, a blueprint, and a repository of changes.

Let's return to those objections to the design process: that it kills the fun of creative coding, and that it is logically impossible to plan a new thing anyway.

When George Lucas was making *Star Wars*, you can bet he had a script, storyboard, and shooting schedule. Everybody on the crew knew what they were supposed to be filming every hour of every day. Do you suppose that killed the fun? Do you suppose having a detailed plan stifled people's creativity? Not a bit. There was room for improvisation. Most famously, in *The Empire Strikes Back*, Han's reply when Leia says she loves him was an idea that Harrison Ford had on the spot. There would have been many other aspects of the movie that were added by various people during shooting, and other ways it would have changed in postproduction. The script wasn't a straitjacket: It was a visionary framework that actually aided creative input.

Remember as I wrote in Chapter 4 that the existence of a design doesn't mean that the designer is necessarily the sole author of the project. Formal design certainly doesn't mean that developers will become serfs toiling without any control of their destiny. Ideas might

Case Study 8.1 Design Saves Time

A couple of years ago, I was working on a sim-type product (which we'll call *Catastrophe)* in which players had to build and manage a kingdom. Early in the design process, I began to consider having a bunch of initially neutral city-states that would declare allegiance according to various factors, including proximity to a player's units (especially army units) and how well each player was managing his economy.

At that stage, the project had just one programmer assigned to it. I asked him to knock up a quick testbed. "Just dots on a screen that change color with allegiance will do," I said. "I want to get a rough idea of how far the allegiance effect will spread, because that feeds back into the player's economy. If we're going to get a runaway effect, I'd rather start building damping factors into the design now—or drop the idea altogether, if it's not workable."

A few days later, he had a display with dots, but they didn't do anything. "I haven't had much time because I've been busy with DirectX," he told me. "But the game engine will be ready in a few months anyway, so can't we test your idea then?"

"I was hoping to be past the purely experimental stage by then. I need to get a guesstimate now to put in the design spec."

"Oh," he said. "Well, we hardly ever stick to the spec anyway, so why bother?"

come from brainstorming sessions in which all can contribute. The design can and will change during development, as the spec is an evolving document.

And what about the difficulty of writing a design when your game is something completely new? Some would argue this is a logical impossibility, but this is evidently not so. If it were, even a description of the new concept would be impossible, because just a five-page treatment is the first step in the design process.

Again, the fallacy derives from a misunderstanding of what the design is supposed to achieve. I have to stress once more that a design (and especially a design for iterative development) is never intended to be 100 percent correct from the start. Instead, initial design provides you with a first "best guess" that, since it typically takes only 12 man-months out of a total development of 160, pays for itself if it's only 15 percent right. (My own estimate is that a good design, even on a highly innovative project, is actually closer to an 80 percent match with the finished product.)

So, to summarize, why document the design? Because the approach of developers to date has been like medieval alchemy. "Creativity can't be planned for!" they gasp. But in fact it can, and as developers we should strive to be scientific and not let ourselves be held back by superstition. From the outset of your design, you can apply principles based on game theory and storytelling techniques. These principles can save hundreds of hours of development time—and that means tens of thousands of dollars.

Why Design Is Fine

The advantages of a good design are that it is good for morale, good for the budget, and good for the game.

Morale

Teams thrive on a shared vision and work with more enthusiasm when given clearly defined goals that reward their efforts.

"When men have a mission, they arrange matters to accomplish it. Without one, they don't."

—Gifts of the Night *(DC Comics, 1999) by Paul Chadwick and John Bolton*

That is what a detailed design is: a shared vision, accessible to the entire team that everyone can analyze and comment on. The tier system of design that this book describes allows the whole team to focus on creating the game in stages. A monthly or bimonthly turnaround means that each tier represents an achievable goal wherein the contributions of all the team members are visible.

This is very different from the kind of process that programmers legitimately fear, where they are simply issued with lists of tasks each week. Incredible as it seems, such a system was in fact applied to all internal developments at a major publisher until very recently. This is the exact opposite of detailed design as I have defined it, as it makes the design opaque and allows none of the coherence and *Gedanken*-experimentation that a tier-based design and development will encourage.

Budget

Robert H. Dunn, in *Software Defect Removal* (1984), estimates that a design error left undetected until testing will take (on average) 10 times longer to fix than one detected at design time. With today's much bigger projects, the statistic is probably even worse. Imagine all those problems showing up a month before your shipping date. Small wonder that some old-time development managers have gotten the idea that games can be completed only by catching catnaps in between coding sessions. But many of those problems could be avoided—and the developers would get better working hours—if things were handled better at the design stage.

Any detailed design allows scheduling, resource inventorization, control, and tracking. Without these, it is impossible to accurately budget a project, and, without an accurate budget, it is unlikely the project will ever be funded—unless you have a rich and very indulgent uncle.

The Game

An iterative or tier-based design is even more vital for any product that has to incorporate new or untried features. If you absolutely, positively have to ship by a certain date, the tier system will let you fit the design to that date. If development is slipping, you may have to trim some features (or even drop them entirely), but the modularity inherent in the design allows you to do so while still keeping control. Case Study 8.2 stresses the importance of keeping all designs up to date.

If you don't have a design, you may find yourself frantically tweaking and changing gameplay the day before shipping. Doing so can never be a good idea. If you didn't get it right earlier, how could an eleventh-hour change do the trick? The advantage of a clear design is that, not only does it describe and plan for the gameplay features you expect, but also it gives you a rational framework within which to make any required changes.

Essentials Of Game Design

Before moving on to consider where entertainment software is headed, let's review some of the essentials of game design. You can rely on a few useful questions as a litmus test.

Is It Original?

Few games are completely original. As we discussed in Chapter 1, *originality* is a relative term in any case. But if your design is worth developing, it has to have some features that no other game of its type has tried before.

Of course, these features are the ones that will give you the most trouble in development. Even if the feature is one that's well understood in another genre, importing it into your game will have new effects—which is precisely why you should identify and consider those features right at the start of the design process. As I have constantly said in this section, development will entail changes to the design, but knowing what your key features are—and anticipating the development difficulties they might create—is far preferable to blundering about with no plan to guide you.

Original features don't have to be gameplay features. You might simply have decided to do a wargame with funny cartoon characters. And why not? After all, look and feel alone can make a game different. As long as there is something to distinguish your game, you will know where to focus your main efforts during development, and you can be sure the finished game will stand apart from others on the market.

Right after the initial treatment stage, compile a list of unique selling points (USPs) that define how your game concept is unlike any other. These are the things that make it special and will justify a development team spending a year or two creating it. If the concept has no original features, junk it. The world just doesn't need another female archaeologist with two big guns. Do it differently, or not at all.

Is It Coherent?

Good game designs are built around a core vision that works like a seed crystal. As the game is built, if changes need to be made, the core vision keeps them targeted on the final goal. It ensures that the game features serve a common thematic purpose. For example, if you

Case Study 8.2 Keep The Design Up To Date

A few years ago, Rachel was brought in as design consultant on a CRPG that we'll call *Golem*. This project had been in development for over a year with no real sign of progress, and the feeling was that it was turning into a house of cards, with no cohesion or robustness in the design. The development director's hope was that, if they could tighten up the design, the software issues might also come under better control.

After chatting to the team and looking at what they had so far, Rachel took the design spec home to read it. When she'd finished, she had a three-page document of queries but wasn't even sure she'd been given the latest version of the spec. "This describes a third-person game," she said to the lead programmer, "but what I've seen is first-person."

"We needed to cut the number of polygons on screen," he explained. "First-person is one less character."

"Fine, but that will change the interface design also."

He agreed. "Bill, the designer, said we'll tweak the interface when we've got the other bits working."

Next, Rachel spoke to Bill. She liked much of his spec and told him so. "There are some great features. I especially liked that the player will be able to prime spells ready for casting. That's a neat tradeoff of versatility against speed."

"Thanks," he said. "Mind you, I can't stand CRPGs. What I really wanted to do was a first-person shooter."

"I thought it was tending that way. Also, one of the artists told me there's a high likelihood of dropping the thief and warrior characters now, so you can only play as a sorcerer?"

"Yes, that's right. The first-person view saves character artwork, but there were too many other issues thrown up, not least being the complication of designing levels that would be challenging to all three character classes."

"It's the old combinatorial explosion problem," Rachel said. "Three character types means nine times the work."

"At least. The new design is a lot simpler."

"Good." They were getting somewhere, she thought. "I was sure there must be a new design. Can you run me off a copy?"

"It's up here!" Bill laughed, tapping his head. "We're so far behind schedule, you didn't think I'd have time to write up every design change, did you?"

The most frightening thing is that Bill wasn't kidding. They never did have any further design documentation from that date, apart from technical specs drawn up by the programmers. Rachel recommended a full retrofit of the game design to date, with further changes to be placed under change control. The company decided against these measures on the basis that they would cost too much time at such a late stage. In fact, it was the failure to implement them that proved costly: About a year and $750,000 later, *Golem* was canned.

intend to make a strategy game that assists the player to plan attacks easily, you might think twice about a multilayered interface that, although original, militates against the core vision of ease-of-use.

A core vision pulls the look and feel of the game together too. Not only do these "chrome" elements assist each other, but also they should enhance the experience of playing the game. When all the elements of the game are working to the same end, you have a product whose internal resonance guarantees aesthetic appeal. On the other hand, a combination of incoherent game features and artistic styles is simply a mess.

Is It Interactive?

Ezra Pound had a saying that he was fond of quoting to poets: "Whatever can be said well in prose can be said better in prose." He was trying to stop poetry from trying to do something it wasn't suited for, to get poets to instead concentrate on the unique strengths of their own medium. In the same way, the entertainment software of the future will hopefully move away from other media like cinema, defining itself by what it can do best—in particular, by offering maximal interactivity.

We discussed specific kinds of interactivity in Chapter 3. A broader but still useful distinction is between high interactivity and low interactivity.

Most computer games today use high interactivity, as the player has a strongly proactive role. The story should unfold directly from what the player sees and does, because the player's expectations are that his role is proactive, which means he will be impatient if forced to sit back and be told a story. The best designs avoid lengthy dialogues, chunks of clumsy exposition, and extended full motion videos (FMVs) that remove control from the player. It is possible to tell a story implicitly and with great economy; you do not need lots of dialogue. Think of entering a drifting spaceship. One of the cryo pods is damaged, and a long-dead body is slumped across a table nearby, a bottle of pills in its hand. You don't need to spell it out; the story is all there.

Low interactivity, on the other hand, is reactive. At its simplest level, it is represented by the audience at a play, hissing and calling out boos and yeahs—as long as the actors take any notice, that is! You use low interactivity when programming a stack of music CDs to play the tracks you want, or when channel-surfing on the TV.

Low interactivity is a way for entertainment software to reach a larger market, since more people choose reactive leisure (such as watching TV or a ball game) over proactive leisure (acting or playing a ball game). In the more story-oriented genres that will evolve out of today's adventure games, we should see flexible narratives that the viewer can dip into with as much interactivity as he wants.

Is It Interesting?

In Chapter 3, we examined Sid Meier's description of a game as "a series of interesting choices." We also saw that interesting choices are difficult choices. One effect of this is that the better designed the game, the harder it is to program the AI, because a good game is a game you win by smart playing. Fortunately, artificial intelligence is getting better, as you can see by the uncannily humanlike behavior of the bots in *Quake*, for instance. This is just as well, because the demands of games in the future will push AI to the limit.

An elementary grasp of logic tells us that just because all interesting choices are difficult doesn't mean that all difficult choices are interesting. Being presented with six treasure chests, five of which are booby-trapped and where there is no clue to guide you, is a difficult choice but distinctly poor gameplay. (And poor storytelling, too.)

So don't include features whose only effect will be to annoy the player. The principle of a good design feature is that it presents the player with an upside and a downside, either of which may vary according to other factors. The choice is thus difficult to make, but, if the player gets it right, he is rewarded by success and a further layer of choice.

Is It Fun?

You can include only so much in a game, so the trick is to make sure that whatever is included will enhance the player's enjoyment.

As an example, consider artificial life, which has hovered around the fringes of the games industry as a buzzword for the last few years. We are now starting to see a clutch of games that make much of their A-life credentials. I'm interested in the technology myself, but a pitfall exists for the overeager designer, because sometimes A-life (like real life) just isn't any fun.

An online RPG world in which all the computer characters are sustaining a real economy is worthless if the player-characters form a subculture that's unconnected to that economy. A strategy game in which you have to keep rounding up your soldiers because they've lost their nerve and deserted isn't clever; it's just witless. In an adventure game, having to remember to keep punishing your hero so that he does what you tell him is...well, actually that could be fun—a true "god game" in the Old Testament style—because it enhances your relationship with the game's central character. But it's for *that* reason that it's worth including, not because it's a nifty example of new technology.

The lesson is that the technology, like everything else, must serve the needs of the game, and thus the needs of the player. Never let yourself get carried away by a cool idea, new technology, or amazing effects. Always ask first: Is this fun?

The Future Of Design

Suppose that, in order to be a game designer, you needed qualifications in business management, artificial intelligence, creative writing, computer science, and game theory. If that were the case, there wouldn't be many game designers, and we wouldn't get the best game concepts possible: We'd just get the best that could be dreamed up by people with more degrees than a thermometer.

Look at it another way. Suppose that the only novelists in history had been people who trained as typesetters as well. Some of them might have written great novels, works of genius, even. But those works would have been fewer, because the talent pool would have been smaller.

In the 1980s, the programmers of a game were most likely the designers as well. (They tended to do the artwork, too, which explains some of those early Spectrum games.) The classic games of the 1980s were created this way, but no one should lament the fact that formalized roles and more-accessible technology mean that it is now possible to be a designer without also having to be a programmer. It just makes the talent pool wider. The creative programmers will continue to design as well, just as some camera operators also write screenplays.

In the future, we should see more individuals such as screenwriters, artists, novelists, and board-game designers enter computer game design, which will revolutionize what we expect from entertainment software. Many of these people will have no idea of the limitations of the technology: It's not the job of the designer to worry about that, at least in the initial design phase. Not knowing what can't be done, they will demand it, and their development teams, rising to the challenge, will deliver games astoundingly different from anything we've seen before.

"Most game designers are programmers and very familiar with technology. Programmers are held back in an artistic, creative way. They know the limits of technology."

—Roberta Williams, creator of King's Quest, *quoted in* Game Design 101

Making Designs More Generic

If there will be one overriding evolution in game design, I would say it will be a move towards starting out with a generic design. This is consistent with (and indeed a logical consequence of) the software factory model. Such designs will allow designers to start arguing from the general to the specific, which will make the design concepts more portable and robust.

Thus, instead of beginning with a design that specified game resources as food, wood, money, and piety, I now begin by defining attributes of resources. I might say that resources can be localized (physically resident somewhere in the game world) or nonlocalized (held intrinsically by the player and therefore not subject to capture by the enemy). They can also be collectable (waiting to be picked up) or creatable (requiring some action to spawn them), and they can be perishable (decaying over time) or indestructible. And so on.

By this model, piety is nonlocalized, creatable, and indestructible, whereas food might be localized, collectable, and perishable. The advantage comes when I move on to my next game—another wargame, but now set in the modern world and involving guerrillas and military juntas. I decide that one of the resources will be morale, which is spent whenever you want to repair damaged buildings. Broadcasting stations generate morale; friendly losses or enemy propaganda reduce it; and it declines over time as long as you have soldiers on your own city streets. Rather than having to design this resource entirely from scratch, the architecture group already has a template for including it: nonlocalized, creatable, and perishable. In practice, the resource template is rather more complicated than that, and with more attributes, because it aims to allow completely customizable resources for any game.

Now, this can mean many attribute slots, but they are actually grouped in classes (attributes involving existence, persistence, and so on). In many games, those attribute slots would never be switched on or would simply default to some higher level of classification. The advantage is that you could, in theory, take units out of the terrorist game and drop them into the first game and they would still be ready to function—which obviously would be handy if you are aiming for any level of reuse.

Nonsymbolic Design

If I throw a ball and take many high-speed photographs of its flight, I'll see that the trajectory the ball took is a parabola. But the ball didn't follow that path because gravity told it to move in a parabola. A parabola is just a symbolic concept in the analytical domain of mathematics, and the universe doesn't know anything about mathematics or analysis or symbols; these are human concepts. In reality, there are just a bunch of physical processes, each of which deals only with the processes and circumstances just before and just after it. So, the ball is at one position, and gravity tells the ball's velocity to change, and the ball's velocity tells its position to change.

This is the opposite approach to that taken in most software applications. There, processing power is at a premium, so the sooner you can go to symbolic constructs, the better. The tradeoff is that software can crash when your symbolic "shortcut" misses something that the one-step-at-a-time approach would have taken in its stride.

Researchers in artificial life have identified an analogous problem:

"The classical AI approach has been criticised because the symbols and symbol structures on which planning and decision making are based are not grounded in the real world. The problem is that unequivocally decoding sensory data into a symbol and turning a command without error into its intended action may be unsolvable."

—Luc Steels, "The Artificial Life Roots of Artificial Intelligence" in Artificial Life *(MIT Press, 1997)*

Here is an example: Suppose I am putting a monster into my new Frankenstein adventure game, and the idea is that it will jump out of its vat when the player enters the laboratory. Instead of putting in a lot of complicated AI to do with detecting humans and having the goal of wanting to kill them, I just choose the shortcut of placing a trigger tile inside the laboratory door. When the player steps on the trigger, the monster will appear and attack.

Okay so far, but what if the player manages to get onto the tower roof, jumps down, and, by some fluke, manages to land safely on the balcony of the laboratory? Now he can explore the lab, get all the power-ups, and read the journal about the monster (an entry that is supposed to be poignant if he's just fought and killed it, but that is meaningless otherwise). Only when the player goes to leave via the door does the monster climb out of its vat and growl, "You shall not steal my master's secrets!"

In the past, the nonsymbolic, step-by-step approach was not practical. The processing capability wasn't available to deal with that and graphics too. But now much of the graphics work is done by the video card, and computers are doubling in power every 18 months or so. At last, it is starting to be possible to create "uncrashable" games by avoiding the need to design using symbolic shortcuts. Case Study 8.3 compares nonsymbolic and symbolic designs.

The Future Of Games

Computer games have been around for approximately 20 years. In the form we know it today, the medium is really only some 10 years old. Nonetheless, throughout this section, I've drawn on references dating back to King Solomon and Aristotle, and through Shakespeare to Orson Welles. I've related computer games not only to the technological leap of the last decade, but to 4,000 years of human culture.

I've done so because I don't see computer games as froth for kids, as mere "brain candy." If I felt that way, I wouldn't be working as a game designer. I believe that games—entertainment software—are potentially the most exciting development in the creative arts since man first drew a bison on the wall of a cave and started to tell a story.

But notice I said "potentially." It's that potential which we really haven't even begun to tap. Everything to date has just been the groundwork. It's in the future that those foundations will grow into an entertainment medium that will rank alongside literature, music, and cinema. And the future starts now.

Over the last decade, computers have revolutionized the way we look at home entertainment. However, the revolution so far has been only experimental. It has yet to give birth to a new medium in the way that the fusion of photography and drama created cinema, for instance.

"No one has ever really looked at what the market wants, or even who it really is. And even when we find out, we often shy away from the lesson. GTI's Deer Hunter*... a slideshow of a game, the US mass market lapped it up, fuelling clones from* Big Game Hunter *to* Turkey Hunt *until the barrel scraping began.*

*"*Deer Hunter *revealed that people were starving for game styles that the industry hadn't even considered making. It also showed that people would buy hunting products. Only one of these lessons was learned."*

—Owain Bennallack, writing in MCV*, 2 July 1999*

Case Study 8.3 Comparing Nonsymbolic And Symbolic Design

In the original *Warcraft*, peasants collected gold by entering a gold mine and bringing sacks back to your town hall. At the start of the game it was always worth spawning peasants because the more peasants you had, the greater your revenue stream. However, there came a point when the peasants started to get in each others' way. Adding more peasants would then lead to "traffic jams" as the peasants encountered each other on the streets of the town and would have to back up to let others get past. The situation was alleviated by leaving wide streets. Additionally, it was not a good idea to place your town hall too close to the gold mine—giving a little more space also helped avoid traffic congestion.

Now, an economist could derive an equation to describe the flow of gold to the town hall. The factors would be the number of peasants, the placement density of the town buildings, and the distance from the town hall to the mine. We can imagine that it would be a pretty complex equation. The point is that the designers of *Warcraft* never needed any such equation. They simply programmed in the basic rules and behaviors and the economic simulation emerged directly from those.

Contrast this with a game like *Caesar 2*, which used underlying equations to create a simulation of an ancient Roman city. This approach is less satisfying because the player is not directly viewing the reasons for success and failure. Instead, when playing a game like *Caesar 2* (or any simulation of its type) you are trying to build an abstract match to the game's underlying equations in your head. The simulated economy and the gameplay are less visible, lessening the sense of immersion.

The designers of the next decade (including, possibly, many of the readers of this book) will take entertainment software from the level of a hobby and make it into a new art form. This is why I have repeatedly said that it doesn't matter if your product is a game. If you like games, all well and good. But, just so long as you create something that people can interact with and enjoy—and that couldn't be done better in any medium other than software—you are doing your job as a designer.

Games on a computer are more attractive, exciting, convenient, and immediate than games played on a board. Multimedia products provide more-interesting presentation and better look-up capability than a reference book. Computer toys let you play with unlimited resources. All these products are worthwhile, but none of them exploits the opportunities inherent in software to create a completely new medium. It is as if we were still at the point where movie theaters showed nothing but short films of onrushing trains and racing meets. What we have to do now is get to the point where a new technology metamorphoses into a new medium.

And what is the really exciting thing about entertainment software? It isn't going to be only *one* new medium; it's going to be a whole bunch of them.

The Next Decade

As the entertainment software industry matures, there will be more formalization, creating a clearer distinction between genres. Why should products as diverse as *Tomb Raider*, *Alpha Centauri*, and *Riven* all be classified as "games"? Hard-core gamers may think there's considerable overlap in the markets for those games, but the wider buying public would find them all quite different.

"Another hugely derided game [is] Riven, *the sequel to* Myst. *'It's not a game!' we cry. 'Then stop giving us games and give us more of this instead,' many punters respond."*

—Owain Bennallack; MCV, *2 July 1999*

We will see an increasing trend towards more-specialized entertainment software magazines and towards defining genres for display in stores. Just as in bookshops, the mass market won't want to search through the equivalent of thrillers, sci-fi, and bodice-rippers to find what they're looking for. You will know the genre you're interested in, and there will be magazines and Web distribution sites devoted to just that genre.

And what will these genres be? We might expect them to be evolutions from the existing game genres, plus a few more that nobody has thought of yet. The demands of a wider market will mean that, in comparison to today's games, they will be:

- *More accessible*—People will want products they can play right away.
- *More flexible*—The user will have more choice in how to use the product.
- *More realistic*—Vastly improved artificial intelligence, physics, and graphics will transform the products of the future.
- *More fun*—No more struggling against the game system; the mass market will not have the patience for underdesigned products.
- *Completely different*—Only the diehards will continue with games as we know them today.

The Strengths Of Software

Let's look at what entertainment software can do really well. If we were compiling a list of USPs for the medium, we could say that it has the edge over other media in terms of:

- *Depth*—The background can be far more fleshed out. The inhabitants of the game world can have their own independent existence.
- *Freedom*—The true payoff of interactivity is that the user can make the product deliver what he wants.
- *Persistence*—You can get engrossed for hundreds of hours, experiencing the ultimate in escapist entertainment.

- *Multiplay*—Entertainment software empowers groups of people with the ability to create a mutual narrative.

These are the areas in which we may expect to see real advances, as entertainment software ("playware"?) defines itself as different from other media. So, we expect to see an increasing trend towards multiplay and for game worlds to feature better artificial intelligence and physics that will enhance the verisimilitude of the setting. A much greater range of interactivity is also required, allowing the player to choose how the game is used. (Better artificial intelligence will assist here, too.)

It's possible even today to wring an additional level of interactivity out of games. That's what we're doing whenever we use cheat codes. Although the cheat codes give some extra degrees of freedom, the downside is that they tend to be used only by the inner cadre of hard-core gamers (the very people who need them least) and are in any case unsupported. In most cases, using cheat codes doesn't enhance the game; it breaks it.

Instead, games should try to empower the user with real choice. My ideal for a strategy game, for example, would be one in which I could choose my own role within the world: commander of an army, ruler of a civilization, or Populous-style god. This way, the same product could be both a wargame and a sim-civilization game. I'd also like to decide the kind of opponents I'd face, both by selection of the computer player AI and by altering constants in the game world. (Changing the likelihood of famine occurring could thus switch a computer player from peaceful farmer to desperate raider.) This is a whole other level of interactivity, letting the player choose *how* to play, instead of constraining them with the preconceptions of the designer. With the release of *Dungeon Keeper 2*, which has several options to let you customize the game you want, we are finally beginning to see this kind of interactivity being made available.

In the case of a storytelling or adventure game of 10 years hence, you might decide one evening to watch a software movie starring Victor Virtual. Later, you could decide to switch characters, or demand longer fight scenes. Or you might interfere more directly, by feeding clues to the hero. So you can experience *The Odyssey*, say, from the hero's own viewpoint, or as Poseidon (the god he had made an enemy of) or as Athena (the goddess who occasionally helped him).

Okay, it's probable that the specifics of these new media won't turn out quite as I've described them, but the principle is clear: Interactivity will be about degrees of choice, as well as the choices themselves.

The Crossroads Of Creativity

To get some idea of the different forms into which computer games will evolve, it's helpful to look at the ways that they entertain.

Games As Stories

I recently heard about several development companies that have hired psychologists to help them inject emotion into their games. In many cases, these are the same companies that are treating development like an art when it should be a science, and now they are treating creativity as a science when it should be an art!

If you want emotion in your game, hire screenwriters, playwrights, novelists, poets, directors, or actors. But don't hire psychologists. This is so idiotic that it's laughable.

In Chapter 6, we looked at some perennial storytelling techniques that can be usefully employed to intensify the gaming experience. However, I have been saying that entertainment software must become a new art form altogether. Simply borrowing the techniques of other media such as cinema will not do the trick.

Famously, Walt Disney made it his goal to produce a cartoon that would make people cry, and he achieved this goal most notably with the death of Bambi's mother. One ending of the adventure game *Outcast* (Appeal) is, if not quite tear-jerking, at least poignant and emotionally mature. However, it achieves this effect entirely through cinematic techniques. The last 10 minutes of the game include a couple of sequences in which the player is proactive, but those sequences have no effect on the final outcome. The story in *Outcast*, although moving, is told by noninteractive cut scenes.

For entertainment software to make its mark, we need to adopt a new approach to interactive storytelling. This will come via improved artificial intelligence and full physics systems that do not *tell* a story but rather allow the player to participate in the creation of a story.

I have said that entertainment software must move away from old models like films, novels, and plays to find a new way to tell stories. In fact, face-to-face role-playing games could provide a useful template.

I have written role-playing games professionally, and I also run them as a hobby. Each week, when preparing a session, I begin by devising a setting—a town by a lake, for example, under quarantine because of a plague. I populate this with the main nonplayer characters (NPCs), whose goals I define. Thus, the notes might read: "Lord Shonu: crafty, cautious, extremely wealthy; wants the Key of Time but isn't prepared to die for it," and so on. When I have all the NPCs, I can infer the story that would occur *if not for the players*. The players' characters (PCs) perturb the situation with their own actions, aiding some NPCs and opposing others. Because I know the NPCs' motivations, goals, and capabilities, I can then decide how they will respond, and so on.

The point is that the role-playing session itself becomes a process of story creation. None of the participants decides the plot in advance. Instead, it emerges from the actions that everybody takes, which means that it would be possible to run the same scenario with two player groups and get completely different stories. (For instance, in one game, the players might kill the bad guys and rescue the princess and the king rewards them. In the other, they act so evil that the bad guys come to work for them, and they jointly collect the ransom.)

This is the kind of storytelling process that we will see in the computer role-playing games (CRPGs) of the next decade and, in modified form, in non-CRPGs also.

Games As Visual Arts

Entertainment software, although rich with unique potential of its own, shares elements in common with other arts. In particular, we might look at two terms used in cinema: *mise en scène*, which is the organization of images in space, and *montage*, which is their respective organization in time. Case Study 8.4 provides an example of *mise en scène*.

To illustrate the difference, consider a very famous movie moment: the shower scene in *Psycho*. The murder scene takes approximately a minute, and there are at least 60 different shots used. This is *montage*. By organizing the shots, Hitchcock creates dislocation and panic. Now suppose he had simply used a single shot for the entire scene. Instead of identifying with the victim, we would become onlookers at the scene of a crime. Instead of empathic terror, we would feel objective horror.

Theater uses *mise en scène* but not montage. Novels use montage as a matter of course, simply because they are forced to describe a scene one point at a time. However, they cannot employ *mise en scène* without evoking montage, because the order of describing objects and people in a room inevitably becomes significant. You would need a picture to detach that from montage. As an extreme simplification of a complex subject, we can say that montage creates narrative and intense emotion, and *mise en scène* creates setting, ambience, and reflexive emotion.

What about computer games? Except in FMVs (which are little movies anyway), the computer game evidently uses only *mise en scène*. This is because montage requires the viewer to be a spectator and not the controller of the action. Montage would work only in a weakly interactive game, say a murder mystery game in which your only choice was which character to follow. In a strongly interactive game, moments of montage can be used very briefly for effect, such as in the marvelous sequence early in *Alone in the Dark* when a monster runs across the lawn and crashes through a window. However, these must be used sparingly, or they cease to work and become only an annoyance. You do not want to keep destroying the feeling of immersion and forcing your player to sit back and wait while he watches snippets of FMV.

The huge advantage that entertainment software has over other visual arts lies in what is going on outside the frame. In an adventure game, I could give a message to a character and he walks off. He later returns with a reply from his lord. This can happen in a film, of course, but there it is a scripted event. In the case of the adventure game, it's possible for me to construct a complete environment so that the character might be waylaid, or lose the message, or give it to the wrong person. (Okay, this wouldn't have been so easy in the past as it would have eaten up a lot of processing power, but we're talking about the next 10 years now.) You get the same effect in a simple way when you see a priest in *Age of Empires* walk out of sight behind a wall and you race units to either end, knowing you have him trapped. It works because, even though the priest has moved "off-screen," you know he's still there.

One of the unique strengths of entertainment software is evoking a world that persists even outside the player's immediate vicinity. This is a cut above the fictional worlds of cinema, which are merely credible. These worlds will be more than credible; they will, in a sense, be real.

Games As Sports

The ability to accommodate multiple participants makes entertainment software perfectly suited for sports. And these don't necessarily have to be real-world sports. Sports that would be impractical because of lethal danger levels (combat golf, lion wrestling) or size and cost (hundred-a-side football) are easy to stage by the medium of software.

Software sports stars may become as well known as real-life baseball and football players, and not everyone need be an active participant. The old game model would insist on a virtual sport in which the user took part, but why shouldn't I be a spectator instead? Perhaps in 10 years' time we might come home from work, get out the beer and pretzels, and connect to view the final of the World Quakeball Tournament.

Games As Toys

A toy is something that we play with in order to have fun, which is why *entertainment software* and *playware* are better terms for what we do than *computer games*. All games are

Case Study 8.4 An Example Of Mise En Scène

About halfway through Appeal's *Outcast*, there is an FMV where the hero, Cutter Slade, responds to his lady friend's parting words, "We'll have words about this later," by saying to himself, "I'm all tingly with anticipation."

Suddenly, he seems to feel he's being watched. He turns to look towards the impregnable fortress in the heart of the city. In one continuous shot, the camera pans up over the wall of the fortress and continues up and up until it finds the villain of the story standing on his balcony, gazing at the city where he suspects Cutter Slade is hiding.

Although FMVs are not really what entertainment software is about, it's impossible to deny that this is a remarkable case of *mise en scène*. To bring us close to both hero and villain in one uncut sequence is something that even cinema would rarely attempt. And, if it happened in a movie, it still would not impress us as being as "real" as in the context of an adventure game where we have at least an illusory sense that these characters are bustling about their lives at all times.

toys, but not all toys are games, and our aim should be to create something that is interactive and fun whether or not it is a game.

I'm not predicting the end of games, as they are a perfectly valid way of having fun. Gameplay will continue to be an absolute priority in the strategy genre, for example. Players of strategy games demand a challenging game experience, and the evidence indicates that they are interested only in the best. This is why the superior strategy games (such as *Starcraft* and *Age of Empires*) are million-sellers while the rest are nowhere. Having found a satisfying game, it seems that strategy gamers will stick with it until something better comes along (*better* in this case being judged purely on the basis of interesting gameplay). Consequently, strategy gamers are loyal consumers, because the better product they are waiting for is usually the sequel to the game they've already enjoyed. To lure them away, you have to pull out all the stops and deliver the very best gameplay experience that the technology allows. (This was my thinking with the design for *Warrior Kings*, incidentally. Time will show if I was correct.)

But is gameplay needed in other genres? At the moment, gameplay is present in a peripheral sense in products like *Ecstatica* when it comes to choosing your weapons and tactics, but gameplay here is only part of a much greater whole: It helps to enhance the product, but it is not central to it. We might suspect that overt gameplay elements are emphasized only in such products by historical accident: Early text adventures like *The Hobbit* found it easier to emulate the form of a game than a story.

The real innovation came with *SimCity*. That was the point in the evolution of entertainment software when people could say, "This is very definitely a toy, it appeals to adults, and it's very popular." Whether it was a game or not didn't enter the equation. (Simulations tend to contain gameplay simply because real life does, and those "interesting choices" are one of the things that make a simulation rewarding. But simulations are not defined by their gameplay content.)

Everybody accepts that software toys (like *Pokemon*, for instance) are fine for children:

"Encourage exploration. Make your environment free and comfortable enough that children will be willing to try things out until hitting on what you want them to do. While they're figuring it out, they'll still be having fun."

—Tzvi Freeman, "Power to the Kids!" in Game Developer*, September 1997*

If you've ever played a game like *Dungeon Keeper* or *Age of Empires* with a small child watching, you'll know that children really appreciate the fun aspects of the game. "Make the lion chase that man," they'll say, or "Pick up the goblin and make him squirm!"

But it isn't just children who respond that way. Adults can enjoy entertainment software in the same way. A friend of mine who doesn't play games enjoys *Age of Empires* because he likes ordering his little men around to build a city. What annoys him is when the enemy players storm in and destroy it. For him, that spoils the fun.

I think we adults like to have gameplay just to make what we're doing seem respectable. We're not quite sure whether it's okay just to play. But play isn't the same thing as tomfoolery. Play can educate the mind, stimulate the imagination, sharpen the wits, gladden the heart, and enrich the soul. In the future, we'll see much more awareness of entertainment software as a new kind of toy, and the products will be all the more diverse and better for it.

The Way Forward

A novelist said to me, "I hate computer games, they're not art."

Well, art isn't a rarefied concept for the elite few. All forms of entertainment give rise to arts. They may not be formal arts, but they are arts nonetheless. Computer games may not be there yet, but it's an inevitable trend.

So far, the technology of entertainment software has overshadowed the art. Now, armed with ever-improving graphics, physics, and artificial intelligence, we can look forward to a decade of exploring the medium's artistic potential. It will move away from the tropes of cinema and literature to define itself in ways that we are only starting to anticipate.

The way forward will come from design because designers are the artists of the new medium, just as medieval architects were the artists of stoneworking. As designers, we must insist that what has been achieved in computer games is not good enough. We must devise new concepts to make us worthy of our role at this, the most exciting moment in the history of human entertainment.

I'd like to end with two quotations. The first is from George Bernard Shaw: "The reasonable man adapts himself to the world; the unreasonable one persists in trying to adapt the world to himself. Therefore all progress depends on the unreasonable man."

The other quotation is from Sir Christopher Cockerell, inventor of the hovercraft: "If it wasn't for the silly chaps, we'd still be in the Stone Age."

Among the readers of this book are, perhaps, those "unreasonable" men and women who will pioneer the transition of entertainment software from a niche hobby to a whole series of brave new media.

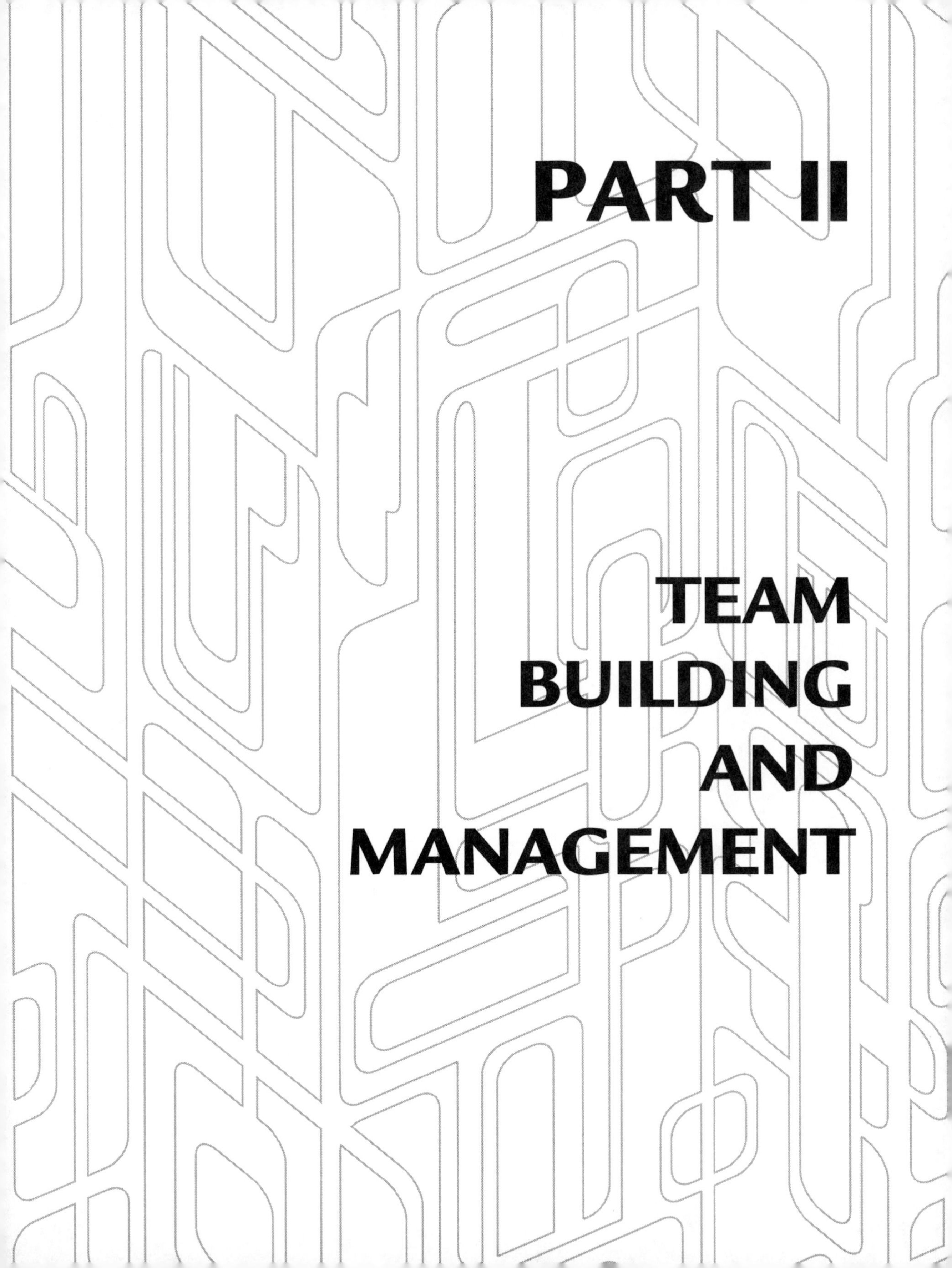

PART II

TEAM BUILDING AND MANAGEMENT

Chapter 9

Current Methods Of Team Management

Key Topics:

- ***Brief history of game development methods***
- ***How games are developed today***
- ***Problems with current methods***
- ***Types of team member***
- ***Exceptions to the rule***

In this chapter, we'll discuss the methods that are currently used to manage the development of games. Although the overall model of game development has changed substantially over the last few years, it still retains much of its initial "spare bedroom" mentality.

This chapter describes the brief history of the techniques that have been used in game development. It draws some parallels with more mature methods that are used outside the games industry (such as those, for example, that are used to develop database software). Although this may sound irrelevant, think of a game as a realtime database with an exciting interface.

Sure, this may be an oversimplification, but the fundamental differences between the two types of development are very small. This rationale will be explained later in this chapter, and we'll look at some examples of the similarities between the two.

The Current Development Model

Except in some of the more enlightened game development firms, the general recipe of software development is as follows:

1. Find four or five developers who are available. Try to make sure that there is a good spread of specialization, such as an AI specialist, a graphics programming expert, a sound expert, a good programmer, and whoever else is available on short notice.

2. Appoint a quirky genius as the lead programmer, usually because he is the sort of person who can code *Quake III* in his sleep, and knows everything about anything. (See Chapter 11.)
3. Put them together in a small room with a staff of artists at their disposal.
4. Allow to simmer for an 18-month period, stirring periodically and adding soft drinks and pizza to taste.
5. Be prepared to allow a little extra cooking time. But also be prepared that the result still may be half baked, or that the developers will have been frazzled to a crisp.

Another oversimplification to be sure, but you would be surprised to know that this is a common method throughout much of the computer games industry. Generally, there are a few more interventions and checks from management, and some sort of plan is occasionally written, but, whatever the intentions, in the end it boils down to the same old "code like hell" methodology.

The Origins Of The Industry

The evolution of the computer games industry can be compared to that of cottage industries, which sprang from individual craftsmen but didn't flourish until the industrial revolution, when they were mechanized and started producing greater output at reduced costs, taking advantage of the economies of scale.

Take the pottery industry as an example.

Note

Don't worry: we'll get back to computers soon enough!

The pottery industry started with individual potters who produced small quantities of pots, plates, and the like, entirely by hand. The more successful of these soon learned that, in order to expand and increase their business, they had to take advantage of the scalability of certain processes. This was not done simply by using more teams of individuals, but was instead achieved by automating and organizing the less individualistic stages of the pottery-making process, and using a central pool of designers.

Of course, a place still remains in the market for the individual manufacturer with a specialized product, but the associated costs per unit are much higher than they would be for a manufacturer who takes advantage of economies of scale allowed by the factory methods. The output of a lone manufacturer cannot simply be a scaled-down version of the output of an efficiently running factory.

That Was Then…

The computer games industry developed out of garages and spare bedrooms all over the world, but mainly in the United States and England. These programmers were enthusiastic amateurs, writing code for machines such as the ZX Spectrum, Commodore 64, and Amstrad 464, all of which are ridiculously underpowered compared to today's computers.

Consequently, the scopes of their game projects were much smaller than those of today.

The limitations were such that one programmer could quite feasibly design and write a game within six weeks, without having to reuse any code from previous projects. Because of the tight memory constraints of early computers, it was often better to rewrite custom code every time to squeeze every last bit of performance and space out of the system. At most, the "team" would consist of one programmer, an artist (if the programmer was artistically challenged), and occasionally a freelance computer musician. Teamwork, such as it was, was merely a group of people who worked on separate parts of the same program and hardly ever needed to touch the work of another team member. It was possible then to hold an entire game design and architecture in your head without once having to set pen to paper.

Hardware was so limited that the emphasis had to be on gameplay rather than on presentation. Similarly, the programming emphasis was on small and efficient code. There was no operating system to interact with, and, due to the universal nature of the hardware, there were no real hardware incompatibilities and abstraction layers to worry about.

This Is Now!

As computers grew more powerful and the industry prospered, we began to see programming teams that remained small enough to manage their projects fairly well and that started to make reasonable use of already written code. However, the computer games industry has always had a "pedal to the metal" attitude working against code reuse. Although this attitude is becoming less prevalent now, it's likely due to necessity rather than volition.

Before the advent of the MS-DOS PC and Macintosh, it was nearly always possible (and sometimes even necessary) to bypass the operating system completely and write directly to hardware in order to gain the maximum speed possible.

Today, trashing the operating system and hitting the metal is certainly foolhardy, if not downright stupid. It's no longer that important to optimize every line of code; the emphasis now is on writing "clean" code for that operating system. To write such code, the operating system Application Programming Interface (API) enforces a certain degree of standardization, and, consequently, with a little extra effort, code can be made reusable and modular, making it ideal for team use.

As industries go, the games industry is still relatively young and developing. Compared to other, more mature programming industries, it simply has not had the time to develop the advanced and proven techniques. It is because of the general nature of games and game development that structured development techniques have become necessary only in the last few years. Games are now being considered as small- to medium-sized projects.

Hardware is also now much more advanced, with virtually unlimited storage space and memory. Operating systems have also become much more prominent and need to be accommodated. Whereas before, the operating system was the first thing to be dumped when development started, it is now advantageous and even necessary to coexist with the operating system.

These technological advances are something of a double-edged sword. The increase in processing power and memory and storage space means that projects have become, over a very short period of time, much larger and exponentially more complex to manage. It is very difficult for developers who are used to the old way of doing things (which was not that long ago) to adjust to the brave new world of advanced development techniques and apply these "sensibly boring" techniques in the wacky world of game development.

Due to the increased project size, the number of people needing to be involved in the development of a game has also increased. To handle the increased need for organization among team members, better-defined management structures and communication channels are being developed. Teamwork is no longer a buzzword: it's an absolute necessity.

The Trouble With Game Developers

The media has a lot to answer for, because they are responsible for the widespread acceptance of programmers and other computer-based workers, elevating them from the ranks of geeks and dorks to being acceptably cool. The media is also partially responsible for the widespread use of computers in nearly every home, office, and school. (These are all good things.)

However, every silver lining has a cloud, and in this case it is that the media has gone too far!

The games industry is now considered the coolest of the cool. You can now introduce yourself at social functions by saying that you develop computer games. Five years ago, you would have ended up sitting in the corner with all the other dorks, discussing the merits of gameplay and assembly-language programming. Now even Dilbert, king of the dorks, is cool.

So, it's only natural to suppose that the industry attracts more than its fair share of gargantuan egos. Does this sound familiar to any of you? How many of your coworkers have egos the size of a minor planet? How many of them are convinced that they are the best coder since Ada Lovelace? How many of them are childishly averse to criticism and protect their code and their ideas with a zeal beyond the rational, even when they are wrong and have been presented with a clearly superior solution (such as yours, of course)?

Game developers also tend to be very individualistic. The games industry tends to feed off this hype by giving the "creative genius" more freedom than is wise, sparking a team dynamic (or more exactly an "antidynamic") that I'm sure you will be familiar with.

Who's The Leader?

When you get a group of egocentric and intelligent people in the same room together, there is usually only one predictable result: trouble.

Due to the individuality and egotism of the typical game developer, there tends to be an elevated level of internal competition, with its attendant "who's the leader?" jockeying to be the top dog. The games industry is the only area of development in which I have seen internal competition to such an envious extent. Of course, competition exists elsewhere, but the type of internal competition that is prevalent in the games industry is of a particularly destructive nature. In other forms of development, the competition is usually of a more cooperative type: developers are mostly keen to learn from others and are open to criticism and new ideas. Okay, so the motivation behind this may be more selfish—being the development of marketable skills to further their career—but the end result is the same: the sharing of skills and ideas raising the average level of skill in the organization.

Note

Microsoft has a name for this: Coopertition, or having the competitive instinct to gain an edge on your colleagues, but only as part of a team.

Sure, gain that edge, but do so in a way that is beneficial to the team. No lone-star mavericks need apply.

This whole "cool factor" is counterproductive. Game development has become ingrained in youth culture. Trying to impose more-mature development techniques and standards is viewed as being stuffy and boring and thus, usually meets varying levels of resistance. Remember that these individuals want to become game developers probably because of the freedom and coolness factors involved (which is probably why game developers get the lowest wages in the whole development industry, but that is another story).

Game developers try to resist the imposition of rigidity in technique; flying by the seat of the pants on the cutting edge of technology is far cooler (even though it is usually as painful as it sounds). You just don't get this sort of problem with spreadsheet programmers! Of course, not all rigidity is good, but in certain areas, it is absolutely essential to have rigidly defined protocols, or the associated risks to development will cause the eventual cancellation of the project…which is not very cool at all. Think of the procedures and practices as padding for the seat of the pants. It makes the ride a bit more comfortable in the long term, even though the extra bulk is a bit more restrictive at first.

Game developers also seem to consider themselves inherently superior to other types of developers. (If you find this doubtful, see Case Study 9.1 for an example.)

Let's look at the classic stereotype. Mr. Hotshot Game Developer is an all-around creative genius who has superior optimization skills and the ability to write fast, tight code, and all before breakfast (which is usually taken at midday while hacking out the greatest code in existence). By contrast, people who program databases are just boring gray suits with no life. Strangely enough, I have found that usually the converse is true. Database developers know that what they are doing is a job that has to be finished within a certain time limit. It is no less creative or difficult than writing a game, and it usually is equally on the cutting edge of technology (just maybe not so glamorous of an edge). More to the point, they have far more of a life than any of the game developers that I know because they know that what they are performing is just a job with standard hours and not an obsession that takes up all their time. Does more money for less work and more free time in which to spend that money sound appealing?

So It's War Then?

The clichéd cutting edge of technology is a fun place to be, and most game development teams feel as if they are right there at the sharp end, pushing the envelope, breaking the limits, and all the other macho stuff. It's all true, of course: they usually are writing for the latest technologies (although often through an insulating API layer, so it's not exactly uncharted territory).

Unfortunately, this fact has shifted the focus to the technology rather than the gameplay This is the biggest problem facing the game industry today. There are dozens of case studies to demonstrate this point, but there is no need too. Just take a stroll down to your local software emporium and check out the games on the shelves.

As technology increases, game production mutates into a technological arms race: bigger, better, faster, more. If this trend continues, then games are going to become less and less fun and more and more like very impressive technology demonstrations. If someone wants to see pretty moving pictures, they go to the theater. If someone wants an entertaining interactive experience, then they play a game. *Quake* suffered from this, being effectively a technology demo with an afterthought of a game tacked on. Fortunately, *Quake II* rectified in great style any deficiencies in the first iteration.

However, this "more technology, less gameplay" is not a trend that I see continuing. Chances are, there will be a backlash in the same way that there was a backlash against the crop of interactive movies that seemed to pollute the software shelves several years back.

It does not mean that games will become technologically challenged. The emphasis will be focused more on the gameplay and stretching the technology will take second place. (At least, this is what I would like to have happen.) It is interesting to note that the biggest selling game of 1998 was Blizzard Software's *StarCraft*, a technologically competent game, but with excellent and well-balanced gameplay and story lines. This should be telling you something.

The aim of this book is to narrow the gap between the games industry and the more mature and reliable development techniques that are used everywhere else. Case Study 9.1 shows what developers are up against.

The document from which this was extracted and modified had some good points, such as a discussion about office layout and space and lighting. (The comments are valid and worthwhile—if a little unrealistic for all but the richest companies—and they could be used as a starting point for something more practical.)

Case Study 9.1 How Game Developers View Themselves

This is a modified extract of a document that was handed in by a group of developers when asked for their opinions on how to improve the development processes used in the company. Names and places have been changed to protect the innocent and the not-so innocent.

The Best Game Development House In The World

- *The Right Environment*—Programmers are not office workers. They are creative. They are obsessive. They are often adolescent.

This means that they get to work late. This means that they often work until 5 A.M. in the morning. This means that they spend all weekend at their computer before realizing that they have spouses, commitments, or lives outside of *The Game*.

A development house is just that: a house. It isn't an office where people work from 9 A.M. to 5 P.M. It is a place where young, talented, driven people spend ridiculous amounts of time creating and playing games. This means that our work area is a bedroom, our coffee room is a kitchen, and our common area is a lounge.

A place like this is where the best games in the world are being written right now. This is the environment we want.

- *The Right Attitude*—Executives want company cars, mobile phones, personal assistants, profit sharing, and international travel.

Developers want games, figurines, T-shirts, toys, and the latest hardware. (Though don't dream of pulling royalties, bonuses, and international travel: it is still a career.)

The point is that a little impulsive silliness goes a long way in games development. *Buy* a seven-foot-tall inflatable weird-looking alien thing: it's cool. Stock a refrigerator with beer for Friday afternoons and supply a games room with consoles and air hockey.

- *The Right People*—The games industry is fiercely competitive, both on the shelves and in the interview room. Skilled developers are in short supply, and *talented* developers are in even shorter supply.
- *The Right Location*—Within five minutes' walk of the nearest train station, pubs and bars, supermarket, pizza delivery, 24-hour shops, banks, car parking, and a gymnasium.
- *The Right Office*—A kitchen, a phone for private calls, a shower, sleeping facilities.
- *The Right Workspace*—No direct lighting, plenty of desk space, wall space for whiteboards, meeting rooms, etc. Chairs should be replaced with sofas, and board tables should be replaced with coffee tables. There should be futons, arcade machines, and a pool table, and computers with Internet and newsgroup access.

It is slightly unfair to just present and criticize the bad points, which is why it is worth mentioning here that the majority of the document discussed office space and development environments, and was for all intents and purposes fairly sensible. Case Study 9.1 represents the worst excesses of the game developer ego.

The claim that programmers are not office workers—but are creative, obsessive, and often adolescent—is wishful thinking. It is the developer ego rattling off. Okay, so they do often act like adolescents. Fine, but you're in the working world now. It's time to accept some responsibility. Programmers are entitled to be creative, but programming is not the place for creativity. Creative programming is better known as hacking, and hacking has no place in a team environment.

Getting to work late is just a lack of self-discipline. What is the point of getting to work several hours late and staying until 5 A.M.? The whole point of being part of a team is to be there when the rest of the team is, which includes management as well. No one is going to thank you for working through the night, producing a lot of unintelligible and hacked-up code that some coder has to spend hours trying to decipher without your help (because you're sleeping off the effects of the all-nighter). This is not good teamwork. Developers such as this hinder teamwork and end up costing a lot more money than a guy who just works his regular 9 A.M. to 5 P.M. like the rest of the team.

The discussions about sleeping accommodation and cooking facilities admirably demonstrate some of the major problems with game development. Why do they automatically assume that they are going to be working in the office for so long that they need to eat and sleep there? That they should even need to consider such arrangements indicates a huge problem with the development process. It seems to be the normal case, rather than the exception. Successful projects don't usually need long hours. In fact, I have seen long hours being worked on unsuccessful projects more often that I have seen them on successful projects. The office is not a home. No one needs a room to sleep in; you have one of those at home.

Developers also most certainly do not need a private phone. (They should have one of those at home, too.) Work is work. You are there to do a job, and it is the job that you are paid for. Pool tables and arcade machines? Get a life! Go home, go out, meet people. Do anything, but don't sit in an office for 12 to 18 hours a day, producing substandard work.

How can you be sure the work will be substandard? It is obvious that no one can concentrate fully on something for 12 hours solid. Exhaustion will set in, and they won't be able to consistently apply their skills to a task for such a duration. A lot of that time will be spent dealing with the issues that they have not had time to do at home. When they come into the office the next day (if they even went home), they will still be tired to commit themselves to the task. Consistently long hours will produce less useful work than a steady reliable conscientious programmer working an 8-hour day, and then going out and clearing his mind of all things work related in the evening. In most cases, the 18-hours-a-day programmer will not produce any more useful work than an 8-hours-a-day programmer.

Of course, the odd spot of overtime is sometimes necessary; in these cases, working longer hours can increase productivity. The danger is that management then assumes that, if a short burst of increased hours produced good results, then allowing (or forcing) developers to work longer hours for longer periods will produce consistently greater results. Sorry, but it just doesn't work like that. The Law of Diminishing Returns kicks in with a vengeance as the developers settle into the new routine, and less work with lower quality and higher costs than before is produced.

If anyone knows what on earth would they want with a seven-foot inflatable alien, please email the authors.

The Typical Game Developer

Clichéd though it may be, it necessary to describe a few of the classic types of game developers.

It may be that this fits some of your team members exactly, or it may be that your team members represent some combination of these stereotypes. Of course, none of them may apply. The problem types of game developer identified are the maverick, the prima donna, the shy guy, the sleeper, and the jack. These guys are initially welcomed into the team, but are capable of causing problems further down the line when their shortcomings become apparent. It is not usually an issue with technical ability, because those with insufficient technical skills are usually weeded out before they can cause any real problems. The problems that these guys cause are usually more subtle and difficult to detect, which is also part of the problem.

These problem types are fairly prevalent in game development teams worldwide. In fact, the game industry actually attracts these sorts of individuals. The only way to avoid them is to interview and screen thoroughly, paying close attention to the personality of the prospect, and maybe even using standard psychological profiling techniques. Follow up any references meticulously. (You can instantly weed out anyone who has worked in the games industry but who doesn't provide any references.) Also, try to find out (if possible) from someone else at the company the particulars of the person acting as the applicant's reference. Sometimes it will be the applicant's best friend!

Now on to the problem types:

The Maverick

The maverick is a talented individual whom everybody trusts and depends on. If you have a tricky job, then the maverick is your man as shown in Figure 9.1.

Figure 9.1
The maverick.

Combining a high level of technical skill with a broad base of knowledge, the maverick enjoys his position as top dog—until something goes wrong. The maverick takes complete ownership of his code, and tries not to let anyone else near it. In the maverick's view, no one else can be trusted to touch his code. No one else would have the skill or the knowledge to do anything other than sully its purity, so it's best not to let them touch it (or so the maverick thinks). This behavior is usually permitted, if not just because the maverick is so competent and confident. Quite often, the code is virtually unreadable by anyone except the maverick. The technical description for this hoarding phenomenon is "job security."

However, when something goes wrong, what happens then? Because no one else knows the code, just sit and sweat it out until the maverick can resolve his difficulties. This means that the team is now waiting on one person. This is a risk, and is not a good situation to be in. If the maverick fails, he takes the whole team down with him.

And what would happen if the maverick quit, leaving a vast quantity of source code that is difficult to even understand, let alone maintain? The only option here would be to try to assign other team members to "reverse engineer" the maverick's code to try to understand it. There are other options, but they are so unpalatable as to be inconsequential (such as rewriting the code from scratch or dropping an entire area of functionality). Unfortunately, this may not always be possible because mavericks tend to be given areas of critical responsibility. If it is not possible or desirable to drop the functionality, then the only option is to stick it out and accept the delays caused by the maverick's departure. (Case Study 11.1 is an example of this choice in effect.)

The Prima Donna

He's the bee's knees. This guy *knows* that he is the best, and anybody who tries to criticize him will suffer his wrath. Everybody must know a prima donna. This is the guy with the huge but fragile ego. His idea is always the best. His code is always perfect. A stereotypical image of the prima donna is shown in Figure 9.2.) Like the maverick, the prima donna also does not know how to take criticism.

The prima donna is usually very intelligent and technically skillful. However, lacking interpersonal skills and the knack of rubbing people the wrong way, are his specialty. He divides the world into two classes: *those who are less intelligent than he is*, and *threats*. He is typically in the leader on projects, because his many talents make him appear invaluable. Unfortunately, it is from this position that the most damage to the team structure can occur.

The prima donna will attack anyone whom he perceives as a threat by insulting their intelligence and their skills. Anybody else who simply is not up to his technical level, will be made to feel completely incompetent. Not everyone (and particularly not introverted programmers) is able to stand up to the attacks, which leads an uncomfortable dynamic within the team. A prima donna is the biggest danger to a team. When a team breaks down as a result of the prima donna's antics, you can expect to lose two or three of your best members.

The prima donna is also basically a control freak who doubts everybody else's ability, and looks with scorn at what they do.

Figure 9.2
The prima donna.

The Shy Guy

The shy guy is the stereotypical computer geek as shown in Figure 9.3. You saw a lot of these guys in computer films from the eighties. (You know the sort: personality-deficient schoolboy/computer geek that saves the world and embarrasses the school football hero.)

The shy guy tends to be very withdrawn, and communication problems of one kind or the other are the order of the day. Taking criticism is also difficult for the shy guy; in fact, taking any kind of advice is difficult, as is the basic communication of ideas. These people seem to be comfortable only with their computers, so maybe the best way of communicating with them would be to send email.

The danger that the shy guy poses to the team is fairly obvious, although there is no direct threat and the shy guy doesn't actively destroy the team. It is just that they never really participate. The biggest problem with their lack of communication is that it drastically decreases the level of project visibility, and hence becomes a great risk to the project at large.

The Sleeper

The sleeper appears just like a normal (or even excellent) member of the team, at least on the surface. Under the surface, they are not so useful, sowing dissent with the management among other team members as shown in Figure 9.4.

There can be many reasons for this. One of the most common reasons is pure anarchy: the sleeper simply has a problem with accepting authority, and so subconsciously seeks to undermine it in any way possible. Other reasons include attempts to poach team members in order to form independent teams, or feeling as if they have been treated badly and wanting to make sure that other team members feel the same way, too.

Figure 9.3
The shy guy.

Figure 9.4
The sleeper.

The sleeper is a dangerous team member because he is also very difficult to detect. The sleeper will not make himself known to management, and will often reveal himself only to a trusted developer who he expects will keep quiet about his level of dissatisfaction. Anonymous reporting channels provide a possible method for detecting this type of problem developer.

The Jack

The jack is the jack of all trades, but the master of none as shown in Figure 9.5.

These are the most useful of the "negative" developer types and, in some cases, can be viewed as positive. Jacks are the only type of problem developer that are worth preserving; as long as they can be taught to overcome their shortcomings, they will then become a useful team member.

The jack's main shortcomings are that they can be very sure of their own skills, which sometimes develops into an overconfidence.

The gap between their skills and their opinion of their skills is usually discovered only when it is too late, after which their credibility is damaged beyond repair. This is because they have managed to sell themselves (which they are very good at) into a position that requires more skill than they actually have. Being unable to admit their failure, they bluff and produce substandard code and technical excuses that tend to be believed by the less technically experienced staff.

Figure 9.5
The jack.

Excessive Long Hours Mean An Unsuccessful Project

If you are expected to work long hours on a project at the expense of a social life, this is an indicator that something is seriously wrong, and it's usually for one of two main reasons (or a combination of both):

1. The project has been badly scheduled. Too much work is being attempted in too little time.
2. The project wasn't badly scheduled to start with, but major developmental problems were not detected and corrected in time, and now the project is attempting to play catch-up.

The first reason is inexcusable. There is no good reason why the development team should have bought into a schedule that was clearly unrealistic. In real life, however, things are not always as they should be. The usual reasons for impossible schedules are pressures from the publisher or, believe it or not, the season.

Let's say the publisher needs the release by a certain date (for any number of reasons: a soccer title needs to released to tie in with the championships, a movie tie-in needs to be released to benefit from the publicity, or the title is part of a lineup required for the release of a new platform). Of course, sometimes there is no good reason for a deadline other than contractual obligations. One company (with which I have worked) had signed themselves into a contract that obligated them to produce a product with nine months—and from a standing start. Fortunately, this was quickly realized to be impossible, and involved much hasty renegotiation of contracts and a change of publishers. In the end, the product was late by more than a year (due to the awful code that had been initially hacked out in the effort to meet the nine-month deadline). This is obviously not a good situation to be in.

Seasonal pressure usually boils down to one thing: Christmas. Everybody wants their game to cash in from loving grannies buying little Johnny a game for his newfangled computer. This also explains the glut of titles in the months before Christmas (and the late arrivals following shortly thereafter) with nothing major appearing during the rest of the year.

In late 1998, a group of publishers got together to see if they could agree to a smoother distribution of releases throughout the year in an attempt to avoid the annual silly season; it will be interesting to see how this is working by the time that this book is published. If this is managed, then the annual nightmare of the Christmas release may be alleviated to some degree (which is a good thing, because nobody can delay Christmas to get a release finished, although I'm sure some people have considered trying).

Exceptions To The Rule

Every rule, though, has some exceptions. In a few rare cases, games development houses have stumbled across development methods that work. These aren't always perfect, and in fact, in most of the examples, the releases were delayed. In these cases, though, the delays were what "positive" delays. For starters, they were anticipated. They also were not caused through incompetence or coding problems or runaway bugcounts. They were caused by the developers refining the gameplay, or fine-tuning the artificial intelligence, and (in one case) by replacing the entire graphics engine.

These companies were lucky. They were in the enviable position of being able to define their own deadlines. They were in the position where they could say, "We are not ready to release this yet. When we are satisfied, we will."

These companies were allowed this freedom because they were the leaders in their fields, the companies that produced the products that everybody else imitated. And this is why they are the exceptions.

The games presented in Case Study 9.2 were either produced on schedule or were produced using good production standards with sensible change-control procedures to ensure that the project was always under control. Why is it that these games are the exception rather than the rule? All three examples were successful games in their own right (particularly *Quake* and *StarCraft*). Is it because a race of superhumans have sent forth their progeny to lead the way in developing games on earth using advanced development techniques beyond the puny understanding of mortal man? (Well, given what I have said about egos, I concede that there is a possibility that they believe this to be the case.)

But it's unlikely. It is more likely that they have a solid grasp of development techniques and the need for good teamwork. Adequate development and change-control procedures had been used, which, in these cases, paid off handsomely.

If these techniques can pay off for these development teams, then there is no reason that they can't for you and your team on your next project.

Case Study 9.2 Quake, StarCraft, and XCOM: Interceptor

These three games are just a few prominent examples of many games that have had successful developments.

Quake (id Software)

The development of *Quake* is a perfect example of how every company would like their development teams to be: no deadlines except those that they imposed on themselves, and publishers chasing after them with the scent of a guaranteed hit in their noses. The team had time to research and perfect the technology. Also, due to the generous amount of funding (available from both the success of *Doom* and the distribution rights of *Quake*), the team was able to employ as much time and as many resources as they needed in order to perfect the product. The team structure placed Jon Romero in charge of the overall architecture and design. He personally resolved any arguments, although there were few of these due to the strictly delineated code ownership. This kind of arrangement wouldn't work, however, for just any team. id Software is truly an exception, and there have been many failed attempts to emulate their style.

StarCraft (Blizzard Software)

StarCraft was developed originally using a similar graphics engine to that used in *Warcraft II*. During development, another division of the company, Blizzard North, developed and released *Diablo*, which used a graphics engine far more advanced than that used by *StarCraft*. The decision was taken by those at Blizzard who were working on *StarCraft* to leverage the experience gained by developing the new graphics engine, so they could improve the appearance of *StarCraft*. This decision was not taken lightly, and added a significant delay to the development of the product. Part of this delay was also due to Blizzard's tweaking the advanced game design and balancing the gameplay. The end result of this calculated risk (as already stated earlier in the chapter) was the biggest-selling game of 1998.

XCOM: Interceptor (Microprose Software)

XCOM: Interceptor was a departure in style for the *XCOM* series. The whole series revolved around the exploits of various aliens trying to take whatever it is that aliens want from humans. The basic game structure involved high-level strategy, researching new weapons and technologies to defeat the alien threat. This was interspersed with varying missions of a more immediate nature. This is how *Interceptor* differed from the previous iterations in the series. *Interceptor* replaced squad-based combat with space-based fighter combat. This game is noticeable because it was produced to a high standard and to a tight schedule. (A boast to this effect even appeared in the end game credits.) The developers were rightly proud of themselves for producing the game on time and on budget: proof of concept that it is possible with a dedicated and focused team.

Chapter 10
Roles And Divisions

Key Topics:

- ***Assigning personnel***
- ***Improving morale and the working environment***
- ***Spreading the risk***

One of the central themes behind this book is that the rapid growth of the games industry has reduced the effectiveness of one-man bands working from bedrooms and garages around the world.

It is no longer possible for one person to design, write, and produce all of the code, artwork, music, and other miscellaneous parts that a game requires. This means that a natural process of specialization has taken place, with certain well-defined roles emerging from the previous uniformity.

Assigning Personnel

A key factor in a project's success or failure is often the personnel who are assigned to it and how those people are divided into functioning groups.

Of course, the roles and divisions we present here are a "best case" scenario. Very few companies in the games industry have anything like this configuration, although it is fairly common outside the games industry. Most game companies have the main divisions, but some of the subsidiary roles do not even exist. It is a sad fact that most coding still begins before any detailed analysis has been made. (In many cases, the analysis is never performed at all.) Outside the games industry, a project such as this would never even get the green light.

The five main personnel divisions each contain a number of roles, and Table 10.1 shows some of the main roles and divisions that are used for project-based development schedules. Note that there are other roles in most companies, but here we are considering only the main ones. (The other roles are mainly support roles that are not directly related to game production, such as network manager, receptionist, and other ancillary staff.)

These roles are adaptable to the software-factory methodology, an efficient software construction technique discussed in Chapter 11.

We'll discuss these divisions and roles in the next few sections, and then we'll compare them to the equivalent roles and divisions that are used in the software factory.

The roles described here are not necessarily positions that one person occupies permanently. Instead, these roles should be viewed as *hats* that someone will wear for a while. People may wear one hat for a long time, while wearing other hats for shorter periods. People can—and often do—fill more than one role (wearing two hats at once). For example, the same person can act as both the software planner and the lead architect.

Management And Design Division

This division includes the levels of management that are directly involved with game production. The lower levels of management do tend to be blurred with the upper levels of technical and design staff, especially in the smaller companies in which everybody is often required to fill a number of roles.

A lot of this crossover, particularly into the area of game design, is mainly due to the most people's unshakable belief that they know how to design games. Many managers and CEOs

Table 10.1 Roles and divisions.

Division	Role
Management and Design	Software planner
	Lead architect
	Project manager
	Game designer
Programming	Lead programmer
	Programmer
Art	Lead artist
	Artist
Music and Miscellaneous	Musician
	Sound effect technicians
	Assorted technicians (such as motion capture)
Support and Quality Assurance	Technical support
	QA lead
	QA technician
	Playtester
	Support technician

believe that they are excellent game designers. A high proportion of these managers and CEOs are the original back-bedroom programmers, the one-man bands that kickstarted the industry back in the 1980s. They designed the games and wrote them as well, so it is only natural that they would want to keep their hand in the design process as they develop their companies.

Of course, some of these guys *do* know how to design games—The Gollop brothers of Mythos Development are good examples—but, for the most part, they are in management positions simply because they have been around the longest and their name is well known within the industry.

However, the more-technical management positions require concrete skills that can't be filled by anybody without some degree of team-management experience or training. Unfortunately, it is not always the case that the right people are put in the right positions. Programmers are too often promoted to management because of their technical proficiency. No consideration is given to how they will be able to interact on an interpersonal level.

Software Planner

The software planner's task is to break down a game design into a set of detailed technical requirements and to estimate the time and effort that are required to implement those features.

The software planner usually works in conjunction with the game designer and the lead architect to prepare the detailed specifications and work them up into a technical architecture document that satisfies the needs of the project.

Lead Architect

The task of the lead architect is to work with the software planner to produce a set of module specifications from the technical requirements.

The lead architect is responsible for the overall architecture of the project. The detailed module design is usually left to the lead programmer. In some cases, this task is further delegated to the programmers in the lead programmer's team.

Note that a software architect is not necessarily the same thing as an experienced programmer, although they are often technically skilled. Usually, the job of the software architect is full time, as modifications of the specs and reviewing the produced code is a long-winded but very necessary job. There is rarely any time for programming.

Project Manager

The project manager's task is to arrange the workload produced by the software planner and the lead architect into an efficient and organized schedule.

The project manager handles interactions between team members and acts as an interface between the project team and the management and marketing departments.

Game Designer

The role of the game designer is to design the games that the team will be producing. The game designer produces the initial game-treatment document, and then goes on to develop this into the detailed game-design document.

The game designer works with the software planner in order to explore the feasibility of the game design.

Programming Division

This division includes the team members who do most of the grunt work for the project. The programming division, on a project-by-project basis at least, tends to be grouped into a small team of programmers working on the one game project.

This team is usually organized into a fairly simple structure, with one lead programmer (responsible for the overall architecture) and an average of four programmers, each of whom specializes in a different area of the program (such as the graphics subsystem, the AI engine, or the control system). Some degree of crossover occurs, but, in most cases, the areas covered by each programmer are pretty well delineated, even to the extent that the lead programmer does not know what is going on in each of the subsystems.

Lead Programmer

The role of the lead programmer is to coordinate and monitor the efforts of the programming team to ensure that the schedule is being maintained.

The lead programmer interfaces with the project manager to ensure than the schedule is being followed and to report progress so the project can be accurately tracked (and any problems can be dealt with as expediently as possible).

The lead programmer is usually the most technically able programmer on the team and is mainly responsible for the overall integrity of the software. Anywhere from half to three-quarters of the lead programmer's time is spent programming, while the rest is spent dealing with administrative and personnel issues (a fact that some lead programmers may find difficult due to their lack of interpersonal skills or managerial experience). Lead programmers are usually selected based on technical prowess and not any other criteria.

Programmer

The role of the programmer is to work in the trenches of the development process. This involves following the detailed technical specifications that are handed down from the lead architect and software planner.

The programmer is usually responsible for working on a particular subsection of the main program, and this is remains his or her area of responsibility for the duration of the project.

The programmer is also responsible for all of the standard programming parts of the development process, such as initial development, unit testing, integration testing, and bug fixing.

The programmer is expected to know his or her craft well enough to implement the most elegant solution without having to waste time on investigating how to implement it. No research is involved here: this is simple conversion of a detailed specification to code.

Art Division

This division comprises of a pool of artists who are usually spread across more than one project at a time.

Art is a suitably relaxed activity (although I know artists who would disagree), so that, in most cases, it is possible for a group of artists to be producing artwork for more than one game at once.

Not all companies function like this, but it is in general more cost efficient to use a centralized pool of artists than it is to assign permanent artists on a per-project basis.

Lead Artist

The role of the lead artist parallels that of the lead programmer, although usually in a much more loosely defined way. The output of an artist is more immediately obvious in quality, and so does not need the close monitoring that a lead programmer would be expected to perform for a programmer.

Consequently, the main role of the lead artist is to interface with the lead programmer and the game designer to ensure that the artwork being produced for the game is suitable.

The lead artist is also expected to ensure that all the artists are producing artwork that is in line with each other and with the overall project vision. The lead artist is sometimes devoted to a single project so that there is at least one constant focus on the artwork being produced for a particular project, even if the artists involved are working on several projects at the same time.

A lead artist should probably be spending approximately 10 to 15 percent of his time on administration tasks and the rest producing artwork.

Artist

The role of the artist is to produce the artwork required for one or more projects.

Artwork, in this sense, can be game artwork, background graphics, manual design, advertising and packaging design, or any other associated tasks.

Usually, the artist will be working on several projects on the same time. Each of these projects has a lead artist who assigns the work among the pool of artists. This means that each artist may have to interface with more than one lead artist, unlike the programmer who is part of a much more tightly knit team.

Music And Miscellaneous Division

This division includes the personnel that produce the miscellaneous bits and pieces that are required to finish a game, such as the music, sound, and the development environment.

Musician

Musicians generally tend to work separately from the main fold of the game development.

Creating music is a very individualistic activity, and, for most cases, the musician can be given an animation or a demo, or even just a description of the mood required, and he or she is then able to produce the music.

If interactive music (which changes in tempo or mood according to what is happening in the game) is required, a closer interaction of the musician and the rest of the team will be necessary. Interactive music usually involves much more detailed specifications of interchangeable themed riffs and loops that can be swapped in and out as required. The role of the musician has become much more prominent than it used to be. As interactive music becomes more frequent in games, the musician's role will become more central to the game-development process.

Sound Effect Technician

All games use sound effects. The role of the sound effect technician is to produce all the incidental sound effects and loops that are required to create the game environment, whether they are gunshots, button blips, or alien death screams.

This is usually a fairly autonomous role. The information required to produce sound effects is pretty much the same as that for music. A list of effects can be created by the game designer, and these can be produced to the required format by the sound effect technician.

In many instances, the common sound effects will have been inserted by the programmers as test cases. (Many of these so-called test cases end up in the final game.)

Assorted Technicians

A variety of other technicians is always required to perform other tasks for a game's completion.

Some of these technicians will be directly involved, while others will be more on the sidelines. Motion-capture technicians, for example, will be heavily involved with the production of animations. Unless the company has a motion-capture studio onsite (which is quite rare), the artists will produce a set of prototype animations that were used during development, and the motion-captured animations will be farmed out to a studio and inserted in the game at a later date.

Other external studios perform similar duties that may not be manageable in-house. However, if these duties can be managed in-house, there will be a technician role in place.

Examples of these sorts of roles include software localization for other countries or actors for Full Motion Video (FMV) films.

Support And Quality Assurance Division

This division includes the testing team that ensures that the game is playable and of release quality. Testing a game is both a qualitative and quantitative process.

It is qualitative in the sense that honing gameplay to perfection is a fine art that very few have a grasp of, as is sadly in evidence from the quality of many games.

The process is quantitative in the sense that the number of bugs can be counted and prioritized. This is the main task of the quality assurance department during the earlier phases of development.

Quality Assurance Lead

The role of the quality assurance lead is to supervise the QA team and to cooperate with the project manager and the game designer to make sure that the game is thoroughly tested, both from the point of view of gameplay and functional coverage.

The quality assurance lead will draw up test plans and assign different areas of coverage to different QA technicians. The empirical results of the testing will usually be reported to the project manager.

Quality Assurance Technician

The role of the quality assurance technician is to test the code written by the programming team. The QA technician is concerned with functional coverage, meaning that the plan he is given by the QA lead should be designed to execute all code paths. All code that is written should be tested: all paths in the code, no matter how simple or trivial, should have a test case written for them.

The QA technician's role is to interact with the programmer responsible for a particular module to ensure that the test plan is written to test every code path.

The QA technician needs a good grasp of the technical details behind the code, so that he or she can better understand exactly what they are testing. This is the most detailed form of testing, and can also be performed by the programmer. This is called "clear-box testing" because the internals of what is being tested are known. The alternative to clear box testing is "black-box testing."

Black-box testing tests the outcome, the visible results of the coding effort. An example would be checking that a polygon-drawing routine draws polygons that are visually correct. Black-box testing can be performed by any tester that has been given a suitable test plan to follow.

Playtester

The role of a playtester is just that: to test how the game plays. Initially, the playtesters are the programmers and artists working on the project.

However, towards the middle and end of the project, the importance of correct playtesting increases. You generally have four options for playtesting, and the one you choose depends upon a number of factors, such as the size of the organization and the amount of money and time available for playtesting.

The first option is to use regular staff, which is not always suitable because they are already too familiar with the project to be objective about it. A useful alternative that many companies use is to pay college students a few dollars an hour to come in and play the games for a while.

The second option is to have permanent playtesting staff. Although this option is most suitable for larger organizations, it can be a cost-effective solution if enough projects are simultaneously in progress. Even if there are not enough projects to keep a team of playtesters constantly busy, the testers can be put to use in other areas of the company.

If a dedicated team of playtesters can't be kept busy due to an inconsistent workload, then the services of an outside playtesting agency can be sought. The advantage of using outside agencies is that they can test across multiple configurations with experienced playtesters who know what to look for in a game. The playtesting agency also performs an excellent job of black-box testing; but, by this stage, the only bugs you want to see are issues with different machine configurations or other such obscure problems.

The fourth option—the public beta test—is the best for most organizations, whether large or small. In a public beta test, a nearly complete version of the software is released to general testing. Other than being a beta version, the software is usually limited in some way (say, by not including the full functionality).

The software to be beta tested can be released with a controlled distribution to a specific group of chosen testers (such as Origin did with *Ultima Online*), or it can be released to the general public for testing by Web or magazine-cover CD-ROM-based distribution (as id Software did with *Quake* and *Quake II*). In the cases where beta testing is limited and controlled, the company may choose to offer an incentive such as receiving a free copy of the final product upon release.

Support Technician

The role of the support technician is to support and maintain the computing environment that is required by the rest of the company.

This responsibility entails maintaining the company network, ensuring that all machines have the correct software installed, and performing hardware upgrades and other such tasks that are required to keep things running smoothly.

Improving Morale And The Working Environment

It should be obvious to even the most antiquated manager that employee morale and the quality of the working environment should be treated as valuable commodities. No single larger factor contributes to the productivity of an employee.

The message here is simple: **Good Morale + Good Environment = Good Work**.

Morale Boosters

What affects the morale of an employee?

Like all good questions, there is more than one answer, and all are equally valid. The surprising thing about morale is that it isn't necessarily fostered by pandering to every whim of an employee. In fact, doing so can hurt morale in the same way that giving a child everything he wants can lead to a spoiled brat.

I have seen a group of developers who feel able to hold a company to ransom just because the developers were so used to getting their own way that, when it was refused, they stopped work until their demands were met. In this case, I am sad to say, the developers got their wishes, and their spoiled behavior damaged the reputation of their company. The project was eventually canned due to lack of progress and the developers were fired. (Maybe there is some justice in the world after all.)

The best approach to maintaining morale (as with a lot of things in life) is to be firm but fair.

Here is a list (in no particular order) of recommendations that I have found to be beneficial to morale:

- Good flow of information
- Minimum level of internal competition
- Realistic schedules
- Fair pay
- Good working relations
- Ground rules
- Pleasant working environment with up-to-date equipment and software
- Dress code
- Regular working hours
- Constructive benefits

Some of these may seem fairly unorthodox as far as the games industry is concerned, so I will discuss each point in the following sections and give reasons for their benefits.

Good Flow Of Information

The whole team should be allowed access to as much information about the project as possible.

There should be no unnecessary secrets; these only breed resentment. All feasible information should be made available either in printed or electronic form, and efforts should be made to ensure that every employee knows how to find the information.

Minimum Level Of Internal Competition

Internal competition between two factions—whether they be single employees or entire teams—is more often destructive than it is constructive.

In most cases, simple competition degenerates into rivalry and sniping at others' backs, while the needs of the rivals overshadow the needs of the project.

Most rivalry arises through insecurities. If an individual or team feels insecure about their position, then they will attack someone else in an effort to improve their standing. This is probably human nature. In some cases, this rivalry can take the form of scape-goating, while in others it is just a propensity to be combative and uncooperative.

If employees feel secure and comfortable, you are more likely to see a healthier competitive dynamic occur: friendly rivalries between groups and individuals to improve the product. This "coopertition" is a great morale booster in its own right, but it also has the added effect of increasing productivity, which further increases morale.

Realistic Schedules

This is a simple point and doesn't need much to say about it. It is covered in other chapters.

A schedule must be realistic. Pitching an overly aggressive schedule at developers and trying to persuade them that it is attainable sends morale sinking like a lead balloon.

Fair Pay

Fair pay means many things to many people. This is what it means to me.

The staff should be paid a fair wage that is based on their experience. When possible, a staff member should receive industry-standard wages based on experience and skill level. By "industry standard," I mean standard of the *computing* industry, and not just the underpaid *games* industry.

Staff should not be expected to work long hours for free. Each hour worked should be paid for, either *pro rata*, or at an agreed overtime rate. Don't subject an employee to the indignity of working a bucket-load of extra hours to get a demo finished for an important client only to be rewarded with a pizza of his or her choice. (This actually happened to me.)

If royalty or stock options are offered, there must be written royalty agreements that are legally binding and clearly state all deductions and clauses in plain language. I have seen and heard enough broken promises to know that, if you want to get your royalties, then get the agreement in writing.

Good Working Relations

This is a simple point. Trust.

The different groups of employees must have a mutual trust and respect for one another. In the situations where this is not the case, the resulting friction is enough to destroy projects and make the working environment a living hell.

Ground Rules

Morale can surprisingly be improved by a clear, simply understood set of ground rules that cover behavioral and professional expectations while on the premises.

These rules should not be draconian or pointless, or rules for the sake of having rules. They should be grounded in basic common sense. They're written down to ensure that everybody has the same concept of what constitutes "reasonable" behavior. Common sense is, unfortunately, not universal.

These rules define the expected behavior of all employees while they are on the premises and being paid by the company. These rules are the great leveler.

With a set of clear guidelines, no employee is likely to feel as if he or she is being unfairly treated if someone is allowed to behave in a different manner (regular long lunches or some other liberty) if it is against the rules. This may sound a bit schoolboyish, but believe me, it is much better than the anarchic alternative.

If the employees are responsible and mature (how many games programmers do *you* know like that?), then they can be relied upon to produce their own set of guidelines for the finer points. Even so, a recommended minimum is general companywide guidelines that define a start time, a finish time, and the allowable range of break and lunch times.

Note that, if the start and finish times are specified, they should be respected. Staff should be encouraged to arrive *and* leave on time.

A Pleasant Working Environment With Up-To-Date Equipment And Software

The importance of a pleasant environment should be self-evident.

Working in a cramped and dimly lit office is demoralizing. In a perfect world, offices would be clean, airy, and spacious, with every employee receiving an office of their own. Not only is this not always feasible, it is, in fact, rarely feasible. (Microsoft allegedly provides all its developers with private offices, but is not exactly short of cash.)

At the very least, the employees should be provided with desks of their own that are spacious enough to provide ample room for all the required equipment. I do not believe that management should have big expensive desks (just because they are management) when the big desk is probably more useful to a programmer with a large computer, a stack of CDs, and two monitors on his desk. But the world is rarely fair like that.

It is not difficult to make an office pleasant to work in. Low-maintenance plants can add ambiance, as can indirect lighting (not overhead fluorescent lights). Natural light should be used wherever possible, but it should also be possible to shut it out. Nothing is more annoying than working with the sun shining directly onto your monitor or into your eyes.

Office design is easy to get right. Aim for an environment that looks professional and, more importantly, makes you *feel* professional.

Dress Code

This one is going to be fun! The games industry is notorious for its lack of dress code, and trying to suggest one is likely to ruffle a few feathers.

However, a dress code should be implemented for a number of reasons. The usual reason trotted out by management is that a dress code (usually shirt and tie in these cases) makes you look more professional to the customers.

Well, this explanation doesn't cut it here. In the case of game development, most employees do not have direct contact with any form of customer, except for shows and, in the case of the deal-making management employees, publishers.

There is, though, a deeper reasoning for a dress code. It is important to differentiate between work and home. If an employee is permitted to wear the same clothes at work as he or she would at home, it blurs the line between home and work. This is a line that should not be blurred: work is work, and home is home.

I am not saying that game developers should wear suits and ties, but it should be at least at the level of "smart casual." The important thing is that what you wear to work should be different to what you would wear at home. What you wear influences how you feel and your attitude to those around you.

Respect is another reason for a dress code. The smarter the dress, the more automatic respect you will get from other employees. If everybody in the company is expected to dress to a certain minimum level, then a lot of interrelational stress is reduced.

Figures 10.1, 10.2, and 10.3 demonstrate the differences that a person's manner and dress can have on how they are perceived.

Figure 10.1 shows the scruffy game developer as an example of what happens without a dress code.

Figure 10.2 shows the minimum recommended level: smart casual. It's smart enough to allow differentiation from what the employee would normally wear, but casual enough to not make him or her feel too out of place or uncomfortable. My idea of smart casual is jeans with a button-down shirt. Go figure.

Figure 10.1
Typical dress of a game developer.

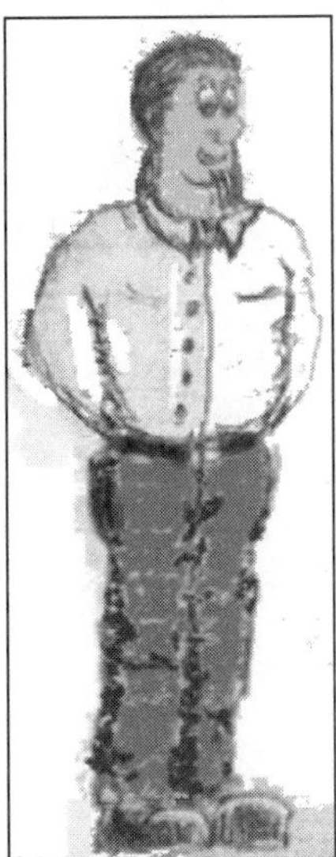

Figure 10.2
Recommended dress code.

Figure 10.3
Over The Top (O.T.T).

Figure 10.3 shows what happens when incompetent management gets hold of a good idea. This would not have a good effect on morale.

Regular Working Hours

In the games industry, there is a tendency to work almost random hours, and all-nighters are not uncommon.

These irregular working hours are, in some cases, the sign of a badly scheduled project. In other cases, it is just the sign of lax management. Whatever the reasons for the lack of regular hours, morale will improve when they are implemented.

This may not seem immediately obvious, but the benefits are soon evident. If everybody works a regular set of hours, you can be sure that all members of the team are available at the times when everybody else is.

There'll be no more cases of missing team members sleeping off the effect of an all-night coding marathon, leaving the morning crew with convoluted code to decipher.

Having a rigidly defined set of core hours also reduces stress on employees. If they are clear that they are required to work only a set number of hours a day, then they can concentrate on working those hours, and leave work at a reasonable time.

By not working ridiculously long hours, the employees will not be fatigued for the following day.

Constructive Benefits

If the company is going to offer benefits to the employees, these benefits should be ones that the employee can appreciate and find useful.

Stock options, guaranteed royalties, free gym membership, training courses, and tickets for relevant shows and free soft drinks are good benefits.

Cups, pens, seven-foot inflatable aliens, posters, and other such cheap detritus are not good benefits.

If you want an employee to feel appreciated, don't make him or her feel as if you think their worth is adequately expressed by the offer of a keyring.

Morale Booster Caveats And Warnings

There are some actions that appear to boost morale in the short term, but that have a detrimental effect on long-term morale.

This has been touched on above, as it is a manifestation of the spoiled-child syndrome. If you give employees enough rope, not only will they hang themselves, they will also tangle up your company as well. This list covers a few of the common morale boosters that are mistakes.

- No dress code
- Freeform hours
- Casual working environment

These measures provide an initial boost in morale, followed by a rapid downward spiral.

No Dress Code

A complete lack of dress code is a morale killer.

At first, of course, it seems pretty cool. Employees feel free to express themselves and their individuality. They feel relaxed and comfortable in the type of clothes that they would wear at home in their free time.

The problem, however, comes in the attitude. Allowing an employee to feel as if they are at home means they will be tempted to behave as if they were at home. For work to feel like a place of work, it is important to differentiate it from home.

Freeform Hours

Some companies and organizations have a remarkably lax attitude towards working hours.

Usually, the situation is that the hours worked are a lot longer than the standard. Twelve to 18 hours a day are not unheard of, and these long days hurt the project in two ways. The first is obvious: no one can consistently produce good work if they are working that much. They will be produce substandard code, and they will be overtired.

Eventually they will burn out. When this happens, they will take more time off and maybe even leave, which damages the team by leaving a lot of legacy code to be maintained. Worse still, they will have been perceived as being a hard-working member of the team, and their departure will affect the morale of the remaining team members.

If they just become ill or overtired and take time off to recover, then this hurts the team, too. The entire team should be working in the same location at the same time for at least a core set of hours. If not, then they are not really a team. They become a collection of individuals working on a common project.

Casual Working Environment

Many game companies have very relaxed rules of workspace and environment, with posters, toys, stereos, seven-foot inflatable aliens, and regular lunchtime *Quake* sessions that last into the afternoon.

In fact, all this does is make the office appear like a teenager's bedroom, which violates the rule about home and office separation. The games industry is viewed as being a fun and cool place, but let's face it, the object of *working* in the games industry is to *write* games, not *play* them.

Okay, so that sounds like sacrilege. I'm not saying that games shouldn't be played, but playing them during work is not productive. It's very difficult to draw the line between "investigating" a new release and just playing it.

The office should be a professional environment, because professional environments create professional employees.

Spreading The Risk

The risk associated with specialized roles is the possibility of losing a staff member who performs that role. The roles defined in this chapter are not job titles; they are merely roles, and one person can fill one or more of these roles as a part of their jobs. The roles should be viewed as *hats* that are worn at different times during the course of an employee's work.

This can be used to the company's advantage as a risk-reduction mechanism.

Chapter 11
The Software Factory

Key Topics:

- ***Problems solved by the software factory***
- ***Setting up a software factory***
- ***Applying a software factory***
- ***Suitability of the software factory***

Chapter 10 covered the roles and divisions that are needed for an efficient development environment. These resources can be organized into many different structures (not all of which are suitable for game development). This chapter explains the roles and divisions of an organizational structure that is particularly suitable for established development houses and demonstrates how this structure can increase performance to an optimum level.

Note

The structure can also be applied to a startup organization, but doing so causes the first project to take longer (or at least it will seem to) as explained later in this chapter.

What Is A Software Factory?

The term *software factory* refers to a methodology of producing software with techniques similar to those used in a standard factory, such as one that manufactures cars. This doesn't mean, however, that all the software produced by this method will be identical, churned out endlessly, and devoid of imagination and flair. Enough companies are already too good at producing creatively bankrupt software. Figure 11.1 shows a rich-looking man (top hat and tails, pocket watch, cigar, and money hanging out of a trouser pockets) turning the handle of a software factory, which looks like a mincing machine. Game designs are fed into the top, and anonymous, identical games come out of the bottom. From inside the machine, a voice can be heard saying, "Come on you fools! Faster! FASTER!" These types of software factories should be avoided at all costs.

Figure 11.1
A creatively bankrupt software factory.

As the computer games industry begins to mature, more sophisticated production methods, such as the software factory, are being implemented to develop new products. The software factory methodology centralizes and simplifies the production of specific common modules that can be used across several products.

It uses the advantages of mass production to make specific tasks both easier and more efficient, and it has the benefit of ensuring that a core set of tools and libraries are well maintained and supported over a series of products. Thus, subsequent products become easier to develop, as they will be supported by a more resourceful library and useful tool set.

The software factory has been proven to work time and time again on series of projects with common functionality. Keep in mind that this the method may not be the most suited for a particular product. (You or your coworkers may have a better methodology scrawled on the back of an envelope!) However, software factories are particularly well-suited for producing a series of products.

"But these are games we're writing! Everyone is unique! There is no way we can rehash the code, change the graphics, and re-release the game!"

This objection is perfectly valid, but how many times do you want to write screen and sound setup code, data file loaders, compression libraries, CD track playing code, finite-state machine code, menu code, or any other chunk of potentially reusable code from a long list of basic modules? Looking at it from a management perspective, how much time and money do you want to spend for specialists to write code that you already have? (Not only does the code have to be written, it also has to be tested, integrated, and debugged.)

Some common tasks that should be placed in reusable modules are as follows:

- Data file loading
- Hardware setup
- Hardware configuration
- Software configuration
- Custom CODECs (compression and decompression)
- Encryption/decryption code
- Windowing and graphics features
- Basic AI components
- User input

The software factory concept eases tasks such as producing common libraries and tool sets, leaving the developers to concentrate on the code bits that *should* be written from scratch. The fastest work is the work that has already been completed and tested for full functionality.

Why Use A Software Factory?

What advantages and disadvantages does the software factory have over other methods of development? Although the answer to this question depends on the particular situation, Table 11.1 lists several key advantages and disadvantages.

As Table 11.1 displays, this method does have its disadvantages, too. However, on the whole, the advantages clearly outweigh the disadvantages over the course of several projects.

Table 11.1 Advantages and disadvantages of a software factory.

Advantages	Disadvantages
Average project length will be shortened.	First project will take longer.
Makes cross-platform releases easier.	Reusable wrapper libraries must be developed for each platform.
Code will be more reliable.	Code will be more generic, and more difficult to develop.
Code is reusable and maintainable	Code takes longer to develop initially.
Knowledge is spread out among all developers.	New developers have to learn unfamiliar libraries.
Increased visibility of project progress.	More administration.
Increased specialization of developers.	Less skill flexibility.

Solving Game Development Issues

The software factory methodology helps to solve a number of common issues in game development, namely platform independence and risk reduction (knowledge spreading, code reuse, and code maintainability, and so on).

Platform Independence

Consider the DOS-compatible PC—an expandable system with a wide variety of possible configurations. If, for performance reasons, you want to write directly to hardware for this PC, how would you choose to do it? You would have to ask yourself what hardware you wish to support and in which machine. The choice would eventually come down to supporting only a limited subset of available hardware, which would eventually reduce your potential sales. You can also bet that the vast majority of support calls would be due to conflicting or incompatible hardware—a logistical nightmare.

Let's look at a specific example. Assume that you have written a 3D space combat game for the DOS-compatible PC. You have been fairly sensible in your architectural design and have isolated all platform-specific code behind interfaces. (Here, the word *platform* indicates a unique hardware configuration for the PC.)

The code behind these interfaces must be rewritten for every platform you want to support. You have chosen to support three popular graphics cards and three sound cards.

Thus, you need to write, debug, and unit test six hardware-specific code interfaces, and then system test nine possible configurations—not to mention the software-only solutions for everybody else who doesn't have one of the chosen graphics and sound cards. To make matters even more difficult, to get the speed required, you have written the libraries in such a way that they must rely on internal knowledge of the game for full functionality. That is a lot of work in anyone's book.

Another common issue to consider is how can you be sure that you have written all of the platform-specific code in the most efficient way possible. It is unlikely that you were able to find enough developers with thorough, in-depth knowledge of each sound and graphic card you wanted to support. Given the amount of code you had to write, it is also unlikely that you have had the time to develop that knowledge.

Of course, this is a contrived example, and has no relevance to the real world. The real world, in fact, is *much* worse.

To promote the production of games on specific platforms and to move the responsibility of hardware support from the game developer to the hardware developer, Microsoft and Apple have independently developed two platform-specific solutions: DirectX and Game Sprockets, respectively. At the time of this writing, DirectX has reached its sixth version and is available from the Microsoft Web site. The Game Sprockets are available from the Apple Web site.

DirectX and Game Sprockets are high-performance, multimedia libraries designed to automatically detect and use any hardware acceleration present on the user's machine. They function by writing to an application programming interface (API) defined by Microsoft or Apple.

These libraries help solve the problem of hardware independence and obviously prevent writing directly to hardware except through the provided standardized mechanisms. (That would be contrary to the spirit of insulating the developer from the underlying hardware.) In the case of DirectX, a common set of features is provided that guarantee to be present in hardware or emulated in software. The acceptance of DirectX by developers was initially slow, but try to find a PC game today that is written without the aid of DirectX.

Of course, DirectX and Game Sprockets are still fairly low level of multimedia libraries and (of course) completely incompatible with each other. To have true platform independence, you must create lightweight wrapper code to present a uniform interface to hardware, no matter whether it is running on a DOS-compatible PC or a Macintosh or some other platform. Even if you are not planning to support more than one platform, the wrapper code is still an excellent idea because it simplifies many common tasks. Creating such wrapper code is one of the main tasks of the factory.

Risk Reduction

One of the problems discussed in Chapter 10 was the loss of key personnel. If one of your team members has a specific, inflexible expertise in a specific area of knowledge or skill set related to the project, then that person becomes a risk.

At this stage you should ask yourself whether you are willing to bet the whole project on that one person. If they ran off to live in communion with the sky in the Tibetan foothills (or even join another games company), would the project survive the loss? If the project can survive, what are the costs in time, money, and functionality? Reducing inflexible expertise is critical to the overall success of the project.

The software factory can help alleviate problems such as losing key personnel by encouraging multiple redundancy and the reuse of code. The scripting engine mentioned in Case Study 11.1 was written specifically for the project. However, as an alternative, it could have been written to an interface, and every scriptable game object would then export methods to support that interface. If these interfaces are designed generically, the ability to reuse and utilize them over many projects comes automatically.

If you are a true dyed-in-the-wool game developer, then you may feel slightly uneasy after reading the last paragraph. Standardized interfaces? Won't that slow things down by adding an extra layer of indirection? Won't it be harder to code, and take much longer?

Well, yes and no. If the interfaces are properly designed, you will be able to get performance at least equal to a custom integrated component. And, because the emphasis of the software factory is on reusability, the scripting engine can be refined and modified over the course of

Case Study 11.1 The Effects Of Losing Key Personnel

According to Jason Regier at Bungie Software, the development of *Myth: The Fallen Lords* suffered a setback when a key programmer left. The individual was responsible for the scripting engine, an important (but fortunately not essential) module that then had to be scrapped. When the programmer left, the scripting code base was incomplete, and no one had sufficient knowledge of the code to continue developing it. Moreover, the *Myth* team was relatively small and consequently was not even able to spare the manpower to learn how the code functioned.

The scripting engine was designed to allow custom unit and map behavior. It had also already been publicly announced as an included feature.

This particular problem was solved simply by dropping the functionality. A scripting engine is a complex undertaking and is usually not a critical path module. In this case, Bungie made the decision to drop it based on a cost/functionality comparison. If the module had been the graphics engine, such a decision would have been impossible.
Source: *Game Developer Magazine* (April 1998)

several projects. For a more detailed treatment of how such a scripting interface could work, see Chapter 19.

In Case Study 11.1, the problem would have been a nonissue if more than one developer had been familiar with the scripting engine and if the code had been fully documented. Documentation is an essential part of the development process and is often (actually, nearly always) overlooked. Why bother to document something if it is only going to be used once? Why document procedures or code when you know the code inside out and are the only one who is going use it?

These are acceptable responses in principle, but it begs the question as to why you are writing throwaway code. If you assume that writing such code can be justified, what happens when you feel a sudden inescapable urge to go to Tibet? How can you be sure that you are the only person who will ever need to read that code?

The ideal path to follow is to reexamine the code being written to see if it can be written with more than one project in mind, and with a full set of documentation.

Why Use A Software Factory?

A software factory is designed to produce a set of reusable core components and tools that evolve over the course of several products. From the very beginning, these tools and components are designed with reusability and future expansion in mind. As much care goes into developing these tools and components as would into the game itself. The development methodology used for these tools and components is rigorously controlled and monitored, and full documentation is made easily available for use in further projects. Any required updates to the tools or components undergo a full requirements analysis and are performed to the same exacting standards. These tools and components are the most important part of the whole process. They are designed to have a shelf life lasting for several projects and are therefore of key importance, as discussed in Case Study 11.2.

The advantages are obvious: code that performs common tasks can be reused again and again, thus saving development time and financial resources. The main disadvantage is that the initial set of tools and components must be developed in the first place, and this will always be a slower process than just hard coding the desired functionality into the project. The gains only begin to materialize on subsequent projects.

One other option is the possibility of incremental improvements to released projects by distributing updated core modules. Use caution on this approach. You don't get something for nothing in this world, and, although ideally all modified components should be backward compatible, this approach may place a large burden on testing. If you are confident that you can do it, then go for it! However, remember all the difficulty that Microsoft had ensuring this sort of backward compatibility with releases of DirectX. Up until version 5, new updates regularly broke what was on the system before the update, rendering the system suboptimal at best, and unusable at worst.

An analogy would be building a sailing ship. If you decided to re-create everything needed from day one, the team would have to go and fell the trees, shape the timbers, season the wood, and then assemble the ship's components. Doing this for multiple ships would soon become overwhelming.

Case Study 11.2 Code Reuse

According to Wyeth Ridgeway of Zombie, the Viper game engine developed for use with their game, *SpecOps: Rangers Lead The Way*, contains no game-specific code. It is a module specifically designed for reuse.

The engine consists of a 3D renderer, an object-scripting module using a LISP-like language, and a sound module, among other things.

Taken by themselves, these components are just tools. The game is composed of the game engine and game-specific resources (graphics, sounds, and object scripts). It is driven by a minimal amount of glue code, consisting mainly of the object scripts and the small amount of game-specific code that is needed to support the scripts and provide a general framework.

The engine has been designed in such a way that, with a different set of resources, one could craft a completely new and exciting game. This ability was demonstrated when a couple of nonprogramming team members were able to create a monster-truck racing demo over the span of a weekend. This shows that with proper planning, a minimal understanding of game development, and detailed and precise documentation, a fully operational and productive software factory can be a realization.

This is the sort of result that the software factory aims for.

Source: *Game Developer Magazine* (June 1998)

Rationally, you might arrange for the initial components to be developed by a production-line process (even from an outside source), and then use the team for assembly only. This combines the advantages of the team model (enthusiasm and motivation) with the advantages of the factory model (efficient use of labor and just-in-time processes).

Organizing A Software Factory

The structure of the software factory is different from what you may be used to. The following sections describe how a software factory is comprised.

A Structural Overview

The core requirements for a minimal software factory are defined in Table 11.2.

Table 11.2 is a basic list of the member groups of the factory. It is not exhaustive or final. Other ancillary roles may be required, but this list defines the core requirements. Granted, not all organizations can fulfill such lofty requirements, but, aside from the software architects (which is a specialized, virtually full-time role), there can be a lot of overlap among groups, as shown in Figure 11.2. Obviously, the more personnel that is available, the less overlap there will be, but some degree of overlap is always desirable to help the spreading of knowledge throughout the team.

The functions and interactions of the core factory teams are described in detail. Figure 11.3 displays the hierarchical structure of the software core factory.

Figure 11.3 is a rough guideline and not a rigid structure. In reality, the situation is much more dynamic than can be shown in a static diagram. What is fairly rigid, however, is the method of interactions among teams. These interactions (or interfaces) help provide the high level of project visibility. Project visibility is the ability to accurately gauge the progress of the project. This ability is very important to everybody concerned with the product, including the investors, the publishers, and the teams themselves. Somewhat surprisingly, a side effect of good project visibility is to reduce the number of team meetings that are necessary. A lot of so-called "progress" meetings turn out to be anything but that, and, unless in the case of projectwide changes, there is very rarely the need to stop development for the

Table 11.2 Essential groups for a software factory's core team.

Group	Comment
Game Designers	Create ideas and produce design documents
Software Architects	Oversee the project architecture and interaction among teams
Tools	Teams of level editors, etc.
Components	Produce low-level, platform-specific code
Projects	Produce actual game code using the output of the components and tools teams
Research	Keep abreast of new technological developments and research new ideas for integration into low-level components

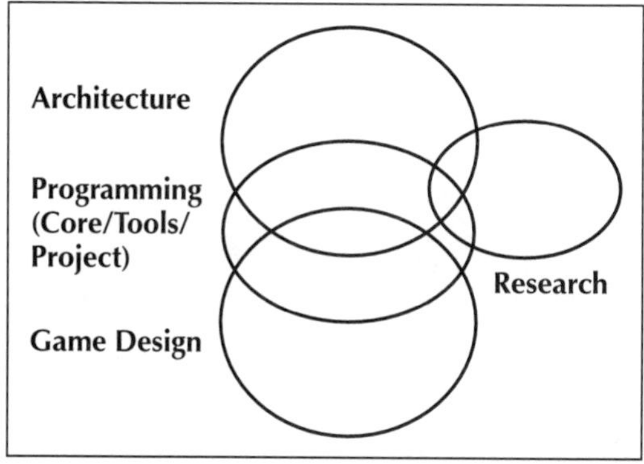

Figure 11.2
Group overlap in a software factory.

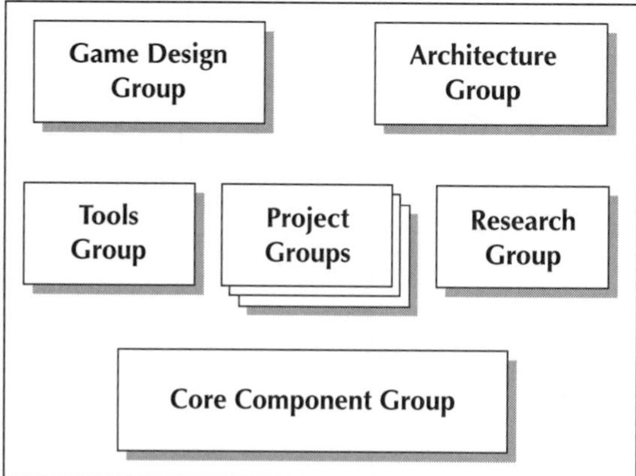

Figure 11.3
Hierarchy of a software core factory.

length of time a typical meeting takes. Such meetings are one of the biggest time killers and are disruptive to the team's focus and work already in progress.

Group Responsibilities And Interactions

Each of the core groups in the software factory has clearly defined roles and tasks. There is little, if any, task overlap, and all important intergroup interaction takes place through rigidly defined channels.

These interactions are based loosely on an internal market system. Each group is the customer of each others' groups and thus, should expect to be treated as valued clients. This means providing exactly the same levels of documentation and product support that would be expected if the software module in question had been sold on the open market to an external client.

This "market system" structure is important to ensure that the progress of the project is tracked correctly. It's always a good idea for the left hand to know what the right hand is doing. Figure 11.4 shows the interactions among groups in a software factory, excluding outside influences. In the figure, the programming groups are positioned together as one large group, because they often will all be the same people. However, for interaction among the separate programming groups, they still have to go through the proper channels. (These channels are described in more detail in Chapter 13.)

Figure 11.4 summarizes the main interactions. At first, this looks restrictive. Here is a list of possible questions that you may have:

- Why is direct contact allowed only with the architecture group?
- How can the game designers influence how the game turns out if they can't talk to the programmers directly?
- Why does the architecture group have to be in the center of everything?
- Why is the research group directly connected to the architecture group?

To answer these questions, you should consider the typical scenario, as presented in Case Study 11.3.

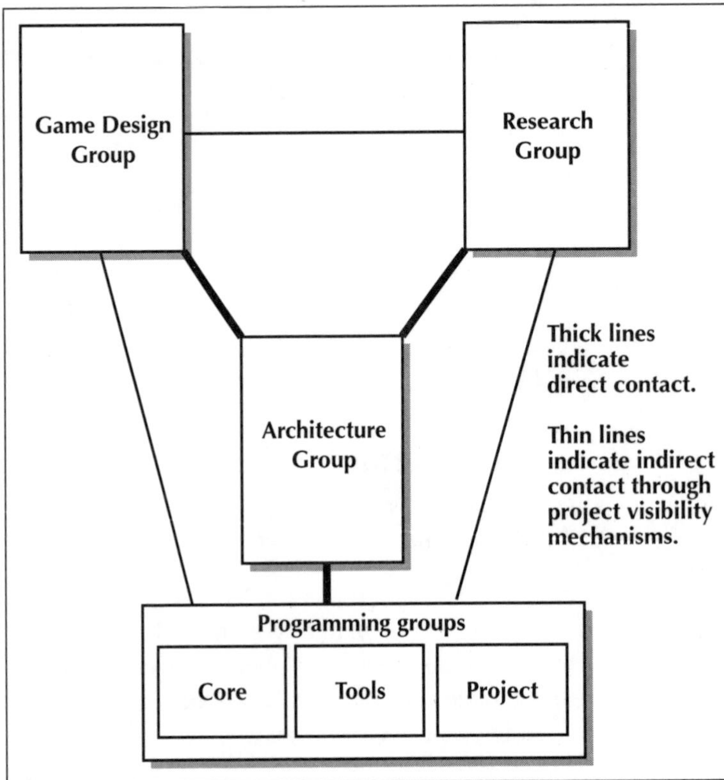

Figure 11.4
Interactions among groups.

Case Study 11.3 Ineffective Problem Handling In Action

Andy, Barry, Chris, Dave, and Eddie are the programming team working on *FlyBusters III, Beyond The Flypaper*, the latest masterpiece by Freddy, a veteran game designer.

Eddie is the lead programmer, a technical genius without many interpersonal skills; Andy is an intern fresh out of college; and Barry, Chris, and Dave are competent programmers who have work experience in the games industry. *FlyBusters III* is their first project together. Andy is new to the world of work, and isn't sure how everything fits together.

While implementing a physics model for the player's ship, he notices that at some angles there is an unpleasant distortion of the landscape. Now, Eddie has a reputation for being somewhat difficult to approach; his favorite response is to imply that his time is being wasted, and that he has much better things to do than listen to team members whining about little problems. (Andy has had his fingers burnt like this before when he mentioned to Eddie that gaps were appearing between polygons when they got close to the viewer. Barry and Dave, the programmers of the polygon engine, had taken great offense at this criticism of the code.)

This time Andy tries a different approach and mentions it directly to Chris, the developer of the landscape engine. Chris, although busy, ponders for a few minutes and suggests that if Andy restricted the player from looking directly down on the landscape, the problem wouldn't be so apparent, because there is no way that the landscape engine can support that particular viewpoint. This is a small modification that will take a couple of hours to put in place, and so Andy gets straight to it. Eddie is particularly busy today and has been giving off a "Do Not Approach" aura, so Andy makes a mental note to tell him tomorrow and gets on with the next task.

A few weeks later, Eddie decides that it is time to implement the bomb view—a special viewpoint that is designed to allow easy targeting of superfly buzzbombs (which have to be dropped with deadly accuracy onto several targets spread across the landscape). When the view has been implemented, Eddie can't quite understand why the bombs do not fall precisely, even though he specified exactly where the bomb was supposed to hit by setting the orientation and position of the player's ship using Andy's physics API. A little investigation soon tells him that the physics engine isn't working properly. After grilling Andy as to whether he has checked his code properly, and verifying that the problem indeed exists, Eddie makes a decision to leave things as they are, seeing as a lot of code has already been written on top of the physics engine, and changing it may break the dependent code.

Two weeks later, during routine testing, Freddy, the game designer, notices that it is too difficult to target bombs correctly. In fact, it seems to be a very "hit and miss" process. (Pardon the pun.) He immediately demands a resolution to the problem, insisting that the bombing strategy is central to the game. The programming team has no choice but to reimplement three areas of code, which delays the project by three months. Andy feels unappreciated and not respected. Chris feels as if he is at fault for not producing a good enough landscape engine. Barry and Dave feel annoyed and irritable that Andy should have criticized their polygon engine. Eddie feels stressed at being held responsible for the delays, and Freddy thinks that the whole team is a bunch of idiots. Team morale sinks, and the game is released six months late to awful reviews mainly because of the badly implemented bombing mode and the outdated technology. In short, it bombs.

With quick and dirty, the dirty will remain long after the quick has been forgotten.

Now let's consider the alternative scenario if a software factory structure is in place, as in Case Study 11.4.

Case Study 11.4 Effective Problem Handling In Action

The same team from Case Study 11.3 is developing the same title, *FlyBusters III*, and after initial resistance, has agreed to adhere to the communication channels in place, at least on a trial basis.

When Andy discovered the polygon-fitting problem, he logged on to the company intranet Web page and submitted an anonymous report detailing the situations in which they occurred. The architecture group examined the problem and discussed it with both Freddy, the game designer, and Eddie. Freddy asked if it could be fixed, and Eddie, after talking to Barry who explains that the symptoms are a deliberate speed optimization, announced that it could be done, but only at the expense of an extra check per scanline per polygon. Freddy asked what that meant in real terms, and Eddie explained that it could mean a substantial drop in frame rate, depending on how large the on-screen object was and how many polygons it contained. Freddy didn't want to lose the smooth-flowing effect of the engine, so he accepted that it didn't particularly affect the gameplay. The problem was resolved as "no action required," and this was logged on the Web site, with a brief explanation.

Andy then came across the problem with the top-down view, and again submitted an anonymous report. This time, however, Freddy insisted that the bombing view was very important to the game play. Eddie, after consultation with Chris, discovered that to implement a true top-down view would involve developing a separate subengine, and that this would take a further three to six months of work. The problem was left "open for investigation," and the architecture group and Freddy went away to think of a solution. After a couple of days of deliberation, Freddy came up with an alternative bomb view that did not need to look directly down on the landscape, and presented it to the architecture group. In the meantime, the architecture group noticed that another project group had developed a top-down map module that would be easy to adapt into the *FlyBusters* project due to the standardized interfaces, but some extra graphics would need to be generated using the accompanying tools. Now, Freddy had two choices as to how to implement the bomb view, and was satisfied.

The solution chosen was then logged onto the project intranet site, and the top-down view was smoothly integrated into the existing project base over a period of a few days, after the architecture group had updated the architecture specifications to include the new functionality. Eddie had been on enough traditional projects to know what would have happened if this procedural approach had not been in place, and was pleasantly surprised to see how quickly and easily the problems were resolved. Andy was quietly pleased that his input was appreciated, even anonymously. Chris was relieved that he didn't have to make a difficult modification to his landscape engine, and Barry was pleased that he was right to implement that optimization in the first place. Team morale improved, and the product was released on time and became a roaring success.

The obvious advantage here is the increased visibility of the project's progress. Problems are dealt with as soon as they arise. The benefit of providing an anonymous channel that can be read by anybody on the project is that it allows everyone to voice their concerns without having to deal with personality clashes and other political problems that so often rear their ugly heads. The main concern should be the success of the project, not the sensibilities of easily offended personnel. The anonymous channel helps to ensure that this is the case. After all, it is not important *where* the information comes from, only that it does come, and that it comes as soon as possible.

With a lot of developers, especially those in the games industry, there is a lot of initial resistance to imposing a more defined team structure such as this, mainly because it's viewed as overly restrictive and creatively stifling. You may get developers saying that these procedures slow down and reduce their productivity. These will usually be the developers who are used to cranking out (almost) working code at high speed and getting things up on screen quickly. These are also the same developers who spend a couple of months fixing bugs when the project slips due to the high defect count. In actuality, what these developers are complaining about is having to do the work that is usually postponed to the end of the project and well past the shipping date. By enforcing the procedural approach, most defects will be caught at an earlier stage.

Tip

It is a well-known statistic in development circles that the earlier a bug is caught (and this can be in any stage of the project), the less time and money it will cost to fix. A bug caught during the architectural stage can cost up to 200 times less to fix than if it were caught during the release preparation phase.

The perceived extra work and delay caused by the extra procedures is only an illusion. For most projects today, this work still has to be done, but it is never scheduled in the project plan and ends up being done later in the development process. Meanwhile, management anxiously awaits the project's release, which has already slipped past shipping date by six months. Late projects damage the morale and credibility of the team and company. Any measures that can be put in place to detect and correct these problems as early as possible becomes indispensable. After all, how many times have you heard after a year and a half of solid programming that a project is 90 percent complete, only to have to wait another year or so for what should have been the remaining 10 percent to be complete, but is instead an additional 90 percent complete?

The following are arguments against the introduction of architecture design procedures: there is no time for all of the delays and paperwork that it will cause, the project is already on an aggressive and tight schedule, and adding all this overhead will only slow things down in the long run. Having seen the poor states of projects that have succumbed to these arguments, the answer is that there is *no* time to implement the measures! Saving time in the long run makes up for any slowdowns in the earlier stages of the project. By developing at a scheduled pace (and foreseeing problems and fixing them as soon as they are discovered), time is saved throughout the remainder of the project.

Note

For more information on communication mechanisms, see Chapter 13.

Now that you know the reasons for restricting the interaction among the various groups, the following sections will briefly explain the mechanisms and channels that are in place. Note that, even though these mechanisms are in place, information will still be transferred in other ways: impromptu corridor meetings and discussions during lunch or breaks are an important mechanism for information transfer. The primary concern is that any issue brought up in these informal meetings must go through the proper channels before any solution or action is performed. This gives everyone concerned the opportunity to have their say.

The Game Designer Group

The game designer group is responsible for producing the initial game designs and subsequently refining any gameplay issues that arise during the development and testing process. As such, members from other groups can be co-opted into the game designer group to contribute ideas and refinements to the game design. However, as discussed previously, game design is generally more complex than it appears, so the generation of the initial designs and specifications are best left in the hands of experienced game designers (or people who have read Part I of this book). Usually, this group is also responsible for end-user documentation, such as the manuals for the game.

The game designer group interacts mainly with the software architect group, and generally tends to rely on the project visibility measures to follow the progress of the project rather than directly approaching the other groups for information.

The majority of this group's time is spent researching new designs and refining designs currently in development. As the tools and components groups get up to speed and various useful tools and components are developed specifically for use by the game designers, this group may find itself with even more "hands-on" experience in the game tweaking and programming process. For example, if a simple AI scripting engine is developed, then the game designers will be able to contribute directly to writing scripts. If the project has been developed using a database to store all commonly tweakable parameters, then the game designers also have the opportunity to tweak parameters to their hearts' content. These parameters are deemed to be *soft architecture*, and can be modified without changing the structure of the project in question, the *hard architecture*. The domain of the game designer group can include direct modification of the soft architecture, but this has to wait until the tools are in place to allow them to do so.

The game designer group also interfaces with the ancillary sound and art groups in order to specify the look and feel of the game.

The Software Architect Group

The software architect group acts as the central hub of the factory and is the main interface between the game designer group and the programming groups (tools, components, projects, and research). The members of this group represent the traditional "lead programmer" for all the programming groups, although they will be doing little, if any, actual programming.

The primary responsibilities of this group are translating the game designs into technical architecture documents, making use of the components and tools that have been developed by the tools group, writing the documents for any necessary modifications to these tools and components needed for the projects, and initiating the development of new tools and components from the results of research projects. The group members also provide feedback to game designers to ensure that the design is feasible, and to advise on technical game design issues related to the game design envisaged by the game designer. The specification of the architecture is an ongoing process. The architecture is progressively refined as the projects progress. Most of the major shake-ups will have been sorted out in the feasibility study and in the prototyping stages, and so any further modifications should ideally be only refinements and clarifications of the existing architecture. It is important to realize that unless you are some kind of all-seeing deity (and the number of these in existence is contained within the set {0,1}—which pretty much rules you out, statistically speaking), then it is impossible to complete more than 80 percent of a given architecture before coding begins. It is this final 20 percent that is worked out during the lifetime of the project. This is known as the 80/20 rule.

The software architect group is in complete control of the overall company standards for architecture and coding. This control encompasses diverse issues such as file formats, interface definition standards, documentation standards, directory structures, source control standards, and other common areas where reuse and maintainability are paramount.

Code reviews are performed by a team member of this group, which ensures that the architectural standards are maintained across projects. The group also oversees the separate system testing of components, tools, and projects.

The software architecture group is generally composed of the most technically skilled members of the company. They are skilled in architectural design and are able to produce detailed specifications that can be followed without ambiguity by a member of one of the three programming groups. Members are technically skilled enough to answer any questions and explain any technical points to the programmers who are following the specifications. If necessary, training should be provided to achieve this, or skilled software architects should be brought into the company.

The Tools Group

The tools group's primary function is the production and maintenance of the tools that will be used by all other development groups. In some cases, the tools will be written in-house, and in other cases the tools will be more general off-the-shelf products such as 3D Studio MAX and Microsoft Visual C++.

When possible, these tools are designed to be used for more than one project. This concept is not as difficult as it sounds. For example, a properly designed map editor can be generalized quite well. After all, a map is a map is a map. In cases where more specialization is needed, it can be defined by providing the information in data files. If true specialization is needed, then custom output modules can be written. Some projects may need genuine throwaway tools, but they should be considered carefully. Maybe they will be useful for future projects, or even as expansion packs for the project that the tool is being written for. In general, however, throwaway tools are rarely necessary, and, even if they are, the coding and documentation standards should remain the same as for the tools designed for reuse, as shown in Case Study 11.5.

The Components Group

The components group generates the low-level modules. These are the interfaces to third-party, platform-specific libraries; common modules such as compression libraries; and other similar modules.

Initially, the modules developed will be obvious and straightforward, but, as the experience of the teams grows, suggestions for extra functionality that can be moved into common libraries will become commonplace. Looking at Case Study 11.2, it is not hard to imagine a situation whereby an entirely different graphics engine (for example, Isometric 3D) could be slotted into place without too much difficulty just by rendering the graphics again.

The most important design goal for the components is that they should do one task and do it well. This does not mean that they should be designed to work for only one specific project. For example, if you have a full-perspective 3D game engine, then it should just provide that service. A 2D map view should be provided by an entirely different module. Each module will have an identical interface. This way, if at a later date it is decided to replace the 2D map view with a 3D isometric map view, then in theory, only the graphics will need to be re-rendered, and the new library will link straight in.

Another example is the sound engine. Under most circumstances, this module should not have both 2D (standard pan left/right) and 3D positional functionality built in. The 3D functionality should be built into a separate module that interfaces with the 2D library. If necessary, the 2D module can be modified to support the additional functionality required by the 3D module, such as recognizing different flags passed to the sound object creation methods, but this should be backward compatible with previous versions of the 2D library.

Remember the overriding design goal of the components is to do one job, and to do it well. This will make it easier to mix and match components during the project building phase.

The Project Group

When a project is first started, the project group is tasked with producing prototypes of the technologies to be used in the game. In most cases, the project cannot get into full swing right away. Beginning a project too quickly is not advisable before prototyping occurs. Unless all the required components have already been developed by the components group, how can the project begin?

Case Study 11.5 The Benefits Of Tool Reuse

According to Swen Vinke of Larian Studios, the game *L.E.D. Wars* was written in a five-month period during the course of another project, *The Lady, The Mage, And The Knight*.

These two game styles are fundamentally different (the former being a realtime strategy game and the latter being a multiplayer role-playing game), but they both had a tile-based map structure. Because of this similarity and some careful framework design on the part of Swen, the two games were able to use a lot of common code. The quality of the application framework that Swen developed allowed him to use that framework across two completely different game types. As a result of this commonality, he was able to use the same editors to create the levels for both games, thus saving on the development of separate tools.

With thought and care this idea can be taken further, and a set of common tools can be developed for use across the projects of the software factory.

Source: *Game Developer Magazine* (October 1997)

The first task once a project begins is to ensure that all necessary components have been developed. This is constant for every project and could mean that, for the first three months after architecture design, nothing but component development and a small amount of prototyping is taking place. This situation has to be handled very carefully, because even the most proactive managers will start to feel a little "twitchy" if there is no actual game of some form after this period of time. The development of a prototype can sometimes allay these fears slightly, but not always. The prototype is also used as a feasibility study. Do the ideas for the game work? Does it look like it will be fun? Are there likely to be any technical difficulties that you will run into at a later date? If so, how will you prepare for these?

After the development of the prototype and components, and assuming that the feasibility studies do not uncover any anomalies that need reworking, then the work on the project can begin in earnest.

The job of the project group is to coordinate the slotting together of the components, the writing of the glue code, and the provision of art and sound effects from the art and the sound groups (see "The Ancillary Groups"). This task is also controlled by the game design group. The input of the project group is to ensure that the output of the art and sound groups is in the desired format for the needs of the project.

The project group coordinates with the testing group to ensure that the project is always shippable. What does "always shippable" mean? It means that the project should always be in a buildable, releasable state. Granted, not all functionality will be there, but it should not crash if the user selects an unimplemented option. The functionality that exists must work properly and be stable. The project is tested constantly, and any problems that are reported are dealt with immediately (with the architecture group being notified if necessary).

The game design group is restricted to interact with the project group through the architecture group and through the defined mechanisms discussed in Chapter 13. This restriction serves a definite purpose: it prevents feature creep, and ensures an attainable schedule.

The game design group is free to tweak the game, and it is possible through the exposed soft architecture. Only changes to the actual program architecture itself require interaction via the architecture group. Changes to the actual program should be a rare event, and so the project group should be shielded from the wild excesses of the game design group.

The Research Group

The research group is loosely directed by the architecture group. The duties of the research group (among other things) include investigating and prototyping new techniques to be included in the core libraries for use by other projects.

These research projects should be carried out with exactly the same thoroughness and attention to detail and procedure that you would expect to find in an important scientific establishment. Detailed journals must be kept of findings, and these should be regularly reviewed and checked. It should also be realized that, by its very nature, it is impossible to plan research based around timelines. To quote Dilbert, "It is logically impossible to schedule for the unknown."

The purpose of the research group is to make the unknown known, and remove the single greatest risk from the development paths of the other groups. Because all of the other groups are using known, documented modules, all open-ended research is removed from the critical development path. If a project actually requires such research, then do not commit to the project before the research has reached a successful conclusion and an accompanying module has been produced by the components group. Either that, or change the project so that it does not depend on the outcome of the research. For example, use a less powerful graphics engine, and then, if the research version is finished in time, switch over to using that version. At least this way, if the graphics research proves fruitless or is not finished in time, you will still have a product to release at the end of the day.

The size of the research group will vary considerably depending upon the requirements of the other teams. Except in the case of dire emergencies, there should always be at least one or two members, and, if you find yourself with any spare programmers (after all other group requirements have been considered), you should assign the spares to research projects.

Note that research doesn't necessarily have to include just researching new techniques. It should also be looked upon as a means of increasing the average skill level of the programmers in your company. Much research implies that the quality of programmers' output tends toward the average skill level within an organization. Obviously, improving the average skill level by concentrating on individual members will produce improvements across the board.

For example, a programmer could be given the task of understanding and improving his knowledge of how some of the core modules function. Or he could be tasked with reading and working through a technical book to improve his skills in that specific area. Thus, time is not wasted. Anything that can raise the bar of experience for the company is a worthwhile pursuit. The research group is the ideal proving ground for such endeavors.

The Ancillary Groups

The ancillary groups are the support groups and are critical to the success of a project. The ancillary groups comprise sound, art, testing, marketing, and management groups, and will usually have less work for any one particular project than will any of the other groups. This does not mean that they are any less important.

The art and sound groups will be providing art and sound or music for the games. This group is directed by the architecture group, and also receives direct input from the project and game design groups, relating directly to the project being worked on. This is mediated by the architecture group if necessary, but it rarely is, unless the art group is being asked to perform a lot of redundant or nonscheduled work.

The testing group is closely linked to the architecture group and is directly controlled by the architecture group. Any testing that the testing group performs is reported to the architecture group. Every piece of released software—be it component, tool, or game—is thoroughly tested, and any obvious defects or faults are submitted via bug reports to be tracked and fixed as necessary. Because of the stringent testing requirements on releasing software that is built into the development process, the main functions of this group will be integration, systems, and compatibility testing.

Note

For more information on these functions, see Part III of this book.

Marketing and management structures already exist in your company. The only reason they are mentioned here is that they need to be considered when developing software using the software factory method. Results are measured differently, and the price to pay for the increase in technical visibility and knowledge of your projects is the lack of *The WOW!* factor. There will not be so many sudden leaps in functionality to amaze and astound upper management, as this development method uses steady, incremental techniques to get to the final product. The lack of apparent progress during development can sometimes panic marketing and management personnel who are unaware of the method. Hopefully, however, this won't be so much of a problem, because presumably some sort of agreement will have been reached by management before embarking on such a program. Management must be aware of the differences between this program and standard game development techniques and of the consequences of these differences.

Applying The Software Factory Structure And Methodology

So, you now know everything you need to know about how the software factory is structured. I guess that by now you'll be itching to know how to get it going—or at least I hope that's the case! The following sections cover the initial stages and the ramping up processes required to get the factory up and running.

Getting Off The Ground

For the purposes of this discussion, assume that you wish to move over from a more traditional development environment to a software factory environment, and that you want it done with the minimum of disruption (with the ability to back out if things are looking shaky or don't go according to plan).

The software factory can be incrementally introduced into your organization by the initial creation of the architecture and research groups. Similar groups may already exist within your organization, particularly in the case of the research group.

What needs to occur first is the creation of companywide development standards and guidelines for coding and documentation. This is mainly common sense, and obviously companywide should mean just that. Code and documents are easier to read and maintain if everybody is whistling to the same tune. This is also the time for implementing some of the project visibility procedures, but at a limited scope. Provide an intranet site so people can see how progress is going on the pilot scheme, such as that shown in Figure 11.5.

Note

See Chapter 13 for more suggestions on achieving consistency.

Once this is done, these groups can begin investigating and prototyping the initial set of component libraries. To begin, the architects should review the projects currently underway, or soon to be underway, to decide what functionality would be suitable for implementing as a core component. Concentrate especially on functionality that is yet to be written in the ongoing projects.

After the feasibility study and testing of the prototype components, the work should begin in earnest on the core components. Form the components team and begin the development of the components researched by the research team. The code should not be developed from the prototypes, because prototype code is no basis for a solid code base. Prototype code is just what it says it is: prototype. Resist the temptation to use it and save yourself the trouble that, chances are, would develop eventually. Throw the code away and start again using the lessons learned while prototyping to develop some killer components.

On completion of the initial set of components, begin leveraging them into the ongoing projects to implement unwritten functionality. It is not wise to try to replace functionality

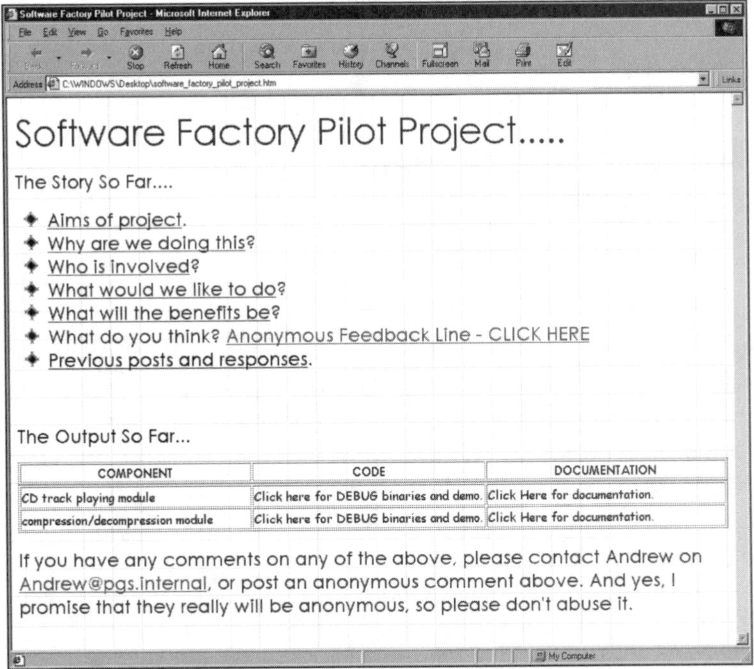

Figure 11.5
An example of a pilot project intranet site.

that is already written, as it will probably involve code rewrites and cause delays to the schedules already in place. If, on the other hand, an ongoing project has yet to implement a CD-playing code, then providing them with a fully documented and tested CD-playing module has got to be a good thing. Make sure that the team understands that all support requests go to the architecture group, and not directly to the programmers in the components group. This shouldn't necessarily be a problem anyway, because the components group won't make any ad hoc modifications without going to the architecture group for confirmation.

Tip

Think, and think again. Think small at first, and think on your feet. Start by providing components that are going to be immediately useful. Once project teams start coming around to your way of thinking, then work can start on the more fundamental and forward-thinking components that will be useful on subsequent projects.

As personnel become available, draft them into the tools group, and start work on the tools to support the more adventurous components.

Now you are already halfway there, and the rest of the process follows naturally, as projects wind up and more developers become available to fill in the other teams, which are incorporated into the communication framework. Also, by now it will have become clear whether the software factory will work for your organization, or whether another approach or combination of approaches would be more suitable.

Knowing When To Use Each Team—A Parallel Development Timeline

Each programming group is assembled on a just-in-time basis. This ensures maximum flexibility and helps to make efficient use of resources.

It is very important to make sure that each group has the correct number of members to support the needs of the dependent teams. These numbers will need to be tweaked according to the needs of your organization. Figure 11.6 shows the group dependencies. If any of the supporting structures are weak, the whole structure will collapse, which is obviously something to avoid. Be aware of the strengths and weaknesses of each group, and avoid overburdening groups by making the structure top heavy. This will only cause trouble further down the line.

So how do these groups work together? Figure 11.7 shows a sample workload against time for a small- to medium-size organization.

When a group has less work, personnel can be moved to groups that require extra staff to encourage knowledge transfer. One of the stranger findings of research into this sort of group dynamics is that the information doesn't always spread as well as one might expect. The information doesn't automatically spread to the new group member in the same way as, for example, the common cold would. This only usually becomes an issue when a member is added late in a project, but, for larger group sizes, the team identity should still be intact. Each member of the team should be made to realize that they are all part of one team. The logical divisions are in place only to make sure that project visibility is maintained to the highest possible level.

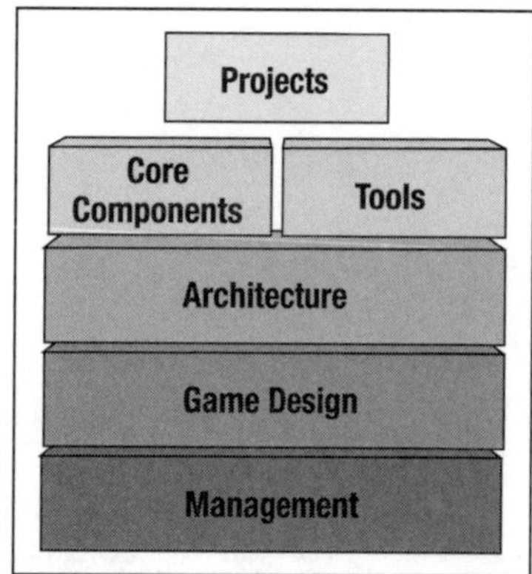

Figure 11.6
The group dependency structure.

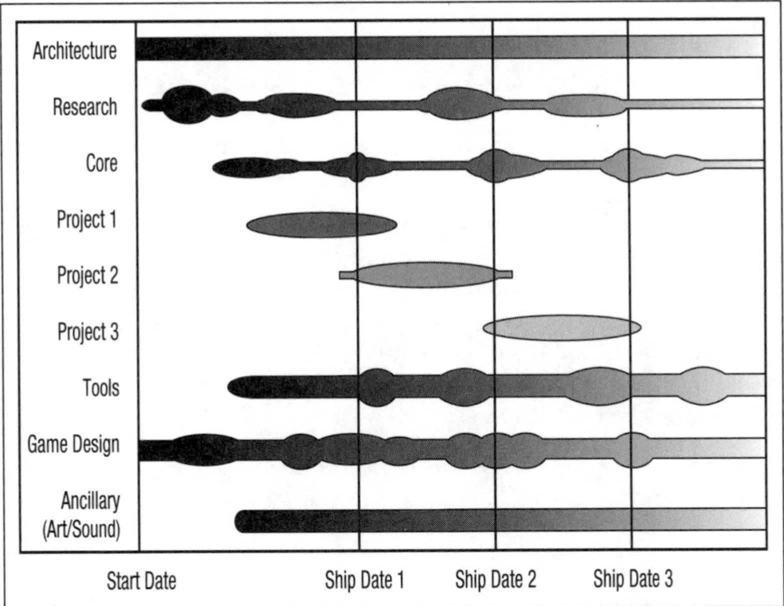

Figure 11.7
A graph of average group workload against time.

For larger organizations, it is possible—and indeed sometimes necessary—to run projects side by side. As long as the supporting infrastructure is strong enough, this will cause no additional problems.

Rotating And Reassigning Team Members

One of the strengths of the software factory is the ability to spread the knowledge among the team members. This is not without its risks, but most of you will already have experienced the greater risks of not doing so, as shown in Case Study 11.6.

By rotating team members, many of problems described in Case Study 11.6 can be avoided before they become a major risk. Regularly rotate members around the different core programming groups, but pick your time carefully—adding a new member toward the end of a project tends to slow things down.

Although this sounds dangerous, it ensures that more than one person has knowledge of any particular area of code, and, because of the documentation procedures in place, the lead-in time for new developers is minimized. What would you rather have: slightly increased development times, or the risk of not being able to complete a project if a key member leaves?

Spread the risk wherever you can, and try not to put all your eggs in one basket.

Case Study 11.6 The Indispensables

On a large multiuser project (not game related) that I have worked on recently, the application being developed was largely dependent on a library developed by an external team, based at another site. This library provided various complicated calculation functions needed by the main application.

One particular section of the library—and I will mention no names, because I do not wish to incriminate the guilty—was often spoken about in hushed whispers and a sense of awe. Why? It was not because that particular area of calculation was more complex than any other. It was because it had been written by one programmer, in a deliberately obtuse style, and no one else in the company had any understanding of how it worked. This particular programmer was solely responsible for this area of code, and had thus far resisted any attempts to force documentation or explanations.

This resistance was because he relished the feeling of power that it gave him, and indeed he was in a very powerful position. He was able to blackmail the company for anything he wanted, because he knew that they were unable to fire him. He was indispensable and had been known to actually say this on occasion.

To handle this problem, I pandered to his ego and recommended promoting him. He was to be provided with an assistant and a private office. The assistant was an object-oriented expert sourced from outside the company, whose coding skills far outreached that of the main developer, and whose task was to learn and document the offending section of code, but as discreetly as possible.

After some initial problems, the developer accepted his newly found power, and made full use of the assistant that had been provided for him. What he didn't realize was that he was undermining his own indispensability. The expert assistant spent six months studying and documenting the code, and soon felt able to rewrite and clean up as necessary.

Over the next few months, the specifications were drawn up for the new functionality, and after being written it was discreetly tested alongside the original functionality. When all bugs had been worked out (including some corrections that had been made to the original code), the announcement was made that the old functionality was going to be replaced by new, superior functionality. Of course, the original developer screamed in horror, but when challenged could not provide a logical argument as to why we should not use the new code. It was clean, object oriented, and, above all, well documented, and it was far superior in quality to the original code.

Somewhat surprisingly, after his power had been removed, the developer became a much more helpful member of the team. He had been told exactly why this course of action had been taken and what would happen to him if he tried to do it again. Thus, he was closely monitored to make sure that he was complying with the demands.

This is not a pleasant course of action to have to take under any circumstances, but sometimes being tough is necessary. The risk to the project and to the company as a whole was too great to depend on that one person.

On a related note, I once knew a developer who had a somewhat "unusual" naming convention for variables. He would start with the letter *a*, and work his way through to *z*. When he ran out of letters, he would begin again at *aa*, and work through to *az*, and so on. The amazing thing was, he remembered what they were all for. Even without any comments in his code, he could come back to it months later and modify it without difficulty. When he left the company, all his code was thrown away and had to be rewritten from scratch. No one had realized that he coded like this until it was too late. They had only been interested in the results, and not in how it had been done.

The Suitability Of A Software Factory

The software factory is suitable for a medium- to large-scale organization. In this example, five or more programmers and the accompanying technical staff are present. This size organization allows the partitioning of teams in an even and balanced way, and allows the rotation of team members to good effect.

The software factory also scales down easily for smaller teams. You will lose some of the parallelism and not be able to have the luxury of separate ancillary teams, but the advantages for the second and subsequent projects will still be evident. This method is the technique that you can use for developing software, and has been honed out of five years of solid C++ development experience for various clients around Europe, in situations in which the speed of development and performance was of great importance. Whenever possible, use software factory construction techniques in all team sizes, and you will be pleased at the consistent results achieved, even if it does take some getting used to on the part of developers who are not used to being so restricted, and on the part of managers who expect to see early results and the bugs fixed later, after the shipping date.

The Final Word

The methodology in this chapter is not a universal panacea. There is no silver bullet in software development. If you have fundamental problems with your development teams, such as a lack of skill and experience, then no amount of methodologies will help before you have tackled the source of the problem.

So don't feel that you have to take this methodology as the letter of the law. Try it out. Experiment with it. See what works for you and what doesn't. Keep the bits that do work and toss the bits that don't. With determination—and a lot of effort—the benefits of this methodology will pay off.

Many other methodologies and techniques are suitable for games design, most of them (including this one) lifted straight from more traditional programming endeavors. This is a system that has been proven to provide quality software, time and time again over a series of staged releases, with each subsequent product cycle converging towards a smaller and smaller release interval.

Game developers in particular are quick to knock anything that places restrictions on the way they can work. Of course, if all projects were delivered up to standard, and within the allotted schedule, there would be no need for such measures.

For a variety of reasons, real life just isn't like that, so the message here should be "Don't knock it until you've tried it!"

After all, you may be pleasantly surprised.

Chapter 12
Milestones And Deadlines

Key Topics:

- ***Scheduling of projects***
- ***Avoiding arbitrary deadlines***
- ***Defuzzification of milestones***
- ***Starting the project***

In Chapter 11, we discussed the software factory method of creating an environment for efficient software development. In this chapter, we will examine how to set this organization into motion. Keep in mind that the ideas presented here are not applicable to just the software factory, but can also be used in any project and team structure.

However much we'd all like to write software while free of constraints and pressures, some milestones and deadlines are a necessity. They are, indeed, a common factor for all nontrivial software projects and, as such, are the bane of many developers' lives.

Given the universal nature of milestones and deadlines, it is surprising how most milestone specifications are set in an arbitrary fashion, and how, in many cases, deadlines are defined on a "wish list" basis rather than on realistic estimates. This peculiarity can be attributed to a number of factors such as marketing influence, inexperienced software managers, and, in some cases, sheer stubbornness. Of course, most people simply do not know how to estimate schedules for software development. To be fair, it is a difficult procedure, and it involves much analysis and calculation to produce any useful results.

Outside the games industry, software companies use a slightly more rigorous approach than "pick a date and hope for the best." Even so, precious little training and guidelines are available on how to define milestones in a sensible manner.

Milestones serve to divide projects into manageable chunks. The undesirable alternative is to present a huge list of desired features that the developers would check off as each is implemented. This, of course, is not recommended practice. Can you imagine how demoralizing it would be, in a project that lasted 18 months, to be able to check off only a few items every week? What sense of achievement could be possible? How would the team maintain focus and enthusiasm? As ridiculous as it seems, some projects are still developed using this system, and they are most likely one of the most joyless experiences in software development.

The method presented here is applicable to all types of software, whether spreadsheets, databases, or shoot-'em-up arcade games. This chapter presents a set of guidelines that is based on these "good practice" techniques for defining milestones and deadlines in a more realistic fashion. Later in the book, we'll explain how these estimates are progressively refined to become increasingly accurate as the project continues. This phenomenon of increasing accuracy is referred to as the *convergence rule*. As well as discussing the overall structure of a project, this chapter also serves as a road map for the chapters ahead. So, this chapter is your first port of call if you are searching for information on the development process.

How Milestones Currently Work

How many times have you had to work to a "fuzzy" milestone? For the uninitiated (and there can't be that many!), a fuzzy milestone is one that has many interpretations and x possible ways to achieve it, where x is any number you like, as long as it is greater than one.

And how do you know if you have *really* reached a fuzzy milestone? If the milestone goals are fuzzy, they are, by default, open to interpretation. So whose interpretation counts? Of course, it usually will be your boss who make the "right" interpretation, and the chances are that it won't be the same as yours.

Try this simple test. Imagine that your boss shows you a piece of paper with five dots arranged in a pentagon and labeled A, B, C, D, and E, as shown in Figure 12.1.

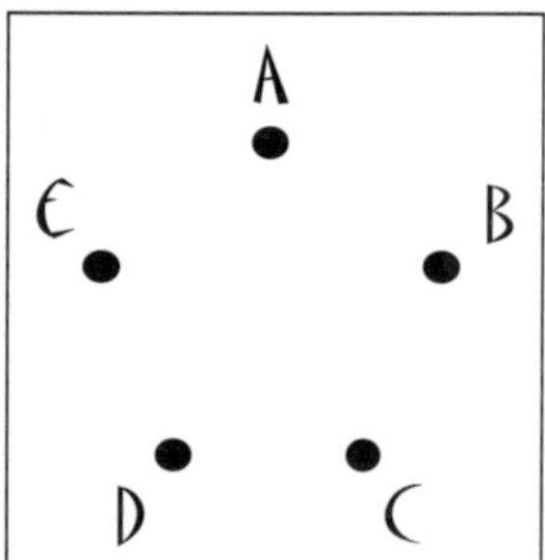

Figure 12.1
The task.

Now imagine your boss says, "I'm very busy today, and I need all this work finished within an hour. I've got lots of people to see, so I can explain only briefly what I need you to do. I'd like you to draw a line between A and B. Have it done by the time I get back from my 'business' lunch."

Three hours later, your boss staggers back into the office and demands his completed document.

If you've drawn a straight line directly between A and B (as in Figure 12.2), then I'm sorry, but you lose. If, however, you have drawn a line between A and E, and have also made sure that it goes through C, D, and B to form the outline of the pentagon (as in Figure 12.3),while leaving the space between A and B blank, then you have hit the milestone correctly.

Okay, so your boss wouldn't you a task as trivial as this. The point is a vague milestone is useless one.

To arrive at your solution, it could be that you have worked too much or too little. In most cases, basic programmer psychology indicates the latter. It's not that good programmers are lazy; it's just a generalization of the axiom that the shortest distance between two points is a straight line. (Most good programmers like to perform the minimum amount of work to produce a given result.)

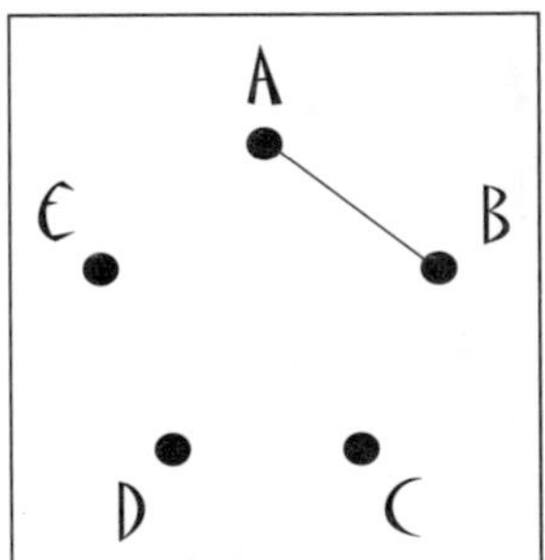

Figure 12.2
The wrong solution.

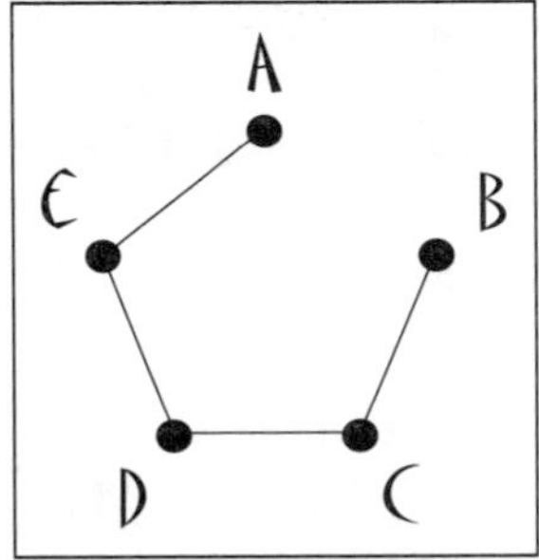

Figure 12.3
The right solution.

However, in cases of the former (too much work), it is also usually the wrong sort of work, meaning that the programmer has overengineered the solution, providing unneeded or unnecessarily complicated functionality.

Ideally, milestones should not give this much room to maneuver, but this sort of situation is unfortunately at the heart of most scheduling problems. On a fair proportion of projects, the milestones were spaced too far apart, and thus allowed a fair degree of drift between them, during which unnecessary work was performed due to a lack of direction and focus.

A milestone should be clear and concise. It should also be obvious at a glance whether the milestone has been achieved or not: black and white, failure or success. It should not accommodate or encourage any ambiguous results or shades of gray. No one should be able to say a milestone is 90 percent complete: a milestone that is 90 percent complete makes as much sense as a light bulb that is 90 percent on. A light is either on or off, and so is a milestone.

This point is critical. The fuzzy milestone is the single most common problem with projects.

You boss's pentagon-dot task should have been specified in the following manner:

1. Prerequisite tools: ruler, and black pen capable of producing consistent thin lines.
2. Connect point A to point E using a thin, straight, black line.
3. Connect point E to point D using a thin, straight, black line.
4. Connect point D to point C using a thin, straight, black line.
5. Connect point C to point B using a thin, straight, black line.

Note: Do not connect points A and B.

This list is comparable to a detailed analysis document. The analysis should be detailed enough as to leave no question or room for doubt as to how the problem will be solved. In this case, there is one optimum solution, and producing that solution is just a case of connecting the dots (pun intended). You may feel that this takes the creativity out of programming, to which I respond that programming is the wrong place for creativity. Another word for "creative programming" is hacking. The time and place for creativity is in the design and architecture. By the time we get around to actually programming the system, the game and architectural designers have finished all the creative parts. This may dent egos, but the job of a programmer is that of simple translation: take a detailed design and turn it into a working computer implementation.

I can already hear the programmers protesting this slur to their creative genius. How dare I reduce them to the level of code monkeys? Well, programmers who only program *are* code monkeys. The actual programming of a design is really just the last small stage in a long and complicated process. It's the finishing touch, a small but important detail. However, programmers usually have more responsibilities other than just writing code. In most cases, they are also responsible for the detailed module design as well as the implementation. This allows the creativity to be shifted to where it belongs, into the *documented* code design, and not directly into the code.

For all those still bristling at the above argument, please re-read Chapter 11, which discusses this point in more detail, and provides justification for my statements and views.

All the good projects that I have worked have deliberately reduced the programming to the level of a simple translation. Without exception, these projects have run smoothly and were completed on time and within budget.

On the contrary, all the bad projects that I have worked on have gone straight from overall architecture design to coding. Without exception, these projects have overrun their allocated budgets and were completed late—if they were completed at all.

As shown in Case Study 12.1, fuzzy milestones cause delays to the project, and consequently sow confusion and distrust among the interested parties that are waiting on those milestones. By not specifying an exact point in which to stop and take stock of progress, you decrease project visibility, which means that no one is exactly sure where the project is. Consequently, delays and problems become endemic. No one intentionally sets out to create a situation such as this. It just happens, unnoticed, one day at a time until it becomes too great to ignore. Statistically, most projects that lose time to slippages are unable to make up the time: slippage begets slippage. Such problems need to be caught early, and the situation rectified as soon as possible.

Fuzzy Milestones

Just as mountaineers are warned not to eat yellow snow, you have been warned not to tolerate fuzzy milestones. This is common sense. Why try to work towards a goal within a fixed deadline when you are not even sure where the goal is, and there is likely to be an argument about the exact position of the goal posts when you get there? Fuzziness is the enemy of software scheduling.

Fuzzy milestones are also the result of completing milestones and schedules before fully defining the specifications of the project. Because not enough is known about the problem domain, milestones are defined with sweeping generalities, and deadlines are divided fairly arbitrarily across the available time using a gut instinct for the difficulty of any particular milestone. Usually too much work is covered by a single milestone, and it is simply too difficult to complete all the separate tasks to hit the milestone. It then becomes a fuzzy milestone, and can be legitimately described as being, for example, half completed (if it depends on two streams of work and only one has been finished).

Cramming too much functionality into a single milestone is counterproductive. Apart from the obvious confusion factor, it can cause other, more subtle problems. The team should get a sense of achievement from completing a milestone. A milestone that drags on for an extended period of time has a detrimental effect on morale, and the attitude of the team

Case Study 12.1 What Fuzzy Milestones Can Do To A Project

For one of the very first game projects I worked on professionally, fresh out of college, I was given what should have been a very simple assignment: write a level editor for the game we were working on using Microsoft's Visual Basic 4.

This is fine for a project title or mission statement, but unfortunately it also became my project milestone.

It is difficult to see how you make a milestone any fuzzier than that. At the time, however, I was inexperienced enough not to see any problems with this.

I was given a deadline of two weeks to finish this particular project. Having a good knowledge of the previous version of Visual Basic, I got cracking.

The first obstacle was a lack of knowledge of the problem domain: I didn't know exactly what was wanted, even though my boss and I thought that we both had the same end product in mind.

The project that I was thinking of (and that I knew I could produce in two weeks) was a tile-based landscape editor that was capable of generating tessellating tiles and a height map for these tiles.

The project that my boss had in mind required a landscape editor with the above capabilities, as well being able to automatically generate landscapes both randomly and from an imported height map, allowing the import of data from *VistaPro* (a commercial landscape-generation package), placement of game objects on the landscape (including autogeneration of formations if groups were placed), automatic import and categorization of the output of the artists, and generation of a complete set of level files with an optimized palette for each level.

Both of the above descriptions are descriptions of level editors, but only one is possible within two weeks, and only one (in my boss's opinion) is the right one. Unfortunately, they aren't both the same one.

Consequently, after two weeks, I had a working landscape editor according to the first specification, hence hitting the project target (as I saw it). I had given no thought to any of the other issues. And given the tightness of the deadline, I had not written the program to take any of these things into account, nor had I even provided for the option of inserting them at a later date. (In other words, I had used the "code like hell" technique of software construction.)

The end result of this was a further 10 weeks of development in order to hit the milestone, and a program that ultimately ran intolerably slow because it was trying to do some very processor-intensive palette calculations using VB4.

transforms into that of trench warfare: us versus them, in a daily slow grind to advance the lines. A team should know at all times how much progress has been made on the project to the nearest percentile.

This is not an impossible task, but it does require more planning than is usually associated with the average game project.

Milestones And Mini-Milestones

As a rule, a good length of time for a milestone is between four and eight weeks. This provides a finite goal and allows the milestone to be reasonably focused. Another problem with large fuzzy milestones is the lack of focus: who cares about a deadline that is four months away? This situation normally degenerates into three months of laid-back programming, followed by a month of coding like hell.

The solution to this (apart from spacing milestones closer together) is to divide each milestone into mini-milestones, or checkpoints, with each lasting approximately a week. Obviously, to be able to do this, you have to have specified the architecture fairly well. If you find yourself in a situation where you cannot set fairly concrete milestones and mini-milestones, then the architecture design is not complete enough to begin coding. In this way, we can help ensure that good practices are followed during the critical period of project startup. If things start well, it is easier to keep them going well than it is repair a situation that had started badly. A good way to divide tasks between milestones and mini-milestones is to specify module completion as mini-milestones, and module integration as the main milestone. (It may sometimes be necessary to divide the mini-milestones even further, but this will depend on the team and the task at hand.)

With a good team, mini-milestones are not always necessary. They wouldn't be necessary, for instance, if the team is experienced enough to know the best way to tackle problems and mature enough to stay focused on an approaching deadline. However, for new teams or for new and unfamiliar projects, then mini-milestones can serve two purposes:

- Keeping the team focused on the task at hand
- Providing increased levels of project visibility during critical times

The first of these is important to avoid the aimless drifting of projects that can occur when milestones are too widely spaced. A good analogy is to imagine that you have been given written directions to a place you have never visited, but you have a rough idea of the general area. You have been asked to draw a map of the route on your way, and to arrive within a certain time limit. As you walk, you spend most of the time drawing your map. Every now and then, you stop and look around to get your bearings.

In this analogy, the milestones are the instances when you stop and check where you are, and the project is the map. The more often you stop and look, the less likely you are to make as many wrong turns or mistakes on your map. Obviously, this method is subject to the Law of Diminishing Returns: if you stop every two steps, not only will it take longer to arrive, but you won't be able to concentrate on drawing the map. Finding the balance is the key. The milestones should not be so frequent that they detract from the amount of useful work performed, but not so far apart that the impetus, momentum, and focus of the project are lost.

A good rule of thumb is to scale the amount of mini-milestones to the level of experience of the team and the familiarity of the subject matter. The absolute minimum spacing of mini-milestones should be one to two days. Any less than this and the amount of administration required would outweigh the benefits of the increased visibility.

When To Use Milestones

In general, every program or module is a separate project, and, for all but the most trivial programs, they should be treated as such and specified, written, and documented accordingly. What exactly makes a program trivial is open to debate, but the recommended guideline is to consider writing a throwaway program only if you can categorically state that there are no other feasible uses, and that developing it in a more general way would generate a ridiculously large project.

An example of a program that fits these criteria is a look-up table generator that is used to create files of pregenerated values to reduce the amount of calculation needed at runtime. (With the advent of faster and faster processors, look-up tables have begun to fall out of favor, but they still have their uses on more-limited systems.) To develop this in a general way would involve writing an expression parser that could read user-defined formulas to produce the tables. In this particular case, it is clear that it would be far better to hard code the required tables.

Making Your Milestones Accurate

In order to improve the accuracy of schedules, we need to remove as many of the uncertainties as possible. Not all can be removed, but one way to minimize the number of uncertainties is to concentrate on avoiding fuzziness in milestones.

In Case Study 12.1, the problem was caused by a mutual misunderstanding and the lack of an in-depth explanation as to what exactly the requirements were. No specification document was followed because no analysis had been performed of the problem domain. Given the tightness of the deadline, it is clear that no thought had been given to gathering the requirements. The boss had just assumed that the knowledge of what he had wanted would be "automagically" transferred from his head to mine. Compounding this, he had assumed that the other team members would be able to explain exactly what they needed within a few minutes.

This clearly doesn't make sense, but you would be amazed and astounded at the number of projects that are run on this basis. Vast sums of money are spent on back-of-the-envelope estimates that do not take into account all the possible factors that could affect the outcome of the project. In some cases, deadlines are set on the basis of demands made by the marketing department, which is probably the least qualified group to make such decisions.

Marketing pressure is obviously important to the release date, but it should never be the deciding factor in scheduling issues. Trying to get teams to respect marketing-defined deadlines is an impossible task, particularly when the team is fully aware that these deadlines are arbitrary and unrealistic, and do not take into account the technical factors involved in the development. If there is a marketing-defined deadline (the infamous Christmas rush), then scale the functionality of the project back to meet the deadline. This reduced functionality must be made completely clear to all concerned. The usual response given in such situations is to ask for time to be shaved off the schedule but for the same amount of work to be done anyway. (The assumption here is that all developers pad the schedule anyway, in order to make their life easier. This is rubbish, and if you succumb to this argument then you are just asking for trouble.) It must be made perfectly clear that the schedule is the optimum time for producing the requested amount of work. If the work must be done in a shorter time, then functionality must be reduced. I have seen too many situations in which project leads have accepted such situations and assumed that they can accomplish 18 months of work in 12. Admittedly, this is just about possible, given enough overtime. Trying to get a team of developers to work solidly for 12 months with tons of overtime is not an easy task (and most certainly not an advisable one). The damage to morale would be very high, and you would stand a good chance of losing most of your skilled developers at the end of the project.

The deadline for the program in Case Study 12.1 was clearly too short under any circumstances for such a nontrivial task. The requirements gathering for this project would have taken at least a week, and, if requirements had been gathered, it would have predicted that a further six weeks would be required for the project. Of course, even this estimate depends upon the progress made by other team members in this period and on their availability to document and explain various areas of their work that the editor needed to take into account. This may or may not have been acceptable to the boss, but at least this knowledge would have allowed him to pursue other options, such as assigning more people to the project, reducing its scope, extending the schedule, giving the project to someone with experience in that area, or firing me!

Before you can even consider planning and scheduling an entire project, certain steps *must* be performed. The first three milestones of a project (shown in Table 12.1) should cover these steps. These will allow a more detailed and accurate analysis of how the time will be spent over the months to come.

These milestones effectively encompass the initial stages of specification and feasibility studies. The cost of these stages is a small part of the project's total cost, and it helps to provide good information on the total cost, duration, and technical feasibility of the overall

Table 12.1 The first three milestones.

Milestone	Checkpoint	Task
1	1.0	General requirements gathering
	1.1	Technological requirements gathering
	1.2	Resource requirements gathering
2	2.0	General feasibility study
	2.1	Technological feasibility study
	2.2	Resource availability study
3	3.0	Draft architecture specification
	3.1	Project initialization

project. At each of these first milestones, the decision makers are in a good position to cancel the project, or allow it to continue to the next milestone. After the third milestone has been completed and the project is given the go-ahead, then the project should be allowed to run to completion (unless it falls into dire straits). The cancellation of a project after a successful feasibility study should be treated as a failure of the feasibility study process and investigated accordingly.

The initial investigative phases of a project are obviously a better place to make this decision than 15 months into development, when a lot more money and effort has been spent and everybody has begun to assume that the project will run to completion. (Does this situation ring any bells with any of you?) The effects on morale of canceling a project increase with the length of time that the project has been in progress. If, however, it is clear to the team members that they are performing feasibility studies to check out the technology and playability requirements, then the damage is minimized: everybody understands that all they are doing is investigating whether the project is worth attempting. This is most effective if the final go-ahead can be relied upon totally. It loses its potency if, even after all the feasibility checking measures have been taken, there is still the risk of random cancellation.

People naturally work better if they feel comfortable and secure in their position. Of course, the risk of a project's premature ending cannot be eliminated entirely, but it can at least be minimized by solving any major issues as early in the process as possible, before a lot of money has been spent and a lot of people have bought into the project. Not only will you lose money and time, you will also lose the respect of the people involved.

In Case Study 12.2, the projects were canceled at different stages in their development. Fortunately, some of these were still at the prototype stage and therefore had not gone too far; even so, $150,000 is a lot of money to spend on a series of prototypes. In reality, I would not expect to spend more than $75,000 on a prototype. It just depends on how you define the term 'prototype.' In these cases, the "prototypes" were not really prototypes in the classic sense, but were merely partially developed versions of the full game. In most cases, the games were being developed as normal, and no effort was being made to separate the prototype (such as it was) from the main development. In these cases, the prototype code would be the actual game code.

However, a prototype should be just that: quick and disposable. It is a mechanism to test ideas and concepts, so don't confuse it with technology research. The purpose of the prototyping stage is to investigate the feasibility of the game's concept. By the end of this stage, the required technology should already be developed (or substitutes should be available). This is not as restrictive as it sounds because these components will have been developed to standardized interfaces. If (or when) a new technology is developed during the actual course of the project, the new component can always be slotted into place at a later date.

The prototype doesn't even need to be written in a compiled language. Often a series of successive prototypes—starting with pencil and paper and progressing to a high-level, rapid-development language such as Basic—are enough to be able to test the rough concepts.

Case Study 12.2 The Costs Of Canceling Projects

Names of individuals, companies and products have been changed to protect the innocent and the not so innocent.

In an interview with Mr. Snow, the CEO of Corporation Y, publishers of the hit *CryptInvader* series, he states that Corporation Y had recently canned approximately 10 projects that weren't measuring up to expectations over the course of a six-month period. These projects were at various stages of development, and had had varying amounts of money spent on them.

Mr. Snow said this was done to maintain the high quality of their software releases, and was therefore sound business sense. According to Mr. Snow, the cost of canceling these projects (including *Fatal Prison II*) varied between $160,000 and $720,000 per project, which he didn't see to be a problem. Some may say that, if you have the sort of money that Corporation Y has available to throw around, then maybe you wouldn't see any problem there, either. However, if you consider that this money could have been used to completely fund up to four other projects (if the early prototyping stages had been performed properly), then it takes on quite a different light. This wasted effort was not only expensive in terms of money, but it also adversely affected the morale of the development teams (potentially up to 100 people).

After all, it's a prototype and not a finished product, and, if it is written in a different language than the final product, it removes all possibility and temptation to use the prototype as a code base for the final product.

Using prototype code at production level is a recipe for disaster, because prototypes usually, by definition, do not feature production-level code. This does not mean that the code is not well written; it just means that the coding priorities are different for a prototype. For example, speed is not a priority in prototype code, but it is the main priority for some production code. Don't underestimate this temptation to use prototype code for the main product. The prospect of saving time by using already written prototype code is a dangerous trap and usually results in significant delays and problems further down the line. It is also not worth attempting to write prototype code to production level, which would be an impossible task and would ultimately impede the development of the prototype.

The milestone schedule presented in Table 12.1 attempts to encompass all the above points and covers the initial stages of a project up to the conclusion of the feasibility studies.

The following sections cover each of these initial milestones in more detail.

Checkpoint 1.0 General Requirements Gathering

This checkpoint answers the following questions:

What Is The Project?

Obviously, it's a game, game component, or a tool to facilitate the production of a game. But what type of game? What is the target audience? Why will it appeal to them? Where and how does the game fit into the company's overall vision. The answers to these questions help to provide a larger focus for the project.

There should be no doubts as to what type of game is being written. For example, the look and feel should be explored, as should all the other issues and concerns that affect the project at its most general level. I personally hate the use of the term *mission statement*, but if ever any of my projects have them, this is where they need to be defined.

What Functionality Do The 'Customers' Expect?

In this case, *customer* can be defined at several levels. The first customer is the company management, the second is the publisher, the third is the press, and last—but most certainly not least—is the buying public.

Each group of these customers must be individually catered to, and, unfortunately, not all of them have the same needs and desires. Each is arguably of equal importance, so the task of pleasing them all becomes a precarious balancing act. For example, the management and the publishers may require regular demonstrations and interim releases for shows and previews. The press will need preview versions, and the buying public needs a finished product! These needs all must be anticipated and built into the schedule (especially the last one.)

What Is The Minimum Functionality Required?

The minimum functionality, surprisingly enough, is the most important consideration. While I do not want to dwell on gloomy thoughts, it must be realized that development, like true love, never runs as smoothly as expected. From the earliest stages in the project, several tiers of functionality must be defined. (These are introduced in Chapter 14 and discussed in more detail in Part III).

The lowest functional tier defines the minimum release requirements: the point at which the software is "complete enough" to be released publicly. The game may not be very good at this point, but at least the core is functional. Reaching this point is the primary goal of the schedule. Once this point has been successfully achieved, additional functionality is added tier by tier until the ideal level of functionality is reached and the product can be released. Of course, if the project has experienced any delays, it may be necessary to release the game before all the desired features have been implemented. In this situation, you will be glad that you took the tiered approach.

In this stage, you'll gather all the overall project requirements, which will serve as the general guidelines for the entire project.

The prerequisite for this stage is the game treatment document, as defined in Part I. To recap, this is a small document that describes the essential feel of the game and the overall idea behind it.

From this initial treatment, you'll develop the game design document, as described in Part I. Once the game design is fully specified (subject of course to the 80/20 rule!), and has been approved by the powers that be, we are ready to proceed to the next phase.

Checkpoint 1.1 Technological Requirements Gathering

This checkpoint answers the following question:

What Techniques And Processes Are Needed?

The ideal situation is to have all the components already developed. This question then becomes much easier to answer. If the components aren't yet available, can they be easily constructed to a fixed timescale, or is research needed in order to define the functionality required?

If research is needed, then the project cannot proceed past the prototype stage. It is very important that you then consider putting it on hold until the research is complete. As soon as you break this rule, you are assuming an unacceptable risk. Remember, the object of these developmental processes is to reduce the ever-present risks as much as possible. Relying on research to a fixed timescale undermines every other measure taken. Don't do it.

If you are sure that the technology to be researched is feasible (and you have a fall-back position), then you may wish to continue developing a prototype. An example of a fall-back situation would be to have a software-based 3D engine that you would like to extend to allow hardware support. Even if the hardware support research fails, you can still use the software engine, so although inconvenient, in this case failure is not fatal. However, you should proceed with caution.

Checkpoint 1.2 Resource Requirements Gathering

This checkpoint answers the following question:

What Resources Will Be Needed For The Project?

Prepare a list of all the software and literature that you don't already have that will be needed to complete the project.

Don't go overboard on this; it's easy to buy everything including the kitchen sink. Instead, be reasonable. You may have a limited budget, and it's Murphy's Law that, as soon as you have depleted your allocated budget, an essential piece of software is released, and you can't purchase it.

Here is a list of recommended useful items (and examples of them):

- Compiler (Microsoft Visual C++)
- Automated error-checking software (NuMega BoundsChecker)
- Profiler (NuMega TrueTime)
- Source-control software (Microsoft Visual SourceSafe)
- Scheduling software (Microsoft Project)
- Word processor (Microsoft Word)

- 3D modeler (Kinetix 3DS Max)
- 2D paint software (Adobe Photoshop)
- Format translation software (Okino Polytrans)

(The contents of this list are obviously just suggestions based on the software that I am most familiar with. It is similar to that used in most development houses today. Some of this software may be a tad expensive, especially for those on a limited budget. Fortunately, there are always other options, and the CD-ROM provided with this book features a range of freeware or shareware alternatives (or pointers to where you can find them). See Appendix B for more details on the included software.)

Tip

Would you like some useful advice, hard won from bitter experience? Never use the latest version of software until it has been out for a while. If you switch versions halfway through a project, it can cause delays. Also, if things do not work out well, "rolling back" the change can be a time-consuming and expensive task. They don't call it the bleeding edge for nothing.

Checkpoint 2.0 General Feasibility Study

This checkpoint answers the following questions:

Is It A Worthwhile Project?

The gameplay and story should be investigated and polished. Obviously, this will not be final, but subject to tweaks and modifications as the development progresses. This is where old ideas are discarded and new ideas discovered.

A word of warning here: beware of feature creep. Many games are delayed or canceled due to underestimating the ease of adding a new feature. Feature creep—and preventative measures—are discussed in Part III.

Is The Market Ready For A Game Such As This?

Does the game fit into the current market? This does not mean that the game should be a derivative of one that is already available. (If this is the case, then you need to rethink the project. Enough companies are producing uninspired and lifeless games without you adding another to the list. Go back and read Part I until you feel more inspired!)

Okay, assuming you are still here, then your game design has passed the first acid test. The next question is whether the proposed game design is completely new or whether it adds and expands to a current genre. If it is completely new, then I would recommend performing a study on how the market is likely to accept it. Initially, try to ask a group of unbiased people for criticisms of the game design. Ask them if it is the sort of game they would play, and then ask them what they like and what they don't like. It is important to get honest (even brutally so) answers, so that rules out family, friends, and colleagues. A common piece of advice is to design a game that you would like to play. There is nothing wrong with that, but you run the strong risk of ending up with a game that only you like playing. Of course, you must design a game that you would enjoy playing, but this cannot be your only guideline.

If the game is an expansion of a currently existing genre, then the above advice still holds. In addition, try to define exactly how your game will improve the genre. A classic example of this is Valve's *Half-life*, a first-person shoot-'em-up built atop the *Quake II* engine. However, it was the best game released in 1998 even though there were other contenders released at roughly the same time (including *Sin* and *Unreal*). *Half-life* considerably added to the genre by including a strong story, incredible adversary AI, and a very carefully constructed playing environment. In *Half-life*, there were usually two solutions to every problem: you could go in with guns blazing and kill everything in sight, or you could think about your next step. This is an example of excellent gameplay. (The thinking element, however, seems to diminish towards the end of the game, relying more on fast reflexes and a high ammo count.)

When you consider releasing a game in an already existing genre, try to improve upon the existing content, rather than following the more conventional "more weapons, more enemies, bigger explosions" route. For examples of how *not* to expand an already existing genre, take a look at the realtime strategy genre. As of December 1998, it was already stagnating, with only a few gems (such as Blizzard's *StarCraft*) adding something new among the muck.

Use your imagination. Try to exploit every possible opportunity to gather opinions and ideas for the design. The general feasibility study is the last point in the development process where major restructuring of the game design can be done cheaply and efficiently, so make the most of it. Don't be afraid to scrap a design if it doesn't make the grade. This may be difficult due to personal attachment and internal politics, but it is better to admit failure privately at this stage than it is to release a poor game and damage the reputation of your company (hence publicly admitting your failure, compounded by the fact that you let a bad game design slip through).

Checkpoint 2.1 Technological Feasibility Study

This checkpoint answers the following question:

What Are The Performance Requirements?

Is the technology required for the game feasible for the configurations and machines of average consumers?

Game developers are lucky. They usually have access to the best equipment, the fastest machines, and the latest hardware. Games really fly when presented on such hardware. The end user, of course, is not so lucky, and they usually have average machines. Research indicates that consumers buy a completely new PC at most once every year. (This is usually the game head who always requires the latest and best hardware.) Your average consumer probably replaces their PC once every two to three years, making do with upgrades in the meantime. This book has been written on my main computer, a two-year-old Pentium 200 MHz MMX. This is still fine for my purposes. I feel no need to upgrade to a Pentium II monster machine, and neither will most normal consumers until it becomes absolutely necessary.

When you target a base machine, you should bear in mind that there is a two- to three-year spread of technology. To maximize potential revenues, you should aim for the center of this spread as the base configuration. If you specify a higher minimum specification, then you should have a good reason (e.g., you are id Software, and are just about to release the *Trinity* engine), or accept the potential loss in sales. Only the most groundbreaking of games can push the envelope and set a new standard base configuration. In general, for the average development timescale (18 months), the top machines of today will be slightly above the average specification by the time the product is released.

Checkpoint 2.2 Resource Availability Study

Checkpoint 1.2 defines the software and literature required for the project. The purpose of checkpoint 2.2 is to consolidate the results of the earlier checkpoint and to choose the initial members of the project group (as defined in Chapter 11). If possible, the project group should be selected from personnel who are most skilled in the type of project being written. The size of the team depends on the size of the project. A group of two or three may be ideal for a small project, but a larger project will require a larger group. Although this seems obvious, assigning a group to a project is always trickier than it appears: too large a group and you risk inefficiencies and extra expense; too small and you risk overworking the team members and causing delays. The idea is to try to get the balance right the first time. Changing things later on is usually more difficult, and always more expensive. (Chapter 21 will discuss this in more detail.)

If it was decided in checkpoint 1.1 that research was needed before the project can be started, then this is the point where it is decided whether or not to start the research project. If not, then this the end of the project. Tough cookies. Look on the bright side: it was most likely ahead of its time anyway. (Where are holographic displays when you need them!) So maybe it can wait for another day. Remember, however, that games should be gameplay oriented rather than technology oriented. That is why they are called *games*.

If it is decided to proceed with the research, then the project spawns one or more research projects. Checkpoints 3.0 and 3.1 (following) still apply, but from there on in we are waiting for the results from the research project(s). (These are discussed in Chapter 11, and again later in this chapter.)

Checkpoint 3.0 Draft Architecture Specification

The first thing to realize is that the architecture is a constantly evolving beast. Despite the continued insistence of some members of the development community, it is impossible to completely specify an architecture before a project is well underway. Our old friend, the 80/20 rule, rears its head yet again.

The best that we can reasonably expect is to complete approximately 80 percent of the project architecture before programming begins. Even this will come as a surprise to most developers in the games industry. Although it is more common to see projects defined to this level outside the games industry, these are generally the projects that succeed, and succeed well. Once the architecture is felt to be approximately 80 percent complete, the project can get underway. The remaining 20 percent will be completed during the course of the project. (This 20 percent usually consists of things that cannot be worked out fully in advance. This is covered in more detail in Part III.)

Checkpoint 3.1 Project Initialization

The 80-percent-complete architecture is enough to allow a preliminary schedule to be created. The work is divided into logical modules and divided among the groups as appropriate. The module is then broken down within the groups into a further schedule. This subschedule is then split into a series of interdependent tasks that are assigned to individual group members.

Development is an intricate set of interdependent tasks that need to be organized to minimize critical path problems. The analysis of these tasks and interdependencies comprise a major proportion of the project management time through development. Like the architecture, the schedule will be constantly updated during development. (This may involve rescaling individual schedules and shifting individual tasks between group members.) The important point is that this is a continuous tracking process that runs throughout the project. It is not to be used just when problems arise. As will be explained in Chapter 14 in Part III, the best troubleshooting is proactive, not reactive.

One of the major mistakes made in development is to treat the schedule as if it were etched in stone. Yet this notion prevails in the games industry. If you think about this for a moment, you will realize how ridiculous it is: how can anyone predict the events of every working day for the next 18 months? Usually, the only time a schedule is modified is in emergency mode: major readjustments are made when the project is in crisis, a case of "too little, too late."

As with navigating a ship, you achieve better results if you make small corrections to your course during the voyage rather than one large adjustment near the destination.

The Next Steps

At this stage, the project is ready to start, so you need to consider where to go next.

The next sections explain how to define the milestones and checkpoints for the rest of the project.

Defining Milestones

A typical game project can be partitioned into various subprojects. Each of these sub-projects will, in turn, have interproject dependencies and (on a more detailed level) intraproject dependencies.

A common mistake made with projects of all shapes and sizes is to assume that a milestone list is just that: a two-dimensional list that charts your progression from milestone A to milestone B, and so on. You should realize that the list is really the collapsed form of a multidimensional web of dependencies. When this web is collapsed into the form of a linear list, you lose all of that interdependency information, and only the end result of all the dependencies remains visible. This can reduce flexibility, so it can be useful to keep these complex interdependencies visible and up to date as long as possible.

Trying to visualize the complex web of information from a mere list of milestones is comparable to trying to construct an intricate, three-dimensional object from looking only at the shadow it casts. The shadow has lost some of the object's dimensionality; consequently, important information is lost in the process. So you can see it's crucial to have access to the project interdependency information while working to a milestone list.

The first step in discovering and defining these dependencies is to create milestone schedules for each of the subprojects. In this way, a multilevel hierarchy diagram of the project can be developed. Remember, a game project is a large and complex problem, and the obvious way to solve such a problem is to break it down into a number of smaller—and simpler—problems. Drawing a hierarchy of the project (and including the subprojects and their respective components) helps you get a good overall picture that you and the team can refer to.

Figure 12.4 shows a template of the overall hierarchy chart format I use. You can easily customized this chart for other structures, but the basic form allows a quick understanding of the position and status of a project within the hierarchy. A chart such as this placed on the company intranet site, as explained in Chapter 11, could also contain hyperlinks to the relevant documentation for each section. Being a hierarchical diagram, it can also act as a link in a bigger hierarchy that connects all the projects in the company, and thus help to define strategies for future development. By acknowledging these dependencies and creating the hierarchy diagram, it is easy to see the big picture and decide how to draw on already available resources, thus reducing unnecessary effort.

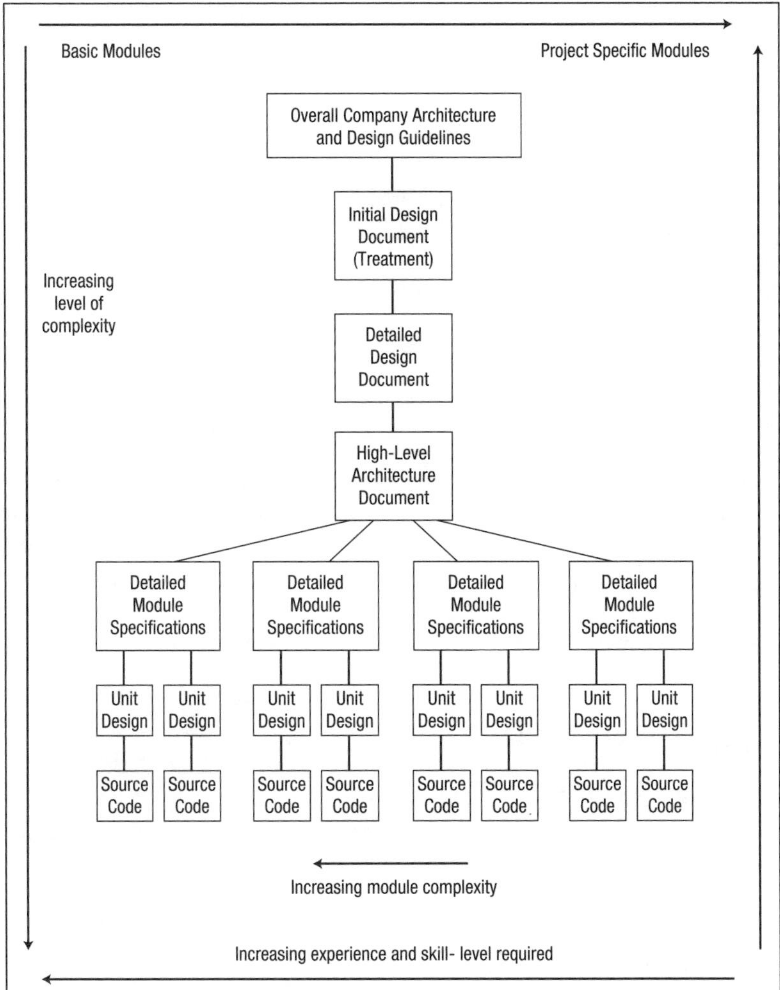

Figure 12.4
Format of a hierarchy chart.

The chief benefit of making this diagram publicly available is that it effectively eliminates the communication barriers within a company. Every member of every team is capable of knowing exactly what every other member of every team is doing. The ability to view this information at a high level, drilling down in detail if necessary, makes the visibility of all progress of the entire project easily available to everyone.

Figure 12.5 shows the hierarchy diagram for the *Balls!* project.

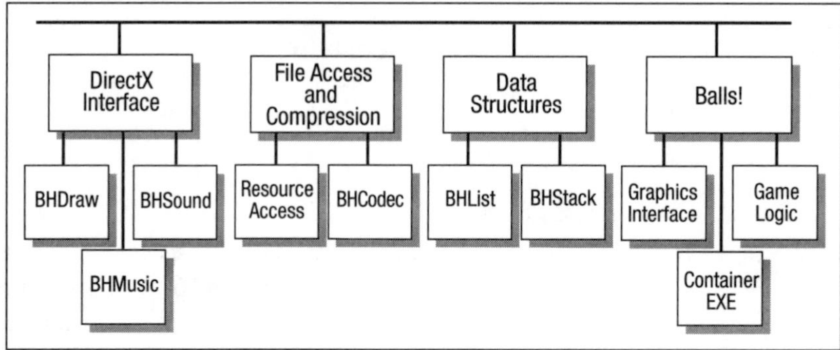

Figure 12.5
The *Balls!* project.

You know now that large projects need to be broken down into milestones. This is usually not too difficult when there is clearly defined functionality, but it is crucial to avoid milestones that encourage cutting corners in order to reach them. Instead, milestones should be defined around architectural points, so that the architectural integrity of the solution is maintained.

To better understand what makes a good milestone, we should pay some attention to what makes a bad one.

Bad Milestones

Bad milestones are those that do not provide any information about the progress of the project. These milestones can be described as fuzzy or are specified to such a superficial level as to be essentially meaningless.

Examples of fuzzy or superficial milestones are:

- Write a Visual Basic level editor to design worlds.
- Convert the graphics engine to 32-bit.
- Integrate two graphics systems so that we can see both on screen at once.
- Have a playable level up and running.
- Have five playable levels.
- Go into alpha testing.

The milestones in the list are real-life milestones taken from various projects. Some are obviously bad, but others are not so obvious. I'll examine each in turn and explain the good points, the bad points, and how the milestone should have been specified.

"Write A Visual Basic Level Editor To Design Worlds..."

This milestone (the same one as specified in Case Study 12.1) was for a flying shoot-'em-up game that featured a fractal-generated landscape. The milestone is far too general; it doesn't provide enough information. This particular milestone should have been changed to something similar to this: *Do the initial requirements gathering and feasibility study for a Visual Basic level editor to design worlds suitable for our game*.

From there, a schedule and a further set of architecture-based milestones should have been developed.

"Convert The Graphics Engine To 32-Bit..."

This is actually one of the better milestones from the list. The full specification was to convert a fully 16-bit set of C and assembly-language modules from a 16-bit architecture to take full advantage of a 32-bit processor. This is no real problem. In fact, it is also fairly clear and concise.

However, the problem is that it covered too large an area of work and didn't specify to what level to convert the code. For example, 16-bit code can be "converted" to 32-bit code by the simple application of a *thunking* layer to call the 16-bit functions from 32-bit code and handle all necessary conversions in the process. Alternatively, the milestone could mean a ground-up rewrite of all the code so that the engine was entirely 32-bit. So we have two solutions, each with advantages and disadvantages. The advantage of thunking is that it is reasonably quick and straightforward to implement. The disadvantages are the extra layer of overhead necessary to convert arguments and return codes for every function call and the fact that the code is still not fully 32-bit (and so may have to use slow memory-management calls to work around 16-bit limitations).

The advantages of the second method are the general improvements that can be achieved by such a conversion. The primary disadvantage is the amount of time such an extensive conversion usually takes.

This milestone should have specified the type of conversion required. In fact, it is also possible that not all the code would need to be converted. (For example, only the most time-critical code would need to be converted, whereas other code—such as loading code—could have used a thunking layer.)

This milestone should have been split into a number of smaller milestones that dealt with the task module by module. Doing so would have allowed a more sensible decision as to how to tackle the conversion, and would also have drastically increased visibility of the progress. In reality, this milestone disappeared from radar for a period of four months while it was being worked on. This is clearly unacceptable risk, and hence would have been well served by the use of checkpoints. In this case however, we were lucky. The programmer working on the engine was very competent and knew the engine inside and out. However, that much reliance on a single team member is a very bad thing (as discussed in Chapter 11).

"Integrate Two Graphics Systems So That We Can See Both Onscreen At Once..."

This is a similar problem to the previous one: there is simply not enough information. However, this milestone involves the source-level integration of two complex modules (meaning that standardized information has to be passed from one engine to the other), and the interfaces for this need to be defined. This milestone describes an entire project in its own right, rather than a small task in a larger project.

Think about the number of steps that are required to perform this task. First, you have to analyze what information you need to export from each engine to allow the other one to function. Which engine is going to have dominance? Is one meant to be a subset of the other? How will they interact? Do they have a shared screen buffer? What modifications will need to be made to the way the engines use the screen buffer? What impact will this have on other modules? How is this likely to affect future integration of modules?

Already you can imagine how the list of milestones and checkpoints could be built up using the guidelines in this chapter. By dividing the problem into atomic chunks, we can increase both the visibility and the accuracy of the project progress indicators. The idea is to attack the problem with enough questions so that the software planner's intent is perfectly clear.

"Have A Playable Level Up And Running..."

This is so fuzzy as to be virtually useless. What is meant exactly by "a playable level"?

I can't even imagine this milestone as being useful in any way. This is not based on any technical or architectural checkpoints; it is instead a visual check to chart progress. This is like an auto mechanic checking out your car by looking at the closed hood. To truly know how things are going, he needs to open the hood and take a look at the engine.

Milestones such as this one encourage shortcuts in order to get a visible result. Milestones that require visible checking such as this one are prone to undermining. Also, how on earth do you estimate how long such a milestone would take?

The obvious solution to this is not to use this type of milestone at all. Make it so that the visible features are the *results* of the milestone and not the *aims* of the milestone.

Applied to this example, this would result in milestones based on architectural goals. The combined effect of completed milestones would result in a playable level.

In this case, the following milestones may allow this to be achieved:

- If the level-editing software is complete, start to load and convert the level files into the internal data format (including all subsequent loading of referenced objects in the level data file and the handling of any unknown objects).
- Correct display of level based on the level data that is loaded from file, including handling of any unknown objects.
- Implement user control using keyboard and/or joystick, including simple menu navigation according to the design document and basic player control consistent with the physics system described in the architecture document.

This certainly is not all that would need to be achieved, but it should give you a rough idea of the difference between the two styles of creating a milestone.

"Have Five Playable Levels..."

This milestone directly followed the previous one. The idea was to ensure that the software was capable of loading generically defined levels (rather than being locked into the single test level of the previous milestone).

Unfortunately, the net result was that the previous milestone contained more hard-coded assumptions than would normally be present, mainly because the programmers could all see that they had been allowed time to clear up their own mess for the next milestone. So they could take all the shortcuts they wanted to hit the original milestone. Needless to say, doing so involved reworking a lot of code that could have been just written correctly in the first place.

The aims of this milestone should have been combined with the previous one and then split into a series of smaller checkpoints based on technical goals, with the net effect of these being to allow the loading of levels.

"Go Into Alpha Testing..."

This milestone is not specified in enough detail. What exactly is "alpha testing"? How do we distinguish "alpha testing" from the standard developer and integration testing that we have been performing throughout the project?

I would define *alpha testing* as the stage in which all components are "interface complete" (all the interfaces to all modules used in the project are implemented). It may not be a useful implementation yet, but at least the components compile without any undefined-link errors. Obviously, there has to be a certain level of functionality present by this stage, but—seeing as the development is likely to have progressed in a method similar to that described in this book—it is likely that there will be a useful level of core functionality.

Why These Milestones Are Flawed

The main underlying problem with these example milestones is their fuzziness. Most are not well specified, and they can be achieved in too many differing ways. Shortcuts can be taken, thus propagating mistakes and misunderstandings around the project and even beyond.

As already stated, these example milestones are okay for general project waypoints, but they leave a lot to be desired as detailed, payable-on-completion milestones. They would need to be split into many micro-milestones, each with a binary, on/off completion criteria.

The next sections cover some ways to define better milestones.

Good Milestones

Having examined what makes a milestone bad, we now turn our attention to what makes a milestone good. Much of this can be deduced from the previous discussion of bad milestones (what isn't bad, must be good), so we'll just summarize the features of a good milestone.

In general, a good milestone leaves no room for doubt. It is clear, concise, specified in technical and architectural terms, and is binary: it is either completely finished or completely unfinished.

Good milestones should be specified in detail. Each should specify in great depth, exactly where the project should be at a specific stage. Estimates should not be based on wishful thinking, but on (brutally) realistic assessments of development time that are based on experience and not on marketing requirements. It doesn't matter how important it is to get something out before Christmas. You cannot change the laws of physics, and equally you cannot change the length of time required to write good solid code. You can, however, attempt to predict and schedule it. This is much more successful than trying to rush the coding to meet an arbitrary deadline, a gamble which in most cases backfires.

Good estimates are achieved by first creating a hierarchy chart that tracks the complete project and all its interdependencies, and then tracing a two-dimensional route from the start to the finish, minimizing the delays due to dependency interlock on the way. Good milestones are specified at the technical level, with each milestone or checkpoint specifying a stage in the completion of an architectural module or submodule. The crisper and more defined the milestone, the better the project visibility. In order to accurately estimate the amount of time required for a milestone, you must divide the milestone into a list of subtasks that are small enough for you to reasonably and accurately estimate the time required to complete them. This usually means breaking the tasks down into those that will take a day or two to complete, providing you with a good basis for submilestone checkpoints if required. This is a skilled process. As you gain experience in the estimation process, you will find it's becoming easier to subdivide the milestones and provide accurate estimations.

A good milestone enhances project visibility and, upon completion, can provide a profound sense of achievement for the individuals involved.

In Case Study 12.3, this particular milestone had been inserted into the schedule after the architecture had been defined. It was a modification to the architecture to increase screen update times for systems with slower graphics cards. (Consider this modification as part of the 20 percent of the architecture that can't be known or guessed.) As you can see, it is unlike the usual sort of project milestone, because it is based on the architecture and is specified in plain English with a minimum of technical jargon. (Any jargon that is there can be easily explained.)

Due to the highly modular nature of the example project, the milestones were usually spaced approximately two weeks apart, and the checkpoints were usually from one to two days apart.

Case Study 12.3 A Real-Life Milestone

Balls!, the example demo project written with this book, was used as a proof of concept for all the development methods presented in this book.

This case study is an examination of one of the actual milestones set for the project and details how it was subdivided into checkpoints. As such, it will demonstrate how to implement a technical milestone.

The milestone:

Overview: Implement an object-level Z-buffer to increase speed update by minimizing unnecessary overdraw per frame.

Note: When performing this milestone, allow for reversion to the standard painters algorithm currently used by surrounding all Z-buffer code with conditional compile directives. When these directives are defined, the Z-buffer code will be activated, or else the code will perform exactly as it did before.

Checkpoint 1.0. Take the standard test levels and activate the timing code in order to time how long each frame is taking to draw. (0.5 days)

Checkpoint 2.0. Categorize the objects into the minimum number of sets. Each set should contain those objects that completely overdraw the others when the two-dimensional screen coordinates are the same. Flag exceptions to the rule (for example, transparent objects should not cause objects behind them to disappear). Provide a separate Z-buffer for each set of objects. (1 day)

Checkpoint 3.0. Implement "check" and "set" Z-buffer members in each of the effective classes. Each game object will have this member, so implement them as pure virtual members of the graphic object base class. Provide a standard implementation that takes a pointer to Z-buffer of the correct object set as a parameter as high up the hierarchy as possible, and override this for specific cases (such as transparent objects) where necessary. (1 day)

Checkpoint 4.0. Insert Z-buffer check and sets in the base class Prepare To Draw and Draw members. Aim to fail the Z-buffer test as soon as possible in the processing stage, so that the minimum amount of work is done on objects that are not going to be displayed. (1 day)

Checkpoint 5.0. Produce new timing information for the test levels and compare with the results achieved in checkpoint 1. Fully update the module design document to reflect the changes, and insert the new timing information. (1 day)

This is a direct transcript (although edited for brevity) of the milestone and checkpoints. I have modified checkpoint 1 as it also concerned reviewing and tidying up the code to ensure that all comments were up to date and that all dead code had been removed (because I hadn't worked on that particular module for some time). This doesn't concern us here, but it accounted for an extra day in the schedule.

Research Vs. Deadlines

At this stage, it is worth digressing into a quick discussion of research milestones.

Let's get the first thing out of the way: *research milestone* is an oxymoron.

A deadline specifies a fixed date and time that were presumably decided upon by a careful and informed consideration of the tasks to be performed. Research, on the other hand, is an investigation of things unknown. How is it possible to accurately schedule for the unknown? It's not, but you try explaining that to your average project manager and see what sort of response you get.

Research in this case should not be confused with requirements gathering. Research is the process of seeking out new techniques and algorithms for implementing an idea. Requirements gathering is the process of finding out what is required to build the product specified in the design document.

The main job of a vanilla programmer, as mentioned in a previous chapter, is to translate a set of detailed technical specifications into a program or program module. It is not to perform on-the-job research to meet a deadline. Research and deadlines are often mutually exclusive entities. If research is needed at this stage in a project, something has gone very wrong with the initial feasibility studies (which should have investigated these possibilities beforehand). All research is a risk: you risk getting no results. The later you are in the project when you take a research risk, the more unacceptable that risk is. In short, avoid all unnecessary research during the course of a project.

Evaluation Of Milestones

When it is time to evaluate a milestone, a number of people need to be able to sign it off as being completed. At the very least, these are the publishers, the company, and the project managers. Because of this, milestones tend to be based around results that can be visually demonstrated. As discussed previously, this is bad. Basing milestones on visual results means you often get just what you deserve: a program with a beautiful exterior and a hollow interior. Like a swan on water, it appears smooth and graceful on the surface, but paddles vigorously underneath. At the moment, this is how milestones are generally evaluated in the games industry. (Maybe this explains to some extent why games are now increasingly a triumph of style over content.)

The whole development life cycle is based around external appearances rather than internal structure. Although this is fine for a painting, it is certainly no good for a complex technical undertaking such as a computer program. Imagine what would happen if these criteria were used to build a bridge: it would be declared complete as soon as the architect liked the color of paint that had been used. So what if it collapsed the first time it was actually crossed?

It is in the best interests of all those who are concerned with evaluating milestones to accept a schedule based around the architecture specifications.

Milestones should be as technical as possible, and act as an integrated statement of the current architecture status. The architecture is the single most important entity in the game development; hence, milestones should be based around it. It's comparable to a skeleton: it needs to be properly developed or the creature will be deformed, no matter how attractive the flesh covering it. (If you've seen the movies *The Fly* and *The Fly II*, then you'll know exactly what I mean here. It's not a pretty sight.)

Even if you cannot avoid using technical terms when writing your milestones, use as much plain and concise English as possible. If you write carefully, even the most nontechnical person can understand the increased benefit and visibility that concrete technical milestones provide to a project. In general, the architect, the game designer, and the publisher are the most important milestone reviewers. It is important to be impartial, and the milestones should also be evaluated primarily from a strong technical standpoint.

The members of the group responsible for the milestone should present their case as to why the milestone is completed, and it is the task of the internal reviewers to act as a devil's advocate and try to prove that the milestone is not complete. Be strict on this: an incomplete milestone that has been flagged as complete tends to rear its head later in the most unexpected and inconvenient way (Murphy's Law of incomplete milestones).

Gaining a complete understanding of what a technical milestone represents is not always immediately straightforward, especially for a nontechnical person. It is the task of the group responsible to present and explain the milestone in such a way as to enable even the office cat to understand the significance and how it fits into the grand plan.

Chapter 13
Procedures And "Process"

Key Topics:

- ***Procedures***
- ***"Process"***
- ***Source control and code reviews***
- ***The importance of information transmission***
- ***Proactive and reactive information***

In this chapter, we'll discuss the procedures and practices that are required for the efficient and cost-effective use of the software factory concept.

These procedures and practices are not, however, restricted to the software factory, as they produce benefits for all nontrivial development. Much software in development (and game software in particular) has no real procedural approach to development. The growth of the average game project tends to be only somewhat organized and very organic in nature.

This chapter covers the aspects of the development process that are relevant to management, the areas in which management is going to want status reports and control. Management's interest is the primary reason for procedures and practices.

Managers want to be able to get accurate information and status reports, and to act on this information without disrupting development. In the same manner, developers don't want managers to be able to indiscriminately wade in and disrupt the development process by asking lots of pointless and time-wasting questions.

These procedures and practices will cover the interfaces and areas of interaction so that information can be transmitted in a timely fashion and defined control paths can be used to steer the course of development.

The "process" doesn't need to be as bad as you may think, as it is mostly a matter of common sense. However, the best sort of common sense is that which is written down so that everyone is clear as to what the local idea of "common sense" is. Common sense breaks down when everyone has a different idea of what it is.

The extent to which these procedures are implemented will depend on the needs of the project. A critical project will need a rigid approach, while a less critical one can afford to be slightly more relaxed.

Procedures

The types of procedures discussed in this chapter are basically controls and measures to minimize wasted effort and to weed out low-quality work before it pollutes the project.

The following list of procedures is recommended to maintain accurate project information and control during the lifetime of the project. Each of the procedures is described in the next few sections.

- design reviews
- document reviews
- technical reviews
- code reviews
- unit testing
- integration testing
- system testing
- configuration testing
- regression testing

Overall, reviews are better at finding defects than is just testing alone, as long as the reviews remain focused on *detecting* defects rather than *correcting* them. An added benefit is that reviews also tend to find different types of errors than those found in testing.

Reviews

The format of a review is roughly the same regardless of the material being reviewed.

The two classes of review are formal and informal. Which class you'll use depends on the nature of the work being reviewed. This is context sensitive, and the ratio of formal to informal reviews will also depend on the situation (all of which is usually decided by the project manager when assigning tasks, but individuals may also be able to contribute to the decision). After all, the project manager knows how complex the work really is, and so he or she should be able to say which type of review would be ideal. The important point is that *no* work should go unchecked. Reviews are usually the first thing to fall by the wayside if the project is suffering from time pressures. This is invariably a mistake. Short-term savings will add up to long-term pain.

It's *not* good enough to just insert unchecked work into the project and assume that it is okay if the whole thing doesn't crash. This "method" does not provide any information on the impact the work will have on the project schedule, or how well the work has been performed. Reviewing weeds out obvious errors at an early stage—before they can get *into* the project—and it is one of the best preventative measures for keeping out substandard and shoddy work.

In projects without review procedures, substandard work can go undetected for a long time. This kind of problem shows up much later, usually when someone else has to maintain or update the affected area. By this time, who knows how far the poison has spread? Later work may have depended on the original, quirky work, and the evil was thus perpetuated.

Reviews have other benefits, too: they allow the sharing and dissemination of information among the employees. Because the work is being discussed and reviewed in a group, the information is naturally transferred among the team, which greatly reduces risk.

Informal Reviews

Informal reviews are very simple, with no real paperwork and no complex and time-consuming meetings.

An informal review involves gathering a couple of team members around your monitor and talking them through your work, giving a demonstration where applicable.

These reviews can be done in several ways. For example, in the case of an informal code or design review, you can choose from a number of different approaches, such as walkthroughs and inspections, although these can also be used for formal reviews as well.

Walkthroughs are directed by the author of the work and are mainly used when the work to be reviewed is fairly simple and easily understood. Walkthroughs have the advantage of being quick and easy, as its purpose is just to bash out the technical quality of the work. It is not really an assessment; it is more of a request for comments (RFC). The walkthrough is also a great opportunity for sharing skills and experience. If a reviewer has a better idea for how to implement the work, it can be passed on to the author. The converse is also true: sometimes the reviewers will learn some new tricks.

Information transmission helps to spread the load of knowledge more evenly, thus reducing the reliance of the team on one person. In theory, every one of the employees should be working to make themselves obsolete. No one person should be critical. Obviously, for this to work, there should be no undue pressure and stress from management. The belief that one can get more work out of people by putting them under undue pressure is false. For people to work their best, they must be as relaxed and secure as possible, while still realizing the importance of what they are doing and the need for deadlines to be met. This is enough pressure without extra arm twisting by the management.

However, all is not rosy with walkthroughs, as they are potentially the least effective way of presenting a review. According to statistics, the effectiveness of walkthroughs alone varies wildly, finding only between 30 and 70 percent of errors.

One of the reviewers is usually your immediate technical manager, and he or she will be able to give your work the seal of approval. Once this is done, and any issues or questions have been discussed and resolved, then the work can be inserted into the project's main repository. The important thing here is that the technical manager should not exert managerial authority, or it soon changes into something else, with the author feeling as if he needs to glorify his work in order to prove himself. It shouldn't be like that. The purpose is just to discuss the work and to detect any obvious defects.

On the other hand, inspections are almost the reverse of a walkthrough. Rather than have the author talk through the work, the technical manager takes the reins and performs the walkthrough himself. This has the advantage that a fresh eye examining the work may be able to spot problems that the author had missed through sheer "overfamiliarity" with the material. The disadvantage of this type of inspection, however, is that it can take longer to perform, but at least it stands a greater chance of finding defects.

If, during the review, someone detected an issue that was later resolved by some action or change, then the work needs to be reviewed again by the original reviewers, including the one who requested the change in the first place. Whether the subsequent review is formal or informal very much depends on the nature of the change. Large changes require formal reviews, but minor tweaks and clarifications merit only another informal review. Change control, a large topic in its own right, is discussed in Chapter 14.

The danger of informal reviews is that they can become *too* informal. Thus, it is always a good idea to make sure that responsible people are in charge of these reviews, and that informal reviews are also combined with a fair proportion of formal reviews. An ineffective informal review can be worse than having no review at all, instilling a false sense of security in the team and causing no end of trouble.

Formal Reviews

Four or five people are usually involved in a review. The members of this review team are chosen by an appropriate group lead and should include the person whose work is being reviewed. Anything less is ineffective and anything more is inefficient.

The author's responsibility is to ensure that all reviewers have the information they need before the review begins, which may involve distributing printed copies of work and answering any questions that the reviewers may have before coming to the review.

The responsibilities of the reviewers are to ensure that they are familiar with the material to be reviewed. The actual purpose of a review meeting is not to *review* the work; this would take up too much time. The purpose of the review meeting is to discuss the reviews that the reviewers performed *before* the meeting.

So, before the meeting, the reviewers should complete a review form that lists the points they intend to raise in the meeting. Depending on the size of the review, they should spend an hour or two reading the material. A sample review form is given in Appendix A, and as an RTF (Rich Text Format) document on the CD-ROM.

Basically, the review form is used as a reminder to the reviewers, so that they don't forget any of the observations. The comments are noted down on the sheet and a severity code is given, with A being the most serious defect and E being the least. (Of course, you can choose your own grading scheme, but this is one of the most common and is simple to understand. It's almost like being back in school!)

The work should be reviewed by a number of criteria, of which "fitness for purpose" is the main one. The work should be what was asked for. Conformance to project and company standards is also important, but functionality is obviously the top priority.

In the meeting, each of the points on the reviewers' review forms is discussed. The meeting starts with a presentation by the person whose work is being reviewed. This presentation will be an overview of the work and the implementation decisions that were involved in it.

One point that many people seem to miss is that criticism in reviews is *not* a personal attack on either the individual or the work performed by that individual. The object of a review is to get second opinions in an attempt to weed out defective work. Focusing a group of minds on the same problem may spot errors more easily. The focus of the reviews needs to be on *finding* the errors; this meeting is not the place to discuss any solutions. Doing so would be a distraction, and solutions do not need to be immediately addressed.

The actual review meeting itself is actually rather insignificant in the search for defects. It just serves as a common point for sharing information from the independent reviews that were performed before the meeting. Ninety percent of defects found in the review process are found *before* the meeting.

Once all the points on the review forms have been discussed, they are given an "action status." Basically, the points are either accepted or rejected. If they are accepted, then the author has to perform the corrective work to the satisfaction of the person who raised the point. In cases in which more than one reviewer raised the same point, only one of them takes "ownership" of it. All the points are then consolidated into an electronic review form, which is stored with the work to be checked. If the changes affect the functionality in a significant way (say, if it affects other areas), then a change control meeting needs to be convened to control and limit any adverse effects.

Depending on the nature of the required changes, another formal review may be necessary. In this case, the same reviewers should be used. If the required changes are minor, then informal reviews should suffice. The author needs to have each reviewer sign off each of their points to be addressed. Once this is accomplished, the work can then be inserted into the main body of the project.

This may all sound like a long-winded process, and—to tell you the truth—it is. However, I have always found that the time saved by preventing substandard work from entering the project outweighs the time spent on reviews.

I have also found that, if someone knows that their work will be reviewed, they will work with more care and attention to detail, and take more pride in what they are doing. This increased attention has a positive benefit for morale. People know that the work going into the project is checked, and the project is therefore of a higher standard (and the risk is also substantially reduced). For these reasons, reviews have been shown to increase productivity by approximately 20 percent. Never underestimate the positive effects that this could have on employee morale and output.

Because of the nature of game development, there is a natural resistance to the imposition of reviews. The most effective way to combat this resistance is to collect statistics about the number of defects found by reviews, and the average time spent finding them. These statistics, compared with the amount of time (and money) that would have been spent fixing these defects later in the development cycle, cannot really be argued with.

Testing In General

While I have seen projects that have no form of review system, I have never seen a project that had no form of *testing* system.

I have seen projects with ineffective testing, and these are usually easy to spot. When a game is released full of bugs, it is usually for one of two reasons: the testing was simply not up to scratch; or the development team had simply run out of time, and the publishers had had enough and published anyway, bugs and all. Here, we are concerned with the first scenario: substandard testing.

Testing is the process of finding errors. How many errors can you expect to find in code? The jury is out on the exact figure, but the industry average is roughly 15 to 50 errors for every thousand lines of code. I would suspect that this is slightly higher for the games industry, although this could be offset by the fact that games tend to be small- and medium-sized projects.

Testing looks for a number of errors that can have occurred at any of the stages of development, but, in general, testing can detect errors at only the prototyping and code implementation stages. Bear in mind that, the longer a defect lies undiscovered, the more expensive it will be to fix. If a defect occurs in the design phase, fixing it when the implementation is half complete is obviously going to much more expensive than if it had been found when it occurred back in the design phase.

In fact, this is the main reason to implement process. It allows you to attempt "phase containment." No, that's not something out of Star Trek (although it could be); phase containment means to detect and correct defects in the phase in which they were created. A standard industry statistic holds that a defect can cost up to 200 times as much to fix if it is not discovered in the same phase that it was created in. Obviously, it makes good sense to detect and fix the defects as soon as possible.

Also remember that testing alone has no direct effect on the quality of the software. Trying to improve the software quality by testing alone is ineffective; it just acts as an *indicator* of the quality. It must be followed up with decisive measures to improve the quality by other means, so that this extra effort can be reflected in the next test cycle.

Testing in this context generally refers to code, and so the following sections are geared towards testing code.

Informal Tests

Informal tests are not in the same league as informal reviews. There's no need to get a group of peers crowded around the monitor, because an informal test is simply any test that a developer does while developing a code module.

Every developer periodically compiles and tests code while developing a program (or at least I hope they do!). This is a good start, but it is not sufficient to prevent bugs creeping into a program—particularly at the module integration stage.

Most game development projects I have seen have used only this sort of testing, along with a healthy dose of playtesting towards the end of the project. This is usually only adequate.

In order to improve informal testing, a number of automatic error-detecting applications (such as NuMega *BoundsChecker*) and programming techniques can be used to catch the obvious errors.

It can work, but, with the addition of at least some formal testing procedures, the risk can be reduced substantially. Although the extent to which formal testing is implemented is dependent upon the nature of the work, all the testing stages that are discussed here should be implemented in one form or the other.

Formal Tests

Formal tests are fairly similar to informal tests except that they are more structured.

A test script is provided for a particular module to exhaustively test all features and functions of that module. The script is usually written by the software planner with the module's developer.

Test scripts are written in a particular way. (A sample test script is given in Appendix A, and an RTF document is included on the CD-ROM.) The tests should be designed so that they exercise *all* the code paths in the module. Because this is quite a difficult task to do correctly, the test script itself is subject to review.

Three main types of testing can be used to do this: *positive*, *negative*, and *ad hoc*.

Positive testing checks for the intended behavior, so these tests are geared to produce the expected results from the module. An example of positive testing is passing sets of valid coordinates to a triangle-drawing module, and expecting to see the correct triangle produced.

Negative testing checks for *un*expected behavior, and these tests are geared to produce exception and error-handling conditions. An example of negative testing is to pass a triangle-drawing module three points with exactly the same value, or three points in a straight line. Boundary conditions should also be tested. What happens when you pass very large values (positive and negative)? What about very small values? Or zero values?

When planning tests, try to consider every type of input into the system, both valid and invalid. The object is to stress the system as much as possible; throw everything you can at it. You may not find all the errors, but you'll weed out all but the trickiest problems.

Ad hoc testing is effectively random. The tester plays with the module and checks whether he or she gets the expected results. These tests are just to throw at the module whatever input the tester feels like. An example is to pass sets of random points to the triangle-drawing module, and check each output triangle to ensure that it appears correctly.

Many organizations use only one of these three methods, but, for truly effective testing, all three should be used. If a test script is written so that the three types of test are segregated, then the tester has the choice of which tests to perform.

When a test script is executed, the results should be recorded in electronic form. The tests should be worded so that the result can be expressed by true or false responses. In some cases, further details are required in order to clarify results (especially if a test fails).

If a test fails, then further action has to be taken. A test can fail for two reasons: a problem with the code, or a problem with the test. The action in both cases is the same. The tester raises a problem report, and the problem-fixing cycle begins again.

Unit Testing

Unit testing is the first wave of testing that the developer performs, and it is a type of clear box testing, in which the tester has full knowledge of the internals of the material being tested. Statistics show that, on average, unit testing can find approximately half of the errors present in a code module.

Unit testing is usually performed with the aid of a *test harness*, a simple program that is designed to exercise every feature of a module. This may be simple and noninteractive, or it may be more advanced and allow the configuration of input parameters.

Unit testing means exactly what it says. It is testing in isolation. This prevents any possible interactions with other, possibly error-prone modules. This is why the test harness is used, and is also why the test harness is as simple as possible. You don't want to spend time debugging the test harness! In a number of cases, when I have found an error in the test results, it has been due to an error in the test data I was using! Having spent hours searching for a phantom problem in the code, finding that the problem was in the test data was incredibly frustrating. (I tried to look at it as an experience-building exercise, I really did, but I would not recommend it as a course of action if you value your sanity.)

Unit testing can operate at several levels. If we take C++ as an example, then unit testing can be performed at the *method* level or at the *object* level. For those unfamiliar with object-oriented technology (where have you been?), an object is a logical package of data and code that acts on that data. The code is divided into methods that are analogous to functions in procedural programming. Object-level testing is black box testing, whereas method-level testing is clear box testing.

Of course, testing cannot prove that a module is free of defects. A test can prove only that a module has errors. The important rule to remember is that if a test indicates that a module is free of defects, then it is much more likely to be due to an inadequacy in the test itself. Maybe not enough cases are being covered, or maybe there is an error in the test.

It is difficult for developers to get themselves into the mindset that is required for testing. A successful test finds broken code; how many developers do you know who actively want to break their code?

Actually, this is a loaded question; the answer should be *all of them*. If not, then the developers are not being thorough. Unfortunately, I am aware of some developers who write code and immediately declare it finished. They seem to have an aversion to finding errors in their own code as this seems to be an indication of weakness.

This is particularly prevalent in the games industry, where the software wolves are out in force. In some companies, showing any sign of weakness is like giving permission to be ripped to pieces, leaving your torn carcass to be picked clean by the vultures.

Everybody makes mistakes. It is completely natural, but what is more of a mistake: finding and correcting an error in your own code (admitting your own fallibility), or refusing to accept that you can make errors, and not even checking fully?

Developers should be actively looking to break their own code. They are required to approach the testing *assuming* that the code is riddled with bugs; in fact, they should actually *want* to find errors. Look at it this way: who would you rather find errors in your code? You, or someone else?

If the assumption is made that there are no problems to be found, chances are none *will* be found. This is not because the errors aren't there; it is because the developer would not have looked long and hard enough at the right places.

Integration Testing

Integration testing is the next level of testing performed by the developer, although it can also be performed by a member of the test team. If a test team member does it, then it is a black box test. If a developer performs the test, then it is a clear box test. (It is preferable to have both the developer and the tester perform the integration testing, but sometimes this is not possible. However, integration testing is a halfway house between unit testing and system testing, so this is not a hard-and-fast rule.)

Integration testing is the act of testing the integration of a new code module with the existing code base. Does it cause compile problems? Are there namespace clashes? Does it even work?

The integration test is—by necessity—less detailed than the unit test, because it is a test of how the module interoperates in the code environment. You could almost say that it is a "field test" of the module.

The focus of the integration test is to resolve technical issues with the integration of the new module. In theory, the module itself should be fairly free of error due to the unit testing. During integration, problems always show up in great style that did not manifest themselves during unit testing. These can be the most frustrating and difficult to find, and they should serve as a good incentive to catch as many errors as possible before this stage. You definitely want to try to find them before the system test stage. If you think that diagnosing errors during integration is difficult, then you should try finding the little buggers during system test!

The test used should be similar to that used in the unit test. A script should be written that exercises each of the code paths.

The one hard-and-fast rule for integration testing is to integrate only one module at a time. It's a simple and obvious rule: it is exponentially more difficult to locate the source of an error if you are integrating two or more untested modules. They may *both* be full of errors, or they may interact with each other in unforeseen ways. Either way, it's territory you don't want to get into.

The good news is that system integration using object-oriented architecture is nowhere near as difficult as it used to be in the bad old days of procedural programming. Object-oriented techniques can make all this much easier. Game development has been slow to catch on to these techniques, mainly because object-oriented applications were considered slow bloatware, and the compilers were considered to create inefficient code.

This may have been valid in the bad old days, but, because we are now in an era in which we have to cooperate with an operating system, consistently wringing every last ounce of performance out of a system is exponentially more difficult than it used to be. Besides, with object-oriented APIs such as DirectX acting as an insulating layer between the game and the underlying hardware, it makes more sense to use a programming language that makes development easier.

Once the integration test is complete, the module can be signed off. It is then considered part of the code base.

System Testing

System testing is something that should be performed at least daily. If this is not possible, then the *absolute* minimum interval is once a week. Any less than this and the system test turnaround becomes ineffective. The code will have changed so much in one week that it becomes difficult to apply fixes to broken code that may have already been modified or had other code built upon it. The frequency of system test turnaround means that, in some cases, not all of the system test can be performed. This usually applies only to the largest projects, and most games should be able to be system tested daily.

In order to facilitate this, the software needs to be buildable every day. In fact, this is a major requirement, irrespective of whether system testing is performed daily or not. The software should always be in a buildable state. This doesn't mean it should be fully functional; subsystems may not be present, in which case they should be stubbed out. Stubbed out is where the interface is defined, but the functionality is not implemented, so it is replaced with 'stub functions' that output a debug message, or throw an error exception, depending on the importance of the interface. The architecture has been completely defined for the most part, so this is within easy reach of the developers.

The build is initially given a *smoke test* by the test team to see if it is stable enough to being testing. A smoke test takes its name from the electronic engineers method of testing newly constructed equipment to see if it is working: they switch it on, and, if it starts smoking, it doesn't work.

The build is rejected if it fails the smoke test. The developers' highest priority then becomes fixing the build. The longer the build remains broken, the more time is wasted for the test team. This is not a good situation.

Once the build is working, it is labeled within the source control system. All good source control software allows you to take a snapshot of the state of the archive so it can be recreated later, even if further files have been added afterwards. Creating at least a daily snapshot is important, because it ensures that the testing team is working with a build that is (at most) one day old.

A sensible daily scheduling system for this is to ensure that all developers have achieved sign-off by midafternoon. The resulting code and modules are then checked into the source control system, and a complete system build is performed.

The smoke test is performed the same afternoon, and the system test is performed by the testers the following day. The frequency of building the game is limited to the length of time required by the system testers to perform all the tests.

The system test should be conducted at two levels. The first level is to run test scripts that check whether all the completed functionality is working as advertised. (This is effectively the *negative* and *positive* testing part of the system test.) These test scripts are most likely written by the software architect; at this level of testing, it is mainly architectural design errors rather than low-level coding errors. Of course, some integration issues that slipped through the integration testing activity are also likely to show up here.

The second level of the system test corresponds to the ad hoc testing. The testers should play the game and test all the features of the program as they would expect an end user to. They should use the manual to install and configure the game, and follow the game instructions therein to see if they can play it.

Doing so serves two purposes: trapping any errors that may be lurking in the code and providing preliminary playtesting information. Obviously, this may not be much help if the game is at a very early stage, but, as the project progresses, it will become increasingly useful.

The results from the system test are recorded electronically, and any defects are reported to the project manager for assignment to the relevant employee.

Configuration Testing

Configuration testing is an extension of the system test. It is the testing of the application on a range of different hardware configurations.

This is particularly important for games as they are usually more dependent on hardware than is a standard application. The range of machines tested should encompass a fair representation of what is in the marketplace: cutting-edge power monsters, weak and feeble Pentiums with low resources, and everything in between.

And, yes, I know that DirectX and other APIs were supposed to solve all the hardware-compatibility problems. But, if you believe that, you're gullible enough to believe anything. (If this is the case, email the authors. Have we got an investment opportunity for you!)

To be honest, this level of configuration testing is usually beyond the resource capability of the average development studio. However, independent testing houses can perform this sort of testing for you.

If resources are not available in-house, then these independent testing houses could be your best option (and is a lot better than releasing a game that works only on your development machines and not on anyone else's).

Regression Testing

Regression testing is not really a type of test in its own right; it is instead a technique that is applied to all the other tests presented here.

Regression testing is the act of re-running the tests using the same test data that was used on previous revisions of the module.

The idea of regression testing is to ensure that the module hasn't regressed to an earlier form. One of the most common types of error is the reintroduction of previous defects. The regression test checks to see whether any old errors have been introduced, and it is applicable to all the previous test types.

"Process"

To begin with, we will examine a general overview of development. At each stage of development, there is a need to generate accurate status information. Hence, there is a need for a set of procedures such as those described previously to make this happen.

Figure 13.1 shows the main phases of development in a vague fashion. In reality, things are more complex, with multiple interweaving strands of the main development phases occurring simultaneously. The diagram does not attempt to show this, but features only the points where an information-transmission interface—and therefore, "process"—is required. The rest of this chapter is devoted to the discussion of how to implement these measures, making method out of the madness.

Process is usually viewed with a high measure of disdain among the development community at large. Within the game-writing sector of the development community, it is viewed with even more scorn. Process is seen as a complete Waste Of Time (WOT) that subtracts from the amount of Really Useful Work (RUW) that can be done.

Examples of WOTs include rewriting old code to be compatible with new code, rewriting of architectures, and uncontrolled revisions and modifications.

These developers believe that process is purely unnecessary overhead. They do not take into account the amount of extra work that is prevented by the processes.

Figure 13.2 shows how they believe the way that work is distributed on a standard project. Project work consists solely of writing new code and fixing old code (RUW), with a small amount of overhead caused by having to deal with team dynamics: meetings, duplication of other people's work, and other WOTs.

Figure 13.3 shows what effect that these developers believe process has on a project. They believe that the process subtracts directly from the RUW in a one-to-one ratio. For every

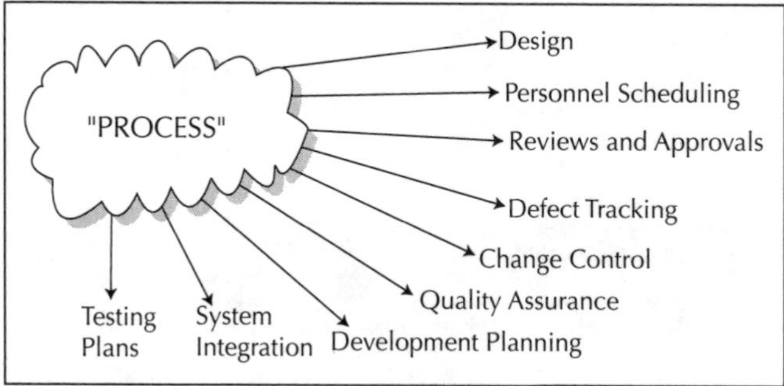

Figure 13.1
What is "Process"?

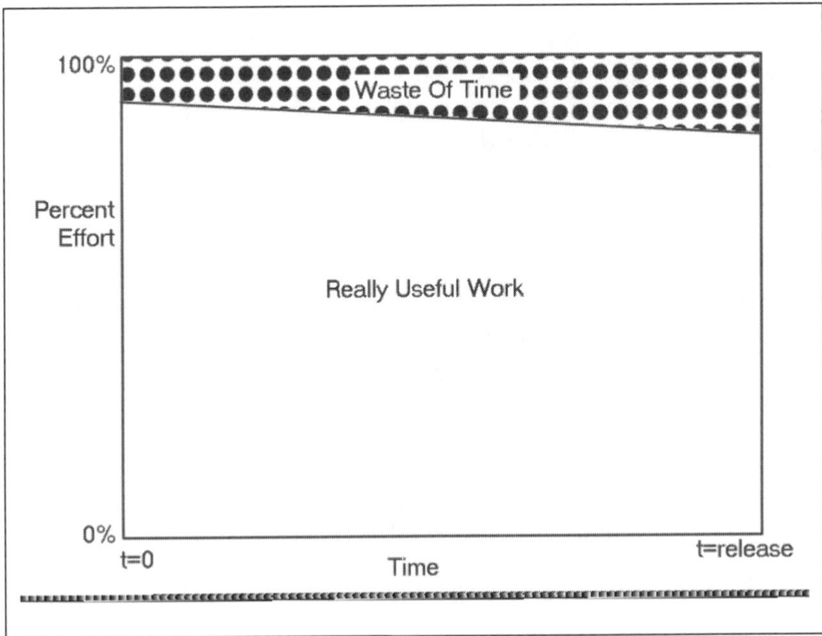

Figure 13.2
Erroneous view of effort expenditure on a project without any process.

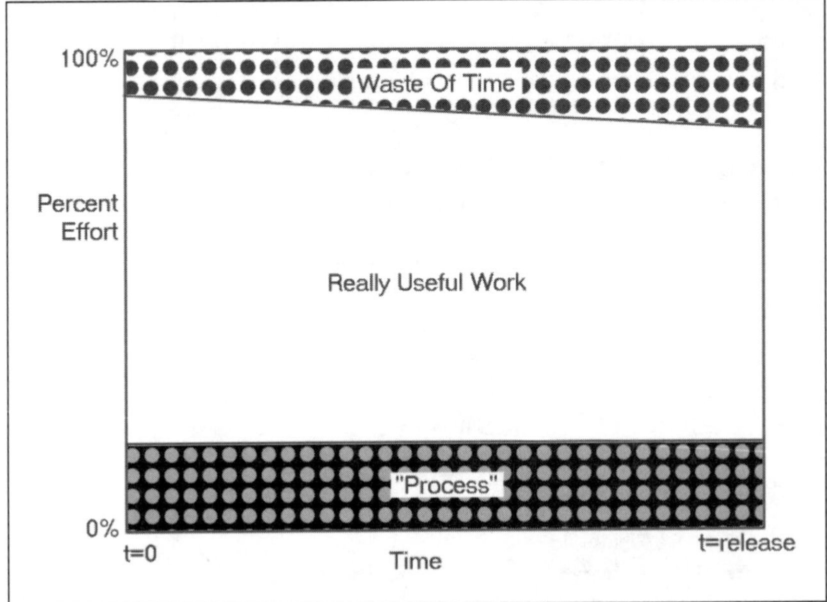

Figure 13.3
Erroneous view of effort expenditure on a project with process.

hour of process endured, the project loses one hour of RUW. This can be true if the process used is badly suited to the project, but, in cases in which it is well suited, the situation portrayed in the diagram is false.

Figure 13.4 shows the true work distribution on a project with no process. As the project becomes bigger and closer to completion, the amount of WOTs increase. The rate of increase depends on the competence of the people working on the project and a fair degree of luck.

Figure 13.4 is shown for the average project. The amount of WOTs increase in proportion with the number of developers on the project. The more potential for interaction between team members, the more potential there is for foul-ups.

The effect of process (Figure 13.5)—if the procedures in use are well chosen for the project—is to increase the efficiency of work and reduce the amount of WOTs. Obviously, these cannot be completely eliminated—there will always be unproductive work—but the verification and cross-checking (as well as the visibility) provided by good procedures will reduce this to the minimum.

The process must scale with the amount of staff on the project. If this is done effectively, then the ratios of process, WOTs, and RUWs remain fairly constant.

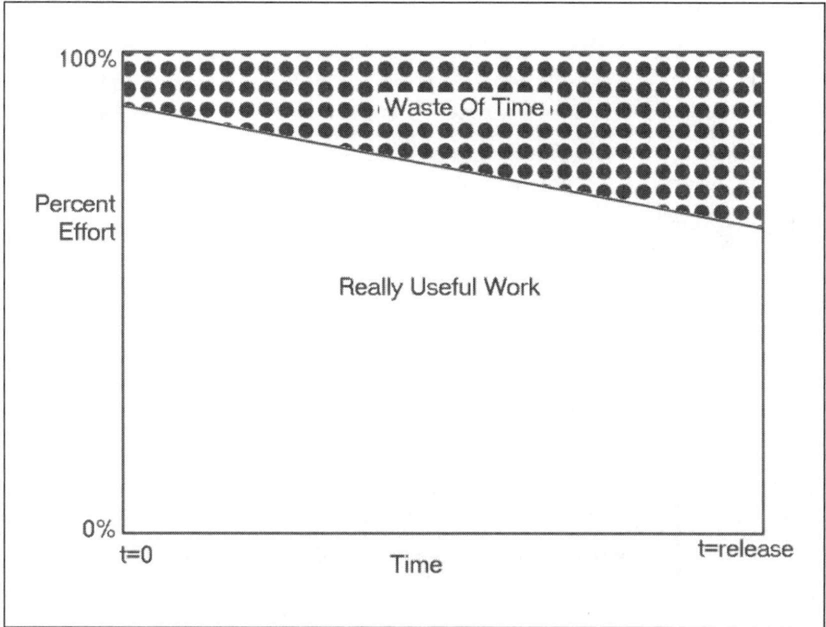

Figure 13.4
Accurate view of effort expenditure on a project without any process.

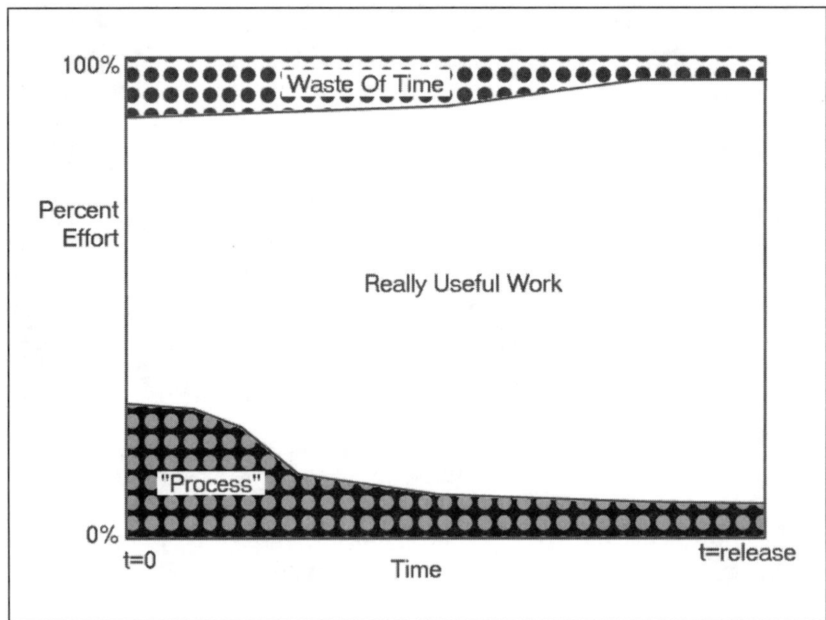

Figure 13.5
Accurate view of effort expenditure on a project with process.

The trouble with process is that it is really difficult to achieve a balance between the amount of process and the amount of work. In many cases, rigid formulaic procedures are used without any account taken of the type of project and the needs of the developers. In such situations, the process is worse than useless, because it has a demoralizing effect on the developers. The process should be there to serve the project team; the project team should not be slaves to the process.

The "knee-jerk" problem in Case Study 13.1 is common. A project that starts without process and then tries to curb the ensuing problems by adding it at a later date is subject to this common ailment.

This situation is shown in Figure 13.6.

The late introduction of the process in combination with the backlogged work grinds the project to a halt. The project is usually cancelled at this point, but, in Case Study 13.1, this was not possible, due to the critical importance of the project. Game development projects are not usually so critical, so such a project would most likely have been cancelled at this point.

Note that Figure 13.6 shows the project actually reaching its release date by the point that process and WOTs consume 100 percent of the expended effort. In this sort of situation, this point can be reached before the projected release date, resulting in a high probability of cancellation unless some fairly major remedial action is taken. This sort of drastic action is covered in Chapter 14.

Case Study 13.1 Process Gone Mad

While working on a large-scale banking project, I discovered that too much process can be as destructive (if not more so) than too little.

The development procedure for the particular suite of applications was fully documented, and there were an intricate set of rules to follow, laid out in a 300-page document.

This is ridiculous! Three hundred pages? What sort of process requires 300 pages to tell a developer how to write code for a specific project? Worse still, the process tracking system had been written in-house using WordBasic (the programming language that comes with Microsoft Word), which was not up to the task.

Maintaining a code module sometimes required more than 20 pages of paperwork, even in the case of a small one-line change. Forms had to be completed in duplicate and sometimes in triplicate. These then had to be printed, distributed to at least five people, and the electronic copies placed in a disparate set of directories, the names of which were constructed using some arcane rules that were defined somewhere in the 300-page manual.

This was just to make a small change to a code module. You can imagine the red tape required to create a new module, and I won't even go into the red tape that bound the testing team.

This was simply too much process. The rules were so arcane and complex that no one person had a complete grasp of the entire procedure. Mistakes were made, shortcuts were taken, and procedures were ignored.

The situation rapidly became worse than if there had been no procedure, because the state of the project was unguessable. Because of the complexity, the status documentation lagged behind the code by approximately three months. Modules would be changed, and documentation would not be updated to match, causing problems for the next poor soul. These problems rapidly compounded to make the whole situation unmanageable.

The history of this project reveals what had happened to make it like this. In the beginning was a small core team with minimal (if any) process. As the complexity of the project increased, more staff had been added, but the structures and processes required to support them had lagged behind. After time, the number of new staff members reached critical mass and caused a crisis whereby the bug count was reaching the high two-thousands, provoking a knee-jerk response: the instigation of the Draconian procedures.

The belief was that these procedures would ensure that no new bugs were introduced while the number of bugs already present were reduced. (This may have been true, but not for the right reasons! The procedures were so complex that they slowed development to a crawl so that no code got written.)

Unfortunately, it was not until new management was brought in that the situation changed. The amount of process was slashed, and each unnecessary and overblown procedure was pared down to the minimum needed to maintain control.

After this, the project started to get back on track, and we were able to fit some useful work in between the procedures.

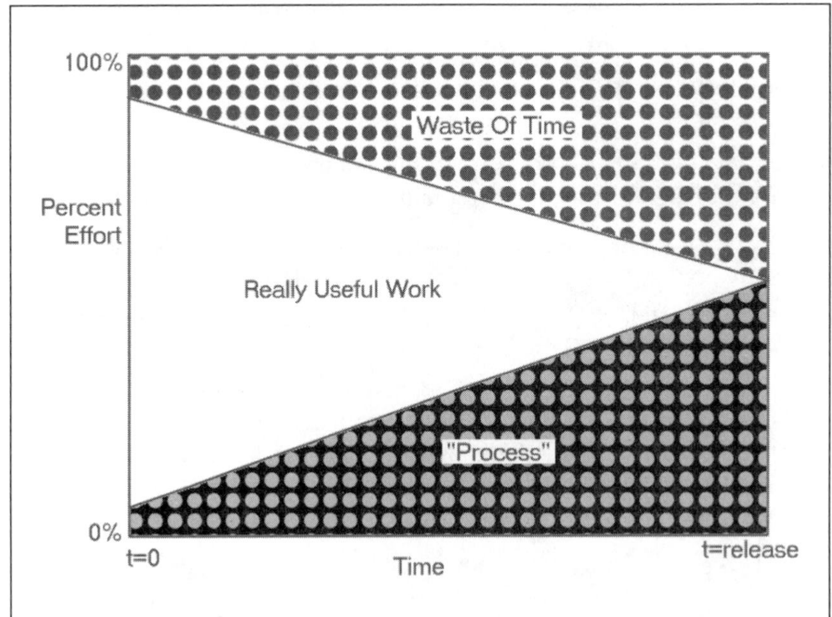

Figure 13.6
The effect of late introduction of process on effort expenditure.

In general, however, the introduction of process to a "virgin team" is likely to cause problems. The main problems are going to arise from a restricted understanding of exactly what process is and what it is for (a mental inertia that takes some time to overcome). There is likely to be resentment and resistance to the enforcement of "unnecessary" procedure. Process is going to be viewed as simple overhead, which, at first, it will be. The benefits of the formal procedures come into their own only when the project has been underway for some time.

So, the solution to the resistance problem is to ask for a little trust. The alternative system, with no real control or procedure, led to an inefficient working environment and poor project visibility. The developers cannot be a law unto themselves. They are working for a company, and the management of that company (the "customers") have every right to know exactly how the project is doing.

By the same token, the development team has the same right, as well as the right to have the management know exactly how the project is going. In this way, preventative steps can be taken if problems arise. If there is no visibility, the only steps that can be taken are usually remedial after the problem has occurred, and are a lot more drastic, in terms of scope, risk, and cost.

Experience has shown me that what generally tends to happen with the introduction of process to a new project is a temporary dip in productivity. It is important to recognize this, or otherwise it could be seized upon as ammunition for an argument as to why process is a bad thing.

There are two main reasons for the dip. The first is that anything new involves a learning curve. The team has to become familiar with the procedures to be able to use them efficiently. The procedures must become second nature to the entire team. This in turn implies that the procedures must be simple and clear enough to be easily memorized. The purpose of each procedure should be obvious to all. Even if the team is not initially enthusiastic about the procedure, they should at least be able to clearly see the potential benefits.

The second reason for the dip in productivity is due to the nature of the initial phases of a project: everything is new, so there is no great capacity for error. Process at the start is effectively pure overhead. The main reason for the procedures is to prevent the sort of errors that occur once a project progresses beyond a certain complexity threshold, and this does not occur in the early stages. (Refer to Figure 13.5 to see this represented graphically.)

Procedures: Where To Use Them?

Figure 13.7 shows the main phases of the module development (left), and the activities associated with each phase (right). Note that the two-boxed activities in the diagram are at phase-transition boundaries. It is possible to insert procedures to control every point of the design, development, test, and release phases, but this is seldom necessary.

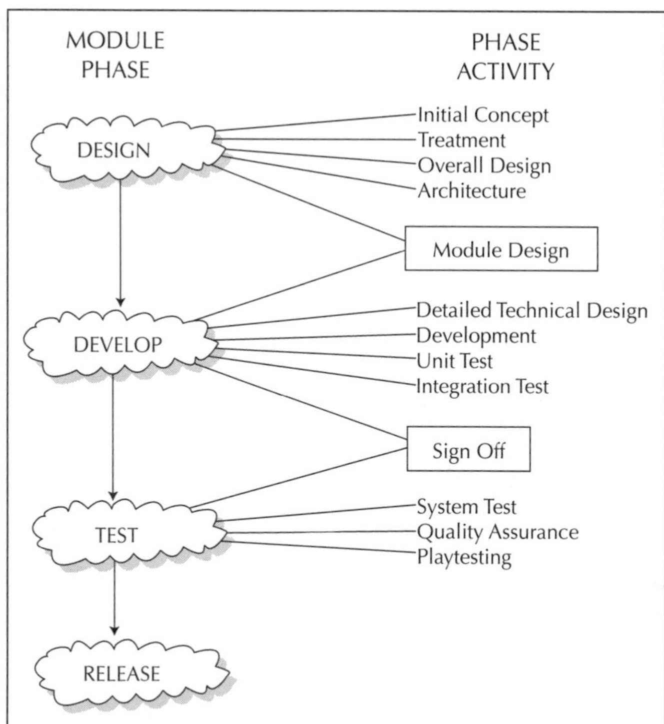

Figure 13.7
Breakdown of project module phases and activities.

A good rule of thumb is that the amount of process needed and the number of points in the development cycle for which it is required scales in proportion with the size of the project. The following sections discuss suggestions for where and which types of procedures to implement.

The Design Phase

The design phase covers the project from the point where the game design is formalized by the game designer up to the point where the overall design for a module is written.

For a single project, this is a one-to-many relationship. There is only one game design, but this leads to many module designs that all have to be consistent with the overall architecture. Figure 13.8 demonstrates this concept.

Initial Concept

There's not much procedure that can be implemented here. The initial concept is too far into the realms of imagination to be controllable. The initial concept for a game (unless marketing gets too involved) is pure creativity.

Fortunately for management, the initial concept tends to be a kick-off point for a project, and there is no shortage of good ideas. (Well, actually it appears that there *is* a shortage of good ideas in the games industry, but only a few game designers have actually noticed this so far!)

Output: Ideas and notes describing the game. Basic concept sketches and diagrams.

Recommended Procedure: Presentation of the idea to stake-holding parties (the management, the development team, the publishers, or even just your coworkers).

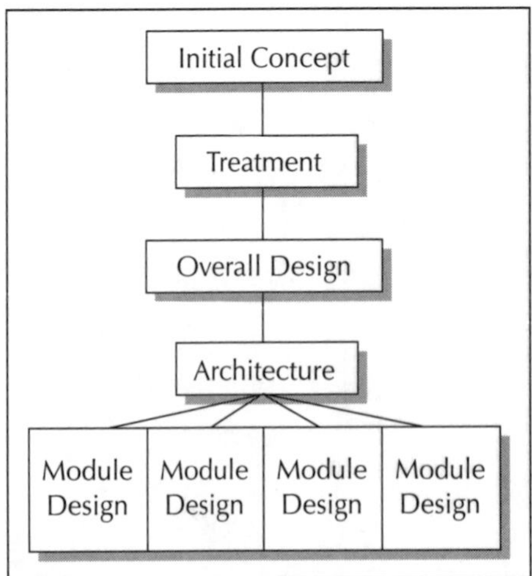

Figure 13.8
One to many: initial concept to module design.

Treatment

The treatment is a proto-manifesto that defines the gameplay, a document that defines the major features of the game and attempts to paint a picture of the game that sets the mood for the team to follow.

Output: A formalized document that describes the game (the story, the look and feel, and the basic mechanics).

Recommended Procedure: Document review by relevant parties (the same parties who reviewed the initial concept). The game design should be thoroughly thrashed out as part of the review procedure, and it should be finalized before the next phase.

Overall Design

The overall design is the first draft of the detailed game design. This constantly evolves during the lifetime of the project, but the baselining of this document is required before any project-specific technical work can begin in earnest. The overall design document is semi-technical and it specifies how the game works, looks, and plays, and how all the game rules and units work in detail.

Output: A detailed specification of all units, characters, plots, physical appearance, mood and setting, controls, and all other details related to the game. This document could be used as a basis for the game manual.

Recommended Procedure: Document review by the entire team, or at least a representative sample.

Architecture

The architecture document is the initial technical document. This document describes how the project will be constructed down to the module level. This should include how the project fits in with the overall company architecture guidelines, including a reuse plan to make optimum use of components that have already been developed.

Output: A document specifying the modules that compose the game and the connections between these modules.

Recommended Procedure: Document review by the programming team, or at least a representative sample.

Module Design

This document is the hand-over document between design and development. One is written for each module. The initial draft is written by a software planner or the game designer, and the subsequent revisions are usually handled by the developers. The document is a fairly high-level technical specification on how a particular module functions, and it is used as a manual for the use of a particular code module. The module design document is used chiefly to provide information for a library of modules, and is an important part of the reuse plans. Note that a module can be of many types, each with varying importance and reusability. For example, code module can be reusable, but an artwork module or a game data file module is not easily reusable.

Output: A document containing detailed instructions on how a particular module functions and what it is used for, containing examples of intended use. It must be maintained along with the module.

Recommended Procedure: Technical document review by the lead programmer (where possible), the software architect, and/or planner (if the document has been completed by a programmer), and at least two other programmers. Where applicable, one of the reviewers should be appointed as a reuse officer to make sure that all opportunities for software reusability are being taken.

The Development Phase

The development phase doesn't just include the writing of code, although many games industry programmers (and even some outside the games industry) seem to feel this way. Even many of the more enlightened programmers feel as if commenting code is sufficient documentation.

The development phase is the most critical phase of the entire cycle, but writing code makes up only a small part of it.

Note that, for the purposes of this discussion, I am concentrating on the code development. I am not including the development of artwork and other modules necessary for the game, although the principles are the same as for code modules.

Detailed Technical Design

Every module is written in tandem with a detailed technical design document. This can be viewed as an extension of the module design document, but with much more detail. This document's aim is to explain to other developers exactly how a module functions, including the reasoning behind design choices and other salient details.

This document effectively becomes a journal of the development of the module, and is considered to be as important as the module itself. The module and the technical design document must always be maintained in tandem.

Output: A document containing detailed technical specifications of a particular module, such as interfaces, algorithms, design choices, test script, and test harness details.

Recommended Procedure: Design review conducted by developers and the software architect.

Development

The module is usually developed from a design document of some form. In the case of artwork, this will usually be the game design in combination with a style guide. Code, on the other hand, will be developed from a detailed technical design document.

Output: A module for the project. This could be a code file, a 3D model, 2D artwork, a text configuration file, or anything to do with the project.

Recommended Procedure: Code review conducted by developers.

Unit Test

Unit testing is the testing of the code written by a developer, and usually by that developer. The unit test follows a script written by the developer as part of the technical design document.

Output: Unit test script results.

Recommended Procedure: The errors found by the unit test are reported to the project manager for assignment. Depending on the nature of the error, errors will usually be assigned back to the original developer.

Integration Test

The integration test is usually the last round of testing that the developer performs. The developer tests the completed module to see if it fits in with the build. Integration testing is considered to be an extension of the unit test, and, as such, the tests used are part of the unit test script in the technical design document.

Output: Integration test script results.

Recommended Procedure: The same as for the unit test.

Sign Off

The sign off is the last phase of the developer's work on the module. Sign off is dependent upon all the tests being completed successfully. If the tests have not been completed successfully, then sign off cannot be obtained.

Output: A tested error-free project module.

Recommended Procedure: Check in to source control.

The Testing Phase

The testing phase involves three critical levels of tests: the system test, the quality assurance test, and playtesting.

System Test

The system testing is performed by the testers as often as possible. It produces much more general information than would be produced by unit and integration testing due to its black box nature.

Output: A system test log.

Recommended Procedure: Errors are reported to the project manager for assessment.

Quality Assurance

Quality assurance is a higher level of testing. This ensures that the program is artistically pleasing. It is not meant to find defects in the program, as they should have all been weeded out by this stage anyway.

The purpose of quality assurance is to make sure that the aesthetics (game atmosphere, menu screens, manual, etc.) are user friendly and self-consistent, while conforming to the game style section of the game design document.

Output: QA report.

Recommended Procedure: The results are reported to both the project manager and the game designer for assessment.

Playtesting

This is the final stage of testing. The total gaming experience is tested. How does it play? Is the manual any good? How is the learning curve? Are there any gameplay issues?

Output: Gameplay report.

Recommended Procedure: Issues are raised with the game designer and the project manager for further assessment.

Source Control And Code Reviews: A Synergy

For those of you who don't regularly read dictionaries, a synergy is defined as the sum of the parts producing a greater output than the parts separately.

The combination of source control with code reviews is a perfect example of a synergy.

In case you are unfamiliar with source control, it is a software application that administers a centralized database of file revisions. It allows a sensible level of control to be maintained over whomever is working with which source code file, and over which revision level of the code is released to testing. If a developer is working on a source code file, all others should be prevented from working on it at the same time. This prevents those horrible configuration errors we used to get before decent source control, in which two people were editing the same file in a mutually incompatible way.

Source control has become an indispensable part of development, capable of acting as both an automated project history log and as a regulating control system for tracking the progress of the review cycle. What surprises me is how slow the games industry has been at catching onto the benefits of source control. Case Study 13.2 provides an example of source control.

Lack of code review procedures is not an uncommon phenomenon in the games industry. Until fairly recently, even source control was an unfamiliar concept. When I started out in the games industry, source control was viewed with distrust. It was considered restrictive

Case Study 13.2 Source Control? We Don' Need No Steenkin' Source Control!

Julian, a seasoned technical lead, had been around the block a few times and had seen how development techniques were maturing outside the games industry before he started work at a fresh young development studio that was started by one of the old-guard veterans of the industry.

When he arrived, he was put in charge of one of the two development teams, working on a team-based sports game. This project had been underway for a few months, and there had been no design phase, just coding, so already a substantial spider's web of badly organized code had been written.

"Okay," said Julian to the team, "Let's talk about source control."

The team looked highly dubious at this. They had never heard of such a thing. It was something that boring gray suits used, when they were writing databases or something equally dull. Source control didn't fit in with the seat-of-the-pants cool image of coding.

"But we don't need source control," one of the team members piped up. "We're doing fine, and we don't need the extra work. It'll just slow us down!"

"But surely you can see the benefits? We'll be able to keep an annotated archive of the source code. We'll know exactly how the work is progressing, and who has done what, when, and why," retorted Julian.

Now it was the turn for another member of the team, John, to comment. John had been a bit insecure about the quality of his code, and didn't like the idea of being "found out."

"So, the management wants to use this software to spy on us, and check up on how much work we are doing, is that it?" he asked, to murmurs of agreement from the team.

The discussion soon degenerated to the point where the programming team absolutely refused to have anything to do with source control.

In the interests of being diplomatic, Julian decided to let the issue go. Instead, he went to a higher level to find out how to proceed.

The general consensus was pretty much the same as the development team. "Why do we want to buy software that the development team feels is unnecessary? Surely they know what they are doing, and if they say it will stifle their creativity, then let's ride with that."

At this point, Julian realized he was facing a losing battle, and decided not to press the point. "Without the support of management, there is no point in me trying to force them to use source control," he surmised.

Development continued as normal until one day, Andy, a junior programmer, shuffled awkwardly up to Julian.

"Julian, we may have a tiny little problem with some of our source code," he mumbled.

Julian sat upright. "What sort of problem?" he asked with growing suspicion.

"Well, I was checking up on one of the core AI files, and I found that there were a few bits that needed tidying up. So, for the past few days, I've been working on that," explained Andy.

"Go on," said Julian, a growing sense of fear crawling up his spine. Bad news was coming. He could feel it.

Andy gulped. "Well, er... It seems as if John was also working on the same area. He started the day after me, but was away from his desk when I asked if anybody was working on that file."

Julian's knuckles whitened, but he didn't say anything.

Andy continued. "It turns out that he was, and he's optimized the core. It now runs at the target speed we were aiming for, but it still has the same algorithm flaws. He'd spent about a week working on it, and I copied my file over his.

Julian pursed his lips and frowned. Andy shifted uncomfortably. "He's lost his work, and he's furious with me. The last backup he has is over a week old."

Julian sat back and sighed. "This is why I wanted source control. This wouldn't have happened if we had used source control procedures."

and unnecessary, an invasion of privacy that tracks who wrote what in a piece of code. Errors could be pinpointed and—*shock horror*—blame could be laid. This was a bad thing. I suspect that this attitude still permeates a few dark pockets of the games industry, but I hope that more-enlightened times are ahead.

Code reviews were discussed in detail earlier in this chapter, so this section concentrates on source control and using it correctly, particularly in conjunction with code reviews.

Like any tool, source control is effective only if used correctly. If used ineffectively, it is worse than useless: source code can be lost, archives can become confused, and no one will be quite sure what the latest version of the project is.

What Should Source Control Be Used For?

The short answer: *Everything!*

The development as a module should be viewed as a package. All electronic material relating to the module—such as design documents, problem reports, and review reports—should be archived. All source control packages allow you to attach comments to the revisions. These should provide a summary explaining the changes made and references to other related areas. An identity code that is unique to every code review could be used to track changes across several files. If this was used, a simple archive search will extract all information relating to a single piece of work.

While it is true that not all organizations need such a detailed audit trail, the small amount of extra effort that this requires can reap rewards later, when the data is later examined.

One important characteristic of the games industry is that few companies ever seem to learn from their mistakes. This may be due to the fact that the information from previous projects is not readily available.

In fact, in most of the projects I have worked on, there has been no real logging activity taking place. No one has really given too much thought to gathering information from a project in order to improve the chances of success in the next project.

This may be for a number of reasons. The games industry has some very peculiar notions about the nature of development. For example, the concept of reuse is anathema to most developers. All games are considered different beasts, and so there is no useful code that can be applied from the previous version. The code used in one game is generally considered to be too old and too slow to be useful in a new version. Whether this is true or not is a moot point.

Developers in the games industry also tend to be rather strange beasts. The typical stereotype for a game developer is that of a twisted genius, petulant and protective of his own code. There can be no sign of weakness, and no one may dare to question the developer's coding ability. In a nutshell, every developer thinks he is the best within the team, and every team thinks they are the best in the industry, if only they were given a chance to produce the game that *they* want to produce.

There's a common joke about programmers. I can't promise that it's funny, but it illustrates the point effectively.

Q: How many programmers does it take to change a light bulb?

A: All of them, one to actually do it, and the rest to say how bad it is, and how they could have done it better.

In fact, this joke would be almost funny if it wasn't true. Case Study 13.3 paints a sorry tale of a common occurrence in the games industry.

The phenomenon shown in Case Study 13.3 is unfortunately rather commonplace. Even I have succumbed to that dreaded temptation.

A number of times when I have had to update code that I have written a few months before, my first instinct usually is that it would be easier to rewrite it from scratch. This is usually because I didn't want to expend the effort required to refamiliarize myself with the old code. What changed my attitude was the cost/effort ratio. If I had commented my code well, and made sure that the associated documents were in line with the code, then it was much less work to modify my old code than it was to rewrite the whole thing from scratch. This is how I learned the importance of documenting and commenting my code effectively.

The team in Case Study 13.3 made the cardinal error of assuming that another aspect of a game is inadequate simply because the development team responsible was not technically capable of doing it better.

Case Study 13.3 Delusions Of Grandeur

A development team is working on a new project for a large publisher. They were discussing their up-and-coming release in comparison with some other similar games that had been released.

Age of Empires was singled out for particular criticism, due to what they considered to be simplistic AI algorithms.

Don, the game designer, was discussing this with Jerry, the project manager who had just come fresh from a meeting with the developers.

"We can do much better than that," said Jerry, "their AI programmer must have been an imbecile! Our guy says that he can do much better than that easily!"

Don was a little more cynical than Jerry. "Okay, let's get him and the rest of the team in here. I want to know why he thinks he can do better." He had heard them speak this way before.

They had always talked about the project in terms of perceived defects in other released games. They had said that the explosions were not good enough in *Starcraft*, the AI was bad in *this* program, the user interface was unfriendly in *that* program, something else was wrong with some other program. Their assumption was that everything would be perfect in their project.

A team meeting is called, and Don asks Chris, the AI programmer, why he thinks he can do better.

"Well it's obvious, isn't it?" asks Chris. "I could do better than that with my eyes closed. We've got plenty of time to do the project, and I can easily work out how to do it better."

"When you say 'work it out', you mean research it, right?", asked Don. "You don't actually know how the overall strategy AI will work right now, but you think you'll be able to figure it out. Do you know how long it will take you?"

Chris thought for a minute and then said, "Hmm. I'd guess that it would take me six weeks give or take a couple."

"On what do you base that assumption?" asked Don.

"I've just got a hunch," replied Chris, with a knowing grin.

"Okay," said Don, "but what is more likely? Did they do it that way simply because they couldn't do it better, or did they do it because it was the simplest solution to a complex problem, given a limited time frame?"

This question was asked of the entire team. After a few moments' thought, Chris piped up, "Well, I reckon that it was because they couldn't do it better."

The rest of the team agreed.

The team thought that they can do something and that it is easy simply *because* they have never done it before, but they have a vague understanding of the general process. Of course, as soon as you hear an idea, it becomes obvious.

This is a clear case of the "That's easy. I could have thought of that" syndrome. If there is one trait that can universally be attributed to programmers, it is an overestimation of their own ability. The best programmers I know are those who are capable of saying, "I don't know how to do this."

As an analogy, consider this: You may be able to tell the difference between a scalpel and a bone saw. You may even know what they are used for and under what circumstances, but only a surgeon actually knows *how* they are used. Would you want somebody who only *claimed* they knew how to perform surgery operating on you?

All development teams assume that their project is going to be perfect. No one considers the compromises that may have to be made. They always assume that they will be able to complete their work in time, and that there will be no problems. The lesson here is that "perfect" is impossible, so "good enough" will have to suffice.

The Importance Of Information Transmission

Information transmission is a sadly overlooked area of development, and is usually never singled out for special attention. The assumption, if it is even considered, is that information transmission simply *happens*.

However, the reality is quite different. If information could just be transferred from brain to brain, then things would be simpler. Maybe somebody somewhere is working on such technology, but I haven't seen it in any shops.

Until then, we are going to have to rely on the good old-fashioned methods of speaking, writing, and distributing information via email and intranet Web sites.

Actually, the order of the communication methods in the previous sentence was no coincidence. The methods are listed in order of efficiency. There is some overlap of course, as email and typed documents can be interchangeable.

Most teams have some form of information transmission, but it is not as effective as it could be. Most information is transmitted verbally, and it is concerned with the day-to-day concerns of the project. The state of the project is effectively maintained verbally, and everybody has their own idea of the project's status. This mismatch of information can cause problems.

In some cases, a token effort is made to keep track of the project status with documentation and regular status meetings. These can vary in effectiveness, depending on the experience level of the project manager who implements these measures. The main problem here is that attracting such talent *into* the games industry tends to be difficult due to the lower wages.

Most of the people promoted to project management tend to be taken from the ranks of programmers. A common management theory relates to this: an employee within an organization is promoted to his or her level of incompetence. It's an obvious side effect of human nature.

If an employee is good in his or her role, he or she is likely to be promoted. Sooner or later, he or she will be in a position in which the job matches or exceeds his or her skill level.

Such employees are then either left to rot in their position until they either leave through boredom, or are forced to look elsewhere due to being "let go."

For these reasons, the sorts of people you tend to find in management positions are not always the best person for the job. If they have been taken from the ranks of the programmers, it could mean that their communication skills are not exactly optimum.

The important point to realize is that the team members must look to the team leader for how to conduct themselves, and the team leader does set the tone for any intrateam communication.

In the best-managed teams, the communication works efficiently on several levels. Not only are the details of day-to-day events spread among the entire team, but skills and experience are also shared.

The net effect is that, as the project progresses, the entire team is raised to a new common level of skill. A fair amount of this is project specific, but a significant portion is an improvement to the general abilities of the individual.

This most effective form of information transmission—the spread of knowledge—relies on a number of factors. The first, and most important, of these is the use of *all* the communication methods mentioned previously. The second of these is *glasnost*—a sense of openness—among the team.

This is less of a problem outside of the insular games industry in which the developers are jealously protective of their own "next big thing." Inside the games industry, this can be combated by promoting a real sense of team.

Before we discuss any of the specific recommendations in detail, a digression on the relative efficiencies of communication is in order.

Figures 13.9 and 13.10 demonstrate the factorial nature of communication lines between team members.

When there are three members in a team, there are three lines of communication. A can speak to B, B can speak to C, and C can speak to A. This is easily manageable. Each developer needs to communicate with only two other team members, which won't take up much of his or her time.

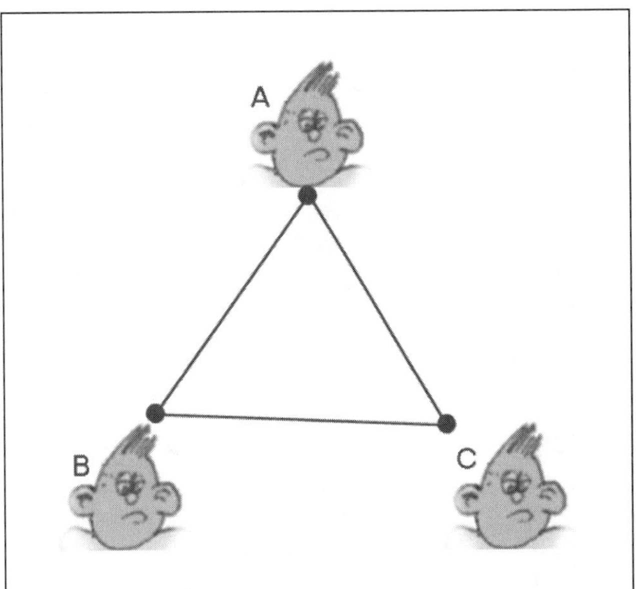

Figure 13.9
Communication lines between three team members.

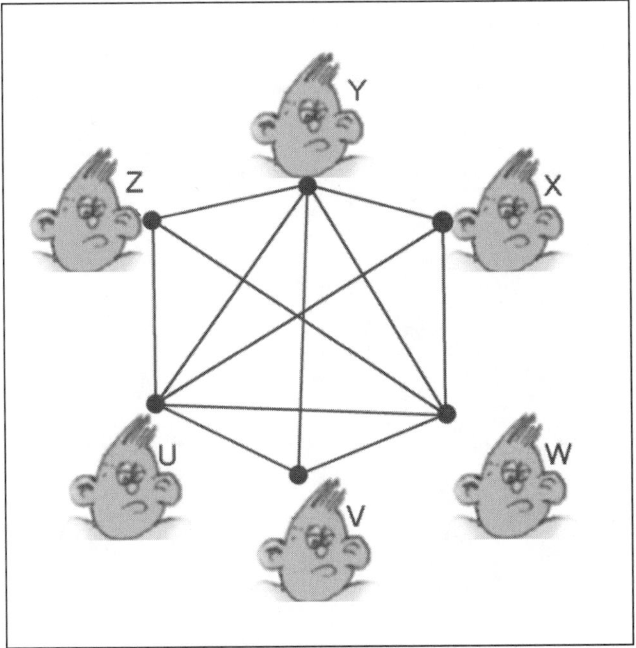

Figure 13.10
Communication lines between six team members.

However, with four, five, or even six team members (as shown in Figure 13.10), the situation becomes horribly complicated.

Figure 13.10 reveals 15 such communication lines. This is substantially more than the original 3, and hence will take up more of an individual developer's time.

Of course, this is a worse-case example, and it doesn't take into account the fact that communication, even in the most lax organizations, is usually more structured than this.

Figure 13.11 shows the sort of situation that usually arises.

One of the reasons for dividing large teams into functional subteams is to optimize communications. With *n* team members, there will be $n(n-1)/2$ communication links.

In Figure 13.11, a team of 24 employees is divided into four subteams of six members each with a team leader (as shown in Figure 13.10). Interteam communication is handled via each of the team leaders, and this helps to reduce the nightmare of communications that would occur otherwise. With this configuration, there are 6 interteam communication links, and four sets of 15 intrateam links, totaling 66 *official* communication links.

Compare this with an undivided team of 24 members. There would be 276 lines of communication. It's clear to see that this would take up a major portion of an individual's time, very little work would get done, and soon the whole thing would collapse into anarchy.

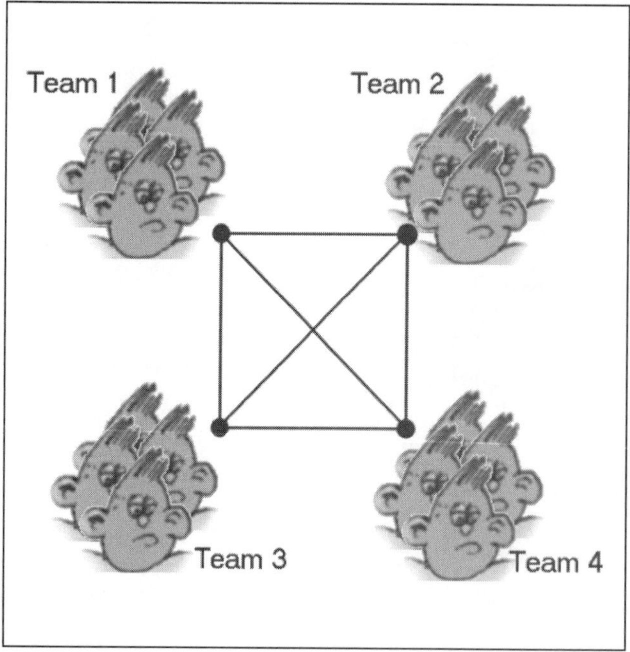

Figure 13.11
Communication lines between four teams.

This system can be used quite efficiently for the transferal of information, but there are more efficient means. This sort of verbal communication is essentially one-to-one, and there are many cases in which one-to-many communication methods are far more effective: meetings, documents, and internal Web sites. Each of these, of course, has its pros and cons.

Meetings, for example, are not usually very efficient. Some managers seem to have a peculiar fondness for meetings. It's almost as if they feel that their lives would not be quite complete if they did not have at least one meeting a day, although preferably more often.

My view is that meetings should generally be called only in exceptional cases, and even then not everybody needs to be automatically included. It seems to be the general case that, when a manager gets an urge to call a meeting, everybody including the tea-boy gets to go along.

Meetings tend to waste a lot of time, and, although they are more efficient than telling the individuals one by one, for the purposes of simple status reports, these can be done much more effectively by the use of an internal Web site or a weekly newspaper (sent out by email).

If everything is going smoothly, meetings are not generally necessary. If there are problems, or changes ahead—for example, proactive news that requires widespread action—then a meeting can become necessary.

Proactive And Reactive Information Transmission

Up to this point, we have given no consideration on whether the information to be transferred is *pro*active or *re*active. What exactly do we mean by that?

Well, proactive news is information that directly affects the future of the project. An example of this would be a large change request. This potentially affects all personnel, and may require the gathering of opinions in order to decide further courses of action.

Proactive information is usually best suited for transmission at meetings. In fact, most of the meetings I would expect to see in a well-run software project will be review meetings, and change control meetings. Except in some specific instances, everything else can be transmitted more efficiently by other means.

Reactive news is effectively everything else. Examples would include project status reports, results from reviews, information on competitors' projects, or any of the 101 humdrum occurrences that are part of any project.

In my experience, I have found that the two best methods to transmit this sort of information is an email newsletter, or a linked web of documents on the intranet Web site (or, better still, *both*). There is a disturbing tendency to call meetings at the drop of a hat, and this combination of email and intranet should provide enough information to make these excessively time-wasting meetings redundant.

Each project should have its own homepage, such as that shown in Figure 13.12.

The exact structure of the home page pretty much depends on personal taste. The sample page shown in Figure 13.13 would be used with the software factory model described in Chapter 11. Note that only the links *from* the main project home page are shown for clarity.

In the ideal system, a weekly email newsletter should be sent out to all employees, containing a digest of updated material every week. Of course, it is the responsibility of the employee to check out the information that applies to him or her.

The one main drawback is that, in larger organizations, they may have to employ a dedicated Web page designer to perform this work. Fortunately, however, most of these companies will already employ such people to maintain their Web sites.

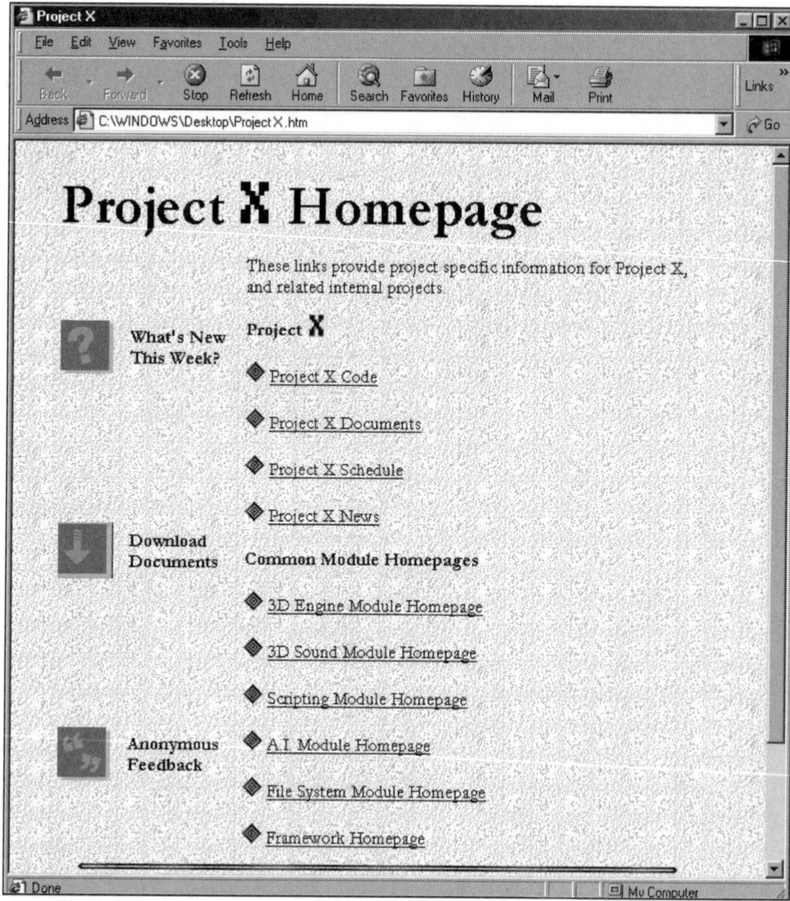

Figure 13.12
Example home page for the fictional Project X.

Moving all the company documents and process records onto an intranet is quite an undertaking. It needs to be carefully designed, and the intranet should have search capability. If this is done properly, then anyone in the company will be able to view the project status.

I have implemented a system such as this on one of the development projects I have worked on, and have extended it to include a project scheduling system so that tasks could be assigned to employees by the management using a simple Web-based interface. The employees were then able to access a customized page that detailed the tasks they had to perform, as well as a personalized schedule of their review and meeting assignments.

Assuming that the home page *is* carefully designed and laid out, it should nullify the classic "But I couldn't find it anywhere" excuse used by nearly every developer (including myself) to avoid reading documentation!

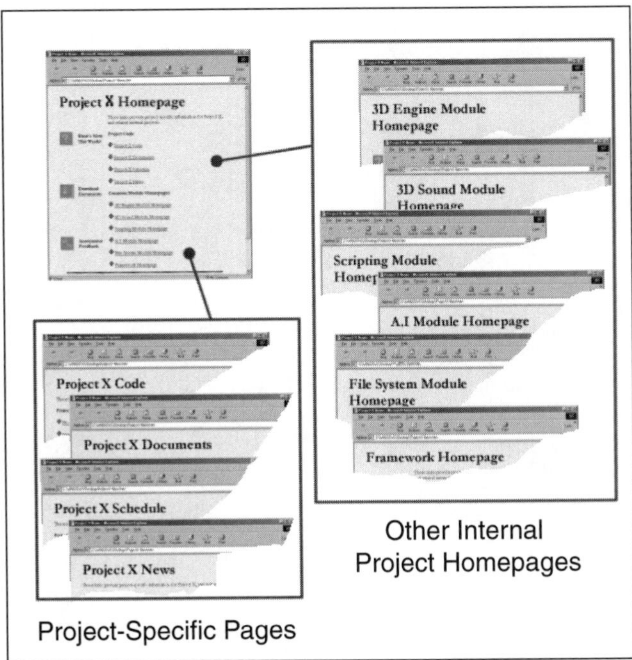

Figure 13.13
Example Web links for software factory model.

Chapter 14

Troubleshooting

Key Topics:

- ***Risks***
- ***Proactive and reactive troubleshooting***
- ***Change control***
- ***Contingency planning—the "Plan B" scenario***
- ***Metrics and information gathering***
- ***Disaster recovery***

In this chapter, we are going to look at what can—and most probably will—go wrong with your project. The average project is simply a catalog of errors just waiting to happen: scheduling errors, coding errors, obsolescence, personnel problems, and illness—you name it, and it can happen. Don't look so surprised! Nothing ever goes according to plan. You can plan the project down to the most meticulous detail, but you cannot plan for the unknown.

Troubleshooting *(noun). Tracing and correcting faults in machinery, etc.*

This chapter may be titled "Troubleshooting," but I'm going to spend most of my time suggesting methods of actually *preventing* the need to troubleshoot. The most cost-effective projects are those that build high-quality software from the outset, rather than those that build low-quality software and then fix the problems afterwards.

Even in the best-run projects, unexpected problems will crop up. What differentiates the successful teams from those that fail is how well they plan for and handle these problems.

Okay, I know what you are saying: how can you plan for the unknown? If you don't know what is going to happen, how can you take measures to fix it? Well, to tell the truth, you can't. If I tried to tell you otherwise, you would know that I was lying.

No one can read the future, so there is no way of knowing what troubles will beset your project. However, you *do* know that *something* is bound to happen. Only the most-naïve project managers assume that a project will run smoothly and free of trouble to completion. Believe it or not, I have found managers like that. I know of one such manager who maintained a belief that an 18-month project could be completed in a 9-month period. He believed this up until the 7th month, at which point a hasty renegotiation of the contract with the publisher was required. The game in question was released one year and two resignations too late.

This sort of undesirable situation occurs more often than is necessary, especially in the games industry. Why? I believe it's a direct consequence of the lack of planning that is endemic in the games industry.

The games industry, as a whole, is still relatively immature. It was still cutting its first teeth when the mainframe world was working on huge projects involving millions of lines of code and vast teams of people. As a testament to the strength and cohesiveness of these teams, many of the results of these large-scale projects are still in use today. Of course, some of the more cynical would attribute this to the fact that the cost of replacing them is more than the cost of keeping them running. This may be true to some extent, but at least they are still working!

However, games are generally not meant to have 20-year lifespans (although I'm sure some designers would like that to be the case), so planning and scheduling hasn't evolved as fully as they have in other disciplines. In fact, due to the short lifespan of the average game, such organized practices have not been as necessary.

But, as the song goes, the times, they are a-changing. Games projects have become bigger and more involved. It's no longer a small undertaking. Few platforms remain where the lone developer can produce anything to match the big boys. Today, it's all motion capture, FMV, movie-quality soundtracks, movie-quality artwork, and more polygons than you can shake a stick at.

There is some talk of comparing the games industry and the contemporary movie industry. It's probably just the romantic talk on the part of a few people who can't accept the idea that they are just software engineers, because the analogy of the two industries breaks down under close examination.

To be fair, I can see the comparisons. Unlike most software projects, however, there is a large artistic element to game development. These particular elements are best suited to a movie-industry style of deployment, but the difference between movies and games is still quite large. Movies are mainly artistic—there is a large technical element to them, but this is handled smoothly and efficiently by outsourcing requirements when needed. In addition, there is no great amount of technical research, unlike game development.

However, the requirements for the production of art, FMV, and music for a game project *do* closely match those of the movie industry, and there would be a point to mimicking the movies in this respect: The movie producers usually outsource their requirements to external companies rather than maintain expensive in-house teams.

If game development can truly be compared to the movie industry, then the movie producers employ new engineers for every project to build new cameras, reinvent celluloid, and redevelop all the software used from scratch. No, the movie industry today is not *yet* a good comparison (although the movie industry of the past, when the technology was young and still being invented *is* a valid comparison).

Today's movie industry has gone through all its teething troubles. It is mature, and there is no real discovery of the fundamental techniques needed anymore. It's all already been done, dusted, and documented. The movie industry has reached a plateau where the technology is essentially stable, and the "target platform" of a cinema screen is generally consistent and unvarying. Think about it: apart from (arguably) small incremental improvements, the cinema has remained virtually unchanged for decades.

The games industry will not reach a similar plateau. The technology is constantly evolving, and, hence, games technology may not ever stabilize, even on the consoles. Every couple of years, it seems, there is a new upheaval in the state of the technology. The advances predicted by Moore's famous "law," (that computing power doubles every 18 months or so) show no signs of relenting. I don't expect that the target platform will ever stabilize, although an insulating layer, such as DirectX, does provide a light buffer, shielding the developer from the immediate effects of the underlying technological changes. However, DirectX is revised every year or so in order to keep up with the technology.

I suppose that, one day, given the way things seem to be moving, there will be an industry-standard game-development kit that contains all the components required (such as graphics engines, AI engines, and scripting engines) to allow relatively nontechnical game designers to direct the production of a game much in the same way as a movie director does with a movie. The game designer will be able to outsource graphics, music, and maybe even buy AI modules in order to augment the game design "script" that he is producing. Even then, there are likely to be different packages available to cover each distinctive genre of game, not to mention the many varying styles of presentation (for example, first-person 3D is not an ideal platform for a multiunit strategy game).

For the moment, however, game development is fundamentally an engineering discipline with artistic aspects. If there were any contemporary discipline that can be effectively compared to the games industry, then it would be bridge building. When building a bridge, the plans are laid out in advance, the work is performed to a schedule, and contingency planning is taken very seriously. Of course, the difference between bridge building and game development is that, if the bridge planning is not meticulously performed, lives can be lost.

Both bridge building and game development are essentially engineering disciplines, both produce "works of art" as output, and both require extensive planning in order to have any hope of being finished on time and on budget (see Figure 14.1).

Of course, no bridge would ever be built if the people responsible for producing games suddenly laid down their tools and became bridge designers. Can you imagine building a

Figure 14.1
The Royal Albert Bridge spanning the river Tamar at Saltash in Cornwall, England.

bridge by getting 100 engineers, giving them several hundred tons of metal and some tools, and telling them to get started, without any planning, and just a rough idea of what the finished bridge should look like, whilst pointing at a vague spot just over the other side of the river? The "build like hell" school of bridge building? I don't think so. That hasn't been used since the dark ages! Maybe if human lives were a factor in game development, more attention would be paid to it!

At any rate, you can deal with problems in generally two ways: after they occur, or before they occur. Now, which sounds better to you?

As much as I would like to lie about this, I must confess that it is not possible to predict and make provisions for every possible problem in advance; to be honest, nor is it recommended. Trying to explain meteor-strike contingencies to the people funding the project may be a little difficult for the average project planner.

Managers sometimes do not understand why you would want to spend money on things that will most probably never happen. They may call you a jinx or a doomsayer. You should stand your ground, however. The extra effort involved in contingency planning acts as a sort of "insurance" for your project.

You should explain to the people in charge that there are certain risks common to nearly every project, past and present, and that ignoring these lessons is the single biggest risk to the success of your project. By expending a small amount of effort to build guarantee resilience to these problems, you are drastically increasing the chances of a successful project.

In searching for potential problem areas, it is better to examine each aspect of the entire project and try to identify where problems may occur. It could be an experimental architecture, a risky or unproven technique, personnel shortages, funding problems, or other such difficulties. (This will be discussed in more detail later in the chapter.)

In the cases in which it is not possible to plan, a sensible general approach to handling problems is necessary.

Some things are just too way-out to plan for, and this has to be considered. The trick is to cover the main bases and to, like the boy scouts, be prepared.

So far, we have ascertained the two types of troubleshooting: proactive and reactive. Proactive troubleshooting is preferable, but is not always possible. Reactive trouble shooting is not always the best approach, but can sometimes be unavoidable.

Reactive troubleshooting is more commonly known as "fire fighting," or any other phrase indicating that a problem is being addressed only after it has surfaced. By this time, of course, the problem has already had an effect on the project. The effectiveness of the troubleshooting depends on your ability to detect the problem before it has had much effect.

Unfortunately, detecting these problems is not always straightforward, and for a number of reasons. The first is blindness through overfamiliarity. When you're working day after day on the same project doing the same set of tasks, it is common to suffer from tunnel vision. Sometimes you just do not notice the problems mounting up around you. Unless the problems are pointed out to you before it is too late you may notice them only when they are too big *not* to notice.

The second reason stems from this and depends very much upon the reputation of the person acting as a manager. Do people want to tell him or her about problems? Does the manager shoot the messenger? This is why being approachable is a very important behavioral facet for a manager.

If this sounds like a manager that you know, then there is a good chance that he or she is not being told about problems at the earliest possible opportunity. This is obviously disadvantageous, as it does not allow the team to get cracking on solving the problem as soon as it would otherwise. An anonymous feedback channel can sometimes circumvent this, but such a system depends on whether the potential contributors trust that it actually is anonymous.

It is a sad fact that project managers do not pay enough attention to contingency planning. The evidence is all around. Games are canceled or delayed, and, when (or even if) they are released, they are often substandard and rife with bugs, requiring several postrelease patches to bring them up to an acceptable standard. These are signs that no contingency planning has been used. Games that are delayed were usually the victims to reactive troubleshooting. No plans had been made to foresee and cope with the problems, and these problems had been hurriedly dealt with *after* they had arisen (a situation more commonly known as shutting the stable door after the horse has bolted).

Worse still, many managers fail to grasp that correctly implemented contingency planning adds very little work to a project. In fact, the aim of contingency planning is to save money and time. By preparing an alternative solution to a potential problem before the problem actually occurs, the impact on the project can be assessed and prepared for. The project thus acquires a built-in resilience.

This chapter aims to set this dismal record right. The advice and guidelines set out here may not save your project if the proverbial "stuff" *really* hits the fan, but it will at least prepare you for ducking out of the flight path when it does.

Risks

The most important things to consider when dealing with your project are the risks that it will inevitably face. Every day of your project, you will face new risks. These risks will need to be carefully monitored and checked. This section will give you some tips on how to implement a sensible and practical risk-management plan in order to avoid these risks when possible, and handle them in situations when this is not possible.

In a fair proportion of software-development projects today, risk management is not practiced effectively, if at all. That is not to say it is not considered. In one way or the other, risks are considered in every project under the sun. However, they are only usually considered as part of another process, and not specifically in their own right. Usually risks are not tackled directly, but are dealt with only as a secondary activity.

In this way, risks remain in the peripheral vision of a project manager and his team, but are never focused on directly until the risks are dire enough to prevent normal work. Because of this lack of focus, risks are managed only if they are covered by another area of work. For example, when a project manager is working on the schedule, he will also be examining the risk from schedule slippage, and to some extent, personnel problems. When a developer is developing code, he is checking for risks from bugs being introduced into the codebase, and checking for any that may already exist. Risks to an area are covered only when that area is being worked on.

However, it is abundantly clear that, because risks are never addressed directly as an area of work in their own right, there is the danger of hitherto unconsidered risks falling through the cracks. This is why the area of risk management is an important one that really *should* be considered in its own right.

By concentrating at least a part of your project's effort onto risk management, you will make the ride a lot smoother than it would be otherwise. On projects that do not attempt to anticipate risks before they occur, the projects (and the team) can often appear to an outside observer to be careening from one crisis to another, before finally running out of momentum, and either failing just short of the finish line, or flopping miserably over it, never to be heard of again. (It can sometimes appear like this to an inside observer too, and then you know the project is *really* in trouble.)

The aim of risk management is to smooth the course of the project, providing as pleasant a ride as possible in the event of rough seas. Figure 14.2 illustrates this point.

Risk management is a field of study in its own right, but, as I have said, it is often overlooked. So how would you go about instigating a risk-management program for your project?

The first thing to consider is where—and how—to look for risks. This is a substantial task, so you should seriously consider assigning the title of "Risk Assessor" to an individual, so that it becomes a fair portion of his or her duties. This position could be rotated among employees on a weekly, biweekly, or monthly basis.

The job of the risk assessor is to keep a weather eye open for any potential threats to the project. The risk assessor should closely monitor each "front" of the project. A good way of doing this is to maintain a "top 10" risk list, which should be updated at least once a week. The risks on this list should be given a priority and rated for their severity.

For a start, the mere psychological effects of this are usually positive. The idea of constantly seeking out risks and dealing with them as they occur will bolster the morale of the team.

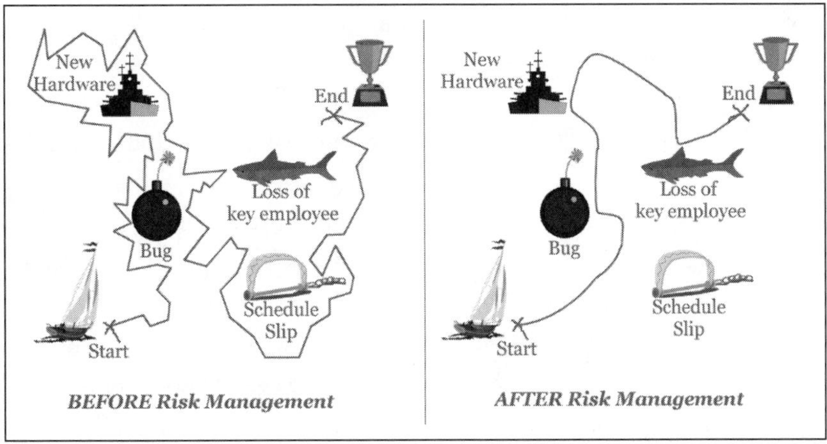

Figure 14.2
The difference that risk management can make to your project.

Anything that can be seen to boost the morale of the team has to be a good thing, even if the effects are not directly measurable.

For each of the high-priority items on the list, a method of resolution should be decided, and it should be the team's priority where possible to tackle and eliminate the risk. In some cases, for the more unexpected and extreme risks, it is necessary to form an "attack team" of employees pulled from their normal work to tackle the problem.

This can be a scary proposition, and it needs to be handled carefully to avoid panicking people. Sometimes, and rather unfortunately, this form of positive action can be viewed in a negative light. Rather than being viewed as an effective way of reacting to the changing needs of the project, it can be viewed by the uninformed as "headless chicken" mode. Anybody who reacts in this way will need to be educated as to what you are trying to achieve.

To be fair, if the risk-management plan is not carefully thought out and implemented, then it *can* degenerate to aimless thrashing. If the risks on the list are only trivial and unnecessary action is taken, it can detract from the real work that is needed in the project. Before any action is taken, the proposed risk-handling plans will have to be ratified by the relevant parties. This could vary depending on the nature of the risk. For example, if the risk involves a change to part of the system, then it is subject to full change control.

The job of the risk assessor can be summed up by saying that he or she is the person who sniffs around the project looking for trouble. It is his or her efficiency at rooting out troubles that will save time, effort, and (more importantly) money further down the line.

The following list is an example of the sort of things that you are likely to see on your top 10 risk list.

Project X Top 10 Risk List

1. Implementation of data packet encryption algorithm is too slow for realtime network use. If we have to remove it, this could leave our peer-to-peer network gameplay open to hacking.
2. Artwork for the main character is taking too long to produce. The animation programmers are being held up by the lack of frames and information pertaining to those frames.
3. The team is being held up by a delayed map design tool. We need to begin designing new levels as soon as possible or we will begin to slip our schedule.
4. A new service pack has just been released for the C++ compiler. This needs to be analyzed to see if it fixes anything that has an impact on our project.
5. There is a bug in the graphics-rendering module causing graphic corruption every few frames. This is not a fatal error, but is noticeable enough to be annoying.
6. There are not enough personnel to cover the amount of work required. We are beginning to work long hours, and this could be detrimental to morale.

7. The compression module we need to use is buggy and difficult to maintain. The tests have shown that it has a low mean time between failure, corrupting 1 in 100 bytes.
8. The 3D rendering module has just been updated by the core team, and we need to make a few code modifications to use it. The advantages of this will be faster and smoother screen updates, and more support for the latest hardware features.
9. We need to bring John, the new team member, up to speed as soon as possible so he can begin to be productive. This should help to alleviate point 6.
10. The test harness for the AI module needs to be updated to test the new features. We would like to make use of the updated fuzzy logic functions that it provides, because this may improve the reaction of the AI opponents to the characters' actions.

Not all of the points on the lists are valid and worth addressing, and the order that they are presented in the list is arguable. Some of the risks may come from the personal opinion of the risk assessor (a good reason to rotate personnel into and out of this position, or at the very least try to find someone who can be unbiased).

The question as to which are worth dealing with and which are not is subjective, depending very much on the status of the project, and different priorities will surface depending on the state of play. For example, the priority might be to complete the game as soon as possible. In this case, the project manager may not want to take the risk of introducing a new technology such as a new 3D engine at this stage (as 3D Realms did when switching *Duke Nukem Forever* from the *Quake II* engine to the *Unreal* Engine). Some managers would consider running a parallel development stream, with one stream using the old engine and one using the new, in order to hedge their bets. If the new engine is successful, then they can proceed with that, assuming that the two codebases have not diverged too much in the interim period. If the codebases have diverged substantially, then the integration then becomes a large risk in its own right. For this reason, I would not recommend anyone take this course of action. The effort needed to maintain two streams of development in this way tends to put off all but the bravest (or most foolish).

However, if the project is not in the final stages, then the new 3D engine may take a much higher priority. By the time the game is likely to be released, technology will have moved on, so it will be commercially advantageous to support the latest technology. Releasing the game with the older engine may make the game look dated compared to any other comparable releases in the shops at the same time. Any problems with the 3D engine will most likely be worked out before release, so this point in the list is likely to receive a higher priority.

The items on the previous list can be grouped into a number of categories, based on the areas that they affect. These areas are not all-inclusive, but instead cover the main types of problems that affect the day-to-day running of a project. Some of these will not be detectable by the risk assessor, because they affect a higher level of management. Someone will need to keep on eye on things at the company level, but that is usually handled without too much difficulty by the management, which is generally meant to keep an eye on these things. The danger areas tend to be more at the project level, where everybody is too busy looking at the trees to be able to see the forest, or even the chainsaw-wielding lumberjacks flitting among them!

The following few sections will discuss some of these risks and giving examples of how they might manifest themselves and how they could be handled.

Design And Architecture Problems

Problems with the design and architecture of a project are the most insidious and difficult to deal with. These are difficulties in the very roots and foundation of a project, and have to be dealt with as expediently as possible.

Potentially, this sort of problem can cause the maximum amount of rework to a project. Obviously, this could be very costly, and so will be something that you want to do your utmost to avoid.

Changes To Baselined Requirements

Changes to requirements once they have been officially signed off can cause problems with integration and mismatched functionality within the project.

These changes can manifest themselves in a number of ways. Sometimes they will be due to "good ideas" from team members (usually those with the most-forceful personalities, and who use these strong personalities to attempt to force their ideas through by garnering popular opinion). The use of change-control boards tends to reduce the powers of forceful personalities, but can also occasionally cause problems with disgruntled personnel when their pet idea has been shot down.

Sometimes, of course, there can be other reasons: the publisher or an external organization (such as a ratings board or a major distributor) could request changes (for example, a request to reduce the amount of blood shown). This sort of request is usually enforced by the imposition of financial penalties, such as the distributor refusing to carry the game, or the publisher or ratings board preventing publication. Either way, usually the only option is to toe the line and make the requested changes, however much the designer and team may not like having their masterwork diluted!

Poorly Defined Requirements

If the requirements are poorly defined, they could well be insufficient for the needs of the project. If this is the case, it is pretty much certain that further requirements will be defined in order to make up for these shortcomings.

This definition and redefinition of the inadequate requirements is most likely to expand the project's scope. If the scope is expanded, then it is possible (and in fact usual) that the work already performed will need some sort of rework in order to accommodate the new requests. Of course, it is never possible to define all the requirements before beginning architecture design, because some of the details can never be known before actually getting your hands dirty with the real work.

The point is that *at least* 80 percent of the requirements should be defined in as much detail as possible before anybody starts work on the architecture. Likewise, at least 80 percent of the architecture should also be defined in detail before construction begins.

Sometimes however, the design and architecture can be well defined, when, out of the blue, additional requirements are added. This can happen for any number of reasons, and I'm sure you can think of many more. Some reasons could be the addition of features due to publisher demand, or a similar game being released with a "must have" feature that will make your product seem out of date if it does not have it. An example would be the addition of multiplayer features, although most games do have this now.

In these sorts of circumstances, there is usually no choice except to buckle down and make the modifications. This can sometimes be virtually impossible without a complete rewrite of most of the code and modules. If such a rewrite is not possible due to financial, contractual, or time constraints, then this is usually the sort of situation that causes projects to be canceled. Sometimes, however, the situation can be salvaged by the promise of an patch update that rectifies the situation. In my opinion, this is no real solution. It is just a quick fix based on a looming emergency; the negative publicity generated in the interim between the forced release of the product and the release of the first patch can damage the reputation of your company. However, if the choice is between releasing a patch at a later date and not releasing a game at all, then in 99 out of 100 cases, (and I won't mention the exception), it is better to published and be damned!

The only real way to prevent this sort of mess occurring is to preempt it by trying to gather most of your requirements in detail before even beginning the architectural design. When doing so, one of the best ways to account for expanding requirements at a later stage is to assign a task force to examine what is in the requirements, and to try to anticipate where expansion may be requested at a later date. This does not mean that these possibilities should be built into the requirements at this stage, but at the very least they should be considered, so that the actual requirement specification will take into account the possibilities, and this should go through into the architectural specifications.

Each potential expansion consideration has three possible outcomes. The first is that the potential requirement may prove to be essential, and so will be included as a concrete requirement. The second outcome is that, although the requirement is not essential, it should be allowed for, and the architecture should be defined to allow expansion in this direction. The third outcome is that the potential requirement adds no real value for effort that would need to be expended to implement it. This is more commonly known as *chrome*, a nice-to-have feature that would superficially improve a product, but the cost/effort ratio is too high to make it worth considering.

Other problems can occur in the design and architecture phase, due to misinterpretation of the 80/20 rule (which states that 80 percent of the work should be complete before starting on the next phase). The reasoning behind this is that it is impossible to completely specify the design and/or architecture, simply because some details will need to be worked out as you go along. Trying to accomplish it all on paper is a fool's game, because there is no way of anticipating all of the possible interactions among components. (Other chapters have already covered plenty of other reasons, too.)

If the 80/20 rule is misinterpreted, it is possible that the next phase would have been started too soon. Vaguely specified areas of the product are generally more time consuming to implement than would be expected.

Vague specifications have a number of knock-on effects. The first and most immediately obvious effect is that the schedule is adversely affected. If the project is on a tight schedule with no room for maneuver, this can be a serious issue. The second negative effect of vaguely specified requirements is the possibility that the proposed solutions may not be compatible with the rest of the system, or may just not work! In this case, a major rework of affected areas may be required.

For some reason, it is the nature of developers to underestimate the time required to implement a feature. A number of reasons contribute to this. Peer pressure is certainly a consideration: being able to perform complex tasks quickly is part of the cool ethos. The second consideration is that managers often do not want to hear what the developer has to say if he tries to give a fair estimate. Case Study 14.1 illustrates "falling on deaf ears."

Case Study 14.1, although not presented in the most historically accurate form, is based upon actual events that are unfortunately a lot more common than they should be.

Despite the fact that it was impossible to accurately estimate the length of time due to lack of knowledge of the detailed specifications and implementation requirements, the developer involved still gave the best estimate possible. The manager chose to accept the lower bound as the correct value mainly because it suited his aims, whilst ignoring the possibility that this was the absolute best-case estimate, and would almost never be achievable without an improbable set of lucky coincidences.

These of course, are not the only difficulties to befall a project in the design or architectural phases. In the previous situation, it was clear that areas of the design or architecture were vague, and that the 80/20 rule was obviously not followed.

Unfortunately, when the designer or architect produces an overly simple design, there is no way to detect it by using the 80/20 rule. An overly simple design is one that fails to adequately deal with the major issues, which inevitably leads to a need to redesign and reimplement the project in a more robust form in order to meet the requirements. This is a difficult problem to detect. It is not always obvious that a design is too simple, especially in the case of game design, where often oversimplification of the game tends to show up fairly late in the process, usually during periods of extended playtesting.

Case Study 14.1 The Case Of The Deaf Manager

"A most intriguing case," said Holmes, "is the Case Of The Deaf Manager."

"That's funny," replied Watson, a confused look clouding his face. "I don't seem to be able to recall that one."

Watson sat back in his chair as Holmes recounted his tale of Fothergill, the senior developer.

"Fothergill was working on some modifications to a complex application for a customer in Europe," continued Holmes.

"Go on," said Watson, scribbling notes furiously.

"This customer had appointed a manager, Snodgrass, who was not known for his technical skills, but was well known for a short temper, and his famous technique of trying to force people to agree with what he was saying by turning purple and spluttering, until they relented, fearing that he may explode.

"One part of the application needed to be expanded, and a whole new module needed to be researched, designed, and written from scratch, and the task fell naturally to Fothergill, being the most senior of the developers.

"The task in hand was assigned to Fothergill by Snodgrass. Fothergill took the notes, glanced over them briefly, and put them to one side on his desk, by reason of the fact that he was busy with some other modifications that were required."

"Interesting, Holmes," said Watson. "And what was the response of Snodgrass to that?"

"Well naturally, Watson, Snodgrass behaved characteristically in this case," replied Holmes. "He demanded to know how long it would take to complete the task."

"And the reply?" asked Watson.

"Fothergill said that he did not know, as he had not looked at it. He asked Snodgrass to ask him tomorrow afternoon, after he had had time to review the documents in question."

"A most sensible answer, Holmes," stated Watson. "This Fothergill is clearly a man of principle."

"Well, indeed," replied Holmes, "but listen to the rest of the case. The following afternoon, Snodgrass did *indeed* approach Fothergill with the same stated request. And—to preempt your question Watson—he replied that, after reviewing the document, he believed that it would be possible to complete the work in three months, with an estimation error of one and a half months. In other words, he said that it would take from a minimum of one and a half months, a maximum of four and a half months, and a most likely completion time of three months."

"Interesting, Holmes. And how did Snodgrass reply to this?" queried Watson.

"He replied thusly," answered Holmes. "Snodgrass smiled, and said how pleased he was that Fothergill would be able to complete the work in one and a half months. Fothergill was naturally aghast at this, but Snodgrass had already departed from the scene of the crime to tell his boss the 'good news.'"

"A most unsatisfactory outcome, Holmes," said Watson, somewhat dismayed. "Were there any further developments after this tawdry affair?"

"Only that Snodgrass got very upset at being made to look stupid in front of his boss when the module took three months and one week to complete," smiled Holmes.

This slightly fictionalized version of a real event illustrates an important point: an unhealthy proportion of people tend to hear what they want to hear, and then blame someone else when their plans, based on what they heard, go wrong.

The only really practical way to detect this before the best part of two years has been spent implementing the game is to make extensive use of prototypes. It is always helpful to make a mockup of the gameplay. It does not have to be extravagant, fast, or detailed. For many of my projects, I have not even bothered using a computer for initial gameplay prototypes. I have used whatever materials come to hand: pencil, paper, building blocks, toy cars, etc.

This technique has also been used successfully in other cases. The exact name of the example doesn't immediately spring to mind, but a certain successful top-down racing game for the PlayStation and PC was designed using toy cars and a large amount of floor space.

While sometimes it can be useful to implement the game prototype as a board game, or as a paper-based role-playing game in order to get the mechanics correct, other options are becoming available. Recently, more-advanced prototyping solutions have been released into the market. These are applications that provide a virtual testbed for interactions and behaviors. A particularly good example (and, in fact, the only one I have used) is *NeMo Dev* by Virtools, details of which are available at their Web site (**www.nemosoftware.com**). This package allows a complete 3D world to be built and actors placed within it using behavioral building blocks that can be expanded, if necessary, by a developer using a C++ interface to the package.

I have not had a chance to use this package as much as I would like, but it does seem to be a new direction in prototyping and it is also touted as being capable of producing the final released product. It is not the only package available: similar packages have been released in the past but have not fared well in the market, even though they were technically superb.

My personal theory on this is based on the nature of game developers. Developers in general—and game developers, in particular—are very competitive. I remember taking a demonstration of a voxel-based graphics technique (which was completely new and had not been done before) to a software company. The managing director of the company had one of his programmers look over the demonstration program. Make no mistake, this was an impressive demonstration for the time—3D accelerators were just a distant blip on the horizon! My technique allowed unprecedented numbers of highly detailed 3D objects to be displayed on screen at once. The programmer's response was to look critically at the demonstration, and make a comment to the effect that he could see how easily that it had been done, and that he had been thinking about doing it himself. My response to this was to ask him, in that case, why had he not done so.

I found out later from the managing director that the particular developer involved wanted to form a development team of his own and work freelance. He resented the idea that anyone was doing so.

The point is that game developers often want to "roll their own." They tend to not trust using code and components that other outside developers have produced. This is more difficult to justify now that all game development (with the exception of small consoles such as the Game Boy) goes through software interfaces, such as DirectX for the PC.

However, although these software interfaces are now unavoidable, a peculiar sort of malaise has afflicted game developers. For these developers, the software interfaces have become the new "metal," the lowest level of the system that they can access. None of them want anyone else getting between them and the lowest-level interfaces of the system application programming interface (API).

Hopefully, this is an attitude that will soften in time, particularly when programmers realize that the external code modules are better than anything they could write themselves in a reasonable period of time.

This is beginning to happen to some extent. Witness the success of the *Quake* and *Quake II* engines. They have been licensed to many developers, and have been used to produce very successful games such as *Half-Life*. However, the *Quake* engines are an exception to the rule. The programmers at id Software are generally considered the best in the industry for 3D engines, and it is this reputation and the success of *Quake* and *Quake II* that caused the widespread demand for these engines.

Hopefully, this sort of snobbery will decrease as development techniques become more mature, and the games industry progresses towards using a model more like that of the movie industry for outsourcing common components. At this moment, we are some way away from that, but it is a clear fact that game development is becoming increasingly complex. Soon, it will become financially impractical to keep rewriting core components, and outsourcing will become a necessity, instead of just an option, for all except the most well-funded development houses. Even then, the larger companies will probably follow suit, just because of the cost efficiencies involved.

It is possible that a new breed of company will be born, specifically producing components to be used by game developers. Virtools is probably one of these. Also, CyberLife (publishers of the *Creatures* series of products) may well serve this role. At the time of writing, they are currently developing *Gaia*, an artificial-life development kit, designed to allow the development of virtual organisms with intelligence, that can hopefully be used in games, as well as for other applications.

If the architecture, as opposed to the design, is overly simple, then this presents an entirely different set of problems. An overly simple architecture is fundamentally broken and needs to be rectified as soon as possible. If the architecture cannot support the functionality required of it, then there is no quick solution. It's not usually possible to simply patch the broken parts and carry on. An overly simple architecture shouldn't have even got through the review stage!

The only real solution is to reevaluate the architecture and reimplement any substandard parts. Depending on the nature of the fault, it may be possible to add any required interfaces and continue the work. A trivial example of this would be a CD playing module that did not allow random access within a track. This functionality would be quite easy to add without breaking existing uses of the module.

However, if the oversimplification was more fundamental, such as an interface for obtaining information about a 2D map needed to be expanded for use in a 3D environment, then the problem is more difficult. In this case, a simple addition of functionality may not be sufficient. The whole structure of the module and its underlying data will need to be reworked in order to meet the new specifications.

The converse of this situation is, of course, overcomplicating the design and/or the architecture. An overcomplicated design seems to be very common in the games market, but just what makes a game design overcomplicated is very subjective.

One man's meat is another man's poison. *Starcraft* may be far too complex for the average gamer (if there is such a beast), but for a hard-core wargamer, it may be too simple.

Games within genres tend to have accepted levels of complexity, which seems to be set by a consensus. This level of complexity increases with each new release within a genre, as more and more developers jump on the bandwagon. Usually, as has become abundantly clear over recent years, once a big-selling genre buster is released, the third-party clones soon follow, with most of these being inferior in design. I can only assume that (and I do have direct evidence of this) the design process revolves around someone looking at the successful game, and saying something like "Wouldn't this be cool if it had more units?" or "Wouldn't it be cool if you were able to control these units in far more detail?"

Invariably, it turned out that it would *not* be cool. Sometimes too much complexity is added, and the game becomes a battle with the user interface. What these designers do not seem to realize is that the interfaces were left deliberately simple because the game worked better letting the computer handle that fine level of control. It was simply a tedious experience for the player. The infamous water pipes from *SimCity 2000* spring to mind at this point. For those who have not played the game, the game required that you switch the view to a subterranean map, and lay water pipes to connect all of the building zones to a pumping station. This feature received lots of criticism in the press and on the Internet. It was simply not necessary, and lessened the enjoyment of the game. It was obvious that water pipes would be needed, so why not just allow them to be laid automatically? Why would someone leave an area unconnected? There's no reason.

Expanding and redefining a genre is not as simple as adding complexity. If that were the case, then, when the realtime strategy game *Warwind* was released sometime after *Warcraft II*, it would have been a huge hit. Sure, *Warwind* had some nice points, but the problem was that it allowed absolute control over almost every aspect of unit development, and with an obscure user interface. This was too much for the average gamer to handle. Press opinions in reviews tended to agree.

Personally, I played *Warwind* for about a day before reverting to *Warcraft II*. Even when *Starcraft* was released, the game mechanics, the user interface, and the method of unit control were virtually unchanged from *Warcraft II*. This would have been a deliberate design decision on the part of Blizzard Software, and it was a good one. Comparing the sales figures of both *Warcraft II* and *Starcraft* to all the other realtime strategy tends to support this view.

This does not mean that you have to oversimplify your game design in order to make it accessible. It just means that you should carefully consider your list of "cool" ideas, and determine if they are cool simply because they would be fun to implement, or whether they would be fun to play. If you can do this objectively, then you may be surprised by how much the list is reduced.

Any complexity in your game needs to be managed. You can do this in any number of ways, such as hiding it behind a user interface or just reducing the complexity to an acceptable level.

The best sort of complexity is emergent complexity, where simple rules combine in order to produce complex outcomes, such as molecules or atoms stacking together to form a crystal. The archetypal example of this would be Conway's *Game of Life*. This probably needs no introduction, but, for those of you who have just landed, I'll describe it briefly. The game is played on a flat field of cells, each of which has eight neighbors. Each cell is either occupied by an organism or is empty. Each game turn produces one generation of cells, and each generation of cells is derived from the previous one according to a set of rules.

The rules for *Game of Life* are as follows:

1. If an occupied cell has two or three neighbors, the organism survives to the next generation.
2. If an occupied cell has any other number of occupied neighbors, the organism dies.
3. If an unoccupied cell has three occupied neighbors, it becomes occupied.

Figure 14.3 illustrates these three rules.

If you are familiar with this game, then you will know that there are many complex constructions that arise from these three simple rules, such as "shooters" and "trackers." This is emergent complexity in action.

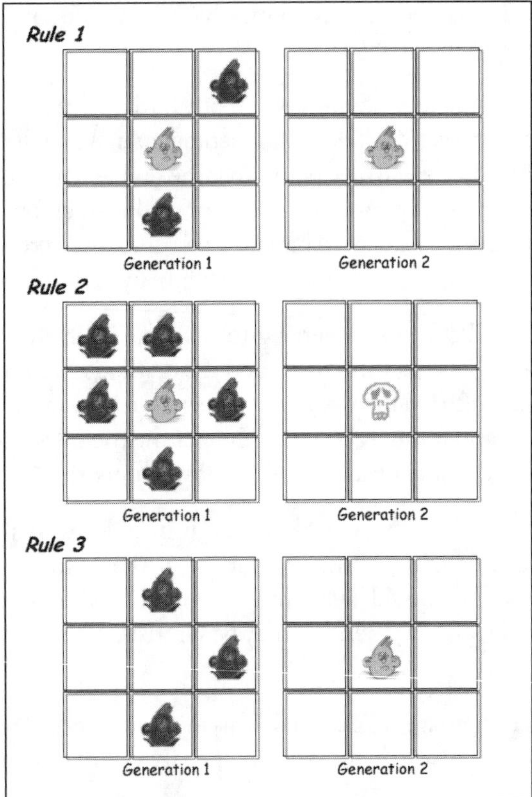

Figure 14.3
The rules of *Game of Life*.

The rules for *Game of Life* appear simple; they are. However, the selection of these rules out of all the possible permutations was a considered process. The rules are very fragile. Any changes and they do not work together as well. Some variations on these rules have been attempted (such as basing organism survival on color, and extensions into 3D), but these rules are neither as simple nor as successful as the originals.

The point of this is to show that complexity in a game is not necessarily a good thing. The process of designing a game *is* complex, but the resulting game design itself should not be. If this were the case, then I would suggest a rewrite. Any complexity in the gameplay would be better off emerging from a set of simple, consistent rules instead of being built in at the design level. You cannot hide an inherently complex system behind a simple user interface without losing something. I strongly suspect there is a strong link between the complexity of the rule base, and the complexity needed in a user interface in a game, and this should be kept in mind during the design process of a game.

An overly complicated architecture is a different kettle of fish entirely, the direct result of which is an increase in errors.

An overly complicated architecture produces unnecessary and unproductive implementation overhead. The architecture is the skeleton of the project, and the code is the flesh on its bones. If the skeleton is misshapen, then you'll get one ugly baby as a result.

By insisting on an overly complex architecture, the architect is reducing the effectiveness of the entire team: more effort will be required to achieve a set level of work. There will be more errors during this effort, and the resulting project will be more difficult to maintain due to increased code complexity. This also means that there will be more "knowledge content" to the project, and it will be correspondingly more difficult for any one developer to comprehend it in its entirety.

Unfamiliar Or Difficult Methodologies, Tools, And Libraries

Use of unfamiliar methodology results in extra training time and in rework to fix first-time misuses of the methodology.

Even the techniques presented in this book will need some take-up time; you cannot expect to be able to instigate a whole host of new procedures and techniques and have the whole team immediately and flawlessly implement them.

When these methodologies are first introduced, there will most likely be a dip in productivity of up to 25 percent. This can be *very* unsettling, and will most likely cause a small outburst of panic among the developers and managers of those implementing the measures. This can often be used as an argument by those who are against the measures. Quite often, developers can be opposed to the imposition of measures designed to track their activities. Game developers seem to be particularly guilty of this, as they like their "free spirit" and carefree existence, and seem to have a healthy disrespect for authority.

Some of the more disaffected developers will oppose the measures from the start, so any evidence that productivity is being compromised will be seized upon as a good reason to return to the warm familiarity of the "old ways." This should be avoided.

You can circumvent this reaction by preparing the development team for this eventuality. For any new methodology, tool, or library, there will be a learning curve. This is inevitable, as there is always a learning curve with any unfamiliar knowledge. Don't let skeptics knock anything new until it has had a sensibly long proving period. Not everything that is tried may work, but you'll never know if it is shot down in flames by a difficult developer.

As an example, if the product (or more likely, part of the project) is implemented in a low-level language (e.g., Assembler), then it is very likely that productivity will be lower than expected. In general, however, for the more powerful machines, Assembler is rarely necessary. Usually the machines are already fast enough to make it a futile aim. In the case of the Pentium processor and particularly when running a multitasking operating system, you can never be exactly sure how long a particular piece of code will take to run.

The only machines where Assembler is really justified are the limited-memory, low-power machines such as the Nintendo Game Boy and other hand-held consoles. Although Nintendo (and other companies) try to keep development information for use only by registered developers, an underground following always seems to spring up. There is even a freeware C compiler available for the Game Boy, and many emulators with excellent debugging facilities.

The development times for these machines with more-limited specifications tends to be shorter than full-blown PC and console projects, mainly because the programs are so much smaller. The Game Boy is about the only platform left where a lone person can be realistically expected to be able to produce a game that can match up to those that the big boys produce.

Architectural Integration Problems

One of the main dangers with developing components separately (as suggested in the software factory model) is that, if the procedure is not managed with the utmost care, there can be difficulties integrating them. Components developed separately cannot be integrated easily, requiring redesign and rework before they can be used.

This is not just a problem that affects just the game industry; it affects the whole of the software industry, which is one of the reasons for the increasing acceptance of object-version technologies such as COM (Component Object Model) and CORBA (Common Object Request Broker Architecture). These would, in theory, be good models to use for game development, except if you were aiming for a multiplatform release.

In the case of PC development, COM is certainly worth considering. There is no need to worry unduly about a performance hit, because the whole of the DirectX library is based on the COM system. Although this will be covered more in the third part of the book, COM allows versioning of objects by requiring that developers guarantee that the behavior of an object interface *must* remain unchanged. All objects would have to be obtained at runtime by calling a standard function with a guaranteed-unique ID number that represented that interface. If the interface needed to be upgraded, then a new interface number would be assigned, and, just as importantly, the old interface would need to be maintained unchanged. This allows upgrading shared components on a machine without breaking applications that use an earlier version of that interface. COM is certainly not a panacea, but it does solve a few of the most common problems with integration of components.

Currently, COM is effectively restricted to Windows-based machines, but Microsoft has stated that it will be promoting COM on other platforms as well. Ignoring any talk about monopolistic tendencies, it's possible that COM will, in the future, become an industry standard, and may be suitable for cross-platform development.

Schedule Threats

Schedule threats are nasty and are often the most insidious type of threat and the most difficult to detect and control.

Often, given the chance, developers will mask slips in their personal schedule in order to save face. It can be very difficult, even for the most experienced and responsible developer to admit that he or she is slipping the schedule. This is not helped by the fact that—although it is no direct fault of the developer—he or she is usually held responsible for the slippage.

Schedule slippages are not necessarily the fault of the developer. The chain of responsibility stretches all the way up the hierarchy of command, and the blame may lie anywhere on that hierarchy. The following sections give some examples of slippage, their causes, and how to deal with them. The main problem with slippage is that it sometimes goes unnoticed. It's only when all the slightly missed deadlines are totaled up that the odd day here and there suddenly turns out to be a schedule slipping by weeks or months.

Too-Tight Schedules

Due to financial and commercial restraints, most schedules are tight. Giving too much time to a team doesn't necessarily produce the pinnacle of perfection you may expect. Even when the financial resources are there for a team to be able to say, "It'll be released when it is ready," a tight control is needed to ensure that time is not squandered.

Deadlines are to provide focus. Nothing focuses the mind of an employee better than the knowledge that he has definite short-term aims to achieve before a certain date and time. Unfortunately, for various reasons, this is sometimes exploited and taken to the extreme by managers who decide that a schedule needs to be impossibly tight in order to prod the "lazy" developers into action. This always has a negative effect. Developers are smart. They wouldn't be developers if that weren't the case.

Schedules can be too tight from the outset for a number of reasons. Sometimes, schedules can have a fixed completion date due to outside reasons, Christmas being the most common. I know that it is supposed to be the season of miracles, but, even so, the number of hopelessly optimistic schedules that spring up at the beginning of a year, trying to get a new hit out in time for the Christmas silly season, never ceases to amaze me.

The only solution to a fixed-schedule problem such as this is to either reduce the product specification, increase the resources available, or to increase the time available. These three attributes (time, resources, and requirements) are in balance. You cannot alter one without a corresponding shift in one or both of the others.

These three attributes can be viewed as three points of a triangle, similar to that shown in Figure 14.4. If you imagine that the triangle is balanced about a point in its center, then it is clear that you cannot alter the "weight" of one of the corners without having to modify the others to balance the change. In order to keep the triangle from collapsing, you have to keep the center of gravity over the actual center of the triangle. So, if you shorten the schedule, you will have to increase the resources or simplify the specifications. If you decrease the resources, the specifications will need to be cut down, or the schedule will need to be lengthened. And so on.

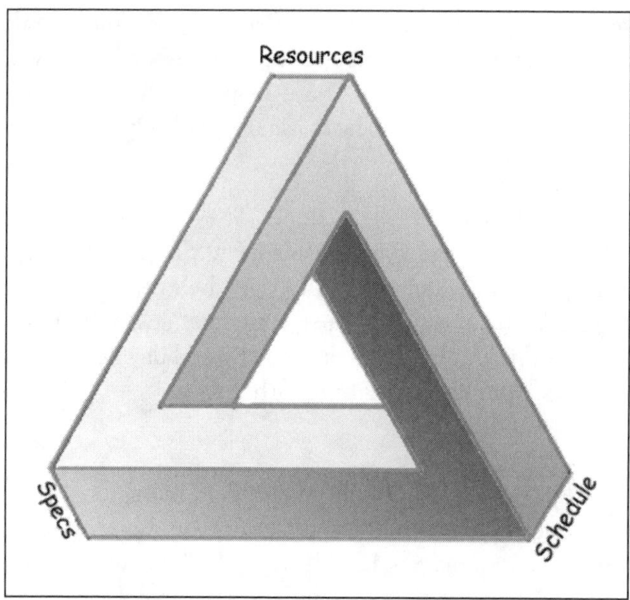

Figure 14.4
The impossible triangle of resources, schedule, and specifications.

This is an immutable law. There *is* no way round it. If the manager does not like this, then tough. Something has to give. Getting employees to work long hours in order to try to meet an impossible schedule is counterproductive. Not only will they begin to burn out, but there will also be a negative effect on morale. They may even leave the company, an outcome that should be held against the manager responsible in the same way as a large financial loss would be.

Another cause for concern is the "barely possible" schedule. This has been hinted at earlier in this chapter (see Case Study 14.1) and is where a schedule has been produced that is fairly accurate, except for the simple fact that it is the optimistic "best-case," rather than a realistic, "expected-case" schedule.

These "barely possible" schedules usually happen for two reasons. The first is that the employee responsible for producing the schedule is inexperienced. In this situation, he or she will usually try to impress management by producing a good schedule that fits what the management would like to see. The schedule is then produced with the assumption that there will be absolutely no problems during the development period. The second—and worse—cause of "barely possible" schedules is that managers will sometimes ask for further cuts to be made to the schedule, and, due to pressure, the scheduler will comply, resulting in an impossible schedule.

This does no favors to anybody, and it is usually the development team that gets the blame for the schedule's slip. There are no simple answers to how to handle this. The only way to really deal with it effectively is for the scheduler to create a realistic schedule in the first place, and then stand his or her ground if management asks them to reduce the length. The assumption usually is that all developers pad their schedules anyway, so they can just cut out some of the padding and produce the "real" schedule. This is an alluring argument that must be resisted at all cost. You cannot just reduce a schedule and expect that the same amount of work will just be produced faster. Something has to give, and that something is either the scope of the project, or the amount of resources assigned to it.

When I am asked to reduce a schedule unreasonably, I try to make the person see things from my point of view. They can have it quickly, but it will cost them more and the functionality will be less, with an accompanying increase in risk. The mention of more money, reduced functionality, and increased risk tends to focus the mind quickly, and usually other compromises will be made.

Incomplete Schedules

Another problem that can occur with inexperienced schedulers is if they omit tasks from the schedule. Maybe they forgot that all the artwork would need additional processing, or maybe they forgot that a game needs an install and an uninstall procedure. But it is very difficult to predict a list of tasks that will need to be performed over a two-year period.

The fact is that, if a task is not on the task list, it will not be scheduled for. This results in the nightmare situation of an incomplete project that, according to the schedule, is actually complete! The only solutions to this are to either buckle down and complete the work, to overshoot the schedule, to allocate extra resources for the extra work, or to reduce the scope of the project. These all come with their own costs and disadvantages, as I've indicated previously.

Unavailable Resources

If the schedule was based on the use of specific team members, and those team members did not become available, then there is a *big* problem.

If a particular team member has skills that are required, and he or she is busy elsewhere, then there is nothing that can be done apart from waiting. More crucially, however, this situation should *never* be allowed to happen. It is extremely dangerous to allow one person to have a monopoly on a particular skill set. What happens if he or she decides to leave? The solution to this is to ensure that you *never* get yourself into this situation, by encouraging the spread of skills between your employees.

Remember that a project has a certain theoretical minimum set of requirements. If you make changes to any one of these, then one or both of the others will need to be adjusted in the opposite direction. This also is an immutable law, so it is not worth trying to abuse it. Doing so will only lead to other problems such as developer burnout, project delay or cancellation, and/or a substandard product.

Overestimation Of Schedule Savings

If certain productivity tools (such as advanced prototyping tools) are used, they are often viewed with a sort of "new-world" style hope and awe.

Often, no doubt dazzled by the multitude of knobs and buttons available, otherwise rational developers become convinced that they can perform superhuman feats, leaping tall buildings in a single bound, rescuing orphans from collapsing buildings, and single-handedly producing a fully working game prototype in a ridiculously short period of time. Okay, so I was lying about the leaping and the rescuing, but the capabilities of wonderful new tools are often overestimated, particularly when they are unlike anything that the team has used before.

Sometimes the tool will appear to have all the features needed to implement whatever it is that needs doing. The problem is that the more "help" a tool gives you, the more it will railroad you into its methods of doing things. Quite often, unless you are extremely lucky, it will not be quite what is wanted, and you will spend your time working around the perceived shortcomings of the tool. Depending on the nature of the tool, the difficulty of doing this can vary from the mildly taxing to the completely impossible. Granted, most serious tools allow a developer to produce an add-in module, but this involves designing a module to fit in with an unfamiliar architecture, learning a new API, and discovering how to actually perform the task within the confines of an unfamiliar design program. This is a seductive task, because it can often be (incorrectly) assumed that, because it is a standard language such as C++ being used to create the add-in, a good C++ programmer should be able to rattle off the add-in fairly quickly. The problem is that the time needed to learn the system being extended is often discounted.

The solution is to either reschedule to allow learning time, or to cut the scope of the use the misnomer, "productivity-enhancing" tool. Of course, you can also drop the idea of using it altogether.

Inaccurate Schedule Estimates

In some circumstances (and I'm sure we've all been there), a schedule can look exactly right. It can have every task labeled, every risk considered, and every developer busy without dependency conflicts. And, yet, when it comes to putting it into practice, one or more areas do not adhere to the schedule. For example, unfamiliar areas of the product may take more time than is expected to design and implement, or a delay in one task may cause cascading delays in dependent tasks

This could be because the product is larger than has been estimated, or the amount of effort required is greater than has been estimated. This assumes that the difficulties are purely due to the technical complexity of the solution, and have nothing to do with on-the-job research being required. If it is the latter, then there is no solution. You just have to sit it out and wait until the research has concluded, or you can cut the functionality. Either solution is usually intolerable, but that is the price you pay for allowing scheduled research. You cannot schedule research: it is an activity that cannot be estimated. How ridiculous would it sound to commit to a schedule of six months, with detailed checkpoints and milestones, for discovering antigravity drives? Ridiculous, right? You would have to have full knowledge of the problem and the solution before you even started to be able to accurately estimate how long it is going to take to complete. Research is, by nature, an investigation of the unknown. Scheduled research? You must be joking!

If, however, the problem is due to unexpected complexity, then there usually are only three solutions to this type of problem. One is to cut the functionality. This solution may or may not be practical depending on your needs. The second is to reschedule the project, making allowances for the extra time required. The third solution, which is based on the software-factory methodology, is to replace the component with a compatible (but maybe less capable) one from the library. This may or may not be suitable for release, but, if all else fails, you will still have a working product. However, that is not the main point. The main point is that even if the slotted-in component does not offer all the functionality needed, it will at least act as a stopgap measure while the new component is being worked on. Other parts of the project can still continue, if a little cautiously, and not as much time will be lost due to having to wait for a critical component to be completed.

Persuading people to work longer hours is another option. If the effort required for a project has been only slightly underestimated, then short bursts of overtime may be a sensible way to get back on schedule, as long as the developers *are paid for it.*

Unfortunately, this system has been long open to abuse within the games industry. I have heard horror stories of developers being forced to work 80-hour weeks for months on end for no extra monetary reward (except maybe a pizza on weekends, and a cheesy award and T-shirt at the end of the project). This is ridiculous. I am a firm believer that people should not be forced to work for longer than eight hours a day for extended periods. It is counterproductive, and you usually end up with a substandard game and a whole bunch of disgruntled, burnt-out developers.

The main excuse used to justify this sort of management abuse (and note that the managers themselves do not usually come in for the weekends) is that writing a game is about sacrifice, or some other related falsehood. Rubbish! It's a job, pure and simple, and anybody who tries to convince you otherwise is deluded (or stands to make a lot of money out of your sacrifice). To summarize, voluntary overtime is okay for short periods, as long as the developer is paid accordingly.

Schedule Adjustment Errors

Adjusting a schedule to account for some unexpected delay is often subject to errors. Sometimes reestimation in response to schedule slips is overly optimistic or ignores the project history or metrics gathered from other projects.

The best way to ensure these errors do not occur is to use past information and metrics on the nature and performance of the employee concerned.

Case Study 14.2 illustrates these procedures in action.

Case Study 14.2 Applied Schedule Readjustment

In one of my roles as a troubleshooter for an overdue project, I was asked to analyze the current schedule and readjust it to estimate an accurate completion based on the state of the project as it was then.

It was not possible to do this without first gathering some metrics from the team. To do this, I observed the tasks that each of them had been assigned, and the time that they had been allocated to do it. First, I assured them that they were not being blamed for the problems with the project, and that I was there to reassess the schedule and produce a more accurate prediction. One of the reasons that the project had run into trouble was that, as the pressure mounted, procedure had been abandoned in an attempt to meet the deadlines. (This is covered later in this chapter.) The result of this was, of course, to compound the problems and cause even more bugs and schedule slips. At this stage, we stopped any new development and were concentrating on bringing the project back up to acceptable levels. This work had been going on for about two months, and was nearly complete.

This was the right time to begin adjusting the schedule, because new development was about to start. If I had tried to do it beforehand, the results would not have been as useful, because extra work would have been needed to work around the problems with the old codebase.

The team members were assigned new tasks, each of which (according to the schedule) was expected to take one or two days to implement. The team was asked to strictly adhere to procedure. I emphasized that this was not a race, and that they were not being assessed for proficiency. Every individual has a different working rate, and just because a coder is fast does not mean that he is necessarily good. I required the information on their rate of work solely because I needed to adjust the schedule to match their rate of work.

With these instructions, I observed and collected metrics from the team over a period of a couple of weeks. I found that, without exception, all of the team failed to hit the scheduled deadlines. The schedule was too aggressive.

For each of the team members, I worked out the ratio between the actual time taken and the scheduled time for the sample activities. Having done this, I took the task list for each individual, and multiplied the scheduled times by this ratio to produce a more accurate estimate of expected times. With the guidance of the team, I then shuffled tasks around to make sure that each individual had a balanced task list.

The whole process was then repeated for another week, and at the end of that week the ratios were again calculated and the tasks reshuffled.

After the third week, we found that the developers were consistently hitting the deadlines, *and* strictly adhering to procedure. Morale, by this stage, had already improved considerably. The team had gone from thinking that they were slow and inefficient to realizing that the schedule they had been working to was unachievable.

The next obstacle was explaining to eager management that the expected time of release for the product according to the new schedule was two months later than they hoped. I was asked if I could trim the schedule somewhere to cut those two months out.

This dismayed me somewhat, because it was this sort of thinking that got them into this mess in the first place. I drew a diagram of a triangle on the whiteboard (similar to that shown in Figure 14.4 and explained the delicate balancing act between resources, specifications, and schedule. I couldn't trim the schedule because there was no room for maneuver. They would either have to add resources or cut functionality and be prepared to deal with the complications that evolved from doing this at such a late stage in a project.

Adding resources or cutting functionality was unacceptable to them because they had a contracted features list and budget, so, in the end, they had no choice but to go with my recommendations.

The project was finished within one week of my newly estimated schedule, and the customers were placated.

The excessive pressure from an unachievable schedule reduces productivity, mainly due to ever-decreasing morale on the part of the developers, as they see themselves slipping constantly behind despite their best efforts to make up lost ground. The only solution to situations such as this is to consider actions such as those presented in Case Study 14.2.

Organizational Problems

Organizational problems are my favorites. However, they are also the most difficult to deal with effectively. They are my favorite because they are usually a direct result of management error, and it is always nice to get one over on the boss! They are the most difficult to deal with because telling your boss that he has made a mistake is usually the quickest route to the door, as shown in Figure 14.5.

These situations have to be handled with the utmost care. Telling your next-most senior manager doesn't usually work, because, if the news is bad, he or she may feel that telling the big boss will be bad for his or her career! Everybody loves to shoot the messenger.

However, put yourself in the boss's position. Would you rather be told about a potential problem a couple of months into initial prototyping, or would you rather be told by a developer several months past the delivery date that he had tried to tell you about the problems over a year ago, but couldn't get it past his immediate manager?

The solution to this particular situation is to have an anonymous channel. In that way, anybody can report problems without fear of repercussions on their career.

Management-Induced Difficulties

Management causes most organizational problems. This statement is not management-bashing; it's just a natural consequence of the fact that management *is* responsible for the organization of a project. Hey, they have to be responsible for something!

Figure 14.5
The easy way out.

For example, management (or even the marketing department) may insist on technical decisions that cause the schedule to be lengthened. It is unfortunate that the market is driven by the technology, but there is not a lot we can do about that. It may be that an OEM deal means that the product has to support a particular graphics card natively, rather than through a more generic API such as DirectX, or something of this ilk.

In some circumstances, management insists on reviewing decisions such as purchasing, budget approval, legal matters, etc. This situation usually occurs when a large publisher owns a stake in a smaller game-development company. One of the conditions these publishers try to impose is the "right of veto." This means that every decision that affects the product has to be ratified by the parent company. If the parent company has many subsidiaries, then the chances are that this could be a significant cause of delay (a cause, you should realize, that the publishers are bound to forget when they are bellowing over the phone at your manager, demanding to know why the game is three months over schedule).

This is the sort of thing that can affect the morale of your team. Other management decisions can also lower the morale, such as extended forced overtime or reduced privileges for no good reason, or an inefficient team structure that further reduces productivity.

Surprisingly, it is also the case that good management decisions can (at least temporarily) reduce morale, such as the imposition of procedure and defined development practices. The root cause of this is that people feel uncomfortable with change. This has to be handled with a "softly-softly" approach, and should not be abused. There is no point in implementing procedures to allow the team to work more efficiently if you are then going to saddle them with compulsory overtime and expect them to work efficiently for 10 hours a day. The whole point of implementing strict development procedures is to make the team more efficient, and save individuals from having to work long hours. If management is going to implement measures that lower the morale of the team, then there had better be an easily visible benefit for the team materializing out of it pretty soon.

Some of the old school of management may not understand the more sedate measured pace that procedure brings. You should remember that the games industry has a decade or more of bad habits behind it, and this it not going to change overnight. Some managers will get nervous at the slow but steady pace and actively discourage it. They may wish to see more cutting-edge heroics, with pretty demos and clearly visible progress rather than steady work that may not show any immediately visible whizzy new effects on screen. If this is the case, then the team will be putting too much effort into only one area of the project in order to satisfy that manager, and the development will become off-balance, resulting in shortcuts and unnecessary compromises further downstream. This sort of off-kilter development, concentrating on external appearances only, prevents accurate status reporting, which undercuts the team's ability to detect and correct problems effectively. This is likely to be compounded by extra pressure as the project attempts to draw to a conclusion and the team finds that important subsystems are either incomplete or missing. In this sort of situation, it is not uncommon that project plans are ignored due to the time pressure, resulting in chaotic, inefficient development, as described in Case Study 14.2.

Contractor Problems

Surprisingly (or maybe not, seeing as how the average games industry wage is much lower than the equivalent paid outside the industry), contractors are not used very much within the games industry. While it is common for an organization outside of the games industry, such as a bank, to hire contract programmers for the duration of a project on a regular basis, this is virtually unheard of in a games company.

The usual use for contractors within the games industry is to allocate complete units of work, such as FMV production, motion capture, playtesting, and configuration testing, the conversion of an already existing game to a different platform, or the production of 3D models.

As I've already said, some of the larger companies enter into contracts with smaller game-development houses, and sometimes you will find that the parent company will ask you to use the engine developed by another subsidiary in order to produce a new product. A number of obvious problems can arise from this.

Late Delivery

If the contractor does not deliver the specified components by the agreed delivery date, then your team will have a problem on its hands. A workaround will have to be found, and this may even put the project on hold.

Penalty clauses for late delivery, although a good idea on paper, tend to have a counterproductive effect. Unless they are sufficiently forbidding, there will be very little incentive to continue work if a penalty is threatened. And, of course, you may not always be in the position to insist on such measures. The best way to prevent this problem is to avoid being in this situation in the first place. If this isn't possible, then you either need to sweat it out and wait, cut your losses, and cancel the agreement (and most likely the project if you cannot find a replacement component), or begin development of your own replacement component.

Poor Quality

Usually, the contractor will have his or her own development standards and practices. There is no way you can guarantee that the work will be delivered on time *and* be of acceptable quality.

In this case, time will need to be added to the schedule in order to allow the quality to be improved. In other words, this is the same as if they were delivered late in the first place. The situation where the work is delivered late *and* is of poor quality is a nightmare that doesn't even bear thinking about.

The solution to this problem is not easy, but some measures that can be taken are explicit quality guarantees built into the initial contract, and a concrete set of specifications. This sort of difficulty sometimes arises when the requirements have not been adequately defined, or there has been some sort of feature creep due to changing requirements. Make sure that your requirements are definite and that there is no danger of misinterpretation. Encourage the contractor to maintain a dialogue with the person who created the specs, so that there can be a constant monitoring and correction process.

Don't just throw the requirements out of the door and expect exactly what you wanted to come rolling back in with a flourish some months later. You will be in for a tragic disappointment if you do.

The other important thing to make sure of is that the contractor has sufficient motivation (usually of the monetary kind) to perform the task required. The danger here is that, if the contractor does not buy into the project due to insufficient motivation, then they are unlikely to provide the level of performance needed.

Personnel Problems

Personnel problems are inevitable. Nobody can be expected to get on with each other all of the time. It's like the old saying, "You can please some of the people all of the time, you can please all of the people some of the time, but you can't please all of the people all of the time."

This is a fact of development life. Get used to it.

Relationships

Developing a game has been compared to giving birth. I don't know whether that is true, because I have never given birth, and neither would I like to. I'm sure that if you asked any woman about the similarities or differences you would probably get a sharp response, which would not be suitable to print here.

Anyway, whether the game-development process can be compared to giving birth or not is not particularly important. The point is to make it clear that development can involve a lot of pain. (This applies to development in general, and not just game development. Any additional pain on the part of game developers tends to indicate masochistic tendencies. Maybe you should see a doctor!)

The pain and stress of the development process can sorely tax relationships between people who have spent every day of the past couple of years in each other's company. Think about it. You are effectively spending a minimum of eight hours a day, five days a week, in the company of a group of (usually) young, headstrong neoadolescents, in a situation of great stress. This is not an environment conducive to peace and harmony. In the natural course of events, there are likely to have been a few arguments and bust-ups along the way, and that is just between team members. This can obviously damage productivity. If the team's members are too busy feuding, work will not get done as efficiently. Worse, if the feuding escalates to open warfare, then there will inevitably be casualties, usually in the form of code sabotage or forced resignations. Sabotage can result in lost work or poor-quality code that requires rework. This is an *incredibly* damaging situation to be in.

Notwithstanding the effects on the project, do any of the people who inflict these situations unilaterally think how it must feel to dread coming into work every day, knowing that they will be subject to abuse as if they were stupid? They should have stopped their bullying at school.

If your company has any employees that use the bullying technique to get their way, then it is not good enough to just say to the victim that he should be able to handle the rough-and-tumble of the working environment. The technique I have used in these situations (when I have been in the position to decide) is borrowed from the American justice system: three strikes and you're out. It can be difficult because the bully is usually a powerful developer within the company, and is quite often a prima donna type, but this sort of behavior cannot and should not be tolerated in a professional environment.

If team members do not work together efficiently, the resulting conflicts cause poor communication, poor designs, interface errors, and extra rework. If the problem team members are not removed from the team as soon as they are detected, then they will continue their antisocial behaviors, damaging overall team motivation.

If this is the sort of damage that employees at the same level can inflict upon each other, then just imagine the abuse that can be heaped upon the employees by an unscrupulous and domineering manager. Poor relationships between developers and management are one of the most detrimental to morale and productivity. This can promote an "us and them" situation, which often has the dubious benefit of uniting the team, but in the wrong way.

The net result of these problems is that low employee motivation and morale reduce productivity. Team members do not buy into the project and consequently do not provide the level of performance needed to make it a success. I shouldn't even need to point out the disastrous events that could ensue if any disgruntled employees leave before the project is complete. This would have an immediate and detrimental effect on the schedule as the team would have to learn and shoulder the responsibilities of the missing member (or members), lengthening the schedule and thrusting increasingly demoralizing levels of stress on the team. One pseudosolution to this would be to add new development personnel. However, if they are added late in the project, the additional training and communications required adds a lot of overhead that reduces the effectiveness of existing team members.

Skills Shortages

Within the games industry, there are a number of perceived developer disciplines (such as a 3D programmer, a physics programmer, an AI programmer, etc.). Whether these divisions are real or imaginary is a moot point and a discussion best left for another time.

Assuming, however, that these divisions are real and necessary, then a skills shortage can arise in even the best-staffed project. Sometimes, a programmer will be called upon to work in an area in which he or she may not have much experience.

This problem does not apply just to developers. In general, when people's assignments do not match their skill set, problems arise. Usually, the lack of specialist knowledge increases the mean number of defects in the work (be it code or otherwise), and the amount of rework needed.

Not all companies have the resources to provide full training to everybody who needs it, and, in fact, there do not seem to be that many training courses specifically designed for game-industry employees, unlike other areas of the software industry.

Three general approaches can be used to solve this sort of problem. The first is to allow extra time for the employees to familiarize themselves with the areas they will be working in. Under some circumstances, this may be practical, but, under others (such as a limited amount of time or money), it may not. The team members selected for this should, at the very least, have the base set of skills to allow them to learn the new material efficiently. For example, there is no real use in asking a nonmathematical programmer to investigate and design a new 3D engine.

The second solution is to encourage knowledge sharing (as in the software factory.) In this way, employees with specialist skills should be encouraged to pass on their knowledge to other employees by direct teaching. An even better approach would be to have a regular set of seminars provided by the more skilled employees with the sole aim of passing on their experiences and skills to other employees. This is cheaper than employing an outside lecturer, and may be more relevant to your company ethos. Employees like to feel as if they are being taken care of, and an optional educational program shows them that their needs are being considered.

The third solution, for those with no time but plenty of money, is to hire an outside contractor with the required skills. This can be an expensive option, but, if you need the skills that badly, then you may have no choice. You can always offset your losses by asking the contractor to teach other employees while he or she is there.

I have said that contractors can be expensive. For long-term use, that is true, but, in situations where you need a small amount of highly specialized work to be done, then employing a contractor is probably the most cost-effective solution. Contractors with the correct skills also tend to be easier to find than permanent employees.

Development Problems

In this section, we are *not* going to focus on coding problems. This book is not about coding. No, here we are going to concentrate on the problems that affect a developer's ability to code.

Developers tend to be an unfussy bunch when it comes to environment. You can sit them down in a darkened office, with only the glow of the monitor to provide light, and, as long as they are undisturbed, they can code quite happily, without worrying about their surroundings. At least, that is the theory; in practice, it is usually altogether different.

Office Facilities

Problems with offices can be a significant contribution to delays. The whole point of an office is to provide a stable working environment for the development.

If, for example, the office facilities are not available on time, then where can the team do its work? Good question, and one that does not have an easy answer. It depends on the office facilities. If the team is part of a large company, then maybe they can relocate to another part of the building. If the team is part of a small company, maybe a startup, then it is possible that the offices that they have rented may not be finished in time. Nobody tends to move offices halfway through a project, so the probability is that the team is about to start a new project (or maybe the first) when the move takes place. This means that the start of the project may be put back, but, if the delay is short, then it shouldn't cause too many problems.

If your company doesn't have an office *at all*, then you may have a bigger problem. You could always take a leaf out of the Yost Group's book. (Yost is the developer of 3D Studio MAX.) The first release of 3D Studio MAX was developed with the entire team in separate locations. The use of a virtual office such as this presented some problems, mainly to do with transmitting large files across a standard modem, but, because of the object-oriented nature of the application, this sort of developer partitioning worked fairly well.

If office facilities are available but are inadequate in some way (for example, there are no phone lines, network wiring, desks and chairs, office supplies, or computers, etc.), then you have a problem. The solution to this type of problem is to take out the checkbook and go buy the stuff, but you didn't need me to tell you that! If you are part of a larger company, then complaining to your manager that the facilities are inadequate may help.

The office could also be noisy or crowded, or disruptive in some other way. Under these circumstances, the imposition of various ground rules should help, such as a clear desk policy (where desks are left clear at the end of each day), and measures to encourage a quiet environment. Provide meeting areas so that people do not have loud discussions where others are trying to work.

Development Tools And Third-Party Libraries

One of the problems with development is that you are invariably dependent on third-party development tools and libraries. If there are problems with these third-party tools and libraries, this can cause problems such as delays or producing mysterious code defects that are difficult to trace.

If the development tools do not work as expected, then developers will need extra time to create workarounds for the defects. This could be because development tools were not chosen for their technical merits, but because they were cheap or had the coolest marketing, and they are not as productive as expected. The only other option, apart from implementing workarounds, is to switch to a new tool (if one is available). Quite often though, this will bring its own new set of problems, not to mention the delay and difficulties caused by transferring the entire project to the new tool.

If code or class libraries are of poor quality, then extra testing, defect correction, and rework will be required. Worse still, problems in an external library are usually hard to find, especially if the source code for the library is not provided. Sometimes, you cannot avoid the use of an external library, so there is no choice but to work around the problems. For example, can you imagine writing a commercial PC game nowadays without the use of DirectX? No? Me, neither! Any problems in DirectX that affect your project will need to be worked around. Reporting the bug may get it fixed, but the chances of it being fixed and released in time for your game release are low. Even if it is fixed, the chances are that many machines will still be using older versions of the library code. Even though you can distribute the runtime of DirectX on your distribution CD, you cannot be sure that everybody has updated their hardware drivers (which are generally released by the manufacture of the hardware). Fortunately, DirectX seems to be working fairly well now, although there were some compatibility horror stories from the early days. However, if a library that you are forced to use is of unacceptably low quality then the code that uses it will require more testing, design, and implementation work to correct than would be expected.

Misinterpretation Of Designs

Even with the best of intentions, developers will sometimes misinterpret design documents and produce output that bears no resemblance to the software that was requested. This misinterpretation may occur by accident or design.

It is possible that the developer simply made a mistake, and did not understand the design correctly. This is understandable, but it is not necessarily excusable. If the developer was unsure of any concepts in the design document, he or she should have asked for clarification before beginning to develop the code. This is an obvious point: a developer shouldn't be developing something he does not fully understand.

A slightly more serious situation is where the "mistake" was a deliberate one on the part of the developer. He or she may have decided to modify or rewrite the design to his or her idea of a superior implementation. It may be only a small change or it may be a large one. The end result, however, is exactly the same: a divergence between documentation and code that cannot be allowed to happen. Even if the developer is conscientious enough to update the design document, the modifications will not have gone through the proper approval procedures and may not be in line with the rest of the project. Worse still, there may be other modules that rely on the original implementation of the code, rather than the new improved version. In these cases, development of the wrong software will require it to be redesigned and rewritten.

Development of extra software functionality that is not required, otherwise known as gold-plating, can extend the schedule. In the case of gold-plating, the developer implements the functionality required, but feels the urge to add extra functionality, because he or she perceives it to be useful and it requires little or no extra effort to implement. The developer implements it because he or she thinks that it is more functionality for free.

There is one lesson that everybody learns sooner or later, and that is that *nothing is free*. Adding extra functionality over and above the specifications may seem free and easy at the time, but the cost will be apparent later during maintenance and bug fixing.

Meeting The Requirements

Requirements may be imposed on the product by the game designer, publishers, marketing, and external organizations such as ratings boards or supermarkets. These constraints may or may not be adhered to depending on the nature of the company's political environment, but, even so, there are bound to be some problems caused by difficult or conflicting requirements.

You may wonder why a supermarket has an influence on a game, but it is a well-known fact that Wal-Mart has made stocking decisions based on game content. Not being stocked by Wal-Mart is viewed quite seriously by most, if not all, publishers. If the man from Wal-Mart says "no," then you can wave goodbye to a large chunk of potential sales. Understandably, many publishers will insist that their products are supermarket friendly.

There could be other more basic requirements that may be difficult to achieve. For example, meeting the product's size or speed requirements may need more time than expected, including the time required for redesign and reimplementation. If a product is fundamentally slow, then optimizing it to meet the speed requirements can be a tedious process.

If the game is developed using a beta version of a necessary library, such as DirectX, then there could be problems when the final version is released. It is possible that not all of the features present in the beta version have made the release, or even that workarounds used to avoid problems with the beta version simply break with the release version.

If there are strict requirements for compatibility with an existing system (for example, a related series of games relying on the same underlying data, or a multiplayer game that needs to cooperate with a third-party online server interface), then the system will require much more testing, design, and implementation than expected. A good example is Blizzard's *Battle.net* server software, which is a free Internet multiplayer server for use with Blizzard's games, *Starcraft* and the two *Diablo* games, amongst others. In general, requirements for interfacing with other systems that may not be under the team's control will result in unforeseen design, implementation, and testing.

If your team is aiming for cross-platform compatibility, then the implementation and testing will take longer. Many things can go wrong with cross-platform development, including subtle differences in so-called "standard" APIs and differences in processor types.

Research: The Consequences

As mentioned before, research, by its nature, cannot be scheduled. You cannot expect to be able to schedule an inherently unpredictable activity. The best you can be expected to do, if you are forced to research as part of the schedule, is to set a cut-off date and make sure you have a contingency plan to fall back on if the research comes to nothing.

That is the main problem with research: pushing the game's state of the art will inevitably and unpredictably lengthen the schedule, and you cannot rely on any guarantees from optimistic developers that it will be finished by a certain date, as seductive as those arguments may seem. The development of a new kind of component that may be unfamiliar to the developers working on it will inevitably take longer than expected, as they must first traverse the learning curve before they will be productive.

Other areas of the project may also be dependent on the module being researched and developed. If no suitable contingency plan is in place, then the only option will be for all the dependent projects to wait for results from the research project, further lengthening the schedule.

The whole point is that you should avoid getting into such a position. Relying on the outcome of research in a scheduled project is just asking for trouble. That is why research should be conducted as an activity outside the schedule.

Process Problems

The previous chapter discussed "process" in great detail, and discussed how it could be used to provide accurate status tracking for your project, and generally make the lives of the people on the team easier (despite their initial protestations on the subject!)

We are going to briefly revisit that subject again here, and discuss how process can be misused, so that it ends up being detrimental to the project, and additionally makes the lives of the team members a misery.

Red Tape And Bureaucracy

Some managers take process to heart…too much so, unfortunately. They will attempt to saddle you with three pieces of paperwork to sign if you wish to sneeze. I once worked for a company that required me to document the time I spent in the lavatory every day, so that they could calculate and subtract the total time from my weekly time sheet! Fortunately, they didn't ask for details of what I did in there!

Process (after an initial learning curve) should never amount to a chore. It is not usually too difficult to do; the only difficulties are the initial shift from a "no process" to a "some process" environment.

In some cases, however, there can be too much paperwork to fill in. If a task generates an inordinate amount of paperwork, then it should be examined to see how it is being streamlined. "Process" is supposed to help the employees, not hinder them. If they are filling in the same information in multiple places, then the information-gathering process should be modified to make this unnecessary. The object is to make the completion of paperwork as simple as possible, so that it is more likely to get done and more likely to be correct. Nobody wants to have to type in the same old information several times for the same task, so make sure the process is as streamlined and free of redundancies as possible. Too much paperwork may well result in slower progress that would otherwise be expected. Care should also be taken to ensure that the employees do not have to spend too much of their time reporting the information to management: instead of scheduling a meeting, which is usually unnecessary for a mere progress report, just send the report by email to all concerned and answer any questions that may arise in the same manner.

Misuse And Metrics

There is no point in having a comprehensive set of procedures in place if they are not going to be used correctly. It is in the nature of developers to try to avoid work that they assume is nonproductive, and this includes quality procedures, unless their benefits are precisely explained.

These can be abused in a number of ways. For example, if the initial upstream quality-assurance activities are not performed properly (the idea being that they are skipping them to "save time"), then the net result is that all the apparently "saved" time (and more) will be spent doing time-consuming rework further downstream in the development.

If the statistics and metrics are not being tracked and reported correctly, then it is possible that early-warning signals may go unnoticed. The inaccurate tracking results in quality problems that affect the schedule being ignored until very late in the project. By this stage, it may be too late.

Metrics should be considered as very important sets of statistics. They are the only consistent way of leveraging knowledge learned in one project so that it may be used to aid the development of the next. This information is too valuable just to be ignored, and should be recorded accurately and consistently. If this data is not being collected adequately, then this will result in not knowing exactly how far behind schedule the development is until late in the project.

If the risk-management program is not making good use of these metrics, then there is a good chance that the half-hearted risk management will fail to detect major project risks before they arise, and the project may founder. There is no point in buying a smoke alarm if you are going to just leave it in its box, without any batteries.

Problems With Formalities

The amount of formality required in the average software project is much more than is usually seen in the games industry, and this is not a good thing for the games industry.

Too little formality (ignoring the development procedures) will result in a lack of communication, poor quality output, and large amounts of rework. Too little formality is usually worse than no formality at all, as it gives the employees a false sense of security. If there is no formality at all, at least they will know what to expect.

The converse situation can also a problem: too much formality (overly bureaucratic insistence of sticking to the letter of the law for procedures and standards) will result in unnecessary and time-consuming overhead. Employees will be spending most of their time completing and processing paperwork.

A certain level of process is definitely a good idea. The benefits that it provides for your project far outweigh any disadvantages from the extra work involved in sticking to a few procedures. The trick is to find the balance.

Chapter 15
The Future Of The Industry

Key Topics:

- ***The hypothetical "mass market"***
- ***Changing management techniques***
- ***The film industry model***
- ***The maturation of the industry***
- ***The online revolution***
- ***The possibility of regulation***

This chapter contains our best guess at what the future holds for the games industry as a whole and what will happen to the games market. As can be seen by the complete failure of the world to end in fire in July of 1999, no one can successfully predict the future—at least not consistently.

I will attempt in this chapter to project some possible directions for the industry based on what I believe will (or at least *should*) happen.

It's entirely possible I will be wrong on every count, but, if the law of averages holds, I should at least get a few of my predictions right. And, at any rate, some of them appear to be fairly inevitable, such as the inexorable rise of the online gaming community.

The games industry is still fairly young. We're through most of the teething troubles and the terrible twos. We've passed through that golden age when everything was feasible and anybody could design and write a hit game. We've even passed through the age of back-bedroom programmers and alleged millionaire teenage programmers (most of which appeared to be unfounded publicity stunts).

Now, we've reached the adolescence of the industry. Everything is still funky and cool, but we're less willing to experiment with the more outlandish ideas, and we're starting to cast an eye to crass commercialism—mainly due to a consolidation of the marketplace, in a similar fashion to the movie industry.

The State Of The Industry

If I'm being completely honest, I have to say that I am fairly disappointed with the current state of the industry. The originality and fire of the early years seems to have been (for the most part) drained out from it.

The latest advances in technology seem to be converging towards a common point. On the latest generation of consoles, all games are starting to look pretty much identical. Three-dimensional polygon systems seem to be the order of the day, even in the most unassuming of systems.

The First Era

Many talented amateurs have built the industry. In the early days, an enterprising enthusiast was able to concoct a game in his spare time and sell it for a reasonable amount of money. These were the days of weird and wacky plot ideas: Literally, any idea would sell—as long as it was a good game.

However, not all companies produced good products. Some attempted to cash in on the new craze for home computer games by releasing shoddy products. As the home-computer market grew, the competitiveness among companies increased, and the less efficient organizations began to get squeezed out of the market.

At first, this was a good thing. The people buying the games were well informed, computer literate, and generally knew what they were buying. Any game companies that consistently produced low-quality merchandise soon found themselves outside the buying loop and pushed into bankruptcy. Quite a few companies fell this way.

This left the fittest and the strongest companies vying for discerning business in a competitive market. These companies had to find a way to differentiate their products from the competitors'—to make it stand out on the shelf and be more desirable.

The most infamous method was the tie-in license: the game or the film or the book. For a while, almost every product released had a license of one form or another. And, almost without exception, all of these releases were mediocre to say the least, products rushed out to catch the wave of the movie's publicity. At the heights of the licensing feeding frenzy, diverse products such as potato chips, breakfast cereals, and soft drinks featured in their own games. In regards to originality, this was one of the worst periods the mainstream industry.

Its one benefit, however, was to further thin out the worst companies, leaving us with only the cream of the crop, producing technically excellent (if unoriginal) products.

This is how things were at the end of the first era of home computer use. With the imminent release of more-powerful desktop machines and mass-market consoles, things were about to change…for the worse.

The Second Era

The advent of the mass-market consoles, such as the Sega Master System and the Nintendo Entertainment System (NES) provided a wider range of platforms and potential sales. Powerful 16 -bit machines such as the Amiga and the Atari ST boosted gaming's prominence in the public mind.

Apart from the endemic licenses, things at first went well for the new consoles. A new wave of original and exciting software hit the market—before the more cynical companies discovered just what type of games these consoles were best for. Then came wave after wave of mediocre platform games that just about killed those markets off.

The same sort of thing happened to the next generation of consoles, such as the Super NES and the Sega Genesis (Megadrive in Europe). It's important to realize that, unlike the more recent consoles, which are geared towards accelerated 3D, these older consoles were less specific in their hardware focus.

However the perennial platform game (as always) proved to be the easiest game to develop for these systems, and the market was flooded again. Maybe in the future this will be the omen for the death of a platform. In a similar way to the banshee of Celtic legend, the death of a platform will be heralded by a glut of platform games (or whatever type of game is easier to produce on that machine).

About the same time, the licensing gold mine began to dry up. The increase in the time required to develop a game made it increasingly difficult to ensure that the game would be released concurrently with the film. Stripped of the benefits of riding on the back of the main publicity, these games had to survive on their own merits. Very few of these made the grade, and most of the companies responsible have disappeared into the void.

The Third Era

The third (and current) era of the industry has seen the inexorable rise of the polygon. 3D technology has captured the mind and hearts of the general public, and mass-market gaming appeal is almost upon us.

The success of the PlayStation (and to some extent the near-universal success of the PC) has made gaming that much more accessible to the mainstream punter.

Witness the success of products such as *Deer Hunter*. The success of this product caught everybody by surprise: All the pundits had quite happily slated it and condemned it to a grisly fate. When it achieved the sales it did, the gaming world had to reevaluate its position.

It seemed that the mass-market gamer—the mythical beast that the gaming industry had been chasing for so long—turned out not to be interested in the technical excesses of glorified demo products and had instead been captured by a simple, averagely executed hunting game. Finally, this was a product that appealed to a totally different market from the dedicated gamer—plus it was cheap. A great gift to give dad for Father's Day or Christmas.

It has been said that if you want a game to sell with the current state of the industry, you're pretty much limited to a small number of genres. Basically, if you want to be sure of a success in the U.S., the theory is that you should write a hunting game or a sports game. The truth may be that you should write a game that is accessible to the mass market, as *Deer Hunter* was, rather than expecting the mass market to take a sudden interest in Elder Gods and plasma cannons.

In the U.K. and Europe, where hunting isn't so popular, your only absolute guarantee of success is the venerable game of soccer. Electronic Arts have had a long-running soccer series tied into a major championship that seems to sell well every year. The less-kind reviewers imply that it is just a minor facelift of the version from the previous year, but this particular soccer series sells to people who wouldn't normally buy games, and it sells because of its tie-in with the high profile Football Association.

The same thing applies with American sports. John Madden's football games have been released with astounding regularity every season, but, again, these have had the same criticisms leveled at them as the series of English soccer games.

Of course, sports and hunting games are not the only ways to marketing success in the current markets. Increasingly, some sectors of the industry have gotten the idea that controversy seems to be a way of selling games. It is a method that has attracted the attention of regulatory bodies across the globe. However, it's likely that the Holy Grail of the mass market is not actually achievable by controversy directly—most people do not want to brutally murder simulated people *or* aliens—but is simply a way of getting the games to penetrate into the general consciousness. Two object lessons in this area are the successes of *Theme Park* and the *SimCity* series. To date, *Theme Park* has sold over four million copies, and *SimCity 3000* alone has sold more than two million, without even considering the sales of the original *SimCity* and *SimCity 2000*.

Celebrity Challenge

A recent trend in computer games is the use of celebrities to promote games. These celebrities can be either real or virtual.

In the case of the virtual celebrity, we have a wide range to choose from: Mario, Sonic, Lara, Link from the *Legend of Zelda* RPG series, Cloud from *Final Fantasy*, and many more. Mario and Sonic were largely responsible for the huge success of Nintendo and Sega, respectively.

Witness the crossover into the mainstream of *Tomb Raider's* Lara. Would the *Tomb Raider* series have been the cultural phenomenon that it has been without Lara Croft and her outstanding assets? If the character of Lara had been replaced with a character more like Indiana Jones, would we be seeing advertisements for Lucozade featuring this more mundane Lara replacement? My guess would be not.

Eidos has far more potential to make money from Lara merchandising and tie-in products than they do from any games. The general press opinion is that *Tomb Raider* as a game series is beginning to lose its shine, but there is still plenty of potential for the merchandising. At the time of writing, a Lara Croft movie is being prepared for production, and, providing that it does not go the way of past game-to-movie transitions (*Mario*, *Street Fighter*, *Mortal Kombat*), then this looks like it will be another golden goose for Eidos.

But for each successful virtual celebrity are heaps of failures. Does anyone remember *Zool* or *Bubsy*? As soon as other companies witnessed the success of *Mario* and *Sonic*, they all wanted a piece of the action. A plethora of cute but arrogant characters appeared, and—fortunately—most of these went the way of the dodo, extinction.

Recently, this trend of generating cute characters has been rekindled by *Rare* with its Banjo the bear, Kazooie the bird, and, more recently, Conker the squirrel. Does this mean that we are going to see a new wave of cute characters?

Well, possibly, although this depends on the success of the Rare products featuring these characters. Cute and recognizable characters such as Mario tend to capture the hearts and minds of the young. However, the quality of the game is by no means irrelevant. Mario and Sonic are strongly defined, likeable characters, but still would not have achieved the success they did if they had not been featured in such excellent games.

"The idea is that if you consume every Mario *artifact you can get your hands on, if you can play the Super NES game in a* Mario Brothers *sweatshirt while scarfing down an individually wrapped* Mario Brothers *snack, then through some mysterious process of celebrity transubstantiation you can become* Mario, *or at least take on some of his abilities. It's kind of like* Pinocchio *in reverse—millions of real boys dreaming of someday turning into a digital marionette."*

—J.C. Hertz, Joystick Nation, 1997

Well, that's the virtual celebrity. What about the real-life celebrity? Discounting the obvious appeal of sports games endorsed by famous athletes (*too* obvious!), we are left to consider the various attempts by other famous figures to break into the games market.

The English heavy metal band, Iron Maiden, recently released a CD that contained a simple first-person shooter featuring their mascot, Eddie. Of course, the British specialist press derided what was by all accounts an average game, for the simple reason that Iron Maiden is no longer trendy.

Note

I've always been of the opinion that members of the British specialist press (with the exception of the more responsible magazines such as Edge*) are not as mature as their American cousins. As part of the research for this book, I have traveled throughout Europe and America, reading the specialist press on the way. I have found that the American press is very adult oriented, with balanced and sensible articles, whilst* *the British press seems to be aimed at prepubescent teenagers, with profanity being the order of the day. This is an aspect the American segment of the industry has done well to avoid, and will certainly do no favors to the mass-market acceptance of gaming in the U.K.*

Douglas Adams, author of the *Hitchhiker's Guide to the Galaxy* novels, recently branched into computer games in a big way by cofounding The Digital Village. This developer's first product was the sprawling adventure game *Starship Titanic*, designed by Adams, which is set on an eponymously named starship heading for disaster.

Tom Clancy, author of many successful political-suspense novels, has also had a hand in the games industry. The relatively successful *Rainbow Six*, a suspense game based on a fictional multinational covert-ops organization, is his contribution to the industry.

These are not the only authors who have decided to dabble: Michael Crichton, famous as the creator of *Jurassic Park*, has made moves into the industry in league with Timeline Studios to produce an as yet unannounced title. You can bet that dinosaurs will feature *somewhere* in the lineup though.

Even old-time pop stars like David Bowie and Queen have tried their luck with *Omikron: The Nomad Soul* (which has now dropped the *Omikron* moniker) and *Queen: The Eye*, respectively.

Is this a valid approach? Is David Bowie the way to attract the punters? Well, time will tell. My view is that entertainment software is a new and very different medium and that it will create its own kind of stars. Just as Valentino and Chaplin were big stars in the silent era but didn't make the transition to talkies. Disney does recruit big names for the voices in *Toy Story*, and other films, but it's just for fun, really. They don't make a big selling point out of Tom Hanks doing the voice of Woody, for example. A big-name star in an animated feature just helps to raise the marketing profile; it doesn't change anyone's mind about seeing it. In Hollywood parlance, the stars who can open a live-action picture don't necessarily open animated features as well.

The stars of the computer-game universe will very often be virtual stars, like Lara Croft, rather than real-life names. Cutter Slade (from *Outcast*) is a character is his own right, and the game would not have been enhanced by getting a big star like Bruce Willis to voice him. If anything, it would have been a jarring note, reminding us that "it's just a game," simply because Bruce Willis' voice is too familiar: We *know* he isn't a game character. Whereas the actor who did voice Slade (David Gasman) did a very good job, and the very fact that he wasn't a celebrity helped us believe in the reality of the character. The requirements of the software medium will probably start trending away from photographically realized characters in any case, towards a more stylized character style such as can be achieved in a good animated feature or a comic book. Think of the *Batman* animated series as opposed to the movies. Or check out the preview shots of Rhama, the stylishly realized hero of *Galleon*, by Toby Gard (who created Lara Croft). This is likely to create a character style and voice-talent requirement quite different from what makes someone a star on the silver screen.

Violence In Games

The question of violence in games has recently become quite a big issue, because, with the increasing power of technology, realistic violence can be graphically depicted for the first time.

Mortal Kombat was a game made notorious for its combination moves that culminated with the death of your opponent by various means. One of the most gruesome of these involved ripping the skull and spine out of your opponent and holding it aloft. The photorealistic nature of this imagery caused uproar among the moral majority.

In the U.K., the first game to receive a rating for viewing content was *Frankenstein* on the ZX Spectrum computer. This was an entirely voluntary effort on the part of the publishers in order to obtain publicity for the game. This (rather cynical) approach has been used on a number of other releases over the years. Games such as *Grand Theft Auto* (an average top-down racer that allowed you to massacre nearly everybody on foot) played on their "18" certification to court notoriety and build sales. Max Clifford, a U.K. public-relations expert, was called in to get publicity for *Grand Theft Auto*. He succeeded in this by securing a series of scathing articles in leading broadsheet newspapers, along the lines of "Ban this filth, now!" Predictably, sales went through the roof.

To promote their mobster game, *Gangsters*, Eidos hired "Mad" Frankie Frazer (a member of the infamous Kray Gang, who was jailed for his crimes in the 1960s) to appear at ECTS, the European Computer Trade Show. This move disgusted the press who saw it as a cheap and distasteful publicity stunt. In response to this, Frazer's involvement in the publicity campaign was quickly downplayed. Whether the adverse publicity generated by forcing *Gangsters* into the public eye has helped or hindered its sales is a matter of debate.

Carmageddon appears to have been inspired by Paul Bartel's film *Death Race 2000*. However, while the film was a satire directed against a society that derives entertainment from violence, the satirical scope of the game was not immediately evident. Initially, the publishers had to replace human pedestrians with zombies oozing green blood, because the censors found the red blood too realistic. They singled out the red tire marks left by your car as being particularly offensive, and refused to allow the release of the game unless this was changed.

The specialist press booed and jeered at this measure, baying for blood and guts in their games. In retrospect, this was not a good idea, as it brought only negative attention to the industry as a whole. If the industry cannot self-regulate, then it will have to submit to external censors, which will neither please the publishers nor provide the consumer with satisfactory products.

The publishers of *Carmageddon* appealed against the censor board's decision, and it was eventually overturned, allowing them to release the full-blooded version. But, seeing as some enterprising person had already "unofficially" released the blood patch, this was all fairly irrelevant. I personally preferred the atmosphere of the zombie version.

Interestingly enough, when Microsoft recently released a rush-hour racing game *Midtown Madness*, there were complaints from the less responsible members of the specialist press in the U.K. that you could not run over pedestrians. They always managed to leap out of the way at the last moment, in the manner of '70s car movies such as *Cannonball Run*.

The game was actually marked down in a number of reviews, and the inability of the player to kill pedestrians was stated as a major disadvantage. It's a bit sick really: The ability to kill pedestrians would not have made it a better game, and it has no bearing on the feel of the driving within the game. If the magazine reviewers feel that their comments are really valid, then they've probably been staring at a computer screen too long. I'd suggest they go out and get a bit of fresh air, smell the real world until they start to feel a little bit better. By contrast, the American press felt the nonlethal nature of the game to be a plus point.

Postal, a game named after an infamous event when a sacked postal worker went into his former workplace with a gun and shot everybody in sight, was a rather tacky attempt at cashing in on the violence debate. Advertisements for this (remarkably average) game involved displaying all of the condemning quotes from the media, and presenting these as a reason to buy it. However, there is no evidence that the media attention gave *Postal* any mass-market appeal—after initial interest, sales soon tapered off.

The granddaddy of all realistically violent games, *Doom*, has been singled out for many of the school shootings in the U.S. This has left the moral majority howling for all violent computer games to be banned, and several class-action lawsuits were launched against a number of publishers.

There is no way a computer game can turn a reasonable human being into a deranged killing machine *without there being something seriously wrong with them in the first place*.

However regrettable and tragic the shootings were, this response is only a knee-jerk reaction. It's only natural when we are outraged and horrified by a great tragedy to cast around for a place to put the blame.

As far as I can tell, most of the population of the planet Earth has played *Doom*. It is one of the most widely played games ever released. I certainly have played more than my fair share, yet I do not feel the urge to go on the rampage with a sawed-off shotgun or a chainsaw.

To reiterate: Games do not *cause* violence. They may be able to reinforce violent feelings in disturbed individuals, but then so could a book, a newspaper article, a TV program, a movie, or any of the hundreds of other stimuli that we are subjected to every day. The fact is that, if someone is disturbed, anything can set them off.

During July of 1999, in Japan, a young man with a knife hijacked an airplane and killed the captain by stabbing him in the throat. Why? Because he wanted to fly under Tokyo's Rainbow Bridge as he had done in Microsoft's *Flight Simulator* '98, and the pilot had refused to do so.

Does this mean that that particular flight simulator should be banned? Should Microsoft be sued for releasing such a dangerous product onto the market?

No. That would be ridiculous. One of the cornerstones of a modern democratic society is that people are responsible for their own actions. Saying "The Devil made me do it" is a defense that should have gone out with the Salem witch trials, and should be just as successful today as it was then. This is basically going to happen every time something new comes along. In seventeenth-century England, the government of Oliver Cromwell closed the theaters because they thought drama was a subversive art form that would lead people astray. In the early days of cinema, gangster movies were attacked because it was believed they glorified violence and would cause problems in society. Howard Hawks' film *Scarface* was held up for two years while extra scenes were added to give it an anti-violent message and thus appease the moral majority. It was finally released in 1932 as *Scarface: Shame of a Nation* and was still widely condemned—yet today it is regarded as a classic. Television and then comic books got the same treatment, being blamed for all society's ills (a critic of the early 1950s referred to television as "an appalling Pandora's box") and now it is the turn of computer games.

Figure 15.1 shows the available markets. The hard-core market that will buy a game on its merits alone form the peak. Then there is the larger base of floating gamers who will buy a game if they become interested in it through other routes, such as related merchandise. The largest area, the mass market, are those who never normally buy games. These are the people

Figure 15.1
The shape of the market.

who the games industry will have to adapt to get the *serious* money—and violent games are not the route. In the same way that the ultraviolent Japanese *Manga* films are not embraced by the mass market, violent action in games is a specialized taste with only cult appeal. It just happens that most gamers at the moment belong to that cult minority. If you want people to invite you into their homes (which is what they do when they buy your game, in effect), you obviously need to make a commitment to entertaining them in a responsible manner. The mass market will never take to games that go out of their way to offend and shock.

The industry is going to have to take realistic portrayal of violence far more seriously in the future. Computer gaming is becoming much more part of mainstream life and consequently is becoming more family oriented. No longer is gaming the sole preserve of the 15-to-20-something males. The fact that traditionally noncomputer-based companies have entered the market with some successful products (such as the *Lego* and *Barbie* products) much to the disgust of the hardcore developer contingent, shows how much the industry has changed over the last couple of years.

The demand for family-oriented content can only increase as time goes by, and this means that violent content will have to be better regulated and more restricted in order to protect the young and to reassure parents.

Releases such as *Kingpin* have shown that the level to which games can portray violence can be far more gritty and realistic than previously supposed. Whether this actually adds to the gameplay is another matter. Personally, however, I'd rather have a game sold on the merits of the gameplay rather than the size of the body count.

I do not have a problem with violence in games if it is appropriate, and as long as it is dealt with properly. For example, in *Outcast* the hero is fighting a military junta that uses violent oppression to control its peaceful citizens. The hero is a Navy SEAL with formidable weapon skills, and it is clear from the backstory that he is no psychopath but rather a responsible soldier who uses violence only because there is no choice. At present, violence in computer games is unbalanced—the moral implications of violence are rarely dealt with, making the violence merely gratuitous. Contrast this with drama or literature, in which violence has consequences for the perpetrator as well as the victim. Violence doesn't come without moral implications, and these should be part of any game that uses violence. (As a side note, presenting the moral consequences of violence does not mean that you necessarily have to punish any use of violence in your games. That's playground morality. A mature art form can present a difficult subject in many ways and explore many themes without having to sermonize.)

"There are two reasons why games have historically relied heavily on violence. First, gameplayers were typically adolescent (or at least the first generation was). Second, the technology limited gaming environments, making more complex interactions impractical.... It's no accident that Sony's next generation PlayStation [2] chip is called the Emotion Engine."

—Demis Hassabis quoted in Edge, *September 1999*

Violence is a part of everyday life. You see it on the television, and you read about it in the newspapers. As a consumer, I don't have a problem with this. What I do have a problem with—and what I think will be a big issue in the future—is the glorification and celebration of violence. This is fine if your target market is a small group of adolescent males, but that's not our market anymore. Our market now includes concerned parents and grandparents, and you can be sure they're not going to be impressed by excessive violence. They're certainly not going to buy *Kingpin* for little Billy's birthday if they take the trouble to find out about the game content.

"At first when the graphics were basic, all you could do was give a character a gun and see how many people he could shoot. As technology becomes more sophisticated, games will have to be more imaginative. There are a lot more interesting scenarios than gratuitous violence."

—Demis Hassabis, creator of Theme Park *and founder of Elixir*

I have to point out that blockbuster movies don't exactly eschew violence, although, in a computer game, the player feels far more involved in what is going on than a person watching a movie. However, computer games probably will be more strictly regulated because, like TV, they are in the homes, and so adults will bother themselves about what their kids are being exposed to. Also, computer games are interactive—when we see violence in a movie, it is only by the director's tricks that we become implicated, whereas, in a computer game (as in life), nobody is responsible for our actions but ourselves.

Children's Products

One area that is currently overlooked in the market is the children's market. Only a few companies are starting to turn onto the possibilities.

This is where I think one of the biggest areas of growth will be. Not with the tacky "edutainment" products—which attempt to educate with such unworthy dreariness—but with the two separate subgenres of children's educational products and entertainment products.

I could be wrong here. Many people seem to like edutainment, but personally I think it is not fair on the kids. Recently, I've had the opportunity to do some research in this area. I sat a two-year-old down in front of a PC with some *Sesame Street* educational software, and left his mother with the software for a couple of weeks. When I came back to check on his progress after the two-week testing period, I was amazed to sit and watch this two-year-old confidently navigating his way around the user interface, clicking on hotspots and thoroughly enjoying himself. However, I was not as amazed as his mother, who told me that he had learned to recognize the digits zero to nine when they appeared on screen.

This is a huge market that is still relatively untapped, and I can confidently predict that the children's market is going to be one of the biggest growth areas over the next few years. No matter how cool you think making adult-oriented games is, this is one area you'll ignore at your peril.

Even companies such as Cyberlife (*Creatures* and *Creatures 2*) are attempting to tap into this market with a simplified version of *Creatures*, called *Creatures Adventures*.

"Creatures Adventures *is designed around the philosophy of free play, the aim being to guide and teach your creatures as they experience the world around them. The product provides the building blocks for you to create their own experiences without forcing them to follow linear play patterns."*

—Ben Simpson, Designer, quoted in Edge *Magazine, September 1999*

Whether they have the right approach or are falling into the "Help Roger Raccoon rescue his presents by jumping on the number logs to complete simple sums" approach remains to be seen, but I have high hopes for this particular product. The artificial-life basis of *Creatures Adventures* means that children should be free to explore and experiment at their own pace, avoiding the regimented structure of what has passed (inadequately) for children's software in the past.

The New Model Developers

Hard times are ahead. A development company that tries to make money by its games alone will have a very hard time. The key to success is leverage. This can be leverage of the technology itself (such as licensing the engine to other games companies or even to nongames companies), as well as leverage of the creative Intellectual Property (IP)—*Kingpin* selling Diesel clothes, Lara Croft appearing in comic books and commercials, and so forth.

At the moment, games based on existing licenses (like *GoldenEye*) outsell character-based games originated in-house (like *Grim Fandango*) by a factor of three (source: *Develop* magazine). However, you have to remember that those bought-in licenses cost money, whereas you can hope that in-house IP will generate money.

A comparison is the fashion industry. The designs that go on the Paris catwalk are never intended to be for mass-market consumption. However, they grab attention, showcase the talent, and depict the trend that the fashion house is taking for the season. It's a bonus if catwalk fashions break even, but it's not vital: Versace could throw all the catwalk outfits away after a show and still make millions.

"I take a good deal of pride in seeing games like Valve's Half-Life. *They've built on our foundation and they've done a spectacular job. I'm not sitting here kicking myself and thinking, 'We could have done that.' Instead we're thinking, 'Hey, we get royalties off this.'"*

—John Carmack, Edge, *April 1999*

Leverage can be internal also. For a small developer, reuse is only marginally practical—you complete one game, by which time much of your technology will be old hat. So consecutive reuse is of little value, but concurrent reuse (applying the same technology, design concepts, or even artwork across several projects in parallel) is more than a bonus, it is an economic necessity.

Obviously, a lone development company with a staff of 20 cannot easily begin to achieve concurrent reuse internally. Therefore, over the next few years, we will begin to see a consolidation within the industry. A few "super publishers" will emerge (we are seeing the first of these already), and there will be a move to a system closer to the way movies are developed. This involves a centralization or pooling of resources.

Two examples of the more enlightened approach are the Gathering of Developers (GoD) coalition system and the satellite scheme originated by Peter Molyneux's company, Lionhead Studios. The approach taken by these two companies is to form a group of favored developers and provide support and assistance to them within a loosely affiliated community of development teams. (See Case Study 15.1 for the GoD Manifesto.)

Case Study 15.1 The Gathering Of Developers' Manifesto

The following extract is quoted from the Web site of the Gathering of Developers (**www.godgames.com**).

Gathering of Developers, a Texas-based computer and video game publishing company, was founded in January, 1998 in response to the industry's need for a publisher who understands and respects independent game developers. Fueled by their past publishing experiences and frustrations, several experienced hit-making development companies bound together to form The Gathering, a relationship-based publisher that treats developers as professional entertainment artists.

Mission Statement

The Gathering's mission is not to build its own brand, but to create value for the company and its partners by promoting the developers and their titles. Our message is simple... brand the developer and its creations so that the consumers can easily recognize a quality product.

Unique Features

With a focus on quality not quantity, The Gathering is able to offer its developers comprehensive AAA marketing campaigns and a favorable sliding scale royalty rate based on unit sales.

Because The Gathering's roots are in game development by virtue of its founding partners, the company offers unparalleled expertise in the areas of title/developer selection and approval as well as determining appropriate development and milestone cycles.

The selection process is determined on merit, track record and technical/commercial feasibility. The company also respects the rights of the developer and encourages them to retain their own intellectual property rights over franchises they've created, an unalienable right which should be afforded game developers.

It would be easy to dismiss this model as hopelessly Utopian, much like the avowedly artistic aims of the founders of United Artists in 1919:

[Film] stars Mary Pickford, Douglas Fairbanks and Charlie Chaplin, and director D W Griffith, founded United Artists as a corporate apparatus for distributing their independent productions. United Artists never owned a production studio; rather, it distributed features made by filmmakers on their own lots or rented facilities.

—Extract from the "United Artists" entry in Cinemania *(Microsoft, 1997)*

To regard the departure of the original founders from United Artists as a failure of its creative vision would miss the point. The advantages of such an alliance are many. Firstly, from a commercial viewpoint, technological resources and management can be shared, so that all participants can benefit from economies of scale. (How many small independent development companies could afford their own motion-capture studio, for example?) Secondly, the umbrella of an established central studio nurtures newcomers into the fold: Even a top-notch team of developers would face many problems at startup (securing investment, convincing a landlord to rent office space, arranging a loan facility at the bank) that being part of a group will alleviate. Thirdly, the central studio can maintain a talent-pool inventory, so that individuals within the scheme are never left idle. Fourthly, by detaching development finance from publishers, the development studio is able to secure higher royalties. (See Case Study 15.2.) And, lastly, the studio guarantees quality control, which is desirable to both the publisher and the consumer (hence, GoD's emphasis on the importance of establishing a brand).

In order to take full advantage of the link-ups within a satellite scheme, the independent teams will have to make use of the full possibilities of shared resources, as suggested by the software factory methodology. Getting a number of independent teams to explicitly cooperate in an expertise-sharing scheme will not be achieved by wishing it so: Formal process is the only way.

This scheme is similar to the film industry development model in that there is a central creative core that kicks off designs and architecture but hires individuals or teams of contractors for the code spadework. However, you wouldn't want to get the modules of your product back from outsourcing and discover that they are way off what you intended. This means:

- The creative core must oversee the project. Somebody from the creative core therefore retains ownership throughout. Traditionally, we might expect this to be the producer of the product, but more probably there will have to be a shift towards design-led control, so we might predict that the project lead will be closer to the director's role on a movie. I'd expect this to work best (people being what they are) if you're either working with an independent team you've used in the past and can trust, or if you bring the contractors to your own location where you have the resources.

Case Study 15.2 *It's Hard For Developers*

A year ago I was involved in putting together the staff roles and design and architecture doctrine for a nascent development company that was assembling a business plan. They were seeking most of their startup finance from a publisher, and it was interesting to see the sales and revenue projections based on the publishing deal they were negotiating.

Their royalty rate began at 20 percent, climbing to 25 percent after 350,000 units. This placed them in profit at around 375,000 units. Contrast that with the publisher, who was set to recoup their investment and go into profit at around 200,000 units.

There is no reason why the publisher should not arrange things this way. The risk was to be theirs, after all—it was their two million dollars! In effect, they were simply building in a self-protection that, in the case of bank investment, would be represented by a rate of return on the investment as a loan or, in the case of venture capital, by equity.

The founders of the company had some creative business ideas of their own. Armed with evidence of firm interest from a publisher, they were able to arrange private investment (from business "angels") in return for a moderate equity share. This would allow them eventually to take a finished product to auction between all the top publishers, thereby securing a royalty closer to 45 percent. The business angels, incidentally, acquired equity in a specific company formed just for the production of that one game, in direct analogy to the Hollywood model, where a new company is formed to create each film. This meant that the development team could also grow to undertake other projects without having to have "sold their souls" right at the beginning.

- There must be a standardization of design methods, libraries, and such. If I'm making a movie, I can show my second unit director the storyboard and discuss the lenses and lighting, and then I'm fairly sure he will shoot it the way I want. We need the equivalent of universal standards in development. Yet (remarkably), some developers are deliberately choosing to define their own unique standards—the equivalent of insisting on speaking only Navajo and then wondering why the Fox network can't find a job for you!

The GoD and Lionhead models seem designed to create the kind of "superdeveloper" model we're discussing. Lionhead's satellites will learn a standard way of doing things (or, at any rate, the potential is there for them to do so): They share resources, and they have mutual trust as to standards of performance. Moreover, the superdesigners like Peter Molyneux could use the scheme to kick off a couple of projects a year as opposed to the current average of maybe one every two years. On the assumption that star quality (the ability to deliver a AAA product) is what publishers will pay for, it makes sense to streamline development so that the guiding genius is not tied up in finalizing every little detail. (This does, of course, require development companies to gain a better understanding of what full design should entail. In particular, they need to recognize that testbeds belong to the design phase, not the development phase.)

The trend towards the superdeveloper has come about principally because publishers (or rather their shareholders) have been asking, "Why is so much of our money tied up in development? We make money from publishing! We're not in the banking business!" A few years ago, many publishers were directly investing in internal development. That meant large development-staff payrolls and at any one time a possible sunk cost, for a medium-scale publisher, in the millions of dollars. Small wonder that the trend has been towards partial funding of independent development studios, or (ideally, from the publishers' viewpoint) just buying a completed game and putting it straight onto the market at no risk.

So, we will see a trend towards the film industry model of finance, with the publisher or main studio providing confidence. The president of Sony was quoted recently as saying there would be only five developers in the world. These superdevelopers will be the equivalent of Universal and Paramount. Those developers will constitute the creative core of talent, like the software factory design and architecture model on a considerably larger scale. Not all need be permanent staff, of course, just as authors can drift from one book publisher to another. If you happen to be in investment banking, the lesson is clear: Sink $25 million into a superdeveloper by all means, but don't waste $2 million on a small development team, because you will never get the return that high risk expects.

Some projects will be originated in-house by the superdeveloper "studio." The advantage of this, as we saw in Case Study 15.2, is that you don't get investors (angels and others) to directly buy a share of your studio. They invest specifically in Shudder, Inc., which is developing the game *Shudder*, on the basis that this doesn't dilute your core equity. (If *Shudder* does very well, they'll reap the rewards of sequels and character licensing, which is the ideal from the investor's viewpoint.)

Other games will be brought to the studio by small nascent teams. For instance, a designer, planner, and lead programmer might present a concept-and-technology demo to the studio bosses just like a director, scriptwriter, and star pitch a deal in Hollywood. Armed with a letter of intent from the studio ("We are very interested in producing this game..."), they will then get finance from a bank to assemble a full team (equivalent to a film crew). This is a perfect example of synergy, or what in economics is called the *principle of cooperative benefit*: The investors have money but no expert knowledge to tell them if it's a good game. The studio has expert knowledge but doesn't want to invest more money than is strictly needed to secure a first refusal. The developers just want startup capital to finish their game.

But how will even superdevelopers make money? Even at a 50 percent royalty, with the gross wholesale price dropping, you will need to sell some 300,000 units before the deal starts looking attractive to serious investors. Well, firstly the income from sales of games is not the only asset the superdeveloper is building; they will own a lot of IP. Additionally, development is cheap for them (the economies of scale again), and they can afford R&D across multiple projects which, for a small developer, would be impossible. Lastly, as we have seen, the creative superstars will be able to kick off more projects by this method. Say that Sid Meier could personally oversee one game every two to three years, or he could mastermind one every six months or so by delegating part of the work to his trusted inner circle. You may think the quality of the games would suffer (I don't happen to think so, if rational development procedures are used), but, even if they did, the marketing muscle of such a name will ensure a healthy market.

And what about the contractors? (These contractors hired by the superdeveloper will be not only individual coders but, more often, small development companies of some 12 to 20 people.) How will they make money? The short answer is they won't (not the big money to be made on royalties, anyway). They'll just get salaries, the upside being that those salaries will be on a par with the mainstream IT industry. We can draw the analogy of session musicians in the music trade or, again, of film crews: The director and producer and stars are the ones who get rich on royalties, but, if you're the camera operator, you must make do with a wage.

And publishers? The advantage to them is that they are brought a product bearing the name of a known creative force. (It could be an individual, like Will Wright, or a well-known brand name guaranteeing quality, like Blizzard). They know it will conform to quality standards and be delivered on time, and the extra trust and absence of risk inherent in the new model are easily worth the doubling of the royalty. The publishers will continue to make good money at very low risk by creaming off whatever retail doesn't take. As fulfillment goes online or to Web-based mail order, however, the publisher's cut will be less and less. Eventually, by strict logic, we will see only one big (Web-based) games publisher.

The Online Revolution

In 10 years' time, I can't see people buying games from shops. If you have a computer (which you presumably must have if you're buying games), then why wouldn't you order straight off the Web? Not only is it easier, but you can filter the genres you want and you'll be able to look at trailer demos, too.

Buying Games Online

Right now, the technology going into games is accelerating faster than the technology required to download them. This is leading to a technology gap. Within two to three years, however, it is probable that retail will begin to fade out of the picture as games are primarily bought and delivered online.

Note

Wireplay, the Internet gaming arm of BT, and ICE, the mail order firm, have been acquired by newly created company ***Gameplay.com****, which will float on the Alternative Investment Market (AIM) within a few months. Gameplay plans to raise $31 million.* ***Gameplay.com*** *will offer consumers a complete online gaming experience. Teaming up with Futuregamer.com, which will promote and provide links to the Gameplay Web site, the new company will allow gamers to compete with others online via Wireplay technology and buy products, which will be shipped via ICE.*

(Source: MCV, 16 July 1999)

Gameplay.com was launched in August 1999 on the AIM and raised $46 million, which was $15 million more than expected. The new company is valued at $79 million and, according to some forecasts, could soon recapitalize at almost twice that. It seems that the financial sector is confident that this is where the future of the industry is going.

Ordering your games online doesn't have to mean receiving them online—nobody in their right mind wants to download and print novels at home, after all, but that doesn't harm Amazon's business. However, direct download from the publisher to the consumer would certainly be the ideal. The online publishers of the future, such as Gameplay, will need to find ways to make the downloading process as quick, simple, and painless as possible. One way is to give sneak previews that can be downloaded quickly. These will not, I suspect, need to be fully playable demos such as you nowadays find on magazine cover disks. The publisher has a lot of product, and they want you to see trailers for as much of it as possible, after all. So we will see the rise of the game trailer to a level more like trailers for a forthcoming movie release—something small but perfectly formed, and crafted to whet your appetite for the full game. The interested consumer will then be guided artfully to reviews, full-scale demos, and whatever else is needed to reel him in.

To solve the problem of downloading time (so as to encourage consumers to buy their games direct), the online publisher needs to establish a basic package of libraries that would be downloaded only once and then used for all games. Consequently, in an ideal case, only the main game logic and artwork should need to be sent for a *Quake*-based game like *Half-Life*, for example. For this to work, it needs an alliance between online publisher and superdeveloper to establish "once and for all" the architecture into which their game modules will fit. At the moment, only Microsoft is capable of a project of this scale.

Playing Games Online

Recently, companies that have set out to specifically provide online content have sprung up like small mammals among the dinosaurs. Maybe they believe that, like the dinosaurs, those who cannot adapt will die.

Perhaps this explains the gradual focusing on providing online content by some companies such as Origin, and providing online-only games such as *Ultima Online*, a huge virtual community set in the fantasy realm of Britannia. However, this is really targeted at the hardcore gamer.

"The hardcore Ultima [Online] *player is putting in six to eight hours a day. You might have eight hours sleep, then some hours at work or school, and the rest is spent online."*

—Richard Garriott ("Lord British"), interviewed in PC Gamer, *September 1999*

Online gaming will initially have a harder time in Europe, where per-minute local phone charges restrict the amount of time people can spend online. However, the phone companies will have to deal: This is business they can get if they lower their prices—and business that they won't get if they are greedy.

The other main disadvantage of online games is that they are difficult to dip in and out of. The mass market is not interested in spending every spare hour online. They want to be able to choose when to play and not be penalized if they don't have time to put the hours in. Online gaming is going to be big, but, because of this restriction, it's not going to be as big as some pundits like to think.

Survival of the Fittest

The only way that game development can be economical in the future is to adopt the processes outlined in this book. We know this because we have applied these techniques to a start up company that as a result received full funding from a major publisher. The only way for development companies in the future to survive—there will be pressure to streamline the process—is to adopt the techniques in this book. These have been tried and tested, and they have been seen to work better than any other processes we have seen so far.

Companies now must start to establish these standards and terminologies or fall by the wayside. There may be resistance to this, but, overall, something has to be done, or it simply isn't economically viable for a development house to operate.

If you have a star name or a star license, you will sell a million copies. If not, the most you are likely to sell is approximately 250,000 copies. Your business plan must show you can make a living on this. If you do the math, you'll see the process has to be streamlined to achieve this. In order to survive, the money has to be saved somewhere while, at the same time, reducing time to market and increasing quality of content.

PART III

GAME ARCHITECTURE

Chapter 16
Current Development Methods

Key Topics:

- ***The history of game development***
- ***Language wars***
- ***Platform Wars***
- ***Optimization and the pedal-to-the-metal***
- ***Monolithic versus component-based development***

This chapter discusses the progression in development languages and methods that have been used in producing home computer games since the early 1980s.

The evolutionary path of game development has taken a slightly different route than the mainstream development world.

While mainstream development generally started on large mainframes and worked its way down to the PC, game development has always started on small computers, with the developers working around the limitations of the system.

These two different approaches have now, for the most part, converged, and little Johnny can play the latest games on the same system that daddy uses to calculate and file his tax returns. This platform convergence (ignoring both consoles and antitrust suits) has to be a good thing. It now means that, ostensibly, both business and game software are written in similar styles. Both are now either coded in C or C++ and generally use the application programming interface of the native operating system and a sprinkling of third-party libraries.

This is good news for companies seeking employees—and for prospective employees seeking work—because it means that the spread of skills required for programming is diminishing. If the skills required for programming a game are essentially the same as those for programming business software, this means that there are more skilled workers available. Some people may say that writing a game is more technically exacting than writing business software, which is considered easier and less innovative. If you put aside any prejudices for a second and think about it objectively, you'll probably realize that this cannot be true. Usually software written for business is just as technically exacting (if not more so) than game software of a similar size. The main difference between the two is that game programming usually requires a correspondingly huge amount of supporting material (in the form of audio and graphical work).

Programming, however, is not the only skill needed to develop game software. Anyone expecting a career in the games industry (or anywhere in the software industry) without secondary areas of knowledge such as mathematics or more game-specific areas such as AI and 3D calculations will find it difficult to progress to anything above the level of code monkey.

This convergence, or homogenization, of skills has in some ways simplified game development. More people with the right skills are readily available for work, and, although the market is tight, there is a wider pool of people to choose from. At least there would be if recruiters could modernize their attitudes. Looking through the job ads in the specialist press, recruiters seem to want only programmers with exactly the right skill set (3D math skills, and so on.) or fresh young graduates; they just want either an off-the-shelf package or the cheapest available.

I can understand this viewpoint, but I am curious to know for how long it can be maintained. I don't know of many game software companies that provide a structured training program for new employees. The reason for this may well be that they are afraid of training programmers only to lose them when, after a couple of successful releases, they leave to create their own "super-team" studio, as has become common over the past couple of years. The money offered to teams with a few successful hits behind them is certainly enticing enough.

Although I honestly don't know what the solution is, the software factory has built-in measures to thwart this phenomenon by organizing the teams in a different way, so no one particular team is responsible for an entire product. With the software factory, no one can say that "their" team developed the game, because they would have developed only a part of the game. The entire game itself would be a product of the effort of the entire company. The simpler option is probably to make sure that the team that developed the game didn't even feel the need to leave. Maybe if the distribution of money for effort expended was more fair, this sort of situation wouldn't occur so often. The distribution of royalties has long been thought to be unfair, and I know of companies who use small print and legal clauses to reduce the amount of royalties they pay to the absolute minimum, which in most cases can be zero.

I once went to the European Computer Trade Show, paying the extra for a Premium Club ticket (which allows you access to a private room where all the top management hang out and discuss their latest deals), and sat for a while listening to the various conversations. The topics varied wildly, but one theme was common: the employees of the software companies were all discussed in terms of how they could be exploited. They were viewed as cattle, to be milked. This was something I had jokingly suspected for some time, but to actually hear it openly discussed was a bit of an eye-opener. It gave me some new insight on the industry. These were the few, living off the back of the toil of the many. For your average Joe Programmer, the industry is not a fair place, and the distribution of wealth is weighted heavily against them. Revolutions have been started for less. The industry has generated its own myths and expectations, and this appears to be one of them. Another is the tales of teenage millionaire programmers from the early 1980s, tales that also proved to be unfounded.

This is not to say that I am advocating for all programmers to overturn their desks, smash their monitors, and storm the management offices. I am just making an observation that the games industry cannot continue in this fashion if it is to become a mature and stable industry. Programming teams are not rock groups, and as soon as people can look through all the artificial glitz and glamour to examine the true situation, the industry will take a big step towards maturity.

The History Of Development Techniques

Back in the early days of game development, the machines were very limited, both in variety and in capabilities. The three home computers that most people think of when asked about this period are the Commodore 64, the Sinclair ZX Spectrum (very similar to the American Timex Sinclair 2048), and the Amstrad 464. These were the three main contenders in Europe during the 1980s.

Of course, these computers were antiquated by today's standards. They had slow, 8-bit processors running at around 4 MHz (for the Spectrum, anyway), limited graphics, and between 48 kilobytes and 64 kilobytes of memory. Three-dimensional graphics were virtually unheard of, and those that did exist were wireframe or solid. Texture mapping didn't exist, as the graphics capabilities and the processor speeds were just not up to the task. Programming for these platforms involved the constant need to work around their limitations in order to produce the best results. All games generally had to be coded in Assembler in order to achieve speed and space requirements. There were no good C compilers then, and the few that did spring up did not produce code small and tight enough to be usable for games. This meant that porting a game to another platform required a complete rewrite. There was no easy conversion method, no compiler switch to change the target from, say, a ZX Spectrum to a Commodore 64 so that you could recompile and have your game targeting multiple platforms.

There were, however, some advantages, such as the fact that there was no variance within the bounds of a platform. You knew that, except in bizarre (and commercially discountable) cases, the machine that you were developing on was exactly the same as the machine that little Johnny had at home. It was a situation similar to that experienced with console programming today: the target machine has exactly the same capabilities as the development machine (although a certain PlayStation game that was developed on the official emulation hardware had to be rewritten when the developers realized that the production hardware came with significantly less memory than that provided by the development kit!).

Developing on exactly the same machine as the target platform means that you didn't repeat a common disaster that has plagued some software developers—producing a game that runs too slowly on the player's machine—because the machines used to develop them were considerably more powerful. Back then, the choice of development language was a no-brainer: you chose Assembler. Anything else just wasn't fast enough.

Because of the restrictions in hardware, the coding priorities then were quite different to those of today. While speed and optimization are still issues today, they are not emphasized as much as they used to be. You had no second chances then; there were no new faster processors coming out to aid your efforts. You were stuck with the limitations of the machine that you were developing for.

In the eyes of the nostalgic, these limitations were not necessarily a bad thing. Because of the restricted memory, graphical capabilities, and sound hardware, more emphasis was placed on the gameplay, and the games simply played better.

This is not what I believe has happened. Apart from the obvious nostalgia trips, gameplay does not seem to have developed on the same scale as have graphics and sound for other reasons, which are covered in the next section.

The Rise And Fall Of The Original Game Idea?

It is true that games are less original than they used to be. Witness some of the titles released back in the early 1980s: *Head over Heels*, *Manic Miner*, *Cliff Hanger*, *Trashman*, and *They Stole a Million* (shown in Figures 16.1 to 16.5).

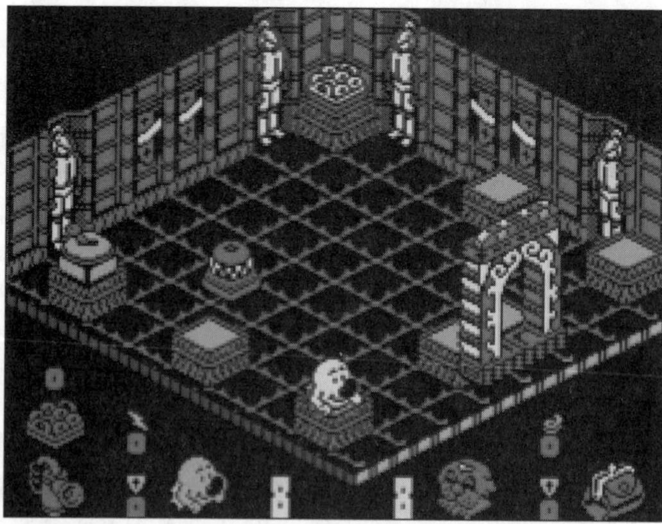

Figure 16.1
Head over Heels.

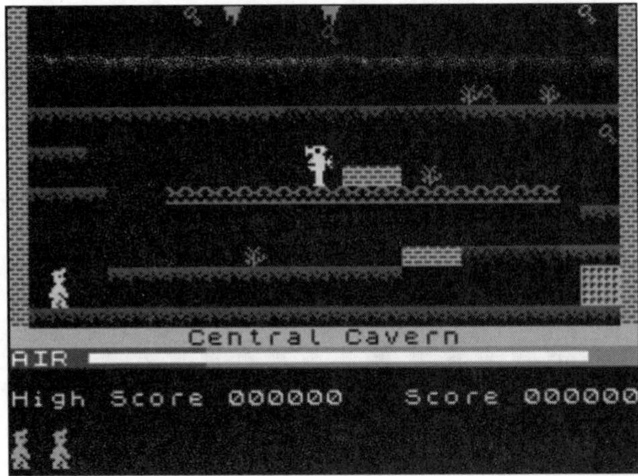

Figure 16.2
Manic Miner.

Figure 16.3
Cliff Hanger.

A plethora of games had odd subject matters and peculiar objectives. For example, in *Cliff Hanger*, you played a cartoon hero who had to kill a gun-toting bandit who was coming over the horizon to shoot up the town, using a Wile E. Coyote-style set of tricks and traps.

In *Trashman*, you played a trashman, collecting the trashcan from each house on the street and emptying it in the back of your truck, before placing it back where you found it. If you did your job well, the house owners would offer you tips. If you performed badly, dogs would chase you.

Similar in style to one of today's role-playing games, *They Stole A Million* put you in charge of planning a robbery: you would select your team, buy plans of a likely target building, pore

Figure 16.4
Trashman.

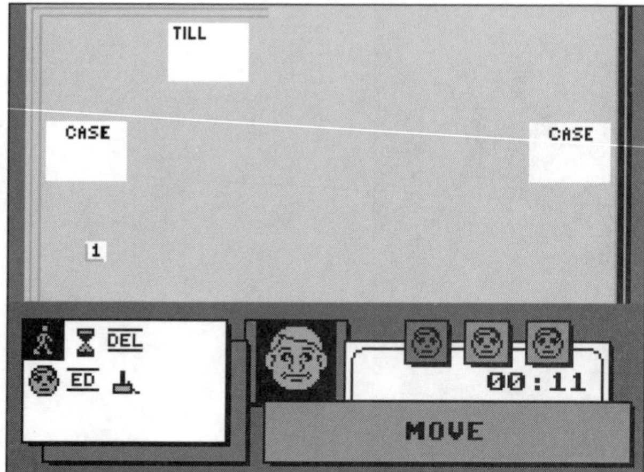

Figure 16.5
They Stole a Million.

over the blueprints marking out elaborate plans, and then send your team off to perform the robbery, stepping in if necessary in order to smooth minor flaws.

Would these concepts be successful today? They may be, because of the burgeoning retro-remake scene. However, it is more likely that they would not be deemed commercial by the marketing department. Because of the pressures of the "mass market" (that may or may not exist), today's games have become very formulaic in their approach. The other aspect of these games is that they were limited by the hardware they were ran on, which would have impacted the gameplay in a lot of cases and forced a deliberate simplicity. However, it was this simplicity that made the gameplay successful. The theory was that, if the game looked bad and sounded worse, then it had better play well!

The fact is that, while graphical capabilities and processing power have increased a hundredfold since the early days, gameplay has not. If anything, gameplay has slightly regressed. We are still playing the same old games, except we are being fooled by the shiny new packaging (a clear case of the emperor's new clothes).

Worse still, we are not even experiencing the best of the old gameplay; we are replaying the average run-of-the-mill games. The games with the best gameplay, such as those mentioned above, are deemed not commercial enough and too "way out." The early days of the industry were very experimental, and there would be games on any subject or combination of subjects you could imagine. They were very original and, in some cases, very strange. There was, of course, a price to be paid for this flexibility: the loss of the hypothetical mass market. One of the reasons given for the increased stagnation and lack of originality of most games today is that the more "way-out" stuff lacks mass-market appeal. Unfortunately, this argument is true, because it is market pressures that have forced the games industry into this state. But how much of it is the tail wagging the dog?

The Development Environment

Back in the 1980s, the development environment consisted of one thing: a glowing screen filled with incomprehensible (to anyone else) hexadecimal digits, and bizarre codes such as LD A, 2Ah.

Nothing much has changed today either, except the incomprehensible hexadecimal digits have been hidden behind several layers of user interface. The code is still there, but it is well hidden behind a bewildering selection of menu options, just in case you might hurt yourself. See Figures 16.6 and 16.7 to see what I mean.

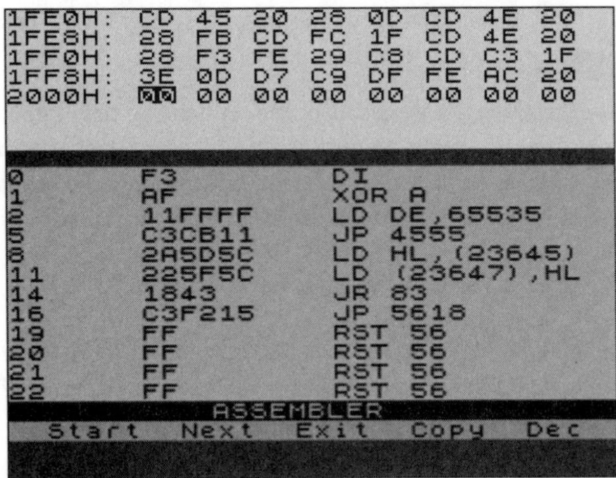

Figure 16.6
A game developer's screen, circa 1983.

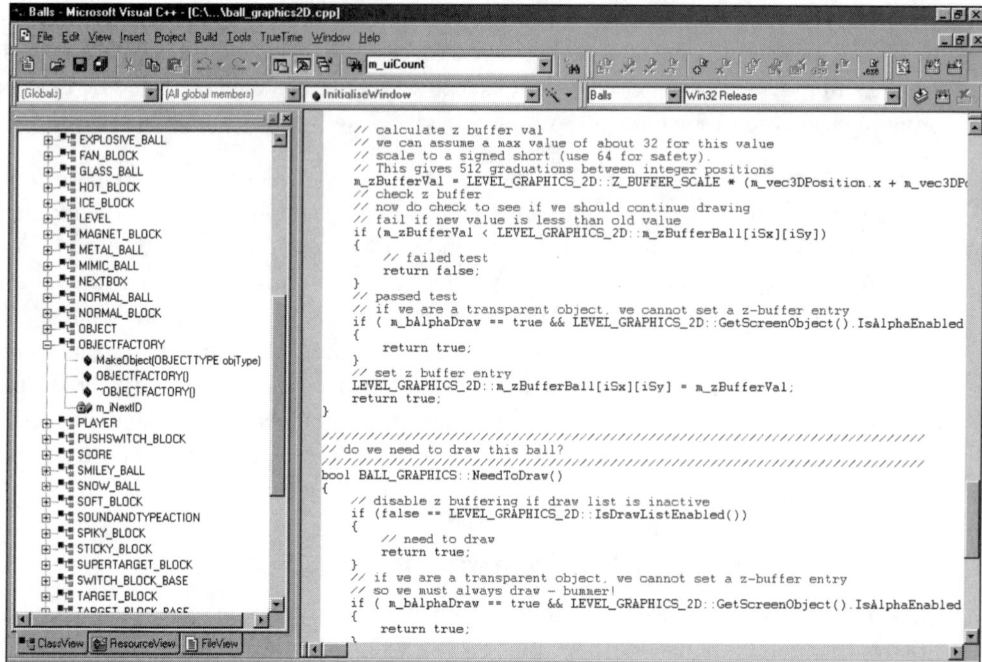

Figure 16.7
A game developer's screen, circa 1999.

Developers have become spoiled in terms of the variety of tools available to them. The life of a game developer has been made easier by a conspiracy of excellent optimizing compilers, game libraries that automatically take advantage of hardware acceleration, remote debugging, multiple-monitor debugging, and, in some cases, the ability to develop the game using an emulator on more-powerful hardware, rather than the target hardware.

In the 1980s, code had to be developed on the target machine. When the first game programmers started out, they were assembling their own programs in their heads. By this, I mean that they were writing down the op-codes (machine language commands) on paper, performing the conversion to hexadecimal, and then typing them into the computer using a simple program (usually self-written) called a *hex loader*, which, as the name suggests, allowed the developer to load hexadecimal codes into memory.

As time progressed, programs called *assemblers* became available. These programs allowed the developer to skip some of the paper stage, and enter the op-codes into the computer program, which would then perform the conversion phase and assemble the program into memory, resolving any references to other parts of the code as it did so.

Although this made some things easier, much was still difficult. A fair amount of juggling was required, because the development was always done on the target machine. The assembler itself took up some of the memory, which meant that, for a game that used all the available memory, it had to be assembled in parts and pasted together.

Debugging was also a restricted and difficult activity, because the debugger itself required some of the system memory, and, hence, it was difficult to fit it all in with the game in memory as well. This difficulty was slightly offset by the fact that the developer usually knew all the code inside out, because the only way to get the required speed was to completely dump the operating system (such that it was) and write to hardware directly. Because all the machines were standard, there were no dangers of intraplatform incompatibility, as there were with (for example) the latter days of DOS PC game programming, where the developer had to take many possible hardware configurations into account.

The main driving force shaping the development of computer games used to be speed and size. This resulted in every game being written in Assembler and addressing the hardware directly. Writing in Assembler allowed the developer to have direct one-to-one control over the size of his or her code. In theory, you could take an Assembler listing and calculate the exact size of the output that would be produced when it was assembled. This is in contrast with a C or C++ compiler, in which the size of the output object file is entirely at the whim of the compiler writer.

This imperative of writing directly to the hardware, and using bit-twiddling optimization gave rise to the expression "writing directly to the metal"—writing code that accesses the hardware of the machine in order to obtain the maximum speed.

The concept of writing to the metal is considered part of the whole game programmer mythology and has become less prevalent. The only way for a programmer to realistically write to the metal today is to become a hardware driver programmer, writing the drivers for audio and sound cards and other computer peripherals. The myth still persists, however, that unless you are writing to the metal you are writing slow and bloated code.

The Development Languages

Assembler is not really used very much nowadays; most products are written in a higher-level language, with only small critical parts being written in Assembler. *Doom*, arguably the most famous computer game of all, was written almost entirely in C. The only parts that were written in Assembler were a couple of vertical and horizontal line-drawing routines.

This shocked many people at the time, and the Internet newsgroups were full of discussions on this new development. People had a hard time believing that it was possible to write a game like *Doom* unless it was completely written in Assembler. You have to remember that, although *Doom* looks pretty clunky by the standards of today, at the time it blew everything else out of the water. It was a turning point in the development of games for the PC; some would even argue that it kick-started the industry. It certainly made people realize what the ugly business machine was actually becoming capable of.

Doom heralded the beginning of the C era of game programming. Watcom, the makers of the C/C++ compiler used to write *Doom*, must have experienced a huge boost in sales as everybody shifted from TASM (Borland Turbo Assembler) and MASM (Microsoft Assembler) to *Watcom C/C++ 10.5*. The main strengths of the Watcom compiler were that it could compile to a 32-bit DOS application and that it produced fast and well-optimized code, whereas the only real competitor, Microsoft Visual C++ 1.5x, could produce only 16-bit DOS (or Windows) applications that were not as well optimized.

The fact that the Watcom compiler produced 32-bit DOS applications was a great boon to game developers. The difference between a 16-bit and a 32-bit application is the memory model. In a 16-bit application, the amount of memory available to the application is limited to 640K (actually 1 megabyte, but the system used the rest), unless you go through a slow and clunky interface to get to the expanded memory (EMS) of the machine. This memory was addressed by using a 20-bit segment:offset system that limited you to address only 64 kilobytes of memory at a time using the 16-bit offset pointer, unless you modified the segment pointer (which was slow). On the whole, it was a nasty system and wasn't really considered fast enough for the needs of game programmers (let alone the fact that it was notoriously difficult to program for).

The move to the 32-bit model solved this at a stroke, as 32-bit pointers allowed the application to directly address four gigabytes of memory, and the segment:offset model became a thing of the past. If the developer wished to allocate 2 megabytes of memory using the C function malloc(), then he could do so without problem. Moreover, the returned pointer was a 32-bit pointer that could address the whole of the 2-megabyte range simply by incrementing it (no messing around with segment pointers to access a different 64-kilobyte block).

With the widespread use of Watcom C/C++, Dos4gw—the DOS extender used to provide 32-bit DPMI (DOS Protected Mode Interface) functionality to DOS executables—became a familiar sight when loading a game. The use of the DOS extender to allow fully 32-bit executables was a watershed for game developers. Now they got the best of both worlds: not only could they write directly to the metal, but they could also use a simple and flexible memory model to do so.

The dominance of Watcom C/C++ in the games industry continued for several years until, a few years later, Microsoft turned its attention to the games market and its reliance on DOS. Microsoft had been trying to quietly kill off DOS for several years by this stage, and had succeeded in promoting Windows (3.1 and NT 3.51) as the platform of the future. All new applications being released for the PC at this time were Windows executables, except for games (which remained as DOS executables, mainly because Windows abstracted the hardware to such an extent that it was impossible to get the speed needed for a computer game). On top of this, the user interface of Windows was, to say the least, visually bland, and designed for homogeneity of application user interfaces. You were strictly limited in your access to the hardware: for example, if you wanted to modify the contents of video memory, you would use the Windows API to request the address of the area in video memory that you wanted to change. Windows would then copy the area from video memory into system memory, and, when you had finished performing your modifications and released the surface lock, the memory would be copied back to the video memory. This is obviously a slow process, mainly because the Windows API calls used to do this were written with flexibility in mind: they were designed to copy all video memory configurations, and were not particularly optimized. They were fast enough for the average application or word processor, but for a game—where the graphics usually change extensively every frame—the speed just was not there.

Microsoft did not want to continue supporting DOS. It saw the future as a 32-bit graphical operating system that was fast enough to support games. In what could be considered to be a practice run, they released WinG, a form of the Game SDK (and a precursor to DirectX), designed to allow faster access to hardware resources on Windows-based machines. I can remember only one game, *SimTower*, that was commercially released using this (although I'm sure that there were probably more), and the game suffered from appallingly slow graphic updates (at least on the 486 DX2 66MHz that I was using, which at the time was the best you could get).

WinG died a quiet death, and, meanwhile, Windows 95 was released with a fair amount of pomp in the closing months of 1995, as I'm sure most of you will remember. Windows 95 sounded the official Microsoft death knell for 16-bit applications. DOS was dead.

Except, that is, if you were writing a game. The games industry practically ignored this new operating system, except to check it for compatibility with their Dos4gw executables. It was not considered then as a serious target for game development. Microsoft, on the other hand, did not want to continue supporting DOS, seeing the games industry as the last bastion of the DOS programmer. If Microsoft could persuade the game developers to begin producing games for Windows 95, it will have achieved its aim of phasing out DOS, and shown the world that Windows 95 was the operating system of the future. To this end, Microsoft developed DirectX, a library to allow the game developer direct access to the hardware if required, and to take advantage of any acceleration provided in the hardware. The ideology behind DirectX was to provide a standard interface to the hardware that was easier to access than had been traditionally possible using DOS. Initially, DirectX was touted by Microsoft as being potentially faster than DOS for graphics, because it would automatically take advantage of any hardware acceleration that was available.

DirectX spawned mild interest (and derision), but it was not until the release of DirectX 2 that people took notice. (Maybe it was the lurid yellow CD with a black radiation warning symbol that caught their eye.) With DirectX 2, the API had just about become usable, and was taking advantage of the newly developed Microsoft Component Object Model technology (COM). COM is an object-oriented technique that allows objects to be easily versioned and (at least in theory) accessible from languages other than that in which the object was originally written.

During this period, Microsoft had not been lazy in updating its C/C++ compilers. It was painfully aware that Visual C++ 2.x (which compiled for 32-bit applications) was showing its age, and, consequently, an update was released in the form of Visual C++ 4. This was a bit of a shock to the industry: a whole "generation" of game programmer had grown up with the concept of "Microsoft = slow, Watcom = fast," and they were surprised to discover that the Microsoft compiler produced faster, tighter code than the Watcom compiler.

The result of this was the gradual transferal of game development from targeting DOS to targeting Windows 95. The first game released as a Windows 95 native executable, taking advantage of DirectX functionality, was a version of the classic Activision game, *Pitfall*. The initial release of DirectX was not fully compatible with the Watcom compiler, forcing anyone who wanted to do serious game development to switch to the Microsoft compiler. I'll leave it for the reader to decide whether this was by accident or design.

With the increasing momentum of Windows 95 game releases, Apple, manufacturers of the Macintosh and PowerPC line of computers couldn't sit back and let its (already tenuous) position be eroded further. More and more games were being released for Windows 95, which further strengthened Windows' position as the operating system for the masses. To fight this onslaught, Apple released the Game Sprockets, a set of components analogous to (but not compatible with) DirectX for the Macintosh operating system. How successful this was still remains to be seen, but, to date, only a handful of companies (Blizzard and Bungie being two examples that spring to mind) are releasing games for both platforms. I'll plead the fifth on whether this is due to the difficulty of writing cross-platform code, or whether it is due to lack of sales on the Macintosh. Recently, however, Apple has reversed its fortune with the relative success of the "designer" computer, the iMac, but whether this will impact the games market in any significant fashion remains to be seen.

This just about brings us up to the present day, at least for home computer development. DirectX has matured through six versions, and there is no serious PC game development done without it. The Microsoft compiler has been substantially enhanced, and now is considered to produce the fastest and most compact code, and have the friendliest user interface. Advantages such as network and multimonitor debugging and "edit and continue" (which lets the developer modify code on the fly without fully recompiling the program) have served to make the life of the game developer easier. At least in some ways.

The growing power and diversity of computer systems have also made the developer's life more difficult. The variety of hardware, and the subsequent complexity of programming the API—compounded by the amount of new information to absorb—is definitely more than before. It's like the development of scientific knowledge: in the eighteenth century, it was possible for one person to know all the areas of science in depth. Now, even after years of study, the best that could be hoped for would be to specialize in a tiny area.

A Note On The Future

The last great taboo of game programming is C++. Up until very recently, C++ was considered too slow to be useful for game programming. The only reason that C was accepted by game programmers was the assurances that you could take a listing from a C program and (with some effort) predict what Assembler language output you would get. With C++, there were all sorts of strange goings-on in the background, and it was not possible to directly relate C++ code to assembly.

Fundamentally, game programmers did not trust the compiler. They assumed that anything the compiler produced was inferior to their own efforts. In the early days, this may have been true (assuming that they were a very skilled Assembler programmer), but now, with the advances in compiler technology and the nondeterministic nature of multitasking operating systems, this argument is invalid. This is the "Not Built Here" (NBH) argument, and it is a particular favorite of the game programmer. This argument is becoming increasingly like pure sophistry: it is impossible to write a game nowadays without using the operating system (somebody else's code)!

Of course, it may well be possible to produce better output than even the best compiler, but the amount of time and money that would have to be expended would be out of reach of all but the richest companies. The last famous example of "It'll be finished when we say so!" was *Quake*, for which Michael Abrash was hired (as he is widely acknowledged as the king of Assembler optimization) to tune and retune their inner loops, although, interestingly enough, the majority of the game was written in C.

Although C++ has become much more prevalent in game programming, there is still one compelling argument for using C: cross-platform compatibility. The implementation of C++ is varied slightly from platform to platform, particularly on the newer features such as templates and namespaces, and this was the reason for *Quake* being written in C. C has been standardized for years, and it is a stable language. You pretty much know that a program written on one platform will recompile and function pretty much as intended on another platform, unless you have made any processor-specific assumptions.

However, the ANSI standard for C++ has recently been ratified. Hopefully, this will mean that C++ will benefit from the source-level cross-platform compatibility currently enjoyed by C. When this happens, there will be no further obstacles to using C++ for the majority of cross-platform game development.

This is the present, but what of the future? There will always be a hard-core contingent that wants to exploit the machine to the max, but there have always been "game maker" packages that attempt to allow nonprogrammers to produce their own games. Nearly without exception, these were universally terrible. The advent of *STOS* (Atari ST) and *AMOS* (Amiga)—programming languages based on Basic with game-specific extensions—were exceptions to this rule. While you couldn't do anything spectacular with these languages—and, although they were easier than learning C, they were still quite technical and had quite an initial learning curve for a nonprogrammer)—they could be giving an indication of what is to come. In fact, the PC incarnation of these took one step forward and two steps back: it allowed the use of dragging and dropping of backdrops and actors to create a game, but this brought inflexibility, and any games created with it tended to look as if they were about five years out of date.

Things have moved along since then. For example, the package *NemoDev* allows the scripting of actors in a virtual 3D environment by dragging and dropping behavior objects onto them. If these behaviors are not sufficient, they can be extended by using C++ to write new behaviors.

While *NemoDev* arguably may not fit the needs of professional game developers, it certainly is the way forward for game design. As it stands, *NemoDev* is certainly suitable for generating advanced prototypes—and you do not need to be too technically proficient to use it successfully—but I am not aware of any commercially released games that use the engine. This is not because the engine is bad; I imagine that it is just another casualty of the NBH syndrome.

Another great concept that has recently come to my attention is the *Universal Save* system by GameLogic. This is so useful, I've been wondering why it is hasn't been thought of before. The *Universal Save* system is a collection of COM objects and utilities that allows the game developer to provide game-save functionality using a standardized database system. This allows other information to be saved as well, such as personal configuration settings, game statistics, and screenshots. A browser utility allows you to browse the saved games and other information and to launch the game with one step.

One of the advantages of the consoles over the PCs is the level of standardization. On the consoles, everything tends to work the same way; on the PC, there is a plethora of different ways to do things. Standardization can make developers' lives easier, and this was the idea behind DirectX. Second-generation products such as the *Universal Save* system can only improve this level of standardization. The use of third-party components such as this not only save development time, they also ensure that the feature is implemented to a higher standard than would usually be possible in the available time.

The Anachronism Of Console Programming

Console development is, at least on the surface, very similar to the way games were developed in the old days. Consoles have been traditionally programmed in Assembler, much in the same way as the old eight-bit computers.

Only the most recent consoles (such as the Sony PlayStation) have broken this pattern and used C as the main programming language. The reason for this is cross-platform compatibility, but not in the usual sense. Sony wanted to be able to guarantee that games would run on later versions of the PlayStation. Sony actively discourages writing directly to the hardware. It has not released the details of the hardware, and recommends that all access goes through the provided libraries.

Before this, the lineage of consoles traced through from the heady days of the Atari 2600 through the Nintendo Entertainment System (NES), Super NES (SNES), Nintendo 64, and the Nintendo Game Boy and Color Game Boy.

The market for console development tools has always effectively been a closed one. The console manufacturer strictly controlled the availability of development kits, and (particularly in the case of Nintendo), there were strict guidelines to follow before you would be granted a development kit. Chris and Tim Stamper, founders of the U.K. software house, Rare Ltd. (producers of classic Nintendo 64 games such as *GoldenEye 007*), revealed in an interview that they had reverse-engineered the NES in order to produce a game to show Nintendo what they were capable of. Nintendo, being duly impressed by the work of the brothers, signed them up as preferred developers and promptly gave them all the information they had figured out by reverse-engineering the console in the first place.

Originally, the choice of development kit was limited to that provided by the console manufacturer. These were usually quite expensive, and were not always the easiest things to use. Pretty soon, however, third-party development kits came onto the market. One of the first was GLAM, which was developed in England and could target a number of different platforms, including the Game Boy, NES, Sega Master System, and a number of arcade boards. (This was the kit used by Rare for many of their products.)

These development kits were never quite as polished as their computer equivalents, probably due to the inherently short lifespan and limited upgrade capacity of most consoles. The development tools usually got only one major development cycle, unlike Microsoft Visual C++, which is currently in its sixth incarnation. Obviously, this has allowed for a lot of polishing and development of new features.

This situation seems to be changing with the increasing prominence of consoles: whereas originally they were seen as toys for small children, the massive success of the Sony marketing machine made the PlayStation into the accessory of choice for young 'n' groovy adults. What Sony started, Lara Croft certainly helped improve.

This mass attention has caused a vast increase in the number of developers wanting to produce console software, which has consequently created a demand for better tools. Metrowerks, producers of *CodeWarrior* for the Macintosh, announced a version of its product for the Nintendo 64.

Microsoft is also (somewhat surprisingly) keen to get in on the act: The Sega Dreamcast uses a version of Windows CE as an operating system, with a specially customized version of DirectX. To facilitate development, Microsoft has released an extension package for Visual Studio, allowing software to be written on PC and compiled for the Dreamcast. The use of DirectX and Visual Studio in this way is meant to allow easy development of cross-platform PC/Dreamcast games. If this works (there is some doubt about the viability of the Dreamcast in the wake of the PlayStation Mk. II), then the future looks bright for the production of cross-platform games.

Over the past few years, there has been a burgeoning interest in writing homebrewed software for the consoles. Usually however, the development tools and hardware manuals are restricted to official developers, and the fee to become an official developer is usually beyond the budget of average individuals. This turned out not to be a problem, as there is a large and active community of people on the Internet who hack the consoles and share the information that they have found. This, coupled with the rise of the emulator scene (you can now emulate practically any machine in existence on your PC, with the Spectrum, the

Commodore 64, the PlayStation, the Nintendo 64, and the Color Game Boy being some examples) meant that pretty soon a lot of free or shareware development kits were written by enthusiastic amateurs. In many cases, these kits are so good that official developers use them in preference to those provided by Sony or Nintendo.

For example, for the Game Boy, you can find full documentation of the hardware, programming tutorials, a fully featured Game Boy assembler, an emulator for the PC that has a built in debugger, and even a C compiler. Using these resources, combined with a cheap cartridge writer, you can set yourself up with a full-blown unofficial Game Boy development kit for less than $100. Similar software and hardware exists for the other major consoles, too. Game Boy programming is an anachronism: due to the limited power of the machine, programming for the Game Boy is the closest experience you can find to the original flavor of programming with the old machines. It is the last computer left on the market for which one person can be expected to be able to write a best-selling game as a single programmer. In the case of the Game Boy, it seems we have come full circle.

This book is not about producing games for the Game Boy, as the techniques presented here would swamp the Game Boy, even if a C++ compiler were available for it. However, the Game Boy does form a valuable part of the still-growing history of game development, and this discussion would be incomplete if it were not mentioned.

By all means, go ahead and produce Game Boy games. It is a good way to learn about producing games with limited hardware, and many game developers would swear that—unless you knew what it meant to have to scrape the bottom of the barrel for that last few bytes of memory, or to hand optimize a critical loop in order to achieve a reasonable frame rate—then you won't be able to appreciate just how easy development is nowadays. Parts I and II of this book are still applicable, of course. Game design and project management are the same, no matter what the platform, but tread carefully when using the techniques in Part III, which may well be a bit too meaty for the Game Boy. The basic structure of a game is the same on any platform, but the amount of work you can delegate to the compiler in order to make your life as a developer easier most certainly is not.

The Present Day

So, where are we now? What is development actually like on the computers and consoles of today? In a word, *easier*. The amount of work that is automatically performed for us by the compiler and the operating systems has increased dramatically.

By producing a few libraries and frameworks to access the hardware interfaces, it has become possible to concentrate more on the game logic, which is the fun part. All the grunt work—machine initialization, joystick detection, hardware setup—has been done for you (or very nearly), and you can concentrate on the task at hand, rather than battling with hundreds of possible hardware configurations.

Reusability

Reusability—the concept of producing software components that are useful for more than one project—appears to be a very difficult concept for the average game developer.

The average game developer believes that using shared components ensures that all the output from the company will be the same. ("We can't keep using the same engine or all our games will look the same!") That may well be true, and the world certainly appears to have enough *Warcraft* and *Quake* clones to support this theory.

This is the difference between monolithic and component-based development and the mindsets that go with them. Monolithic development is the practice of developing a program in one large "lump." This lump may consist of separate parts, but the parts are so interwoven that they are inseparable. Each part of the system is interdependent on the other parts, and the parts rely on internal knowledge of how they function, rather than using the published interface. This reliance on internal knowledge means that these parts are effectively immovable: it's as if they have extended tendrils deep into the hearts of the other parts, and have tangled each other up irretrievably. Figure 16.8 portrays a monolithic system.

The contrast of a monolithic system is (obviously) a component-based system, the sort of thing that Microsoft has been touting for quite a while with its COM-based system. Figure 16.9 illustrates a component-based system. Just because Microsoft has suggested it doesn't mean that it is automatically a bad idea, although it is a little bit heavyweight and is not yet supported fully on all platforms. You can't rely on it if you want automatic cross-platform capabilities. This may change in the future, but, for the time being, COM is strictly Windows only.

Most game developers consider COM too slow. In most cases, this is simply a gut feeling, based on the (incorrect) assumption that anything C++—and especially everything C++

Figure 16.8
The structure of a monolithic system.

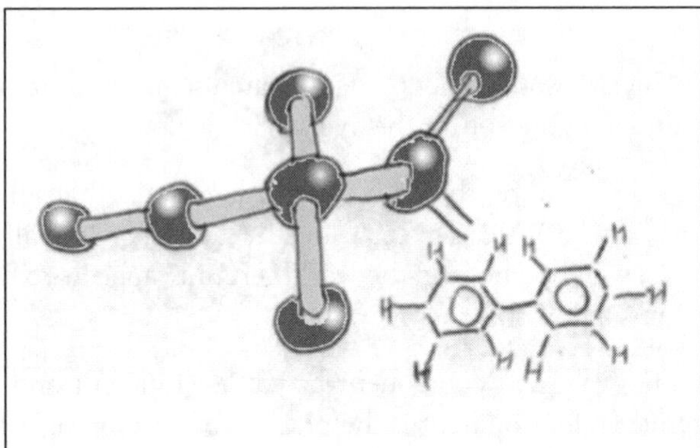

Figure 16.9
The structure of a component-based system.

and Microsoft—must be slow. This may or may not be true, but, in any case, it is not safe to make such assumptions without using a profiler to test the speeds.

I have not found any particular problems with COM, and neither have most PC game developers; whether they know it or not, DirectX is a collection of COM objects, and they have been using those for a while now!

The arguments for and against using COM are not as simple as "Is it fast enough?"

A much more fundamental concern needs to be considered first, and that is whether you actually *need* to use it. COM is very powerful, and, for a lot of game development, it is using a sledgehammer to crack an egg. COM is useful for designing operating system components, because all details to the location of the object are stored in the system registry (a sort of database that contains all the settings for the operating system), but how often will you need to run your game out of a bunch of different directories?

The major advantage of COM is easy versioning. A COM object can export one or more interfaces to a client. COM objects always export at least one interface, **IUnknown**. This is the daddy of all COM interfaces, and supports just three main operations: incrementing a reference count, deincrementing a reference count, and querying for an interface. This is not very useful on its own, so a nontrivial COM object will export more than just the one standard interface. These extra interfaces are obtained by first obtaining a pointer to **IUnknown**, and then asking it to provide a pointer to the interface that you want to use, using the **QueryInterface** method. The golden rule of COM objects is that, once an interface is published, it *cannot* be changed. If you need to add extra functionality to an interface that is already being used by other programs, then you do it by adding a new interface to the object. This interface can support all of the old functionality, and can also support the new features that you wish to add. That way, both old programs and new programs are served adequately. For example, if you had an older game that used the interface **IAIEngine**, and then you released an updated and/or expanded version, you would probably name the new interface **IAIEngine2**. *Any* change to the functionality of an already published COM object requires a new interface. It is best to do this, even if you have changed only the internal functioning and have not modified the external interface (unless you can absolutely guarantee that the way the object appears to behave externally has not been changed at all).

Another advantage of COM—at least in theory—is that the objects are easily accessible from other languages. For example, I use a COM object that I have written that exports the interface, **IBHCodecCOM**. This is a compression/decompression object that can compress or decompress to and from areas of memory, resources built into the executable file, or files on the hard disk.

I have written a number of programs that use this object to decompress files, and they all use it from C++. The COM object can be treated just like a normal C++ object, and there is no difference in syntax, except for a call to **CoInitialize** to initialize the COM system. Sometime after writing this object, it occurred to me that it would be useful to have a graphical browser of archive files, so I could check and update the contents.

What did I do? Did I spend a couple of weeks writing an MFC graphical browser? No, I fired up Visual Basic and wrote a user interface similar to WinZip in a couple of hours. While it wasn't the prettiest thing in the world, it did the trick, and was usable enough to release to other people as an internal tool. Accessing a COM object in Visual Basic is as simple as referencing the type library (a library of interface information built at compile time), declaring a new object, and using the methods provided just like you would with any other Visual Basic object. The highlighted lines in Listing 16.1 shows how this works. Listing 16.2 shows the usage of the same object in Visual C++.

Listing 16.1 Accessing a COM object from Visual Basic.

```
Dim BHCodec As New BHCodecCom   ' compression/extraction object
''''''''''''''''''''''''''''''''''''''
' function to add a file to an archive
''''''''''''''''''''''''''''''''''''''
Private Sub AddChunk(strFile As String)
    ' check that an archive has been selected
    If BHCodec.ArchiveFile = "" Then Exit Sub

    ' set busy mousepointer
    FormBHCODECViewer.MousePointer = vbHourglass
    ' select compression type based on user input
    If OptCodecType(0).Value = True Then
        BHCodec.CompressionType = BHCodec.BHC
    ElseIf OptCodecType(1).Value = True Then
        BHCodec.CompressionType = BHCodec.ZLB
    ElseIf OptCodecType(2).Value = True Then
        BHCodec.CompressionType = BHCodec.NONE
    End If
```

```
    On Error GoTo adderror  ' set up error handling
    BHCodec.Add (strFile)   ' add the file to the archive
    On Error GoTo 0         ' switch off error handling

    ' set normal mousepointer
    FormBHCODECViewer.MousePointer = vbArrow

    ' successful compression
    Exit Sub

' error handling (on error jumps here)
adderror:
    FormBHCODECViewer.MousePointer = vbArrow    ' restore mousepointer
    ' display error
    Call MsgBox(BHCodec.Error, vbOKCancel + vbCritical)
End Sub
```

Let's examine this snippet of code more carefully. (Don't worry. There won't be an overreliance on code samples in this book. It is more about design and architecture than it is about code, but a few examples will be necessary to understand key points. Where we use code samples, we will dissect and discuss each sample to ensure that any tricky parts can be understood.)

In Listing 16.1, the **BHCodecCom** object has been specified in the project options as a reference. This means that the type library (a small library of information about supported interfaces of that object) has been included, and the Visual Basic compiler knows where to look for it. This code snippet is taken from the archive viewer utility I wrote to examine the archives created by the compression object. As you can see in the code, it is very simple to use a COM object from Visual Basic: the lines that show the object in use are highlighted. The highlighting indicates the lines that we are interested in for the following discussion.

The first action performed by the code is to create a new instance of the compression/decompression object. This is performed globally, so it can be accessed by any procedure.

The **AddChunk** takes a file name to compress to the archive.

The assumption is made that the object has been initialized with an archive name. If not, the function will return without performing any actions.

The compression type (selectable from the user interface) is then checked and assigned to the **BHCodecCom.CompressionType** property.

Error handling is initialized to allow jumping to the **adderror** label in the case of an error during the compression.

The specified file is then added to the archive. If there is an error, a description of the error will be displayed, and the function will exit.

In there is no error, error handling is turned off, and the function exits normally.

The next code snippet shows a similar function in C++.

Listing 16.2 Accessing a COM object from Visual C++.

```
// import the type library so the compiler knows about the COM object
#import "c:\msdev\projects\bhcodec\bhcdcshl\bhcdcshl.tlb" no_namespace

// standard includes
#include <stdio.h>
#include <iostream.h>

//////////////////////////////////////////////////////////////////////////////
// This function will add an file to an archive.
// Note that _bstr_t is a class provided by Microsoft that implements
// COM compatible strings.
//////////////////////////////////////////////////////////////////////////////
void AddFile(_bstr_t bstrFilenameToCompress, _bstr_t bstrArchive)
{
    // Initialise COM
    CoInitialize(NULL);

    // create compression COM object
    IBHCodecComPtr lpBHCodec(__uuidof(BHCodecCom));
    // set archive file name
    lpBHCodec->ArchiveFile = bstrArchive;

    // add the file to the archive (using default compression type)
    lpBHCodec->Add(strFilenameToCompress);
    // release compression object
    lpBHCodec = NULL;

    // Unitialise COM
    CoUninitialize();
}
```

The code needed to set up and use a COM object in C++ is slightly more complex than in Visual Basic.

Note

The code in Listing 16.2 is not production code. In reality, you would not initialize and then uninitialize COM every time you wanted to add a chunk to the archive. It is shown in this way for simplicity. A far more sensible usage would be to initialize COM when the program starts, and then uninitialize it when the program exits.

The first line in the listing imports the type library so that the compiler can recognize the compression object. This is analogous to the references required in Visual Basic. The **no_namespace** directive at the end of the **#import** statement is for simplicity. This ensures that I don't have to use any complex syntax to access my object. The only situation where I would require the namespace is if I were using lots of objects in a large project and I wanted to avoid any danger of namespace collision. The act of including this type library generates some C++ code behind the scenes that creates a smart pointer wrapper to the COM object, so that we can use it as we would any other C++ object. Usually with COM, you have to be sure that you keep the reference count correct in order to have the object deleted correctly at the end of its life. Using the smart pointer wrapper, most of this is handled automatically.

The compression function itself takes the name of the archive and the file to compress into it as parameters. First, COM is initialized (it is shut down at the end of the function, as described in the note above). This sort of thing is handled automatically in Visual Basic, but Visual C++ gives us more flexibility and control, so we have to do it ourselves.

In the following line, the compression object is instantiated. This is similar to the way it is done in Visual Basic, except the syntax is slightly more complex. We are declaring an object of type **IBHCodecComPtr** and initializing it with the Universally Unique ID (UUID) of the compression object. Each interface that a COM object supports has a UUID, generated at compile time. This number is guaranteed to be unique and unchanging for any particular interface, and is used to identify the interface by the COM system. All the initialization information for the COM object is stored in the system registry under this UUID, and the system uses this to instantiate the object.

Note

UUIDs used to be known as Globally Unique Identifiers (GUIDs). Then someone decided that mankind would be colonizing other worlds in the near future—hence the more space-age friendly term "Universal."

The next two lines are simple. We set the archive name, and call the **Add** method of the object to compress the file into the archive. Note that I have not included any error checking here for the sake of simplicity.

We have now finished with the COM object, so it is released. One of the benefits of the smart pointer class is that it has overloaded the assignment operator (**operator=** for the C++ minded). Assigning **NULL** to the object actually causes the reference count to be decremented by one. If it reaches zero, the object is deleted. In our case, we have not explicitly increased the reference count, so we know that the smart pointer class will have initialized the count to one. Hence, when we assign **NULL** to the object's smart pointer wrapper, it will be deleted.

We can see from these two examples that, although platform specific, COM can be incredibly useful for the game developer. The power to be able to use the object from a number of different languages makes the development process much smoother. For example, I could write a COM object that handles the loading and saving of level data. This object could then be used by the level editor (written in a high-level language such as Visual Basic) and by the game itself (typically written in C++).

A word on the speed of COM objects: the typical response of game developers to suggestions of COM is that it will be too slow for "real" use. Of course, it depends how you define "real." While I wouldn't suggest that it be used in the most critical inner loop of your game, everywhere else would be fine. With a good compiler, there is not much more overhead to using a COM object compared to using a standard C++ object. And don't forget that all of DirectX is based on COM, so you are most likely using a number of COM objects in your everyday development anyway.

The only fly in the ointment is the lack of real cross-platform support. A COM system for the Macintosh would be ideal, and I understand that some third parties are working on this. Unfortunately, because these COM systems are third party, they are unlikely to be included as part of the operating system, as it is with Windows.

COM will be covered in later chapters of this book, and I will provide some guidelines about their suitability and where they could be used in your project.

Chapter 17
Initial Design

Key Topics:

- *The importance of a good architecture design*
- *Platform considerations*
- *The problem domain*
- *Tokenization*
- *Token interaction*
- *Finite-state machines*
- *Events, states, transitions, and properties*

Part I of this book covered the game design process, from taking the germ of an idea through to a fully fledged game design, with some interesting detours into what a game actually is. This chapter picks up where Part I left off. You have your cool game design nicely specified, and now you'll turn it into the killer game you've been aiming for. Okay, guys; get coding!

Well, that's what usually happens.

If you've been paying careful attention so far, you will have noticed that most game development goes directly from a game design to the programming phase. You also will have noticed that the games industry is the only place where this occurs. Why? Because the games industry hasn't yet caught up with modern development techniques. Current thinking is that the games industry is some eight years behind the rest of the industry. Okay, so the programming itself is up to date, but the techniques are a bit behind the times, much like building a car using period techniques (but modern tools). Eight years in this industry is a long time.

Developers do not write technical design documents because it helps them kill some time. Rather, they write technical designs as roadmaps of the way ahead. The technical designs improve project visibility and allow someone who has a view of the bigger picture to see how the work fits in with the overall company plans. There's no point in having a developer beaver away for weeks on a CD-playing module if the team next door produced one a couple of months ago, or if the company bought one and it's on the shelf gathering dust behind the office copy of *Quake II*. There is also not much use in building a module that nobody else knows about.

The technical design is an advertisement. It tells people what you are doing, so they can fit their work around yours. It helps to prevent unnecessary duplication of work, and it improves the overall visibility of the development process. No production-level coding should start until the technical design is complete (subject to the 80/20 rule). Of course, a number of intermediary phases must be gone through first. Before the coding can begin, the design has to progress from the biggest picture (the initial game design) right down to the smallest picture (the technical design for an individual module). So put away your coding hat—which you're not going to need for a while—and pull out your architect's hard hat, and read on.

This chapter covers the initial phases of the technical design process, and its aim is to take a well-specified game design and produce from it a well-specified overall architectural design.

As stated before, the ubiquitous 80/20 rule again comes into play. It is not possible to fully complete an architectural design before beginning coding. You should, however be able to complete approximately 80 percent; the remaining 20 percent will be modified and rewritten as the project progresses. An important point to realize is that the architectural design is never "finished," but will be constantly evolving as development proceeds. There is nothing wrong with this; in fact, it's the sign of a healthy project. It's impossible to be able to predict with 100 percent certainty what will be needed before you've actually got your hands dirty with the code, but, with a good design, the amount of rewriting will be minimized. It will then be a simple process of refinement and clarification of the document. At this point, I must stress the importance of keeping the documentation in line with the code. (This has been covered before: the documentation work should be considered an integral part of the development work. The code itself is just a small—but important—detail tacked onto the end.)

The classic argument against having to do all this "boring" documentation is that the code is the best documentation possible. That can be true, of course, but it shouldn't be, because, if code is the "best" documentation, then the documentation is for all intents and purposes, nonexistent. This is a chicken-and-egg scenario, as the code is the best documentation, because nobody bothers keeping the real documentation up to date. What you must consider is that you will not be the only person reading this documentation. In theory, anyone who wants or needs to know exactly how the project is going—anyone from another member of the technical team to the game designer to the company president.

Another classic response is that the code is the only documentation required, and anybody who can't read it probably doesn't need to. If you really believe that, I cannot help you. Maybe you should choose a new career—a more solitary one, in which you won't have to interact with people, such as a lighthouse keeper.

Then again, if you tell your company president that she should be able to read the code for herself when she asks for a technical design document to check the progress, the decision to choose another career may be already made for you!

The Beginning

A lot of hard work has gone into your game thus far. The game design has had to jump a fair number of hurdles before reaching the stage it is at now. It has satisfied the company management, the marketing department, and the game designer's peers that it is a game worth developing. It's been through a number of iterations and refinements, and will continue to do so throughout the development process. The sign of a good design is that these refinements will become increasingly minor as the technical phases begin. Radically redesigning a game halfway through development does not tend to make for happy developers.

In this chapter, we will consider three game designs, and how we would take them from the design phase through to the architectural phase.

Everybody should be familiar with two of these games, and the other one, *Balls!*, is the game written as a testbed for some of the concepts in this book (a demo version of which is included on the CD-ROM).

Before we even consider these, however, we must consider something else that is even more fundamental. We must take into account the platform(s) on which the software is running. The architecture of a game has two main aspects: the hardware abstraction interface and the game abstraction itself. The hardware abstraction interface is conceptually easier to deal with, because the architect is providing an abstraction for something that already exists. There is no real point in providing concrete abstractions for phantom hardware, although it's not a bad idea to try to take consider future developments at least in the interface design.

The second aspect is the game itself. All games share a few standard aspects—which almost count as hardware interfaces themselves—such as the menu and options system, and, on a lower level, the main game loop. When we venture out of this familiar territory, we are on our own (or nearly so, as there are very few problems in modern computing that someone else hasn't already solved). Game developers tend to like the feeling that they are pioneering uncharted territory, or that they are boldly going where only a few have gone before (and that they are doing it better). Of course, they can't all be right. The "Not Built Here" syndrome is endemic within the games industry, and even the developers who licensed the *Quake II* engine proudly boast about how many modifications they have made. It's almost as if they cannot admit that they used an engine "as is," because that would make them seem like lesser developers—or worse still, little more than glorified level designers. The trouble is, that whatever these guys do with the *Quake II* engine, the games are going to look inherently similar anyway. The problem is in the hardware: any given 3D card tends to produce similar looking output, no matter what graphics engine is forcing the polygons through it.

The game itself—the way the game world is defined, and how the objects contained within that world act and interact—is effectively an uncharted area of design. Sure, there are a few standard guidelines and ideas, but only you, as the architect, will have an intimate knowledge of the game world, its inhabitants, and their interactions. This knowledge can be put to good use simplifying the design, as we'll see later. The balancing act comes in making sure that the simplification does not turn into a restriction if new elements that had not previously been considered are inserted into the game. Some of the ugliest hacks in history have been directly due to this. (I should know, as I'm responsible for a couple of them.)

The software factory methodology (described in Part II of this book) recommends producing components that perform common functionality so that they could be reused in future projects. One of the things about game development that amazes me the most is the almost total abhorrence of reuse. In fact, the only reuse I've ever seen has been of the less-than-useless cut-and-paste variety.

Even though certain tasks are common to *all* games, and in fact, to all possible platforms, this code is rewritten for each new project. This is just plain ridiculous. How many times do you need to rewrite screen-initialization or sound-system code, or in fact any other code that abstracts the hardware? In fact, with careful design, you can produce an abstraction that maps nicely onto multiple platforms, making the task of porting easier.

I can already hear the seasoned game developers scoffing that, if you abstract a system to be cross-platform, you'll lose too much in speed. It'll be unworkable, they are thinking. These people might find it helpful to read Case Study 17.1 in order to gain a fresh perspective on just what is possible with a sensible design.

Hardware Abstraction

Hardware abstraction is very useful in game development. Apart from the obvious, the main benefits are the homogenization of the development environment and the development of reusable components that allow easy setup of the hardware without all the grunt work that's usually associated with it. One of the reasons for all the grunt work—even with libraries such as DirectX—is that APIs are designed to be as flexible as possible. Millions of people use DirectX, and they all probably have different uses in mind. The main result of this in-built flexibility is increased complexity.

A company that knows the plans for its next few releases can take advantage of this knowledge by producing a hardware abstraction library that takes into account the needs of the future releases.

For example, you may develop a screen-handling library that supports a common range of resolutions, double or triple buffering, bitmapped and TrueType fonts, and sprites. I know that most games now use 3D, but let's keep this example simple for the time being, and anyway, 3D is just a presentation method. Many games that are presented in 3D nowadays would work just as well (if not better) in 2D, but marketing pressures say otherwise. At least *some* developers nowadays are realizing that 3D isn't everything, and are not trying to shoehorn 3D into places where it doesn't belong.

Case Study 17.1 Abstraction In Quake II

Quake II, by id Software, caused a huge stir when it was released a few years ago. Pretty soon after the original release, the game was also released on a number of other platforms, including Linux, a free version of Unix for the PC.

This was made possible due the advanced design of the software. *Quake II*, fundamentally designed as a multiplayer game, was based around the client-server architecture model.

Client-server architecture is a process whereby the majority of the functionality (AI calculations, game mechanics, etc.) takes place in a server process, and the results of the processing are made available to the clients.

In *Quake II*, the responsibility of the client was to send user input to the server and to render the output of the server. The server had done all the hard work making the game run, and now the client had to display a representation of that world, accept user input, and forward it to the server for processing.

As you can imagine, this made the multiplayer capability easier to develop than, for example, a peer-to-peer system, in which each of the machines involved in the game accepts input from all of the others and runs its own AI calculations. With a client-server setup, all of this is centralized, and so all the client has to do is to connect to the server to upload and download data.

All very impressive, but what does this have to do with cross-platform capabilities?

The server was written in mainly portable C, in a machine-independent fashion. This allowed it to be easily ported to another platform. Any platform-specific code was partitioned out into a separate library. The client itself was written in a similar fashion, interfacing with the server through a platform-independent interface.

This is how the single player game worked: as far as the server is concerned, it does not know whether the client is on the same machine, or half a world away across the Internet. Any platform-specific code was also hidden behind an interface.

For example, the graphics renderer just receives a pointer to a block of memory to draw to. There is no reliance on platform-specific architecture. This method is repeated throughout the code wherever an interface is needed with the hardware.

The example of *Quake II* shows that platform independence through abstraction is possible, and doesn't necessarily have to impact performance. Nobody seems to complain about the performance of *Quake II*.

Graphics Hardware Abstraction

So let's take a closer look at our example. For *Balls!*, I developed a simple graphics library that performs all of this setup for me. I needed only basic functionality: a screen setup, bitmapped font support, sprite support, transparency and translucency, and some temporary working buffers for compositing some of the more complex graphics. Bear in mind that, when I wrote this, I aimed to provide only the level of functionality required for *Balls!*. For more information, read the game design documents included in the appendix.

The graphics abstraction solution I decided upon is shown in Figure 17.1

The graphics abstraction layer shown in Figure 17.1 is fairly simple, and has lots of room for improvement. However, it is a good demonstration of the sort of thinking that goes into abstraction.

When I was designing my abstraction, I thought in terms of a console. I didn't want to do anything overly flashy with the system, so this was a suitable solution.

The actual hardware of the graphics card itself is wrapped by a class called **CDisplayCardObject**. This class is private and is used internally by the rest of the graphics classes. The only access to this class that is externally provided is an initialization function that creates a systemwide

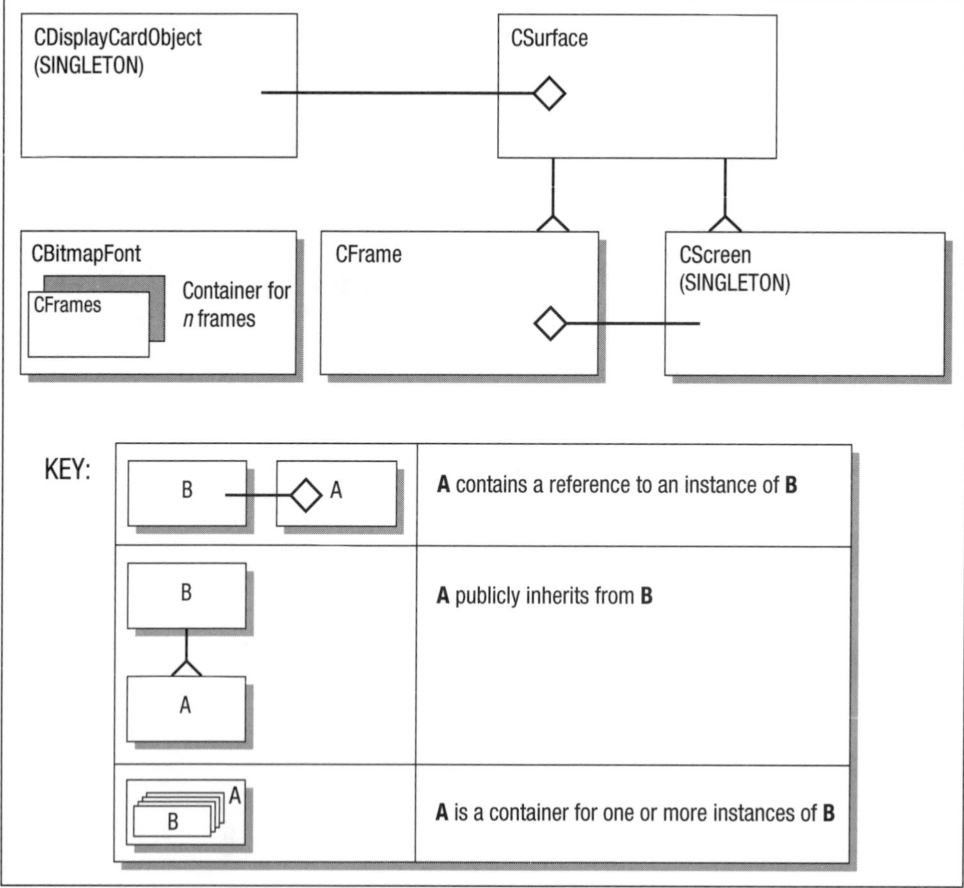

Figure 17.1
The graphics abstraction layer.

singleton that is globally accessible. (A singleton is an object that is instantiated only once per process.) The initialization function is needed because the system needs to know to which window all output will be directed.

I took as my root the concept of a *drawable surface*, encapsulated by the class **CSurface**, a surface that can receive graphical output. (In reality, it's just an area of memory that DirectX knows about.) A graphical surface can be created in two types of memory: system memory or video memory (local or nonlocal). The class **CSurface** provides functionality that is common to all surfaces, such as initialization. The surface-initialization member takes parameters that indicate the height, width, and bit depth of the surface, whether it is 3D capable, and where it is to be located in memory.

Other private members provide error reporting, and placeholders for restore capabilities and surface-release capabilities. The class **CSurface** is never instantiated directly, because not all functionality has been implemented. That must be done in derived classes. (**CSurface** is technically known as an *abstract base class*.) All other surface classes derive from it and provide or override the needed functionality as necessary.

The only publicly available members of the **CSurface** class are those for querying the height, width, and bit depth of the surface.

The **CScreen** class derives from the **CSurface** object. **CScreen** is a singleton. (As most games still tend to run on one screen, this is not a particular problem.) If I ever decide that I need two or more screens, then a number of small modifications will allow this.

The **CScreen** class provides a wrapper for a double- or triple-buffered surface that is displayed on the physical screen. It can operate in window or full-screen mode completely transparently to the user. Even though there are some subtle differences (when using DirectX) between windowed mode programming and full screen, these differences are taken care of in the class, and both modes appear programmatically identical.

The rest of the functionality of the screen class is fairly simple. Debug text output is provided, as is pixel-setting capabilities, although they are slow. The usual array of surface-querying functions are available, such as querying for width, height, bit depth, or transparency capabilities. Support is also given for screen or area clearing, buffer flipping, and copying areas of the screen to another surface, so that they can be modified elsewhere, and then redisplayed.

The **CFrame** class encapsulates sprites and working surfaces that are to be displayed on the screen. (The name ***CFrame*** was taken from the animation frame concept, because I felt that the word *sprite* didn't describe the functionality too well.) One of the important things in this sort of design is naming. Make sure that the name of an object aptly describes its function.

The first important thing about the **CFrame** class is that there are three methods of initialization. Note that no initialization can be performed until the **CScreen** object has been created. This is because all **CFrame**s are dependent on the screen, and an internal pointer to the **CScreen** object is statically maintained within the **CFrame** class.

The first—and simplest—initialization member lets you create a frame with read/write functionality, initialized to a given color. You can specify whether you would like the frame to be created in system memory or video memory. Usually, although video memory is faster to display, it is slower to modify than system memory and is often a limited resource.

The second initialization function allows you to create a read-only frame initialized with a given image. This image can be located in a file or resource and can be retrieved from a compressed archive. The decompression and loading is encapsulated in another class and is transparent to the user. Because the **CFrame** class keeps track of what images have been loaded, it does not unnecessarily duplicate images in memory. If an image has already been loaded, then any attempts to reload it will cause the encapsulating **CFrame** object to reference the original surface rather than create a new one. This conserves resources and provides useful tracking and debugging functionality. The developer does not have to worry about managing surfaces because they are automatically taken care of. All of this grunt work occurs during initialization, so there is no worry about the game being slowed by extra overhead, even if it means that surfaces initialized from bitmaps have to be read only, because writing to the surface of one **CFrame** object would otherwise affect all of the other **CFrame** objects that referenced it. If you want to have a write-enabled bitmap, you can load it as normal, and then copy it onto a frame initialized using the first initialization method. This is okay, because you would usually want a backup copy of any bitmap you are going to modify on the fly anyway.

The third initialization function lets you specify a source **CFrame** instance, an (x, y) offset into that surface, and the width and height of the new surface. This creates a read-only surface that is merely a window onto the larger surface. The most common application of this is displaying individual sprite frames that have been loaded onto a larger surface, because this is faster and more efficient. Figure 17.2 illustrates how this works. The sprite frame is a window that shows a small portion of the larger surface.

Other functions provided by the frame class include a draw member that draws the sprite to the screen (with transparent areas if required), an alpha drawing member that allows the sprite to be drawn to the screen and be translucent so that anything behind it can be partially seen, and a member that allows the frame to be copied to a blank frame for modification. This last member is necessary, because, by default, a picture is loaded as read only, as explained above.

The **CBitmapFont** class is simply a collection of **CFrames** that have been initialized with a set of ASCII character bitmaps. Because fonts are not usually drawn to the screen as frequently as most other types of graphics, the underlying surfaces are created in system memory to conserve precious video memory. The **CBitmapFont** class has a print member that will take a text string as a parameter and output it to the screen at the specified coordinates, allowing you to center the text vertically and/or horizontally, and query a string to get the length in pixels.

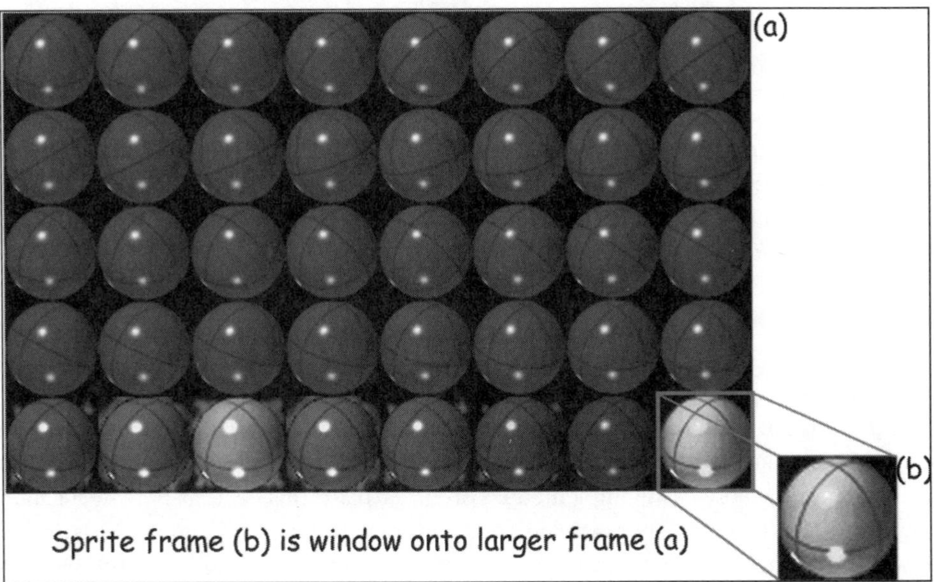
(a)
(b)
Sprite frame (b) is window onto larger frame (a)

Figure 17.2
Sprites packed onto a large surface.

The above example, although simplistic, allows me to explain to you the reasoning behind the abstraction. For my project, I wanted a simple interface to screens and drawable surfaces. I didn't want to have to worry about whether I had drawn a picture to the wrong buffer, and I didn't want to have to specify which buffer I wanted to draw to every time I needed to. I also wanted a consistent interface, whether I was drawing into a window or was using full-screen mode.

The class library I designed solved those problems. Setting up the hardware is as simple as calling a global initialization function, creating a screen object, and then initializing it with width, height, bit depth, and whether it should be double or triple buffered and windowed or not. Then I create some frames, call their draw members to draw them onto the back buffer of the screen object, and call the buffer-flipping member of the screen object to flip the back buffer to the front position, making it visible.

The DirectX setup code behind this is rather complicated, but that is not a problem. All of the complex (and thus slow) code is away from the critical execution path. What do I mean by critical execution path? Well, if you ran the code through a code-profiling utility, such as *TrueTime* (NuMega), the critical execution path would be the functions that are called most frequently and take up the lion's share of the execution time.

For example, the initialization code for each instance of an object is always going to be called only once, so nobody really cares whether it is lightning fast or not (unless you are calling it thousands of times, in which case some optimization work may be required). On the other hand, the screen-flipping and frame-drawing members are going to be called very frequently, and so these need to be as fast as possible. In my code, I strive to ensure that the object is fully set up and checked for errors during the initialization phase, so that there is a minimum of error checking during the execution of the most frequently called members.

A common complaint by game developers is that hardware interfaces such as those described above restrict flexibility and provide too much overhead. This complaint may well be valid, but, on the whole, the time spent calling the member functions of the class interface is will be minimal compared to the amount of time actually doing the real work within them. Your game will be spending most of its time in system calls. The perceived lack of flexibility is no real problem either. The underlying library is most likely *too* flexible for your needs; after all, it has been designed to be applicable to *every* possible use a developer could want. Haven't you ever heard of the expression "too much rope…"? What is the problem with trashing parts of the functionality that you are never going to use, and making your life simpler by producing an easy-to-use interface module? Even more importantly, a simple interface can be more easily implemented on other platforms, so that porting a game to a new platform involves only rewriting your hardware interfaces. Compare this to having liberal sprinklings of DirectX throughout your code. Are you going to rewrite DirectX for the Macintosh and PlayStation? (If you are, be sure to send me your source code!) By writing your own cross-platform interface, you may have to provide simple capability querying functions (similar to those in DirectX except much simplified) for some of your more advanced functionality, but most of the current platforms have very impressive and (fortunately) similar core capabilities, even though the underlying hardware and the programming interfaces are radically different.

Sound Hardware Abstraction

The sound hardware abstraction is based on a similar model to the graphics system. A good idea for component design is to aim for a basic similarity of structure across different modules. This means that new modules can be learned easily from experience with current modules.

Again, a similar approach was taken to the sound hardware as was with the graphic hardware. The **CSoundCardObject** directly wraps the sound card object, a private singleton accessed through an initialization function. There is no sound-hardware analogy to the screen object of the graphics abstraction, as it is pretty much included in the **CSoundCardObject** object.

The **CSound** object wraps the sound. The usual range of member functions are provided: playing, pausing, stopping, changing volume and frequency, and specifying the position of the sound in 3D space. The initialization function provides parameters for dictating which of this functionality you want enabled in the object.

A similar system to that used with the graphics object prevents loading of duplicate sounds. Instead, a new object is created that refers to the original data.

If a sound file is too large (and the size limit can be set using a **CSoundCardObject** member function), a small buffer is created that loads the sound, piece by piece, on demand when it needs to be played. The small overhead for doing this has so far not been a problem.

Figure 17.3 shows the similarity between the abstraction for the graphics hardware and that for the sound hardware. This theme can be extended for most of the hardware that is present on a machine. The use of abstraction in this fashion almost creates a virtual machine, providing a consistent interface that can be written to, whatever the platform. The windows implementation of the libraries used for *Balls!* performs a lot of WIN32 and DirectX jiggery-pokery behind the scenes, but none of this leaks out beyond the watertight interfaces. In theory, if the libraries were implemented on other platforms such as the Macintosh or the N64, then the main body of the source code could be recompiled without too many changes. Unless your company wants to fund two or more separate teams to produce versions for different platforms, then the abstraction library is probably the best way to go.

The important thing about hardware interfacing is that it can be viewed as building upon an essentially stable platform. Even though new features are being added to DirectX and other libraries with every release, they are usually backward compatible. By building an interface, you are effectively consolidating and simplifying the original interface, providing functionality that is suitable for your projects and ignoring the rest. As I've already stated, most of these APIs are very general, designed to be useful to the widest possible developer base. By wrapping this stuff up in an easy-to-use interface, it becomes more specific and more suitable to the requirements of your project.

Other Hardware Considerations

With a little thought, I'm sure that you can design simpler interfaces for the other aspects of the hardware needed for a game.

For example, on top of my sound object, I have a **CJukeBox** object that plays the in-game music and operates in a similar fashion to a normal jukebox (except I don't have to insert money). It can play selected tracks, use autorepeat over a number of tracks, or just randomly select tracks to play. In order to set the tracks to be played, a member function is provided that allows the insertion and removal of tracks (analogous to which records are placed in the jukebox). The tracks that can be played are MIDI files, CD tracks, or MOD files (a

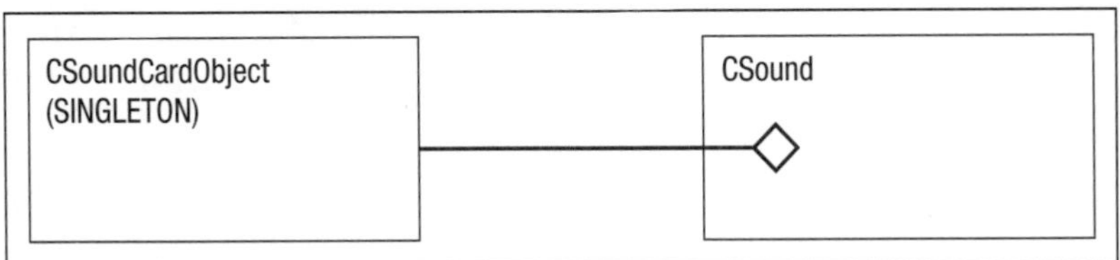

Figure 17.3
The sound hardware abstraction layer.

music format that originated on the Commodore Amiga). To support these different types of music are three separate classes, all derived from the base class **CTrack**. This base class provides an interface that the jukebox uses (for querying the track name and controlling play, pause, and fading the track's volume in and out). All the **CJukeBox** object needs to do is call the correct member of the **CTrack** object, and the tune will play, irrespective of the underlying format. The jukebox doesn't care what it is, as long as it provides the **CTrack** interface. The jukebox itself is just a fancy collection object that allows the selection of tracks and ensures that only one is played at a time.

A similar library has been built to take care of user input from diverse sources. These resources include the obvious (keyboard, mouse, joystick, and joypad) and the not-so obvious (such as network and scripting).

These last two options are not suitable for all situations. The network interface merely allows user input across a network. The scripting interface, which will be discussed in more detail later, is very useful for a number of diverse situations, such as AI interfacing, attract modes, and automated testing. At the core of this system, each object that needs to be moved (such as the player) and all the mobile game objects implement a control interface. This control interface does not know what is driving it, be it network, player, AI script, or whatever. As such, it would be easily possible to allow the player to control *any* object that provides this interface. I'm not going to talk about this in too much detail here, because I want to cover this in a lot more detail later. This is a very important point however, and you should be beginning to get a realization of just how powerful these architectural techniques can be.

All games, no matter how trivial, require a timer of some sort. In the early days, the timer would be the machine itself. The main loop of the game would simply run as fast as possible, and tie itself in to the clock speed of the processor. This was because the early machines were lacking in power, and there generally was never time to spare. Another consideration was that all machines were identical, and so there was no need to normalize timing, unlike today's PC, where your game could be expected to run on any system across the vast range of speeds available. It would be no good if your game ran at different speeds on different computers (unless it's a turn-based game such as *Sid Meier's Alpha Centauri*), although, amazingly, a lot of the earlier PC games did so.

When game developers were initially faced with this new problem, they took a fairly simplistic approach. What has surprised me the most is that, even up until comparatively recently, this approach has still been advocated—and not always by amateurs. Every now and then, I still see it suggested as a solution to the timing problem.

These game developers attempted to use the frame rate as a timer. They would choose a frame rate (possibly dictated by the hardware)—say, thirty frames per second (fps)—and construct all their game logic around that. There would be one AI tick every frame, so, doing the math, you can see that each game object would be updated to move the distance it could normally move in each thirtieth of a second. Note that this technique is still used with platforms that are limited in power and universally identical, such as the Game Boy. This technique has the least overhead. No special effort is required to dynamically adjust the timing parameters. This is shown in Figure 17.4.

This was all fine and good, but there were two main problems. The first was that owners of faster machines weren't too pleased that their brand-new game didn't take advantage of their machine's speed, and that the game looked exactly the same on their friend's machine that had a processor half as fast.

The second (and rather more serious) problem was that, below a certain threshold level of processing power, the game would suddenly halve in speed. If the AI tick took just longer than one frame to calculate, then every other frame would be skipped, resulting in a drop in speed. The same sort of thing could happen if a frame took too long to draw. All in all, a bit of a disaster.

Fortunately, some thinking was done on the subject, and a couple of suitable solutions were developed. I'll call them *semi-decoupling* and *full decoupling*.

Semi-decoupling is the simpler of the two solutions. The trick is to decouple the frame rate update from the AI ticks. This technique is suitable for games that don't particularly stretch the hardware of the average midrange machine, but also want to run acceptably well on the lower-end machines. The concept is shown in Figure 17.5.

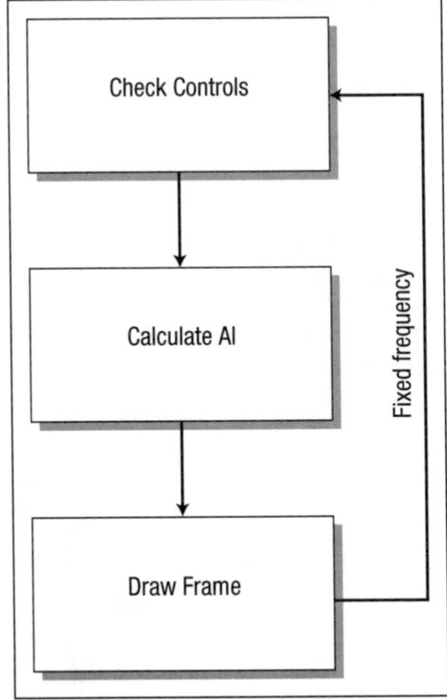

Figure 17.4
Ye olde game loope.

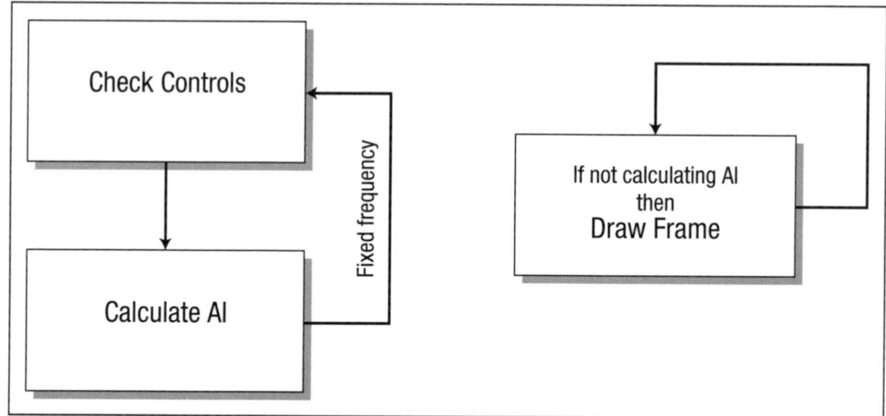

Figure 17.5
A semi-decoupling game loop.

The AI runs at a fixed rate as before, but the frame rate just runs as fast as it possibly can. Assuming the AI is running at 30 ticks per second as before. A separate loop draws each frame, and then waits for the next AI tick to be complete before drawing the next one. This means that, if the frame takes too long to draw, it would not be such a disaster as before. The AI loop would continue independently, because it wouldn't be stalled waiting for the frame to complete, and the next frame to be drawn would be correct. The player may notice a drop in frame rate, and some of the animation may be slightly jerkier, but the important thing is that the internal AI would still be running correctly. The main disadvantage of this technique is that your maximum frame rate is limited to the fixed tick rate of the AI loop. There is no point in updating the screen if nothing has changed in the AI, so the drawing loop will be idle while this is going on. This technique is fine, if you are sure that your AI is going to run at a constant rate and you don't mind being limited to that rate. But what if you want your frame rate to be the maximum possible, irrespective of the speed of the AI loop? This is where full decoupling comes in. Most games today use this technique.

Full decoupling, as shown in Figure 17.6, attempts to run the AI loop as fast as possible. A reference timer is used to adjust the changes in game object states per AI tick, so that the game does not appear to speed up and slow down. This means that, on faster machines, there will be more AI ticks per second, so, for each tick, the delta value (which is the reciprocal of the length of the tick) will be smaller. On slower machines, ticks will take longer, and so the delta value will be larger. Imagine that we are animating a clockface that has one hand. This hand rotates once every second. Internally, the AI tick updates this clock according to the delta value. The clock is drawn at the end of each AI tick. Obviously, the smoothness of the animation depends on the frequency of the AI ticks. The animation will still show the hand performing a full rotation every second, but the smoothness of the animation will vary. This is illustrated in Figure 17.7.

This is a pretty smart technique that allows a program to max out frame rates, but it is not *true* full decoupling. The frame rate is still limited by the rate of AI ticks. It is impossible to

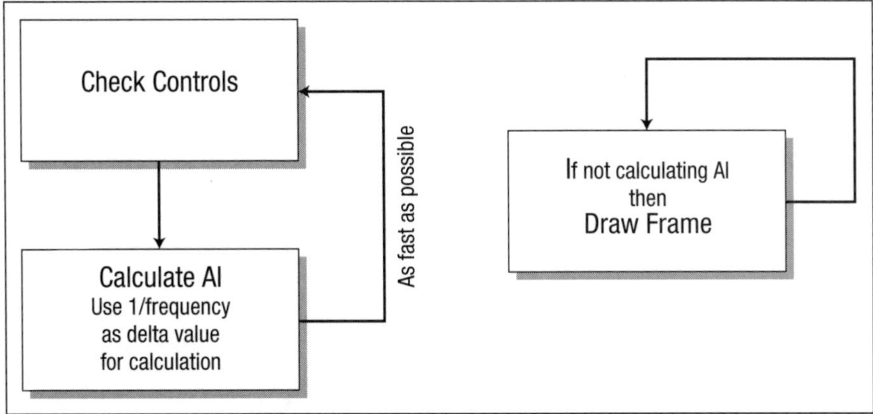

Figure 17.6
The full decoupling game loop.

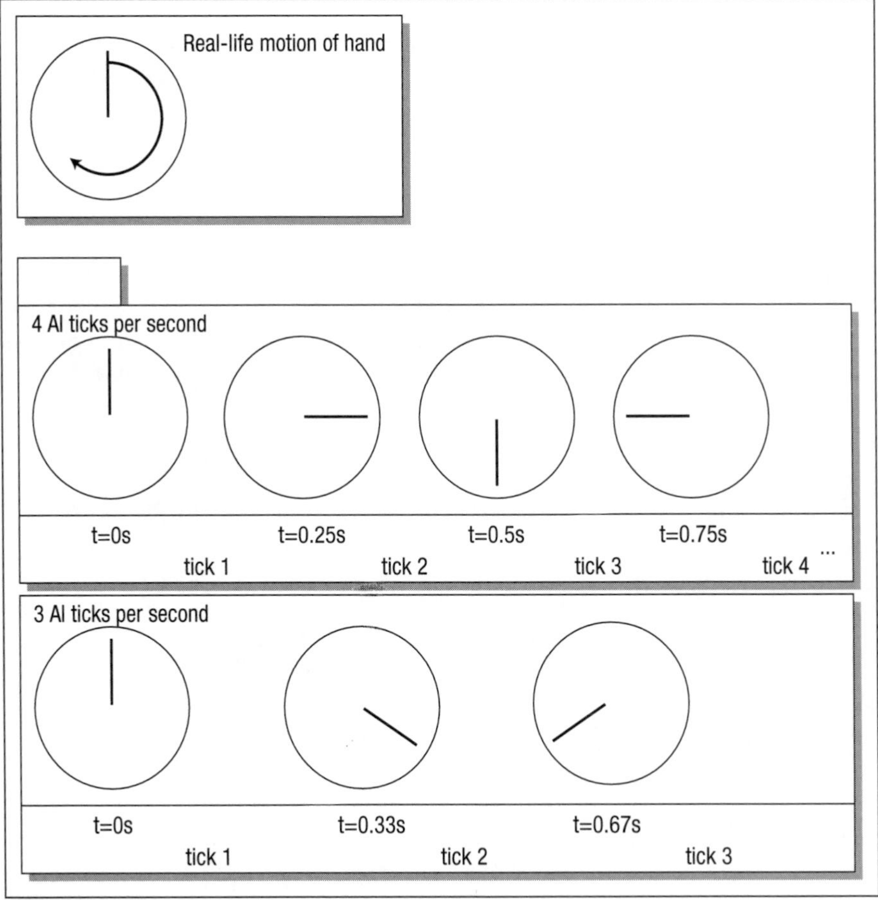

Figure 17.7
The effect of tick length on screen updates.

have more than that. To achieve full decoupling would be difficult, but possible. To do this, the AI loop and the frame-update loop run completely separately, most likely in separate threads. Then the frame loop is given the ability to take a "snapshot" of the state of the AI loop whenever it likes (assuming that it is not so often that it chokes the AI loop), as long as at least one visible object has been processed. Care has to be taken to make sure that an object is not halfway through being processed when the snapshot is taken (it may be in an internally inconsistent state), and the easiest way to achieve this is to set the snapshot granularity to the object level.

I'll explain this concept in slightly more detail. Let's assume that we are processing 50 AI objects per tick. Let's also assume that the graphics hardware is powerful enough to take a snapshot three times per tick. This means that we will get a request for a snapshot every 16.67 objects. Because we are only two-thirds of the way through processing a particular object at this stage, it may not be a good idea to allow the snapshot to be taken. In this case, we delay the snapshot until we have finished the current object, allow the snapshot to be taken, and then continue with the next object. This is shown in Figure 17.8.

When used well, this technique will allow some truly phenomenal frame rates to be achieved on powerful hardware. For most purposes though, semi-decoupling is good enough.

A timer object has been built for *Balls!* that attempts to use the best timing facilities available on the given machine. If these are not available, then the next best is used, and so on until all possible options are exhausted (an unlikely occurrence). Despite all of this complexity, the class that provides this functionality, **CTimer**, has a simple design based on handshaking. This class provides an initialization function that allows you to specify the timing interval, and where you would like the timer to notify when triggered. Pause, resume, and stop functionality is provided, as would be expected. When a message is received from the timer, there is a requirement to call the timer message acknowledge function. The

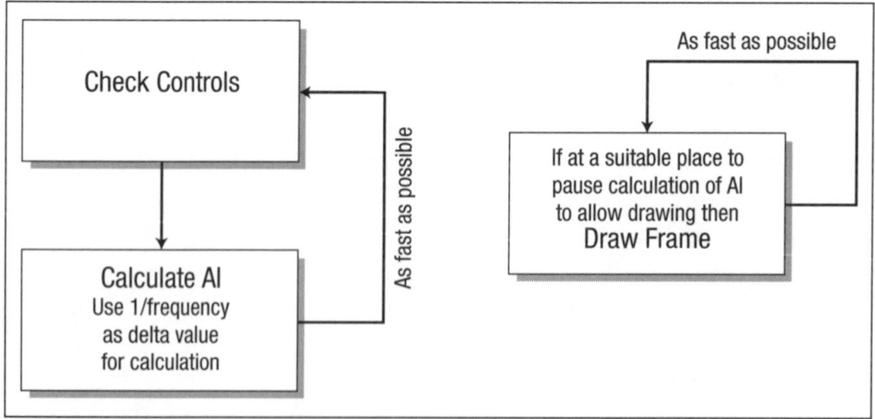

Figure 17.8
The real McCoy!

class then times the interval between when it sent the message and when the receipt was acknowledged. This information is then packaged and sent with the next timer message. This allows for some pretty accurate delta timing, and is suitable for all three of the techniques mentioned above.

"Not Built Here" Can Be Better

Although the proverbial "seasoned" game developer may scoff at these ideas, he or she may not be able to in the future. The new generation of machines from the likes of Sony and Sega are becoming incredibly powerful. Today, many game development organizations typically work in teams of 10 to 15 for a period of 18 months at a time. And this is just to fill a standard CD with a typical game!

What are these development teams going to do with these new machines, where there is about seven times the storage space? It won't be possible to extend the development time accordingly. No one wants to wait 14 years for a game to be produced, and most certainly no sane person would want to work on one for that long.

There are fears that this will mean that only the largest and most cash-rich development houses will be able to afford development, and that the smaller development houses will either disband or be swallowed up by these corporate giants. The fears are that the destruction of these smaller houses will drown us all in a wave of corporate mediocrity.

The development community at large, however, is proposing a solution, driven by a mixture of market pressure and industry consensus. As an example, Sony is actively acquiring third-party technologies in order to augment the libraries provided as an interface to the hardware of the PlayStation 2. A number of smaller companies are producing third-party modules that can be used in your development. Modules such as physics engines have recently become the vogue. These engines provide a full, realistic physics system that produce realistic collisions and mechanics. MathEngine, a small company with offices in Oxford, England, and San Francisco, have produced such an engine (which has been licensed by Sony).

These sorts of modules are going to become increasingly essential as the hardware increases in power. It is pure fantasy to expect a small team of developers to be able to compete against the big boys in terms of technology. Those days are (sadly) gone. The main problem, I think, with the increasing technology is that the gameplay is becoming less important. When a development team has to spend most of the time developing ways to harness the technology, it doesn't leave much time for developing the gameplay. This is why bringing in third-party modules is going to become more and more essential if a development house wants to be able to bring out a technically excellent—and, more importantly, playable—product. *Half-Life*, by Valve, is a perfect example of this. For *Half-Life*, the developers brought in the *Quake II* engine, made some modifications to suit their purposes, and then spent the rest of the time developing the sophisticated AI and storyline. In doing so, they probably saved themselves 12 to 18 months of development.

Even the artwork required for these engines is becoming more detailed and time consuming to produce. As the power of the technology grows exponentially, so does the effort required to produce cutting-edge games for it. What can be done? If an increasing amount of time is spent on harnessing the technology, obviously a decreasing amount of time is being spent on the gameplay. The provision and use of third-party components such as 3D engines and physics engines is really the only way of staving off this disaster waiting to happen.

But it doesn't stop there. Music, sound, and artwork can also be bought off the shelf. Libraries of 3D objects are available from companies such as Viewpoint Datalabs and have been used in games such as Activision's *Interstate '82* and Microsoft's *Combat Flight Simulator*. Viewpoint supplies ready-made and animated models, and this can cut months off a tight schedule. Why pay artists to produce a perfect reproduction of a town hall, when you can buy a ready-made version that can slot directly into your game?

You can hire a musician to produce cool music for your game, and you can also buy CDs full of top-quality, royalty-free samples. These products all go some way towards reducing the development time—and, consequently, the development costs—of a game.

"Engines are just a set of paints, and game developers are painters. It's what they do with the paints that determines the outcome." - Mark Rein, Epic.

Edge Magazine, June 1999

It is unfortunate that game developers remained bogged down in the past. It is usually a matter of pride that developers will not want to use third-party engines. They will always consider that they can do better. Maybe they can, but if they have to extend the schedule by 12 months in order to do so (with no guarantee of success), then surely it makes more sense to use the third-party offerings.

As soon as developers begin to realize this, they will make more use of these third-party components. All of the basic functionality—the graphics engine, sound system, music, save game system, AI system, artwork, and music—will be brought in off the shelf. This will allow the game developers to concentrate on what is *really* important—the gameplay.

I feel only sorry for those developers who don't realize this in time. Many developers may have their heads in the sand, and they are going to miss the technological revolution that is coming to the game development world. Unless they are in there right from the start, they will have a difficult time catching up.

The Twilight Zone

But what of things that are pretty much common to all games, but not part of the game itself and not part of the hardware either? I'm talking about setup programs (where applicable), loading and saving of games and data, and menu systems that allow you to configure the game.

These intermediate-level components can be reusably implemented in many ways. They can be frameworks that support the internal structures required to implement the features required. For example, most games employ some sort of menu system that allows starting new games, configuring settings such as sound or music volume, redefining controls and screen resolutions, and the like. This is one of the most obvious areas to target for reuse. In virtually all projects I have seen, the time required to implement the menus and other supporting areas that aren't part of the actual game engine itself has always been severely underestimated; consequently, it is usually rushed through at the last minute. With a little more thought, it would be possible to create a generic framework that allowed menu screens, option screens, volume screens, and any other "out of game" screens to be constructed quickly and easily. I'm sure that *some* companies must have done this, but whoever they are, they have either done it so well and their framework is so configurable that each new product just *looks* like there is completely different code driving the user interface. Or maybe they just hack out new code each time. Given the current state of game development techniques, I'll leave the jury out on that one.

Of course, I've already intimated that you don't necessarily have to write your own framework: you can use one that another company has developed. And, let's face it, if another company is marketing a framework or component for a particular purpose, they are likely to have expended much more effort on making it applicable to that purpose. In short, it's likely to be a lot better than whatever you or your team are going to be able to produce in a reasonable amount of time, given that you are at the same time focused on producing the game itself. Another point to consider is that the developer of the component or framework may also have a view of the bigger picture, and you can benefit from this. The classic example would be DirectX. If you're developing a game for the PC, do you write your own interface to the hardware, or do you just use those provided by DirectX? This one's a no-brainer.

A great example of the sort of thing I am talking about is the *Universal Save* system mentioned in the previous chapter. This system provides a unified interface that all games can use to store their saved games. A browser interface is provided so that the player can launch a saved game in a familiar fashion, and, as far as users are concerned, familiarity makes their lives easier. If a system such as this is adopted as a de facto standard, then, not only does it make the development process easier, it can also act as a selling point. The *Universal Save* system is such a useful concept that I would not be surprised to see it absorbed into DirectX at some stage to emerge as "DirectSave."

The Problem Domain

With the hardware interfacing taken care of, it is time to look at the interesting part. This is the only part that is unique to your game (or at least should be). All of the rest of it is *not* unique. Everybody is developing for it. Some can do it better than others, but that is not so important any more. The power that is now available in hardware (where previously it would have been written in software by the developer) is now available to all. The "indefinable" quality that makes your game different is the game itself.

The game design itself was taken care of in the first part of the book. Here is where we start taking this game design and converting it into something workable that a developer can understand, and that will be easy to expand, debug, and maintain over the coming months.

A good design can turn technical "issues" into complete nonissues. With a good architecture, questions such as "How could we do this?" can become less and less frequent. The object of a good architecture design (accompanied with the good dissemination of information) is to make it obvious how to do something: the only way possible—the best way.

So what is a problem domain?

A problem domain is what we need to explore when we convert our game design into a technical architecture. The architecture is a map of the problem domain and will serve to guide developers through this uncharted area of problem space.

Earlier in the book, I introduced the concept of "hard" architecture and "soft" architecture. Up until now, we have been discussing the hard architecture: the interface with the hardware, and the various housekeeping tasks, such as the game loop, that virtually all games perform.

Now we are into a much more fuzzy area—the soft architecture, the part of the game that is (or should be) unique to the game. Just because something is unique does not mean that the framework that it is based on need be disposable. We should strive to achieve reusability here, too.

How can we do this? Well, for a start, we can exploit certain factors that are common to the soft architecture of virtually *all* games. This is akin to game theory (which was examined in the first part of this book).

Okay, so what are these factors? How can we be sure that they are common to all games we could do? And how can we be sure that building within such a framework won't impede our development?

What Is A Game? (Revisited)

Let's take a random walk through a list of games and see if we can spot any commonality:

Pong, Frogger, Pac-Man, Elite, The Sentinel, Missile Command, Tetris, The Legend of Zelda, Virtua Fighter, Carmageddon, Defender, Chess, Warcraft, Zork, Doom, FreeCell, Scrabble, Tennis, Balls!.

What do all these games have in common? The first thing is that they all have a player. A game without a player is not a game: it's a movie.

All games also have discrete elements that are directly or indirectly manipulated by the player. For the time being, we shall call these *tokens*. These tokens are the elements of the game that are supervised and managed by the computer. For example, let us consider *Pong*, as shown in Figure 17.9. What are the tokens in this game?

Pong has two players (represented by bats and a score), a ball, and some walls. Which of these are tokens? Conceptually, they all are. Each player controls a bat, and the players' prowess with this bat will improve their score. Therefore, it could be said that the players' bat and score are subtokens of the token representing the player. The ball is another token, as it is indirectly influenced by the players and, aside from small interactions, is essentially managed by the computer. The walls of the play area themselves are tokens. They interact with both the bats and the ball, in order to prevent them escaping from the top and bottom of the screen.

What about the goal areas? These are the areas that the ball travels to when the player has failed to deflect the ball in time. When the ball reaches here, a point is awarded to the opposing player, and the game begins again. These are tokens too—although they are defined by area and have no visibile representation.

All the games mentioned above (in fact, empirically speaking, *all* games) can be described in terms of players and tokens. We don't have the space or the time to go into why all the games can be decomposed into players and tokens, but we have yet to find a game that cannot. We're going to cover two more in this chapter (*Pac-Man* and *Balls!*) and leave the rest as a proverbial "exercise for the reader." I'd be interested in hearing if anybody can find a game that cannot be decomposed in this way. This argument is an important one, so I hope you are playing close attention, because the next section will develop these ideas further.

Thinking In Tokens

We can also consider these tokens to be arranged in a form of hierarchical structure. The playing area, or game world, in itself is at the top of the hierarchy. From then on in, it is an essentially flat hierarchy. This is shown in Figure 17.10.

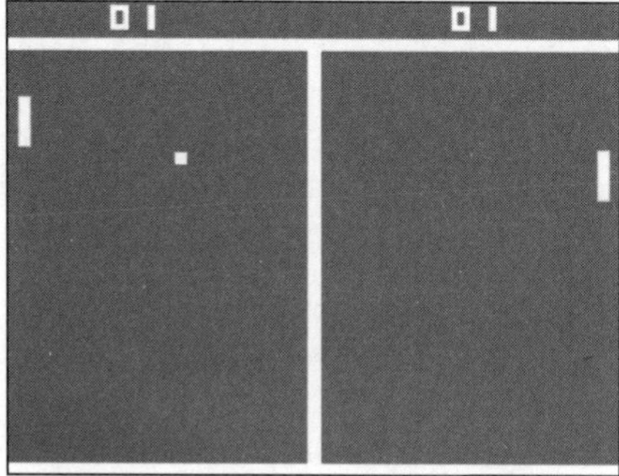

Figure 17.9
Pong.

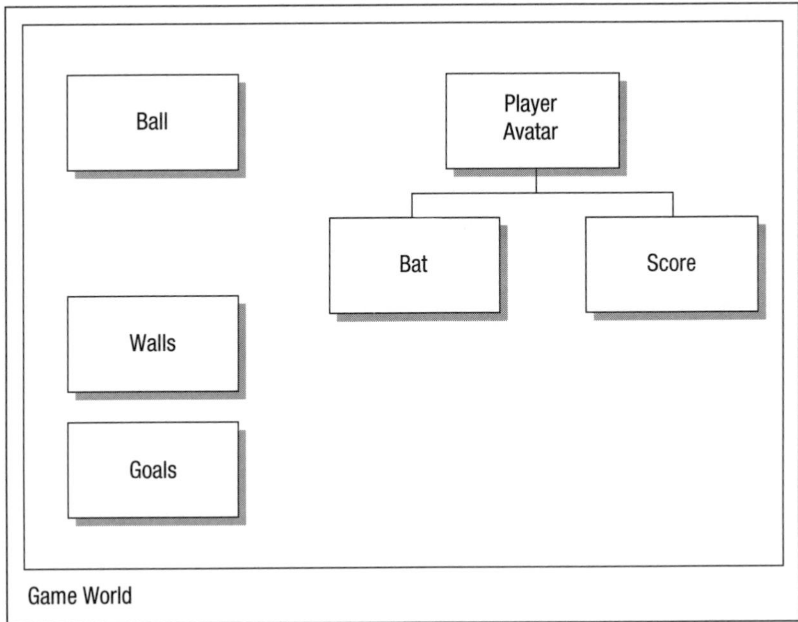

Figure 17.10
The *Pong* token hierarchy.

The game world token contains all the other tokens. This is a nonstatement. Obviously, every token has to operate within the game world in order to form a part of the game. The player avatar token is the representation of the player within the game world. It is effectively a channel for the user interface between the player and the game. The player avatar for *Pong* is very simple; it is merely a bat and a score. These are how the player is represented in *Pong*. The other tokens—those manipulated by the computer—are the ball, the walls, and the goal zones.

Now it's time for a little sleight of hand of the sort that is possible with only the written word. Reread the paragraph about the tokens in *Pong*, and, for every instance of the word "token," read it as "object."

So, if I was just talking about objects all along, why didn't I just use the word "object" to start with? The first reason is that, by using a nonstandard yet familiar term, I could introduce what is undoubtedly a familiar (and maybe unwelcome to some) paradigm without instantly bringing to mind object-oriented methodologies and all the prejudices that tend to accompany them in the games industry.

The second reason—and why I particularly like the use of the word *token* and why I will continue using it from here on in—is that these conceptual tokens may not have a one-to-one mapping with the programming language objects (e.g., in C++) that are defined by the programmers. What we are trying to do is to break down the game design into conceptual objects that will eventually be translated into programming language objects. This *tokenization* process is an intermediary stage in the production of a decent architecture. In order to describe this without causing confusion, I need to use different terminology for each type of "object."

Tokenization Of *Pong*

The tokenization of a game design such as *Pong* is fairly trivial, and there's really only one way to do it. In spite of this, it makes an excellent example to try to demonstrate the thought processes behind tokenization. Not all games will be so trivial, and, for some more complex games, there may be many ways, all of which are equally valid.

So now we have a set of tokens. On their own, they are not very exciting, as they do not interact with one another. But, as we know, in *Pong* there are all sorts of interactions going on. Well, one anyway: collisions.

We can now define an event—the collision event. Let's say that a collision event is generated when two tokens collide. The net result of this event is that each token receives a message telling it that a collision has occurred, and the type of object it has collided with.

The token interaction matrix, shown in Figure 17.11 is a very important construct. It is a chart of all the interactions that take place in the game. Note that, for very large games (or basically anything that's slightly more complicated than *Pong*), these matrices can become more complex (even three-dimensional), and there can be more than one of them. The way to prevent this is to produce several levels of token category matrix, where similarly behaving tokens are lumped into a category. This reduces the number of effectively duplicate entries.

Okay, so let's look at the *Pong* token interaction matrix. The matrix is arranged in a triangular format, with each token listed along the side and the bottom. An unusual feature of *Pong* is that tokens do not come into contact with other tokens of the same type. This immediately means that the token-token interactions for *bat-bat*, *ball-ball*, *wall-wall*, *goal-goal*, and *score-score* can be discounted. Due to the nature of the game, the following interactions can also be discounted: *bat-goal*, *wall-goal*, *score-bat*, *score-ball*, and *score-wall*.

There are two main types of interaction in the matrix: symmetric and asymmetric. Symmetric interactions are the same both ways. For example, the behavior of the ball and the bat are not different depending on how we consider the collision. That is, if we say that the ball collides with the bat, we would expect exactly the same results to occur as if we had said the bat collides with the ball. The semantics do not matter. Symmetric interactions are shown as squares in the matrix.

Asymmetric interactions are shown in the matrix as a square split into two triangles. An asymmetric interaction is different depending on the direction. In this case, the semantics do matter. Each triangle represents one direction of the interaction. Taking the solitary case

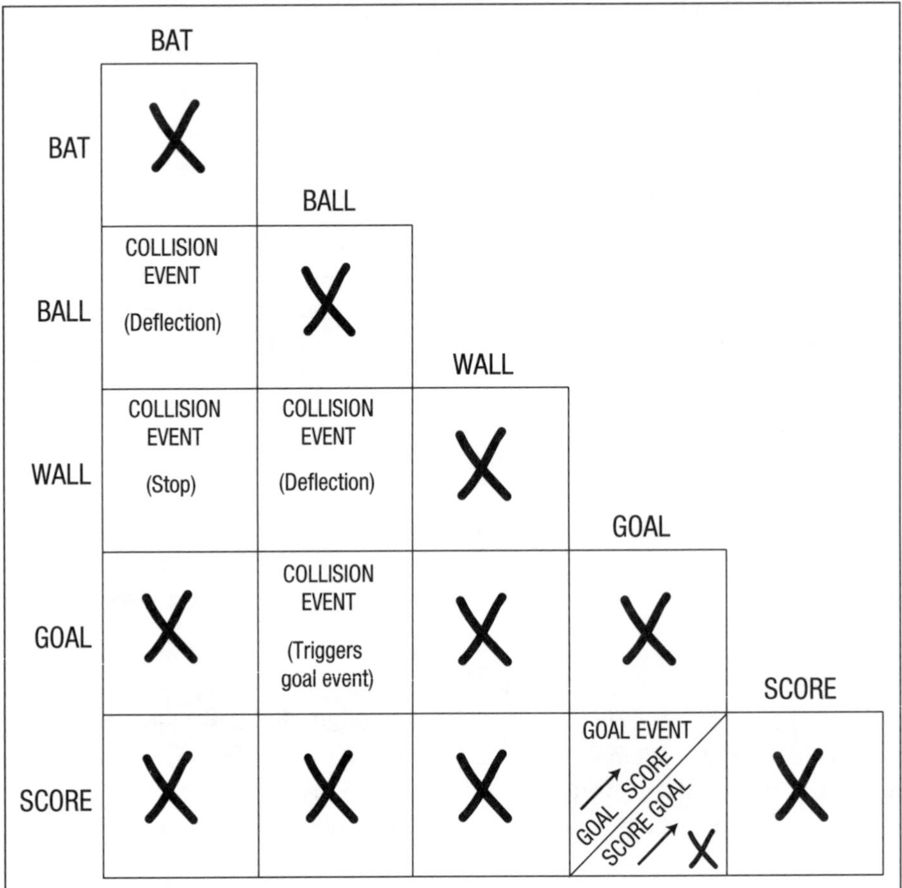

Figure 17.11
The *Pong* token interaction matrix.

from the *Pong* matrix as an example, we could say that a goal causes the score to increment by one, but the score incrementing by one does not cause a goal to occur. This is not much use in this case (because the only way to increment the score is by scoring a goal), but let's assume that there were another way of incrementing the score (maybe a secret cheat mode). Then, we would not want to generate a goal event (and the associated resetting of the playfield) every time one player decided to cheat. For a start, it would be far too noticeable!

So what can we use this matrix for? The matrix allows us to perform a visual check on our interactions. We can check that they are what we would expect, and we can see if we have missed any or made any errors. We may be able to spot unexpected chain reactions (the sort of things that in some cases will enhance a game, but in other cases will render it virtually unplayable). These things will be picked up in playtesting, but the sooner it is spotted, the cheaper it is to fix.

One token that is not included in Figure 17.11 is the game world itself. This can be considered a token and, for games more complex than *Pong*, probably would be included in the matrix. This is because the game world token needs to be informed of certain events, so that it can act as an intermediary between different tokens and also respond to certain events itself (such as the goal event in order to reset the game). Figure 17.12 shows how the game world token would respond to the goal event.

Why would we want the game world token to perform this task instead of the individual tokens directly contacting all the others? Wouldn't it be faster if there were just direct

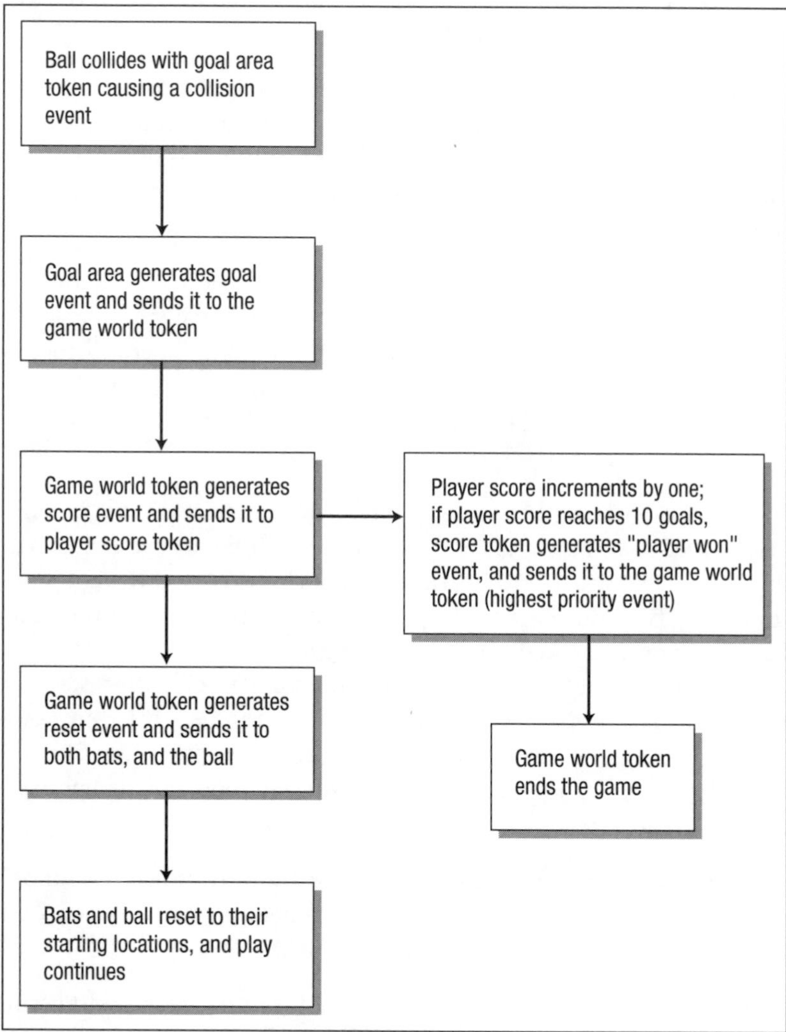

Figure 17.12
Propagation of events when a goal is scored.

communication? Well, yes, and, for a trivial game, I certainly would consider having direct inter-token communication. However, for a more complex game, this is a bad design decision because it means that tokens have to have intimate knowledge of the other tokens they are likely to encounter. From a coding point of view, this causes unnecessary complexity. The game world token can act as an intermediary if this helps to simplify the coding effort. The primary aim is to make sure the tokens respond only to necessary events that are transmitted to them, and not rely on internal knowledge of the other tokens in order to decide how to behave. A generalized system of event handling helps this, and one of the roles of the game world token is to act as an event broker and arbitrator. Events can percolate up and down the token hierarchy and be trapped by any token that needs to respond, overseen by the top-level game world token.

If the game designer wanted to add a new token, he could do so fairly easily and not cause the developers the headache of having to touch loads of modules in order to implement the new token. As long as the token's behaviors can be described in terms of existing events, then adding it in is simplicity itself. Even if new events have to be added, it is still simpler than the alternative of spreading them out throughout a wide code base.

This sort of organization also helps with certain technical issues such as deciding what to draw and how to update the AI for the tokens. For example, if we can determine whether a token is not within visible range of the player (impossible in *Pong*, where all tokens are visible), then we can either discount that token in further processing, or process it in a faster but less rigorous fashion. As will be seen later in the book, this allows some further optimizations to be taken.

Another reason is that the game world token can often have information that is denied to the other tokens: knowledge at the global level. By definition, it knows the contents of the entire game world. This means that it can perform filtering of events: if there is an event that it can determine will have no effect on the participants, then it need not transmit it at all. For example, the game world token could do filtering based on location and not transmit events to other tokens that are too far away to be affected. After all, the fastest code is code that is never executed. This sort of optimization has to be handled with care, however, in case a token is later changed to react to an event that has been previously filtered out. This is quite a difficult concept to describe, so the following sections will attempt to clarify the issue with some examples.

The token interaction matrix can also be used to figure out how to structure your object-oriented architecture and (with practice) can be used to help produce a pretty optimal result. Let's do this now for *Pong*.

Before we can get started, we have to decide what other features we would like in our version of *Pong*. Bear in mind that this is most certainly not how it would have been originally designed, but it is a game that is simple enough so that the design itself is not going to get in the way of my explanation of the architecture. I am going to start talking about objects (in the programming sense) as well as tokens, so pay attention at the back there!

Let us assume that we would like to do an update of the classic *Pong*. We are not going to change the gameplay, but we may like to spruce up the graphics slightly, and we want to flex our new object-oriented muscles to give them a bit of a workout.

For our design, we are going to take the *Quake II* approach and operate on a client-server model. This will be reflected by the provision of a scripting interface for each of our game objects. (A word about object inheritance is needed here. Although object-oriented languages have been with us for some time, new and improved ways of using them are constantly being developed and invented. Apparently, we are currently in the third "wave" of object-oriented design, but there are already too many surfing analogies in the world of computing, so I'm not going to mention it again, suffice to say that we will be using a mixture of the old and the new.)

What this means to us is that we are going to use inheritance in two different ways. The classic way to use inheritance is to ensure that all objects with common behavior inherit from a base class that implements that behavior. The derived class augments or overrides that behavior in order to implement its specific functionality. An example would be the ghosts in *Pac-Man*. They all share the same fundamental behavior (for example, chase Pac-Man), and this would be implemented in the base class, but they have specific individual quirks that are implemented in the derived classes: the pink ghost is fast, the blue ghost is shy, the red ghost is stubborn, and the orange ghost is, well, orange, I guess.

The second way inheritance is used is for *interface inheritance*. Interface inheritance is a method of providing functionality that is not necessarily in the nature of the object itself. Usually, the class that the interface is being inherited from will be abstract; that is, it will not provide any implementation. The implementation must be provided for each derived class. In other cases, an implementation will be provided. The best way to explain this is by example. For *Pong*, we have an amount of common functionality that all objects need to implement. They need to be drawable (so that we can see them), and they need to be scriptable (so that we can position them). We may also want to be able to output debug information. To allow this, the base class for our objects will multiply inherit from the following three classes: **IDrawableObject**, **IScriptableObject**, and **ILoggableObject**. The **I** in front of these class names (as opposed to the more usual C), indicates that these classes are being inherited for their interface. This is not the sort of thing that is usually included in the standard class hierarchy and could be confusing (hence, the different naming conventions).

Let's take a quick look at how these interface classes would be declared, shown in Listing 17.1. Note that no internal details are shown—just the interface members themselves. The member functions labeled as "pure virtual" are just declarations. A pure virtual function signifies that any class deriving from the class containing the pure virtual *must* implement the member. In C++, pure virtual members are denoted by the **virtual** specifier, and the '= 0' tacked onto the end of the function-member specification. Without the '= 0', the function is merely a virtual function. A virtual function is one that provides an implementation but is safely overridable in derived classes. This is in contrast with a normal member function, which cannot be safely overridden. (This is to do with accessing derived classes through base class pointers, but, as this is not a programming book, I'm not going to go into it here. Any good book on C++ will explain this fully.)

Listing 17.1 Interface classes.

```
/////////////////////////////////////////////////////////////////////////////
// Interface classes
/////////////////////////////////////////////////////////////////////////////
// IDrawableObject is used to provide an interface that allows an object
// to be drawn. It is an abstract class that must be implemented in any
// derived class.

Class IDrawableObject
{
public:
    // draw the object to the screen in its current state
    // returns true if the object was drawn, or false if it
    // was not drawn (this is not necessarily an error - the
    // object may have determined that it was obscured by others"
    virtual bool Draw() = 0;             // pure virtual

    // returns false if the object does not need to be drawn (i.e. off screen)
    virtual bool NeedToDraw() = 0;       // pure virtual
};

/////////////////////////////////////////////////////////////////////////////
// IScriptableObject allows the object to be driven by a script. It provides a
// default implementation for the ExecuteScript member which logs the
// unexecuted script directly to a logging file

class IScriptableObject
{
public:
    // override this and handle object specific scripts here. If your class
    // handles the script then return true, else delegate the script to
    // the base class, returning the result.
    virtual bool ExecuteScript(string sCommand);
};

/////////////////////////////////////////////////////////////////////////////
// ILoggableObject allows data to be logged during run time.

Class ILoggableObject
{
```

```
    public:
    // The default implementation simply logs a message
    // to the debug window
    //
    virtual bool LogMessage(string s);
};
```

These interface classes make use of a much-maligned area of object-oriented languages: multiple inheritance. Multiple inheritance does not have many legitimate uses, but interface inheritance is one of them. The important thing about interfaces is that you are inheriting the class primarily for its interface, and not for its implementation.

If you are really not keen on multiple inheritance, you can simulate the same effect by making instantiations of concrete classes (derived from interface classes) member variables of the class that you are working on. Then you can provide casting operators to return references to the encapsulated classes. If you don't understand what I am on about here, don't worry: this is a nasty method. If you do understand, you'll already know that multiple inheritance is usually the best solution for this problem.

So, how do we use these interface classes? Well, before we can go into that, we need to decide what the concrete classes are that will be representing our tokens. I will give you a general overview of the main class hierarchy. In later chapters, we will go into much more detail of the classes themselves and, in particular, how they interface.

The best place to start is with the game world token. We can give this a class to itself, which we will call **CGameWorld**. This class (among other things) will act as a container and manager for all the objects within the game world.

For convenience, we shall derive all of the game tokens from a common class. We can call this class **CToken**. **CToken** is multiply derived from the interface classes described above. It's basically a "flag of convenience" base class that we can use to refer to all our game tokens by, as a pointer to this base class. Okay, so that's the basis of our object-oriented hierarchy sorted out—now to get on with the details.

Referring back to the token interaction matrix, we can attempt to work out the best way to implement our class hierarchy. One way to approach this (and there are many others) is to look at the behaviors that need to be implemented for each object and group them by behavior. This may or may not be appropriate, depending on your point of view, in which case, you may decide to group them by some other criteria.

Nonetheless, I have always found that the best way to do this is to group by behavioral traits. In *Pong*, we can notice some striking commonality between seemingly different elements. In particular, if we look at the behavior of a bat compared to the behavior of a wall, we notice that they behave identically (except for wall-wall collisions, because they cannot occur). This in turn means that we could consider the bat itself to be a mobile piece of wall!

If wall-wall collisions were then defined as causing both collision members to stop dead, then the comparison would be perfect. We could legitimately treat the bat as a mobile piece of wall. If we had not drawn the interaction matrix, then we may not have spotted this right away, if at all.

The rest of the tokens are pretty much direct token-to-object mappings, as shown in Figure 17.13. Something as simple as *Pong* doesn't have many possible variations for a class hierarchy. The only interesting quirk in my suggested hierarchy is the derivation of the bat class from the wall class, but, as I have already explained, that is because I think that the bat is merely a specialized form of mobile wall. (Nurse! Quickly! The medication!)

At the top of the figure are the three interface classes that feed into the **CToken** class. Although this class multiply inherits from the interface classes (interface inheritance), it can be considered to be the true base class here. This is because it sits at the top of the tree as far as implementation inheritance is concerned.

The **CToken** class would be expected to implement all the functionality that is common to all the tokens, and the subclasses would specialize behaviors in order to implement each token type. The next few chapters of the book will develop this theme more fully, and we will get the opportunity to look at what we would put into classes such as these, how they

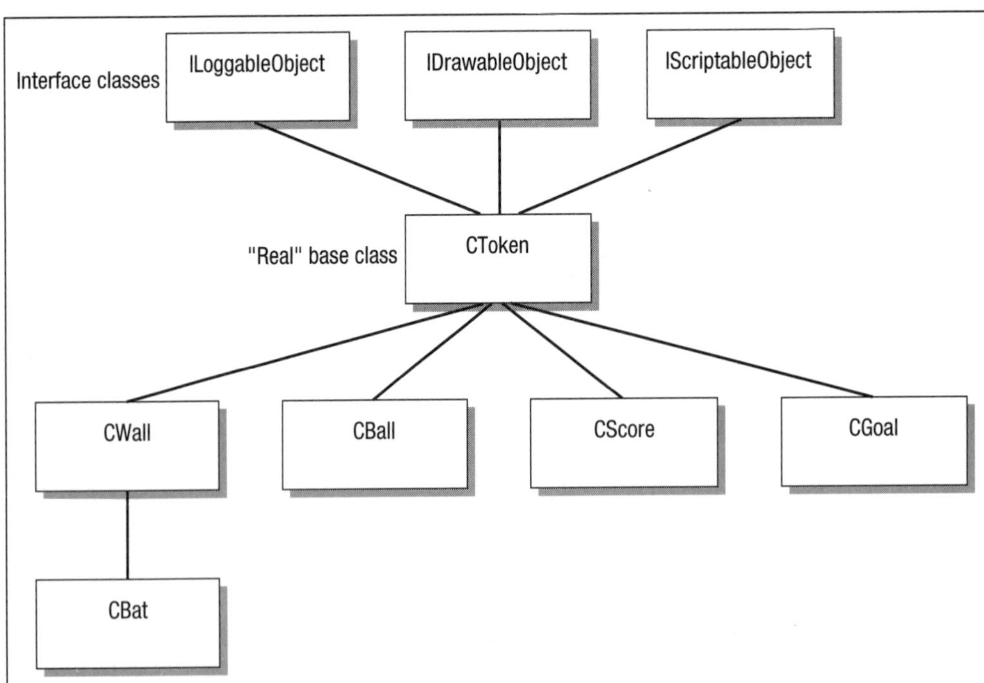

Figure 17.13
Suggested token class hierarchy for *Pong*.

would be managed, and how to effectively use the interfaces to make the development simpler. Reaching this point concludes the initial design phases for the *Pong* project. We have started from the game design, examined all the behaviors inherent in the game, and compiled this information into a form that allows us to hack out an initial class hierarchy for the tokens. A number of standard support type classes go with these, the "soft" architecture, and these will be examined in more detail in the next few chapters.

Tokenization Of *Pac-Man*

For most of the rest of this chapter, we will run through the same process for another well-known game, *Pac-Man* as shown in Figure 17.14.

Everybody must be familiar with this game, so it requires no introduction. On the other hand, if you've been living in a Tibetan monastery for the last 15 years, then you may not be aware of *Pac-Man*. For these readers, here is a brief description of the game: You play a greedy, little, round, yellow, blob-thing called *Pac-Man* and have to travel around a maze, eating all the pellets. The maze has warp tunnels on the left and the right so that you can leave the screen on the left to reappear on the right, and vice-versa. You are being chased by four ghosts. Each ghost is differently colored and each has his own individual personality. If they catch the Pac-Man, he deflates and dies. If, however, the Pac-Man manages to eat one of the four "power pills" in each maze, then the ghosts turn blue, and, for a short time, he can eat them. Every so often, a bonus fruit will appear that can be eaten for varying amounts of points. Once the maze is cleared of pellets, the level is over, and another level commences, (identical to the last, except for being slightly faster and having a different fruit). Every five or so levels, an amusing cut scene takes place as a reward for the player.

The attempt at a token interaction matrix for *Pac-Man*, shown in Figure 17.15, is significantly more complex than that for *Pong*. This is because the tokens may exist in one or more *states*, and the interactions between tokens depend on the state of the token. For example, the ghosts can be in one of three states (hunter, hunted, or eaten).

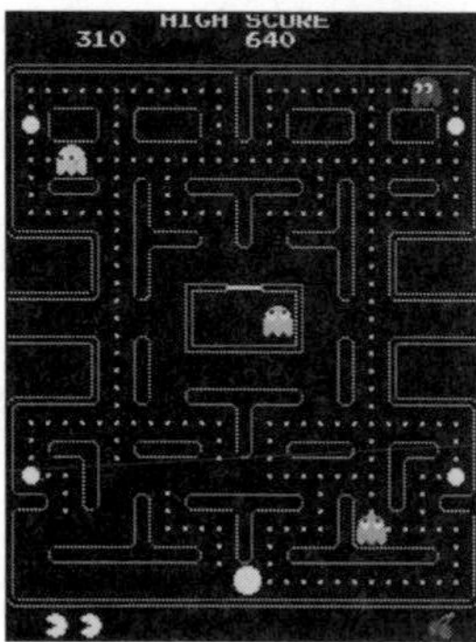

Figure 17.14
Pac-Man.

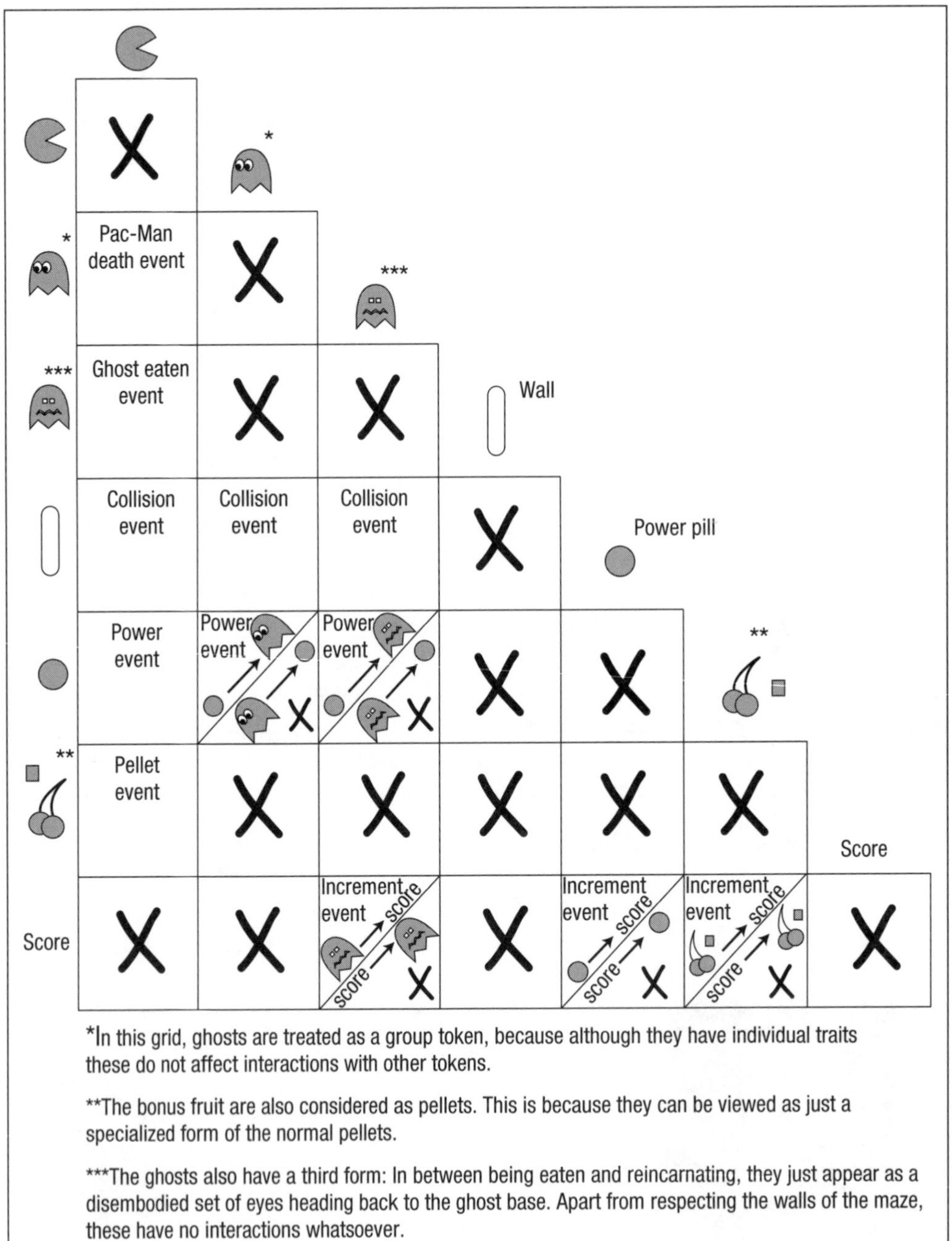

Figure 17.15
First attempt at a token interaction matrix for *Pac-Man*.

Some events are not directly included on the matrix itself, and, during the course of the following few paragraphs, we will be discussing some modifications we might like to make. The most important event that is not included is the *resurrect event*, which is experienced by a ghost that has been eaten on returning to base. To simplify the diagram slightly, I left out the "eaten" ghost token. I have also left out the ghost homebase (which we are going to add later, because we will discover that we need to beef up the abilities of the homebase). The ghost homebase acts as a resurrection point for ghosts once they have been eaten. Once resurrected, they stay there for a small while before rejoining the chase. The only other item of note is the door to the ghost homebase, which allows passage for the ghosts, but not for the Pac-Man himself. These could also be dealt with using separate diagrams that portray the way events affect the token. These are known as finite-state machine diagrams. A finite-state machine is a system that is commonly used in game AI (and lots of other systems). This will be discussed further in this, and later, chapters.

This *Pac-Man* example is more sophisticated than the *Pong* example, where we were concerned only with events. Events had instantaneous effects and did not force any of the tokens into different states. Essentially, *Pong* is a stateless environment. However, in *Pac-Man*, the events that affect the tokens can cause them to shift into different states. We have moved from a purely event-based model (the E model) to an event and state-based model (the ES model).

If we look at the interaction matrix in Figure 17.15 in more detail, we can describe in more detail through some of the more complicated interactions. Most of the events in the matrix are pretty straightforward (if you're familiar with *Pac-Man*), but some require a little more explanation. For example, the interaction of the "power pill" with the ghosts. When the Pac-Man eats a power pill, this generates a power pill event. The game world token then disseminates this event to all the ghosts. If a ghost is in the "hunter" state, then it immediately switches into the "hunted" state for a defined period of time. If a ghost is already in the "hunted" state, (i.e., if the Pac-Man has eaten a power pill recently), then the ghost reenters the "hunted" state, and the state timer is reset.

The other interactions that require some description are those involving the score token. The power pills, food pellets, and fruits are fairly simple: when these are eaten by the Pac-Man, a score event is generated and routed to the score token. The amount added to the score does not vary for the pellets. The ghosts, however, are a different story. The score for a ghost depends on how many others have been eaten: 200 for the first ghost, 400 for the second, and 800 and 1600 for the third and fourth. This is reset when the Pac-Man eats another power pill.

It is not easy to handle this situation with the interaction matrix in its current form. Instead, we need to modify it by adding another token to the matrix that would represent the homebase of the ghosts. Then, when a ghost is eaten, instead of sending a score event, it sends an "I've been eaten" event to the ghost homebase. When a power pill has been eaten, the homebase also receives the event (meaning that the homebase knows how many ghosts have been eaten since it received the last power-pill event. With this information, the homebase can calculate the score for eating that ghost, and it forwards the information on as a score-increment event to the score token. In the game itself, the score for the ghost is displayed briefly where the ghost was eaten, so an event would also need to be sent to the ghost telling it how much it was worth. If this was not the case, then the homebase would need to know where the ghosts were when they were eaten, and this sort of thing does not make for a clean architecture. All of this indicates the importance of thinking through the game design fully: an incorrect interaction matrix will not help you produce the best possible architecture. If you build on shaky foundations, then your building is likely to fall down.

The Machine In The Ghost

As can be seen from Figure 17.15, that—even for a relatively simple-seeming game such as *Pac-Man*—the interaction matrix can be quite complex. Finite-state machine (FSM) diagrams can help to show some of the interrelationships more clearly than just the interaction matrix alone.

The strength of the interaction matrix is that it allows you to focus on the big picture, whereas the advantage of an annotated FSM diagram is that it allows you to focus more clearly on a specific area of the matrix. It's a different way of looking at the same information. The interaction matrix looks at the system from the viewpoint of the interactions between tokens, and the FSM diagram looks at the system from the viewpoint of a single token and how the rest of the system interacts with it. Figure 17.16 shows the FSM diagram for the ghosts.

The notation in the FSM diagram in Figure 17.16 makes it slightly easier to read and removes any ambiguity in the interpretation. I have not come across any standard notation for FSM diagrams that isn't too complex for my needs (i.e., requiring an engineering degree to understand), so I use a simple notation that I devised specifically for this purpose.

Each individual state of a token is shown in a box. Incoming events are shown as large circles. A line leads from an event and terminates at a state box. The smaller "connector" circle at the end of the line acts as an identifier in the case of two or more events entering the same state box: each event will have a uniquely marked connector circle. The usual effect of an event is to cause a shift in state. A line will lead from the current state to the new state. In cases with more than one event leading into the state box, the correct state shift line will be the one that has the same color connector circle as that of the incoming event. The only other symbol of note is the circular arrow with the "mini" event. The event is one that can cause entry into that state. This notation indicates that, if that event occurs, the state is reset to new, even though we are already in that state. If there were no such notation, then, unless explicitly shown, the state would not be affected by further events of the same type. Note also that we have not included events such as collisions with the maze wall, as these are more-generic events that affect every object, and do not cause a state change. (This is true at least for *Pac-Man*: if this were a car racing game, we may expect the

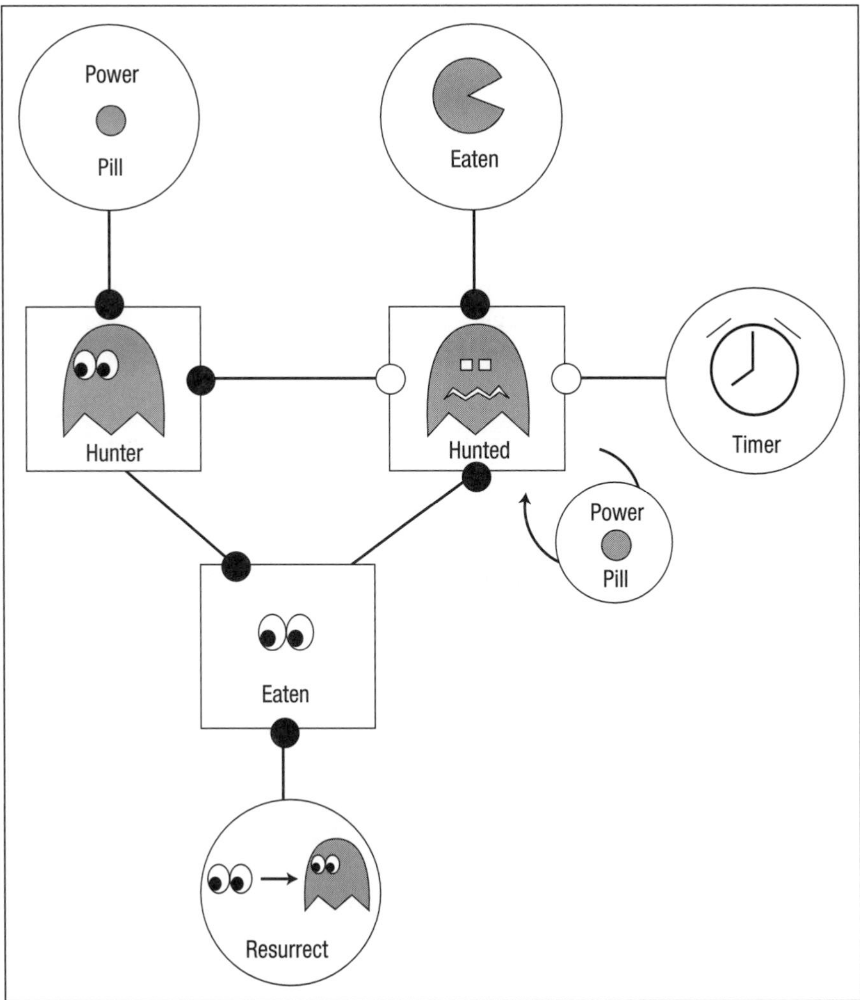

Figure 17.16
Finite-state machine diagram for the ghosts.

collision event to cause damage, in which case it would probably be shown in the FSM diagram.)

So let's examine the FSM diagram in Figure 17.16 in more detail. The first thing to notice is that we have not included any events that are *triggered* by the ghost. For example, when the ghost is eaten, it will trigger a score event. This is not indicated on the diagram due to personal preference. I prefer my FSM diagrams to show only incoming events. There is no reason not to include them, apart from increased clutter, but I would show the ghost-eaten event as an incoming event in the FSM diagram for the score token.

Okay, back to the ghost FSM diagram: the three state boxes indicate the ghost in the "hunter," "hunted," and "eaten" states.

Look first at the "hunter" state. In this case, the event is Pac-Man eating the power pill. The power pill event has a black connector, so we look at the "hunter" state box to see which outgoing connection has the same connector. Following this connection leads to the "hunted" state. The only other connection for the "hunter" state does not have a connector circle, indicating that it is incoming only.

The "hunted" state is slightly more complex. Two events can affect the ghost while it is in the hunted state: a timer event, which happens when the power pill runs out (shown by a white connector), and the "eaten by Pac-Man" event (black connector). Tracing the event route for the timer event shows that the ghost reverts back to the "hunter" state when this event is triggered. The "eaten by Pac-Man" event puts the ghost into the "eaten" state.

The circular arrow indicates the effects of Pac-Man eating a power pill while the ghost is already in the "hunted" state. In this case, the countdown for the timer event will reset to zero, so the ghost remains in the "hunted" state for a longer period.

The "eaten" state is fairly simple, as there is only one event that affects the ghost in this state. As soon as a ghost is eaten, it heads straight for the ghost homebase. When the ghost reaches homebase, it receives a "resurrect" event, which causes it to reenter the "hunted" state.

This is a *closed* FSM diagram, meaning that there are no dead ends: there is no state that a ghost can enter from which it cannot escape. We should contrast this with the FSM diagram for the Pac-Man, shown in Figure 17.17.

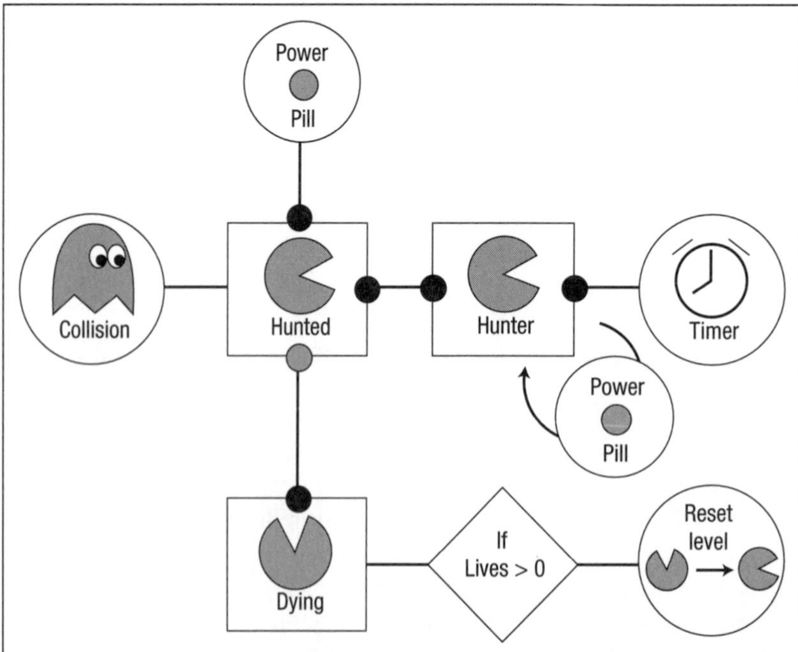

Figure 17.17
Finite-state machine diagram for the Pac-Man.

You should be able to follow this FSM diagram yourself. (It's very similar to the ghost FSM diagram.) The difference is that there are only a limited amount of "resurrect" events for the Pac-Man. Once he is dead, he *is* dead, unlike the ghosts. This is an example of an *open* FSM diagram, because there is a way to escape the state network during the game. This FSM diagram is actually pivotal to the entire game: it represents the transitions in state for the main player token. Most of the events that occur in this FSM will also be handled by the game world token. For example, it will reset the level when the Pac-Man loses a life and will end the game when all lives have run out.

I have not covered a lot of stuff here, such as the score-event handling, but these things are all fairly trivial to work out. The most important token not yet covered is the game world token, and the FSM diagram for this is shown in Figure 17.18. This isn't as pretty as the other diagrams, but it does show how the ES model translates nicely to the nongame aspects of the game design. This game world token need not be specific to *Pac-Man*. In fact, on a fairly general level, most games use this model for their user interface. The specifics of the options screen or the cut scenes may vary, but the essential structure shown in the FSM diagram is the same for most games.

This is the most complex FSM diagram that we have looked at so far. It introduces the concept of modeling the majority of the game as a finite-state machine. This is not as ridiculous as it may sound. On analysis, most games can be broken down into a hierarchical set of finite-state machines—large finite-state machines in which each state is a smaller finite-state machine in its own right, and so on, down to the finest granular level. Managed correctly, these diagrams, in combination with the interactivity matrix, can be used to document and design the architecture for the most complex undertakings. Once the notation is learned, these sorts of charts and diagrams help developers to visualize what is needed far better than any amount of dry prose.

State Transitions And Properties

In order to increase the flexibility of this technique to allow the description of even the most complex designs, we need to introduce two more concepts: *state transitions* and *properties*.

We are going to use *Balls!* as the example to describe these concepts. The game design for *Balls!* is in Appendix A. If you are not already familiar with this, then it may be worth a cursory glance. We will not be doing a full in-depth study here, so there is no need to learn the game design by rote, but, just to be able to follow the discussion, it would be useful to familiarize yourself with the basics of the game.

So far, we have assumed that state transitions take place instantaneously. In reality, of course, this is not always the case. A token generally will not instantaneously flick from one state to another. Aesthetically, this would not be acceptable: we would expect to see some form of transformation process. For example, if we were playing a character that could transform into a werewolf, then obviously you would want to see the whole gory process of change from man to wolf. Just flicking instantaneously into the wolf form would ruin the

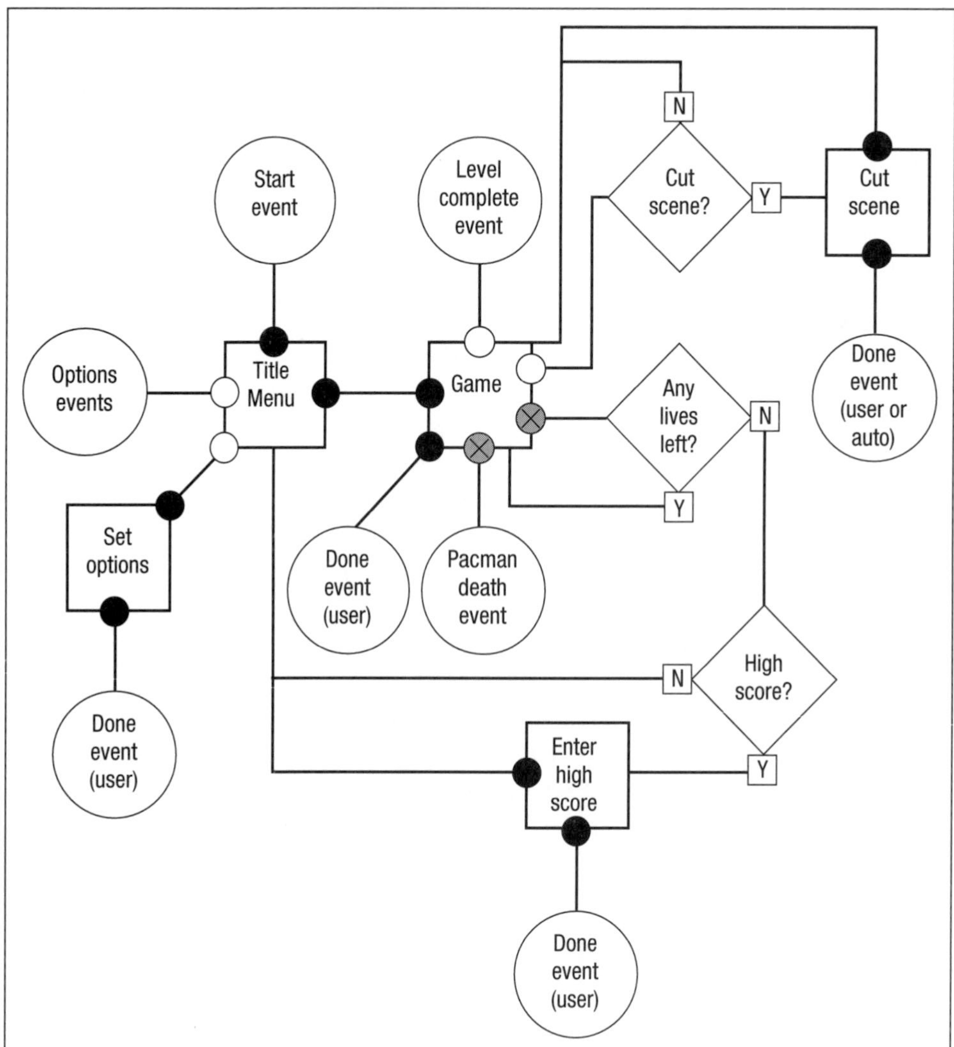

Figure 17.18
Finite-state machine diagram for the game world token.

suspension of disbelief and sense of immersion that the game had thus far built up. This means that we want the state transition to take a finite amount of time, and it consequently has to be included in the FSM model. The state transition can be viewed as a state in its own right, one that the token passes through for a short time in order to reach the destination state.

Let's look at a couple of specific examples from *Balls!* to demonstrate this more fully. We will consider a collision between a heated metal ball and a snowball. When a hot ball collides with a snowball, the hot ball cools down to a metal ball, and the snowball melts.

Figure 17.19 shows the sections of the FSM diagrams for the hot ball and the snowball concerning this interaction. The transitional states are indicated by the broken-edged state boxes.

As you can see from the figure, the hot ball does not instantly cool to the metal ball, and the snowball is not instantly destroyed by the collision. They both go through a transitional state: the snowball melts and the hot ball gradually cools.

This is all well and good, but we are missing a dimension of information. Consider the situation in which two events affect the same token *exactly* simultaneously. In most cases, it only makes sense for a token to respond to one event at a time, or you can get nonsensical

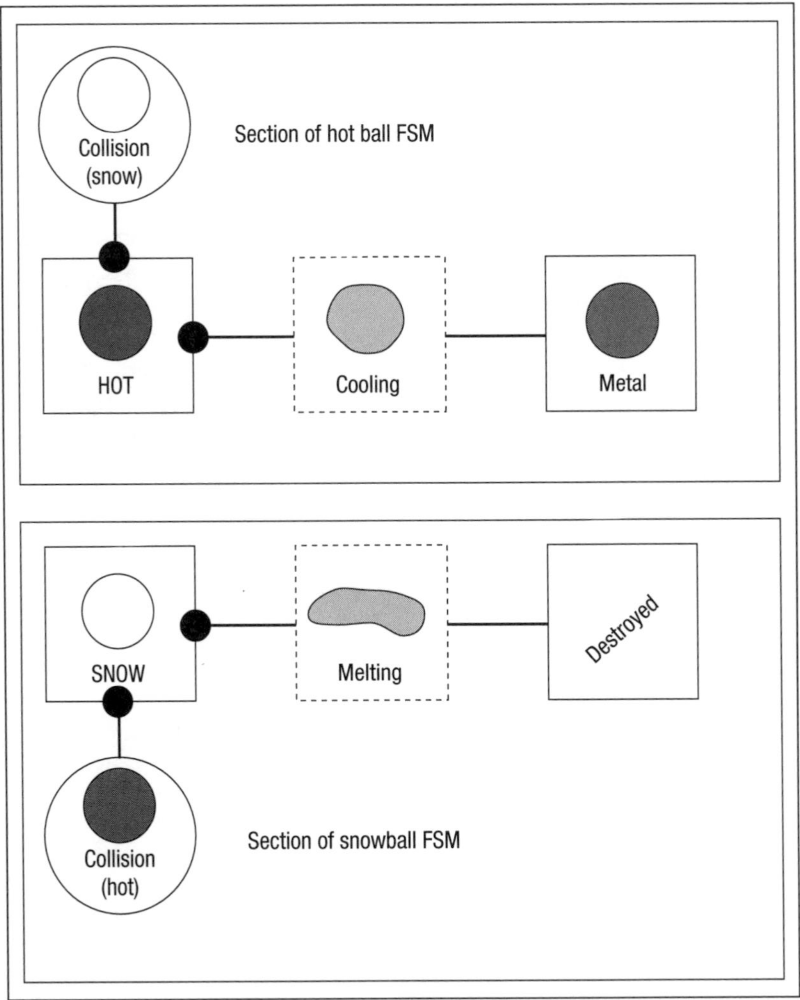

Figure 17.19
Part of the finite-state machine diagram for the hot ball and the snowball.

occurrences, such as a ball trying to heat and cool simultaneously. Handling this sort of thing generally requires lots of nasty special cases in the code, and all sorts of priority trickery. For example, when handling several simultaneous collision events, it is common to sum the collision vectors to produce a net result. You would also have to keep track of all the collision members so that extra effects such as heating and cooling could be resolved. Okay, so that is not too much of a problem if you never plan on adding or removing any tokens from the game design, but what if the game designer wants to add another type of ball, a cross between the hot ball and the balloon ball? How would this be handled as a collision member? How would it be implemented? Well, you could multiply derive the new ball from the hot ball and the balloon ball, which may give you the functionality you need, but this would not solve the collision-member problem. Would you treat it as a hot ball in some cases? Or as a balloon ball in others? Or maybe you would just bite the bullet and implement new handlers for the hot balloon type? Either way, it means that a whole lot of new code would have to be written and tested across several modules, and that is not one of the signs of a well-structured architecture, as the response to collision members would have to be hard coded. Case study 17.2 shows the disastrous consequences of such an arrangement in a real-world example.

The problem in case study 17.2 is the same as we have with our addition of a hot balloon ball. The architecture is not flexible enough to allow a new token to be easily added, and so a lot of extra code had to be written. This pretty much circumvents all the reasons for designing the architecture in the first place. (Although in the project in case study 17.2, architectural design is a nonissue. There wasn't one!). Reuse and expandability are the main aims of all the effort expended on the design, and so circumventing all these measures the first time a problem occurs by hacking extra code on top of what is already there just does not cut it. We should be able to add a new token with minimal changes to the "hard" architecture (the code itself). No, the majority of the work should be put into the soft architecture, the data that drives the game.

Happily, a solution to the problem of the hot balloon ball is at hand. If we assume that the token has a set of properties that are transmitted along with the event, then our problems are solved. The best way to demonstrate this is by example.

Let's define a set of properties that can be applied to the hot ball, the snowball, and the hot balloon ball.

We can give the hot ball an intrinsic property of *WARM*. The *WARM* property indicates that the token exhibiting this property will melt any *COLD* or *COOL* objects that come into contact with it, but it is not hot enough to transmit heat to any other heat-accepting object to the *WARM* or *HOT* properties. The *HOT* property is the same as the *WARM* property, except that it will allow heat to be transmitted to other heat-accepting objects, such as the metal ball. This use of properties meant that I was able to define a hot ball as a metal ball with the *WARM* property set. When cooled, the metal ball exhibits the *METAL* property. During the transition from a hot to a metal ball, the token has no properties (indicated by *NONE*).

Case Study 17.2 The Inflexibility Trap

In a recent (commercial) project, the development team decided to take some shortcuts in their implementation of world interactions. The game was based in an underground dungeon from which the player has to escape, preferably loaded down with treasure.

Initially, the developers didn't anticipate having locked doors, but they did have trigger tiles. When the player stepped on a trigger tile, he or she changed the on/off state of the trigger, and this opened or closed the door.

They later decided that they wanted to put in locked doors. They decided that the easiest way to do this would be to put the key floating above a trigger tile. When the player stepped on the tile to get the key, this also set the door to "unlocked." This was fine, because normally the player wouldn't retrace his or her steps on a level. (If he or she did, however, the door would be reset to locked, which would cause much confusion.)

Then there came a level on which there was a door with two locks. The player needed to have found both keys for the door to be unlocked. However, if the player arrived at the door having found only the obvious key, then he or she had to go back searching for the other one. This search could easily result in the player stepping on the original trigger tile, thus resetting the first lock. The player would then return after finding the second key and have no idea why the door still wouldn't open.

One solution was to set the trigger tiles to deactivate after one use; for example, they would only unlock the door and stepping on them again would do nothing. This would have been easy if the design had been object oriented: you could just have a new subclass of trigger tile. But, unfortunately, the design wasn't object oriented. A lot of new code had to be written. Worse still, this whole solution hung on a very tenuous thread: it equated finding a key with unlocking the door to which the key corresponded. Suppose they had then added a multiplayer version? So, when the player found a key, the door would unlock for all the other players, too. Or suppose they had wanted players to exchange items? (The proposed—and now canceled—sequel was to be more of a role-playing game.) They couldn't have used the trigger tile trick then!

What we discovered from this was, don't shortcut in the design, at least to begin with. Shortcuts lead to headaches later. That is why, in *Warrior Kings,* I got the developers to specifically deal with the peasant collecting the wood from the fallen log, then delivering it to the manor, then the manor handing it to a cart, then the cart delivering it to the Palace, and the Palace delivering it to the "global stocks" object rather than magically going straight from the peasant to the global stocks. We could take shortcuts later on, but only with the benefit of hindsight. Hindsight is always 20/20, so it's a good idea to use it when it is possible to do so without compromising the development efforts.

The snowball is very similar. This is given a property of *COOL*, which means that it will cool any *WARM* or *HOT* object. During the time it is melting, the snowball has no properties (indicated by *NONE*). Look at Figure 17.20, which shows the same FSM diagram section as before, except with properties attached to the state boxes. This allows us to see how the properties change with the collision. The FSM diagram shown in Figure 17.20 is the most

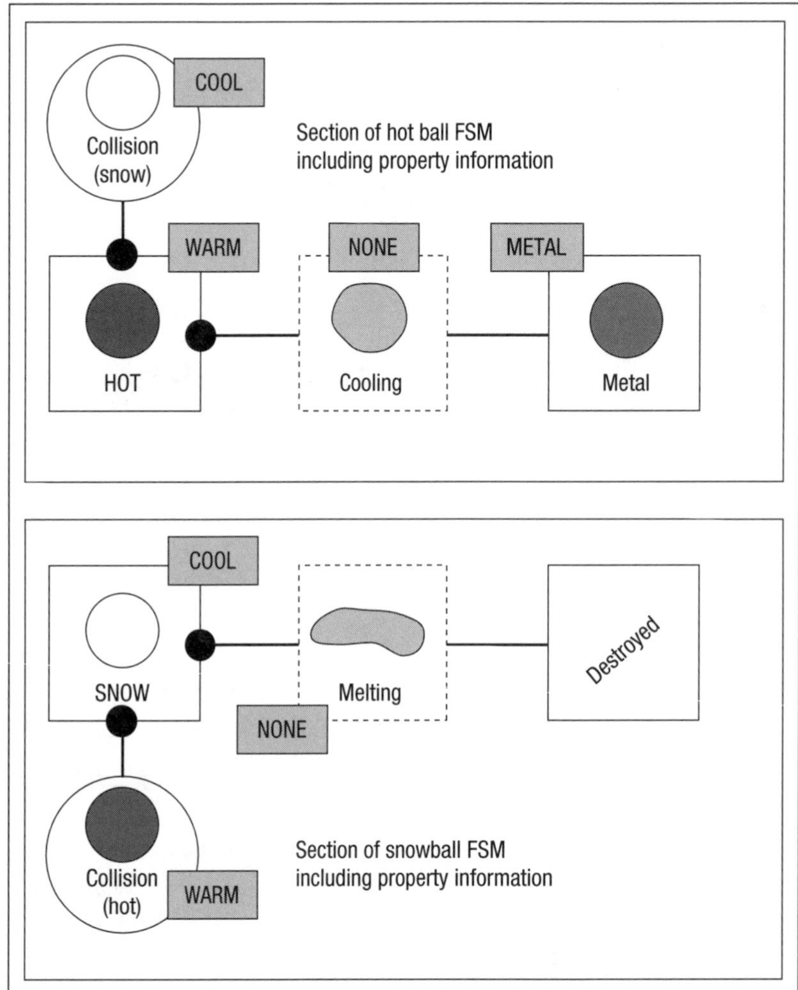

Figure 17.20
Part of the finite-state machine diagram for the hot ball and the snowball, including properties.

complex type of FSM diagram I use, because it includes everything: events, states, properties, and transitions (the ESPT model).

When the collision event occurs, all the properties of the tokens involved in the collision are stored in the net collision event, which effectively frees us of any dependencies on the actual collision object. As long as we have designed a rich enough vocabulary of properties, then we do not need to add any more code, except that which controls the hot balloon ball itself. How is this possible? Well, the hot ball has the *WARM* property, and the normal balloon ball has the *LIGHT* property. Consequently, our hot balloon ball would have the *WARM* and *LIGHT* properties, as shown in Figure 17.21. This in turn means that it would

Figure 17.21
The elusive hot balloon ball.

automatically behave correctly with all tokens that already respond to the *WARM* and *LIGHT* properties.

In *Balls!*, I started out with more properties than I needed. This wasn't a problem, because it gave me all the flexibility I needed to implement new tokens. When the token base was stabilized, I removed the unused properties. Even if I needed to add in another property, this is still less work than modifying the code to respond to a specific token, such as the hot balloon ball. It has another advantage, also: if I had hard coded the interactions to use the *type* of the token rather than its properties, what would have happened if I later decided that I wanted to add a hot balloon ball with a metal coating? With properties, I would have just added the *METAL* property and everything would be handled automatically, but if I were using the token type rather than the properties, I would have to modify every piece of code that reacts to the metal ball, the balloon ball, and the hot ball in order to get it to recognize the new hot metal balloon ball. By using a rich vocabulary of events, states, properties, and transitions, we can effectively remove any direct token-interaction interdependencies, creating a more structured overall architecture, and making the development process a lot smoother and cleaner. The next few chapters will develop these ideas further.

Bear in mind that this is not the only approach that can be used for architecture design. I'm not trying to sell this to you as the only way to do things. There is no one true way. You may have a technique that works better for your ideas, and you may not even agree with what I have said. That's one of the things that makes development (in whatever discipline) fun! Hopefully, though, you will find these ideas useful for your project. At the very least, it should improve your repertoire of techniques. Flexibility in approach is important. The latest methodology is too often presented as a cure-all wonder, suitable for every purpose, which it invariably is not.

After all, if your only tool is a hammer, then your whole world will look like a nail.

Chapter 18
Use Of Technology

Key Topics:

- ***The current (sorry) state of the art***
- ***Blue-sky research***
- ***Reinventing the wheel***
- ***Use of object technology***
- ***The advantages and disadvantages of abstraction***

The last chapter discussed methods for producing the initial architectural design for your hot game project. To illustrate these points, we took two well-known video game examples, and specified an architecture based on the analysis of the gameplay elements. Although the examples were simple, this did not affect the validity of the techniques presented, and these techniques are at the core of nearly all game designs. In the last chapter, we deliberately skipped over the technological considerations in order to focus on the actual mechanics of the game itself, the soft architecture. In this and subsequent chapters, we begin to focus on the technology itself, and later we will begin combining the two concepts to see how the complete architecture could be structured.

I have been very careful to specify that the architectural design is not a detailed technical design, and I will reiterate it here. Technical design is part of the actual programming cycle, and, as I have said before, this is not a book on programming. For this reason, we will not be going into the specifics of programming in any great detail. By the time we get to the end of Part III, we will have covered all of the architectural and technical aspects (except for the actual programming). You can find plenty of books on programming, bit twiddling, and Assembler-level optimizations, but this is not one of them! And all the bit-twiddling skills in the world won't save your project if you don't know how to structure your architecture in a logical and coherent fashion. A main cause of failing projects is spaghetti architecture, and later chapters will cover this and other potential problems in detail.

The conceptual "objects" in the architectural design are not the same as programming language objects. For this reason, I used the term *tokens* for the design-level objects, so they cannot be confused with programming language objects. From this point on, when I refer to *tokens* I am referring to conceptual architectural objects, and the word *object* will be used as expected for programming language objects.

Note

The terms object *and* token *will become increasingly important as we progress, so you may want to review the last chapter to make sure you understand the distinction.*

In the last chapter, the *Pong* example briefly touched upon the mapping of an architectural design to an actual technical design. *Pong* was a very trivial example that illustrated some of the main points behind the theory, but it did not really provide any detail. However, the value of simple examples such as this cannot be underestimated—if we take a common and simple game design to apply our theories to, then, assuming that these ideas are scalable, we will have a universally understood common ground. This is one of the most important tenets of game design: we must speak a common language all the way through the chain of responsibility, from the project manager and game designer to the programmer, artist, and musician.

This chapter will describe some of the types and possible applications of object technologies and how they can affect the development of the architectural design. Like most powerful tools, object-oriented techniques can be dangerous in the hands of the novice. Alexander Pope said "a little learning is a dangerous thing," and he certainly knew what he was talking about.

The usual reaction of new object converts is to start seeing their entire world in terms of objects: this is known as the golden-hammer syndrome, as mentioned in the last chapter.

The subtle danger of object-oriented techniques is that they appear to be so intuitive: Anybody can think in "objects." After all, we all do, don't we? Well, this is true—in a way—but this is also why I introduced tokens in the last chapter. Broadly speaking (and abbreviating many theories of human thought process into one simplistic conjecture), we all think using abstract tokens, not programming language objects.

Most novice object designers cannot make the distinction between objects and tokens, and their architectures tend to reflect this. This can lead to overly complex architectures that, to the untrained eye, look right but that are actually difficult to maintain.

The architecture is the skeleton of your project. Unless you want to end up with a deformed, misshapen monster (however pretty the flesh slapped on top is), it is best to get this skeleton right in the first place. There is no simple way to teach this, and the best methods are to read a lot of books written by acknowledged object technology experts (Booch, Meyer, et al.), and to get lots of experience.

However, I wouldn't necessarily recommend reading other peoples' code. Unless you happen to be close friends with the above-mentioned acknowledged experts, and you can persuade them to lend you their code, time, and expertise to explain their architecture, then any code you read is not likely to be that well designed or written. Many common programming errors are propagated in this fashion.

For an example of this, take a look at the samples that come with the DirectX SDK. Although these have become slowly better with recent releases, the general standard of coding and design for the samples has been universally panned in the past.

Although object-oriented techniques are the current flavor of the month, and can indeed be used to solve most problems that you are likely to come across, they are not suitable for all purposes.

For example, it would have to be a pretty heavy-duty file converter that required a true object-based design. Part of my work a few years ago required me to write a series of fairly complex parsers and converters for a diverse range of files. In these cases, it was quicker and easier for me to write the converters in plain old ANSI C than to try to implement a fully object-based design, and attempt to provide any sort of reusability. Maybe this is a decision I will come to regret if I ever get asked to write another extended series of file converters, but I always attempt to follow the same rule of thumb when designing software: do not make it more complex than is absolutely necessary.

One of the most common software-analyst errors is to overengineer the solution. What is the point of implementing a full object-based design for a program that never exceeds more than a couple of hundred lines of code? We, as developers, seem to find it very difficult to resist the urge to gold-plate, polish, tweak, and modify above and beyond the call of duty.

The most valuable skill a software analyst develops (especially one who is paid by the hour) is to know when to stop. Knowing when a design is done and dusted is what separates the real analysts from the wanna-be newcomer.

This chapter will focus on the current uses of technology in the games industry and will attempt to gently lead you into an object-oriented approach to game design. Games in particular lend themselves to an object-oriented design more than any other particular type of application, mainly due to the fairly direct mapping of tokens to objects.

In your average business application, this mapping may not be so immediately obvious. After all, trying to visualize a space containing tax returns, billing receipts, and bank accounts with transactions zipping through the ether does not come as easily to the average human being as imagining a space full of spacecraft with lasers flashing between them. Of course, the token-to-object mapping may not always be so trivial; it can be deceptive.

Games are generally more intuitive and comprehensible than business applications. It's one of the things that makes them fun. The average player has to be able to relate to the world within the game; otherwise, it is not fun. If the world within the game is easy for a wide range of people to relate to, then it is most probably expressed in terms of understandable concepts and entities.

The tokens in the game can be easily mapped to real (or imaginary) life equivalents, and the interactions between these tokens can be implicitly understood and predicted.

Of course, this does not apply to all games or business applications. We know of enough games that are not fun—and enough business applications that are—to support this last point.

Business applications and games have two different agendas. A business application has no real goal: it is merely a tool to use to complete a task. You don't get three attempts at creating your spreadsheet before you have to go back to the beginning and start again (although with the early buggy releases of a certain famous spreadsheet application, it certainly seemed that way). A good game is meant to provide a challenge. A good business application is not.

The State Of The Art

The games industry has always prided itself on being on the cutting edge of technology. Whenever a new processor, graphics card, or any other cool peripheral appears on the market and garners enough support, the game developers are there in force to provide that support.

Although game developers may perceive themselves as being on the cutting edge of technology, this position is debatable. Who is to say whether the latest 3D game or the latest multiterrabyte database software is the most advanced?

I've helped design and write some financial analysis software using calculations many times more complex than those you'd find in even the most complex 3D games. Which are the more advanced? It's not an easy comparison to make: like comparing two fine wines, each has its own individual nuances, and you cannot easily say which is superior.

Undoubtedly, in terms of technical complexity, a database such as SQL Server 7 is more advanced than any game currently on the market. But it's just not as *enticing*, and the coolness factor associated with games and game development only helps to feed the hype.

In conclusion, I would say that, although game developers are not on the cutting edge of technology, they are most definitely world leaders in the art of fast approximation of simulated real-world systems.

Why fast approximations? Well, until home computers get much more powerful than they are today, there is no way we would be able to model an immersive world full of complex dynamics and interactions in realtime, without taking a few shortcuts to save time. Even if Moore's Law holds true, and raw computer processing power doubles every 18 months or so, it is doubtful that anybody will be able to make a truly accurate to-the-molecule simulation of a world for a very long time. (And, unless they were molecular engineers, nor would they want to.)

As computers get faster and faster, these approximations will become increasingly accurate. Nowhere is this more evident than in the graphics engines for today's games. The lineage of the 3D graphics engine can be traced back to the early days.

The Rise And Fall Of The 3D Engine

The first famous 3D game was *Battlezone*, as shown Figure 18.1, in the arcades. This simple tank simulation used low-polygon-count wireframe graphics to portray a simple landscape interspersed with cubes, pyramids, and tanks. No hidden-line removal was attempted (that is, objects appeared as if they were made of glass and you could see the hidden edges on the far side of the object).

The next famous one was the BBC version of *Elite*, as shown in Figure 18.2, by David Braben and Ian Bell. (See Chapter 7.) This incredibly immersive game involved trading goods between different star systems. The 3D engine represented each star system as a single sun (as a filled circle with perturbed edges) and a single planet (as an outlined circle). Ships were drawn in wireframe and benefited from intraobject hidden-line removal (that is, you couldn't see the far side of a ship through its infrastructure, but you would be able to see if another ship was behind it).

As processing power increased, so did the number of polygons used, as well as the complexity of the drawing techniques. First came filled polygons, such as those seen in the Archimedes version of *Elite*, as shown in Figure 18.3. These polygons were simply colored a flat shade of a single color.

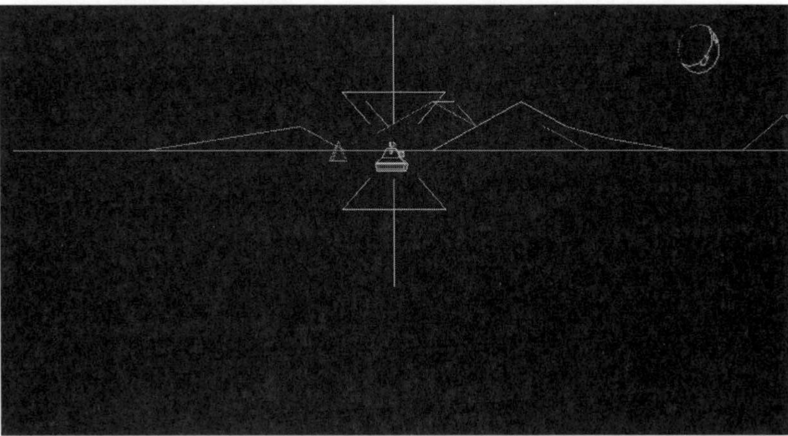

Figure 18.1
Battlezone.

Figure 18.2
BBC *Elite*.

Figure 18.3
Archimedes *Elite*.

Soon after, simple flat shading was added to the polygons, and these would change in illumination according to a light source, as demonstrated in *Zarch* (known as *Virus* on other systems), as shown in Figure 18.4. This was usually a simple directional light source; anything else would have been too computationally expensive.

This was closely followed by Gouraud shading, a technique whereby the illumination was calculated at the vertices of the polygon and simply linearly interpolated over the interior of the polygon, as in *Little Big Adventure* (known as *Relentless* in the U.S.) shown in Figure 18.5.

The next development in the saga of the polygon was texture mapping: projecting a picture onto the surface of the polygon so that it appeared that the polygon was textured. *Ultima Underworld II*, as shown in Figure 18.6, was one of the first examples of this.

Later developments—such as *Wolfenstein 3D* (which introduced ray casting) shown in Figure 18.7, *Doom* (which introduced binary space partitioning (BSP) trees) shown in Figure 18.8, and *Descent*—brought more advances to light sources, with explosions providing directional point sources, and laser fire dynamically lighting walls as it streaked past.

Figure 18.4
Zarch.

Figure 18.5
Little Big Adventure.

Figure 18.6
Ultima Underworld II.

Figure 18.7
Wolfenstein 3D.

Figure 18.8
Doom.

At this stage, 3D was still the exception rather than the rule. Most games were still being developed in 2D, and 3D was only just beginning to become the mainstream. *Quake* (as shown in Figure 18.9) heralded in this new era of game development.

What caused the great turnaround was the introduction of the first 3D accelerators into the market. 3D products with huge polygon counts, advanced lighting, texture mapping (such as *Quake III Arena* shown in Figure 18.10), and all the latest whizzy features now jostle for position on the shelf, but try to find one of these products that uses the 3D technology in an original and innovative fashion. (*That* should reduce the number of worthy candidates a bit.)

Too many games make their 3D engine the game, rather than use it as a tool for presenting their game. That is one of the main problems of the industry today: the focus is on the technology and not on the solutions provided by the technology. The tail is wagging the dog.

To be fair, this is not all the fault of the tech-head developers. Consumer expectation contributes to it, also. These two factors feed off each other, additionally fueled by other outside influences such as the expectations created by the public perception of what computers should be, and the hard-core gaming contingent (mainly adolescent males), who until recently were the *only* purchasers of computer games.

Figure 18.9
Quake.

Figure 18.10
Quake III Arena.

Now that gaming is becoming more mainstream and acceptable, a whole set of different subtle factors are coming into play. However, the main factor—the one that has been there from the start: the infamous "wow" factor, perhaps the most ostentatious role of the technology. Does it make you exclaim "wow!" when you first set eyes on it?

The Perception Of Technology

In games, as in most things in life, first impressions count. Often the first impression we get of a new game comes from magazine reviewers, many of whom are hard-core gamers. They are susceptible to the "wow" factor in the same way that the rest of us are, it is does not help that they are generally under pressure to review the game and get it into the magazine as soon as possible. Consequently there is a tendency for reviews to be superficial, as shown in Case Study 18.1.

A lot of the very best games do not have this initial "wow" factor: the presentation may be slightly bland, or the graphics may be slightly outdated or not quite up there with the rest of the competition. This can be a problem when it comes to getting good scores in the reviews, because gameplay (no matter how great) is rarely evident on first impression.

The corollary is that games that are technically impressive but lacking in gameplay get ridiculously high marks in reviews. In some magazines *Quake* scored 100 percent, implying that it could not be bettered! And when *Capture the Flag* was introduced, you had the same reviewers saying, "This makes *Quake* even better!" (Better than 100 percent? Doh!)

Now *Quake* was a great technology demo, and the multiplayer game was pretty good. Single play, however, left much to be desired, but it still got fantastic reviews. It's unfair to single *Quake* out in this manner: there are many worse games that have had high scores just by having a great technology and by looking pretty: the "bimbos" of the computer game world.

Case Study 18.1 A First Impression

When Blizzard's *Warcraft 2* was released a few years back, the reviews that it received in the specialist press ranged from average to good, but the reviewers never wrote anything really stunning said about it.

Opinions seemed to vary, but the general consensus was that the game was a cartoon-like derivative of *Dune II*, with average looks and gameplay, and, overall, it was considered to be an "okay" game, but nothing special—and certainly not "hit" material.

Warcraft 2 is not a game that appears impressive on the first playing. It takes time for the hidden depths and the intricate game balance to reveal themselves. It has no flashy technology to immediately impress the time-pressured reviewer.

The problem is that reviewers have a lot of games to review in a fairly short amount of time: If a game doesn't show the blatant "wow" factor within the first few minutes of play, then it stands a good chance of getting a poorer review than a game that has the initial "wow" factor but inferior gameplay.

The reviewers didn't even learn their lesson by the time that *Starcraft* was released. Only a few of the magazines rated this game highly, with the rest giving it only average reviews. Both games were the best-selling games of their respective years despite the average reviews, so obviously the game-playing public saw the potential in both of these sleeper hits.

This "inconsistent review" phenomenon could be due to any number of reasons. One of these could be that, although the game looks beautiful, it doesn't stand up well to repeated playing. (It has low longevity.) Another of these reasons is that the game publisher wants the review to be read by people before or at about the same time as when the game hits the shelf.

Whatever the reasons, the outcome is the same: in many cases, poor games are slipping through the net and getting high marks (and hence sales) because they look pretty enough to create a great first impression, and some of the better games get lower marks because not enough time was devoted to them to allow the reviewer to experience the richness of the game play.

Take, for example, *The 7th Guest*. Now, I'll admit that this was a truly stunning experience, but it was not a game in the same way that a jigsaw puzzle is not a game.

It was a series of simple puzzles linked by a sequence of beautifully orchestrated movies. It got high marks in reviews simply because it was so beautiful to look at. There was virtually no gameplay, but it made a great showcase for the brand-new CD ROM drive that Johnny's dad had installed in the family PC.

Interestingly, reviewers had got wise to this particular style by the time the sequel was released. Consequently, the sequel, *11th Hour*—and the later re-release of *The 7th Guest*—did not achieve such high marks, being recognized as distinctly average puzzle games. However, why did the reviewers not notice this the first time round?

If reviewers are supposed to be impartial judges of games, how could they fail to notice that *The 7th Guest* was just a computer-rendered animation with limited interaction? They are susceptible to being dazzled by eye candy just like the rest of us.

So it really depends what sort of sales curve you want. If you want high initial sales followed by a tiny trickle, then make your game more stunningly beautiful and graphically showy than anything else out there. Style before content is a valid approach (you can fleece the sheep before anyone notices that you left out the actual game) but it can backfire when you come to release your next product.

This is getting harder to do now that the hardware is enforcing a homogeneity of style, and some reviewers are beginning to wise up. For example, *Incoming* (Rage Software) was an amazing-looking product. It generated a lot of pre-release publicity owing to its special attention to detail in the shape of big, pretty explosions. But when it was actually released, the gameplay was deemed to be pretty shallow. (Even so, it managed to sell quite a few copies, and it got bundled as an OEM deal with some 3D cards as a pretty and easily accessible demonstration of what the card was capable of.)

Despite protestations to the contrary, the majority of commercial developments today put presentation before gameplay. This is a fundamental mistake that can only worsen the public perception of the industry, in a similar way to the public perception of big Hollywood movies such as *Independence Day*—very pretty to look at, but not much meat (just like nouvelle cuisine except possibly more expensive).

Doing It Properly

You don't have to be a slave to the "wow" factor. There is another approach to game development, which is simply to concentrate on the gameplay first, spending many hours balancing and perfecting the interactions between tokens. This does not mean you neglect the technology (that would be commercial suicide). You just make sure that technology is a priority but the design is *an even bigger* priority.

For example, the freeware game *Rogue* has an ASCII graphics interface and is very playable and involving. However, it was the souped-up graphical version called *Diablo* that got all the coverage. Even though *Rogue* is free, I am pretty sure that more people have bought *Diablo* than have played *Rogue*. *Diablo* debuted at number one in the computer game charts.

The key approach here is to assign the correct priorities to the elements of the game. Gameplay is the highest priority, closely followed by accessibility and appearance.

Take *Starcraft* as an example. This game was clearly developed on a gameplay first basis. Early development work used the same graphics engine as its predecessor, *Warcraft 2*. This was a pleasant-enough graphics engine, but it was not technologically stunning.

Later in development, after the release of *Diablo* by the same company, they ripped out the *Warcraft 2* graphics engine and replaced it with an engine similar to the *Diablo* graphics engine. Again, this was still not a stunning engine by the standards of the time, and it could be argued that *Total Annihilation* by Cavedog looked better, but that is not the point.

Even though the graphics engine had taken a major overhaul halfway through development, the gameplay had remained consistent throughout. It would seem that they attributed more importance to the gameplay, because, in any sensible development, ripping out and replacing a graphics engine should be seen as a risky but noncritical undertaking. Ripping out and replacing the gameplay should be seen as a failure: you're effectively beginning a new game.

The approach that Blizzard took with *Starcraft* is the path less trodden. The gameplay was the primary concern, with the presentation coming a close second. This diligence and attention to detail paid off admirably, and *Starcraft* achieved consistently strong sales.

Even the original release of *Quake* succumbed to the "technology first, gameplay second" school of thought, especially in single-player mode. For *Quake II*, the majority of the technology was already there, so they had more time to explore the gameplay and story line.

The pinnacle of the first-person shooter genre, interestingly enough, has always been achieved by licensees of the engines, with *Half-Life* being a good example of this. Since Valve was licensing the engine, the whole question of technology was out of the way; consequently, they could concentrate on the gameplay and ambience—which was universally acknowledged as very successful.

Some of the other licensees were not so diligent: they saw the *Quake* engine as the opportunity to tack a pretty first-person shooter onto the back of it in an attempt to make a fast buck.

The Cart Before The Horse

Die by the Sword is a particularly interesting example of a technology-led game. This was a third-person action adventure, where the player was a sword-wielding adventurer on some quest of great importance.... (Oh, you already heard that story?)

It came with all the usual accoutrements, such as a nice 3D engine and music, but its main feature was more interesting. The intriguing thing about this game, and its main USP (unique selling point), was considered to be the implementation of a realtime inverse kinematics engine.

For those of you who are not exactly familiar with inverse kinematics, I'll quickly explain the principle. Imagine that you have a computer model of a man standing up, with his arms down by his side. Imagine now that you want him to raise his arm, as if he was giving you a friendly wave. How would this be done?

Well, there are a number of approaches. The first is obvious: you could script it by either using calculated or motion-captured data. Alternatively, you could start at the shoulder, and rotate the top of the arm to the correct position. From there, you would rotate the forearm about the elbow, and the hand about the wrist until it was in the correct position. This, more or less, is forward kinematics.

The other option, which is more intuitive, is to move the hand to the position you wanted, and expect the forearm, upper arm, and shoulder to move naturally to support it. This is not as trivial as it sounds: the calculations have to take into account the natural rotation range of the joints and other such factors in order to ensure that the man does not look like every bone in his body is broken. Inverse kinematics is commonly seen as a method of calculating animation in packages such as *3D Studio* MAX, where it is not usually done in realtime.

Die by the Sword allowed you to do things such as swing on a rope and cut through it with your sword while you were on it. This was not scripted behavior: it was all handled dynamically by the engine itself. Once skilled enough, the player would be able to perform amazing feats such as leaping through the air, turning head over heels, and dispatching an enemy with a smart sword blow to the top of the head while doing so. (Although it is unlikely that anyone would be able to do this in real life, in the game it was a pretty handy trick!)

But therein lies the problem. Picture the story: you are the hero who is supposed to be already proficient with the sword, so starting the game as a complete amateur somewhat destroys the suspension of disbelief. Why then, did they make you learn how to control the sword as if you were a complete beginner?

Well, in fact, they didn't. They provided some scripted moves that the player could execute. So, why didn't they just do this in the first place? The question must be asked: did the inverse kinematics add that much to the game? In my opinion, shared by many reviewers, it did not.

You are playing a great swordsman, so you should be able to start the game with the skill of a great swordsman. However, you don't: you start the game having to actually learn to use the sword, and it takes weeks before you can do anything useful. The developers realized this and had to add some animations of sword sweeps to make the game easier to use. So all that technology finally came to the point where they had to put in the animations, bringing them back to the point where games had been for years, and they might as well not have bothered.

This is one of those cases in which the technology took priority over the game itself. If the game designers had asked themselves the right questions, they may have realized that the inverse kinematics engine was unnecessary to the game; a simpler motion capture with an interpolation-based engine may have been a more suitable option. The inherent "cool factor" of the technology proved to be their downfall.

As a side note, I'd also be interested to know whether their inverse kinematics engine was a reusable component, or whether it was integrated inseparably into the game to allow the maximum amount of context-specific optimizations. Whatever the situation, the result was clear: the effort spent on the technology did not produce comparable rewards. I have not heard of it being used since.

Although I do have reservations about the way technology is currently used within the games industry, I cannot deny that having a good technology is essential to success. For example, you could not now release a game that would have been considered the state of the art five years ago and expect anything but a dismal commercial failure.

Where's The Game?

Technology certainly has its place, but its importance is distorted at the moment. Technological innovation, like mountain climbing, is attempted "just because it's there." Let me give you a possible example.

Black & White is a game being developed by Peter Molyneux's development company, Lionhead. It is being realized as a fully 3D game, with all sorts of technical wizardry allowing a detailed 3D perspective, true shadows to be cast on the landscape, and other such marvels.

Knowing the attention that Peter Molyneux pays to gameplay, it will undoubtedly be an excellent product, but, from reading the gameplay description, I can't help wondering if a fully 3D view is even necessary. Is it the best way of presenting the game and managing the information within it?

Take *Dungeon Keeper*, a game that uses a primarily isometric top-down view, although it provides the ability to take over a creature and use a first-person 3D view. This was rarely necessary however, and sometimes it was not even desirable. It will be interesting to see how Peter Molyneux overcomes the difficulties of interacting with the 3D engine, and the need to know the events that are happening over a wide area simultaneously.

These are some examples of how technology is currently (mis)used in the industry. The rest of the chapter details some more common mistakes, and suggests alternative approaches to the role that technology plays in today's games.

Blue-Sky Research

We would all love to spend all day in front of a computer chewing on pizza and guzzling soda pop, just engaging our creativity and researching whatever we like. Some companies do allow this, and have active (if somewhat variable) research departments. That's a good thing. Research is essential to the survival of a company. It's *blue-sky* research you have to be careful about.

By definition, any technology present in games currently available in the shops is about 18 months behind what is currently being worked on by the best design houses. This constant advance of technology can lead rather seductively to certain common pitfalls that can have a greatly detrimental effect on the schedule. In some cases, the project can even fail.

Blue-sky research is one of the common dangers. Undirected research—where developers are given a free hand to research whatever interests them most—is little more than a gamble, and usually at very long odds.

This is tantamount to putting a hundred code monkeys in a room and expecting them to produce *Shakespeare—The Adventure Game*. In other words, even with the best will in the world, it is statistically unlikely that anything remotely useful will be achieved, except a rather tragic comedy of errors.

When a game project depends on the outcome of research that has not been completed, that project is in great danger. Putting anything in the critical path for which the outcome cannot be predicted is sheer idiocy; but, for some reason—whether greed, stupidity, or just plain ignorance—development teams do this on a regular basis.

I'm not advocating that research should be abolished; that would be a Draconian measure and would lead to further stagnation of the industry. I'm saying that there is a time for research and a time for development, and that the two should never overlap. Any research that is instigated should be directed research. It should have an aim.

An example would be the design and development of a library useful in fuzzy-logic calculations. For sure, there would be a fair amount of research involved, but this would be research into ways of optimizing and improving on known techniques. The alternative—commonly known as *blue-sky research*—is looking for a completely new method of doing things. Fortunately, there is very little you can imagine doing with a computer that hasn't been already done by someone somewhere. If you're very lucky, then they have published their results.

Building on the work of others, although less glamorous, is a surer way of getting good results. Besides, if you wanted glamour, why did you become a developer?

When your team is researching, set a strict time limit and stick to it ruthlessly. Run with what you physically have at the end of the research period, not with what you are promised at the beginning. The time allocated for research should also factor in the time necessary to bring the research project to a successful conclusion and with a stable and well-documented component.

As the research progresses, more and more unknowns will become quantifiable, so, as soon as the fundamental technique being researched is working, a mini-schedule can be drawn up to allow for this tidying-up procedure.

If the game design depends on this research, then this is the single most critical point of the whole development. The project will succeed or fail—right here, right now—dependent on the success of this research project. Obviously, this is not a good idea: gambling the whole project on blue-sky research is a game that only the very foolhardy or the extremely desperate would play.

Wherever possible, a backup plan should be in place: even if Blizzard had failed to integrate the new graphics engine into *Starcraft*, it still would have been able to fall back on the original one.

Remember: any safety net is better than no safety net. If no safety net is possible, then "make-or-break" research should be avoided. It's too much of a risk, no matter how cool the developer doing the research is. Under most circumstances, releasing the product is better than canning it.

Only the most cash-rich companies will be able to afford internal research such as that used during the development processes of *Die by the Sword* and *Outcast*. Not so many companies are able to afford the protracted development times and the risks that are associated with research of this nature.

If your company doesn't have the sort of cash available to finance a research department, you still have a few options open.

The first, and most undesirable, is to avoid projects that require R&D. This is only really acceptable for the "ticking-over-and-we-know-we'll-only-sell-a-couple-of-hundred-thousand-or-so" type of company. This is a viable option, but it isn't going to go anywhere fast.

For the less-affluent companies, another option is to form links with academia. Forming a loose relationship with universities and their computing departments can provide some good technology at some very good prices. A company I have worked for in Belgium used their local university as a source of cutting-edge cryptography algorithms and regularly tested their latest algorithm designs by letting the university researchers loose on them. The theory was that any implementations of algorithms that these university cryptography experts couldn't crack were pretty much guaranteed to be secure. (This cryptography software is used by the Bank of England, the European Commission, and several important Swiss Banks—so I would have to say that it must be pretty secure.)

If you use the "external research" system, then this also simplifies some other company decisions. Form a liaison with academia: a good relationship means that they get to publish and you get to use their new ideas.

The best part about this is the cost: academics are not expensive. Ten thousand dollars is a lot of cash to an academic, and it is a very cheap price to pay for an expert researcher. The only drawback is that it is best to make sure that your aims and the researcher's coincide. There's no point giving money to a cryptography researcher if you want to get a voxel landscape engine! Also, bear in mind that there is no guarantee of results (but, then again, if you had a similar researcher in-house, you'd have no guarantee of results either, and he or she would be likely to cost much more). Academics and researchers tend to be code mavericks, but they are also excellent at documentation. So, even if the code is tricky to understand (they will have their own coding standards, as their code is designed to be read by their professors), it will be thoroughly documented. This is fine, as long as you have solid and dependable people in-house to compensate for the maverick-style researchers.

Yet another option is to be part of a large conglomerate, either using the Hollywood studio model (an option that I prefer) or the loose alliance model typified by Lionhead's satellites and Gathering of Developers (GoD). The latter may not be an optimal system given the way all human institutions tend to evolve. To optimize it you need to ensure that the separate development teams are aware of and able to share each other's technology. Also you would ideally organize collateral R&D so that two companies don't waste time on the same tasks. All of which is best achieved by appointing a resource investigation unit to interface between all the projects in development. A loose development alliance can work, therefore, but it needs structure.

Research Types

Research can be divided into several different types, and, as in the physical sciences, each type has a different approach. Not all of the techniques suitable for quantum research would be suitable for researching archaic laws, but all types of research do share a common factor: the recording of results.

Research without meticulously recorded results is close to useless. We need the records in order to determine the path taken by the researcher. The notes themselves may inspire further research or refinements to the current research. It's not just our opposable thumb that sets human beings apart from the animals: it's our ability to collect and distribute information. Imagine if we as a species had not learned to record and distribute results—then millions of people all over the world would have to start each new day by rediscovering fire!

Now let's take a look at the current state of the games industry. Each company has their own proprietary version of a standard technique. Each individual within the company jealously guards his own technology. Each company regularly reinvents the wheel by duplicating already existing code. They may well do research, but it would usually be of the hacking type: "Hey, let's hack some code around until something cool happens." Ring any bells?

I'm not suggesting that games companies should give away all their company secrets and assemble annually at Woodstock for an international knowledge-share fest. But, in general, information sharing can only be a good thing for the company. This may well be restricted to inside the company only, but it is better than nothing and is the first step to creating a powerful research synergy.

Even sharing knowledge outside the company isn't as fatal as it sounds. Michael Abrash spent some time at id software optimizing the core code of the *Quake* engine. He wrote several magazine articles on the inner workings of the code and the techniques used within the engine. These also appear in his book, *The Black Book of Graphics Programming*, which is also published by The Coriolis Group.

Why did he give away "company secrets?" Was he disgruntled with his employers? Did he want to sabotage *Quake* before it even hit the stores? No. It was none of these reasons, and id software did not suffer at all by the publication of the techniques: in fact, they were most probably helped by it. Techniques are nothing without implementation, and they had already done the hard work of the implementation. No one would be catching up for a while at least.

This may be a slightly cynical view, but it's certainly likely that they released the information because they knew that no other companies would be able to catch up in time. This may well be true, but the sharing of the information allowed other companies and individuals to take the ideas and run with them. Of course, the downside of this is that we are now completely swamped with first-person shooters. Oh well, at least they all have nice engines.

Let's now examine the different areas of technology research that will be required for the average "cutting-edge" game product.

- "What's out there?" research
- Target market research
- Gameplay research
- Technology research

"What's Out There?" Research

The first type of research is the commonest. It involves finding out what is already out there? Are there any products similar to your proposed game in any combination of the other research areas: **target market** (in a niche market), **story line** (you can only have so many evil galactic empires before it gets boring), **gameplay** (it's like *Warcraft*—only with meerkats), or **technology** (we've got this great idea for an A-Life engine like it's never been done before).

Based on the outcome of your survey, you may want to modify your initial ideas and evaluate how your proposed game compares to the competition. After all, only the most cynical or desperate company will release a game knowing it to be inferior to other similar products either already on, or about to hit, the market.

This research is usually the domain of the marketers: the guys who will be abreast of the changing market. They will know what's out there and be in a good position to evaluate the competition. That's true to some extent of almost anybody on the team, of course, but the marketers will also be able to provide useful statistics.

You should also keep a weather eye open for up and coming releases that encroach on the same territory as your game. Imagine releasing a realtime interstellar wargame game around the same time that *Starcraft* hit the market. Unless your game had the best technology *and* artwork *and* game design in the business (and maybe not even then) you would simply be blown away.

Admittedly it is difficult to develop your own games and at the same time keep an eye on what the competition is doing. Take a look at Case Study 18.2 for another example.

Target Market Research

The second type of research—researching the target market—will help gauge what sort of sales your game might achieve, and the likely spread of machine configuration your players will have.

Obviously, you want these sales to be as high as possible, but what is the likelihood of this? Is your design aimed at the mass market, or is it aimed at a more specific market? If so, what is the typical machine possessed by your market? If you are aiming at the mass market, then you are aiming for a wide spread.

If you are aiming for a niche market (such as flight simulation), then you can probably rely on the fact that dedicated flight simulator fans are usually decked out with all the required gear.

Target markets are notoriously difficult to define, especially in the game development world where, unless you are targeting twenty-something males (which comprise the majority of game players), you are really on your own in terms of targeting content.

For example, targeting the young-girl section of the market (or, with the current game industry situation, *creating* a young-girl section of the market) would involve much more than just creating a game that they would like. You have to break down the acceptance barrier. Computers are still perceived as toys for boys, and it takes a big-name license such as Barbie to break down these prejudices.

Case Study 18.2 Losing Sight Of The Ball

A few years back, Arthur, a young graduate and an avid gamer, began working at a games company as a junior programmer. He played a lot of games and had a fairly good handle on what sort of games sell and which do not. As gamers go, he was fairly mainstream in his tastes.

James was Arthur's boss. He had been in the gaming industry since the beginning and he knew the industry inside out. He had boundless enthusiasm for projects he was supervising, sometimes overlooking their shortcomings.

A normal topic of conversation in any games company is to discuss the games that have been released—comparing their relative merits, and predicting how well they will do in terms of sales.

Arthur had been playing the newly released *Command & Conquer* by Westwood Studios, and was very impressed. He mentioned this to James, adding that he believed that it would be one of the biggest selling games of the year.

"You don't know much do you?" James retorted. "C&C is just not mass market. They'll just about break even on it, if they're lucky."

"Really?" said Arthur. "Well—we'll see at the end of the year."

Skipping forward to the end of the year, the press reported that *Command & Conquer* was one of the biggest selling games of the year. James said nothing and Arthur could not resist going as far to say that the newly released *Warcraft 2* will do the same thing.

Again, James was unimpressed and refuted the claim, saying that the puzzle game that he had recently produced would take the honors—that it would, in fact, be bigger than *Tetris*.

Of course the rest is history—*Warcraft 2* went on to do phenomenally well. And the puzzle game? You probably won't have heard of it.

A few months later Freddy, the lead game designer, spoke to Arthur. Freddy, although senior in the company, was less certain of himself than Arthur's boss. He liked to get everyone's opinion. "You're a *Warcraft 2* fan," he said to Arthur. "What do you think—would it be worth us licensing the *Warcraft 2* engine to produce a realtime strategy game of our own?"

As an office junior, Arthur wasn't used to being asked such a pivotal question. With some diplomacy he replied: "If you think that you have something new to add to the genre, and won't just be producing a rip-off then sure, it's a great idea. The only difficulty will be that Blizzard did such a fine job with *Warcraft 2*. It's already been done and done well. What can you add?"

Freddy agreed and the idea was rapidly dropped.

Listening to the little guy is important: sometimes they have a better overall picture of things that you would give them credit for. After all it is hard to keep track of the market when you're managing companies, doing deals, and entertaining potential investors at expensive lunches. Useful insight can come from the most unexpected sources.

This doesn't mean that you should concentrate on the core market of twenty-something males, which would cause further stagnation of the market. There must always be attempts to break into the (much overhyped) theoretical mass market. When this happens, it will not be a game such as *Quake* X that scoops up the honors: it will be something completely unexpected. The last game that effectively broke into mass-market territory (a feat that has been unsuccessfully attempted ever since) was *Tetris* when it was released on the Game Boy. *Tetris* was responsible for the majority of the 60,000,000 Game Boy sales worldwide.

Gameplay Research

The gameplay could have an impact on the technology needed for the game. For example, the game's user interface may require investigation of certain types of controller.

Other aspects of the gameplay may require active research. For example, in the case of strategy games, plenty of information is available if you're prepared to do a little digging: game theory from the War Studies Group is readily available on the Web, as are analyses commissioned by the U.S. Navy and the Pentagon. Looking at history also indicates where different factors have contributed to the payoff matrices of a real situation, such as why the Aztecs became so powerful, and how, in spite of this, they were beaten by Cortés.

For researching the gameplay of a puzzle game like *Tetris* or *Balls!*, you could look at psychological work on types of reasoning. A satisfying puzzle game like *Tetris* or *Puzzle Bobble* will include spatial and temporal reasoning (the "story" part) as well as logical reasoning using the manipulation of abstract concepts mapped to concrete entities (the "planning" part) and the pleasurable payoff of watching where all that leads, and learning something more about the way the game rules operate (the "play" or "learning curve" part.)

Obviously, you can find more genres of games, but the point I am making here is that you don't necessarily have to look in the standard or clichéd places for gameplay ideas, such as novels, films, and other games. There is a whole world of information out there, and a lot of it can be applied to gameplay, even if it does not seem immediately obvious.

After all, the idea for *Tetris* was drawn from the field of mathematics.

Technology Research

The last kind of research involves researching the technology that is required to actually implement the game. Are you going to be using any new techniques, or breaking into uncharted waters?

This sort of research is what id Software spends most of its time doing. id Software has lots of money. This is no coincidence: without lots of cash backing you up, research has to be more focused and specific. You can't just go wandering through your ideas randomly, idly daubing code "paint" on the "canvas" of your compiler without someone being willing to pay the bills.

The fact is that this sort of research takes a lot of time and a lot of money. This is where the real research is, and where the bulk of the budget of time and money will be invested. In an ideal world, your company would have enough money to allow unrestricted research into new technology.

Unfortunately, unless you are id Software, then this is very unlikely. There will always be commercial pressures breathing down your necks, and the company management will be expecting results. In previous chapters, we have pointed out the dangers of depending on concrete results from research. I'll not repeat those warnings here.

Research is an unpredictable activity, and research into new technologies is particularly difficult. For every *Quake* engine, there are probably hundreds of failed attempts. Worse still, a fair proportion of these failed attempts will have been for game projects that had to be canned due to the failure of the underlying technology. id Software had no problem with this: for the original release of *Quake*, the focus was on the technology and not so much on the game.

Sure, there was a minimal game there, but it only really became evident in multiplayer mode. This wasn't really a conscious gameplay effort on the part of id Software, but was more a consequence of the nature of the *Quake* engine. *Quake* was effectively a technology demo, which became evident with the disjointed nature of the themes used in the game.

In contrast, *Quake II* was much less of a technological advance over *Quake* than *Quake* was over *Doom*. A few refinements were made to the engine, but most of the effort appeared to have gone into refining the gameplay and the storyline. *Quake III Arena* seems to have reverted to the original *Quake* model: concentrating on the gameplay emerging from the technology (which has been improved by the addition of quadratic curve rendering).

This is an interesting approach that appears to defy conventional game theory. Even the single-player game is a multiplayer game, with all the other players controlled by the computer. I'd go as far to say that there is no real gameplay in a multiplayer game: it's more a simulation set in a fantasy environment. It's too close to reality (albeit a fictional reality) for it to be considered a game. It's an accurate simulation of future combat. Case Study 18.3 provides a caveat to *Tetris*.

You may be getting the impression that I am against technology in some way. That's not true. I am against the gratuitous use of technology in the same way as I am against gratuitous violence. It's unnecessary and is, in some cases, quite disturbing. The whole industry (with few exceptions) appears to be putting technology before gameplay, and this is a dismal and worrying prospect. I've lost count of the number of games I have seen that have lost gameplay value because the developers wanted to showcase their latest technologies. Case Study 18.4 gives details of a much-welcome exception to this pattern.

Case Study 18.3 Tetris: A Caveat

There's hardly a developer on the planet who doesn't wish he had thought of *Tetris*.

Tetris is one of life's enigmas. It's hard to meet anyone who is not impressed by *Tetris*: it is available on almost any machine, and was largely responsible for the success of the original Game Boy.

Tetris was low-tech: nothing in the gameplay of *Tetris* couldn't have been done 10 years earlier. Nevertheless, it was still a resounding success due to its simple but addictive gameplay. The technology is a nonissue, but *Tetris* has still sold more copies worldwide than virtually any other game.

One of the most common responses I have heard from game developers when they have been asked which game they would have liked to have been responsible for, one of the top answers in *Tetris*. They then go on to qualify this by saying that they could have written it in an afternoon.

And they're probably right.

I have thought this also. I wish I'd had the clarity of mind to think of a concept like *Tetris*. (Then maybe I would be lounging on my yacht in the Caribbean instead of writing this.)

The important point is that technology bears very little influence on what makes good gameplay. *Tetris* performed equally well on all machines, and, interestingly enough, when technology was applied to the problem of producing a sequel, none of the sequels did well.

For example, *WellTris* was a 3D extension to *Tetris* with the player stacking blocks falling down into a well. The Nintendo 64 had a similar game, *Tetrisphere*, which had the blocks raining down onto the surface of a sphere. There were many others: *Pac Panic, Columns, Dr. Mario*, and so on.

None of these derivatives and sequels did well. What was their mistake? Well, apart from trying to improve something that did not need improving in the first place, the fundamental flaw in most of these derivatives was that they did not understand the holistic nature of the gameplay of *Tetris*.

Tetris is a thing of beauty: a perfectly balanced game. You cannot just add technology and expect to produce a better product. The appeal of *Tetris* was the gameplay. All of the sequels strayed from the purity of the original, and paid the price in reduced sales.

Even Nintendo seem to have learnt its lesson: The Game Boy Color was released with an enhanced version of *Tetris* called *Tetris DX*. What had changed? There were a couple of extra gameplay modes, the blocks were in color, and you could save your high scores across sessions.

Technology does not make a game. It will allow you to make a very pretty graphics demonstration, but so far there is no technology in existence that helps you make gameplay. This involves creative thought and a lot of luck and judgment. Maybe this is why most companies find it easier to produce games with far more style than content. *Tetris* is an object lesson in this case.

Case Study 18.4 Outcast: Good Use Of Technology

Outcast, released by Infogrames in June of 1999, is a game that had been hotly anticipated for the four years that it had been in development.

Usually, a four-year development cycle indicates major problems in development and that the game will be outdated immediately on release (a common complaint in reviews of *Heart of Darkness*, an animated cartoon platform adventure released in 1998 after a lengthy five years in development).

However, in the case of *Outcast*, the lengthy development seems to have paid off well. Rather than go down the standard path of using 3D polygon accelerators, the developers have spent the best part of the development cycle perfecting a voxel-based landscape engine. The end result is purely stunning and has to be seen to be believed.

If the industry pattern had been followed accurately, you would expect *Outcast* to be a technology demo (which it excels at) with an afterthought of a game tacked on top.

This is not the case, because the game is a beautifully detailed adventure, with a strong and consistent story line.

The important point is that the technology is a vehicle for the game and not vice versa (as in most cases in which new technology is showcased). The main benefit that the landscape engine brings to *Outcast* is ambience. The sense of immersion generated is almost too real, and it is a rare game that manages to achieve that.

An interesting point is that the game clearly came first in the priority list. The developers were not satisfied with a quick excuse of a game bolted onto a graphics showcase, and they instead spent the extra time needed to produce a playable game. (This is interesting because the game would be strong enough to survive without the advanced technology it is attached to.)

Could the same be said for the original *Quake*? If you displaced the game logic of *Quake* into another graphics engine (such as a 3D isometric engine like that used in *Diablo*), would the gameplay have stood on in its own? The answer is probably not. It may well have been diverting for a short period due to the multiplayer aspects, but it most certainly would not have been the success that it was. The main attraction of *Quake* was the amazing technology, and, when you looked behind that, the gameplay was fairly nonexistent. The sense of immersion provided by the 3D engine made up for that.

If the gameplay from *Outcast* was similarly transplanted, then—although it would not have been such a big success—it still would have been a solid game in its own right. If I were to compare this theoretical isometric *Outcast* to current games, then I would say that it would probably fall between games such as *Diablo* and *Fallout* or *Baldur's Gate*, which are all very successful games.

Outcast is a great example: it's a game that combines stunning technology with a solid game. This didn't come without a price: four years in development is a long time and a big risk to take. The longer a product is in development, the more likely it is that someone else will beat you to the prize. However, if you consider that they probably spent anything up to two-thirds of that time developing the engine, then obviously any further development projects using that engine will take less time and be more cost effective. This could have very well been a case of blue-sky research made good.

On a related note, a similar landscape engine has been adapted for mapping applications, and can be seen as a very impressive demo on **www.mobilemaps.com**.

Keeping A Journal

Research should be treated with as much seriousness as you would find in a top laboratory. Everything should be documented. Every thought, every procedure, and every result—even the wrong ones—needs to be recorded. This is serious stuff. Research is the lifeblood of your company. You need to research in order to keep up with the fast-changing pace of technology. If not, you risk being left behind in the rush.

I have recommended that a written journal be kept of research. Each member of the research group should be issued with a suitable notebook (spiral-bound graph paper is usually ideal), and they should be expected to take notes as they work. There is a common preconception in the industry that being assigned to research is pretty cool, because you get to play with all the latest toys and play around with code to drive them. In the cases that I have seen, the only output (when there was some) was a finished module—finished in the sense that it was feature complete, but not in any other sense.

That's great. It's nice to get a result, but, if you produce only a finished product, then you lose so much of the process. If notes have been made during the research, then this allows the amount of work to be quantified. It provides a learning opportunity for the other developers, who can read the notes and follow the thought processes. At best, this may stimulate them into improving the system, and suggest modifications that the original researcher may not have thought of.

At worst, it will allow them to understand the thought processes behind the research and give them a deeper understanding of the design motives. This knowledge will be invaluable when these developers come to maintain the codebase at a later date, as they will be more likely to make modifications in harmony with the design motives, rather than simply implementing a crude hack.

Some of the worst code I have had to work with was written like this. A number of developers had sequentially modified the code without having a full understanding of what the previous coder was trying to achieve. This resulted in overcomplicated code full of dead lava flows that had solidified.

A lava flow is an area of code that is thought to be unused, but is left in the codebase because nobody is quite sure if there is any other code dependent on it. The thinking is that it is safer to leave it in than it would be to remove it. Lava flows and other such phenomena are discussed in more detail in later chapters. If a journal had been kept, then the developers would have known that they could remove the excess code as they went along. This was done eventually due to sheer necessity, but only as a long and expensive process of reverse engineering and architecture mining.

In summary, the most important part of research is not the result: it's how you got there. Even if there are no concrete results from the research itself, then other people can learn from the route you took. Using the research journal, they may be able to see another way around the problem that you didn't see—or, failing that, then at least they know which areas of research have already been covered and written off as dead ends.

Reinventing The Wheel

The most common problem I have come across with game developers is the "Not Built Here" syndrome. It's bizarre: I've only found this in the games industry. Outside of the games industry, developers aren't so picky. They seem to be capable of understanding that other third-party developers are capable of producing good code, and they are consequently more disposed to using third-party libraries.

Contrast this to game developers, who seem to feel that the need to use a third-party library is an admission of failure: if they need to use somebody else's code, then it must be due to their own failure. They're just not good enough to cut it in the big bad world of game development.

Note

"A few months in the laboratory can frequently save a few hours in the library."

It's funny, but, for some reason I guess I'm not smart enough to work out, this only applies to the "coolest" areas of code (graphics libraries, AI, physics systems, 3D engines, and so on), except where the developers are obviously far beyond what could reasonably be achieved in a set time period.

Yet, strangely, nobody seems to have any problems with buying third-party libraries for their sound routines, install procedures, or FMV players.

This is a situation full of contradictions. Either third-party code is good enough or it is not. And, if it is not, you should probably rewrite the operating system—it won't be fast enough—and, while you're at it, recode the microkernel of the processor, too.

This parochial attitude to other people's code is slowly dying. As the complexity of game machines increase, it is no longer possible to expect a team to write all of the code required in a reasonable period of time.

The "Level Of Sameness"

It used to be that you could write directly to the hardware of a machine, knowing that all machines the software would be running on would be functionally identical. Then, with increasing complexity came variations of design, and there was a need for an operating system to mask this and present a uniform interface. In a way, the operating system can be viewed as a second-level computer.

If we define "the level of sameness" as being the conceptual level at which all machines of that type appear programmatically identical, then we can see that this level has been slowly rising over the years. It began at the same level as the hardware itself: each machine was identical at the level of chips and PCBs. Then more complexity was added: machines had expansion ports, and these could contain a variety of hardware.

The "level of sameness" had to rise slightly in order to account for these differences and the primitive "operating system" was born. Soon came further developments—different processor configurations and speeds, and wildly different hardware—that caused the operating system to develop into the heavyweight beast that it is today, and the "level of sameness" rose yet higher.

Recently, people have begun to catch on to the idea of providing a consistent interface in order to increase their hardware sales. I'm sure that the Game Boy Color wouldn't have sold quite as well initially if it hadn't have been able to play the vast majority of the old grayscale Game Boy releases.

Early reports indicate that Sony's PlayStation 2 will be able to play all of the original PlayStation games. The PlayStation 2 wouldn't be taken up so quickly if it weren't backwardly compatible with the old PlayStation. In this way, it becomes a seamless transition. Picture the scene: you are walking into a shop to buy a new console. Would you buy a PlayStation or a PlayStation 2? Both run the same core software base, but the PlayStation 2 also has software specifically targeted for it that takes advantage of the advanced features of the hardware. Most people would walk out with the PlayStation 2 under their arms.

So, this is where the "level of sameness" is now. New machines are being produced that are virtually compatible with their predecessors, meaning that new users are able to keep their old software. Planned obsolescence is a thing of the past: the consumer is wise to it, and would rather switch brands than be trapped.

For example, the Game Boy Color allows three types of game to be played: the old grayscale games designed for the original Game Boy (the majority of the user base), the dual-mode type of games (that detect which type of Game Boy they are running on and execute different code accordingly), and the color-only games (which take advantage of features of the Game Boy Color that would be impossible for the older hardware to handle or substitute for, such as the double-speed mode of the processor).

The "level of sameness" has pretty much reached its zenith now, and, for various (commercial) reasons, it is unlikely to rise any further. Why is this? Well, two paths can be traveled to increase the level: emulation and a common operating system. Both are fairly difficult to orchestrate, relying as they do on cooperation between competitors.

Emulation

One way to increase the level is by emulation, and this is fraught with difficulties, both technical and legal. Depending on the circumstances, manufacturers will either turn a blind eye towards emulator writers, or else they will pursue them vigorously through the courts for breach of copyright.

The producers of a Macintosh PlayStation emulator recently felt the wrath of Sony's lawyers, and a similar barrage of legal flak is most likely being prepared for the developers of *Bleem*, a PlayStation emulator for the PC.

Neither of these emulators promote piracy, because they require an original PlayStation CD to function. Nonetheless, Sony is not happy—which is quite strange, because, as is the usual practice, it didn't make any real money from the sales of the hardware. Most of the money comes from licensing and duplication fees from third-party developers that want to produce games for the PlayStation.

Nintendo hasn't escaped emulation either: Many emulators are available for its older consoles, and there are even Game Boy Color emulators, the best and most accurate being *No$GMB* by Martin Korth (**www.work.de/nocash/gmb.htm**), with its built-in debugger and developer tools. But it was only on the release of *UltraHLE*, a Nintendo 64 emulator for the PC, that Nintendo began to get upset, and possibly with good reason, too.

The Nintendo 64 uses cartridge, rather than CD-based storage. Consequently, games are smaller. This means that downloading them from the Internet is a reasonable proposition, and this directly threatens Nintendo's revenue stream. In fact, downloading them from the Internet (or using special hardware to copy cartridges to your computer) is the only way to play N64 games on *UltraHLE*. This means that it can be argued against on the grounds that it promotes piracy.

Even APIs aren't free of emulation! Glide is the API for direct programming of 3D graphics cards based on the 3Dfx chipset. Recently, some clever developer wrote an emulator for that API that interfaced with DirectX and released it on the Web.

This meant that games that were 3Dfx specific could be run on any DirectX-compliant graphics cards, including those that were specifically commissioned for the 3Dfx chipset. The producers of the 3Dfx chipset were understandably displeased with this, and demanded that the API emulation be removed.

Recently, this has gone a step further: Creative, which produces 3D accelerators based on the nVidia TNT chipset, has also produced a similar wrapper to the Glide API. It's titled

Unified, and it allows 3Dfx-specific games to be played using TNT-based cards by mapping the Glide API calls to DirectX calls. At present, these drivers are TNT specific, so they won't work with any other DirectX-compatible cards. 3Dfx is less than happy about this and is taking measures to clamp down on wrapper writers, claiming that their copyright has been breached and that the Glide API is being misused.

It could be argued that the Sony PlayStation 2 is an emulator of the original PlayStation, and that the Game Boy Color is capable of emulating the older grayscale version. This is a moot point, however, as the PlayStation 2 provides the same API (in a binary-compatible format) as the older PlayStation, while the Game Boy Color is compatible at the hardware level. Here, the line between emulation and backward compatibility is blurred.

In general, as a method of raising the level of sameness, emulation has a bleak future, mainly because it inhabits a legal gray area. Emulation is really a distraction: it is not a major consideration in achieving multiplatform release, but it is merely an interesting diversion that can be useful for tests during development.

The other major stumbling point of emulation is that it is also very asymmetrical. Only the most powerful machines can emulate other less-powerful machines: you can play a Nintendo 64 game on a PC as well as (and in some cases better) than on the Nintendo 64. The converse, however, is not true: you cannot play a PC game on a Nintendo 64.

Common Operating Systems

The other way of raising the level of sameness is by using a common operating system across all the platforms. This is more likely to come about than widespread emulation—but, again, commercial reasons conspire against it. The only "open" standards on the market are the PC and the Macintosh (and Linux, but that is not a mainstream consumer choice). These are arguably the most powerful, and are certainly the most versatile.

The idea of emulating a home computer's operating system on a console—even just the game-playing portion of the operating system—is quite unlikely. The range of input controllers and configurations available make this a very tricky proposition, and probably not even commercially viable.

However, there is nothing to stop the console makers using an industry-standard operating system: the glimmerings of this new frontier are beginning to appear with the Sega Dreamcast, which is the first (and hopefully not the last) console to use a Microsoft operating system.

The Sega Dreamcast uses Windows CE for the core operating system, with an implementation of DirectX included (unlike the majority of Windows CE machines). This does not make it an emulation of a Windows PC, because the code needs modifications and recompilation—it is not binary compatible—but it certainly eases the process of producing cross-platform products. In theory, a game can be produced for the Dreamcast, and then recompiled with little modification to run on the PC.

How easy this is in practice depends very much on the differences between Windows CE (which was designed from the ground up as a 32-bit operating system) and the desktop Windows family (which is uncharitably referred to as a 32-bit patch on a 16-bit operating system). While it would be great for us developers if all the competing game-machine companies held hands and settled on a common operating system for all their consoles, we should realize this is very unlikely. If they all have the same operating system, then the only thing that differentiates them is their underlying hardware.

This has obvious advantages for Sega. Sega has been having difficulties since the release of the ill-fated 32X expansion for the Sega Genesis (known as the MegaDrive in Europe). Their subsequent console, the Saturn, also foundered in the face of strong competition from Sony's PlayStation and Nintendo's N64.

The other issue that will determine how successful the Dreamcast is (apart from competition from Sony and Nintendo) is the ease of conversion of developed software from PC to Dreamcast. It may not be a simple matter of recompilation: PCs are increasing in power and specifications constantly, whereas a console does not. One of Sega's arguments for the Dreamcast is that titles will always be available for it because of the ease of conversion from PC. This may be fairly easy now, but this clearly will not always be the case. As PCs grow more powerful, the gap between the two systems will widen, and the conversion work will involve a lot more that just a simple recompilation. The principles of scalability (which are discussed later in the book) will alleviate this to some degree, but these principles are only just beginning to be taken up by the more progressive members of the industry.

One of the major difficulties with a new console is the lack of experienced developers. In general, each console has a unique architecture that must be learned by the developer. This knowledge is difficult to come by and rapidly becomes a legacy skill—consoles have a limited lifespan—and nobody wants to back a lame horse by investing their time and energy learning to program a console that will not be successful.

Sega has attempted to give its new console an advantage by making it Win32/DirectX compliant: it is able to tap into the vast numbers of PC developers already in the marketplace. PC-development skills are far more durable than the limited-lifespan skills for console development and are consequently more widespread. If you want to attract new development to your console, then what better way to ensure this than to make use of skills that are already present in abundance?

If this approach were to become more widespread, then this would mean that new games could be released on all game machines simultaneously, given that the developers had taken scalability issues successfully into account.

Unfortunately, this is unlikely to ever happen, because the manufacturers of the consoles would not be happy at losing their exclusivity. One of the factors that made Nintendo so successful is that *Mario* was available only on Nintendo consoles. Not that Nintendo would consider allowing other console companies to use them if they still had a viable console in the marketplace, but there would be nothing to stop third-party developers doing a simultaneous release across all the compatible platforms.

Each manufacturer wants its own console to be the best and most popular. If it is in a powerful enough position to start with (such as that which Sony has attained), then why should it support a common standard when its own will become the de facto standard, assuming that its console is popular enough? This is the approach that Sony appears to be taking with the PlayStation 2, and why shouldn't it? After all, Microsoft has done exactly the same thing with its operating systems.

So far, this discussion has been on a very general level. The next few sections begin to focus on the application of object technology to the development of games.

Use Of Object Technology

Object-oriented techniques have been viewed with suspicion by the games industry. While the rest of the developing world had moved on to C++ and even Java, the games industry generally used C and Assembler for their development right up to a couple of years ago.

The general perception was that C++ wasn't fast enough, and you couldn't tell what it was doing behind the scenes. Game developers liked to know what their compiler was producing and were not at all keen on the fact that C++ produced a lot of extra code behind the scenes to handle the object-oriented nature of the language.

I seem to remember that one of the most common complaints was that virtual functions were slow because they required an extra address lookup. This is true under some circumstances—they do require an extra lookup—but, compared to the amount of other stuff going on in the system, this is no great hardship. In fact, in some cases, an optimizing compiler can optimize this out. But that's not the point: the point is that the people spouting these complaints had never actually programmed using C++, and knew very little about the language except that it was object oriented (whatever *that* was!) and was supposed to be slow because of the extra overhead. These people had very little idea of what a virtual function was, and when and why they are necessary.

Note

Virtual functions are important only when a derived class is accessed through a base class pointer. If this doesn't happen, then most modern compilers will optimize away the "virtualness."

That in itself is not a problem. Many people don't know the ins and outs of virtual functions when it comes down to it. It's nothing to be ashamed of—unless you happen to be one of the people who condemned C++ because virtual functions required lookup tables.

To be fair, at first, C++ was a bit slower than it should have been. The initial compilers were literally just front-ends to C compilers that converted C++ code into an intermediary (and virtually unreadable) C that was then compiled directly by the C compiler. This way of doing things missed out of a whole slew of optimizations that could be performed only by a compiler with built-in knowledge of the object-oriented paradigm. This is why the original C++ compilers were thought to produce code that was fat and slow compared to the C compiler from the same companies.

Optimization: Computer Vs. Human

One of the big skills a game developer needed in the old days was Assembler-level optimization. The compilers could not be trusted to produce the fastest or most efficient code, and so key routines were hand written and optimized in Assembler by skilled programmers. The graphics engine for the original *Quake* was written in this fashion, with id Software hiring Michael Abrash, an industry acknowledged expert in optimization strategies, to perform the task.

Technology has moved on since then, and optimization technologies have become much more advanced. It is still possible for an exceedingly skilled programmer to produce better Assembler output than even the best compiler, but it is very close. In terms of effort per unit time, the compiler wins hands down.

In other words, a skilled developer can produce a faster hand-tuned routine than a compiler in most cases, but the developer will spend a few hours (or longer) and the compiler will spend a few seconds. The difference between the speed of the two routines is likely to be fairly minimal, but the difference in cost is huge.

If you find that you absolutely have to have that hand-tuned Assembler routine, then it is likely to be for one of two reasons: your algorithm is too slow and needs rethinking, or your design is too ambitious.

Note

*You can never say never, but in 999 cases out of 1,000 (*Quake *being the most recent exception), assembly just isn't necessary in modern game development.*

One of the faults of the generic developer is a failure to see the wood for the trees. If a routine is too slow, then he or she immediately thinks in terms of programming optimizations—tweaking and rearranging the code to make it faster.

However, there are two levels of optimization:

- Code optimization—bit twiddling and code tweaking
- Algorithm optimization—investigating a faster algorithm

Code optimization is a lost battle: the computer is rapidly gaining ground on a skilled human, and will soon be on equal par. Of course, a computer cannot simulate human ingenuity, but it is very good at following a complex set of rules, such as those required to efficiently optimize Assembler code.

So, unless you really have no choice, structural optimization is a waste of time: you *can* produce marginally better results than the compiler, but the amount of effort that you have to put in to do so is very great, and possibly too much so to warrant. And, with the advent of multitasking operating systems, all the familiar optimization rules have changed, because you cannot rely on the processor executing your code without being interrupted to go and execute code for someone else. This makes instruction counting and processor cache calculation very difficult. You have to make assumptions about what else the user may be running on the machine.

Fortunately, not all is lost. There is an area of optimization in which (for the foreseeable future) humans will always excel. Algorithmic optimization is something that computers just cannot do. It requires lateral thinking and a spark of ingenuity to redesign an algorithm. In fact, this is now the most effective form of optimization.

Let's consider a simple example of what I mean by algorithmic optimization:

Imagine that I have a list of data that needs to be sorted as quickly as possible.

Initially, in order to get the code working, I implement a BubbleSort. This is a simple sort that compares adjacent elements, and swaps them if they are in the wrong order. It's not very efficient, but it's simple and easy to write (one less thing to go wrong when I'm coding).

When testing, I decide that the sorting code isn't fast enough and that it needs optimization. There is no point in trying to improve the speed of the BubbleSort—the problem lies in the technique. It is an $O(n^2)$ algorithm (read as "Order *n* squared"). That is, for a list containing *n* items, it requires a period of time proportional to the square of *n* to complete. I could optimize this slightly by allowing the sort to terminate when all items are sorted, but this would not improve things as much as I would like.

The obvious thing to do is to select a faster algorithm. Leafing through a handy book of algorithms, I come across a promising-looking search algorithm. It's even got an encouraging name: the QuickSort!

Hoare's QuickSort is a fairly efficient algorithm. Other algorithms perform slightly better, but performance varies according to the nature of the input data. The best case for the QuickSort is $O(n \log n)$, and the worst is $O(n^2)$, the same as the BubbleSort.

This seems like a suitable algorithm, so I replace the BubbleSort with the QuickSort, and perform some timing tests. To my dismay, I find that, although the performance is improved, the performance is nowhere near any of my predictions.

This could be due to any number of reasons, such as the nature of the input data or the difference in structure of the new code. Maybe the old BubbleSort was small enough to fit in the processor cache and take advantage of the boost in memory access speed, but my QuickSort algorithm implementation is too large to benefit from this. Whatever the reason, the end result is the same: it's back to square one.

At this stage, I'm thoroughly fed up with staring at a monitor, so I take a short break in order to clear my head. There's no point in sitting staring at the monitor if I'm stuck. I'll get up and walk around in order to get those analytical juices going while thinking about the nature of the data to be sorted, which is a list of tokens that need to be drawn in *z*-sorted order, as shown in Figure 18.11.

I have realized that I have been sorting it for every frame drawn, and this may not be necessary. The list contains two classes of objects: static tokens and dynamic tokens. In fact, I realize that I need to perform a full sort in only a few circumstances: when the list is created and when the viewing angle changes.

The list needs to be created only once per level. On creation, I already know what is contained within the level, and the static objects do not move, so they will need to be sorted only once.

The user can also change the viewing angle in 90-degree increments. This means that all the static tokens will change their relative distance from the camera, and hence the list will need to be resorted.

This leaves the dynamic tokens to be dealt with. Their *z* coordinate changes as they move, so they will need to modify their position in the list. There are always many more static tokens than dynamic tokens, so I can afford to take more time in dealing with them.

Figure 18.11
Balls!

The optimal solution to this problem is to use a simple insertion sort for the dynamic tokens every frame. At the beginning of each frame, the dynamic tokens insert themselves into the list in the correct position. That is, they iterate through the sorted list of static objects and insert themselves at the correct position to be drawn correctly.

At the end of each frame, the dynamic tokens remove themselves from the list. This proved to be a much faster solution than sorting the entire list, but it still wasn't quite perfect. Too much work remained to be done—particularly in the case of overdraw. Due to the nature of the isometric view, tokens can completely obscure other tokens behind them on screen. On a large level, this meant that as many as 400 tokens were being drawn when they were going to be obscured by other tokens closer to the camera, but this is one of the drawbacks of this technique, known as the "Painter's Algorithm." It is called this because you start drawing at the furthest point from the camera, and closer objects overdraw those behind. This is a very inefficient algorithm.

If I could think of a way to prevent this unnecessary drawing, then the frame rate would be much faster, and the game would spend less time drawing (which was taking up the majority of the time at this stage.)

The solution I chose was to implement a token-based *z*-buffer. To be more efficient, I wanted tokens to fail the *z*-buffer test as often as possible. Failing this test means that they do not have to be drawn.

When I first implemented the test, I did not change the way the tokens were sorted, and it took me approximately twenty minutes to figure out why no tokens were failing the test. Then I remembered that the code used the Painter's Algorithm. I was drawing the tokens in order of decreasing distance from the camera, which meant that they never failed the *z* test.

The solution to this was to simply reverse the order of the sort, which meant that the tokens closest to the camera were drawn first, causing the *z* test to fail with tokens that were further away and obscured.

The net result of all these optimizations was a 90 percent decrease in the average time taken to draw a frame.

The point of all this is to draw attention to the fact that, in most cases, superior optimization can be achieved by looking at your data structures and algorithms. You have more knowledge of your data than it is possible for the compiler to have, and you can make use of this knowledge in order to perform great optimizations.

No compiler on the planet could have performed the optimizations that I performed: A compiler could not have looked at my code and replaced the BubbleSort with a QuickSort. Even if I had spent months hand-coding my original system in highly optimized Assembler, I doubt I could have shaved more than ten percent from the frame-drawing time.

The Pros And Cons Of Abstraction

Abstraction is a method of separating the interface from implementation. This means that all the hard work is going on behind the scenes, and we don't care how it functions as long as it provides a consistent way of using it. This is similar to driving a car: Under the hood, they are all different, but the driving method remains the same. They all have a steering wheel, doors, foot pedals, and wheels.

If we take the previous example on sorting as our starting point, when I needed to replace the sorting algorithm, I could have taken two routes depending on how I had structured the code.

If I had mixed the sorting algorithm in with the code that required it and had coded it specifically for the situation in hand, then I would have had to rip it out and start again. This is not the solution I chose.

All sorts have common features: You want to be able to add a member to the list, delete a member in the list, insert a member in a certain position, iterate through the list, and (obviously) sort the list.

When designing the architecture, I had assumed that I would want to be able to change the sort algorithm with minimal (if any) changes of code. For this reason, I spent some time designing an abstract interface, **ISort**, which allowed all the above operations.

From this base interface, I derived two concrete subclasses, **CBubbleSort** and **CQuickSort**. I used the template support provided by C++ to ensure that these classes were type safe. In a nutshell, templates can be viewed as an advanced form of macro that allow you to define a type-independent skeleton of a class, and then instantiate it where needed for a type-safe version. Any good book on C++ will tell you more about templates and their advantages.

Replacing the sort in my code simply involved me changing one line of code to instantiate a different class and recompiling. This is obviously much less effort than changing a lot of custom-written code. I could have gone one step further: If I had stored the type of sort in an external file and made the code read this configuration file to find out which type of sort to use, then I could have changed the sort type as much as I wanted, without the need to recompile.

One of the chief advantages of this sort of abstraction is the localization of code. A program is much easier to understand in small bite-sized chunks, and object-oriented abstractions allow this sort of partitioning in a natural and easily comprehendible form. When bugs occur, they can be traced more easily because the developer is able to focus on the problem code in isolation, without having to worry so much about what is going on in the background.

This sounds great, but what are the disadvantages? Well, the first is that a good abstraction is hard to do. Object-oriented design skills are very difficult to develop. One of the problems is that it appears to be deceptively easy, but it is not always the case.

Another disadvantage of abstraction—and particularly the more advanced forms of abstraction—is that it can add overhead to a program. For example, by partitioning code into well-separated modules, you lose some opportunities for advanced bit-twiddling optimization (whether performed by the compiler or by an Assembly programmer), but, as I have already stated, I do not consider this to be too much of a drawback.

Another disadvantage is the implementation overhead needed internal to the program in order to manage the object-oriented architecture. This is where the dreaded virtual functions come into play, but unless the developer is going for a soft architecture that is configurable at run time rather than fixed during the compile, then a lot of these can be optimized out by the compiler.

Of course, some moderation is required. It is probably not a good idea to have objects permeating your code all the way down to the tightest inner loop, because the overhead of the object management would begin to become a liability at this level. This begins to touch on the concept of granularity, which will be covered in more detail in the next few chapters.

Chapter 19
Building Blocks

Key Topics:

- ***Reusability in software***
- ***Types of reusability***
- ***Design patterns***
- ***Application of patterns***

Object-oriented design has been successful (at least outside the games industry) for a number of reasons, but chiefly because it allows you to create much larger systems than is traditionally possible using procedural programming techniques.

Statistics show that a program written with a procedural language such as C can reach (on average) approximately 25,000 lines of code before it becomes difficult to maintain due to the size. A similar C++ program can reach upwards of 100,000 lines of code before it succumbs to the same problem. This problem is exacerbated, depending on the number of developers working on the code. (The more developers, the more difficult it is to keep track of all the interacting subsystems of the project.)

Object-oriented design has helped alleviate this problem by providing language-based support for partitioning subsystems. This is all very well, but they're not much good if you don't use them. The best burglar alarm in the world won't help if you leave your back door open.

This chapter discusses the prevalent industry methods for helping to ensure that an object-oriented application doesn't fall victim to these problems. The games industry is not renowned for the use of standard techniques and methodologies (or in fact *any* of the industry standard best-practice measures), but—as I've pointed out in previous chapters—this is mainly due to the reluctance of many developers to use third-party code, preferring instead to "roll their own" wherever possible. And don't even try mentioning formal process to your average hack-meister game programmer!

Even so, even the biggest hacker must be aware that there are many smart people whose expertise is available for use and reuse by an enterprising developer. One of the strengths of the average game developer (if there is such a beast) is that they are generally excellent coders, capable of getting things working quickly. Unfortunately, the prevailing industry winds place much less of an emphasis on doing things properly.

Games are, by nature, very sense oriented. By this, I mean they are designed to stimulate the senses, principally hearing and vision. This emphasis means that coders are under pressure to produce visible (and audible) results quickly, and shortcuts often have to be taken to get the results. Sometimes (in fact, usually) any attempt at a decent underlying architecture gets trampled underfoot in the rush. This state of affairs can be compared to a swan: smooth and beautiful on the surface, and paddling like hell underneath.

I have been fortunate enough to work in both types of environment. I have worked in situations in which the emphasis was on producing results regardless of the method (and they were usually hideous experiences). I have also been in situations in which the customer was happy to let me take the time to do things properly. (This was a much more pleasant situation, and it made for a very rewarding work experience, especially when it came to the integration and maintenance phases of the projects.) In the end, when you take into account the maintenance phases (which are much more unpleasant in a project that has been rushed in the initial stages) the total development time equals out.

If the games industry took the plunge and migrated to this latter mode of development, then it's just possible that development times and bug counts may come down. This chapter is intended to present some of the more advanced concepts of object-oriented designs, and specifically their possible applications within games.

"When a game slips, you're going to need to add features to stay current. The only way to do that, on the programming side, is to take the hit from day one, always doing things correctly instead of doing things quickly."

—Jamie Fristrom of Treyarch talking about Die by the Sword

One reason for the success of the object-oriented paradigm is that it is more aligned to the way we think. Objects are inherently simpler to understand than procedural techniques: areas of functionality can be neatly partitioned and packaged together, isolated from the other subsystems of a project. This is difficult to achieve with procedural programming.

One of the disadvantages of large systems, even when written in an object-oriented language is that sometimes work can be duplicated, even within the same organization. As mentioned in the previous chapter, reinventing the wheel is a common problem.

Object-oriented design allows the developer to package components into reusable modules. This has been one of the holy grails of development for some time and, up until now, has been very difficult to achieve. We are still a long way from achieving it consistently, but, with component-based technology, we are at least on the right track.

Reusability In Software

Reusability is difficult enough to achieve *within* an organization, let alone *among* organizations. How could we possibly achieve reusability throughout the industry?

To know exactly how to tackle this problem, we need to define exactly what we mean by reusability. The two main types of reusability in development are code reuse and design reuse.

Code Reuse

Code reuse is pretty much taken care of in the industry. In some ways, at least. What do I mean by this?

Although the level of code reuse between projects leaves a little to be desired (a lot of unnecessary code is rewritten between projects because it is no longer cool enough or flexible enough to allow for reuse), there is still a surprising level of "unseen" reuse in the industry.

For example, how many developers have produced games based on one of the *Quake* engines? I've lost count of the licensees for these (although they all claim to have performed substantial tweaking under the hood—simple reuse is just not good enough for them!).

But there is an even more fundamental example of reuse that may not be immediately obvious.

Microsoft has provided us with six major releases of DirectX, a multimedia SDK, and each version has been (more or less) compatible with the previous version. This is a remarkable achievement considering the task's level of complexity. Not only did Microsoft provide an API that handles the needs of most game developers, it also made the API flexible enough for use in a wide range of applications. Virtually all PC games in production today make use of DirectX, and this is a prime example of reuse that game developers would do well to remember.

The next step in code reuse is to provide core components for common functionality across projects, and this is what the software factory methodology, described in Chapter 11, is meant to achieve. Case Study 19.1 provides an example argument for reusing engines.

"The data-driven approach worked so well that, through much of our development, Thief *and* System Shock 2 *(two very different games) used the same executable and simply chose a different object hierarchy and data set at run time."*

—Tom Leonard, lead programmer on Thief, *quoted from* Gamasutra, *July 1999*

Code reuse has already been covered, and so the rest of this chapter is going to focus on a more fundamental type of reuse.

Case Study 19.1 Reuse Of Engines

Numerical Design, the company responsible for the game engine, Netimmerse, presented a compelling argument as to the validity of using third-party engines.

According to CEO John Austin, certain key factors impact the life-cycle cost of the average game. His research has found that the cost of developing a proprietary 3D engine for a game takes from between 40 to 70 percent of the total development budget.

Of course, developing your own 3D engine rather than buying one will add substantially to the length of development. Newly developed code has an additional problem: the amount of testing it will have been able to receive is likely to be much less than that for a third-party engine that has already been used in a number of games. The maintenance and development of the engine is handed off to a third party. Moving the maintenance off site (and particularly where more than one group is using the engine) ensures that the engine will develop more stably and rapidly than it would if it were being developed in-house for a single game. In most cases, support for the latest hardware is also added faster than it could be by your in-house development team. More to the point, it is absolutely crucial to the company publishing the engine to be able to keep up with the latest standards. By taking a fully featured engine, right from the start, a large part of the development cycle is short-circuited, allowing the team to get up and running faster.

One of the difficulties with software reuse in general—and particularly in the case of game engines—is knowing at what level to pitch the engine. Too low and it misses many reuse opportunities by forcing developers to rewrite a lot of midlevel boilerplate code; too high a level and you force the developers into a particular genre of game, such as first-person 3D. Obviously, you also benefit from requiring fewer team members, as you already have a 3D engine.

Two types of commercial engine are available for licensing today: the general engine, which provides a good range of cutting-edge features but tends to require more work to use than the second type of engine, which is more specific in its application, such as the *Quake* engine. If the source code is provided with the engine and it is readable, it can be a great help during development. Modifications can be made to the source, and any functionality that is not provided by the basic engine can be added in.

If the cerebral arguments of Mr. Austin don't convince you, then consider the fact that the cost of using the NetImmerse engine is substantially less than the cost in time and money of developing your own. Refer to the NetImmerse Web site (**www.ndl.com**) for further details and a detailed cost breakdown. So far, the NetImmerse engine has been used to reduce the development time for *Prince of Persia 3D* from Red Orb Entertainment.

—Information drawn from the Numerical Design, Ltd., white paper on the business case for using a third-party engine, rather than an in-house effort.

Design Reuse: Patterns

One of the most useful methods of reuse is design reuse. In the computing world, many common problems are solved again and again.

For example, before the introduction of the Standard Template Library (STL) in C++, constructs such as linked lists tended to be rewritten from scratch every time they were needed. Now, for a simple construct such as the linked list, this is not a particular problem. Once a developer has knocked out one batch of linked-list code, writing another is about five minutes of work. But that is not the point. If a developer has already written perfectly good code, why should he or she write it again?

"I remember a conversation with Jon Blossom at a Computer Game Developer conference in which he asked me if we were using STL. I said, "No, we've pretty much internalized how to do a linked list." The very next week I wrote a linked list with a stupid bug. The next day I switched to STL."

—Jamie Fristrom of Treyarch talking about Die by the Sword

It gets worse too. What if the module to be written is more complex? In some cases, especially with game development in the past (and sometimes still today), modules have to be intricately tied in with the application (for speed). Fortunately, this isn't so necessary now, but historical reasons (and prejudices) still cause it to happen.

An experienced game developer will often try to use solutions that have worked well in the past. Unfortunately, this limits game developers to choose solutions that they are familiar with or to design a solution completely from scratch.

For example, what about the situation in which a company decides it wants to write a scripting engine, and the company never needed one before? Does the developer have to do all the work designing the thing from scratch even though other companies and individuals have already written a million and one scripting engines? Using their code is impossible, because that would involve industrial spying and theft on a grand scale (unless the code is free, and that has its own problems). Licensing in a generic scripting engine such as VBScript or the Java runtime wouldn't necessarily be a good idea, either; maybe the requirements aren't as demanding as that, or maybe the licensing fees are too high.

Integrating a fully featured scripting engine such as VBScript would be overkill for even the most ambitious game. So, it looks like our developer has to design and build a scripting engine from scratch, which could be a bit of a problem if he has never written one before. Maybe he could do a search of the Web for a solution, but this is fraught with difficulties. The problem with the Web is that there is no guarantee of the validity of the information you obtain. I've found "definitive" methods of implementing designs on the Web that were fundamentally flawed. Even the newsgroups aren't much help in these cases. Everyone has their own individual "definitive" methods, and trying to pick and choose between them is almost as difficult as trying to understand all the different terminology and variable-quality code samples used to describe them. Interfacing a freely available scripting language such as Python (**www.python.org**) may be one answer, but this also could be too heavyweight for many situations. In any case, Python is included on the accompanying CD-ROM, so you can investigate for yourself.

So how *do* we share fundamental design knowledge? Well, first, we need an easy and consistent way to describe that knowledge to others. One of the most important requirements for good communication is a common language.

One type of answer to this problem is design patterns, a (comparatively) recently developed method for describing optimal design solutions to problems that crop up in everyday development.

One of the most important things to remember as a developer is that you are not alone. In almost all cases, hundreds, if not thousands, of other developers have already faced the technical design decisions that you are going to have to make today, and have already produced optimal solutions. Design patterns are the distillation of this experience into a common form that can be easily understood and applied to your project.

Using design patterns specific to the problem domain you are trying to tackle can help you understand the problem at a fairly high level, and understand the effects it may have on your design before you get down to the tech-level detail.

All this object-oriented design will not have any appreciable impact on the execution speed of a game if the architecture is designed properly. Primarily, the area affected is not in the critical execution path. In any case, with the advanced multithreading operating systems of today, an element of chaos is introduced into program execution. You cannot be sure when your code will execute or what other code the processor will attempt to execute concurrently. The fastest code is still the code that isn't executed, and this can only be achieved with good design.

In this chapter, I will present some common design patterns that are applicable to games and give examples of their application. The discussion will be necessarily brief, but it should whet your appetite to the potential of these techniques for disseminating information. Once you have applied design patterns successfully to a project, the benefits become clear. These solutions have been tried and tested in a wide range of common problems, and as such, they are gold dust to a beleaguered developer. If you wish to read in more detail about design patterns, then the widely acknowledged standard textbook on the subject is *Design Patterns, Elements of Reusable Object-Oriented Software* by Gamma, Helme, Johnson, and Vlissides (the "gang of four"), published by Addison-Wesley.

Where possible for the following design pattern examples, I have used the same terminology as that used in the design patterns book, as there's no point having a common design language if everybody uses different words for the same thing. The design patterns book is obviously tailored towards "serious" application development. The patterns presented here are tailored more towards game development, and I have tried to give examples of uses related to the technical aspects of game development.

Figure 19.1 shows the conventions used in the slightly augmented Object Modeling Technique (OMT) defined by the authors of the design patterns book. These notations and conventions will be used for the examples in this chapter, and I would also recommend using them in your own technical documentation, as they are based on a de facto industry standard, and are hence more accessible than any home-brewed object standards.

The design patterns described here are all suitable for use with a number of common game development problems that you are most likely to be familiar with. However, you may not be used to seeing them presented in this way.

This chapter contains rather more code than I would like it to have. However, in some cases, the easiest way to demonstrate a practical application of a pattern is to supply some sample source code. However, where I have done so, I have also described how the code functions in plain English.

Pattern 1: The Object Factory

The object factory is a class whose sole purpose is to allow the creation of families of objects. This means that the code creating the objects is not tied in specifically to the objects that it is creating. Usually, all the objects created by the factory derive from the same abstract base

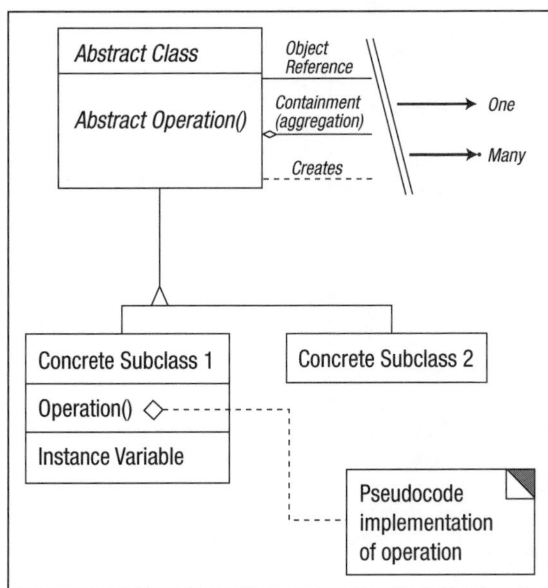

Figure 19.1
Notation for augmented OMT diagrams.

class, and are returned to the requesting client as a reference to this class. You could also have multiple methods, MakeXXXX(), each returning a different base class, but personally I prefer to have one factory per object family.

For example, in *Balls!*, all of the tokens are created by an object factory. Among other things, this makes the loading of levels very simple. Each token type has a unique ID, and loading a level is a simple matter of passing that ID to the object factory, and making use of the pointer returned.

One of the other advantages of this is low-cost garbage collection and memory tracking. The object factory can keep track of all the objects that it allocates, inserting them into a list. When these objects are deleted, they remove themselves from this list. If, at the end of the level, any of these objects have not been freed, then they can either be cleaned up automatically or reported as errors. This helped me find quite a few insidious little bugs in the code.

Figure 19.2 shows the class relationships. This describes how the objects are related to each other programmatically.

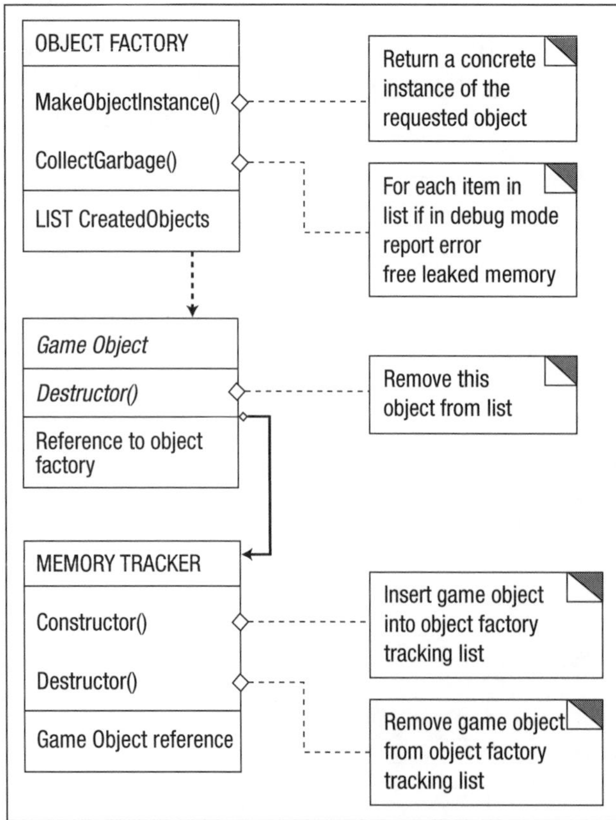

Figure 19.2
Class relationships for the game object factory.

In Figure 19.2, the "game object factory" receives requests from clients to create a specific "game object." This factory class is responsible for creating all objects representing tokens within a level, and keeps track of them by using a related class, the "memory tracker" class. The factory class produces instantiations of the requested object, which are returned to the client as a pointer to the base class of all in-game token classes, the game object class.

The game object class contains a memory tracker class as an instantiated member variable. When a game object class is instantiated, the memory tracker member is also instantiated as part of it. When instantiated, the constructor of this class stores a reference to its owner (the enclosing game object), and inserts itself into the list within the factory class.

When the enclosing game object is deleted, the destructor of the member memory tracker is invoked, which removes the reference to itself from the list within the factory class. When the factory object is itself destroyed, it checks through the list to see if any remaining game objects have not been deleted. These can be either freed automatically, or (preferably) reported as errors, to be tracked down later.

This sort of dynamic object creation is very flexible: with judicious use of the object factory, the structure of whole applications can be determined at runtime. As long as all the objects returned by a specific factory conform to the same interface and behavioral contracts, then it is possible to (for example) configure levels dynamically with fairly simple code, allow customization of the user interface, release game expansions that don't need to modify the original game code, or accomplish any number of tasks that would be tricky by other means.

The code samples in Listings 19.1 and 19.2 show how the object factory can be used and implemented.

Listing 19.1 Client code, which uses an object factory.

```
bool  CLevel::LoadLevel(std::string& strLevelName)
{
    // note: most error checking removed for clarity
    // open file and read header
    CLevelFile lf;
    if (false == lf.Open(strLevelName)
    {
        // report error and return
        return false;
    }

    // loop through file, reading in coordinates and object type
    CVector3D vec3D;                        // 3D vector class
    CGameObject::typObjectType objType;     // object type enumeration
    CGameObject *lpGameObject = NULL;
    For (unsigned int n = 0; n < lf.lfHeader.uiNumberOfObjects; n++)
    {
```

```
        lf.GetObjectDetails(n, objType, vec3D);     // gets detail of object
                                                    // 'n' into objType and
                                                    // vec3D

        // make object and insert it into level object
        lpGameObject = CObjectFactory::MakeObject(objType);
        this->InsertObject(objType, vec3D);         // 'this->' for clarity
    }
    return true;
}
```

This code in Listing 19.1 is an excerpt from the level-loading code. The function takes a name of a level file as a parameter, and uses it to initialize a CLevelFile object, which has the task of loading and parsing the level file.

The routine then loops round, extracting all the relevant details from the level file. The token type is passed to the object factory in order to create the correct object, which is then inserted into the level at the correct coordinates.

Listing 19.2 Factory code.

```
CGameObject *CObjectFactory::MakeObject(CGameObject::typObjectType objType)
{
    // act on requested type
    switch (objType)
    {
    // if it's a normal ball ...
    case CGameObject::typNormalBall:
        {
            // return new normal ball (derived from CGameObject)
            return new CNormalBall();
        }

    // lots more objects here

    // . . .

    // . . .

    default:
        {
            // flag error for unknown object requested and return NULL
            // (another option is to throw an exception)
            return NULL;
        }
    }
}
```

The factory code itself is very simple. It takes an object type as an input, and, if it knows about the type of object, it will return a pointer to a newly constructed instance of that object. If not, it will return a **NULL** pointer, which can be checked for by the client.

Pattern 2: The Singleton

The singleton pattern ensures that only one instance of a particular object can exist in your application.

This can be important in certain applications. For example, in most situations you will want only one systemwide instance of an object factory for a particular family of objects. Another example would be an object wrapping the sound card or the graphics card functionality (given that most machines only have one of each).

The singleton pattern is probably one of the most familiar in use, because it is needed in everyday situations. It's really more of a proto-pattern, because it is a fundamental building block required for other more complex patterns, such as the object factory pattern and the flyweight pattern.

There are several ways to implement the singleton pattern, varying when the object is instantiated. Which one you choose depends on how you expect it to be used.

The most straightforward implementation is the singleton that instantiates on program initialization. Skeleton code for this is shown in Listing 19.3.

Listing 19.3 Singleton that instantiates at program initialization.

```
#include <iostream>          //include stream library

using namespace std;         // so we don't need to put std:: in front of
                             // all uses of the stream library functions

// minimal class - doesn't do anything useful
// instantiation on program initialization
class CSingleton
{
    public:
    // in a multi-threaded system this should be
    // protected with a critical section.
    static CSingleton& GetInstance()
    {
        cout << "Entering CSingleton::GetInstance" << endl;
        cout << "Leaving CSingleton::GetInstance" << endl;
        return ms_sof;
    }

    // function that does something
    void DoSomething()
    {
```

```
        cout << "Doing something" << endl;
    }

    protected:
    // protected constructor
    CSingleton ()
    {
        // initialization
        cout << "CSingleton construction" << endl;
    }
    // single instance
    static CSingleton ms_sof;
};

// define the static member
CSingleton CSingleton::ms_sof;

// usage
void main ()
{
    cout << "main() starting" << endl;
    CSingleton::GetInstance().DoSomething();
    cout << "main() ending" << endl;
}
```

Listing 19.4 Singleton that instantiates on first use.

```
#include <iostream>         //include stream library

using namespace std;        // so we don't need to put std:: in front of
                            // all uses of the stream library functions

// minimal class - doesn't do anything useful
// instantiation on program initialization
class CSingleton
{
    public:
    // in a multi-threaded system this should be
    // protected with a critical section.
    static CSingleton& GetInstance()
    {
        // instantiated on first call of GetInstance
        // in a multi-threaded system this should be
        // protected with a critical section.
        cout << "Entering CSingleton::GetInstance" << endl;
        static CSingleton sSof;
```

```
        cout << "Leaving CSingleton::GetInstance" << endl;
        return sSof;
    }

    // function that does something
    void DoSomething()
    {
        cout << "Doing something" << endl;
    }

    protected:
    // protected constructor
    CSingleton ()
    {
        // initialization
        cout << "CSingleton construction" << endl;
    }
    // single instance
    static CSingleton ms_sof;
};


// usage
void main ()
{
    cout << "main() starting" << endl;
    cout << "First call" << endl;
    CSingleton::GetInstance().DoSomething();
    cout << "Second call" << endl;
    CSingleton::GetInstance().DoSomething();
    cout << "main() ending" << endl;
}
```

The code in Listing 19.3 shows the implementation of a singleton that instantiates when the program containing it first initializes. This would be more useful in the circumstances in which the instantiation of the singleton could be expected to take some time. Consequently, it would be desirable to prepare it before it is needed. The static modifier indicates that only one instance of the **CSingleton** exists. Because it is a member of the class, it will be instantiated when the program is started.

Listing 19.4 shows a first-use instantiation singleton class. Because the static **CSingleton** is declared as part of the **GetInstance()** function, it will be instantiated only when that function is first called. This is best suited for situations in which it is acceptable to defer the initialization of the singleton. An example would be for a class that reads and writes a configuration or data file. You would want only one access at a time to such a file, and the time it would take (and the circumstances where it would be used) are not very significant.

The outputs from the two listings are subtly different.

Listing 19.3 produces:

```
CSingleton construction
main() starting
First Call
Entering CSingleton::GetInstance
Leaving CSingleton::GetInstance
Doing something
Second Call
Entering CSingleton::GetInstance
Leaving CSingleton::GetInstance
Doing something
main() ending
```

Listing 19.4 produces:

```
main() starting
First Call
Entering CSingleton::GetInstance
CSingleton construction
Leaving CSingleton::GetInstance
Doing something
Second Call
Entering CSingleton::GetInstance
Leaving CSingleton::GetInstance
Doing something
main() ending
```

In the first set of output, the constructor of the singleton is called before the **main()** function is called. In the second, however, it is clear that the constructor of the singleton is not called until the **DoSomething()** member is called. Hence, if your program does not call **DoSomething()**, then the singleton will never be instantiated.

This is the advantage of the second approach. With instantiation upon demand, the singleton isn't instantiated if it is not used. For a trivial singleton such as this, this is not a problem, but most singletons will not be so lightweight. This could make a difference to the startup time and runtime memory footprint of projects that make extensive use of singletons.

Pattern 3: The Flyweight

The flyweight pattern is often used in conjunction with a singleton. The flyweight allows the user to instantiate multiple instances of a class, which all refer to a common component, shared between them all. Only individual configuration data is stored within the flyweight object.

In *Balls!*, the flyweight pattern is used to manage the graphics. Each graphic object is a singleton that contains the frames of animation, and the individual token classes contain references to the graphic objects, as well as independent state information to allow them to be rendered correctly to the screen. This is shown in the code snippet in Listing 19.5.

Listing 19.5 Use of the flyweight pattern.

```
// simple use of a flyweight
class CStarGraphic : public CGameGraphic
{
    public:
    CStarGraphic();
    virtual ~CStarGraphic();

    protected:
        // flyweight part (unique for each instance)
        CVector2D m_vec2DscreenPosition;


        // shared among all instances of this class
        static CFrame m_frStar;
};
```

In Listing 19.5, the static qualifier on the **CFrame** member variable indicates that there is only one instance of this variable shared among all instances of the class.

Hence, each flyweight object contains a reference to the singleton graphics object and has its own local copy of state variables such as position and other internal variables. Figure 19.3 shows how this concept works.

The flyweight pattern has the advantage of saving machine resources (which are limited on even on the most powerful machines). Obviously, sharing one copy of a resource can alleviate this problem. This technique is applicable only to read-only resources. It's no good if you want to make local modifications to the global resource.

In *Balls!*, this was a requirement for some situations, and it was dealt with by the provision of a deep cloning mechanism that allowed a temporary copy to be made of the underlying resource. This is useful only in some circumstances, however, and is an extension to—rather than an integral part of—the flyweight pattern.

Pattern 4: The Chain Of Responsibility

This pattern sets up a chain of objects that receive notification of an event in order to avoid direct coupling between an event signaler and a whole slew of interested objects. It allows all of the objects in the chain to have a chance at handling that event.

Several ways can be used to implement the chain of responsibility. Two of these are linked to the class hierarchy and the object (runtime) hierarchy respectively.

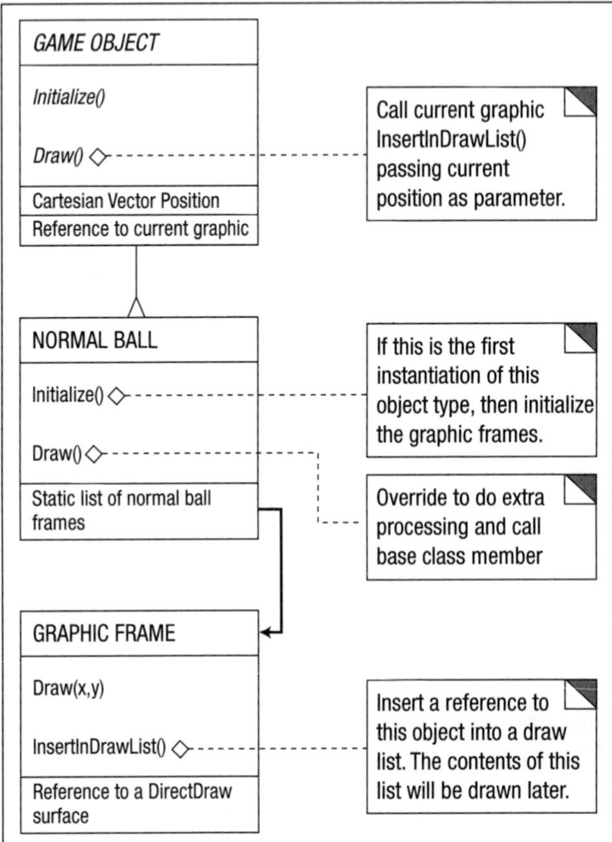

Figure 19.3
Class relationships for a generic game object.

Whichever you choose to use depends on the particular circumstances. Let's look at each of these mechanisms in turn. The first option (based around the class hierarchy) is used for the propagation of events in *Balls!*

A sample class hierarchy is shown in Figure 19.4. This shows how the "hot ball" is derived from the root-level game object.

The CHotBall class derives from the CBall class, which in turn derives from the CGameObject class. Each of these classes has functionality that become more specific the farther down the class hierarchy the object is. Here, the CGameObject class knows how to react to gravity, the CBall class knows how to behave like a simple ball, and the CHotBall class knows how to be hot. Specifically, each class adds upon the functionality of the base class with increasingly specialized behaviors.

In the game world, each token receives events and generates events based on its reaction to those it received. To facilitate this, each token's class has a member function **HandleEvent()**

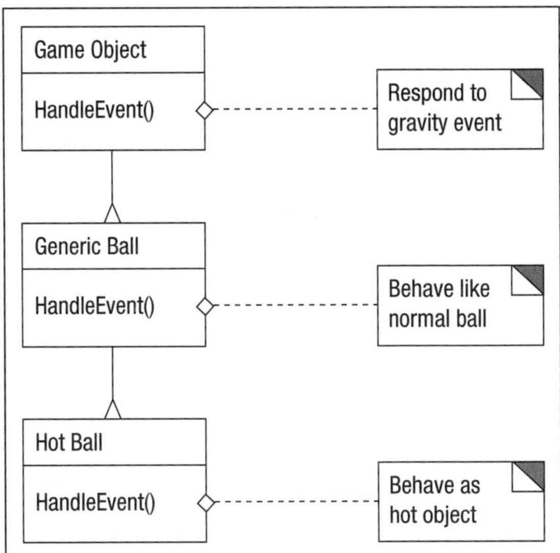

Figure 19.4
Sample class hierarchy for tokens in *Balls!*

that (eponymously) calculates how the token reacts to an event, changes the internal state of the token, and broadcasts any new events that may have been generated by this reaction.

Take the specific case that the hot ball receives a collision event with cold property. This is just the "techie" way of saying that the hot ball hits something cold. The first event handler that gets the chance to react to this is the hot ball's handler. It looks at the event and its properties, finds that it has hit something cold, and sets its internal state to "cooling."

Then, because it hasn't handled the actual collision event and only the properties accompanying the event, it gives the base class a chance to handle this part of the event. Fortunately, the ball's handler knows how to collide and rebound, and so it handles the event. Now all the events have been handled, there is no more work to do, and the chain terminates.

It is possible to design chains that require all members to have a chance at responding. Although this sometimes makes for cleaner code, it can be slower than terminating earlier. In general, you need to balance the decision by deciding whether speed is required, or whether you prefer maintainable code. In the case of *Balls!*, I got the best of both worlds. I designed it so that I could keep the code clean and cut short the chain when the event had been handled. This was possible because each derived class specialized the base class in a very specific way, and there was no overlap in functionality, which is the usual cause of difficulty resulting from attempting to optimize this pattern.

The main disadvantage of linking the chain directly with the class hierarchy is the inflexibility. The chain is fixed at compile time rather than at runtime. In many circumstances, you will want to be able to modify this chain during the course of execution, inserting members here, deleting members there, and maybe even changing the order that members appear in the list.

A trivial example: you are writing a role-playing game with a party of four adventurers (something like *Dungeon Master*, the original 3D role-playing game initially released on the Atari ST and Amiga computers), and you decide you want to implement their ability to react to events by their reaction time. You could do this by inserting each of the party members into a chain of responsibility in decreasing order of ability. In this fashion, the party member with the highest reactions in combination with the best positioning gets the first chance to react, and so on, down to the party member with the lowest reactions combined with the worst positioning getting the raw end of the deal.

This would be very difficult to implement using the class-based system, because that relies on a fixed hierarchical relationship between tokens. It would be very poor coding if we required each of our party member tokens to be derived from another in order to implement a chain of command. This would mean a very fixed and rigid game. And there's another problem: imagine that the slowest member of the team finds an agility potion that, when drunk, boosts his reactions to superhuman levels. How would we modify the chain of responsibility in order to allow him to react first?

This is where the second way of implementing a chain of responsibility becomes useful. For the runtime implementation, each token that is interested in a specific event adds itself into a linked list that forms the chain. In the example mentioned above, when the heroic (but slow) team member drinks the performance-enhancing potion, he can change his position in the chain in order to be notified before the others in the chain of any incoming events. When the potion wears off, the character can be restored to his rightful place in the chain. This is shown in more detail in Figure 19.5.

Another good use for the chain of responsibility pattern is in the building of a filter system. Let's assume that you have a large list of objects that you want to apply a number of filters to and that you may wish to dynamically configure these filters at runtime. Obvious

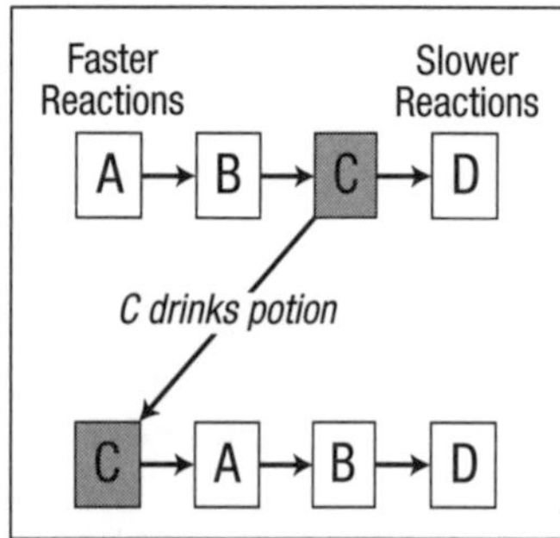

Figure 19.5
A runtime configurable chain of responsibility for a hypothetical role-playing game.

applications for this technique include various types of polygon filtering for 3D engines, but I'm going to discuss a far simpler example here. In fact, it won't even involve computers.

Assume that you have been given a large bag of multicolored blocks. These blocks are of various configurations (tetrahedral, cubic, and so on) and made of different materials.

If we wanted to apply a filter to the contents of the bag—say, for example, to take out all except green blocks—then we would sit down and examine the blocks in the bag, one by one, until we had discarded all except the green ones.

Now let's say that we are given another similar bag containing a similar random selection of blocks. This time we are asked to apply two filters. We are asked to extract all except the cubic green blocks. Traditionally, in computer programming, we would tackle this by examining each object and discarding it if it was "NOT (cubic AND green)".

This is an example of Boolean logic. While this may fine for a fairly simple example such as this, what if we were then asked to apply a much more complex filter? Maybe we are asked to remove all except those that have six or more faces, are made of plastic, and are green. We also need to consider that we may be asked to change our filter criteria at any moment. Would we construct a Boolean logic statement for each possible combination of filters and then hard code them into our application. Well, I suppose we could, but, to be honest, I'd rather not, and I'd certainly not employ anyone who did.

If we had to do this in real life, it's possible that we could sift through the bag and examine each shape one at a time to see if it fit the requirements. This would be tedious and time consuming and not much fun at all, even if you liked playing with shapes. On the other hand, if we got two friends to help us, then the job would be much simpler.

We could stand in a chain formation. The person at the head of the chain would hold the bag and remove the objects one by one. He would be responsible for checking the easiest of the rejection criteria. This means that many objects would be discarded with the minimal amount of effort. In our case, the easiest feature to determine is the color. As he takes the shapes out of the bag, he checks the color. If it is green, he passes it along to his friend; otherwise, he discards it. Note that it's possible that color isn't the best criterion to observe. It does depend on the relative distribution of object criteria among the objects. For example, if there are a low proportion of plastic objects, it may be easier to reject objects on whether they are plastic before considering color. In a development situation, this will depend on prior knowledge of the data set you wish to filter.

For this example, we will assume that there are equal distributions, so that color is the easiest to spot. Our friend who has been handed the green object now checks to see if the object is made of plastic. If it is not plastic, he discards it, or else he passes it along to the last person in the chain, who counts the faces. By being the last in the chain, he will receive the smallest amount of objects.

Counting the faces is probably the hardest job of all, so it makes sense to try to remove as many objects as possible in order to minimize the amount of objects that need to be examined.

This last person counts the number of faces. If any objects have six or more faces, he places them to one side; otherwise, they are discarded.

This specialization of roles allows the filtering to take place much more efficiently than it could if the same person was looking at each object for all three criteria at the same time. More relevant is that, by implementing a chain of responsibility with each link in the chain responsible for a particular criterion, the code becomes much more manageable, understandable, and (more importantly) flexible than it would be if the standard monolithic approach had been taken.

Pattern 5: The Iterator And Reverse Iterator

The iterator and reverse iterator are patterns that are deceptive in their simplicity. The iterator's apparent simplicity belies an astoundingly flexible and useful construct.

Iterators and reverse iterators allow the developer to dramatically simplify and generalize algorithms that rely on iterating through a list of items without any great loss of speed.

The excerpt in Listing 19.6 shows how an iterator and a reverse iterator would be defined for a simple class. Note that the implementation of the classes is removed for brevity and clarity, but you should be able to follow the code.

Listing 19.6 Use of the iterators.

```
#include <iostream>
using namespace std;

////////////////////////////////////////////////////////////////////////////
// iterator abstract base class
// acts as interface for ALL iterators
////////////////////////////////////////////////////////////////////////////
template <class TItem> class IIterator
{
public:
    virtual void First() = 0;
    virtual void Next() = 0;
    virtual bool IsEnd() = 0;
    virtual TItem CurrentItem() = 0;
};

////////////////////////////////////////////////////////////////////////////
// class header for list class demonstrating
// use of iterators
////////////////////////////////////////////////////////////////////////////
```

```
template <class TItem> class CList
{
// public functions
public:
    // constructor
    CList(){};
    // destructor
    ~CList(){};
    // insert a list item
    bool Insert(TItem listItem);
    // get a list item
    TItem Get(unsigned int index);

    // iterator base class
    class CListIterator : public IIterator<TItem>
    {
    public:
        CListIterator(CList<TItem>& list);
    protected:
        CList<TItem>& m_list;
        void* operator new(size_t nSize);
        void operator delete(void * vpToDelete, size_t nSize);
    };

    // forward iterator
    class CForwardIterator : public CListIterator
    {
    public:
        CForwardIterator(CList<TItem>& list);
        void First();
        void Next();
        bool IsEnd();
        TItem CurrentItem();
    };

    // forward iterator
    class CReverseIterator : public CListIterator
    {
    public:
        CReverseIterator(CList<TItem>& list);
        void First();
        void Next();
        bool IsEnd();
        TItem CurrentItem();
    };
};
```

```
///////////////////////////////////////////////////////////////////////////////
///////////////////////////////////////////////////////////////////////////////
template <class TItem> void IterateTest(IIterator<TItem>& it)
{
    for (it.First(); !it.IsEnd(); it.Next() )
    {
        // this works as long as the class represented by TItem supports the <<
        // operator, or there'll be a compile error.
        cout << it.CurrentItem() << endl;
    }
}

///////////////////////////////////////////////////////////////////////////////
///////////////////////////////////////////////////////////////////////////////
void main(void)
{
    // declare list of ints and two iterators
    CList<int> iLstTest;
    CList<int>::CForwardIterator fIt(iLstTest);
    CList<int>::CReverseIterator rIt(iLstTest);

    // fill list
    for (int i = 0; i < 10; i ++)
    {
        iLstTest.Insert(i);
    }

    // forward iteration
    IterateTest<int>(fIt);

    // reward iteration
    IterateTest<int>(rIt);
}
```

Listing 19.6 is quite a big chunk of code to take in all in one go. I'll break the class declaration down into smaller parts as I discuss it in order to make it clearer.

The first part of the code is the class declaration for the list itself, CList. This is a very simple list class (almost useless, in fact), with the obvious **Insert()** and **Get()** members that allow insertion and retrieval of list members. Inserting an object tacks it onto the end of the list, and specifying an index can retrieve an object. This is not a very good way of accessing the list, but how do you specify which *type* of object goes into the list? The template parameter **TItem** allows customization of this list to a specific object type. (I'm not going to go into detail about how that works here. If you want to know the details, get yourself a good book on C++.)

Outside of the list class declaration, an iterator abstract base class is defined. This defines the interface for an iterator and allows iterators for all collection classes (not just lists, as shown here) to be referred to by a common base class. Two concrete iterators follow, **CForwardIterator** and **CReverseIterator**, defined within the CList class, that allow forward and reverse iteration through the list using the **First()**, **Next()**, and **IsEnd()** members that move to the first item in the list and the next member in the list, and test to see if the end of the list has been reached.

A template function, **IterateTest()**, takes an iterator interface as a parameter and uses that iterator to step through the list, displaying each list member as it does so.

The test program demonstrates this by instantiating an integer list and then iterating through it twice using a forward and a reverse iterator.

The output of the program is as follows:

```
Forward iteration
0, 1, 2, 3, 4, 5, 6, 7, 8, 9

Reverse iteration
9, 8, 7, 6, 5, 4, 3, 2, 1, 0
```

The main benefit of the iterator class is to efficiently allow iteration through a collection of objects. The iterator doesn't necessarily have to just iterate forwards or backwards. For example, I could create an iterator that will iterate through a list of game objects, and returns them in order of distance from the camera. This means that a standard set of generic algorithms could be used to process a collection of objects in a number of different ways.

Pattern 6: The Template And Strategy Methods

The template and strategy methods are discussed because they are fundamentally similar. The strategy method allows the dynamic selection of entire algorithms while the template method allows a finer grain of replacement: individual parts of a generic algorithm can be replaced.

For example, a computer-controlled character in a fighting game could use the strategy method to allow for differing fighting styles. This would allow the coders to implement a generic fighter controller class to be used among all computer-controlled characters and just attach new fighting strategies at runtime to customize the individual characters. This would promote good code reuse within the project, and it efficiently segregates code into well-defined modular compartments. Figure 19.6 shows how this could work.

In our fighting-game example, the strategy method could be extended to provide more modules to allow fighting styles to vary with different levels of aggression. However, this is probably not advised. It would produce a large number of classes per fighting style, and these would be difficult to manage and maintain.

A finer level of graduation can be obtained by the use of the template method, which can be used in combination with the coarser strategy method if necessary. The different fighting styles can be selected using the strategy method, and individual variations within the style (such as those caused by differing aggression levels) can be applied by using the template method as shown in Figure 19.7. Pattern 12, the state method could also be used for this too.

The template method is used extensively throughout *Balls!* Despite its name, it is not implemented using templates, the C++ mechanism for allowing generic-type independent implementations of algorithms. It is called the *template method* because, although the base

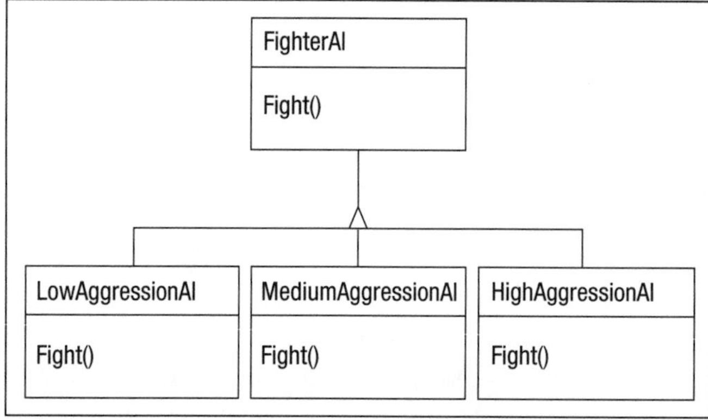

Figure 19.6
Class diagram for the strategy method applied to a fighting game.

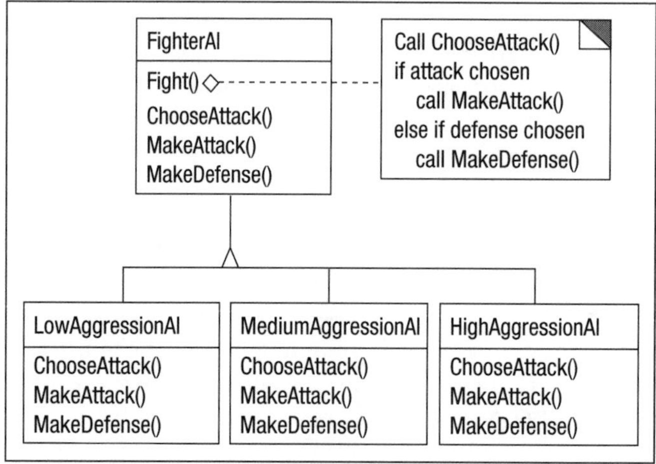

Figure 19.7
Class diagram for the template method applied to a fighting game.

class defines the order of the steps of an algorithm, the derived classes are free to change the individual steps in the algorithm (albeit in a consistent fashion with the rest of the algorithm).

To implement this, an algorithm is split up into a number of parts, and each part is implemented as a virtual function. This allows subclasses to specialize each aspect of the algorithm, even though the algorithm itself is used in the base class. To see how this works in more detail, take a look at Listing 19.7.

Listing 19.7 Use of the template method.

```
class CGraphicObject
{
public:
    // template method Draw() defines a skeleton for the
    // graphic object drawing algorithm and requires
    // the individual steps to be defined by subclasses
    bool Draw()
    {
        // see if we need to draw the token
        if (true == NeedToDraw() && true == CheckAndSetZBuffer())
        {
            // insert this object into the draw list
            return InsertIntoDrawList();
        }

        // not necessary to draw token
        return false;
    }

    // insert this token into the draw list
    void InsertIntoDrawList();

protected:
    // signatures of templates to be overridden

    // defined in derived classes: returns false
    // if it is not necessary to draw this object
    virtual bool NeedToDraw() = 0;

    // defined in derived classes: returns false
    // if this object fails a z buffer test
    virtual bool CheckAndSetZBuffer() = 0;
};
```

Listing 19.7 is an excerpt from the *Balls!* graphics-rendering framework. Each derived class gets the opportunity to override the two pure virtual functions, **CheckAndSetZBuffer()** and **NeedToDraw()** that are called in the Draw() base class concrete function in order to take into account the shape, size, and transparency of both themselves and other objects that may need to be drawn.

Pattern 7: The Observer

The observer pattern allows a one-to-many dependency between objects so that, when the observed object changes in some way, all the observers can be notified as and when this happens.

For example, let's assume that we are writing a realtime strategy game that requires a minimap to display troop units over a wide area, and also display them in a standard playing area in a zoomed-in part of the minimap, rather like that used in *Warcraft II*.

Furthermore, assume that we want to be able to filter out certain units on our minimap, such as nonmilitary units. Classically, this sort of object interaction has involved tight coupling between the units and the views. This means that it can be quite laborious and time consuming to add in new units. Object orientation is also violated, which increases the difficulty of understanding and maintaining the architecture.

The observer pattern (also known as the publish-subscribe model) could be used as a method of implementing this, without violating the object-oriented nature of the system.

The object representing the minimap is the observer. It observes all the units in the game. Each unit registers with the minimap, allowing itself to be observed. The minimap is notified when there is a change in unit state, for example, if the position changes. The minimap then uses this information to display the state of the game world. In the case of our realtime strategy game, the minimap will be the graphical representation of the game world token (discussed in Chapter 17).

The minimap itself is then in turn observed by the main view. The viewing window is defined by a small rectangle on the minimap that can be dragged around by the player.

When the view position is changed on the minimap, then the main view is notified and is sent a list of the contents of the view. This chain of notification is a very efficient method of information transferal without violating the object-oriented tenets.

This system is shown in Figure 19.8.

In some ways, this is similar to the chain-of-responsibility pattern, except that, in this case, there is usually only one level of interaction rather than a long chain. The chain of command is usually used with a long sequence of one-to-one, or one-to-a-few interactions, while the observer pattern is used as a means of propagating information in a one-to-many model, while abstracting the interactions between objects, thus reducing their coupling.

One of the disadvantages of the observer pattern is that the object being observed has no way of knowing who is observing it. Although this allows the integrity of the object-oriented system to be maintained, it reduces the possibility of filtering at source to prevent too many messages being sent out.

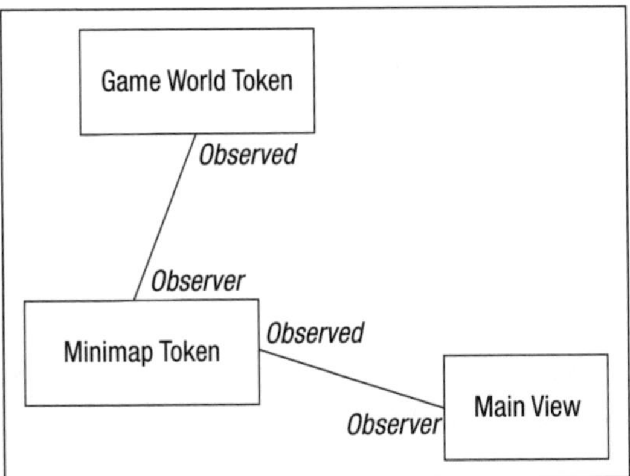

Figure 19.8
Implementation of a network of observers.

In a real situation, such as writing a game, the need to maintain the object-oriented nature of the system must be balanced with the need for speed. This should be done very carefully however, because, if this is used indiscriminately, you'll end up causing more problems than the observer pattern solves. In the case of our strategy game, I would make use of this by loosely coupling the main view and the minimap, so that the minimap could apply a filter on the information it sends to the main view. In this way, the main view would receive information only on tokens visible within the view. This would be achieved by allowing the main view to subscribe with a filter condition, possibly by passing in a filter object that could be used by the minimap notification mechanism to determine which information to send to the main view.

The minimap could of course perform its own filtering, but this would be inefficient. Many more messages than necessary would be sent, and the minimap knows the position of the main view anyway, and hence can legitimately perform the filtering. This filtering can also be performed with a chain-of-responsibility construct.

Pattern 8: The Command

The command pattern allows the encapsulation of commands. Commands can be passed around as objects.

An event is encapsulated as an object and is passed around by means of a reference to this object. This piece of technical trickery allows us to implement command queues and undoable lists. This pattern can also be used in conjunction with other patterns such as the chain of responsibility, the state pattern, and the object factory.

Let's look at some examples. In many current games, the trend is to implement AI by using scripts. This has become more feasible because of the increase of processing power. The AI is traditionally the most complex part of a game. Producing a good AI is very much an art form, and generally requires a lot of tweaking and manipulating in order to get it working properly. If this is all hard coded, then there are many tweak-recompile-test cycles to achieve. By scripting the AI, the compilation phase can be cut from this cycle.

By using scripting engines in this manner, the AI can be updated and maintained much more flexibly. If the script-updating system is designed to be user friendly, then people with no programming knowledge can perform the scripting modification. This allows a much more hands-on approach from the game designers, removing a layer of indirection from the route between the game designers and the game itself.

To implement this, the scripts can be supplied in a text file and used in conjunction with an object factory to create the command objects specified in the text file and the linkages between them.

This approach is useful for sequences of commands like those that might script complex behaviors such as those that deal with animation or behavioral sequences.

For example, the commands can be used in conjunction with the state patterns to implement dynamic finite-state machines (FSMs), which are the principal techniques used to implement convincing AI in games. FSMs were discussed in some detail in Chapter 17.

Figure 19.9 show how this system could be implemented using commands.

In *Balls!*, I designed the player avatar to be controlled by command objects. This means that these commands can originate from a number of sources. The first, and most obvious, would be from user input. The other sources of command are the demo-mode player module and the network proxy module, which accepts input from a player across the network.

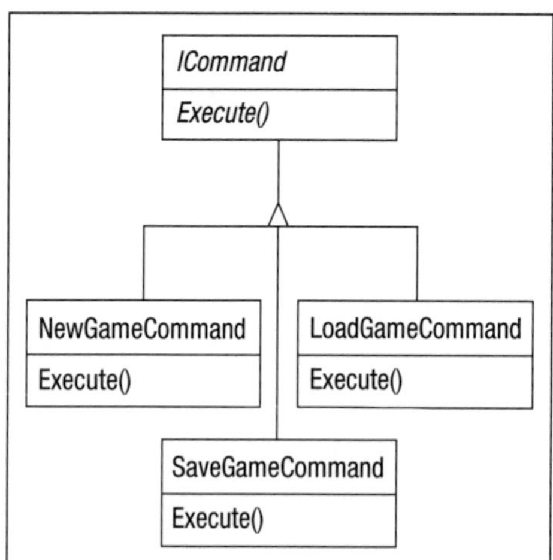

Figure 19.9
Class diagram for the command pattern.

Note

For fast-action twitch games, using network proxies to relay player-input information is not a reliable technique if used on its own. Some sort of dead-reckoning algorithm and/or guaranteed messaging should be used to take into account the possibility of high network transmission times and lost messages.

All *Balls!* command-object providers adhere to a common interface and are isolated in components that are enumerated at runtime. This makes the possibility of adding in other controllers at a later stage. Granted, this may not be that useful for input controllers (most of which are taken care of by DirectInput anyhow), but this was intended as a dry run of the dynamic enumeration process. This general technique can be applied in other areas of game design, and one example that immediately springs to mind would be to add new game tokens. *Creatures* and *Creatures 2* from Cyberlife use a similar approach to dynamically add new objects into their simulated world.

Another use for the command pattern is to implement a menu skeleton system Let's face it: most games use menus in one form or another, and although menu code is generally considered to be fairly easy to write, it is constantly rewritten, project after project. Developers talk of knocking up the menu code in a few days or, in some (rather exaggerated) cases, 10 minutes.

If the command pattern is applied to this problem, then you can build a menu framework that is reusable from project to project. This could be achieved by allowing the client software (the game) to register a menu structure (perhaps contained within a text file, specifying menu links and graphics) with the menuing system, and registering a series of game specific commands derived from a menuing system provided interface, such as **IMenuCommand**, which would have the method **Execute()**. When a menu item is selected, the command is executed and the game knows how to respond to the request.

Okay, so this will take longer to write initially than just hacking out the menu code, but it provides a reusable module that can be used across all your products. In the long term, this will save a lot of time and money.

Pattern 9: The Decorator

The decorator is a formalization and extension of a wrapper class, with which everybody should be familiar. A wrapper class wraps an interface around another class, in order to provide extra functionality that is not provided in the wrapped class.

This could also be done using straightforward inheritance, but this is not always desirable. The larger and more branched the class hierarchy, the more difficult it is to understand. Sometimes, we would wish to be able to customize our classes to a very fine level, and, in these cases, the decorator pattern is often more flexible and efficient than just subclassing for every possible combination of features we would require.

Let's look at an example of how this could be used. In *Starcraft*, the user interface is customized depending on the type of unit that you play. For the Terrans, the user interface is very mechanical and based on near-future technology; for the Zerg, the interface is an organic living entity; and, for the Protoss, the interface is a very ethereal and high-concept implementation. These three interfaces are shown in Figure 19.10.

Now, it's very unlikely that the *Starcraft* implements these interfaces using the decorator pattern, but if I were going to implement a similar system, then I would use this system to do it. The basic user interface, showing common features such as the map and the main view screen, would be "decorated" using three decorator classes that apply the individual user interface as shown in Figure 19.11.

Listing 19.8 shows a skeleton that could be used to implement this.

Listing 19.8 Use of decorators.

```
#include <iostream>
using namespace std;
/////////////////////////////////////////////////////////////////////
// plain user interface class
/////////////////////////////////////////////////////////////////////
class CUserInterface
{
public:
    void DrawPlayField()    // draw the playing area
    {
        cout << "Drawing playing field" << endl;
    }
};


/////////////////////////////////////////////////////////////////////
// decorator interface
/////////////////////////////////////////////////////////////////////
class IDecorator
{
public:
    // draw decorated interface
    virtual void Draw() = 0;
protected:
    virtual void DrawDecoration() = 0; // pure virtual
};

/////////////////////////////////////////////////////////////////////
// decorator base class
/////////////////////////////////////////////////////////////////////
class CDecorator : public IDecorator
{
```

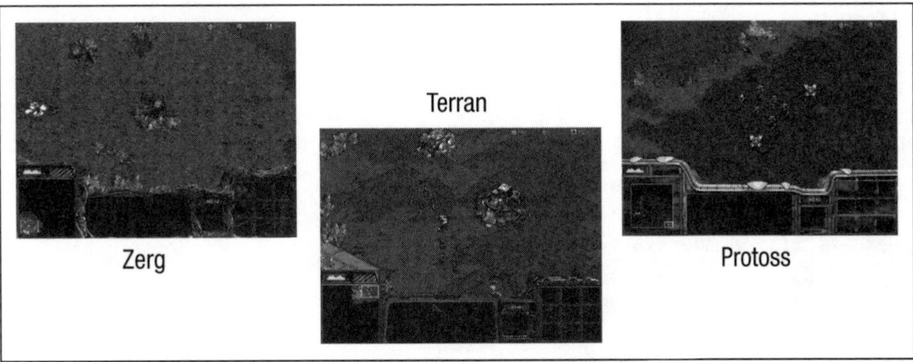

Figure 19.10
The *Starcraft* user interfaces.

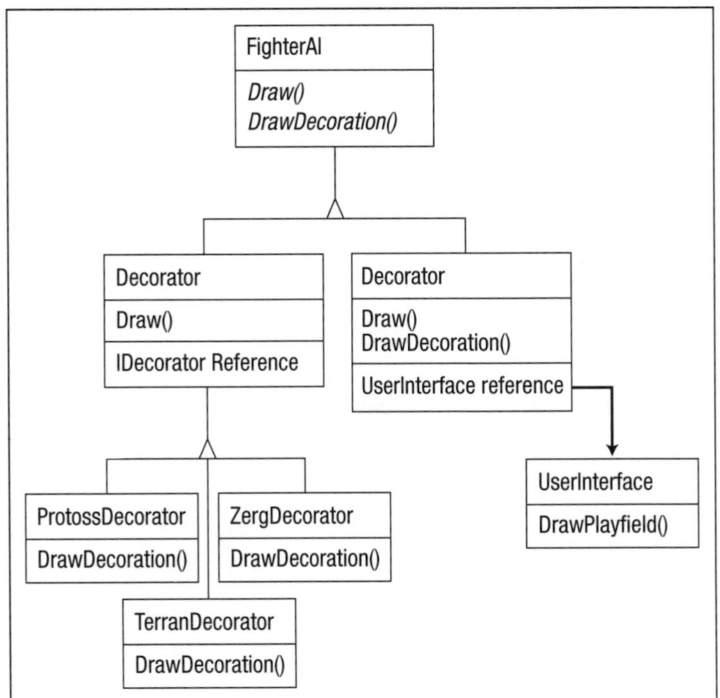

Figure 19.11
Using the decorator pattern to implement a variable user interface.

```
public:
    CDecorator(IDecorator& decorator)
    : m_decorator(decorator)
    {}
    // draw decorated interface
    void Draw()
    {
        // draw member variable decorator
        m_decorator.Draw();
        // draw decoration for this object
        DrawDecoration();
    }
protected:
    // member variable
    IDecorator& m_decorator;
};

//////////////////////////////////////////////////////////////////////
// root user interface decorator
//////////////////////////////////////////////////////////////////////
// The root that accepts the initial object to be decorated.
// This is a simple example of the adaptor pattern
// (Design Patterns book, page 139)
//////////////////////////////////////////////////////////////////////
class CRootDecorator : public IDecorator
{
public:
    CRootDecorator(CUserInterface& userInterface)
    : m_userInterface(userInterface)
    {}
protected:
    void DrawDecoration()
    {
        Draw();
    }
    // draw decorated interface
    void Draw()
    {
        m_userInterface.DrawPlayField();
    }

    CUserInterface& m_userInterface;
};

//////////////////////////////////////////////////////////////////////
// zerg user interface decorator
```

```
///////////////////////////////////////////////////////////////////////
class CZergDecorator : public CDecorator
{
public:
    CZergDecorator(IDecorator& decorator)
    : CDecorator(decorator)
    {}
protected:
    void DrawDecoration()
    {
        cout << "Drawing zerg decorations" << endl;
    }
};

///////////////////////////////////////////////////////////////////////
// terran user interface decorator
///////////////////////////////////////////////////////////////////////
class CTerranDecorator : public CDecorator
{
public:
    CTerranDecorator(IDecorator& decorator)
    : CDecorator(decorator)
    {}
protected:
    void DrawDecoration()
    {
        cout << "Drawing terran decorations" << endl;
    }
};

///////////////////////////////////////////////////////////////////////
// protoss user interface decorator
///////////////////////////////////////////////////////////////////////
class CProtossDecorator : public CDecorator
{
public:
    CProtossDecorator(IDecorator& decorator)
    : CDecorator(decorator)
    {}
protected:
    void DrawDecoration()
    {
        cout << "Drawing protoss decorations" << endl;
    }
};

///////////////////////////////////////////////////////////////////////
```

```
// example of use. Obviously in reality, it's
// slightly more complex than this(!)
////////////////////////////////////////////////////////////////////
void main()
{
    // user interface
    CUserInterface userInterface;

    // user interface adaptor (this makes the code more flexible
    // for extensions)
    CRootDecorator rootDecorator(userInterface);

    // let's assume we want to be terran,
    // but we could have a switch statement here
    CTerranDecorator terranDecorator(rootDecorator);

    //draw user interface
    terranDecorator.Draw();
}
```

The code in Listing 19.8, although it looks fairly complex, is actually quite simple.

The **main()** routines sets up an undecorated user interface object, **CUserInterface**, and adapts it to conform to the decorator interface using the **CRootDecorator** object. This performs no explicit decoration of the user interface, except to allow the user interface to be used as a decorator. This simplifies the coding and makes the implementation more flexible. This technique is an example of the adapter pattern, which is discussed more fully in the software patterns book. You may ask why I didn't just make the user interface CUserInterface class conform to the CDecorator interface by design. I could have done this, but in real-world situations this is not always possible or desirable, so I used the adapter pattern to perform the coercion.

In our example, we have chosen to be patriotic and have explicitly coded to be terrans. This is just for the simplicity of the example. Quite clearly, we could have had some form of selective code here, allowing the players to choose the race that they would like to play. The CTerranDecorator class is instantiated taking the **CRootDecorator** as a parameter.

The CDecorator base class provides the **DrawDecoration()** interface that must be implemented by each decorator. Calling the concrete **Draw()** calls first the **DrawDecoration()** interface of the encapsulated class, followed by the **DrawDecoration()** member of the enclosing class.

The output from the listing 19.8 is as follows.

```
Drawing playing field
Drawing terran decorations
```

Okay, so it's not quite as polished as *Starcraft*, but I'm sure that you get the picture (or the text, in this case).

The useful thing about this technique is that you can continually chain decorators in order to produce more-complex effects. For example, say we were writing a licensed extension to *Starcraft* that required us to implement static on the screen when the communications array was under attack. With the decorator system, we would just define a new decorator, CStaticDecorator that drew interference on the screen and insert it in at the head of the chain. Listing 19.9 shows how the CStaticDecorator and new **main()** function would look.

Listing 19.9 Chained decorators—the static decorator.

```
/////////////////////////////////////////////////////////////////////
// assume this class is inserted into listing 19.8
/////////////////////////////////////////////////////////////////////

/////////////////////////////////////////////////////////////////////
// static decorator
/////////////////////////////////////////////////////////////////////
class CStaticDecorator : public CDecorator
{
public:
    CStaticDecorator(IDecorator& decorator)
    : CDecorator(decorator)
    {}
protected:
    void DrawDecoration()
    {
        cout << "BZZT! Drawing static BZZT!" << endl;
    }
};

/////////////////////////////////////////////////////////////////////
// this replaces the main() in listing 19.8
/////////////////////////////////////////////////////////////////////
void main()
{
    // user interface
    CUserInterface userInterface;

    // user interface adaptor (this makes the code more flexible
    // for extensions)
    CRootDecorator rootDecorator(userInterface);

    // let's assume we want to be terran,
    // but we could have a switch statement here
    CTerranDecorator terranDecorator(rootDecorator);
```

```
    CStaticDecorator staticDecorator(terranDecorator);

    //draw user interface
    staticDecorator.Draw();
}
```

The excerpt in Listing 19.9 simply adds an extra class, the CStaticDecorator class, and inserts it in the decoration chain.

The output from this is as follows.

```
Drawing playing field
Drawing terran decorations
BZZT! Drawing static BZZT!
```

Although this is a fairly trivial example (and has been coded rather inflexibly), compare the use of the decorator technique with the alternative of defining classes for each user-interface element and extending these by use of inheritance. With enough combinations, the resulting combinatorial explosion would produce enough classes to make code maintenance a hideous experience. The advantage of using the decorator technique is that it keeps code down to a minimum while maintaining the object-oriented design. It also provides maximum flexibility for runtime configuration of the decorator chain.

Pattern 10: The Facade

The facade provides a simplified interface to a set of related classes in a subsystem. This is intended to make the subsystem easier to use. It also increases the level of encapsulation within the code, while reducing the complexity.

By ensuring all communication between a client and a subsystem all go through a common interface, the act of code maintenance is simplified, so there are fewer places where bugs can occur. The difference a facade can make are shown in Figures 19.12 and 19.13.

The main use of the facade pattern within *Balls!* was in the wrapping of the DirectX objects. DirectX provides a high level of abstraction that, while allowing for very flexible code, also can cause the code to become very complex. For *Balls!*, I provided a simpler set of interfaces based around the functionality needed to set up a screen mode and display sprites. The CScreen object is a facade that encapsulates the IDirectDraw and IDirectDrawSurface interfaces representing the graphics card and the screen. This is shown in Figure 19.14.

A similar facade was used with the other DirectX interfaces, such as the DirectSound, DirectInput, and DirectPlay components of DirectX. The simplification of the game code that this provided for allowed the code to be much clearer and easier to understand. The facade could also be used as an interface to similar libraries on other systems, such as the Macintosh, meaning that the same client source code could be used cross platform as long as the facade had been implemented correctly on all target systems.

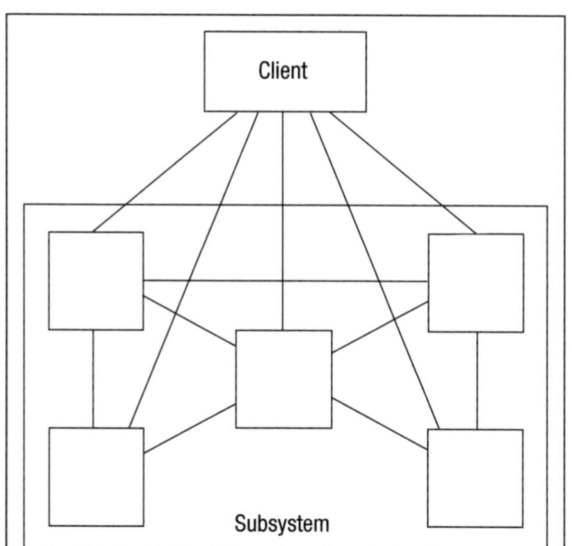

Figure 19.12
Interfacing to a set of subsystems *without* the use of a facade.

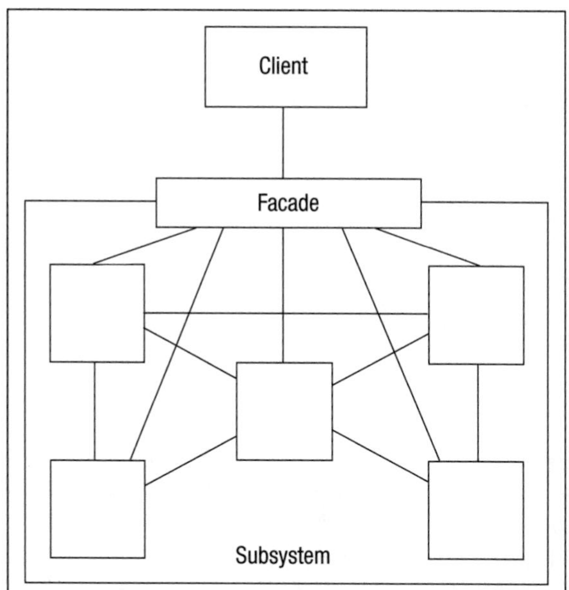

Figure 19.13
Interfacing to a set of subsystems *with* the use of a facade.

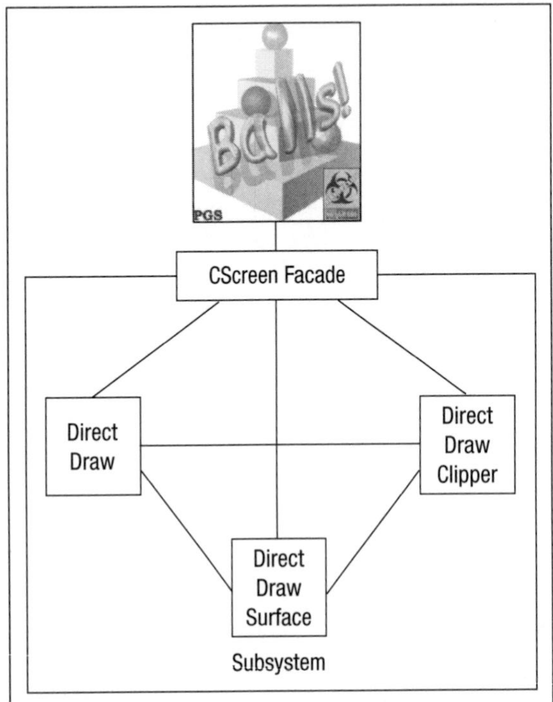

Figure 19.14
A facade for the *Balls!* graphics subsystems.

In *Balls!*, all of the subsystems interfacing with the operating system are behind a facade, which (in theory at least) makes the possibility of porting to another platform feasible—or at least a lot more feasible than it would be if the facade pattern was not used. Maybe certain specific issues such a big- or little-endian processor assumptions would have to be dealt with, but this is generally only if you have used processor-specific manipulation on numbers in your application.

Pattern 11: The Mediator

If initial appearances are anything to go by, then the mediator seems to be closely related to the facade pattern. The main difference is the level of involvement with the encapsulated member objects. The facade acts as an interface between a client and a set of subsystems, whereas a mediator concentrates on managing the interactions among the subsystems. It may well provide an external interface, in a similar way to the facade pattern, but this is not the main purpose of the pattern.

The communication pathways in the facade are essentially one way only, but, with the mediator, the communication is bidirectional. The mediator both receives information from and relays responses to the enclosed objects.

The main purpose of this pattern is to encapsulate the interactions between a set of objects. This pattern promotes loose coupling among the objects within the set by removing the need for the mediated objects to hold references to one another. This has a set of further benefits, the chief one being that with this system the mediated objects can vary independently from one another as long as they conform to the interface rules defined by the mediator.

The mediator is usually implemented as an observer. It observes the mediated objects and responds to events raised by them. This process is covered in the discussion of the object pattern. Figure 19.15 shows how this pattern is implemented.

The one glaring example of the use of a mediator object in games is the "game world token" discussed in Chapter 17. We will use this as our example.

The game world token is the controlling object of a game. It encapsulates the entire artificial universe of your game and mediates interactions between the tokens contained therein.

This allows a fair degree of intelligence in the generation of events, because the game world token has the legitimate knowledge of how to apply filters to these events so that the minimum number of events are flying around the system. This filtering is very important, and so a lot of attention should be paid to it. Each unnecessary event will exact a price. Remember, the fastest code is that which is never executed, so paying attention to algorithmic optimization event generation can pay great dividends. This is the system that *Balls!* uses. No extraneous events are sent to tokens. Granted, with *Balls!*, which doesn't exactly stretch the capabilities of today's PCs, this doesn't make much difference (although, as I've already pointed out on enough occasions, technology does not gameplay make), but it's easy to

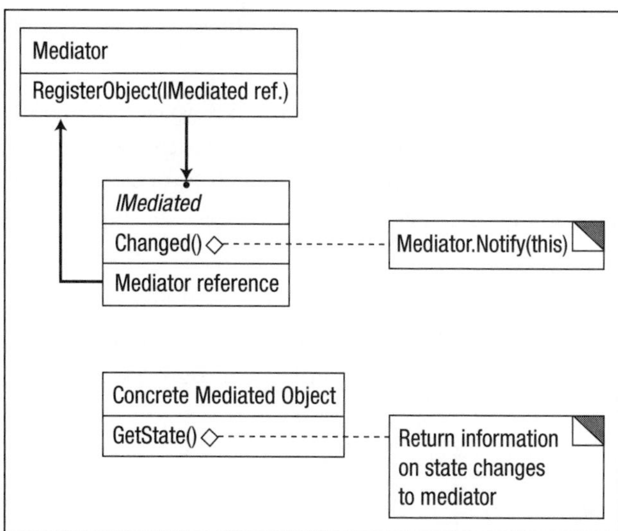

Figure 19.15
Class diagram for the mediator.

imagine a situation in which this would be important. In fact, the average program can afford to spend quite a lot of time on avoiding work in this fashion. Make sure you test all your timings, though. Sometimes you can spend more time avoiding the work than you would if you'd actually buckled down and done it in the first place! A bit like the average programmer really.

This pattern was applied to the game world token, which was discussed in great detail back in Chapter 17, and so we won't cover the same information here.

Pattern 12: The State

Allow an object to alter its behavior when its internal state changes. The object will appear to change its class.

The fighting-game example introduced in Pattern 6, the template and strategy methods, could also make use of states in order to provide more variation in fighter response.

Let's assume that we have our generic fighter framework class. For the sake of our discussion, we will discount the template and strategy methods and just look at how the state pattern could be used to create variety in play.

Our example fighter is a rigid fellow in that he has only three distinct modes of combat: "angry," "very angry," and "absolutely furious" (designated as mild, medium, and hot). In each of these distinct modes, the fighter uses a slightly different set of moves. The angrier the fighter gets, the more powerful and impressive the moves become. This leads to an interesting gameplay dilemma as to whether it is worth allowing your opponent to slap you around a bit in order to get angry and increase your power, or to just wade in there and risk your opponent beating you because his anger at being beaten makes him more powerful than you.

Our game designer expresses a bit of dissatisfaction at this and has asked whether there is any way we can implement more variety. Could we take into account where a fighter has been hit and "downgrade" that body part to a weaker move until it has recovered? (This is analogous to being hit in the arm and getting a dead arm: until your arm stops hurting you can't retaliate as effectively.)

So, clearly, each body part needs to have its "anger level" individually set. We can do this using state objects. Take a look at Listing 19.10 to see how this could be done. This is a very simplistic code snippet (it makes no distinction between left and right for a start), but it illustrates the main point.

Listing 19.10 Use of states.

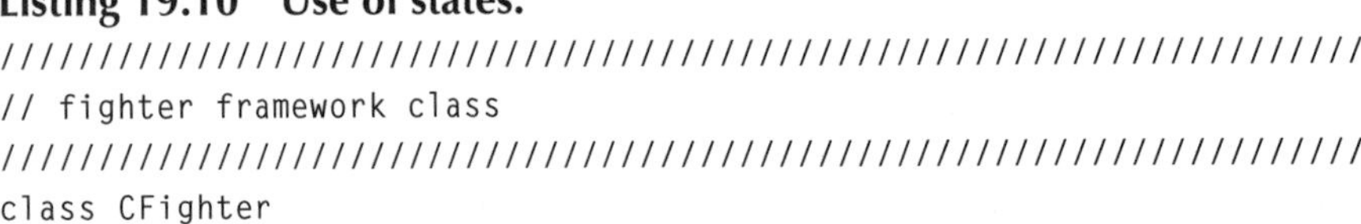

```
//////////////////////////////////////////////////////////////////////
// fighter framework class
//////////////////////////////////////////////////////////////////////
class CFighter
```

```
{
public:
    // kick using the current punch object
    bool Kick();
    {
        m_kick.Execute();
    }
    // punch using the current punch object
    bool Punch();
    {
        m_punch.Execute();
    }
    // perform a head butt using the current butt object
    bool Butt();
    {
        m_butt.Execute();
    }

protected:
    CKick&    m_kick;
    CPunch&   m_punch;
    CButt&    m_butt;
};

//////////////////////////////////////////////////////////////////////
// command interface - see command pattern
// abstract base class
//////////////////////////////////////////////////////////////////////
ICommand
{
public:
    virtual bool Execute() = 0;
};

//////////////////////////////////////////////////////////////////////
// concrete commands (forward references)
// commands come in three flavors:
// mild, medium and hot!
//////////////////////////////////////////////////////////////////////
//////////////////////////////////////////////////////////////////////
// kicks
class CKick : public ICommand // abstract base class
{
    // if we derived the concrete kick subclasses directly from
    // ICommand then it's possible to mix references up with
    // other commands. By defining a further specialized class that
```

```
    // all kicks derive from, we can avoid confusion.
};

// forward references
class CMildKick   : public CKick;
class CMediumKick : public CKick;
class CHotKick    : public CKick;

//////////////////////////////////////////////////////////////////////
// punches
class CPunch : public ICommand // abstract base class
{
    // see comment in CKick
};

// forward references
class CMildPunch   : public CPunch;
class CMediumPunch : public CPunch;
class CHotPunch    : public CPunch;

//////////////////////////////////////////////////////////////////////
// head butts
class CButt : public ICommand // abstract base class
{
    // see comment in CKick
};

// forward references
class CMildButt   : public CButt;
class CMediumButt : public CButt;
class CHotButt    : public CButt;
```

The code snippet shown in Listing 19.10 is very much simplified. Don't expect to see any production code based on it appearing in stores near you.

By segregating the actions for fighting in this way, it is now simple to add in our features to implement the effects of injury. If our fighter is using the hot punch and his opponent hits him in the arm, then we can downgrade the punch to a mild punch.

The fighter class CFighter is fairly simple. It supports three members, Kick(), Punch(), and Butt(). These act by calling the Execute() methods on the member variables that are references to the concrete implementations of CKick, CPunch, and CButt. These are base classes for each of the three subtypes of the attack types; they are implemented according to the command pattern, and they derive from the ICommand interface. Of course, it would have been possible just to derive all the concrete subclasses (CMildXXXX, CMediumXXXX and

CHotXXXX) directly from ICommand rather than going through the intermediary classes, CKick, CPunch, and CButt, but this would not be a good idea.

Why? Well, if we (heaven forbid) had made a coding error, this means that we could incorrectly cause the CFighter member variables that reference the action types to refer to the wrong types. If it wasn't for the intermediary classes, all of these member variables would have to be ICommand references. This would result in such "amusing" errors as the m_kick referring to one of the CXXXXPunch objects. Whenever the fighter wanted to kick, he would end up punching. By using the intermediary classes, this possibility is avoided. Trying to use an incompatible class with one of the member references will cause a compilation error.

Figure 19.16 shows how this pattern would be constructed for our hypothetical fighting game.

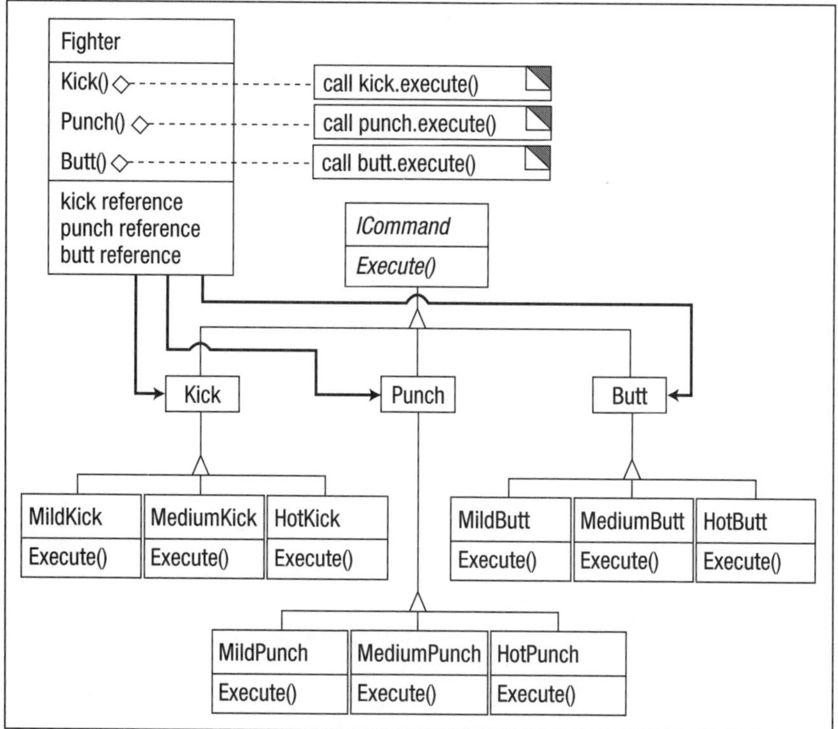

Figure 19.16
Class diagram for the state pattern applied to a fighting game.

Game-Specific Patterns

Design patterns are not the perfect solution to all problems. However, they have proved themselves to be extremely effective as a method of documenting common design solutions.

On the whole, design patterns are extremely generic solutions, tailored to a wide range of applications; consequently, not all of them will be suitable for application to game development.

What I'd really like to see in a couple of years is a set of documented patterns that is specifically tailored for games. This isn't so far fetched as it may initially seem. At the architecture level, all games are inherently similar. Anything that can help reduce the spiraling development costs for games should be seized upon and applied wherever possible. Maybe company management should aid in this process, by setting procedures in place to architecture mine and document the patterns (however corrupted) that may already be used in the existing codebase. These can then be "purified" wherever possible, using the correct form of the pattern.

In this chapter, I have identified design patterns as one area in which costs can be reduced. I hope that other members of the development community will develop this initial exposition further.

Chapter 20
Initial Architecture Design

Key Topics:

- ***Why we need architecture***
- ***Teamwork and architecture***
- ***Hard and soft architectures***
- ***Architecture granularity***
- ***Tier systems***
- ***Prototyping***
- ***System architecture/game architecture orthogonality***

This chapter begins to integrate what we have been discussing in the last three chapters.

Chapter 17 discussed the architecture of a game from the point of view of the game itself. We took a long, hard look at how to produce a set of state diagrams and other documents that accurately described how the game worked in terms of the tokens within it.

Chapter 18 discussed the use of technology for games and examined how the latest hardware is being used (in some cases) to improve games, making them more immersive and believable. We made a clear distinction, however, between technology and gameplay. I argued that the two concepts are coupled only very loosely, contrary to popular industry opinion, which seems to be that gameplay is led by technology.

Chapter 19 provided a discussion of patterns, a set of powerful techniques for reusable, object-oriented design that can be applied to the architecture of your game project.

In this chapter, we will look at the big picture—the overall architectural design. We will consider how to control the growth and development of the architecture, so that we can effectively manage our time and minimize the amount of any rework and backtracking.

Being able to design and construct part of a system doesn't automatically confer the ability to oversee and construct an entire system. This is a very complex job that requires an overview of the entire system, and this overall knowledge may not be compatible with knowing the lowest levels of the system: When you're considering the shape of the forest, it can be difficult to consider the shape of the leaves simultaneously.

The Birth Of An Architecture

In the bad old days, architecture was something concerned only with buildings. Old-school game developers never bothered with architectures, because they were trying to squeeze every last ounce of speed out of the system. This sort of coding often frustrates attempts to build a consistent architecture. Fortunately, the scale of the projects in the past has not been the multimillion-dollar epics of today: the average program fit into less than one-sixteenth of a megabyte and was worked on by only the one person.

But this was the stone age of game development. Our games then were the computer equivalents of mud huts. Today, we're nimbler and faster, and we no longer drag our knuckles along the ground when we walk. But we're not necessarily smarter.

One of the problems presented by the explosion of game size is the increase in the number of people that is required to produce a good product. This means that, like it or not, in most professional game-development roles, we are going to be expected to work as a team. And teams mean that other people have to be able to read your code and understand your design. This, in turn, means architecture. Today, our games are skyscrapers.

"The first team was a collection of talented individuals, while the second was a talented team."

—Dave Perry, quoted from a Game Developer Magazine *postmortem of* Wild 9, *lamenting the difficulties in development.*

Many industry people have said that most game-development teams are just a collection of talented individuals rather than a closely-knit team. This may well be true in many cases, but it will become less so in the future. Games are big business now, and budgets and game size keep increasing. Survival of the fittest ensures that all but the best meshed of teams will be weeded out, and for two reasons. The first is that dysfunctional teams tend to be self-destructive, and the second reason is money.

The day is coming—and it won't be long now—when game development suddenly shifts away from using the maverick skunkworks game-development model (the current rule which *should* be the exception) to a more orderly and planned "corporate" development style (the exception that *should* be the rule.)

You may scoff at this. You may say that game development will never "sell out" to the corporate-slave model. You may even believe that. However, the day will come, and the final decision will be down to the money. At present, companies investing in games are still fooled by the mystique inherent in game design. Companies are prepared to accept slippage and unprofessional attitudes, simply because "that is how game developers are." After all, schedule slippage is the norm in game development.

Soon, however, companies will start to notice that game development is not the only creative industry. For example, the film industry is just as creative as the games industry, but the schedule slippages are the exception, not the rule. Consider that George Lucas knew to the nearest month exactly how long it would take to write and produce *Star Wars: Episode 1*. More tellingly, he also had a schedule drawn up for the second film specifying the exact month in which it would be finished, in order to release it in time for summer.

The main differences between the film industry (which can predict schedules accurately) and the games industry (which can't) are experience and structure. The film industry has had nearly a century to work these things out. The games industry has had a little over 15 years. (This is not much excuse, because the software industry in general hasn't been around much longer than that, and that is fairly well organized.)

As the game industry becomes more valuable and mass market, we will have two choices: adopt industry standard practices willingly, or have them thrust upon us. I doubt the games industry will ever go as far as requiring ISO9001 quality certification, but you never know!

Note

ISO9001 certifies that your company adheres to certain best-business practices that (amongst other things) ensure that a full software-development audit trail is available.

The games of the future will require large teams to produce them, even with the use of "middleware." The larger the team, the greater the importance of teamwork. Teamwork involves a common vision of the project, and a common vision implies an architecture.

Teamwork needs architecture to survive.

Architectural Concepts

Now that we have ascertained the need for an architecture, we should go into more detail as to what we actually mean by the term *architecture*.

In short, architecture is the structure of a program, but there's more to it than that (otherwise this would be a very small chapter). Architecture also encompasses the structures and flow of the data, and it defines the interactions between all the components of the system.

The act of defining an architecture is the reduction of a monolithic system into a set of discrete logical subsystems. The system architect examines the problem domain from a number of different perspectives and produces a model of the system based on criteria such as data flow, natural partitions, and resource availability.

Architecture is not just a static creature. It can be specified in stages, using a tier system. The architecture can be specified to differing degrees at different tiers, and each tier builds on—rather than replaces—what has gone before. The tier-based model of architecture development is advocated in this book. This model of development, sometimes known as the *spiral model*, has been shown to be fairly reliable under most circumstances. We will discuss this in more detail later.

We have noticed that, when trying to design and impose an architecture on a project, developers are often very concerned with the validity of the approach. They ask, "Why bother specifying an architecture when we don't stick to it? The game will change as it goes along anyway."

This is a perfectly valid point and, given the classic view of architectural design, could be a good reason *not* to use architecture. Or at least it would be a good reason if we were going to use the classical model of architectural design. We're not. We're going to make great efforts so that our architecture is flexible and expandable.

A properly designed architecture allows for flexibility of code and algorithm. All danger areas (those that we expect to change substantially) are hidden behind consistent interfaces. The architectural design breaks the game down into systems and subsystems that can be built in stages, with a functioning model being the ultimate aim of each stage. Each stage provides more functionality than the previous stage, without breaking the interface, which is defined from "Tier One" onwards. Why is this desirable? By reducing the design into its discrete components, you segregate the areas of responsibility. It is much easier to understand a system composed of many small modules than it is to understand a monolithic system, which are prone to bugs and very susceptible to change. Even an apparently small change in such a system can cause large ripples (which in turn cause schedule slippage).

Rotating developers between tiers prevents a "developer monopoly," thus ensuring that the knowledge of a system is spread around the team and helping to reduce the impact of losing a team member. Another side benefit is that no team can claim to have been responsible for an entire game: this may reduce the "super-team" effect that has plagued the industry recently, in which a reasonably novice team with a couple of hit titles behind it can break away and form its own company, taking all your best ideas. This phenomenon can be only harmful to the industry as a whole, because, in most cases (and there are a few exceptions), these super teams end up costing a whole lot of money without producing any great amount of output. This damages the reputation of the industry with investors and may ultimately reduce the amount of money flowing into the industry, making it harder for start-ups to get off the ground.

By using modular components, the developer can concentrate on the correct level of granularity: he doesn't need to worry about whether his work will break other parts of the system (as long as he adheres to the specifications of the published interface). Each module is self-contained and requires no knowledge of surrounding modules in order to function correctly.

In fact, the module would be tested using a custom-written harness that tests all possible uses of the module. A custom test harness serves two purposes. The first is to allow for consistent testing between modifications. A module should be backwardly compatible with the previous version of the module, and regression testing is a good way of showing this. Of course, the test harness will have to be modified to include any new functionality, but this should be done in a way that won't invalidate the older tests.

The second use of the test harness is to demonstrate how a module is used. While this is not a substitute for good documentation, sometimes a developer needs to examine working code in order to get a handle on how to use a particular component.

Test harnesses are discussed in more detail in the next chapter.

"Hard" And "Soft" Architectures

For the purposes of game design, architecture comes in two flavors. There is the "physical" architecture, such as the subsystems that interface with the computer hardware, and the player (the input/output architecture). This is the *hard* architecture.

Such hardware is pretty much invariant in architecture design, especially with the continuing success of game development APIs such as DirectX.

In proper design terms, we would refer to the hard architecture in a project as the *horizontal solution*, because the hard architecture is actually a fairly generic framework (at least within a platform) that doesn't unnecessarily straitjacket the type of game produced upon it. An example of hard architecture would be a module that interfaced with an aspect of DirectX, such as the graphic and sound cards.

The hard architecture interfaces with outside systems, and, by definition, it is reliant on the interfaces provided by those systems. This brings with it a certain rigidity of architecture, and, because there are only a few sensible ways of interfacing with any given system, this is why it is called the hard architecture.

The converse of the horizontal solution is the vertical solution. This is the soft architecture of a project, the part that actually makes the game. The terms *vertical* and *horizontal* imply a sort of orthogonality that I like. It's true: although the soft and hard architecture intersect at certain points, they are generally orthogonal to each other. Look at it another way: if the soft architecture is the king, then the hard architecture is the red carpet he is walking on.

Soft architecture is domain specific and generally is not reusable between projects. The soft architecture is effectively isolated from the outside world, sitting atop the hard architecture and making use of the services provided. An explicit example of soft architecture would be the configurable menu system discussed in Chapter 19.

All of this implies that the architecture for a game is a bit like an M&M: crunchy on the outside, and soft on the inside, as shown in Figure 20.1.

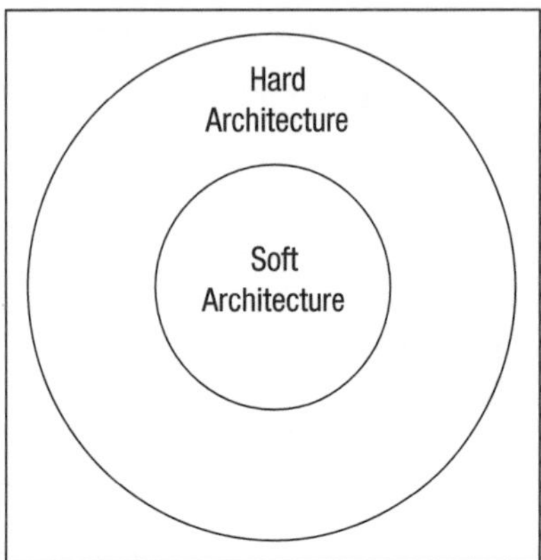

Figure 20.1
Generic game architecture.

Architecture Granularity

The granularity of an architecture is an important consideration in deciding how to approach the design of the subsystems.

But what exactly do we mean by *granularity*?

As we go from the lowest level to the highest level of a development project, the code becomes less generic and more specific to the task at hand (the ultimate being a completely soft architecture as used in *Thief* and *System Shock II*). This is still quite specific (being a scriptable 3D engine), but it is a sensible level of abstraction, although there were many complaints about level-loading times. Because it was completely soft architecture oriented, it had to virtually load the soft architecture of the entire level and configure it at runtime.

The number of discrete elements that are visible at the layer being examined defines the granularity of a system. This concept is best explained by analogy.

Let's take a boat as the system we wish to examine. We will examine it from the top down, and we will look at the boat as a hierarchical list of elements, as shown in Figure 20.2.

Okay, so what is the top-level element of the hierarchy? The boat itself. This is granularity level 1.

At the next level down, we can consider the larger-scale components of the boat: the hull, the cabin, and the engine. Further still, we can subdivide and specialize. The hull can be broken down into a collection of different-shaped pieces of fiberglass. The cabin can be broken down into a further set of hierarchies based on the equipment contained within it, and the engine can be broken down into a set of pistons and cylinders and so on.

At these levels, the granularity is moderate, but not so unacceptably high.

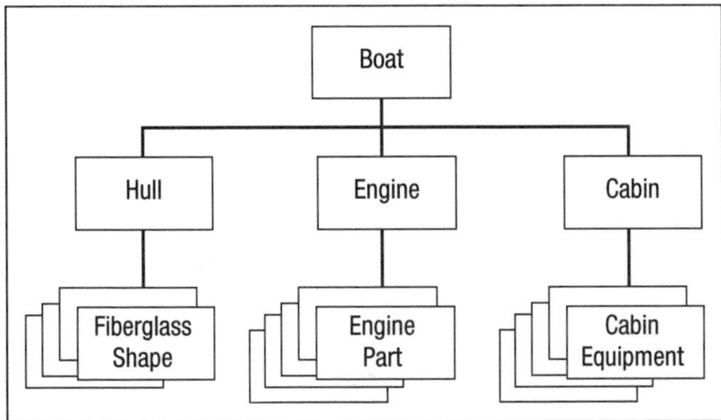

Figure 20.2
The granularity of a boat.

We can go still further. We could traverse down the hierarchy until we reach the atomic level: the level at which things all start to look the same. We have approached the granularity singularity, which is a sign that we have gone too far. You may find the odd programmer down at this level, but, for the most part, they all operate a couple of levels up.

The hierarchical-granularity diagram of a boat directly parallels that of software architecture. But why are we so interested in granularity? It may be interesting from an analysis point of view, but how does it apply directly to what we need to do?

To answer this question, we need to consider the nature of object-oriented programming.

When using object-oriented techniques, a certain amount of overhead is associated with an object's creation and use. Each object created must have memory allocated and initialized for it, and each call to a member function involves a pointer lookup that may significantly impact the time taken for the function to execute. This process doesn't even begin to consider that the increased code size due to using object-oriented techniques may detrimentally affect cache efficiency.

Let's take a specific example: the hypothetical class CPixel. (This is a fairly trivial example, but it makes our point admirably.)

The job of CPixel is to allow the setting of a pixel on screen. It is a very low-level class and consequently doesn't do much, as shown in Listing 20.1.

Listing 20.1 The CPixel class.

```
////////////////////////////////////////////////////////////////////////////
// global screen buffer
////////////////////////////////////////////////////////////////////////////
unsigned char g_auchScreen[640][480];
```

```
//////////////////////////////////////////////////////////////////////////////
// class to handle the drawing of a pixel
//////////////////////////////////////////////////////////////////////////////
class CPixel
{
public:
    void DrawPixel(int ix, int iy, unsigned char uchColor)
    {
        // set the pixel in the screen buffer
        g_auchScreen[ix][iy] = uchColor;
    }
};
```

Looking at the code in Listing 20.1, it's clear that the **DrawPixel** member function is fairly simple. It doesn't do much. Let's take a look at how it may be reduced by the compiler into simpler instructions. Let's take the first line of the member function. This shows us how the function would be called, and we can make a rough guess as to how many time units it would require.

```
void DrawPixel(int ix, int iy, unsigned char uchColor)
```

We have three parameters to pass: **ix**, **iy**, and **uchColor**. Let's assume they each take one time unit to pass.

The next line does the calculation itself:

```
g_uachScreen[ix][iy] = uchColor;
```

The correct screen address has two calculations (one for **ix** and one for **iy**), each of which takes one time unit. Then there is the color assignment itself, which also takes one time unit.

This gives us a grand total of six time units. But we've missed something. We haven't taken the overhead caused by object orientation into account. When we call a member function of an object, an implicit parameter containing a pointer to the object is also passed, making the function call in actuality a little more like this:

```
void DrawPixel(CPixel* this, int ix, int iy, unsigned char uchColor)
```

and the extra parameter passed means that we are taking up an extra time unit—seven instead of six. This is a whopping 17 percent increase in the time taken to call the **DrawPixel** function, and this doesn't even take into account the cost of instantiating the object, and deleting it when we've finished.

Note

This is only a first-level approximation of the true situation. It's not intended to show, or even be proportional to, real values. All we can show is that using objects at this level would have a significant impact on speed. In reality, to get an accurate reading, you would have to measure the code itself using a profiling tool such as NuMega's TrueTime. *This sort of analysis can be a useful first-level check though.*

Object-oriented techniques do have an impact on the speed of the code, but, as long as the body of the member function takes significantly longer that the overhead caused by the object member function call, then this impact is negligible. This is why the level of granularity within the system is important: we need to know where to draw the object-oriented line. We need to know the point at which applying object-oriented techniques becomes a liability rather than a help.

Clearly, the CPixel class described above is a terrible idea, and only a fool would use it in a time-critical situation. That's not to say we couldn't find a use for it (in a slightly augmented form), just not in a time-critical portion of a game.

The Tier System

One of the most effective development models for game development is the "waterfall," "spiral," or "tier-based" method (and variations thereof). This method has many slightly different versions, but (and don't tell anyone I said this) they are all essentially the same thing.

Although this will be discussed in more detail in Chapter 21, suffice it to say that these methods reduce the development into discrete tiers, with each tier taking into account what was built before, and what will be built ahead.

Thus, we approach the architecture design in a holistic fashion. By this, I mean that, even as we split the architecture into a series of tiers, we still keep an eye on the whole architecture.

When designing the architecture of a module, we first try to define the interface that will be required. The best starting approach is to build the skeleton of what we will need. Implementing this skeleton is the main aim of the first tier, and subsequent tiers concentrate on fleshing out the framework, filling in and replacing stubbed-out functionality with the real deal.

Tier Zero: The Prototype

Of course, it would be difficult to leap straight in and implement the skeleton correctly the first time you try, so we need to take this into account when designing the architecture. We do this via prototyping techniques. In fact, the prototype is really the very first part of defining the architecture. We could say that the prototype is Tier Zero in the development model.

Tier Zero is really a special case, before we get into the architecture proper. We need to be able to test our game design ideas, refine them, and work out what we need to do in order to efficiently implement our tier-based architecture.

This tier of our project isn't really one of the main tiers. It's really a "pre-project" investigation. How are we going to put our architecture together? What will work? What doesn't? How does our game design hold up to interrogation under the harsh light of critical analysis?

What Is A Prototype?

Before we can begin to consider this, we should consider what a prototype is. A prototype is basically an extended project-specific test harness. It is written to allow us to examine the game mechanics and to easily change and modify them. Prototyping is a risk-reduction mechanism, allowing us to explore and evaluate simulated risks before we have to tackle them for real (when our money, and our development, is on the line).

In fact, prototyping is the passage between the academic world of research and the here-and-now world of production code.

A game prototype doesn't have to be advanced. Prototypes can be made in any way that you see fit: a paper-and-pencil RPG, a set of models and toys, a board game, a simple Visual Basic application, or anything else that allows you to model the processes going on within your game.

Although the definition of what may be called a prototype varies wildly, there is one thing that all prototypes are not: they are not, under any circumstances, to be used as a codebase for the game development itself. Any development based on prototype code is doomed to fail or, at the very least, doomed to have lots of irritating little teething problems caused by using inappropriate material.

Prototypes do not use the same development criteria as games. They are not developed for speed or efficiency, and usually a significant amount of rework is required before they are useful as part of the game code. A cleaner and more efficient system can be up and running in less time than it takes to clean up and convert prototype code to production code. Nevertheless, the temptation is still there to make use of prototype code. After all, it's just sitting there, waiting to be used, and you know that it works.

For this reason, I advocate writing any code prototypes in an entirely different language to the main project itself. For example, if I am writing the main project in C++ (with no COM trickery), I will use VB for my prototype. The two systems are mutually incompatible, and—no matter how tempted I am—I simply cannot use the prototype code in the production codebase.

Types Of Prototype

The many different kinds of prototypes all contribute to the overall architecture. So far, we have discussed the gameplay prototype, and, indeed, this is the main use for prototyping. It's not the only use for prototyping, however, and you will find instances where it is useful throughout your project.

We will be considering four main types in varying levels of detail:

- Gameplay prototypes: the most important consideration!
- User-interface prototypes: How does the game interact with the player?
- Subsystem prototypes: How do all the subsystems interact with each other? What interfaces do they export for use with other systems?
- Algorithm prototypes: What is the best algorithm to use for a given situation? Is it suitable to be abstracted behind an interface so that we can literally "plug and play" the algorithm?

These prototypes will live and develop with the project. For example, I would fully expect the gameplay prototype (in whatever form it may take) to develop parallel to the game itself. As new ideas are added to the game design, they should first be field tested in the game design prototype.

The user-interface prototype may be nothing more than a set of sketches in a notebook or a VB application defining how the user interface will operate, both in the game and out of it. User interfaces are a much-neglected area of design, and they really need to be worked on until they are perfect. Because the user interface is the main junction between the player and the game world, its strength can make or break a game. A good user interface doesn't intrude into the world of the player, and it plays a major part in the suspension of disbelief. Without suspension of disbelief, the game is nothing.

Subsystem (or module) prototypes are often developed into the test harnesses for a module. As I've already stated, it is sometimes hard to design a module correctly the first time, and these tend to grow organically. Unless it is properly managed, organic growth can be more trouble that it is worth: your module can become weed ridden and overgrown. By prototyping the module interface and using a test harness to try to use all the functionality that you think will be required, you at least stand a chance of thrashing out a fairly good first-order approximation of what you will need.

As part of the module prototype, you will have developed a suitable test harness that can be used to test the functionality of the module and that can take any changes into account. We will discuss test harnesses further in Chapter 21.

On a lower level of granularity than module prototypes, the algorithm prototype is useful for testing out different algorithms. Sometimes a complex algorithm that is specific to the domain of your game is necessary, and this may require some prototyping in order to perfect. Even if the algorithm itself is merely a composition of more-standard components, these components can sometimes interact in unexpected ways to cause bottlenecks or, if you are lucky, to provide opportunities for optimization. As long as the algorithm you are prototyping is hidden behind a consistent interface, then you are free to explore other options. I would still recommend not using prototype code in a live situation, however. Where possible, stick to the golden rule of developing the prototype in a different language (such as VB or Java) and then converting to the target language when the algorithm is finalized. I appreciate that this is not always possible, particularly if you are trying to fine-tune an algorithm, but fine-tuning generally comes well after the prototyping stage, so this should not really be a problem in most cases.

Why Use A Prototype?

This is a good question. With an experienced team of game developers, is it really necessary to prototype? After all, they all know their stuff really well and mesh like a well-oiled machine. You know the sort of thing: "Prototype? We don' need no steenkin' prototype!" Yeah, right, whatever.

In most cases, teams do not run "like a well-oiled machine," and there will inevitably be problems and miscommunications during the development process. While it's not a complete solution, the prototype can be viewed as a dress rehearsal for difficult aspects of the real development. With code prototypes, tricky algorithms and subsystem interactions can be explored in anticipation for when they are needed. However, I would expect that, in general, code prototyping goes on throughout the lifetime of the project, at least in a small way. When a new module is implemented, I would expect there to be some degree of prototyping first.

Only the most sweeping coding aspects should be dealt with during the Tier Zero prototyping. The main purpose of Tier Zero is to investigate the potential for the gameplay and the architecture as a whole.

Prototyping allows you to explore difficult aspects before you have to implement them for real. (One of the most difficult aspects is gameplay balance, and any attention paid to this pays dividends at a later date.)

A prototype is designed to be very easily changeable. This means that gameplay balance can be chopped and changed as much as the game designer likes. The design of the prototype means that this is the simplest place to do this. The whole ethos of the prototype design is to allow the game design to be examined, tweaked, and modified. This is clearly a lot harder to achieve in the full game. The prototype itself is the place to do this tweaking, leaving only last-minute refinements in the game itself when the time comes to prepare for shipping.

Of the types of prototypes we have mentioned, only the game design prototype needs to be covered in more detail. The other types of prototype are self-explanatory and need no further detail other than what we have already provided.

Preparing A Prototype

Preparing a prototype isn't always as simple as just sitting down and hacking some code out (although it can be in some situations in which you already have a pretty good idea of what will be required).

Undirected effort is usually wasteful at whatever level of development. Nowhere is this truer than with prototypes. By their very nature, prototypes can involve a lot of meandering and sidetracking development. So, in order to minimize the loss of development momentum, it is essential to consider exactly what needs prototyping.

As I have already stated, prototyping is a risk-reduction mechanism, and you should keep this foremost in mind when considering where to focus our prototyping attentions.

For example, as far as I am concerned, the biggest risk in any game project is the gameplay itself. This is the make-or-break point: you can have the best architecture in the world, but, if the gameplay isn't there, you end up with an expensive slide show.

Getting a gameplay testbed up and running is the single most important thing. Whether it is a paper-and-pencil mockup, a primitive board game, or a crude graphical representation, the important thing is to investigate it. These investigations are a lot cheaper to perform with a prototype than they are within the game itself, 18 months into the development cycle. Some cash-rich companies (such as Blizzard) can get away with this approach (as seen in Chapter 7), so it cannot be completely discounted. Unless you happen to be in a very financially secure position and very experienced in the field, then the prototype is the best place to do these refinements, at least at the first level. Subsequent fine-tuning may be required within the game itself.

Other areas of risk can also be prototyped, especially in the areas we have already described. In this way, the prototype serves as a useful risk reducer. Think of it as a low-cost model that allows us to approximate the problem to the first order of complexity. An analog would be NASA training astronauts for weightlessness: it's a lot cheaper to put them in a swimming pool than it is to ship them into space for their weightlessness training.

In essence, the prototype should be prepared in the same way as any other part of the project. The key goals of the prototype are flexibility and low cost. It doesn't matter if it looks like a 10-year-old text game. It doesn't even matter if it crashes every half hour or so, as long as it doesn't lose data (although you'd hope it wouldn't.)

You are going to throw the prototype away anyway (you *are*!), so, as long as it was cheap to develop and was flexible enough to serve your needs, no less and no more, then it was worthwhile. All that matters is that it allows you to thoroughly explore the problem domain that you are prototyping.

Note that a testbed doesn't have to be hard coded using a custom-written program. Off-the-shelf packages such as *NeMo Dev* by Virtools (a demo of which is included on the CD-ROM) are excellent for creating good-looking prototypes that allow for drag-and-drop specification of complex behaviors. These can be great for developing prototypes so advanced that they could pass for the game itself, but then care has to be taken not to get so wrapped up in creating a great-looking prototype that the game itself suffers. Of course, *NeMo Dev* can be used as the basis of a game—the engine is licensable—but this is not a decision to be taken lightly. It is certainly suitable for this, but the learning curve of new technology should be taken into account. Certainly, it still would be easier than developing a new game engine from scratch, but you may find that you need to augment the system with custom-written add-ons.

NeMo Dev (and to some extent, *NetImmerse*, described in Chapter 19) are the ultimate in soft architectures. They attempt to define a complete game framework that can be used to create a quality 3D game. How successful this is will be revealed by the tests of the marketplace, but the future certainly looks promising for this sort of product.

Even in-house equivalents, such as those used to produce the game engine for *Thief* and *System Shock II* are steps in the right direction. The more game-specific functionality that can be implemented as soft architecture, the more reusable and generic the hard architecture will be. This is what we've been aiming for all along. (We will be discussing soft architecture and hard architecture in much more detail later in the chapter.)

Driving A Prototype Using Soft Architecture

One of the best ways of allowing a game designer to actively tweak his game design is to run the prototype using a soft-architecture back end.

For example, the testbed of *Age of Empires* (by Ensemble and published by Microsoft) used a back-end database to hold the unit type information, as described in Case Study 20.1.

By using an interface class to the database access, both the prototype and the main game can share access to exactly the same data. More to the point, when the final parameters are

Case Study 20.1 A Database-Driven Approach

Age of Empires was developed using the soft-architecture approach.

According to Matt Pritchard of Ensemble, the advantages of an object-oriented design paid off, especially as the project approached 220,000 lines of C++ at its peak.

Almost nothing about any object in *Age of Empires* is hard coded into the program. Huge tables of information describe every characteristic of every object that appears in the game. The game designers used a system of over 40 Paradox database tables to control and shape the game. As a result, they were able to constantly update and tweak the game, and then test their changes without having to involve a programmer.

—Source: *Game Developer Magazine*, (March 1998)

frozen, then the data can be moved to a permanent data file, and then only the code *behind* the data access interface needs to be changed in order to make it read from the custom storage.

This technique is useful in a number of situations, the golden rule (yes, another one!) being: the more architecture that is soft, the more flexible and adaptable the game engine will be.

Tier One And Beyond

Once all the prototyping has produced useful results, it's time to get down to the real meat of the architecture design.

Hopefully, if you've been adhering to the software factory methodology described in Chapter 11 and following the discussion of milestones and deadlines in Chapter 12, then you'll be able to see where all this is leading.

Tier One of the development process takes the results of the prototyping we have done and unifies the results into a single framework design. The good thing about this is that this framework will be designed to be reusable. Because we are using the software factory methodology, a large proportion of this initial Tier One work will be reusable for other concurrent or future projects.

In Tier One, the developers concentrate their efforts on producing the hard-architecture components that will be required in the game project.

Usually, unless there is a pressing reason otherwise, Tier One begins at the lower granularity levels, and the work involves producing components such as hardware-interfacing modules and the basic game framework code.

Subsequent tiers involve filling in this framework with hard and/or soft architecture. This could mean adding or refining features in the hard architecture or adding more functionality to the soft architecture. The later tiers will concentrate more on the soft architecture: by this stage, the hard architecture should be pretty much done and dusted. This is unlike the usual industry process whereby the hard architecture is still being added right up until the close of play. With the power of computers today, there is really no excuse for the use of this development model anymore. Even *Balls!*, which is being developed as a demonstration of the techniques used in this book (and hence is not expected to be developed further), makes extensive use of the soft-architecture approach. The hard architecture (the hardware-interface components and the menuing system components) were the first to be finished. The rest of the project has involved implementing the game logic within the soft-architecture framework provided.

At each tier, the game should be shippable. What do we mean by this?

Shippable means that we could theoretically release the product. Not all the functionality would be there, and a lot would be stubbed out and inoperative, but at least the program will build and be stable. There would be no crashes, and the product would be essentially free of bugs.

This "always shippable" concept is one of the most important tenets of development. By mandating that the product be always shippable, we effectively restrict additional development until the current codebase is working properly. This has a number of benefits, such as the prevention of feature creep and developer gold-plating. It also helps prevent the famous "demo rush" syndrome, wherein developers rush and take shortcuts with the codebase in order to get a demo ready for an imminent show—as long as the project manager can keep his nerve long enough to avoid taking self-destructive shortcuts in order to squeeze in new features.

Usually, when time is taken out of the schedule to get a demo ready, all the patchwork code that has been written to get the demo out of the door has to be discarded in order to continue work. At least it should be: it will have been rushed and will not be of the highest quality. This removal process can often delay the schedule, as can fixing the many bugs that will have most likely been introduced by the forced insertion and removal of large quantities of substandard code. (I'm talking from personal experience here.)

By ensuring that the project is always ready to ship, it is also always ready to demo. Okay, so the demo may not be as slick and high powered as the publishers would always like, but, as long as they realize that the emphasis of these techniques is on slow and steady progress—and they can see the benefits of this approach on the usual mad demo-rush cycle—then they will be appeased. Slow and steady progress is not as sexy as the mad-rush effect, but it will produce greater benefits to the project as a whole.

All Games Are The Same

Under the hood, all games are essentially the same. Sure, there are local differences, but, when it comes down to it, they are pretty similar in internal design.

"A game is just a real-time database with a pretty front end."

—Dave Roderick, U.K. consultant

When I first heard the above quote, I scoffed at it. I distinctly remember arguing with the guy for several hours over it. How could he make such a blanket statement? After all, he wasn't even directly associated with the games industry. What did *he* know?

However, the more I thought about it, the more I realized that he had a point. At the most basic level, a game consists of the following primary subsystems:

- user interface
- bidirectional event handler
- data engine (graphics, level, and miscellaneous data)

- dynamics system (collisions and general physics)
- logic engine (the heart of the game)
- graphics engine
- sound engine
- hardware abstraction layers (interfaces with graphics, sound, and controller hardware)

and one or more of the following secondary subsystems

- game configuration system
- menuing system
- online instructions and help system
- music system

This second list is not all inclusive. I'm sure that there are lots of other things that you can think of that could go here. (See Figure 20.3.)

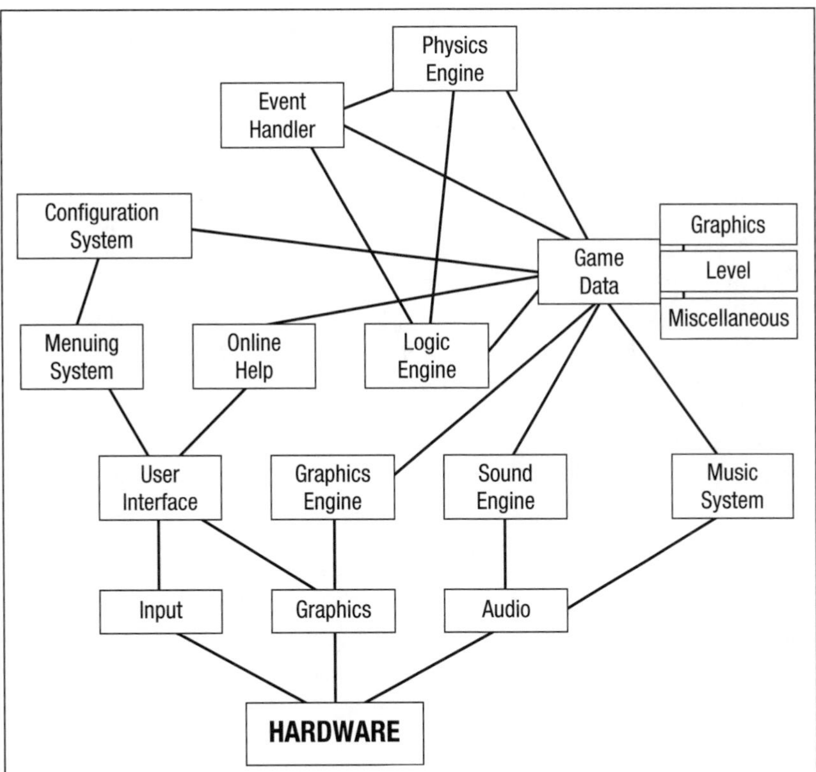

Figure 20.3
The architecture of a game.

Note

Figure 20.3 is quite a complex diagram: in reality, it would not be as complex. The main cause of the complexity is that I have lumped all the data access in as one module. This is how it would be best done within the architecture, but it doesn't make for a very pretty picture.

The important thing to consider is that each of these subsystems (both primary and secondary) can be implemented as a component that can be reused from project to project. With many of these, it should be possible to implement similar interfaces so that one type of component can be substituted for another with the minimum of (programmatic) effort. Of course, in reality, there would be a lot more work involved: the data used by the component may need to be reproduced in a more suitable format (for example, a switch from an isometric 3D to a full 3D graphics engine requires a switch from a sprite-based to a polygon-based graphics—clearly *not* a five-minute job).

Components

When developing the components for the game (and we are still talking within the realms of the hard architecture here), then we should be drawing on the components developed by the software factory system.

When building the architecture, we should take into account whether we can make use of already existing components, whether they be in-house or not. Increasingly, it seems that the biggest factor in game development seems to be the time to market, so any use of existing components that can shave precious time off the schedule should be seriously considered.

The buzzwords that we need to keep in mind are *component-based architecture*. If we build our architecture up piece by piece, selecting each piece from a virtual catalog (as the Victorian English did when they built their houses from pattern books), then we should end up with a cleaner and more segmented architecture.

Even big players such as Sony have seen the benefits of this scheme—which has been dubbed *middleware*—and are leveraging those benefits by licensing third-party physics engines and other components to incorporate into their developer SDK for the PlayStation 2.

In the situations in which we have to develop a *new* component for our project, then we should consider the potential for reuse. Most game platforms nowadays are powerful enough so that we simply do not need to put any of the game-specific code into hard-architecture modules. There really is no excuse for missing reuse opportunities, because the major opportunities for reuse are going to be at the level of the hardware interface and general algorithm.

It's quite easy to imagine reusing a graphics engine or a sound engine, which are at the lowest level of granularity within our architecture, but with a little effort we can also reuse components from higher in the hierarchy. For example, with careful design, we can produce a menuing system that can be used across a number of projects. This is not such a strange concept: after all, a large part of Windows itself is taken up by a common user interface that can be used across projects. Of course, this does not mean that we'd want our games to conform to the Windows user interface, because we would consider them boring, but the concept can be stolen and used to provide a simple configurable menu system that we could happily use across an entire range of projects without the customers even noticing that we had reused the code.

This is not the only opportunity within the architecture for reuse. You'll find plenty more as computers become more powerful and are able to take up the slack required to support the extended demands of a completely soft architecture.

Architecture Design

When we begin to consider the actual architecture of the game, we need also to consider how to construct it around the planning needs of the schedule. A scheduling system based on the milestone system is discussed in Chapter 12.

Assuming that we are following this scheme, then it is sensible to assume that we will map tier completion to milestones. Each milestone will specify the technical requirements to complete a particular tier. This nicely fits the requirement that Chapter 12 laid out for technical milestones.

As we have been discussing, the architecture is specified in three main stages, each of which expands into a number of tiers.

These three stages are:

- prototyping
- hard-architecture design
- soft-architecture design

The prototyping stage allows us to have a dress rehearsal of the full architecture, allowing us to tackle any tricky points and difficulties that we might encounter. Of course, this doesn't mean that we are going to be able to cover all of these difficulties, but we can tackle at least the more obvious ones, and, of course, we will be able to explore gameplay issues sooner than we would be able to otherwise. Traditionally, gameplay is dealt with as a last-minute rush before the final product is shoved out of the door, and, in a lot of cases, it suffers for this. This should be enough of a reason to make prototyping an essential part of any project.

The hard-architecture design stage involves the laying of the game framework. For the first few projects, this will be a major part of the design. However, the point of using a component-based design is to produce a set of generic components that can be used across projects. Only after a few projects have been undertaken will we see any benefits from reusing in-house components. That's not to say we cannot take immediate advantage of the benefits of component-based reuse from day one: we can import third-party tools from other companies, such as *NeMo Dev* or *NetImmerse*, in order to speed up our development. Once a few projects have been completed, we will also be able to use our own components, such as a menuing system or a game configuration module, as described earlier. In Chapter 11, we mentioned that the software factory architecture caused an apparent drop in productivity for the first project developed using it, but this was more than repaid on the development of second and subsequent projects. This initial component development is where we will take the hit, although this increase in required time is also slightly offset within the scope of the project, by applying more-structured development methods that reduce the amount of time spent on backtracking and unnecessary rework.

The soft architecture is the area where we are truly on our own. This is pretty much unique for any project, and this is as it should be, for within the soft architecture is the unique spark that makes your game stand out from the rest. By using the soft-architecture system, we are taking advantage of all the groundwork that has already been done for us. It makes no sense whatsoever to keep running over the same old ground, reinventing the wheel, and rewriting components that we have written countless times before. In essence, we are heading for a state of Nirvana—the sort of effortless perfection that allows us to create a new game just by defining the new content that is required. In reality, of course, this would be quite difficult to achieve. Hard-architecture components would need to be upgraded and augmented in order to keep up with emerging technology, but, with a sensible set of interfaces, the disruption caused by this continual upgrade (*not* replacement) process would be minimal.

The soft architecture defines the game-specific functionality and data required, such as in game graphics, music, and other data. In fact, the soft architecture is essentially data driven. By expending such careful effort on the design of the hard architecture, we have effectively produced a data-driven game engine. This is the approach taken by a number of successful companies, and it has paid dividends on the reuse stakes. Look at the number of total conversions available for *Quake* (such as *Quake Football*, *Quake Chess*, *Quake Rally*, and many other even stranger efforts), and you'll see the benefits of providing a soft architecture: if gifted amateurs can use the hard-architecture framework to convert a game such as *Quake* to a completely different game, then just imagine what your own in-house team would be able to achieve with the company code. They would have the advantage of having access to the source code of the components, and hence be able to modify them if absolutely necessary (a benefit that the total-conversion guys just don't have).

Figure 20.4 shows a set of idealized curves for the amount of effort expended on each of the three aspects of architecture over the course of a few projects. This doesn't take into account any sudden unexpected events, such as the release of a new killer platform or technology.

We can see from the graph that the effort expended on soft-architecture development remains fairly consistent, as you'd expect. The effort spent on hard architecture decreases with time. This reflects the construction of a library of reusable components that can be

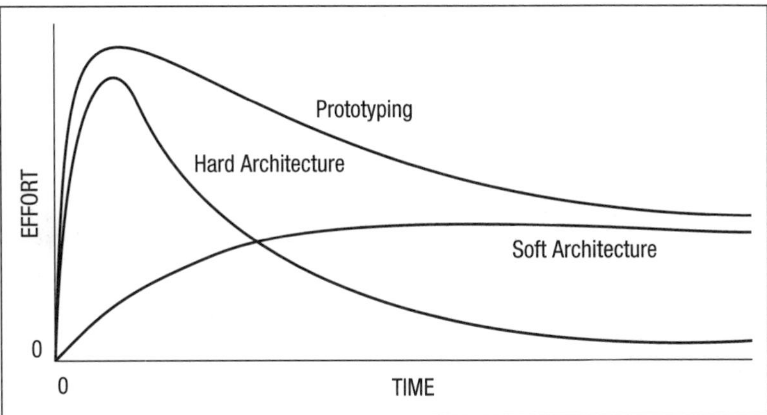

Figure 20.4
Effort expenditure against time for a set of projects.

sourced for use in further projects. The graph assumes that we develop everything in-house and don't make any use of external components (hence the high initial development). The effort spent prototyping also starts off high and decreases with time, but not to the same extent as the hard-architecture effort. This reflects the fact that prototyping will always be a part of the development of both the hard and soft architecture.

Applying The Tier-Based Approach To Architecture Design

To apply the tier-based approach to our architecture design, we need to slice our subsystems up in a number of different ways.

First, we need to slice them by functionality. Imagine we have a bunch of onions, tangled together by their roots and leaves: our complete system. Each onion is a separate component-based subsystem, and we extract the components by separating out the onions.

This is good: we have our components, but how were they built? If we slice our hypothetical onions in two, then we see that they comprise layers. These layers represent the tiers of functionality that have been built up over time. We can peel these layers back, and we still have a functional onion (that is, it still tastes disgusting), but the functionality is restricted (the onion is smaller).

Okay, so now we know how a bunch of onions is constructed, how do we apply this to building our architecture? You are probably thinking that the strain has been too much for me, and that I have finally snapped—talking about onions and all that—but I'm about to restore your faith by making a concise and valid point: games are like a bunch of onions.

Actually, that's not exactly the point I was going to make, but it serves its purpose. In fact, games are more like a bunch of *bionic* onions. We have to build them from scratch. And, yes, we *do* have the technology to rebuild them, as long as it doesn't cost us 6 million dollars.

Hopefully, you will have been able to divine much significance from my dalliance into the structure of onions, because this is how we are going to subdivide the first phase of our architecture design: by components, and then by tiers.

These two subdivisions are orthogonal to one another. For the first tier, we build the framework, providing minimal functionality for all of the required components, and then subsequent tiers concentrate on filling in the missing functionality in controlled stages as shown in Figure 20.5.

To enable us to incrementally update parts of a system without affecting other parts of the same system, we should have a consistent interface between the subsystems.

The aim of the first tier is to define all of these interfaces (as far as possible subject to the 80/20 rule) so that minimum disruption will occur when adding functionality for later tiers in the development process. Of course, unless you are extremely fortunate, it is unlikely that you will completely avoid having to make modifications to the interfaces at later tiers, but a careful thought as to what is needed will minimize the changes required. As long as the interface is reasonably flexible, then this should be the case. Chapter 19 is the place to look for interface discussions.

Interfaces are the most important aspect of the technical design. Make sure that you design them to be generic enough to take future tiers into account. (See Case Study 20.2.)

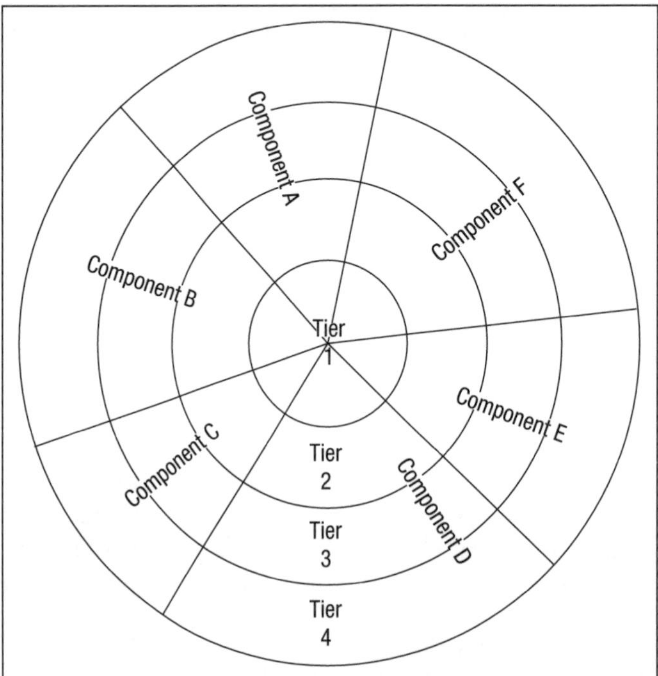

Figure 20.5
Tier-based component design of a game architecture.

Case Study 20.2 Discussing The Architecture Of Warbots

Warbots is a fictional real-time strategy game first discussed in Case Study 4.3. Previously, Peter, the designer, had been discussing some aspects of the tier-based development model with Nick (lead programmer), Victoria (AI programmer), and some other members of the development team.

After explaining what he wants, Peter has left Victoria and Nick to discuss the more technical aspects of the requested functionality, and we join them as they are discussing how to partition the architecture across the tiers.

"Okay," says Nick, "I think we can probably abstract this route finding to some degree. The team developing *Genishore*, our Manga-influenced seashell collecting game, has produced a generic route-finding module. We can patch into that. It implements all the algorithms we were planning on using."

"But what about the route-finding module we already have in place?" asks Victoria. "I spent a couple of weeks on it, and I think it could be augmented fairly easily to cover what we need."

Nick interjects, "Yes, that's true, and it does a good-enough job for the current tier, but that's why I specified the interface you needed to write to. It would take you another few weeks to design, implement, and test all the other functionality we require—and I'm sure you'd rather be working on the 'bot AI than bog-standard route-finding algorithms, so I've planned it so that we can drop their newly finished module into place, hopefully without any teething problems. That's what I'll be taking care of today."

"Good point! Anything that saves me making unnecessary effort has to be a good thing as far as I'm concerned," smiles Victoria.

"Right. Now we've got that settled, let's go on to the next issue. The visibility constraints." Nick consults his daily "to-do" list. "We need to begin adding the visibility filters into the next tier. We already have the stubbed code in place for that. It's just a filter based on the 'chain of responsibility' pattern, which currently implements a clear filter."

"I take it that just passes the data straight through unchanged, so that all 'bots are visible no matter what the external conditions?" asks Victoria.

"That's right. We need to write some filters that take into account the position of the querying 'bot and the effects of smoke for restricting visibility and metal wreckage for radar impairment," explained Nick.

"Don't forget the cloaked unit filter," interjects Charles, the level designer, who has been listening from his desk.

A lightbulb appears above Victoria's head. "I see. That explains why you asked me to ensure the 'bot passes his filter criteria to the visibility engine even though those filter criteria are currently not used. The engine can tailor the filter to that 'bot and pass back the correctly filtered data. This could replace my idea of visibility fields! We could just have the filter build up the data on request."

"Yes, it could, but I'm not sure whether we want to do that. We'll have to knock up an algorithm prototype and run some tests. It could be that building up the list on demand is too processor intensive. We may want to use your visibility fields, or something like them, to spread the workload out more evenly," says Nick, making a few extra notes on his list.

"That sounds good. Shall I get started on that algorithm prototype?" asks Victoria.

"Okay, but don't do any coding yet. I want to know how you are planning on implementing it so I can be sure it fits in with the overall architecture plans. Do you think you can bring me a technical design by later today?" Nick asks Victoria.

Victoria nods. "Sure, no problem. I'll draw up a design that includes the two possible systems, and present it to you with a set of augmented OMT diagrams. If you okay those, I'll begin the implementation tomorrow and update the documentation. Can we fix a meeting for later this afternoon?"

Each tier level must be technically specified, taking into account the requirements of higher tiers. The tier system may influence module design, as there will be some effects on modules. Maybe some will be included, and maybe some will not. There will be stubs or less functional versions in place of the modules in this case. The interface will have to be implemented to take into account all tiers, but, at the lower tiers, a lot of functions will be stubbed out, returning trivial or fudged values.

For example, if a complex algorithm is required, a simple brute-force approach could be used as a placeholder, such as a bubble sort instead of a quick sort, or the provision of a set of valid (but dummy) data.

The architecture itself is fairly independent of the tier system, but the tier system is a useful way of subdividing the work in a quantifiable manner. Clearly, the architecture is a prerequisite of the tier approach: we must have the architecture defined before we can partition it into tiers. Although it is likely that it will change somewhat during the development process, these changes should not be major. Minor refinement is to be expected. In fact, it's inevitable, mainly because the 80/20 rule always comes into play at some point.

Architecture Orthogonality

The project tiers are generally split into three sections. The first, Tier Zero, is the prototyping stage. The subsequent few tiers cover the specifications of the hard architecture, while the remaining tiers of development wrap up the hard architecture and implement the soft architecture.

The hard and soft architecture do have a fair degree of overlap in terms of their conceptual design. The hard architecture is more concerned with the design of the system, while the soft architecture is more concerned with the design of the game. This is summarized as follows:

- system architecture (relationships between components)
- game design architecture (relationships between tokens)

In most systems, unless you have managed to achieve a complete separation between the soft and the hard architecture, then there will be some overlap between the two.

For example, in *Balls!* the soft architecture scripts the behavior of the balls, but the actual behavior code is implemented as a C++ dynamic link library. I would have preferred to have implemented the behavior as a soft-architecture component, but, because *Balls!* was a one-off project, I couldn't see any reason to expend the extra time on a component I was unlikely to reuse in the near future.

This is more likely to be the mode of development that you will be using. Although, in an ideal world, it would be great to be able to design and develop a completely generic game engine so that creating a new game was simply a matter of developing new content and scripts, we are some way away from that point at the moment.

That is not to say we cannot make inroads into the process. The more of the game-specific functionality that can be moved into game-specific soft architecture backed up by a generic hard-architecture framework, the easier our lives will become in the future. In a few years' time, we may find ourselves freed from the drudgework of game design, and able to concentrate on the content rather than the technology.

Chapter 21
Development

Key Topics:

- *Creativity in coding*
- *Code quality*
- *Coding standards*
- *Coding priorities*
- *Debugging and code completion*
- *The seven golden gambits and the three lead balloons*

The actual development of a game—and by this I mean getting the developers to sit down and begin writing the code—is a small part of the entire process. However, it is also one of the most important parts, which is why your team doesn't want to make any costly mistakes that can cause delays and potential cancellation. I wrote earlier in this book that the actual coding is just a small but important last step in the entire development process. In this chapter, we will concentrate on how to reduce risk in this area of development.

There's no room for such mistakes here—and you'll soon run out of second chances to get it right—so it's imperative to get it right the first time. This is why, up until now, the book has been mainly concerned with the preparation for the development process. Everything up to here has been the dress rehearsal, and now it's time for the passion play.

An important consideration when developing a game is the nature and location of creativity. Creativity—inventiveness and inspiration—obviously has its place in games, but, when it manifests in the wrong places, the consequences can be disastrous.

Creativity is a double-edged sword, and it can hinder as much as it can help. In the wrong place, creativity will cause delays and problems more than it will help. For real progress to be made, we need to recognize that creativity can have negative aspects too, when it interferes with getting the job done. Creativity, like any asset, needs to be applied only in the proper place. In this chapter, I will expand upon why the actual code-development phase is the worst possible place for improvisation and creativity. We will focus on the reasons for keeping creativity out of the actual coding and leaving it where it belongs, which is in the design and research phases.

This may sound like anathema to a lot of current game developers, especially those who feel that their creativity is their greatest asset. If I am saying that they are not to use their creativity while developing, then I am effectively rendering them useless, robbing them of the ability to use their greatest skills. This is usually the reaction of the more inexperienced developers—those that believe that coding is the be-all and end-all of development—and that there is nothing else of relevance in the entire process.

However, more-experienced developers, those who understand that there is more to developing a game than just coding the darn thing (which is the central message of this book), have found that creative coding (or hacking) is a major cause of delays and other problems.

The Development Process

In most current game projects, the development process is the area that needs the most attention. Looking at many recent projects, it can be seen that there has been no real development model used. The entire project was just one large, amorphous phase with no effective delineation between phase boundaries.

As we have already discussed, this lack of structure had never previously been a problem in game development, because projects were small enough not to need any formal process or structured approaches.

Unfortunately, a problem has arisen with the explosive increase in power and capabilities of the latest-generation game platforms. At the moment, the games industry as a whole is clinging to the hope that the techniques of the past will still work. The industry has always had a maverick image, and, in order to preserve this image, it has resisted the imposition of formal process, which is just not cool enough. It's probable that a couple of years ago any company attempting to unilaterally implement formal process without a general move by the industry would be labeled as a "square" company to work for, and suffered within the industry as a result. Times are changing now, but not really quickly enough.

Unfortunately, the industry is discovering that the old ways simply aren't scalable to the current size of the average game project. It's no longer single individuals or small teams of two or three; they just can't produce all the content required for an acceptable game today. The increase in team size requires more-formal process to manage the interactions between team members. This has already been discussed in the second part of the book. What we will focus on in this chapter is how the development itself—comprising the technical design and the actual code—has been affected by the increase in team sizes and various measures and techniques that can be used to manage the increased complexity without the entire project descending into anarchy.

Most (if not all) of the techniques discussed in this chapter are already in common use in other areas of the software development industry. These code-management techniques attempt to ensure that the code produced for a project is of a consistently high quality.

It is not a good indicator that the games industry is still reluctant to wholeheartedly adopt these techniques now that the size of the average game project has begun to approach the size of a small-to-medium "typical" industry project. Even though the consensus is that the imposition of processes and controls on the development process is "restrictive" and "boring," I personally would much rather be "bored" and "restricted" while working a standard 8-hour day on a smoothly running project than having to work a run of 20-hour days on a "free" and "interesting" project.

I'm reminded of a Chinese curse: "May you live in interesting times." To our crude Western ears, this doesn't sound like much of an insult. In fact, it could even be construed as a compliment. However, "interesting times" is a metaphor for difficult times—such as periods of civil unrest and personal danger, and this malediction is applicable to software development, too. "Interesting" projects are troubled projects.

I've certainly had enough of working on interesting projects, and nowadays most of my projects are not interesting in that sense. Rather, they are interesting in the more positive way. I don't have to worry about internal politics, backstabbing, or rapidly impending impossible-to-achieve deadlines because all the planning stages have been performed and signed off before the start of development.

The one feature that all these successful projects had in common was excellent planning and management. Once we had begun producing code, it was a simple matter of constructing the code in accordance with the blueprints. Not very exciting or "interesting" I'm sure you'll agree, but the project was completed on time, with no requirements for overtime, so all the developers were able to go home on time and have a life outside of work for the duration of the project. This was not a game project, but the same concepts are still applicable. As I have already maintained, the only difference between a game project and a non-game project is the amount of content that needs to be created. However, content creation is the domain of the game designer, the artists, and the musicians. It has little to do with coding. If you take away all the graphics and just look at plain source code, you would have difficulty telling the difference between the internals of a great game engine and those of the latest spreadsheet calculation engine. (Except the latter will probably be a larger project that is better written, more complex, and have more comments than the game project.)

One thing I'm having difficulty understanding is the insistence by some game industry luminaries that there is a difference between software development in the games industry and that in other industries. This is plain rubbish. Software is software is software. Within the majority of game development, any supposed "differences" are mainly due to the incompetence of the developers. I didn't believe this either until I had experienced it firsthand. The reason that many games companies' development style is different from that of the mainstream software industry is because their development style is notably inferior. While the rest of the software industry has grown up and moved on, the development processes used by these companies remain firmly rooted in the past, and this past doesn't consider the present's marked increase in project size. The problem is further exacerbated by their failure to realize that the old techniques simply are not scalable. Like the dinosaurs of history, they won't survive if they can't or won't adapt.

But, even recently, some of the more forward-thinking members of the games industry have been paying lip service to formalizing development processes. Some have even attempted to implement a full methodology, just not very effectively.

Why does this area need attention in most cases? Well, for one, these token levels of controls are more counterproductive than they are useful. If source control is used, it is rarely used to full potential, and so it instead becomes more of a thinking man's backup system rather than a powerful quality assurance tool in its own right, especially when backed up by some level of code review.

In some cases, full and formal code reviews are considered to be quite an extreme measure. It depends on the relative skill levels of the developers concerned and the amount of risk the project is under. Assuming that the developers are competent, then more of the code reviews can be informal. However, the reviews cannot be dropped altogether and should be treated as a vital part of the development process.

As stated, the only difference between game projects and mainstream projects is the amount of content. Moreover, game engines can be divided into a number of distinct types, and it's not difficult to see that in some cases the only difference between certain games is the content.

For example, it's not hard to imagine that *Command & Conquer* and *Warcraft 2* could have been produced using the same engine even though different companies have written them and the code is most certainly different. I don't mean that they look like they have actually been produced using the same engine; instead, I mean that it's not outside the realms of theoretical possibility.

It's the same thing with all the *Quake* clones—not the ones using the *Quake* engine (there were several different engines floating around at one point, such as the *Unreal* engine, but there may as well have just been the one). The difference between them all was minimal to the average punter.

So that's where the future is: off-the-shelf game engines, minimal game code development, and more focus on content creation. Chapter 24 will expand our ideas for the future.

Now, let's look at the life cycle of code, from inception to check-in. As has been already stated many times in this book, this is not a book on C++ or game code development specifically. You won't find long listings of "type-your-own" 3D engines in this chapter. In fact, the most complex code snippet is probably a three-line **if** statement. What is covered, however, is a number of general techniques that can be applied throughout the development cycle—from the beginning of coding to the system integration.

You also won't find much game-specific material in this chapter: all the advice here applies to any type of software project. But is this any surprise? Throughout the book, we have been adamant that the difference between the development phases of games and those of other software is due to differing levels of professionalism, despite the romantic talk of games being a creative medium. Games *are* a creative medium, but that's no excuse for sloppy development.

Code Quality

Source code of good quality is too often just assumed in all parts of the software industry. After all, we are all professionals, and we are all supposed to write good code. Unfortunately, we don't live in a perfect world, and people write code of varying quality and with varying techniques. Even among the best developers, there is a wide range of different styles.

In fact, the subject of coding styles is almost a question of personal liberty for many developers, and attempting to enforce a uniform style is a recipe for trouble. I've lost count of the number of arguments I've had with other developers over the placement of curly braces in code.

The coding wars used to be about which language to use. With that decision largely decided, the only arguments left concern how to use those languages.

I'm not about to impose my own particular coding style on you. I know how much trouble that would cause, and I'd probably still be receiving hate mail 10 years from now arguing about the correct positioning of curly braces. I have my own coding style, and, if anybody uses a different one, then that is fine by me—except when I am in charge of a project, and my prime concern is to make sure the coding style is uniform. With this in mind, this section will present some coding tips and advice that can be applied to team development to minimize potential risks and avoid certain difficulties that may otherwise arise. This book—I'll say again—is not about programming, but its advice does intend to make code easier to maintain. Its aim is to ensure that the development process doesn't expose itself to unnecessary risks, and the examples cover general issues that are applicable to any programming language at a very general level.

Coding Standards

As long as you write functioning and robust code that you can understand, the coding style shouldn't be that important. Unfortunately, as part of a team, your code needs to be understood by its other members—and not just you. This fact prompts the enforcement of coding standards, stylistic edicts that affect various aspects of code.

Ideally, you would want your team-developed product to look like a consistent unified whole and not some Frankenstein's monster of stitched-together body parts.

For example, the software factory model suggests creating modules that can be used over the course of a number of projects. For this to work as effectively as possible, it would be sensible to ensure that the style of the programming interface is consistent for all the modules released to the project teams. It would only confuse matters if all the modules sported radically different interfaces and usage methods, especially with modules that support similar functionality.

Amongst other issues, the following coding points should be addressed:

- Layout
- Commenting and documentation
- Naming and coding conventions
- Data-access conventions

Let's look at all these points in turn and consider some suggestions as to how they could be handled. These are just specific examples, not hard-and-fast rules. So don't feel that I am forcing you to follow them. You don't have to implement them as is, but it is important to understand the ideas behind the suggestions.

Layout

When considering layout, you need to be aware of several issues.

We need to consider the various aspects of the constructs within the programming language and how to regulate their usage. For example, a language like C++ has many powerful features—in fact, too many powerful features. C++ gives you enough rope to hang yourself, and, unless you avoid using some of the more way-out features such as multiple implementation inheritance—and restrict yourself to what has become known as the *sane subset*—then you are just asking for trouble.

When writing code, you need to consider certain things, for example, the maximum number of lines that are allowed per file, per class, and per method or functions. Certain resolutions should be in place governing the allowable complexity of code. By this, I mean that even the most talented programmers can sometimes get into a sort of "I'm-going-to-get-it-all-done-in-this-method" mentality when they find that the required functionality for that method will take code that is more complex than they initially thought. Instead of doing the logical thing and subdividing the code into another set of smaller methods, they would attempt to cram all the functionality into the one method originally planned, much like packing a suitcase for a holiday.

This can be prevented by implementing these guidelines and those covering the complexity of the code, such as the level of nesting allowed, the allowable complexity of logical constructs, and the calling conventions and protocols used across the projects.

Another useful guideline is to restrict the way that code is laid out. For example, the restriction of one C++ class per source file is pretty much an industry standard. It appears to be an unspoken agreement, and, when I have seen code that spreads C++ classes out among several files, I have found it very difficult to read and get a handle on at first. Anyhow, it is not good programming practice, and unless you have lots of small closely related classes that logically belong in the one file, it should not be used.

This topic is covered in more detail in the next few sections.

Commenting And Documentation

Commenting goes hand in hand with the layout of the code, but it is so important that it gets a section of its own.

Commenting is one of the more emotive issues in the great style wars. The subject and style of comments have caused much argument in the development community. Personally, I prefer minimal commenting. Here is my personal formula for writing and commenting code, and it's the one I recommend for use at work:

- Write the code clearly enough not to need comments. Any sections of code that are tricky enough to require comments should be rewritten so that they are clear enough for their function to be understood without comments.
- Comment it all anyway.

But what is a comment exactly? And what makes a good comment over a bad comment? Again, this is a very emotive issue, but there are some obvious guidelines, the main one being that a comment should say *how* the code does its job, rather than telling the reader *what* it does. Let me give you an example of what I mean, as shown in Listing 21.1.

Listing 21.1 Bad commenting style.

```
void DoAIPreparation(unsigned int uiModeFlag)
{
    // set AI mode flag
    m_uiAIModeFlag = uiModeFlag;
    // . . .
    // Do other stuff
}
```

What does the first comment in Listing 21.1 tell you? Nothing that the code itself doesn't tell you. This sort of comment is all too common. It's deceptive in that it appears to tell you what is going on, but it really tells you nothing. It's redundant information. Comments such as this mean nothing unless you already know what the code does, and how the infrastructure works with the flag.

Compare this with the code snippet shown in Listing 21.2.

Listing 21.2 Better commenting style.

```
void CGameObject::DoAIPreparation(unsigned int uiModeFlag)
{
    // set how this object reacts to incoming AI events.
    // the higher the value, the more aggressive the response
    m_uiAIModeFlag = uiModeFlag;
    // . . .
    // Do other stuff
}
```

In Listing 21.2, we have provided much more information in the comment. The comment doesn't just blithely state the function of the line of code, but instead explains a little of the background. The Listing 21.2 comment explains what the effect of that line of code is on the rest of the object, and it is clearly likely to be much more useful in the context of the object concerned.

If used well, commenting can actually help prevent bugs and promote understanding of the code. For example, when I am writing code, I use several standard techniques in order to make my code more readable.

For each file, I include a standard header, as shown in Listing 21.3.

Listing 21.3 Standard file header.

```
///////////////////////////////////////////////////////////////////////////////
// File:     "ball.cpp"
//
// Related Header File:      "ball.h"
//
// Original Author:          Andrew Rollings (AR)
//
// Creation Date:            22 Jul 98
//
// Specification Document:  "http://PGS.internal.net\specs\modules\ball.htm"
//
// Purpose:                  Implements the basic CBall class, which defines
//                           functionality common to all balls.
//                           This class is not intended to be instantiated as
//                           a concrete class. Derive from it to instantiate
//                           new ball types.
//
///////////////////////////////////////////////////////////////////////////////
// $Log: $
///////////////////////////////////////////////////////////////////////////////
```

The header above is fairly obvious in its structure. Two issues of note are the "Specification Document" field, and the strange **$Log: $** structure.

The first of these refers to the specification document that this file was created from. It is included here as a quote-delimited Uniform Resource Locator (URL), because I do the majority of my development using Microsoft's Visual Studio, and this allows you to right-click on a URL in this format and open it within the development environment. As we have discussed previously, documentation of your project is very important as a risk-reduction mechanism, and this can be kept on an intranet Web site. This feature of Visual Studio (assuming you are developing for PC or Sega Dreamcast) can be very useful for quick access to documentation.

The second point, the **$Log: $** construct, is a source control embedded control code used by Visual SourceSafe. This tells the source control system to embed the check-in comment entered when a developer checks in this source file directly into the file itself as a comment. Source control is a topic we will be covering in more detail later in this chapter.

The other fields are fairly straightforward. The "File" field is obviously the file name. The "Related Header File" field is the name of the header file containing the class declaration. These are also quote delimited so that I can take advantage of the automatic file-opening features of Visual Studio (in the same way as the URL for the specification document). Then come the "Original Author" and "Creation Date" fields, which are filled in with the name of the developer who originally created the file (as well as the acronym he uses to label his "TODO" comments in code—"AR" in this case), and the date it was created.

The "Purpose" field is filled in with a brief description of the functionality of the code in the file. This is the place to point out any peculiarities or caveats for using the file contents.

At the next level is the function header, which gives an overview of each particular function or member function. (See Listing 21.4.)

Listing 21.4 Standard function header.

```
//////////////////////////////////////////////////////////////////////////////
// Function:                CBall::CBall
//
// Last Modified by:        Davey Jones
//
// Last Modified:           21 Aug 99
//
// Function:                Performs initialization of the ball object.
//                          Sets up "per instance" member variables, and loads
//                          "per class" graphics if they are not already
//                          loaded.
//
// Inputs:                  None.
//
// Outputs:                 None.
//
// Returns:                 None.
//////////////////////////////////////////////////////////////////////////////
```

The function header shown in Listing 21.4 is fairly straightforward, and there is nothing that really needs explaining in great detail. The function field contains the fully qualified function name. In this case, we are labeling the constructor for the CBall class. The "last modified by" field contains the name of the developer who last worked on the function. The "Function" field provided a plain language description of *what* the function does, not *how* it does it. "Inputs" and "Outputs" describes the functions of input and output variables respectively, and "Returns" described the meaning of the return value.

Another trick I use is to comment a routine before I actually write it. I then use the comments to marshal my thoughts as I write the code. The comments are usually taken directly from the pseudocode described in the technical specification. This is how code should be written on all large projects: The developer writes the comments with his Technical Architect hat on, then writes the code with his Programmer hat on.

I have stated that good commenting, used effectively, helps to reduce the number of errors in the code. Unfortunately, within the games industry, there appears to be a sort of "machismo" that comments are for wimps. If you can't understand the code without comments, then you're no coder. In other cases, developers have deliberately not commented their code in order to make it as difficult to understand as possible—in order to protect their "secrets." Hopefully, this sort of attitude will begin to die out, but, in the meanwhile, the best approach is simply not to employ people who can't or won't comment their code. After all, comments acknowledge that, on a team project, the guy who has to check the code is often not the guy who wrote it in the first place. A lot of time can be lost if a developer has to spend days deciphering another person's uncommented code. A developer who is not prepared to share ideas has no place as part of a team, and well-commented code is one of the best ways of sharing information in a team of skilled developers.

Note

I once knew a developer who would write copious amounts of comments. He never had any problems in doing this. This would have been a good thing, except he used the comments as a sort of personal diary. Rather than write about how the code worked, he would write about how he felt that day and what he had had for breakfast that morning. He was a great developer, but his comments were worse than useless.

Commenting is also important for code reviews. Comments show what the developer intended to do: If the code differs from what the comments say it should do, the comments are usually correct. Without this extra information, the reviewers would have to consistently refer to the technical specification document. The comments in the code give some insight into the thought processes of the developer, and they act as a source for extra information to cross-reference with the code.

The last crucially important aspect of commenting is for marking areas of work in progress, so that it can be located later when searching through the code. (This is the only recommendation I'm going to make that really isn't optional!) When a developer is working on an area of code and has to interrupt the work for any reason (fixing a bug elsewhere, a telephone call, lunch, end of work, or whatever), then it should be labeled as such. Many errors can be caused by a developer forgetting a small but important detail that he left undone in the code just before clocking off, originally meaning to have finished it off the following morning. This can be avoided by inserting a simple "TODO" comment in the code. This should include an identifier to identify the developer and the date and rough time of the comment. If the area of code to be fixed comprises a block, then a matching pair of beginning and end blocks can be used, as shown in Listing 21.6 in the next section.

Naming And Coding Conventions

This is another great subject for arguments and holy wars.

Naming and coding conventions cover two main areas:

- Files and directory structures
- Classes, functions, and variables

It's clear that it is important for variable, class, and function naming to provide some information about the type of information you are dealing with. For instance, can you tell what the code in Listing 21.5 does?

Listing 21.5 Bad code.

```
/////////////////////////////////////////////////////////////////////////////
/////////////////////////////////////////////////////////////////////////////
void D::pd(B* b, bool& x)
{
    x = false;
    if (!b)
        return;
    bool bb = b->ntd();
    if (false == bb){
        static char t[64];
        sprintf(t, "%p : bb false\n", b);
        ::OutputDebugString(t);
        return; }
    n++;
    x = i(b);
}
```

In fact, even though I tried to give the variables vague names and obscure the purpose of the code in Listing 21.5 (to make it difficult to understand), I have seen code like this in production systems. In fact, I have seen code that is worse.

How could it be worse, you ask?

Well, in Listing 21.5, although the code is difficult to read, at least the indentation represents the logical structure of the code. But, although it is easy to see what is going on in terms of the logic, you will have no idea as to what the function of the above code snippet is. About the only statement in the entire snippet that is clear in purpose (if not in meaning) is the call to **OutputDebugString**, which is a Microsoft defined function. The message being output is not much help though: It doesn't tell you anything the code doesn't already tell you.

Listing 21.6 Better code.

```
//////////////////////////////////////////////////////////////////////////////
// Function:                CDrawlist::Draw
//
// Last Modified by:        Andrew Rollings
//
// Last Modified:           21 Jul 99
//
// Function:                Prepares the object (supporting the IDrawable
//                          interface passed as a parameter) for drawing by
//                          checking first if it needs to be drawn, and then
//                          inserting the member graphics object into the draw
//                          list, which is then drawn when all objects have
//                          been processed.
//
// Inputs:                  c_pDrawableObject_ : valid const pointer to the
//                          object to be drawn - must support the IDrawable
//                          interface (see "Drawable.h")
//
// Outputs:                 bSuccess_ : reference to a Boolean variable that
//                          is set to true if the object c_pDrawableObject_ is
//                          drawn, and false if it was not necessary to draw
//                          the object.
//
// Returns:                 Nothing.
//////////////////////////////////////////////////////////////////////////////
void CDrawList::PrepareDraw(const IDrawable* c_pDrawableObject_,
                          bool& rbSuccess_)
{
    rbSuccess_ = false;    // assume default result fails
    // check input validity
    if (NULL == c_pDrawableObject_)
    {
        return;
    }
    // check if we need to draw the object. It may be obscured by
    // closer objects.
    bool bNeedToDraw = c_pDrawableObject_->NeedToDraw();
```

```
    if ( false == bNeedToDraw)
    {
        // begin ARTODO: 22/07/99 : remove (temporary diagnostics)
        static char s_szBuf[64];
        sprintf(s_szBuf, "%p : Draw not required\n", c_pDrawableObject_);
        ::OutputDebugString(s_szBuf);
        // end ARTODO
        return;
    }
    m_uiNumberOfObjectsToDraw ++;
    // passed test, so we need to draw the object
    rbSuccess_ = InsertIntoDrawList(c_pDrawableObject_);
}
```

Apart from a sensible naming scheme (which makes the purpose of variable and functions a lot easier to understand), Listings 21.5 and 21.6 are identical. To the compiler, (assuming that, as most modern compilers do, it optimizes logical comparisons to their simplest possible form), there is absolutely no difference, and both listings will produce identical compiled output (except—for the pedantic among you—the formatting of the text string displayed by the **OutputDebugString** function). It is, however, pretty clear which is easier to read.

Secondly, this is not production code. It is not at all optimized, primarily because I need to cram a lot of examples of coding conventions into a clear and concise listing.

Let me explain some of the notation and terminology I have used in the example. Most well-organized companies and individuals use some variation on these techniques, so unless you are a relic from the stone age of computing, the concepts will not be unfamiliar to you.

The function header, introduced in the previous section, contains a description of the purpose of the function, valid inputs to the function, expected outputs, and return values.

The function parameters are indicated with a trailing underscore, such as **rbSuccess_**, to ensure differentiation from local variables, such as **bNeedToDraw**, which is used to store the return value from the **NeedToDraw** member of the object to be drawn.

The return value, **rbSuccess_**, is passed as a reference parameter rather than being specified as a traditional return value. There is a good reason for this: It's a lot easier to ignore a return value returned in the usual fashion than it is to ignore one that has to be passed as a parameter. If the caller of the function is forced to go to the effort of setting up a variable to hold the return value, then they may as well check the return value when it comes back. If the return value is just returned in the usual fashion, there is no compulsion (apart from asking nicely) for the caller to even acknowledge the fact that there is a return value, let alone check it.

When using this style of calling, passing all values including return values as parameters, it is customary to place input-only variables (such as **pDrawableObject_**) on the left and the output on the right. Mixed input/output variables (where the input value is used and set to a new value for output) should be placed somewhere in the middle.

Within the **if** statement, I have placed some debug code. There are two areas of interest here. First of all, as described in the previous section, I have included a "TODO" comment block and prefixed it with my initials (AR) to mark the modification. This means that, at a later date, I (or someone else) can perform a multifile search for all the TODOs remaining for the entire project or for a single individual.

The second area of interest is that I have explicitly used the global scope operator (**::**) to mark the use of the global function, **OutputDebugString**. This is not at all necessary unless the class has an identically named member function, but it is useful to tell at a glance whether a function is a class member or not. If it has the global scope operator, then it is global; if not, it is local (such as the **InsertIntoDrawList** member function used later in the code snippet).

This also protects against the (admittedly unlikely) possibility of accidentally naming a member function with the same name as a global function that is already used within the class. However, the primary purpose is to allow at-a-glance distinguishing of global and member functions. For larger classes with lots of members (have you taken a look at MFC lately?), this can be essential.

One of the classic errors in C and C++ is using an assignment operator instead of an equality operator. Listing 21.7 shows this in action.

Listing 21.7 Assignment instead of equality.

```
if (pObject = NULL) // this line sets pObject to NULL, which is always "true".
{
    // code here will always get executed
    ::OutputDebugString("I am always executed\n");
}
```

The correct code is shown in Listing 21.8

Listing 21.8 Correct but unsafe equality testing.

```
if (pObject == NULL) // note the '==' - easy to get wrong!
{
    ::OutputDebugString("I am executed if pObject is NULL\n");
}
```

However, relying on the developer to always type this correctly is not safe. Even the best programmers still make this mistake. Fortunately, there are two ways of getting the compiler to spot the error and refuse to compile. (Visual C++ 6 issues a warning for the above code, but it's all too easy to ignore warnings.)

One method is suitable for all situations, and is shown in Listing 21.9. The other, which is to declare the pointer as **const**, prevents the assignment in Listing 21.7 from compiling, but is not always possible depending on the nature of the code.

Listing 21.9 Correct and safe equality testing.

```
if (NULL == pObject)
{
    ::OutputDebugString("I am executed if pObject is NULL\n");
}
```

By reversing the order of the equality test and putting the constant **NULL** on the left, it is impossible to make the error. If the developer mistypes the equality test by using the assignment operator, then the code will automatically refuse to compile because you cannot assign a value to a constant. If you can use the compiler to automatically trap errors such as this, then you should take advantage of it in order to save yourself the stress of looking for nasty little bugs such as this.

Another similar problem that sometimes catches even the best programmers (although somewhat less than the above example) is the one-line **if** clause.

Take a look at the code in Listing 21.10.

Listing 21.10 The if statement problem—setup.

```
if (NULL != pObject)
    pObject->DoSomething();
```

Although this is perfectly legal C (and C++) code, it is fraught with dangers. If a developer needs to add an extra statement to the **if** clause, then it is not unheard of for the situation shown in Listing 21.11 to occur.

Listing 21.11 The if statement problem—compounded.

```
if (NULL != pObject)
    pObject->DoSomething();
    pObject->DoSomethingElse();
```

Now, because I've led you up to this and you can see the code in isolation rather than in its natural environment, surrounded by other code, you will immediately spot what is wrong in Listing 21.11. The unbracketed **if** statement refers only to the line immediately following it. The line where the member function **DoSomethingElse()** is called will always execute, whether **pObject** is **NULL** or not. If the value of **pObject** is **NULL**, then this will cause a memory-access violation, and the program will crash. Depending on the frequency that **pObject** is **NULL**, this would be quite easy to spot. If you are using C++ exception handling (which I don't recommend using for this purpose, especially in debug builds), then the problem will become much harder to spot.

Similarly, the problem could be made worse if no such error is thrown. Take a look at Listing 21.12.

Listing 21.12 The if statement problem—mark 2.

```
if (true == pObject->ReadyToProcess())
    pObject->Process();
    pObject->MarkAsProcessed();
```

Listing 21.12 is potentially disastrous. This code will mark the object as processed regardless of the return value of the **ReadyToProcess()** member function call. This sort of error could be extremely difficult to find without stepping through the code line by line. But, then again, how can we be sure that the original developer didn't intend that in the first place and hadn't just made an indentation error? The real error could be elsewhere! And, worse still, if the developer accidentally put a semicolon after the **if** statement, like this

```
if (true == pObject->ReadyToProcess());
```

then this is an empty **if** statement. Both of the subsequent lines will be executed, regardless of the result of the test.

The remedy to this problem is simple—two or three extra keystrokes—and is shown in Listing 21.13.

Listing 21.13 The if statement problem—solved!

```
if (true == pObject->ReadyToProcess())
{
    pObject->Process();
}
```

By enclosing the **if** clause with curly braces, we have made it abundantly clear what we mean. This is defensive coding in action. Listings 21.14 and 21.15 show how this coding style can answer the question as to what a developer means.

Listing 21.14 The if statement solution—part 1.

```
// the developer only wants objects to be marked as processed
// if they are actually processed
if (true == pObject->ReadyToProcess())
{
    pObject->Process();
    pObject->MarkAsProcessed();
}
```

In Listing 21.14, it is completely clear what the developer wanted. The object is only to be marked as processed if it actually has been. Listing 21.15 deals with the alternative scenario.

Listing 21.15 The if statement solution—part 2.

```
// the developer wants objects to be marked as processed
// whether they actually are or not
if (true == pObject->ReadyToProcess())
{
    pObject->Process();
}
pObject->MarkAsProcessed();
```

In Listing 21.15, the developer clearly wants the object to be marked as processed, whether it is ready to be processed or not. Looking back at Listing 21.12, it is impossible to tell which of Listing 21.14 or 21.15 the original developer intended to write. Even if you only ever intend an **if** statement to be a one-liner, you can never tell what will be necessary in the future. Why tempt fate, when three extra keystrokes could potentially save a lot of difficulty later in the project?

The above guideline has one exception, and that is what I call a real one-liner. This (and the alternative I sometimes use) is shown in Listing 21.16.

Listing 21.16 The if statement solution—epilog.

```
// the developer only intends the following statement to be a
// one-liner - or maybe he just wants to fit it on one line
if ( true == pObject->ReadyToProcess() ) pObject->Process();

// this is the way I would write the preceding line. Note
// the curly braces.
if ( true == pObject->ReadyToProcess() ) { pObject->Process(); }
```

Sensible naming conventions are also used within the code. Aside from certain conventions with the prefixes and suffixes (which I will be discussing next), all the functions and variables used have concise, descriptive names that give a clue as to what they are used for. Generally, the verb/noun format is used for this sort of naming, but, in the cases in which functionality is difficult to describe, don't try to force it. A function called **DoCalculation** helps nobody. I tend to use internal capitalization in order to differentiate the words within the function or variable name, and this is a pretty consistent standard within the development industry. Compare this with Java, where the accepted standard is to capitalize only the second and subsequent words in a function: for example, **needToDraw()**. Which you use (if any) is—as always—a matter of personal preference, but my preference is to use capitalization throughout.

As can be seen in Listing 21.6, I tend to use a certain set of conventions in variable names. For example, function parameters have a trailing underscore, and member variables are preceded by "**m_**".

This is a Microsoft convention. On Unix, member variables tend to be prefixed just by an underscore, but I don't like the Unix notation as much, as it tends to make code more difficult to read, especially when function parameters are being mixed with member variables. (This is just a personal opinion, however.)

Table 21.1 shows a table of prefixes used for class naming conventions.

The indicators in Table 21.1 are not used for variable names but only for actual class declarations and definitions. If it is necessary for a variable to indicate whether it is a class, interface, or structure, then it is usually included as a suffix as described later. Usually however, this is not necessary, because the other information provided within the context of the code is enough to locate the type of the variable.

Table 21.2 shows the prefixes and suffixes used to denote variable scope.

As shown in the last entry of Table 21.2, if an object is of multiple types, then each of the indicators is used sequentially before the underscore. For example, a global static constant could be defined as **gsc_uiRefCount**.

Table 21.3 shows a table of prefixes used for variable type indications.

Note that, for types that already have a prefix taken from Table 21.2 (scope indicators), then that prefix appears first, followed by the prefix from Table 21.3 (type indicators). For example, an unsigned integer class member variable would be denoted as **m_uiRefCount**.

Note

Classes, structures, and interfaces are unadorned. If you wish to indicate that one of these is being used (if it is not already obvious from the context of the code), then append the type to the end of the variable: for example, ***pDrawableObjectIface*****,** ***pAIHandlerClass,*** *or* ***pConfigStruct****. Usually this level of detail is not necessary because, by using the other recommendations, the reader can easily determine whether the variable is a local variable, a passed parameter, or a class member variable—which considerably narrows down the hunt for the declaration of the variable type.*

You could also use the single letter values directly from Table 21.1. For example, the above variable names would become ***pDrawableObjectI****,* ***pAIHandlerC****, and* ***pConfigS****. Decide on one of these formats and stick to it, however, or much confusion will result.*

So, from Tables 21.1, 21.2, and 21.3, we can conclude that the general format (which is based on the Microsoft version of Hungarian notation) for a variable name is

<scope>_<type><Name><Class/Struct/Interface><_ = parameter>

where

<scope> is one of the values taken from Table 21.2.

Table 21.1 Class naming conventions.

Category	Name Prefix	Example	Notes
Class name	C	CBall	In C++ a class has all members private by default. See Structure name.
Interface name	I	IDrawable	
Structure name	S	SConfig	In C++ a struct is a class with all members public by default.

Table 21.2 Variable scope indicators.

Scope	Indicator	Prefix/Suffix Affects	Example	Notes
Global	g_	prefix to variable	g_uiRefCount	
Class member	m_	prefix to variable	m_uiRefCount	
Static	s_	prefix to variable	s_uiRefCount	This isn't really a scope indicator.
Const	c_	prefix to variable	c_uiInitialValue	This isn't really a scope indicator.
Enumeration	e	prefix to variable	eStateOK	
Static class member	ms_	prefix to variable	ms_uiRefCount	

Table 21.3 Variable type indicators.

Type	Indicator	Example	Notes
Signed integer	i or n	iXPos, nLoopcount	n is usually used for loop variables or counters.
Unsigned integer	ui or n	uiRefCount, nLoopcount	n is usually used for loop variables or counters.
Signed char	ch	chKeyInput	
Unsigned char	uch	uchInputVal	'b' was used before the **bool** type was defined in C++.
Signed short	s	sXPos	
Unsigned short	us	usScore	
Signed long	l	lBallCount	
Unsigned long	ul	ulBallIndex	
Boolean	b	bNeedToDraw	
Array	a	achMap[200]	See "Zero Terminated String."
Pointer	p	pchChoice	
Pointer to array	pa	pachMatrix	
Array of pointers	ap	apLookups	
Reference	r	rConfigStruct	
Parameter	_	rbSuccess_	This follows the variable name.
Zero terminated string	sz	szOutput	This is usually an array of characters.
Unicode characters	w	wszOutput	This is usually an array of shorts.

<type> is one of the values taken from Table 21.3 (separated from **<scope>** by an underscore).

<Name> is the internally capitalized variable name.

<Class/Struct/Interface> is taken from Table 21.1 and either used in full or just with the initial capital (**C**, **S**, or **I**).

<_ = parameter> indicates that an underscore is appended if the variable is a function parameter.

Now, although this is the naming convention I use and enforce and has become second nature to me, I must state that I am not trying to force it upon you. It is entirely your choice as to whether you use it or not. You may have another scheme—more complex or simpler—that suits your team, or you may not use one at all.

In general, although the importance of coding standards is great, it's not worth going to war over it. Is it really going to hurt the productivity (or the feelings) of a developer that much to be told where to put his curly braces? It's not worth getting excited about. It's not just about where the curly braces should be: It's also about avoidance of unsafe and risky practices and improving the code quality and readability (for example, the use of references instead of pointers to avoid the need for pointer-checking code).

The consistent use of a naming system helps immensely in increasing the understandability of the code. With practice, this variable naming system becomes second nature and prevents any of those "What type is this variable?" questions and bugs that crop up. If you add all the extra time taken on this sort of unnecessary investigation over the course of a project, it will become clear why sensible naming is of paramount importance, regardless of whatever naming scheme you use.

I couldn't write a book about computers without including something about the **goto** statement. Programmers are divided about the use of **goto**, although most believe that it is a "bad thing," because it produces spaghetti code. This is true enough if it is used badly, but, used in the right place, it can be useful. The only good place I've found for the **goto** statement is the one-shot error cleanup. Take a look at the code in Listing 21.17, which seems to have been written by a programmer with a religious aversion to the **goto** statement.

Listing 21.17 Error cleanup without the use of the goto statement.

```
bool CObject::FuncThatLocksAResource(COperand* pOperandC_)
{
    // lock resource
    m_resource.Lock();
    // do something with object
    bool bRet = DoSomethingWithObject(pOperandC_);
    if (false == bRet)
    {
```

```
        // unlock resource and return result
        m_resource.Unlock();
        return bRet;
    }
    // do something else with object
    bRet = DoSomethingElseWithObject(pOperandC_);
    if (false == bRet)
    {
        // unlock resource and return result
        m_resource.Unlock();
        return bRet;
    }
    // do last thing with object
    bRet = DoLastThingWithObject(pOperandC_);
    if (false == bRet)
    {
        // unlock resource and return result
        m_resource.Unlock();
        return bRet;
    }
    // finished with object, and processing was successful
    bRet = pOperandC_->SetState(COperand::eFinishedOK);
    // unlock resource and return result
    m_resource.Unlock();
    return bRet;
}
```

Functions such as those shown in Listing 21.17 are fairly commonplace with coders who believe that the **goto** statement is the manifestation of true evil on Earth. The highlighted sections shows four instances in which code has been duplicated unnecessarily. Multiple areas of duplicated code (more commonly known as cut-and-paste programming) are a maintenance nightmare and should rightfully be rejected in any code review.

Listing 21.18 shows the way that this routine could be made much clearer with the use of a **goto** statement.

Listing 21.18 Legitimate use of the goto statement—one-shot error cleanup.

```
bool CObject::FuncThatLocksAResource(COperand* pOperandC_)
{
    // lock resource
    m_resource.Lock();
    // do something with object
    bool bRet = DoSomethingWithObject(pOperandC_);
    if (false == bRet)
    {
        goto cleanup;
```

```
    }
    // do something else with object
    bRet = DoSomethingElseWithObject(pOperandC_);
    if (false == bRet)
    {
        goto cleanup;
    }
    // do last thing with object
    bRet = DoLastThingWithObject(pOperandC_);
    if (false == bRet)
    {
        goto cleanup;
    }
    // finished with object, and processing was successful
    bRet = pOperandC_->SetState(COperand::eFinishedOK);

    // unlock resource and return result
    cleanup:
    m_resource.Unlock();
    return bRet;
}
```

The code in Listing 21.18 is much clearer than that of Listing 21.17. The cleanup code is in just one place, and the use of the **goto** statement to jump to the cleanup code is much simpler than the previous method. Also, if the cleanup code needs to be changed, which version is going to be the simpler: the version with the cleanup repeated four times or the function where it is only in one place?

Of course, this is the standard argument for the judicious use of the **goto** statement. You won't find anything here that hasn't already been repeated in every programming textbook released in the last 20 years. There is another issue, however—one that you won't find mentioned in many places, because it's not so immediately obvious.

Using **goto** in conjunction with exceptions is not a good idea. Take a look at Listing 21.19.

Listing 21.19 Caveats of the goto statement.

```
void main()
{
    CObject object;
    object.Initialize();
    // then go on to do other stuff with object that requires the ability
    // to lock the internal resource
}

/////////////////////////////////////////////////////////////////////////////
/////////////////////////////////////////////////////////////////////////////
```

```
void CObject::Initialize()
{
    COperand* pOperand = new COperand();
    If (false == FuncThatLocksAResource(pOperand))
    {
        // if an unexpected exception is thrown in FuncThatLocksAResource
        // then the cleanup code will not be executed, and the resource
        // will still be locked. The object then becomes unusable.
        // This code will not be executed, because the exception will
        // be passed up the call stack until it finds a handler
        ::OutputDebugString("CObject::Initialize() failed\n");
    }
}

//////////////////////////////////////////////////////////////////////////////
//////////////////////////////////////////////////////////////////////////////
bool CObject::FuncThatLocksAResource(COperand* pOperandC_)
{
    // lock resource
    m_resource.Lock();
    // do something with object
    bool bRet = DoSomethingWithObject(pOperandC_);
    if (false == bRet)
    {
        goto cleanup;
    }
    // do something else with object
    bRet = DoSomethingElseWithObject(pOperandC_);
    if (false == bRet)
    {
        goto cleanup;
    }
    // do last thing with object
    bRet = DoLastThingWithObject(pOperandC_); // unexpected exception thrown
    if (false == bRet)
    {
        goto cleanup;
    }
    // finished with object, and processing was successful
    bRet = pOperandC_->SetState(COperand::eFinishedOK);

    // unlock resource and return result
    cleanup:
    m_resource.Unlock();
    return bRet;
}
```

The code in Listing 21.19 contains a bug. If an exception is thrown anywhere between the locking of the resource and the unlocking of the resource (for example, by the highlighted line in the listing), then the resource will not be unlocked. The "correct" solution would be to include exception-handling code to free the resource, using **try** and **catch** statements within the **FuncThatLocksAResource** function. However, including exception handling in every possible situation that an exception could possibly occur is an unreasonable expectation, and would make the code unnecessarily more complex and difficult to maintain. There is also quite a bit of overhead associated with setting up the exception handling mechanism, so this is not something you would want to do at the higher granularity levels of the program (because this would cause unacceptable slowdowns).

Okay, that's one solution, but there is another. It has less overhead, and it doesn't require that you place exception-handling code in the higher granularity levels of your application. Instead, it can be left where it belongs in the lower levels. Take a look at Listing 21.20.

Listing 21.20 Avoiding use of the goto statement—one-shot error cleanup.

```
///////////////////////////////////////////////////////////////////////////////
// CResourceLock is an autolock for the resource. It locks the resource on
// construction, and unlocks the resource on destruction
///////////////////////////////////////////////////////////////////////////////
class CResourceLock
{
    public:
    CResourceLock(CResource& resource) : m_resource(resource)
    {
        m_resourceToLock.Lock();
    }
    ~CResourceLock()
    {
        m_resourceToLock.Unlock();
    }

    private:
    CResource& m_resourceToLock;
};

///////////////////////////////////////////////////////////////////////////////
///////////////////////////////////////////////////////////////////////////////
bool CObject::FuncThatLocksAResource(COperand* pOperandC_)
{
    // set up resource autolock/unlock
    CResourceLock reslock(m_resource);

    // do something with object
    bool bRet = DoSomethingWithObject(pOperandC_);
```

```
    if (false == bRet)
    {
        return false;
    }
    // do something else with object
    bRet = DoSomethingElseWithObject(pOperandC_);
    if (false == bRet)
    {
        return false;
    }
    // do last thing with object
    bRet = DoLastThingWithObject(pOperandC_);
    if (false == bRet)
    {
        return false;
    }
    // finished with object, and processing was successful
    return pOperandC_->SetState(COperand::eFinishedOK);
}
```

Listing 21.20 places the resource handling code into a separate object. This is cleaner from an object-oriented point of view, immeasurably improving the clarity of the code, although it does raise some concerns over performance. However, resource locking (of whatever type) is usually a fairly slow process compared to the small amount of time it takes to create and destroy the **CResourceLock** object.

The best thing about using the auto-lock object is that the error-handling code in the function, **FuncThatLocksAResource**, is much simpler. When the function is exited (for whatever reason) the **CResourceLock** will be destructed and the destructor will be invoked even if an exception has been thrown. In my code, I tend to use auto-lock objects to lock screen updates. With a double-buffered screen, the constructor of the auto-lock object locks the screen for writing, and the destructor unlocks the object and flips the buffer. This auto-lock object is defined as a protected local class within the CScreen class.

Of course, it is debatable whether it is worth doing this if this is the only place we will ever have to lock this particular resource. It's a lot of extra effort to write a new class just for one instance of code. If this is the case, then it's probably better to use standard exception-handling techniques, and to unlock the resource normally in the **catch** part of a **try/catch** statement. For situations in which the lock is needed in multiple places, (such as locking a screen for writing), then this is an invaluable technique.

For a book that purportedly states that it is not about coding, there is an awful lot of code in this chapter. That's okay. I still haven't lied: the book is not about coding. The examples presented here are showing how to use language features to minimize risk, and minimizing risk is one of the main topics that this book is about.

Coding Priorities

At each level of project development, certain priorities drive the process. These priorities will almost certainly differ for certain areas of the project. For example, the priorities for the code to provide a menuing system is likely to have wildly different priorities than the code for a 3D engine would have. (If they don't, then there is something seriously wrong with the project.)

You need a project edict to establish coding priorities as part of the technical design, and the coder needs to follow these priorities. Otherwise, time is wasted reimplementing code that is not suitable for the purpose.

These priorities cannot be ignored, as they are the low-level forces that govern the direction of the project. At the highest level, project goals drive the project, but, at the lowest levels—where all the action is—coding priorities drive code implementation.

What do we need to know about priorities? What sort of considerations need to be taken into account?

- Speed
- Size
- Flexibility
- Portability
- Maintainability

Let's look at each of these issues in turn, and briefly discuss them.

Speed

The need for speed is foremost in the minds of the majority of game developers. Games have to be fast. Each function needs to be pared down to the absolute minimum. Each needs to be optimized to the max.

Well, that's what a lot of developers believe. And, if they are working on restricted platforms such as the Color Game Boy, with its relatively low-powered processor, then they will be right. Of course, some code (such as menuing code) wouldn't set such a high priority on speed. As an example, on the Game Boy, the next highest priority would be system architecture considerations and size.

On more-powerful platforms, including the PC and Macintosh, the quest for speed is a bit of a wild goose chase. It simply isn't possible to optimize down to the instruction level in a reasonable period. The processors that these machines use (and the software they run) tend to be so complex that the execution speed of any particular block of code is pretty nondeterministic at the lowest levels of granularity. The only way to measure speed with any accuracy is to use stochastic method; that is, run the code to be tested several thousand times and take the average execution time.

You could do this sort of thing manually, but this doesn't provide you with much application-level information. The best solution is to use a package such as NuMega *TrueTime* on PC (shown in Figure 21.1), which instruments the application and collects information as it is running. The resulting database can be reviewed in a hierarchical form, and you can see which functions are taking up the most time, as a percentage of either program execution time or the execution time for the calling routine.

The main use of this sort of program is not just to tell you how effective your optimizations are, but also to tell you *where* to optimize. It's a standard statistic that your program spends 90 percent of the time in just 10 percent of the code. Well, that's a good place to start optimization, and profiling applications such as NuMega *TrueTime* allow you to determine this information quickly and easily.

It's just not worth focusing your attentions on areas of code that simply aren't executed that often. You'll get much better results by focusing on the 10 percent of commonly executed code than you will by working on the rest. Sure, you might have the fastest-appearing menu in the West, but who's going to notice if the main game loop runs like a lethargic slug?

In regards to optimization, it should begin at the algorithm level and end at the op-code level only as a last resort. You'll get much better optimization results if you take a long, hard look at the algorithms you're using than you will by concentrating on the op-code level, which is the highest granularity level in the system. Only when all the lower granularity level options have been exhausted should you shift up a granularity level.

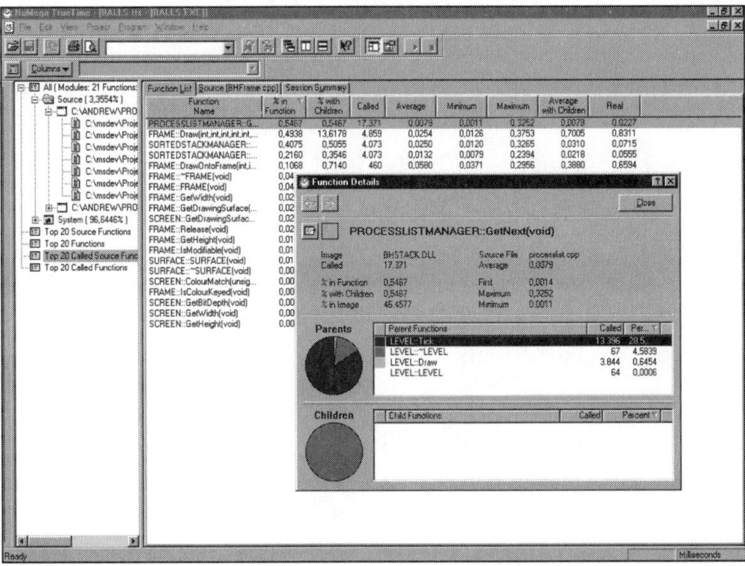

Figure 21.1
NuMega *TrueTime* in action.

Size

Size is less of a priority on the more powerful platforms. This is because the amount of system resources available to the programmer are usually exhausted by other means long before code size becomes an issue. On a typical CD-ROM game for the PC, the program files themselves take up less than two or three megabytes of space. The data for the game—comprising the artwork, the music, and the game data—take up the major part of the space on the CD-ROM.

On the PC or Macintosh, unless you are coding for a specific purpose (such as components that are to be download over the Internet uncompressed), then code size is never a consideration, because the available level of local read/write storage is usually much more than a typical game requires. The only size limitation on the PC (and these are rapidly disappearing) is the amount of memory on the graphics cards, but, again, this is a matter of data rather than of code. The bottleneck here is how much data can be shifted across the card bus and how much of that data will fit in the card's memory.

Even processor cache considerations are for the most part redundant. It's no longer important to try and tune assembly loops so that they fit comfortably inside the processor's first-level cache. The last famous program that took these things into consideration was the original *Quake*, but this was written before the advent of the powerful 3D graphics acceleration cards.

However, on space-limited platforms that do not have large amounts of fast, on-board storage (such as the PlayStation or the Nintendo 64), then code size becomes a much more important consideration.

The PlayStation has a CD-ROM that allows slow-access, read-only storage of approximately 600 megabytes, but it has only a small amount of system RAM. You don't really want to have to frustrate the player by continually having to page code into memory from the CD-ROM, so it is important to consider overall size.

The Nintendo 64 is even more limited in terms of space, because it relies on cartridges rather than CD-ROMs to store the game code and data and has similar system limitations to the PlayStation. Although the cartridge access times are for all intents and purposes instantaneous, they generally tend to only have about 100th of the storage space of a CD-ROM.

Space considerations are more of a concern, but, because you usually write for these consoles in a language such as C (even though Metrowerks provides a C++ compiler for the Nintendo 64) and are discouraged from programming the hardware directly (especially on the PlayStation), you have slightly less control over the size of the code than you would otherwise. There is a rough correlation between the C and the assembly, but it is not exact.

On platforms that are even more limited, such as the Color Game Boy, the code size is one of the most important considerations. Because of the hardware limitations, most of the important code has to fit in a small area, although other code can be paged in from the cartridge as necessary. With the Game Boy platform, which has a relatively weak processor, the majority of programs are coded in Game Boy Assembler, which allows precise control over the code size.

Flexibility

Code flexibility depends on where and how it is intended to be used.

For example, linked lists are generally useful in many situations, so, if you wanted to implement a linked list, it would make sense to use templates that allow it to be customized for use in other modules by instantiating a type-specific version of the code where required.

Note

If you wanted linked list code, I would normally recommend STL, because it is likely to be a better and faster implementation than the average developer can manage. However the Microsoft implementation of STL that is available with Visual Studio 6 is flawed and cannot be exported from a DLL without crashing the application due to incorrect use of static data within the STL library. In cases such as these—where the compiler vendors are at fault—the only option is to find another implementation of the library (such as Hewlett Packard's or Rogue Wave's) or, if one is not available, to roll your own.

Where reuse is a consideration, flexibility of code is also important. The rule to follow when considering flexibility is that the lower the level—and the more generic the functionality—the more important it is to make flexibility a priority.

Portability

For portability to be a consideration, the platforms being targeted must be broadly similar in capabilities. For example, it would not make sense to attempt to write C code that would be portable from the PC down to the Color Game Boy because of the huge difference in power between the two platforms. The concept of portability here is meaningless.

However, between platforms of arguably similar capabilities—such as the PlayStation, Dreamcast, and Nintendo 64 (and to some extent the PC)—the potential for cross-platform libraries is much greater. The similar power and capabilities of these platforms lend themselves to some degree of abstraction, meaning that common game code could be written in a portable style using a consistent interface to platform-specific code on each machine.

Maintainability

Maintainability—the readability and ease of modification—of code is usually one of the most important concerns, especially when the code is designed to be modified by more than one person.

The software factory methodology places maintainability very high on the list of important priorities.

Maintainability is usually enforceable everywhere, but, sometimes, when code is optimized for speed or size—or even to work around a bug, such as the Microsoft STL bug mentioned earlier—the maintainability can suffer slightly.

In general, it is best to mandate that code should be as maintainable as possible, except in cases in which the maintainability affects another higher priority, in which case augmenting the documentation should make up this deficit.

Debugging And Module Completion

Once you've written your code (and of course updated your documentation in line with the code), you need to test it. Most developers regularly test their code to some degree, although we've all dashed off that last minute, one-liner modification that we barely even bothered to compile—let alone test—only to find we've broken the build.

However, all developer testing is not equal. Some are more equal than others. You can get all kinds of advice on testing from many different books. Without exception, they all blithely state that, when debugging, you must step through each line of code, including (and especially!) any error-handling code whether you expect it to ever be called or not.

In practice, only a small handful of developers actually do this. Most just cannot be bothered with the hassle. Why is this? There are usually two reasons: They are either very confident that they have tested their code thoroughly during development, or they find they don't have the time for it.

However, I am one of the (as far as I can tell) small handful of developers who actually steps through each line of code, and, although my code is perfect (of course!), I regularly find obscure bugs and problems by doing this. Despite the inconvenience and perceived disruption to workflow, this method of testing is an invaluable part of development.

The problem is that usually, by this stage of the development, the developer is sick of even the sight of the code, and wants to get it signed off and checked in to source control as soon as humanly possible. This haste can cause them to skimp on these final, crucial stages. This haste is not a good thing and so should be avoided by implementing a sign-off "checklist."

Depending on the nature of the developers in the team, this checklist may have to be made mandatory. It is important enough to do so. Spend half an hour stepping through the code line by line in a debugger before merging it with the master source in the source control database; you can frequently save days of bug fixing towards the end of the project. No one is infallible. Consequently, time spent on this during development is not wasted, because the alternative is to find your team saddled with a host of previously undetected problems in the crucial release-preparation phases.

Ideally, of course, all the developers on the team should believe that the quality of the code is paramount and happily take on any reasonable measure that ensures that this is as high as possible. It is hard to convey the importance of this until the end of a project, when (with the benefit of hindsight) everybody can see that a code-fix in time could have saved nine.

Bugs must be fixed as soon as they are created and should not be allowed to accumulate until some mystical "fix-it-all" end phase. This just doesn't work, because in 99 percent of projects there never *is* a "fix-it-all" phase. According to Steve Maguire in his book, *Debugging the Development Process*, this used to be the standard Microsoft technique, and it resulted in huge delays and cancellations. Microsoft learned from their mistakes–why shouldn't the games industry learn from them too?

When possible, bugs should be fixed by the same programmers that caused them. This is an important point for a number of reasons.

Fixing bugs as you go along acts as negative feedback for fast but careless programmers. By implementing an automatic "fix-it-as-you-go" rule, you prevent them working on new features until the old stuff is implemented bug-free. No half-implemented features are allowed. The information gained from this will allow you to determine if a programmer needs extra training. Another reason for fixing bugs as you go along is that old chestnut of project visibility. Bugs are the unknown. Even if you think that you know what is causing a bug, you just cannot estimate with accuracy how long it will take to investigate and fix them. Multiply this by a few hundred—or even a few thousand—bugs, and that adds up to a whole lot of time left in limbo. Here lies madness and schedule slips. You just cannot tell the progress of a buggy project. By fixing the bugs as you go along, you keep the bug count as close to zero as possible.

Types Of Bugs

The general scale for bugs marks them as A, B, and C, depending on severity.

Class A bugs are the most severe. These are showstoppers as they prevent the use of the program correctly. An example would be an install procedure that bombed out halfway through, or a game that always crashed just as you were about to get off the first level.

Class B bugs are the next severity level. These do not cause the game to crash, but severely restrict the use of it. These are bugs that affect the quality of game. For example, as the monster approaches, the gun you are carrying disappears or will not fire.

Class C bugs are minor cosmetic bugs, such as user-interface glitches or spelling mistakes. These are nice to fix if there is enough time.

The categorization of these bugs is quite important, as it is according to these that you will assign priorities to the bugs, thereby deciding which is fixed first. Class A bugs have the potential to hold up the entire project and would need to be fixed immediately. Class B bugs are still serious. They could hold up the testers and thus delay the discovery of bugs in other modules. Class C bugs are minor annoyances, but they should still be fixed as soon as possible, because they affect the polish of the product.

However, while the final word on this categorization should be done by the people in charge of the actual project, this isn't always the case, as the cautionary tale in Case Study 21.1 shows.

There's no shame in making a mistake once, but you wouldn't want to make the same mistake again. This is another reason for fixing bugs as you go along: if one kind of bug is occurring continually, the team members can spot it and learn to avoid it. Leaving bugs to be fixed later can hide other bugs, and, later in the project, the developers will probably be less familiar with a certain area of code. Also, there may already be workarounds for earlier bugs that will need further workarounds. In short, if the bugs are left until later, the codebase will become a complete mess.

The message here is that "Bugs are serious, so don't ignore them!" Okay, so this is obvious advice, but you'd be surprised (or maybe not) by the number of developers who feel that they are above the law in this respect.

The bug-fixing process doesn't just end there. By fixing a bug—even a trivial bug—a developer can learn more than if he had just coded it correctly in the first place. We learn by experience, and we also learn by our mistakes. Don't take this as a big "okay" for you to write bug-ridden code in order to learn by experience, but we can turn our mistakes to our advantage in a small way. When fixing a bug in code, a developer needs to ask himself the following questions. How could I have avoided this bug? How can I avoid it in the future? What can I learn from this?

The approach to searching for bugs in code is also important, and the following two statements can sum it up. A novice programmer will finish a piece of code and say, "Okay. It compiles without error and appears to run. I'm done." An experienced programmer will say, "It compiles without error and appears to run. I must have done something wrong!"

Bug-free code is almost impossible to achieve. Many developers believe that they can write completely bug-free code. They can't. It's as simple as that, so they should take advantage of every possible means for automatically detecting bugs, whether this be by adding in specific debugging code or by using automated testing programs such as NuMega *BoundsChecker* and *TrueCoverage*, as shown in Figures 21.2 and 21.3. *BoundsChecker* and similar tools have already been covered in this book. Using *TrueCoverage* as a testing tool will be covered in the next section.

Within the bug categories defined above, there are three main types of bug: logical errors, programming errors, and data errors.

Logical errors are (obviously) errors in the logic of your program. The code is correct, the structure is correct, but the actual logical flow through the program is incorrect. This sort of bug is the most difficult to detect, because there is no off-the-shelf automatic tool capable of

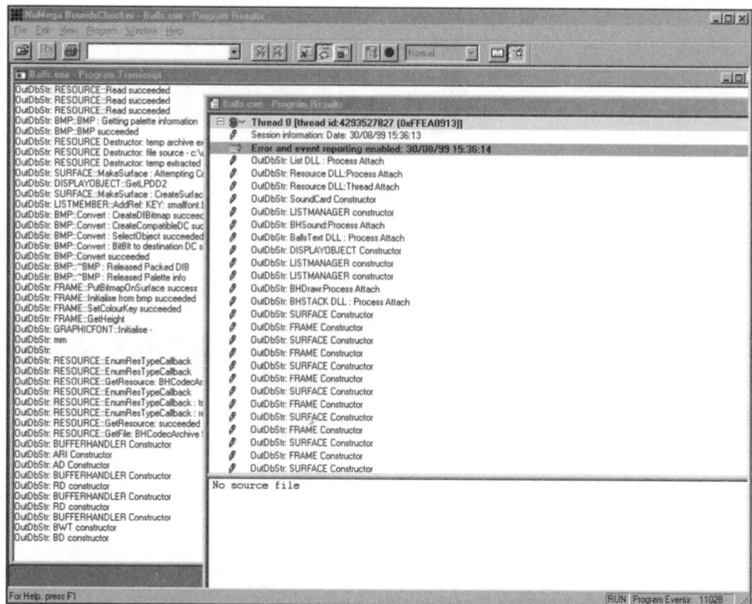

Figure 21.2
NuMega *BoundsChecker* in action.

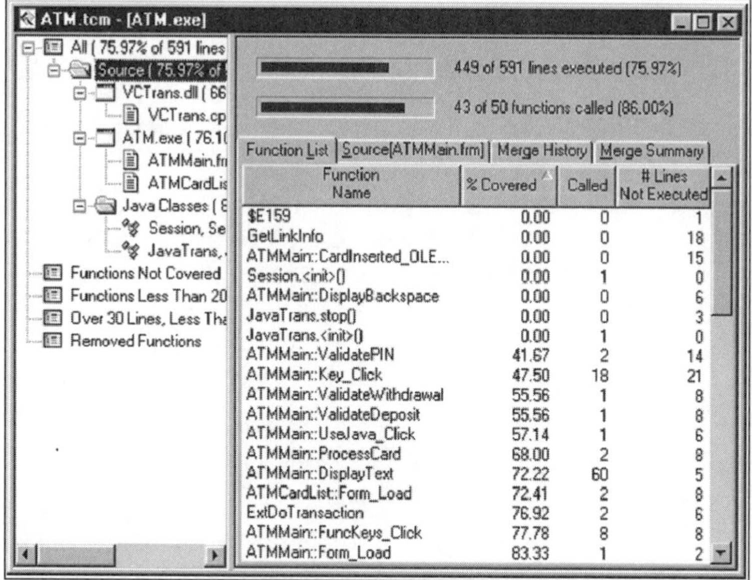

Figure 21.3
NuMega *TrueCoverage* in action.

Case Study 21.1 Class A Bugs Or Not?

Oubliette is a real game whose name we have changed for legal reasons. Inspired by *Prince of Persia*, the game was a platform-based adventure game set in an isometric dungeon environment.

In the run-up to release, the beta was sent to the publisher for evaluation by the QA department. After a while, Mike, the project manager, had bad news for his team. "The publisher has sent a long list of Class A bugs. We've got to pull out all the stops to get these fixed by the shipping date."

Sandy, the designer, had been looking over the list before the meeting. "I don't agree these are all bugs. For example, how about this: 'Wraiths on the cathedral level are invisible and cannot be targeted without the Jack-o-Lantern spell.' What are they talking about? The player will obviously use the Jack-o-Lantern spell to light up the wraiths, won't he?"

"Well, I guess their testers must have used up all their magic by the time they got to that level," said Cathy, a programmer.

The lead programmer, Duncan, agreed with Sandy. "But they're saying this is a Class A bug! Like, you can't play the game if this is in there. Suppose I was down to one hit point and had no healing potions on the pandemonium level. I'd be dead for sure. Is that a Class A bug, too?"

"I think you'd go back to an earlier save if things got so bad that you only had one hit left," Cathy said.

"And you wouldn't revert to an earlier save if you were slap out of magic? It's going to say on the box, you know, 'Wield the mystical secrets of ages past to battle your way through timeless vaults...' Whatever. You wouldn't figure that being a sorcerer without magic was a bad idea?"

"Absolutely right!" said Sandy impatiently. "The intent was that Jack-o-Lantern reveals invisible creatures and hidden doors. The downside is that it costs magic points and also attracts the attention of some monsters, whereas the oil lamp has no special advantages or disadvantages. So that's exactly why it's in the game—to help you fight things like wraiths."

"We can fix this, can't we?" said Mike. "All you have to do is make the wraiths visible all the time, whether the player has cast Jack-o-Lantern or not. Don't tell me that's going to take more than five seconds."

Sandy flung up his hands. "So why have the Jack-o-Lantern spell at all? We might just as well take it out altogether if it doesn't have any gameplay value."

"For what it's worth, I agree with you," said Mike. "We're being forced to downgrade the gameplay because some guy in the client's QA department is an idiot. But they are the client, and they pay all our salaries, so we swallow it and move on."

Oubliette was released a couple of months later, complete with a Jack-o-Lantern spell that now had become a feature with no upside—effectively just the same as the oil lamp except that it cost magical energy and attracted wandering monsters.

detecting these: finding the errors is dependent on knowing the system. These can be found only by specialized debug code written by the developer and by single-stepping through the source in a debugger.

The second class of error, programming errors, is the easier of the two to detect. Programming errors can be as simple as incorrect syntax or misspelled keywords, which cause the compilation to fail. Or the errors can be more complex and insidious, such as the one I had in *Balls!*, in which I was sporadically overwriting a block of statically allocated memory by one byte. Because of the way the object that contained this memory was laid out, the vtable (virtual function table—an internal table of pointers to virtual functions within the class hierarchy for the object in question) was overwritten by that one byte. This caused the pointer to the base class destructor function to point elsewhere, resulting in a bizarre crash whenever an object of this type was destructed. This was a very difficult problem to track down, and it remained in the source code for some time. This bug was detected only when I ran the program against *BoundsChecker*, which highlights the importance of such tools for finding such insidious little problems automatically.

The third class of error, the data error (where some of the game data is incorrect) can also be very difficult to detect because generic tools wouldn't know how to tackle such a specific problem. An example would be a table of characteristics for an RTS strategy game that gave a lowly peon 1 million hit points instead of 10 hit points.

Data errors are usually derived from and related to code and logic errors in the program that was used to produce the data (usually an in-house tool). Of course, if you are using a soft architecture model for your game, then there is a blurring between data errors and the other two error forms. For example, is an error in the scripting code a data error or a code error? The answer, of course, is who cares, as long as it's fixed?

As a last note on debugging and debug code, it is important to always follow this rule: add lots of debug code. Lots and lots. If developers say that it takes too much time to write debug code, tell them it takes too much time if they *don't*. Finding bugs automatically is demonstrably much more reliable than relying on a developer to manually search through the code, by either reading it or stepping through it with a debugger. The automatic tools will find many of the common-but-obscure bugs, leaving the developers to solve the logic bugs, which are more difficult to automatically detect using a generic tool.

Test Harnesses

The previous section mentioned using off-the-shelf packages to diagnose problems with the code. The conclusion that we came to was that, of the three main types of error (code, data, and logical errors), code errors are the easiest to detect.

However, expecting developers and testers to manually check for these other classes of error without a little help is just asking for trouble—which is where test harnesses come in. Now, a lot of lip service has been paid to the use of test harnesses by developers, but I'm not sure how many of them realize what a test harness actually is, and who the target audience is.

At this stage, we should define exactly what a test harness isn't. Once we have dispelled all the common myths and misconceptions, we'll get onto the real meat of what a test harness actually *is*.

First of all, the test harness is not the game itself. There's no purpose in using the game code as a test harness unless you want your customers to be the guinea pigs. The whole point of testing a component is to test it in isolation, free of other interacting components. While such clean-room conditions are not available in reality, the best we can hope for is to rig up a test harness that tests the module. This isn't completely testing it in isolation because there is always the possibility that the test harness itself is flawed. It should be considered a part of the code module itself and should be maintained just as seriously. The temptation is just to use the actual codebase itself to do the checking, but this does not test the application in isolation. When testing, standard scientific theory says to reduce the number of variables (in the scientific sense) to a minimum.

Also, the test harness is not a few hacked-out lines of code calling a few functions and hoping for the best. This does not allow tester interaction or even exercise all the possibilities. The best approach is to provide a graphical user interface allowing the tester to exercise all the possible functions. A generic test harness that can be used to provide the classes of inputs such as random and boundary conditions (as discussed in Chapter 13) can be constructed by the tools group. This can then be customized for each module to be tested, either by recompiling a new test harness for each application, or by taking the approach that I tend to use, which is soft architecture. On WIN32 architectures, I construct most of my modules as either COM objects or just plain DLLs, and use the dynamic loading capabilities of the operating system to make the test harness configurable (to some degree) at runtime.

The test harness application I have developed also integrates with the source control system to store old test results in order to provide an auditable history of tests. This also facilitates easy regression testing, as old results can be compared with new results to check for any bugs that have been introduced (or even reintroduced) into previously working modules. The testing harness could also be scripted, so that it can automatically run a whole series of tests overnight, comparing the new results with the results of the previous tests, and producing a summary document of any anomalies to be tackled the following morning. Commercial packages are starting to appear: for Java programmers, there's an automated class tester, called "jtest!," that will bombard the class with inputs, performing black-box testing, regression testing, and, of course, user-defined testing. Hopefully, a C++ version of this type of application will become commonly available at some stage.

Note

The CEO of Parasoft, the producers of "jtest!," makes a comparison between the U.S. and Japanese car industries of the 1970s. Both had high levels of defects in their cars, but the only difference in their approach to solving the problem was that the Americans believed it was not possible to make a zero-defect car, while the Japanese believed it was.

Hence, their approaches to solving the problems differed: the American car manufacturers placed more people at the end of the production line, hoping to catch more errors. Of course, they caught more errors, but a large number of defects still slipped through.

The Japanese, however, tackled the problem at its roots. They statistically analyzed the production process to see at which stages the errors were introduced and improved the processes to prevent those errors. Japanese cars streaked way ahead of American cars in terms of reliability.

A car is a frighteningly complex piece of modular engineering—more so than software—and the lessons learned by the Japanese and Americans can be directly applied to software development. Writing virtually defect-free software is possible, but not if you don't test it effectively.

One of the best things about computers that developers in particular seem to forget is that computers are perfectly capable of running by themselves. Some tasks require human interaction (such as programming), and some tasks do not (such as running through a test script). If you can leverage your time so that you don't waste unnecessary time doing jobs that with a little extra initial outlay could be done adequately by the computer, then the developers and testers will be able to spend their time more effectively. Instead of running the tests, they can be analyzing results and designing new tests to catch more errors.

The golden rule of testing is that it must be done. It is at least as important as the actual writing of the code. Testing is time well spent. You can never do too much testing, because code is rarely free of bugs. The differing types of testing, unit testing, system testing, and integration testing are discussed in Chapter 13.

The Seven Golden Gambits And The Three Lead Balloons

This section covers some of the classic dos and don'ts of development. Although these are general considerations, they should nevertheless always be on top of your mind to guide you through the development process.

The following gambits are the distilled wisdom of many thousands of man-years of development around the world, so I guess you should pay attention now.

- Gambit 1: Plan for reuse. Don't reinvent the wheel.
- Gambit 2: Document. Don't keep it in your head.
- Gambit 3: Design first; develop second.
- Gambit 4: Schedule. Make sure everybody knows the targets.
- Gambit 5: Catch mistakes as you go along.

- Gambit 6: Control the degree of R&D.
- Gambit 7: Know when to draw the line.

Let's look at these gambits in more detail.

Reuse

The transition of any cottage industry to a major industry comes when you achieve reuse. In game development, this doesn't have to mean only component reuse.

Potentially even more useful are the foundation classes that can be carried over from game to game. We already discussed design patterns, whose value is that they enable a design to be built rapidly and in a form that is already largely understood at the supermodular level. Chapter 24 also discusses metadesign: the extension of these concepts to the point of a generic system from which all games can be derived.

Developers often disdain plug-in modules because of the "Not Built Here" syndrome. Frequently, even a perfectly good in-house module (a route-finding algorithm, for instance) is not used merely because it was created by a different team in the same company. At the very least, plug-ins should be used in the early stages. If you genuinely feel there's a better route-finding algorithm, you can always write it later if you happen to experience that miracle development where the game is finished ahead of schedule.

Reusable components require a standardized architecture, of course, and you need to know the format that each module's inputs and outputs will take. Then, you can refine the interior of the module as a black box without having to change the rest of the system. (See Case Study 21.2.)

Documentation

Once I was talking to a development manager who was lamenting the loss of a project that had been running smoothly for nine months. "It was a dream," he said. "It was on schedule, they had a good demo, the whole team got on, and the concept was a winner, too."

"What went wrong? Let me guess—the publisher just didn't get it?"

"No, the publisher was behind it all the way! The trouble was the lead programmer went off to a new job in Atlanta, and nobody else can complete his engine."

Documentation won't always save you from situations like that one. Documentation aims to make individuals less dispensable, but it can't always make them indispensable. However, look at it like an airbag in your car: it's not guaranteed to save your life, but it sure helps with the odds.

Documentation has another great value also. It allows other team members to know what your work is about. The payoff to the whole team is that developers don't have to keep interrupting each other's work with minor questions: they can go to the documentation.

Case Study 21.2 Reusable Architecture

Not long ago, I was working on a PC game. The technical manager was drawing up the detailed architecture of the project, and he wanted to know if there would be a Mac version of the game. "If I design the architecture to fit the Mac as well," he explained, "it would have the knock-on advantage that a Dreamcast conversion would be much easier."

I went to the publishers who were funding the game and asked if they had thought about a Mac version. "It's early days," they said. "Let's see how the Mac does as a games platform first."

The Catch-22 was this: if I advised the development company to plan the architecture to include the Mac (and by extension the Dreamcast), it would delay the project by at least a month, which was the technical manager's estimate of the time required for the broader architecture. If the decision was left until later, though, development of the Mac version would require another separate architecture of its own, and that would eat up much more work.

There was no obvious solution. Putting in a little extra effort up front was more rational than spending more time later, but the publisher would not commit to even a short delay. As a result, development had to press ahead, and a valuable opportunity to build in reuse was lost.

And it isn't just for other team members, either: documentation often reminds you of a train of thought you might have forgotten. (See Case Study 4.2.)

Remember, every time you document something, it's one less thing you have to juggle inside your head.

Design First

Design comes first, and development comes second. Be careful with that dictum, though. It doesn't mean that design stops and then development begins. Design is an ongoing process, which we've estimated is roughly 80 percent complete at the commencement of development and which is further refined as time goes on.

In Chapter 7, Glenn Corpes implies that approximately 20 man-months went into the original *Populous* game. Technology has moved on since then, forcing games to get bigger, and it's possible that the latest *Populous* game took more than 200 man-months. However, there would be nothing to stop the first 10 percent of that time being spent on a throwaway testbed (effectively, a predevelopment design phase). The gameplay of *Populous 3* is not so far advanced beyond the original, if at all, and SDKs like *NeMo* make testbeds very easy to create.

Schedule

Sticking to the schedule is all important. But, if you've read this far, then you'll already know this. Let's hammer the point home.

"Teams make plans and then routinely abandon them when they run into schedule trouble. The problem isn't so much in abandoning the plan as in failing to create a substitute, and then falling into code-and-fix instead."

—Steve McConnell, Rapid Development *(Microsoft Press)*

Just like plans, you can't always stick to your first schedule, but you can try to recalibrate the schedule as you go on. Suppose you had to get to an interview at noon and in the morning you're planning to get your haircut and buy a new suit. Only you leave the house late. What do you do? Just press on with all your tasks and hope you still make the meeting at noon? Of course not! Yet this "hope to catch up" approach is common in development teams.

Instead, you replan the schedule, trimming nonessential tasks or finding ways around them. In this example, maybe you'd find a hairdresser nearer to the tailor's—not your favorite hairdresser, but it'll have to do. Or maybe you'd try to reschedule the interview. The point is that you would hopefully realize that the worst thing to do would be to run around aimlessly without any kind of schedule. That way lies panic.

Catch Mistakes As You Go Along

This has been discussed in this chapter, as applied to code, but of course it applies everywhere in the project. The longer an error is allowed to fester untouched, the higher the cost of repair (in terms of both time and money) when it is finally tackled. This could make the difference between a successful project and a cancellation.

Limit R&D

This has also been covered in great detail in the second half of this book. R&D is effectively open ended and virtually impossible to schedule for, especially if you are dependent on the results. The rule is to perform R&D outside the scope of the project and to make sure that the success of the project is not dependent on the outcome. Always have a backup plan.

Know When To Draw The Line

When is it "good enough"? The average game developer will say "Never! Or at least not until I've optimized every last function down the max." Sometimes developers are just too focused to know when to stop and look at the bigger picture. This is a very difficult skill for a developer, who is generally used to focusing in at a very detailed level of construction. Usually a project planner is the individual responsible for keeping the developers focused in the right areas and for the right periods, but this role can fall to other team members, too.

Knowing when to draw the line prevents feature creep, one of the three lead balloons (covered in the next section) that can affect a project.

The Three Lead Balloons

Okay, so we've covered the good things to do: now we need to emphasize the key things to avoid. These are the things that will cause your project to sink like the proverbial lead balloon.

- Lead Balloon 1: Bad management
- Lead Balloon 2: Feature creep
- Lead Balloon 3: Coder insularity

Bad Management

Bad management occurs when ownership of the project is vested in the wrong people. Team methodologies are not about finding ways to manage people, but about building a process into the team itself so that imposed management becomes unnecessary.

In the past, teams were customarily managed by a team member, often the lead programmer. In trying to "professionalize," many development companies are now bringing in managers to impose schedules from above. This is actually worse. Good management is invisible: it facilitates the activity of the team and intervenes only when needed. The leadership comes from within the team and is a single individual with ownership and creative vision, someone who is equivalent to the director of a movie.

Feature Creep

Feature creep is the insidious addition of features to the specification, because someone thought it would be cool to have them. Feature creep is a major cause of delays to projects because it takes work away from the main body of the project and uses it to implement specialized and unnecessary features.

This is a big danger, because it is so easy to slip into the habit of implementing just a couple of extra features because they are easy to do, and they practically drop out of the framework for free.

Unfortunately, nothing is free. When you add up how much time it takes to maintain and test this "free" functionality, you will realize that it wasn't free after all.

Coder Insularity

Games are a holistic creative process. Yet, too often, coders judge a person's value solely by his coding ability. This tendency directly contradicts the need of game development to draw on a fusion of talent from authors, designers, artists, and musicians as well as coders.

The bad habit grew out of the fact that many games coders are self-taught loners. Possibly unpopular as children, they developed the coping mechanism of regarding only their own area of expertise as having any value. You will rarely see the sullen one-upmanship (at one time common in coders) among the artists on a team. Artists almost never seem to bother with a pecking order: they all respect each other's work, and that's the attitude that makes a great team.

How can you shake coders out of an insular approach? To some extent, it's happening with time anyway: younger coders no longer suffer the stigma of having been considered a nerdy kid. Programming and Computer Science are now respected skills in our society. Also, it is possible to get those insular coders to open up. If you have an abrasive individual on your team and no one else can work with him, it's a fair bet he's actually the most insecure. Showing that he is valued as a person and a colleague as well as for his coding skills is a good start.

A very talented and enthusiastic young programmer said to one of us a while ago: "I'm not going to use the terms *coder* and *artist* anymore. From now on, as far as I'm concerned, we're all just *developers*, and I hope other people will start to see it that way because it will make us a better team."

Chapter 22
The Run-Up To Release

Key Topics:

- ***Late evaluation***
- ***Localization and foreign markets***
- ***Playable demos and playtesting***
- ***Public beta testing***
- ***The Web site***
- ***The gold master***
- ***Patch preparation***

Towards the scheduled end of the project, you need to address and verify certain issues—one of these being that the project *is* on schedule to complete on time, of course! This chapter covers these issues. Most of them will have already been taken care of (or at least thoroughly prepared for) as an ongoing process throughout the project, but some of them really are last-minute issues.

The issues covered in this chapter include those related to localization and foreign markets, focus groups, the release of playable demos, playtesting, and responding to criticisms from playtesting. These criticisms may result in a need for changes, and this has to be handled very carefully at such a late stage in development.

Other relevant material in this chapter includes a discussion of public beta testing—including its advantages and disadvantages—and also of ensuring that the testing is actually effective.

When release day actually comes (which will hopefully be as originally scheduled, barring outside interference—which will be discussed later) and the gold master is placed in the sticky little hands of the producer, the development is still not over. Unless you are exceedingly lucky, there will be a requirement for patches of some sort, and you will need a mechanism for distributing these patches, such as a game Web site (which can also serve as useful advertising and publicity for the game).

Generally, the run-up to release involves a number of distinct stages, all coming in close succession. Before this, the prototype and alpha stages conclude about one-third of the way through the project. "Alpha 1" and "Alpha 2" generally require that the publisher receives general background information on the program, other material such as early screenshots (chosen for their suitability for promotional activities), and a detailed profile of the developer and the expertise and experience of each member of the team including any games they have worked on in the past. All of this information will provide the fuel for the early publicity machine.

Towards the end of the process, we reach the beta stage. The usual stipulation for the "Beta 1" software is roughly for a playable version of the program (with all known bugs removed) that demonstrates how the program functions and that showcases the program's unique selling points (at least one of which should be functional and demonstrable). The basic game concept should be apparent, although it doesn't necessarily have to be playable. Usually, the publisher will also require more screenshots and possibly some high-resolution renders for publicity purposes.

The "Beta 2" stage is generally accepted to be a good quality demo of the program, one suitable for presentation of the program to magazine reviewers and investors for publicity and funding purposes and, of course, exhibition at shows. With some negotiation, some publishers may accept a rolling demo at this stage.

The "Beta 3" stage is accepted to be a completed version of the program ready to be submitted to the final acceptance-testing process. This is followed shortly by the gold mastering stage. At this stage, many companies will require a playable cover mount demo in freeware or shareware format with all bugs removed.

Late Evaluation

Late evaluation means that, at this stage in the development—when the game is nearly completed and the final shape of the product can be seen fairly clearly—we should take a close look at the product, examining it objectively to see how well it matches our initial project vision.

Depending on the outcome of these investigations, we (or the publisher and producer) may want to take certain actions in order to rectify any perceived shortcomings or to take advantage of any areas that are wildly successful.

Final Analysis

The following sections cover some of the questions that should be asked when performing this investigation. If necessary, the responses to each of these questions should be used to adjust the final approach technique.

Look at it as if your project is an aircraft coming in for a landing. You may have to adjust the course to take into account local weather conditions and other factors such as the runway length and the ground topography. Inconvenient as it may be, if you want to get down in one piece, these checks and adjustments just have to be made.

Is The Game Better Than Was Expected?

If the game has excelled in one or more areas, then the product will need further examination to make sure that other areas of the project are also up to scratch and don't stand out as being out of place.

Imagine that we are working on a project for which the original specification called for monaural eight-bit, 22 kHz sampled sound throughout the game. This sound is used in two ways. The hero character uses sampled speech to make pertinent comments at key points during the game. The incidental nonplayer characters that the player has to interact with do not use sampled speech. Instead, they use a clever phonetics-based system that strings together alien words from sampled phonemes, creating sounds on the fly.

Assume that some previously unresolved technical problem had prevented us from having higher-quality sound, but that problem has now been fixed, allowing us to have 16-bit 44 kHz stereo samples for the main hero character. Now, all the nonplayer characters sound tinny and robotic in comparison. The mean level of acceptability has now been raised, and what was previously acceptable now stands out as substandard.

Consider another, more visual, example. Assume that we have a game that uses 3D polygonal characters that have all been carefully hand-animated by our artist. However, our plan stated that we were going to have motion capture for the main character, but the motion capture studio wasn't available when we needed. It's going to be a while before we can book some more studio time, so we asked the artist to also do the animations for the main character. Everything looks great in the game.

Eventually, we get our studio time, and we insert our motion-captured animations in for the player character. Now the player character looks great, but every other character in the game looks robotic and stiff by comparison. Again, the mean level of acceptability has been raised, and this makes other modules look inferior by comparison.

This phenomenon often affects projects in their late stages because it is in precisely these stages that many temporary stopgap measures are removed and replaced with the final working versions. Now many surprises like those mentioned above—and others—will rear their ugly heads. Of course, sometimes these imbalances just occur naturally during development. Maybe one part of a game just doesn't match up to the other parts, or the presentation of certain areas isn't up to par.

The question is what should we do about these problems. One pseudosolution would be to ignore the imbalance and release the game anyway. For sure, many games do this, and they get slaughtered in the reviews because of it. Nothing is more jarring than a mismatched feature set.

This situation, which occurs more often than we might like, is not always predictable. The only real solution (and one that is not palatable but can be sometimes acceptable to publishing houses) is to consider whether it might be worth holding up the game while the substandard areas are given a real polish. Remember that the situation we have here is that a certain feature of the game has exceeded expectations, and we want to take advantage of this in order to maximize the potential of the entire game, and consequently maximize sales.

The results of a couple of months' extra work can make the difference between an average title and an AAA success. This was the approach taken by Blizzard Software with *Starcraft*, which, as we've already seen elsewhere in the book, paid off handsomely for the company.

Is The Game Up To Scratch?

What, however, if the game does not measure up to expectations and it doesn't fulfill the expectations of the publishers? If we take the approach of trying to improve all the substandard areas (as mentioned above), then we are effectively rewriting the entire game. This is not the sort of thing that can be fixed with a couple of months of polishing.

Sometimes, despite all the best efforts from everyone concerned, last-minute disasters may threaten the project.

Sometimes these will be self-inflicted, as in the rather amusing Case Study 22.1. However, the approaches for tackling this problem are not straightforward, and, for a team of developers who have spent the best part of two years working on the product, it will be difficult for them to separate objective analysis from the sort of love/hate relationship they will have developed with their work.

If the game is simply not up to scratch, you effectively have four options.

The first is to release it anyway, which is exactly what some companies do. I'm not going to mention any examples here, but I'm sure that we can think of many games that have just been released regardless of their quality, just because the publisher did not want to wait any more. For responsible publishers who want to protect their reputation and their revenue stream, this is *not* an option.

The second option is to cancel the project. Nobody wants to do this, but this can be a sound financial decision under some circumstances. You are only as good as your last release, so releasing a true stinker of a game can have a negative impact on the games released afterwards. It can sometimes be better *not* to release a game than to release it, make the marketing spend, achieve zero sales, and—adding insult to injury—scare people off buying your next game because your last one was so poor.

The third and fourth options are applicable if the game simply must be released and cancellation is not an option. The third option is to simply bite the bullet and rework the game.

Case Study 22.1 A Self-Inflicted Disaster

This Case Study concerns an unnamed company releasing a cartridge for a console system a few years back.

To save money on the cartridge product, the publisher decided that, rather than going to an official supplier—it would design and manufacture its own plastic game cartridges and the associated internal circuit board.

The 12,000 cartridge cases, circuit boards, and manuals were sent to the packing company for assembly. Three days before release—on the Friday, with the release date being the following Monday—a fully assembled product was tested at the publisher's Quality Assurance department.

Unfortunately, the game cartridge did not fit in the slot. The person who designed it forgot to design in a locating groove. Over the next two days 12,000 grooves were gouged—by hand—into the plastic cases to make them fit. Everyone from the company, including the MD, turned up to help. Thus was the spirit in those days: unpack, gouge, and repack the cartridge.

Everyone, that is, with the exception of the chap who fouled up in the first place.

But all this to save a few pennies per product.

This may involve a further lengthy development process to correct all the deficiencies, but at least this gives you the chance to modify the game design to take into account later developments. Look ahead to Case Study 22.2 to see how this may take place.

The fourth and final option is to reconsider the pricing strategy and the target market—equivalent to straight-to-video in the film industry. Maybe a budget release is right for the project, whereas the previous full price would not be. This is still no excuse for releasing a stinker: a stinker is a stinker, whether it is low priced or not, and your company's reputation will suffer accordingly.

Has The Market Shifted?

What about situations in which the target market demographic has shifted since the start of development? This used to happen more in the early days of computers, when topical games were more common.

In the U.K. in the1980s, for example, certain topical events were parodied in games. Obviously, these types of product have a very narrow market time, as the events they are based on soon become old news. Delays in production can make the difference between big sales and zero sales.

It doesn't have to be just topical events causing the problems, however. Other issues can be involved. Movie tie-ins are one area in which this can occur, as are general shifts in the public's interest. Releasing a football game out of season is nowhere near as effective as releasing it in the early days of the season. Not only do you get add-on benefits from the media coverage (free advertising), but you also have a captive audience: a large portion of the target market is going to have the topic of your game as the foremost thought in their minds. Now all you have to do is to make sure it is the best of the many other football games that will be around at the time.

But what if you have a game that is applicable only to a small market, and you want to increase the appeal? Short of rewriting the entire game, you need to consider if there is a low-cost way to adapt the product to appeal to a wider market. This technique is more commonly known as "bandwagon jumping."

An excellent example of this would be Eidos renaming its game *Tartan Army*, a game about Scottish battles, *Braveheart*, acquiring the license to the film and automatically increasing the awareness level to hundreds of thousands of potential buyers. After all, if you asked me what a game called *Tartan Army* was about, I would assume it was a game about Scottish soccer supporters, but, if you told me about a game called *Braveheart*, I'd immediately have some idea as to what it may be about.

How To Recover From Near Disaster

Okay, so we are approaching the end of development, and we are having a near disaster. Everything is going wrong, and the publisher is going to condemn us to one of the inner circles of hell if we don't manage to pull this one off. What should we do?

The answer is simple. Keep calm, and go back to the plan. There is no point in panicking, which is wasted effort and achieves nothing. If you have been using the methodologies we've presented in this book, then we will already have adequate disaster planning.

The tier system is designed to cope with late problems like slippage in the best way possible: it aims for a degree of completion at six-week intervals so that the client has the option to ship a product.

Developers worry this means a substandard product might be given a premature birth. In truth, the extra confidence the client gets from interactive, incremental development means they are more likely to say, "Okay, we can see it's taking shape. We're going to give you some extra time."

To see this in action, take a look at Case Study 22.2, which is based on a real situation that occurred during the troubled development of a project a couple of years ago.

Of course it's easy to give in to the panic and mess things up completely. If panic sets in, then all sorts of nightmarish scenarios are freed to run riot. The plan could be abandoned, and free-for-all development could become the order of the day. Extended long hours and weekend working for more than a couple of occasions will sap the morale of already over-worked and stressed-out developers, encouraging them take shortcuts of the kind that hurt long-term productivity.

Case Study 22.2 A Recovery Plan

This document is part of the recovery plan for a project that began to find itself in difficulties as the release date approached. Names and faces have been altered to protect the innocent and the guilty.

SUBJECT: Development on the *Lyonesse* project

PROPOSAL: A seven-point recovery system

Lyonesse was supposed to be a two-year project but is now likely to require another year before release. The causative factors are:

(1) Lack of a constantly updated game design, depriving the team of focus.

(2) Time wasted on frequent demos of only peripheral value to the project.

(3) Undue bureaucratic workload placed on the team leader.

(4) Lack of planning, preventing critical path analysis and concurrency of tasks.

(5) Demoralization resulting from recent redundancies, summary cancellation of other games, and uncertainty about the future direction of in-house development.

The proposals put forward here deal explicitly with points 1 to 4. The issue of demoralization begins to be solved by the mere fact of swift, decisive action now, backed up by arranging tasks to give the team a succession of easy victories over the next couple of months.

Prospects for *Lyonesse*

Before looking at what needs to be done, it's important to see the strengths of the work so far. Let's take a look at the *Age of Empires* credits by comparison. That's a game with three designers, eight programmers, and eight artists. Even so, it was almost two years in development. Meantime, *Lyonesse* has struggled on with a six-man team.

Our lead programmer has produced a 3D engine that is admired throughout the industry. The character animations and interiors are mostly completed. Route finding and other micro-level AI are already in place. A fully completed toolset means that time-boxing is now a feasible option. Only the gameplay is lacking, and this is because a designer has not been engaged on the project on an ongoing basis.

The building blocks of *Lyonesse* are mostly there. The task over the next nine months will be to assemble them into a completed game.

Steps we intend to take to turn the project around are:

(1) Recruit an assistant for the lead programmer.

Creative talent must be given the freedom to create. The team is led by one of the very best games programmers in the world, but, up until now, he has been saddled with a wide range of management tasks—interfacing with the publisher, interviewing recruits for other projects, scheduling, and so fourth. In addition, he has had to do the bulk of the coding single-handedly. He needs someone he can delegate to, someone who can do the job without requiring constant micromanagement.

This individual must have the experience and expertise to swiftly adopt the lead's technical refinements and put them across to the team. He doesn't have to be able to invent a better mousetrap—just to build it once it's explained to him.

We're thinking of John Doe for this role. We've worked with him, he is easy to get on with, and he commands respect for his games experience as well as his track record in industrial work. And he has the lead programmer's full approval.

(2) Appoint a project coordinator.
The project coordinator is a middle-management position whose function is to remove the organizational workload from the lead programmer. The lead programmer retains ownership and continues to provide the creative thrust of the project—crucially, as he is the one team member who has been on the project from the start and understands the vision.

We have an existing staff member in mind for this role: Tom Brown. Although not imaginative, he is dependable, hard working, and a good team player.

(3) Completely overhaul and revise the design.
The original *Lyonesse* spec is now two years old. In that time there have been quite a few changes in the adventure/RPG genre.

Specifically, games such as *Dark Earth* have shown us how far the adventure game can move beyond mere puzzle-solving or the micromanagement of weapons and items, towards being a truly immersive, interactive story. At the same time, other games have stuck to the old CRPG model, misusing the advances in technology to create a dinosaur of data management. We will learn from their mistakes, refine our design, removing emphasis from the development-heavy elements whose worth is dubious and instead focusing on the areas of proven value.

For these reasons, a full-time designer is essential in game development. It is absurd that *Lyonesse* has continued with a locked-down design for two years and no designer on the staff to update it. We will bring the original designer back in to work with the team leader on a new gameplay spec.

(4) Draw up a detailed project plan.
The revised design will make it possible to divide the development process into discrete stages of the prototyping. This will form the basis of a new project plan.

The project plan will describe the game in its idealized form, which will provide the team with a focus for their efforts. Additionally, and more importantly, by breaking the project into monthly (and smaller) milestones, we ensure that the team is always provided with specific targets to set their sights on.

Our aim is to get a full beta of the game within 8 months. This will allow the designer to exhaustively test and tweak the gameplay and write the scenarios, while the team gets another 6 months in which they can put a graphical polish on the product and stomp any remaining bugs. *Lyonesse* will be ready to ship in 14 months.

(5) Avoid unnecessary demos.
Demos are flashy but do very little to advance the project. Time spent by the team to produce three-monthly demos is 75 percent wasted time. It is as if the director of a movie kept having to stop filming in order to edit the movie's trailer.

But naturally the publisher needs assurance and confidence that work is progressing. We will achieve this by defining keystone elements of the product in the form of time-boxes. Under the new review process, the project coordinator will report on the team's behalf to senior management and the client and will demo ongoing modules to show that functionality is being continually improved. The module demos may not be colorful and flashy, but they will be useful to the project.

(6) Use time-boxing to keep development on track.
Lyonesse must be released by next spring to put us comfortably ahead of the main contender in the genre. Our aim now is to structure all further work on the game around a fixed timeframe with a view to having the game in releasable form by then.

Time-boxing means that we are certain to complete each step in the development process to at least a minimum functioning point. We cannot guarantee that the version of *Lyonesse* ready by next spring will have all the chrome we would ideally like: it might well have, but that depends on how much time is free at the end. What it will be at that point is a good, well-designed, bug-free game that embodies the innovative gameplay promised in the high concept.

(7) Restore enthusiasm and morale.
An army suffers lowered morale when it experiences setbacks, casualties, and what is seen as arbitrary judgments from senior command. Inadvertently, this is what has happened to the *Lyonesse* team.

Morale is to some extent restored simply by giving the team confidence that the company is fully committed to their project. Remember that if this team were to take their talents to another development house, the cost to us and the publisher would not merely be the $400,000 so far invested, it would be the $8 million or more (based on the client's own projections) that another publisher would make from their game.

The development personnel are the fundamental resource of the company, and they must be treated in a way that reflects their value. Any judgments that affect them must be explained so they understand the company's reasons. A team that is alienated from its company cannot be expected to work at full efficiency.

A commander restores his army's morale by giving them easy victories. Similarly, development cannot be allowed to stretch into a two-year highway with no signposts. It must be organized in bite-sized chunks so that the team is constantly rewarded with wins. This again is ensured by the time-boxing process.

Summary
The graphics are already there to be seen; all that remains is to build this around Smith's new design.

In a sense, the delay in *Lyonesse's* development, whatever its causes, can be turned to our advantage. As mentioned above, other adventure games have made mistakes that will guide our redesign. At the same time, the market has been broadened. Thanks to *Tomb Raider*, adventure games are nowadays featured in the mass media. With full commitment, *Lyonesse* will be out for next spring and will show profits comfortably over $8-10 million.

Our belief is that the company now has the opportunity to harness a world-beater team on a product that will dominate the adventure game market. If senior management has any doubts—if there's anyone thinking that it might sell only 100,000 units—then cancel it now. Everyone involved can go on to better things. But, if you have the confidence and conviction that this project and this team deserve, then give *Lyonesse* all your backing and let's make it so.

In fact, any unauthorized or unplanned activity is likely to damage the project prospects. Although there is the romantic image of the "skunk works" development, where all the developers muck in and ad lib the project to completion, I have to tell you that there are far more failed skunk works than there are successful skunk works. It's just that you don't hear about the failures as much as you do the successes.

The following guidelines cover most of the issues that can occur at this stage.

When things are going wrong:

- Don't misjudge the cost of future time. If you waste an hour now, you'll regret it six months down the line.
- Don't get hung up on doing tasks in the wrong order. (Stick to the plan; it's your best friend.)
- Don't keep trying to polish a feature when you're supposed to move on to something else.
- Don't try to throw more people at a project: it never works, and they just cost you more time.
- Don't be unrealistic. Some people (especially managers) sometimes get into berserker mode, saying, "This has cost so much that we can't abandon it now." Wrong! Sunk costs are sunk costs. Sometimes you just have to retreat: it's more rational to abandon the battle but salvage what you can than to go down fighting pointlessly.
- Don't allow targets to conglomerate into an unmanageable mass. When the schedule is slipping, it's easy for many tasks to turn into one big deadline. But (just like in a game) people thrive on small, continuous rewards. "We have five weeks to get all this done," is an invitation to panic, whereas, "I have two days to rewrite the character rendering code," is a challenge.

Sometimes the situation can appear overwhelming, as in Case Study 22.3, in which the modifications forced on the product were caused by clauses in the contract. However, careful application of the techniques in this book could have prevented the situation becoming

Case Study 22.3 Licensing Hell

A superhero license on the Super NES and Megadrive...

Three months before the release date, the comic company, in an attempt to revitalize comic sales, redefined its hero characters and the enemy characters. Overnight, the superhero featured in the game went from being a good guy to a bad guy and all his previous enemies were killed off. The license contract was such that the developer had to follow suit. A year of work had to be redone, both in game design and artwork.

Much of the code for the enemy characters also had to be thrown out the door as it was hard coded per character.

The product became confused, the team lost enthusiasm, and the result was a very poor product.

a complete disaster, so that changing the license at such a late stage wouldn't have been such a huge problem.

Time doesn't solve problems. Common sense solves problems. This means that you may need to take a step back and look at how you've been spending your time. It's often a case of more haste, less speed. The best way to solve a problem is to plan to avoid it in the first place. Take a look as Case Study 22.4.

When coping with change, most last-minute changes could and should be dealt with sooner, even at the predevelopment stage. Change control has been the principal topic within this book, and I'll cover some of the main issues here in order to put this into context.

In the initial design phases, you should've planned to accommodate a degree of ongoing change within an allowed envelope. For example, an RPG interface or even some character artwork might change, but there's no way it is going to suddenly become a platform adventure halfway down the line.

Genuine eleventh-hour changes must be a last resort; that is, if you're sure that it's broken, you might as well bounce it off the floor and see if that fixes it! This is technically known as percussive maintenance: drop-kick it to see if it will work. After all, if you have nothing to lose, you may as well try drastic action to fix it.

But what if the technology changes? Try to make it so that you don't have to guess the typical spec of machines at release time. "We're aiming for minimum spec P160, but it'll go best on a PIII-550," should become, "It'll run on a P160 at minimum and the better the machine above that, the better it'll look," which means writing modules that scale with the technology available. This is precisely what *Messiah* (headed by Dave Perry of Shiny Entertainment) purports to do.

Case Study 22.4 Last-Minute Madness

Frank had just returned from presenting a beta demo of *Bughunter Squad* to the publisher. "You look down in the mouth," said Caroline, the finance director. "Didn't it go well?"

"It was fine. They liked it. But I really goofed. I wanted to show off what the graphics engine could do, so I switched it to the *Tomb Raider* mode."

"Is that bad?"

"It is, because now they want it to run with the *Tomb Raider* view as default, that is, close in just behind the selected character. But the game is designed around a zoomed-out, high-angle mode where you get a wide field of view."

"And does it run slower in the other mode?" asked Caroline.

"No, it's just as fast, but what works well for *Tomb Raider* doesn't necessarily work in *Bughunter Squad*. The player is constantly flipping between characters, so you need to have a high-angle shot to play effectively."

"How about leaving it up to the player to choose?"

Frank shook his head. "Suppose 50 percent of people start off playing using the *Tomb Raider* view—actually it'll be more, because the publisher wants it to be the default, but say it's only 50 percent. A good proportion of those people will find the gameplay unmanageable in that mode, and they'll give up on the game. It's certainly enough for reviewers to dock us a couple of points, and that could be make or break."

"I have an idea." Caroline leaned out of the office door and called across to the lead level designer. "Hey, Bill. Any chance of slotting in a couple of extra levels with just a single character, to give the *Tomb Raider* view a chance to shine?"

"It's lucky you're a lady," said Bill without looking up from his work.

Frank groaned. "I'm an idiot. Why did I have to show off like that? They were quite happy with the game as it was. Wait a minute. What was that you said about the engine speed?"

Caroline was perplexed. "Well, I asked if the *Tomb Raider* view slowed the game down, but you said…"

Frank was already dialing the game's producer. "Hi, Danny. Yeah, I thought it went well, too. Listen, I jumped the gun showing you that *Tomb Raider* mode. I'm just sitting here with my lead programmer, and he's saying there are some bugs to be ironed out there. It won't make it into *Bughunter*, I'm afraid, but give us a couple months and I'll demo you something new that'll really show it off to advantage."

Was this an ideal solution? We can't fully condone ignoring the requests of the client (in this case, the publisher who was funding the game). However, publishers frequently have little idea of what development involves. Famously, they are unable to find the solution to the problem: "You can have it in time, or you can have it with those extra features." And so, as in this case, the trick is sometimes to deliver the game that they really want, rather than the game they think they want.

Late Localization

Of course, localization issues need to be considered as part of the initial design. Anything else is a complete recipe for disaster. However, as the project draws to an end, the issue of localization needs some final attention in order to make sure everything is still okay.

One of the main things we need to consider is the current climate in the market we are considering. For example, in reviewing the localization issues, we should look to see if anything has changed that may affect our game, such as the release of a movie on the same theme, a topical event, or a change in the law.

Some things you should've known from the start, and these should've been factored into planning as the project has progressed.

For example, some countries have cultural differences that mean a game has to be substantially modified in order to be acceptable for release. For instance, a game in Germany is very limited in the amount of violence it can incorporate. Nazi imagery is completely forbidden, as is blood and realistic violence. *Wolfenstein 3D*, *Doom*, and *Carmageddon*, all fell foul of this and were either completely banned or heavily modified for release.

When Microsoft decided that it was going to release *Age of Empires* in Asian territories, the developers made the late design decision to incorporate an entirely new Asian race into the mix, so that it would appeal to the market. Furthermore, according to the localization department at Microsoft, *Age of Empires* was the easiest game it had to localize. This wouldn't have been the case if the initial design hadn't considered the fact that the same phrase can be many different lengths in different languages.

Licenses

Also, you must consider that, just because a license is big in the country of origin, does not mean that the product will be able to take advantage of it in all the target countries. For example, an NFL title may not do as well in Europe as it would in its native America.

In fact, this is more likely to be the rule than the exception. There are so few truly global brands and identities. I can think of only *James Bond*, *Coca-Cola*, *Pepsi-Cola*, *McDonalds*, and *Star Wars* as being truly global. Maybe *Pokémon*, *Furbies*, *Tetris*, *Tamagotchi*, and *Snickers* bars also come close, but you should also consider how many global licenses are really worth the money.

It really depends on what it costs you. In an extreme case, imagine a license where you and the toy/movie company both benefit and no money changes hands (which is admittedly unlikely). However, what won't work are licenses where the brand is just tagged onto the game as an afterthought. Everybody agreed that *GoldenEye* was a good license because the concept really worked off the character.

Also, if what you're after is the "special shine" in a brand (that is, what makes it an interesting idea as opposed to just the value of prior publicity), then you can always just use the concept. After all, Lara is nothing more than Tank Girl meets Indiana Jones. If you can capture the essence of a license without infringing any intellectual property rights, then you're onto a winner. Lara has now become hot property in her own right.

Languages

The most obvious aspect of localization is, of course, the language. Both text and speech have to be handled and translated.

Text

Text is the trickiest to convert across the language boundary, because so many different glyphs must be taken into account.

For example, in some languages, such as Japanese, text has to be displayed as graphics due to the wide variety of characters available.

Even languages such as German and French that are lexically much closer to home have a high degree of redundancy compared to English. German is 40 percent less efficient in terms of space and succinctness than English is. Graphics screens and screen text must take into account these multiple languages and should provide the ability to display them in different ways. In fact, it may even be possible to take advantage of operating system support for this (Windows has a great deal of localization support), but this has not been the case so far. Maybe there is a market for a localization middleware module in the same way as there is for sound and graphics middleware.

In the past, the big joke in localization used to be American games companies. They used to just tack localization right onto the end of a project and get in all sorts of messes. The line, "Well, you never said it was going to be sold in France!" has been used as a line of defense with respect to incorporating multiple language screens on a console product and therefore running out of space on the cartridge.

Speech

Speech presents its own translation problems. By default, all text in games is *usually* spoken in English. This causes difficulties when translating into other languages, because spoken sentences are usually longer in other languages.

Trying to play and synchronize multiple languages (all of which are of different lengths) is no easy proposition. For example, you try dubbing German on English!

Also the cheap way is for a U.K. (or U.S.) company to get a U.K. (or U.S.) translation company to do the work. This is always a problem. The only way to do voice translations and to record voices is to use professionals from the country in question. This means using local actors and scriptwriters to add the right nuances in the right places. Otherwise, you end up with all sorts of strange and stilted speech.

For example, the Italian version of Geoff Crammond's *Grand Prix II* (Microprose) was incorrect in several places, indicating that someone with a patchy understanding of Italian had performed the translation.

But it's not only the language that can cause the problems. Sometimes cultural colloquialisms can cause problems too. Many years ago, Ocean Software had an action game called *Jelly Boy*. The main character, Jelly Boy, deformed to overcome certain tests and problems. For example, in one section, he turned into a ball to roll down a hill and in another he became a hammer to hit things. If missiles or objects were coming towards him, the player would push down on the joy-pad, and he would duck down so that the object would miss. The problem was that to duck he physically turned into a duck (the aquatic bird). Of course, this was very amusing if you are English speaking, but everyone else is just confused.

The localization issue has cropped up in much the same form at many different publishers.

However, when localization was discussed about halfway through development (already too late—it should have come prior to and during the design phase), the response from the teams was "nobody said there were to be foreign-language versions."

The problem of localization requiring extra screens is more appropriate to cartridge games for which memory is at a premium, but also for CD-ROMs where graphics consume a lot of space.

Demos

Demos are the bane of a developer's life. They take time out of an already busy schedule to produce what is essentially throwaway work. Of course, it is very important work, as it publicizes and demonstrates the progress of the project "so far" to publishers, producers, and the general public.

In fact, the demo can also serve to show the developers how far they have gotten. The only danger is that demos do tend to encourage developers into bad habits. Deadlines for demos are usually very short, and a large amount of work is attempted in a fairly short period. This is the perfect breeding ground for such nasties as quick code hacks and shortcuts.

So, in the case of demos—and especially magazine cover demos (which require a higher standard)—how do you deal with the fact that the need for these usually comes at the most hectic point of development? Would it be worth having a separate, small group within the company that is dedicated to making demos, the same way that a movie director usually doesn't have to do his own trailers?

Well, in some cases, demos could indeed be just a movie. This is fine, but it does not show you how the game feels. Demos must use the original code and play as the game would play. The problem is that, although every one knows demos are needed and even when, such as for major shows and just before release, they are not usually planned as part of the schedule, and usually involve lots of unproductive work in a very short period of time that will be thrown away after the demo date. It would be better to incorporate them into the plan to start with, so that the amount of unnecessary work is minimized.

Care needs to be taken in producing demos with original code, as shown in Case Study 22.5.

The reason why demos are a problem is that they are not considered at the beginning of the project in the initial planning phases. The more planning and more modular the code, the easier demos become. Having an extra artist and programmer would be a benefit for producing demos, but they would have to be part of the team.

Of course, one of the key indicators that the gaming cognoscenti take as an initial indicator of the quality of a game is whether a publicly available demo is released.

You also have to be careful exactly what you give away. An example of the perfect demo is the *Doom* demo. It was almost a complete game, except that the punter got only the first of three episodes. The experience lasted long enough to get the player hooked, but not long enough to really satisfy. This, coupled with the huge buzz surrounding *Doom*, and the excellent Internet distribution resulted in huge sales (although it was still a tiny percentage of the total number of downloads) and resulted in a string of Ferraris sitting outside John Carmack's house.

Take a look at Case Study 22.6 to see how *not* to produce a teaser demo.

Case Study 22.5 Giving The Game Away

A company doing a cover disk demo of a game wanted to release just one level.

However, nobody realized that the person putting the CD-ROM together had merely deleted the files that loaded the other levels from the appropriate directories. The directory images were then copied to the master disk used for the CD-ROM, and the CD-ROM was created directly from that master disk.

Unfortunately, as any Windows user knows, when you delete a file, it is still really there. It's just marked as free space so that the operating system knows that it can overwrite the space when needed.

Because no new files had been written before pressing the CD-ROMs, all the punters had to do was run a restore on the directories to reinstate the deleted files, and they then had the full game.

Result: Zero sales.

Case Study 22.6 Keep Something Back

This case study concerns an unnamed racing game.

The publisher decided to release the network multiplayer version on a cover disk.

The retail product was just the single-player game, which got panned in the press when it was reviewed. The single-player game was just not much fun at all.

Unfortunately for the publisher, the best part of the product was the multiplayer section, which they had just given away free to everyone.

Result: Zero sales.

Playtesting

Playtesting is arguably the most important of the final stages of a project. Without playtesting, you have no idea whether your game is a game or just a pretty slideshow.

I have to assume that all games *are* tested in this way, but, judging by some of the games that are released, they are either not tested extensively enough or they are tested well and the problems are spotted, but the designer does not know how to fix the problems effectively.

In the latter case, it's possible that playtesting was not performed early enough. Remember that the full game does not have to be finished before the gameplay can be examined. It makes far more sense to use the scientific method, testing the gameplay component in isolation as far as possible, in much the same way as you have tested the code components.

After all, if the gameplay stands up in its own right, without the chrome of the graphics and sound supporting it, you can be sure you've got a fairly good game. Look at the game mechanics of something like *Doom*. This is a game that is essentially a first-person view of *Gauntlet*, a 2D collect-the-keys-and-kill-the-monsters game. The gameplay could have been refined using a simple 2D maze view, without having to wait for the 3D engine. Of course, the 3D engine is one of the things that really made the game the success it was, but the game mechanics are pretty sound without it. You can test gameplay throughout the project using a simple testbed. It doesn't have to be the true game engine.

Playtesting should be an integral part of the test and review phases of each tier ("target, build, test, review," and so on).

The other important question about playtesting is how much should be directed at finding bugs and how much should be directed at refining the gameplay or deciding if the product is fun? At what point should playtesting begin? Three months before release, four months, or something else?

I like to get testers involved at the design stage if possible (but they are rushed people). A tester should be assigned to the project all the way through. Testers play tons and tons of games and have the experience to know what works and where the problems normally are.

Initially, testing at the beginning (whenever the game can be played, even if the levels and game mechanics are only partially complete) is a mixture of fixing bugs and gameplay refining.

Towards the end, one to four weeks out from the projected finish date, it becomes an issue of fixing the critical bugs because of the inevitable sales pressure that this will cause.

But what about using professional testers from external testing companies as opposed to using your own in-house testers?

I think using professional testers is a good idea, because the more testing there is the better the product will be. But, again, you must ask the question, "Why?" Do not underestimate an internal test department. If run correctly, it will not be able to be pressured by sales/marketing into passing a substandard game.

Public beta testing is another option that has worked for many games, such as *Ultima Online* and the *Quake* series. But what are the pros and cons of public beta testing?

It is simple to arrange public testing: you can either release a limited demo on the Internet and solicit responses from the users, or you can place an ad in a local paper or get people in from schools or any other suitable source. But this is not always a good solution. One of the problems is that these people are not trained to test. Origin's (publishers of *Ultima Online*) and Microsoft's principle is that, if you have enough dumb people using the product, you will get all the bugs out. This is true, but the sample rate is astronomic. Also, the product must be one that people want to buy once they have been a beta tester. For example, who is going to beta test *Driver* and then want to pay to play it? For games such as this, the larger the beta test sample, then the lower the sales will be. Of course, products such as Microsoft Word and massive online games are the exception to this rule. The former because it is essentially a business application, and most businesses buy software to stay legal and get the publisher technical support, and the latter because online games constantly evolve, and you have to pay to keep playing.

Case Study 22.7 is a good example of a situation in which independent testing may be useful.

Case Study 22.7 How Did They Miss These!?

This case study concerns an unnamed educational product.

Most programmers like to hide little things that spring out of nowhere to amuse a surprised audience. Called *Easter eggs*, these bits of code just sit there and may never get noticed, but sometimes they do.

On this particular occasion, the educational product was basically a questions-and-answers session set in a classroom. If you got a question wrong, a schoolchild would go to the corner and put on a dunce's hat (which means that there was a big game design mistake there to start with, because negative reinforcement is bad in any game, especially for kids).

Occasionally, the school kid standing in the corner would do something very rude. Unfortunately, a parent discovered this, and 20,000 units had to be recalled from distribution. But tens of thousands of parents have not yet discovered this "unexpected" behavior.

Of course, this isn't the only example: other products (game and nongame) have fatal flaws that testing should have caught. These are a just a small sample of many.

WordStar 4 and _WordStar 5_ by MicroPro International Ltd.

If you asked the spelling checker to check the word "Stop," that is exactly what happened. The computer stopped and hung, and you had to reboot.

Messenger by MicroPro International Ltd.

This first email-type product bombed due to bad marketing and lack of understanding of the concept. When a sales manager was asked at the Compec Computer show what *Messenger* actually did, the answer was, "It sends messages."

Sadly, this was all the understanding that the salesman had and no one on the sales team could elaborate further.

Designer Power Pack by Soft Key International

The first version of this replaced all the Windows icons with a screen with the Designer Power Pack icon only. Rebooting did not always restore, and some users had to reinstall Windows.

Oxford Interactive Encyclopedia by The Learning Company

The first version had an entry: Sir Anthony Hopkins (the Welsh actor best known for his role as Hannibal Lector in The Silence of the Lambs) as being from New South Wales, in Australia, not Wales, in Britain. A member of his fan club pointed out the error to Sir Anthony's secretary.

Compton's World Atlas by Compton's New Media

This had many U.K. inland cities moved to the coast. I know that the U.K. is small compared to the U.S., but it's not that small!

***Key Home Gourmet 10,000* by Softkey**

This had a recipe for a Caribbean rice dish that had the line "take one cup of poo...."

***The Oxford Encyclopedia* by The Learning Company**

Version 1 had the wrong year for Marilyn Monroe's death.

***The Genius of Edison* by Compton's New Media**

The first version shipped without an EXE file so it could not be installed. This had passed by Compton's U.S. Q&A department.

***Outcast* by Infogrames**

The first release of *Outcast* would randomly crash back to the desktop at inopportune times and would fail to read on some DVD drives. This latter problem doesn't just affect *Outcast*. Other games have fallen foul of the DVD read trap, but this is still inexcusable nowadays, seeing that the majority of new PCs include DVD drives.

Focus Groups

Focus groups are a group of individuals who are selected to be a good representative sample of the target audience.

However, it's not as simple as just grabbing a group of likely looking suspects from the street and putting them in a room to play the game.

Before considering a focus group, decide what you want to know. If you don't know what you want to know, it will be a waste of time. The problem is that it is all about gameplay, so the focus group is involved only at the end. The testing department acts as the first focus group in this respect (albeit a very biased one).

Focus groups will work, but you need people running it who understand people. Many psychological and sociological issues must be overcome to get honest truthful results from focus groups. It is in the nature of people to tell you what you want to hear, especially if you have put them on the spot by putting them in a focus group. The quandary is that a professional focus group defeats the object of the exercise, but amateurs off the street do not know what is expected of them.

You can get the best from focus groups in a variety of ways. For example, Nintendo uses one-way mirrors to observe players. Freed from expectations, the results and reactions received from the players are more honest and natural.

Focus groups are undoubtedly of value, however. Lego uses focus groups to evaluate its software. In fact, based on focus group findings, the company even canceled the release of a project and started a complete rewrite one month before it was due to be released. The product was duly rewritten and released one year later.

Focus groups do not have to wait until the product is complete. Useful feedback can be gained from early evaluation of the product. You can start them on screenshots, concepts, and UI evaluation early, and use the results from this early feedback to tailor the look and feel of the game while it costs the least to do so.

The Web Site

A standard feature of most games released nowadays is an associated Web site. Even *Balls!* has a Web site (**dspace.dial.pipex.com/a.rollings/balls.html**) where the latest version in progress can be downloaded, a link to which can be found on the CD-ROM.

The Web site for *Balls!* is not the typical game Web site, mainly because it is a companion site for this book. The *Balls!* development diary and notes can be found there, as can the full version of the software at the latest stage of development. Although *Balls!* is not a commercial project, it served as a useful testbed to refine some of the concepts presented in this book.

Of course, commercial game sites are an entirely different kettle of fish. The purpose of a commercial site is to publicize the game, providing an introduction to the company and the game. A good Web site will provide a bulletin board for players of the game. For an example of an excellent Web site, check out the Blizzard Web site at **www.blizzard.com**, which has the latest news on Blizzard products, downloadable demos, game expansions, and patches (which will be discussed later), as well as their online gaming system, battle.net.

Another example of a great Web site is the Cavedog Web site at **www.cavedog.com**. This Web site was largely responsible for the great sales of their game, *Total Annihilation*. After an initial slow start, the online support provided in the form of extra units and maps helped create extra sales. This use of a Web site to create sales leverage was unprecedented, and it shows the power that a well-applied Web site can have in boosting sales. Cavedog has now started posting extra units for its new game, *Total Annihilation: Kingdoms*.

Other developers have followed up after release with such additions to the core product, helping to make the experience of playing the game more of an ongoing experience. Sports Interactive has a particularly good reputation for fostering "community spirit" with its free monthly updates for *Championship Manager*.

Many other excellent Web sites can be found: just check the box of your favorite games, and go to the Web site. Do some research and find out what makes a good Web site. It's no longer good enough just to throw together some HTML and slap it up on the site. That may work for an internal site, but your external site is your interface with the world. There are two main rules: make it slick, and make it fast. Too many Web sites are graphics heavy, and do not take into account that downloading over phone lines is boring, time consuming, and—if you live in Europe—expensive. If a Web site takes too long to load, (that is, more than 30 seconds), then I click away to another site. Which brings me on to another no-no:

music. Don't add music or sound effects on Web sites! How am I supposed to be able browse them at work if music blares out every 10 minutes! (This actually happened to me when I was researching this book during a quiet moment. It took some explaining as to why the *Pacman* music came blaring out of my machine in the middle of a customer site.)

Make sure that your Web site is ready for the buzz when it begins. Unless you are absolutely huge, then don't give away too much design detail on the Web site. The aim is to intrigue and whet the appetite. A good magician keeps some things up his sleeve.

Getting Ready For The Gold Master

Well, this is it—the final moments. It's time for the team to wish a cheerful goodbye to their baby. The next time they will see it, it will be packaged on the shelves of their local software emporium.

Well, that's the theory, anyway. In practice, other last-minute tasks need to be accomplished before the gold master can be pressed.

For example, when distributing demos in an increasingly crowded market, how can publishers make sure their products get enough coverage?

The answer is to have a good PR and marketing department! Also, it does help if development actually talks to marketing/PR and achieves the milestones it promised them. This is a good reason why realistic schedules are vitally important.

One of the main problems with product placement is hitting the shipping dates. Miss a magazine cover, and you pass a lot of grief onto the magazine editor. He or she will then likely be far less receptive in the future, especially considering that, in some cases, the magazine will have been proofed before the demo software has been delivered. If you fail to deliver, he is not going to be pleased.

One thing that can be done is to hold back all early publicity until you are sure of the release date. The problem is that you need to book magazine covers, editorial space, and feature space approximately two to three months in advance. So, hold back as long as possible, but not so long that the game appears in the shops long before any magazine coverage appears. You need to try and time the two to appear simultaneously.

Once a game has been released, it is not always the end of the story. If a game exercises a particular piece of hardware particularly effectively, then it's possible that the manufacturer of that equipment may want to bundle your software with that hardware as a technology demo. In fact, sometimes hardware manufacturers like to include games software with their hardware just to catch the eye of casual shoppers. This is known as an OEM (original equipment manufacture) bundling release, and it can be great for your company.

Take the following hypothetical example. Assume that a hardware company takes 500,000 copies of your game and puts one inside each of their products. As it is a guaranteed sale, you get cost plus royalty automatically and a further audience for your products.

When I bought my new computer, it came with a whole slew of bundled games, such as *Hexen II* and *Asteroids*. These were bundled to show off the hardware capabilities of the machine, and they were factored in as part of my decision to purchase from that manufacturer. As you can see, OEM bundling releases are good for the hardware manufacturer, and they are a good source of guaranteed income for your company.

Well. That's the gold master pressed and out of the door. In theory, that should be it, but unfortunately that is not usually the case, so what comes next?

Patches

So what is it with patches? Why are so many games released in a buggy state, and then patched a few days after release? (I won't even mention games that are released buggy, and then *not* patched!) Is it the release dates? Are they unrealistic? Just why is it that so many products are released only to need a follow-up patch a few days later?

This happens for many reasons, and pressure from quarterly accounting and optimum release periods (such as Christmas) all eat into the schedule.

Patches are a form of product support. But, at some point, product support has to wind down. There is a finite amount of time before the team is told, "Stop fixing what's wrong with the last game and start working on the next."

The length of this period varies per product, but, usually, the entire team will continue working on the game for about a month after it hits the shops. If a game needs further patches, then the publisher will either completely abandon it, or use a skeleton team of two or three members to maintain the product.

The methodologies in this book allow some degree of maintenance to take place automatically. By developing reusable components, older products can be automatically patched to some degree when the modules are upgraded for new products, assuming that backward compatibility is an issue (which it should be).

A novel way of patching software used by online games such as *Ultima Online*, *Everquest*, *Half-Life*, *Diablo*, and *Starcraft* is to automatically download software patches when the player connects to the multiplayer game server. When we get faster net access (such as ADSL), this will be an even more practical solution, especially considering that the support is built directly into the latest Microsoft operating systems. Even they can download patches and upgrades when the user connects to the Web, via the Windows update site.

In most cases, patches are fixes for the bugs that you know about but did not have time to fix. Patches very rarely contain bugs that users have found, with the exception being machine-configuration problems and when new sound or graphics cards have been released.

Failing to control development time cycles means that the product that is ready at the time of release is more often little more than a beta version containing hidden bugs, rather than a finished and fully robust product.

Crash bugs (Class A) are the worst bugs. The console manufacturers tend to run a tight ship, especially with regard to crash bugs, because releasing a critically bugged product would impact very badly on their good name (not to mention that the cost of releasing a patched console cartridge is considerably more than the PC equivalent).

Developers and publishers of PC products can afford to be less careful—both because there is no manufacturer breathing down their necks and because PC users will typically be quite ready to go online to find a patch. (Also, of course, consoles do not suffer from the compatibility problems that beset the PC market with its near-infinite range of drivers, cards, and hardware specifications.)

Here are some examples of patches that really should have been in the first release of the respective products.

Sin (Ritual Entertainment) took ages to load saved games because it apparently reloaded the whole level—even though it used the *Quake II* engine, which doesn't require that by default! An 18Mb executable was later made available for downloading to fix this.

Braveheart was held back by Eidos to get class A bugs fixed. *Edge* magazine reported problems with the DVD-ROM drive: "After installation, it is suggested that first-time players read a provided text file. Among other concerns, it suggests that owners of DVD-ROM drives may encounter difficulties. The proffered solution? To disable the game port on your sound card." According to *Edge* magazine in their October 1999 edition, this task was duly performed, yet, even with the music off, *Braveheart* continued to spin its CD-ROM at high speed.

Many people reported problems with *Outcast*, including that the game would throw you out into Windows during one of the (four different) endings. Two patches (totaling 10Mb) have been released by Appeal, which appear to solve the problem. However, many reviewers went by the bugged beta (pre-patches), and this may have been the reason why *Outcast*, surely one of the greatest games ever, received some poor reviews.

The dilemma for publishers is either to release a product on the due date even though it's not ready, or hold it back until the bugs are ironed out. Unfortunately, consumers are too forgiving. The financial equation is made easy for the publishers, because it seems that consumers would rather get the game on time, even with the bugs, than be made to wait longer. Most consumers will soon download or circulate the necessary patches.

What are the problems with this scenario? One is that developers cannot get on with the next product while they are fixing problems on the last one. (To a large extent, you can trace this back to the mistake of planning big and scaling down during development, which we earlier pointed out is the wrong way round.)

The other problem is that hard-core gamers may be willing to wait for patches, but, if you're aiming for a wider market, you can expect them to be less patient. If they have to fix the game by downloading a patch, they will regard it as a broken product and they may not buy your later releases. (They may take the same dim view of being charged money for a strategy guide, incidentally. Imagine buying a book of puzzles that didn't have the answers in the back!)

Sometimes patches are packaged with a little extra functionality and extra levels or units and sold as add-ons to the main game. However, game players aren't that easy to fool. The company that tries to release an add-on that, in fact, adds nothing except bug fixes and some token goodies will lose credibility. By contrast, look at how Valve benefited by releasing the *Team Fortress Classic* download for free. This enhanced the original product (*Half-Life*) and ensures players remain interested and eager for future *Half-Life* releases.

Chapter 23
Postmortem

Key Topics:

- ***The project postmortem***
- ***Learning from your mistakes***
- ***Applying lessons learnt to new projects***

According to the old saying that you can't steer a ship by looking at its wake, there is nothing to be learned from studying the past. However, the opposite view recognizes that the past is the best repository of case studies you are going to find. Therefore, reviewing the whole development cycle with the benefit of hindsight does have value.

In this chapter, you'll discover why I've been urging you to make sure that each developer keeps a project journal or diary for the project. In analyzing a past project, it's much easier and more accurate to refer to hard facts that have been written down rather than to rely on the distorted vagaries of memory. Memories will most likely be distorted by the current views of the developer. For example, if the developer feels bad about the project—maybe it was late, and working on it was like a march to hell—then the opinions of the developer will be skewed. He will paint a worse picture than it really was, and it will be hard to find the signal for the noise. Even on a bad project, some things are likely to have gone well. Also, with the doom-and-gloom approach, the real causes of the failures may be hidden among a wealth of useless and misleading information.

Likewise, if the project *appeared* to go well and is currently riding on a wave of good reviews, the developer is likely to view it through rose-tinted glasses. The opinions of the developer will be skewed in the other direction. Worse still, attempting to analyze the project for faults may cause offence—"Hey man! It was a great project! Stop trying to find fault, even when we do something right!"

Obviously, it makes more sense to keep journals, which will be a day-by-day account of how the project went. After the fact, no one can argue with what was written down, and you'll get a far more accurate picture of the project progress (however well or badly it turned out in the end).

Game Developer Magazine, which is pretty much considered a great source of contemporary game development information by those in the know, regularly runs a feature in which a developer on a recently completed project performs a postmortem of it. For me, this is the most interesting and informative part of the entire magazine, and the part that I usually read first when I receive my copy.

In the articles, a developer reviews the project on a point-by-point basis in three main sections.

First, a general overview of the project serves as an introduction—what the game was about, who it was for, and why the postmortem is justified.

Second comes great detail about what went right with the project—what parts of the team worked well together and which processes went like a dream. This section makes interesting and instructive reading.

It is not, however, as instructive as the third section, which is a detailed discussion of what went wrong with the project. Interestingly, this section is usually longer than the second, perhaps for a number of reasons. It may be because the general, uncontrolled state of game development causes more things to go wrong than right, or it may have to do with the very human urge to pick over the bones of mistakes that have been made. Personally, I suspect that it is a combination of both.

One thing that particularly stands out in almost all the articles is that the developer professes a desire to learn from his mistakes, adamantly stating that the problems will not be allowed to occur on the next project. Indeed, this is the very purpose of the articles. By examining the corpses of released games, the aim is to educate the reader of the pitfalls and errors that can occur in the development process. I'd guess that they haven't been that successful in that particular aim: after all, they still run a new postmortem article each issue.

In fact, it's worse than that. Not only do the articles keep appearing, but the list of things that have gone wrong tend to be the same every month. Only the specifics are different. I would bet that the majority of developers could take the "What Went Wrong?" sections of the postmortems, plug in the name of their last project, and find a scary level of correlation between what had happened to them. It probably would be virtually identical.

But what does this mean?

It means that game developers as a community are not learning from their shared mistakes. This is strange, and you may be wondering how this could be so. After all, the answers are all in front of them, and they can make use of their experience of past projects (and the experiences of others) to refine the development processes on each successive project.

Surely if they had been doing this, the art of game development would be reaching a Zen-like perfection by now. We learn by our mistakes and those of others, and there have certainly been enough failures to educate developers to a very high level. Everybody has been on a stinker project, and we all know what the problems are. So why do they keep occurring? Are we so pig-headed and arrogant that we can't—or won't—learn from our mistakes?

One answer, of course, would be "Yes, in many cases, we *are* too pig-headed and arrogant," but that is not a complete answer. We need to dig deeper than that to look at the true causes, because the solutions to these problems are not immediately obvious. Remember, there are no easy fixes, and that is one of the reasons for this book.

Case Study 23.1 is a good example of the sort of situations in which things have gone horribly wrong. A productive postmortem would be a good idea to help solve some of the problems. Suggested solutions are given at the end of the case study.

Team Dynamics

Before we get into specifics, let's look at a general area that will demand some special attention. A group of individuals will have worked together on a single project for the best part of two years or more. Only a very naïve person will imagine that they would get on perfectly for that entire period without some arguments and temper tantrums along the way.

The postmortem is arguably the most important learning experience in the whole development process. It's here that the battle-weary developers get to sit back and take stock of their work over the past couple of years. This process is best done individually at first. Each person involved in the project can compile a list of how he or she believes it went. The nature of some of these problems means that this is best done as an anonymous process. The results can then be collated and discussed in a group without fear of recrimination (because it's entirely possible that some of the problems are due to individuals—although not necessarily in the obvious way).

For example, if someone complains about one or more team members, and these complaints aren't backed up with supporting testimonies from others, then this could indicate a problem with the individual who is making the complaint. It may not necessarily be the case. Indeed, there could be a problem with the individual that the complaint is against, but we should at least take into account the possibility of a disgruntled developer making spurious complaints.

If, however, more than one complaint is leveled against a particular individual, this probably indicates that this individual may be causing a problem in the team. Again, this may not be the case—maybe that particular developer upset some people for an issue that wasn't related to the project and they are getting their revenge in a coordinated fashion (if only the team would gel that well normally!)—but this situation should happen so rarely that we can discount this in most cases.

Case Study 23.1 A Tale Of Two Projects

Ludotek Studios was developing two games concurrently. One, *Waste Lands*, was a strategy/RPG crossover set in an underworld kingdom. The other, *King Kestrel*, was a flying game with weapons, in a similar vein to *Magic Carpet*.

Recently, the president of Ludotek set up an internal technology unit that he was keen for new projects to draw on. "It will save the developers time to concentrate on gameplay," he told his staff.

The first thing that the technology unit unveiled was a new 3D engine. *King Kestrel* had been in development for some time and already had a reasonably good graphics engine, so Jenny, the project leader, was reluctant to switch horses. "I agree with the idea of the technology group, and I'll use its output in the future," she told the company president, "but it'd just hold us up if we were to rip out the existing engine now."

Waste Lands, on the other hand, was still in the preproduction phase. The company president got the team leader, Richard, to look at the new engine.

"Well, I'd be interested to see it when it's finished," commented Richard dryly.

"What do you mean, *finished*?" asked Mike, the head of the technology unit. "This is it, done and dusted! We're moving on to work on a new physics engine now."

Richard was still reluctant, but the company president was losing patience. He had shown this graphics engine to investors, and they had all been very impressed. "Use it," he told Richard.

Fast forward six months. By now, both projects are in trouble—a different kind of trouble in each case. On the *Waste Lands* team, using the technology unit's engine was referred to as "polygon fishing." In the absence of an adequate tool set, levels had to be painstakingly assembled in a text editor, compiled, and then imported into the graphics engine to see if they hit sorting problems. Often, placing too many vertices would cause the engine to chug as it shifted data across to the graphics card.

Richard had quit the project, all his warnings having been ignored. The new lead, Marty, realized they were slipping behind schedule. He knew he could either halt development while they cleaned up the engine, redesigned the API, and wrote proper tools—or he could push ahead and hope to make up lost time with hard work. Unfortunately, having seen what happened to Richard, he took the decision that he knew he would regret. It was soon obvious that the level designers would never be able to put together a level without constant demands on the programmers' time. One of the programmers flatly refused to do anything with the graphics engine. "It's the worst code I've seen," he told Mike, a week before resigning to work at the company that Richard had moved to.

Every day, *Waste Lands* was slipping further behind, but the company president refused to accept excuses. "That engine is going to be the pride of the industry," he told Marty. "The problem isn't with the technology. It's that you people won't take the time to understand it."

Marty confided all to Richard when the two met for a drink shortly afterwards. "*Waste Lands*?" he said bitterly. "We should rename it *Wasted Lives*."

And what of *King Kestrel*? It had originally been a model project, but the fanfare surrounding *Waste Lands* and the new graphics engine impacted it badly. Jenny took the hint after the second meeting at which her graphics engine had been unfavorably compared with Mike's. "I can do better than that," she told her team.

"But we don't need to be better," pointed out Ralph, the lead designer. "*Waste Lands* is set in a huge dungeon environment. In *Kestrel*, you never need to get close to the ground, so why bother with detail that the player doesn't need?"

Jenny was adamant. "It's not so simple. Every time there's a meeting, I can see those SOBs looking at our demo and thinking, `It's not nearly as cool as the technology unit's stuff. Maybe we should pull the plug.' You and I know that engine is a millstone, not an asset, but even if the president finally cottoned on to that, do you think he'd admit it? The technology unit was his idea, after all. No, we have to outshine them to survive."

So, while Marty was driving his team to cope with an inadequately finished engine, Jenny spent her time continually refining the *King Kestrel* engine just to save her project from being canceled.

The fault was not in having a technology unit—a good idea, in principle—but in failing to structure it properly. The technology unit's customers were in fact the development teams. Therefore, Richard should have been able to specify his requirements for a graphics engine, including the tools. If Mike were reluctant to waste his people's time on writing tools, he should've got another unit set up to write tools—a unit whose customer would be the technology unit.

Instead, the technology unit had been structured into the company as though their client wasn't the *Waste Lands* team, but the president. This meant that the code they were handing to the development team was not based on the requirements of the game, but on what looked good at meetings with investors (again, a legitimate use of the technology unit but not one that was congruent with the goals of development).

In the run-up to release, of course, the problems only intensified. Jenny couldn't make any headway on her game because she had fallen into a cycle of continual refinement. *Waste Lands* was losing staff, suffering the effect of hundreds of bugs, and having to cut whole levels out of the game to have any chance of meeting the due date.

The worst thing was that the wrong lessons were learned.

Looking back, Jenny said, "I should have seen the writing on the wall and used their damned engine like they wanted." She should have said, "I just should've gone with the engine we had to begin with. I knew it was fine."

Richard said, "I'm not working in the games industry anymore. The bosses are all idiots." But he should have said, "Next time, at least I'll have the facts to back up my gut feeling."

Marty said, "I've learned the hard way that being team leader isn't about programming or game design. It's about politics!" Whereas he should have said, "I should've pushed for extra team members to fix the problem early, instead of letting it get on top of us."

Mike said, "We're researchers. We can't be expected to waste time on menial stuff that the development teams can do." It would have been better if he'd said, "It's a waste of our time, but it's a waste of theirs, too. Let's set up a tools unit to finesse our leading-edge stuff to a point where it meets the developers' requirements."

The end result of these two situations is the same: we need to investigate why the problems are there. It may help us at this point to see if we can map problem reports about team members to the developer types discussed in Chapter 9.

Case Study 23.2 shows some postmortem reports from a completed project. Issues relating to team dynamics are raised, so let's see if you can decide which developer type each team member is.

Case Study 23.2 also discusses a pretty dysfunctional team. This team didn't start out dysfunctional; it became that way after things started to go wrong on the project and were not remedied quickly. For the rest of this chapter, we will examine the postmortem of the fictional *FlyBusters III* and discuss how the results could be used to prevent the same mistakes from happening again. Remember, hindsight has 20/20 vision: it's easy to spot mistakes *after* they have already happened, but it is not so easy to prevent them happening again in the next project.

When we have a complete list of areas of problems that affected the project, we can begin to look at ways to prevent them in the future.

Concept

What about a postmortem of the concept itself? Surely the game concept must have been essentially sound, or the project wouldn't have been given the green light in the first place.

Well, the evidence is fairly clear that this is not the case. Just wander into any software store and count the number of lame concepts that you can see—games that should have never got off the drawing board because the concept behind them was so wholly inappropriate to the industry climate.

It may not have even been the fault of the designer. The climate in this industry can change faster than the weather in England. Blink and you've just missed a demographic shift. Spend 18 months to two years writing a game, and you've missed an entire ice age.

So, in order to perform a postmortem of the concept, what issues do we need to consider? We've just touched upon one of the issues: misjudging the climate.

Climate

This is not a simple issue at all. Being able to predict what the market is going to be like two years from now is not easy. If it were, everybody would be doing it.

However, misjudging this completely doesn't happen often. Usually, the general concept is in the right area, but occasionally a game will completely miss the mark. To be fair though, games that miss the mark are often seen as being ahead of their time. I suspect that this is because anything else that is wide of the mark is usually canned or rewritten before it hits the market.

Case Study 23.2 It's All Gone Horribly Wrong!

For this case study, we are going to revisit a team from an earlier case study, presented way back in Chapter 11.

Andy, Barry, Chris, Dave, and Eddie are the programming team who worked on *FlyBusters III—Beyond the Flypaper*, the latest masterpiece by Freddy, a veteran game designer. In Chapter 11, we presented two possible scenarios: a good outcome and a bad outcome. Here, we carry on the scenario from the bad outcome.

Still reeling from the abysmal reviews and poor sales, the *FlyBusters* team has resolved to examine what went wrong with their project, so that they won't make such a costly and demoralizing mistake on their next project.

Each member of the team compiled their individual postmortem report, and they are ready for collating by Jan, another member of the company who wasn't involved in the *FlyBusters* project.

Jan is reading the team-dynamic sections of the postmortem reports.

Andy: I felt that I was not taken seriously because of my inexperience. I am technically competent enough, but, because this is my first project, and I have not "made my bones" on as many projects as the others. Even when I made valid suggestions, I was overridden or ignored on a number of points. I found it difficult to communicate with the other members of the team, particularly in the case of Eddie, who didn't seem to have the time of day as far as I was concerned. This disheartened me, and I found it difficult to feel as if I were part of the team.

Chris: I found that I wasn't allowed enough creative freedom by Eddie to implement my landscape engine. He was always breathing down my neck when I was trying to get work done on the system, and I found that this impacted my time, causing me to be delayed in my work. Barry and Chris kept annoying me by asking me for unnecessary features to support their polygon engine, when they could have worked the answers out for themselves quite easily. I found that Andy was okay, although again he asked me questions that he could have easily answered himself.

Barry: I worked mainly with Dave, and, as such, I had no real problems with the team. Chris sometimes needed a bit of pestering to get him to explain the landscape engine fully so we could integrate the polygon system, and Andy was alright, although a little inexperienced. This meant he sometimes bit off a bit more than he could chew, and it took time out of our schedule to help him out. He didn't always talk about his problems immediately, preferring to try and solve them himself before asking for help, and this sometimes caused further complications. For the most part, Eddie was a good team leader, although he could be a bit distant at times if he was stuck into his code and he sometimes came down a bit hard if things weren't going as well as he liked.

Dave: Because I worked directly with Barry for most of the time, I had no big problems with the rest of the team. On the few occasions when I did need to interact, only Chris really caused problems, because he appeared to deliberately obstruct us when we tried to integrate with his landscape engine. I found Andy to be extremely difficult to work with, because, at the start of the project, he acted as if he knew more about polygon engines than I did, even though I have been working in the industry for much longer than he has. He tried to make Barry and me look bad by criticizing the polygon engine before we had even finished the first beta.

Eddie: I've never worked with such a team of incompetent idiots. They needed hand-holding throughout the entire process. Granted, Barry and Dave were okay at times, if a little slow, but Andy and Chris were intolerable. I felt it was completely unfair that I got the blame for the delays caused by the poor code produced by these two unmanageable idiots. Don't put me in charge of a project with those two developers again, or I won't be held responsible for the consequences. Incidentally, on the next project, if you put me in charge of the development of the polygon engine, I'll be able to fix up the errors and optimize the code that Barry and Dave produced, and I can move them on to other stuff.

From these comments, Jan has a pretty shrewd idea of what has happened within this team, and which type of developers she thinks comprise the team.

She thinks that Andy started out at a disadvantage. He was effectively the token learner on a project that did not have room for a learner. In her opinion, Andy was put there because they needed to fill a seat. Unfortunately, this particular project had not taken Andy's learning curve into account. It was an entirely unsuitable project, seeing as the deadlines were too tight to allow for the sort of errors that a learner can make. The conclusion that Jan came to was that Andy has been damaged by his experiences on this project. His self-esteem has been shattered, and he has gone from being an enthusiastic, if inexperienced, developer to an introverted and withdrawn shy-guy developer type. Of course, if the schedule hadn't been so tight and the team environment had been such that a learner would be tolerated more, then this might not have occurred, but unfortunately the other developers were less than helpful at answering Andy's question. It is doubtful whether Andy will fully recover from the experience, but her recommendation is to place him on a few solo (or paired) developer confidence-building projects, such as small (but not trivial), self-contained modules and tools, or maybe provide him with some training courses. Care is needed to ensure that he doesn't feel as if he is being shunted off into a corner where he can't do any harm to the more "important" work, because that will just exacerbate the problem, and could cause Andy to quit.

Chris, she has decided, is a classic maverick. He exhibits all the signs, from the need for creative freedom to the misplaced ownership of code (*his* landscape engine, rather than the *team's* landscape engine.) This isn't necessarily a bad thing, although he does have a tendency to lose the correct focus and concentrate on the more interesting, but less important, areas of code. This causes problems because, in this case, his failure to provide an interface to the polygon engine (which was due to a combination of it not being interesting enough, and of his not wanting to have to "pollute" his code with outside work) caused significant delays to the progress of Barry and Dave. Her conclusion was that Chris has the potential to be an excellent team player and that he is certainly a skilled and creative developer, but he needs to learn the importance of team work—there's no "I" in team. He would also respond well to a more laid-back management style. When Chris began to lose focus, Eddie responded by trying to micromanage him—an entirely inappropriate response to Chris's personality type. A better approach would have been to apply gentle course corrections at key points with the use of smaller milestones specified by a software planner rather than breathing down his neck until he got back on track—an approach that had entirely the opposite effect to that which was intended.

As far as Jan is concerned, Barry is a good developer, although tending towards the "jack" developer type. He is conscientious and thorough, if lacking in a little imagination. From reading his comments, she feels that he has painted the most accurate picture of what life was like on the project. Barry seems to be a fairly relaxed individual, and he has probably come out of this project unscathed. He has enough experience of other projects to be able to separate his work from his feelings. Jan feels that Barry needs to be a bit more open to other developers' suggestions and not take criticism of his code so personally.

Jan recognizes Eddie's type immediately: a prima donna. There are absolutely no questions about the level of Eddie's technical knowledge. He is a technical wizard. However, there is no way he should have been team lead. It's a classic mistake: The management chose the team leader solely on the basis of technical ability and took no account of his temperament or lack of management skills. Too often, an accomplished technical genius in such a position sees it as his job to make sure everybody knows their place. Instead of guiding team members, he may assume that their failure to match his programming competence marks them out as stupid. Worse still, if another person has knowledge that the prima donna does not, that person is liable to be viewed as a threat, and their knowledge will from then on dismissed as obscure and irrelevant.

It seems to Jan that, when things started to go wrong, Eddie blamed everyone but himself. She comes to the conclusion that it would be best not to try and use him as a member of a team in future—still less as the team leader. In view of his technical skills, she recommends that he is moved to the company's research group. This allows him to focus on his own projects but ensures that his expert knowledge is still available to the entire company in the form of consultancy on projects in development.

Let's continue with the postmortem of *FlyBusters III* to examine this problem further. Take a look at Case Study 23.3.

The issues examined in Case Study 23.3 are a fictional amalgamation of situations that have occurred in real projects. Misjudging the climate can occur in other ways, too—not just those mentioned here.

As stated, the consequences of this can be serious, but for the most part this is a very difficult thing to get wrong. Why do I say this? Usually because a game that misjudges the climate often gets singled out for specialist attention in the press and ridiculed accordingly. If this weren't such a rare occurrence, then the games wouldn't be singled out for this special level of attention. I would estimate that only about six or seven games a year misjudge the climate badly enough to be noticed in this way. The rest probably don't even get released or are delayed until they fit the bill. Sometimes the misjudging isn't too serious. For example,

Case Study 23.3 Misjudging The Climate

Jan continues reading the postmortem document, focusing next on the "Climate" section.

Andy: I felt the initial concept was strong. After all, it was the third game in a fairly successful series, but I guess the general feeling was that it was a bit long-in-the-tooth.

Chris: The game concept was fairly sound. It was sufficiently different from the previous version to be considered more than just a plain update, while still retaining the features that made the previous games popular. The bio-organic ship was a big favorite from the previous version, and the latest version was just as good, if not better. I don't think there were any problems with the concept.

Barry: I never liked the previous two versions that much. It's not that they weren't good—it's just that I'm not a big fan of 3D flying/shooting-type games. I much prefer RTS (realtime strategy) games. I think that the strategy elements in the concept could have been given more emphasis, but apart from that the concept was okay.

Dave: I think that we misjudged the massive growth in multiplayer and online gaming. We have no real support for multiplayer (a two-player, head-to-head mode only), and we had no Internet support. This meant that we were releasing effectively a single-player game, when everyone else was releasing single-player games with strong multiplayer aspects. This may not have been as bad if we'd got it out on time.

Eddie: There were too many similar games on the market at the same time. In fact, one month before we managed to release it, two other companies released similar (but superior) games.

Freddy: There was nothing wrong with the concept of my game. It built well on the foundations of the previous products and expanded them well, introducing some classic concepts from old games and modernizing them appropriately. This has always been a successful concept in the past. We used the same approach with *FlyBusters II*, and that did really well. Why didn't the same concept apply here?

Jan recognized the points raised in the reports as all caused by classic problems. The main one of these was the lateness to market. If it had come out when originally intended, six months earlier, then the other two competitors mentioned by Eddie would not have been present. Unless a gamer is a complete fanatic, he is not going to buy a game similar to one that he already has, unless it is clearly superior. *FlyBusters III* would have been great—but only if it had arrived on time. Because the other two projects had been started later and had been completed roughly on time, they had started six months after *FlyBusters III*. In six months, many things can change. One of the biggest changes was the sudden increase in the number of good 3D cards. *FlyBusters III* had been caught short by this (it happened about a year into the development cycle), but the other two had been able to predict and adapt, and featured full 3D card support. *FlyBusters III* did not, and consequently appeared dated even before release.

Another area that the team failed to pick up on was the rapid growth of online and multiplayer gaming. The game design had only ever supported the concept of two players. Any more would have destroyed the balance and made it a frustrating free-for-all. Unfortunately, most other games at the time of release were supporting 8 to 32 players. The two-player game could have been salvaged slightly by allowing Internet play, but unfortunately this hadn't been considered. Only network play was supported (not even direct cable link), and this was suitable only for real hard-core gamers. Your average punter does not have a home network setup.

Barry felt that the concept was a bit stale. Jan could agree with this to some extent. Although the previous two outings had done exceptionally well, she couldn't help but feel that the new version didn't offer anything particularly new and exciting. Sure, strategy was being considered more, so this wasn't just a pure arcade blast, but there can sometimes be a problem there, too. Attempting to straddle genres has been one of the classic targets for some time. For example, Activision's *BattleZone*, attempted to merge a first person 3D shoot-em-up like *Quake* with a tactical realtime strategy game similar to *Command & Conquer*. They did a great job of the interpretation and got great reviews, but the sales were not that great. They had fallen into the classic trap of trying to appeal to two incompatible demographics, and, instead of crossing the boundaries and appealing to both, they appealed to neither. More specifically, they appealed to the intersection of the two sets: those players who liked both realtime strategy games *and* first-person shooters.

Jan found Freddy's comments to be a bit strange. What made him so sure that the concept was a sure-fire winner when most of the other members of the team seem to be of the opinion that the game design was a bit tired and worn out? She wonders whether Freddy may be losing his touch slightly. This would be a difficult subject to broach with him, so a more subtle approach would be required. Another alternative is that he is just becoming jaded with the series. It was his initial conception, but the decision to produce a third game was not his. The marketing department and managing directors of the company had decided that a third game was required, after the runaway success of the first two. This means that he's been working on the same game series for the best part of six years. Maybe it's time to give him something else to work on, so that he can exercise his imagination again and get a fresh look at things.

if a game has a poor multiplayer mode but an excellent single-player game, this can sometimes offset the weaknesses. The game will be marked down in reviews, but it won't suffer too much if the rest of it is solid. It may make the difference between a game of the month and an "okay" review (and of course this makes a difference to sales).

You may be wondering why I am covering this subject if I state that only six or seven games a year are released that have misjudged the climate. After all, it's a very small figure to concern ourselves with. However, as I've already said, many more games are affected by this: they are just either canned or redesigned before release.

This means that the symptoms are easy to spot *after* they have occurred, but this is too late. By this stage, a lot of money will already have been wasted in redesign. Or, if it is cancelled, much more money will have been wasted, because there is no chance of reclaiming some of the costs back from sales revenue. In a postmortem of your project, you should leave no stone unturned. You can't afford to miss a trick.

Accessibility

Accessibility is a contentious issue. The hard-core gaming contingency often complains about the "dumbing down" of gaming. These complaints usually come from the same people who lament the lack of appeal their games have to the mass market.

Well, as the saying goes, if the mountain won't come to Mohammed, then Mohammed must go to the mountain. The mass market isn't going to change that easily. If you want to get the mass market, you need to cater to the mass market, because it certainly is not going to cater to you.

Originally games were simple beasts, and this simplicity was part of their appeal. Usually they were games of conflict, because this was the easiest to represent on limited hardware. This, and the abstractness imposed by the hardware—realism simply wasn't possible. Conflict is a key ingredient of the best stories. Because of the way computers have developed over the years, violence is the simplest and easiest action to show. On the early games machines, it was about all you could do to get some graphics together that represented a man with a gun, and a bevy of enemies, such as *Space Invaders*. The power was just not there for anything else. You cannot imagine a *Space Invaders* machine having a "Negotiate" button placed within convenient reach of the fire button. Even if the game developer had come up with such a radical concept, the hardware certainly wouldn't have been able to support the advanced interactivity required.

Today, of course, we don't have that excuse. So why are we forced to accept games in which the only advance since *Space Invaders* is a wider selection of weapons, the ability to move in more than two directions, and more realistic deaths?

Appealing to the mass market doesn't necessarily mean "dumbing down," either. Witness the success of *Driver*, or *Command & Conquer: Tiberian Sun*. These are both very respectable games in their own right and have achieved stupendous sales. These high-quality products don't actually quite achieve mass market appeal, but they go some way towards it—and they've done this without any "dumbing down." How?

These games are accessible, but why? What exactly is accessibility? What makes one game more accessible than another? Let's first look at the immediate factors that promote accessibility in a game.

First of all (from the consumer's viewpoint) there are the packaging and supporting materials. How do you make sure your product stands out on the shelf? Examine the design of the packaging of the shelves of your local software store. Does anything stand out in particular? If so, why? Does it stand out because it is well designed and stands above the rest, or does it stand out for another reason, such as being particularly graphic or tasteless?

In fact, accessibility has a far wider range than this, and we must step back and look at the big picture. A product's accessibility starts with its advertising. How much advertising was there? How effective was it? Did the advertising successfully publicize the product, or did it fall on its face? Owing to regulations, American advertising is usually substantially different from the equivalent U.K. advertising in that American ads are allowed to draw direct comparison with competing products.

In the U.K., this just does not happen. Personally, I doubt the effectiveness of this form of comparison (especially the derogatory kind), but I guess that it does draw attention to the genre of the game. Maybe it's just because, as a Brit, I'm not used to that sort of advertising, but, in general, I like to be able to draw my own conclusions about a particular product. After all, it's not difficult for me to work out that one game is similar to another game.

Anyhow, would you really want people to buy your game just because it is like another? (Of course, the answer to this is that really you don't care why someone buys your game, as long as they buy it. However, we are assuming you are reading this book because you want to improve your game design skills, and not just create derivative rip-offs.)

So, we can see that, before we've even looked at the game, the question of accessibility has cropped up. As I've stated before, we have to look at all the angles when performing a postmortem. The results can sometimes be surprising.

The overall polish of a game—the friendliness of the interface and the amount of chrome—has an important impact.

Microsoft spends a lot of money on user-interface research. The result of this, of course, was Windows 95 (and later 98 and 2000). You may scoff, but—although Windows has its foibles—it's still arguably the friendliest operating system out there. You can take their hard-earned research and apply it to your products. Work out where your interface falls down, and look at something that works in order to rectify it.

It's not difficult to work out where things have gone wrong. All you need to do is just sit down with a group of testers who are unfamiliar with the proposed interface and observe their reactions. Any tricky points in the interface will soon be discovered. Of course, this is all obvious stuff. I shouldn't need to spell any of this out, but you'd be surprised to learn how often projects go into headless-chicken mode when problems crop up, and common-sense advice such as this is ignored.

The interface is the main way the user interacts with your game, and as such it is the most important feature. If it's poor, players will give up and play something else. It's as simple as that.

Treyarch, developers of *Die by the Sword*, noted in their postmortem, which was published in the January 1999 edition of *Game Developer Magazine* that they had completely misjudged the learning curve. The tutorial contained jumping puzzles that were almost as difficult as those towards the middle of the game. According to Treyarch, from this the developers learned two things. One of these is the (rather obvious) observation that levels should be arranged so that easy stuff comes first (that should have been spotted at the playtesting stage). The other is that the separate tutorial/game model does not work. "Users should learn skills gradually as they progress through the game, rather than learning them all at once."

However, *Half-Life* took this approach, and didn't seem to suffer too much for it. (I still prefer the gradual-progression model however.) Perhaps the only reason that it did not grate too much in *Half-Life* is that the interface was very similar to every other first-person shoot-em-up game out there. People already knew how to use it. Only one of the moves, the long jump, was different, and it took me ages to learn. However, the training course was presented as part of the game, under the pretext that you had to learn how to use the hazardous environment suit provided as part of your new job.

This "learn the skills as you go along" approach was taken by the famous game designer, Shigeru Miyamoto of Nintendo. He was responsible for *Mario* and the *Legend of Zelda* games. His approach to game design is exemplary, particularly in the case of the *Zelda* series. When playing these, you'll notice that the game designer carefully leads you down a fairly linear path in such a way so that you do not notice. One of his favorite tricks seems to be fooling you into thinking that you need an object to complete a level, and then providing it to you as a reward for completing that level. Then you realize how much easier it would have been to complete the level *with* the object. Frustrating? Yes, and also ingenious. This approach provided an excellent addictive hook, and provided a seamless way of learning new skills. The object you had won in the level would undoubtedly be crucial for the next level. Yes, this is unrealistic, but real life is not as well structured, and that's why people play games—to be entertained by the game designer in a consistent and well-structured world.

Development

Problems in the initial concept and game design are usually rarer than problems in development. For the majority of postmortems, the problems will be in the actual development phase of the project, and for two reasons.

The first is that this is usually the longest and most intense stage of the project: there is simply more to go wrong. The second is that the development is also the most complex stage, and generally involves the most number of people at once. Problems are harder to spot because there is a lot of other simultaneous activity, and also because of the technical nature of the work.

For this section, we will briefly look at the main phases of development in turn: software planning, coding, and testing. At each stage, certain questions can be asked as to what went wrong, how it should have been dealt with at the time, and how we can prevent it from happening (or at least to minimize the effects) in the *next* project.

Software Planning

The software planning aspects of a project come early on. Any mistakes here will multiply and compound themselves during the development phases. More importantly, the cost of fixing such mistakes later can be up to 200 times more expensive than fixing them early on, soon after they are introduced.

To put this in real terms, getting the software planning phases wrong—for example, by making a huge error with the architecture—will cost much more in terms of time and money to fix during development than it would if it were spotted and fixed during the design of the architecture. Bluntly, this could make the difference between a minor blip on the project timeline and complete cancellation.

"There are two ways of constructing a software design. One way is to make it so simple that there are obviously no deficiencies, and the other is to make it so complicated that there are no obvious deficiencies."

—Charles Anthony Richard Hoare

It is clearly important to spot and fix mistakes early on, and, with the benefit of hindsight, it is easy to see how this could be done. Unfortunately, we don't have the benefit of hindsight before we actually perform the work, which is why we use postmortems of previous projects to extrapolate results to our new project.

Phase breakdown and project planning are the processes whereby you calculate and divide up amongst the available resources the actual work that is needed to produce the finished product.

These are the stages where the milestones and mini-milestones are created. The work is then allocated to individual developers on a schedule plan, creating a complex web of dependencies (and of course creating lots of opportunities for error).

Note

You will make mistakes, but formal process makes sure you won't make the same mistake again. Formalizing the methodology means that the team learns from an individual's mistakes.

Case Study 23.4 illustrates a problem associated with software planning in which the differing underlying architecture of two separate target platforms was not taken into account when designing a game.

Planning errors usually occur early in the project, so they are worth looking at carefully. According to the April 1999 postmortem of Multitude's multiplayer Internet game, *FireTeam*, Art Min states that defining project constraints in the planning stage of the project—defining what the project should and should not be—helped keep the project on track and

Case Study 23.4 Oubliette

On a project that we shall call *Oubliette,* the publisher had taken 2 months doing an evaluation of the PlayStation conversion, and it was determined that the conversion would be 3 months' work. The *Oubliette* team leader, however, estimated that it would be 12 months' work. It turned out to be 18 months.

Here's why.

Development had already been going on for a year. The PC game map creation process was well under way, but no planning had gone into understanding what the maps were and how the characters would move around the maps (route finding, AI, and so on).

In fact, the design did not even refer to the AI. Everyone initially thought that the maps could just be cut up into sections for the PlayStation and loaded on demand, but this turned out to be impractical for various reasons.

Consequently, the PlayStation version had to become more linear within the large plan of things, even though on the smaller scale the maps were not linear.

Because of memory limitations, keeping track of variables became a real problem, as did saving and loading the game: on the PC, you save to hard drive which (usually) has plenty of space, but on the PlayStation you have to save to a very small memory cartridge.

focused. This degree of planning allowed them to spend more time developing the tools required for building the game. Too often, tools are hacked together quickly in order to get things moving.

In the November 1998 postmortem of DreamForge's *Sanitarium*, Chris Pasetto talks about its modular design. The project was constructed in defined modules. This meant that they could construct the game in blocks that improved the gameplay and the storyline, but would not otherwise affect the quality of the game if any of them were not completed. This approach proved to be very successful, as in the end only a few parts didn't make it into the final product.

This can often be a false move, as the developers of *Die by the Sword* discovered (postmortem, January 1999). They found that they had not developed their level-designing tools to a high-enough quality. Rather than taking time out to modify and improve their tools, they instead fired artists who could not adapt to them. Those artists who were able to use the tools took much longer to complete levels than they would have otherwise.

One thing that the planning phase should be able to clamp down on is the amount of feature creep in the project. This problem affects many projects, and it is a direct result of a couple of developers beginning a conversation with the phrase, "Wouldn't it be cool if...."

Sometimes their discussion may well unearth a valuable and needed addition to the project, but this doesn't always come without consequences. The addition needs to be thoroughly evaluated to see if it is worth adding in—and taking any hit to the schedule that may be associated with it. Remember, you don't get something for nothing. You may not pay for it immediately, but believe me, you will pay eventually…and usually at the most inopportune time.

Die by the Sword also suffered from rampant feature creep. They documented a recurrent pattern of slippage and creeping. As the developers fell behind schedule in an area, they would succumb to the temptation to add some new features when the publisher agreed to the slippage. After all, they reasoned, we've got a bit more time; let's improve the area while we are there. This is a seductive argument, but adding features when the project is slipping is only asking for yet more slippage. It seems that they consistently underestimated the time required to implement new features. These results highlight the need for discipline and sticking to what's in the schedule. This can be summed up with the following harsh advice: if it's not down on the plan, then it's not going in! This is the extreme view: if the suggested feature really does add significant value to the project, then at the very least examine the prospects of slippage thoroughly.

Overcomplicated designs can also be a cause of problems. With *Sin*, the developers wanted to make the game as expandable as possible and attempted to generalize the source code (in effect creating a soft architecture). Unfortunately, they discovered that writing such generalized source code is much more difficult than specifically hard-coding functionality. In the *Sin* postmortem, they noted that this added a lot of extra development time to the project.

Coding

The coding phase of a project is usually where most of the errors occur. This is not necessarily because it is the most difficult part (although it can be.) More often the actual coding (including the technical design) is the longest and most protracted phase of the project.

As I've stated before, the actual typing in of code is only a small but important part of the entire process. *Coding* in the context I am presenting it here also included the detailed technical design process, which should be performed before even touching the computer. Of course, this is the real world, and, until people know better (that is, after they've read this book), then many projects will have been written this way, going straight from a general architecture design to coding, thereby making the coding segment the largest part of the project. This process is also very prone to error. You can't rely on the developers themselves to spot the errors that easily, because they will be focusing on the code in a high degree of detail and won't be worrying about general concerns that much.

Problems with tools seem to be more common than not. In the March 1999 postmortem of Ritual Entertainment's *Sin*—a first-person shooter using the *Quake II* engine—the developers reportedly had problems using the tools provided with the engine. They attributed this to the late inclusion of the *Quake II* engine in the project. They had originally started out with the *Quake* engine, and the second engine became available at some later stage in the project. In order to port the code to the second engine, they had to rewrite some of the major subsystems. In some cases, they were rewritten more than once. Clearly, the wisdom of switching over to the second engine at such a critical stage in the project needed to be examined closely to see how it could be performed much more smoothly—or altogether avoided—in the future.

Testing

Judging by the number of patches required for games (virtually every game ever released requires a patch), testing is an area that needs a lot of close attention.

Is there something fundamentally wrong with testing techniques, or is the problem a little more complicated than that? In some cases, problems are simply due to inadequate testing, but in others, more complex factors come in to play.

When a game is released, it inevitably requires a patch of some kind. The sloppier games require big fixes (due to laziness on the parts of the developers, or impatience on the part of the publishers).

Even the better-tested games have compatibility issues. On the PC platform, it is impossible to test every possible configuration of machine.

The developers of *Sin* had a bad experience with testing. They did not test with enough hardware configurations, and, when a problem was found, instead of releasing a quick fix, they gathered up all of the fixes into one mammoth patch of about 20 megabytes. This is a lot to download in one go, so the publishers, Activision, offered a free CD-ROM to anyone who requested it.

Business Aspects

Whether you would include business aspects as part of a project postmortem depends very much on the nature of your company. Whatever the reason, in most cases this would be performed away from the main postmortem.

After all, financial information is generally company sensitive, and, unless you are running some sort of cooperative, then this would not be discussed outside of select management circles. Although financial matters are beyond the scope of this book, Case Study 23.5 may prove a useful starting point for your financial postmortem.

Of course, the best advice when dealing with financial matters and contracts is to consult a lawyer who knows the business. The most important thing—and something that both authors of this book have learned the hard way—is to make sure that you have everything in writing. Not everybody in the industry is an unscrupulous fiend, but there are certainly more than our fair share. A good place to look for tips on arranging financial matters is to consult the Gathering of Developer's Web site (**www.godgames.com**) or Gamasutra (**www.gamasutra.com**) where you will find a wide array of advice in this area.

Case Study 23.5 Secure Your Revenue Stream

Bertrand and Vito ran Force du Jeu Studios, a small development company that was working on *Hard Won*, a racing game. Recently, a new CEO had taken over at the publisher that was funding the game. After he had paid them a visit, Bertrand and Vito were anxious to hear his opinion of their game, which was now only four months from completion.

What they didn't know was that the CEO had made his decision about *Hard Won* even before he was back at his office. "It's okay, but too similar to another one we have in development in Milan," he told his marketing director.

"Which should we keep?" wondered the marketing director.

"The Milan game. There's a good chance they can coincide with the re-release of *The Italian Job*—you know, that movie with Michael Caine. So I'm going to have to pull the plug on *Hard Won*."

A few weeks later, the marketing director stopped by the CEO's office with an invoice. "Force du Jeu has billed us for this month's payment on *Hard Won*," he said. "I thought we were canning it."

"We are," said the CEO. "Whose job is it to tell them? Oh, never mind, I'll do it myself." He reached for the phone.

"It has to be in writing," said the publishing director. "And I'm still going to have to pay this invoice."

At Force du Jeu, Bertrand received the news with shock, but to his surprise Vito wasn't fazed. "Now they've told us in writing that they're pulling the funding, they still have to make two more monthly payments as long as we made our last milestone—which we did."

"That still leaves us with the last month's wages to pay—and funding on our next game has yet to be finalized."

"It's not a problem," insisted Vito. "I arranged this with our bank manager right at the start. Basically, as long as we hit our milestones, he agreed to step in with a bridging loan of up to three months' operating costs."

Suddenly it hit Bertrand too, and he was laughing. "So the publisher is going to end up funding us right to within one month of completion, then our bank steps in to tide us over! You realize this frees us from the publishing agreement? We won't be tied to 25 percent royalties. We can go shopping around."

"We still have to pay back the original funding if we get a new deal elsewhere," pointed out Vito. "But yes, I agree it's pretty sweet."

Ironically, the publisher's movie tie-in fell through and they were one of the companies bidding for the completed *Hard Won*. Even though they had provided the original funding, it was their unilateral choice to pull out of the contract, and so Force du Jeu was able to ask for and get an additional 10 points on the royalty rate. On the other hand, if Vito hadn't had that talk with his bank manager when work on the game began, it would have been a very different story. Funding isn't easy to arrange in a hurry, and they might have had to give up all rights in the game.

The Postmortem Postmortem

A postmortem is a critical examination of a past project in an attempt to figure out where mistakes were made and where they could have been avoided.

This is all very interesting from a historical point of view, but, for it to become more than an extended navel-gazing session, the lessons must be registered and applied to new projects.

It's not enough just to say, "Oh yeah! We see what we did wrong. We won't do it again," because, if you do, then you *will* do it again. Instead, you must actively take steps to prevent it (and things like it) from happening next time around.

The software plan of the next project should actually include measures to prevent it from happening.

If not, then you will be doomed to repeat your mistakes over and over again–like Sisyphus, pushing a rock up a hill, without a break, for all eternity.

Chapter 24

The Future Of Game Development

Key Topics:

- ***The structure of future development***
- ***Psychology of team dynamics***
- ***Metadesign***
- ***A glimpse forward***

We concluded the earlier sections of this book with a forecast of how things might be in the next 10 years if the methods we have discussed were to be put into widespread use. In the case of development, one prognosis can be made with crystal clarity: development has to undergo a revolutionary change. Overmanaged projects destroy morale. Still more common, the undermanaged model is worse: it leads to chaos, slipped deadlines, wasted effort, and, all too often, project cancellation.

We have advocated a formal process operating within the development team, the purpose of which is to ensure that the design is maintained and refined in parallel with the build. Our development model controls everything through the design and architecture of the project to prevent runaway change and inaccurate focus on requirements. The method we have recommended—and which we have seen yield best results—is to produce a thorough design and then conduct development in phases, or tiers, in which new features are incorporated in successive iterations. Each iteration ends with a revision of the design, which is the target that development is always converging towards.

The development company that switches to design-led development experiences many benefits. One is that the collateral reuse of technology is made easier when you have a well-maintained architecture. A repository of plug-in modules affords the company with the toolkit required for cost-effective development. Metadesigns establish a generic framework so that development time can be spent on perfecting gameplay instead of infinitesimally tweaking basic routines. We have predicted that these trends will eventually lead to the consolidation of a few "super developers"—extended design and architecture groups that may usually hire the programmers, artists, and other team workers on a per-project basis.

In this final chapter, we'll first look at how the structure of the architecture-driven developer will affect working practices. Marshalling big teams will call for accurate planning to ensure that the work of the "creative core"—the visionary personnel at the heart of the project—is enhanced and not diluted. You can hire and fire freelance workers interchangeably, but the people who provide the unique creative spark are all important. Replace them, and you have a different game. Thus, knowing where your company's added value lies is vital in order to maximize creative innovation. (An analogy is the creation of an animated movie: the main artists produce key frames, and the rest are tweeked by assistants.) The trend in this environment will be towards clearly defined, specialist roles. Thus, we will see the era of the professional designer, planner, and programmer as distinct from the all-rounder teams of the past.

After discussing the structure of the super developer, we'll then examine more-scientific ways to forge and motivate teams. Lastly, we will speculate wildly as to the ways in which a rational, streamlined development methodology will transform the way that games are made.

Development In Context

Game development is not an isolated endeavor. Rather, it is a single (although supremely important) element of a larger commercial process. Even today, you will still hear designers say something like this: "We just develop the games we like, and we figure that the buyers will like them, too." Yet it is naïve to think that creativity cannot be harnessed or directed: a truly great artist creates what he likes *as well as* pleases the customer. Therefore, it is essential to know who your customers are. To understand how development must change, we will begin by stepping back and looking at the entire process so as to understand game development's place in the commercial environment.

Any commercial activity can be represented as a network of discrete business units, as in Figure 24.1. Here, the arrows point from supplier to customer. It is useful to know your direct customer in the network because they are the people you need to please. Except at the end of the chain, there will be further customers for whom your customer is the supplier; indirectly, they are your customers as well. Thus, you need to have their requirements in mind in a strategic sense, but first your product must satisfy your immediate customer.

Each of those business units does not have to be an independent company. Figure 24.1 shows one way that the business units (black outlines) are often grouped into companies (gray outlines). Contrast this with Figure 24.2, which shows the structure that was more typical a few years ago, when it was quite common for the publisher to contain virtually all steps in the process. Moreover, there was less differentiation between the units (although it is not shown in this diagram). In particular, as we have discussed in earlier chapters, development in the past was often based upon an informal methodology and less clearly defined roles.

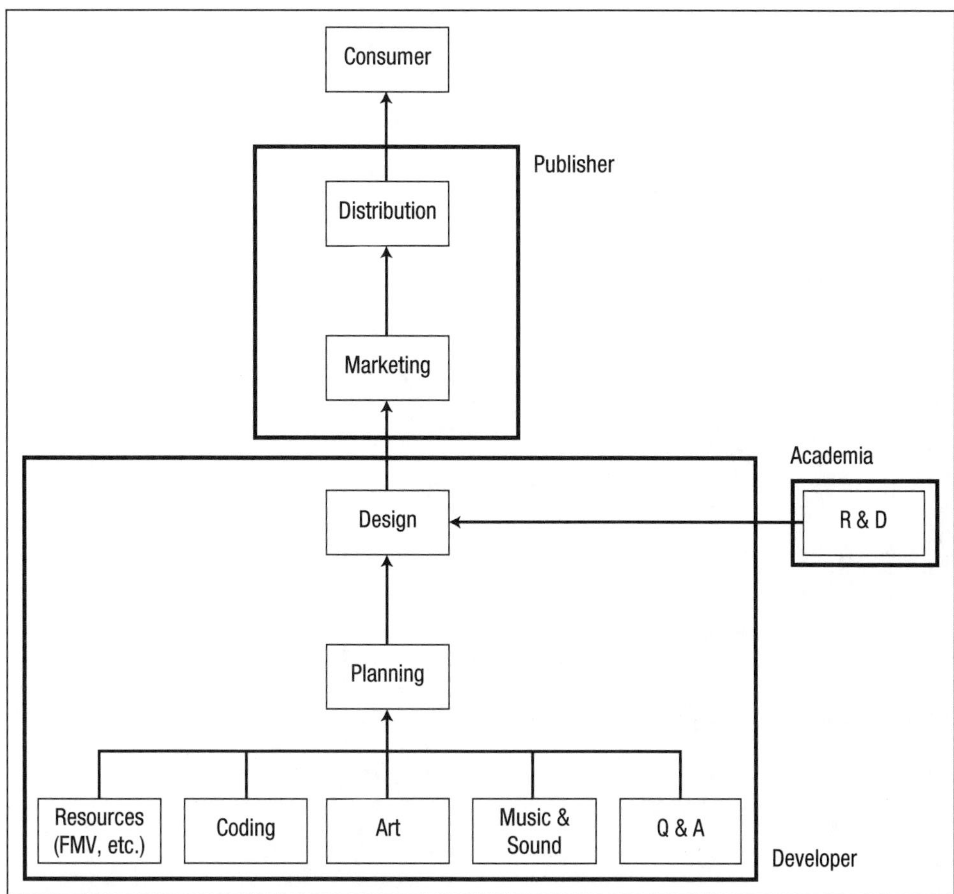

Figure 24.1
A current representation of the game industry.

The trend in development has been towards specialization, whereby each business unit becomes more clearly defined as a separate entity. At the same time, the industry has moved towards consolidation. In other words, big is beautiful. We shall examine the trend and speculate on its impact on development in the future. This trend is quite commonly seen in a maturing industry, but it would be simplistic to anticipate it as an axiomatic symptom of maturation. In fact, it is the result of real-world economies of scale coupled with diseconomies of scope (which we looked at in Chapter 3 with respect to gameplay). A similar effect is often observed in zoology and is known as Cope's Rule—the tendency, when environmental factors are stable, for most species to get larger and more specialized over time. It is an extremely simplified analysis that allows us to see a rhinoceros as a small, underspecialized triceratops, for example. However, biologist Stephen Jay Gould remarks of Cope's Rule merely that it is a "generality that works more often than it fails," an important reminder that one should always be skeptical of such rules of thumb. Industries are subject to catastrophe theory just as ecosystems are. And, in a field in which technology continues to advance at an accelerating rate, we would be well advised to take all predictions with a pinch of salt.

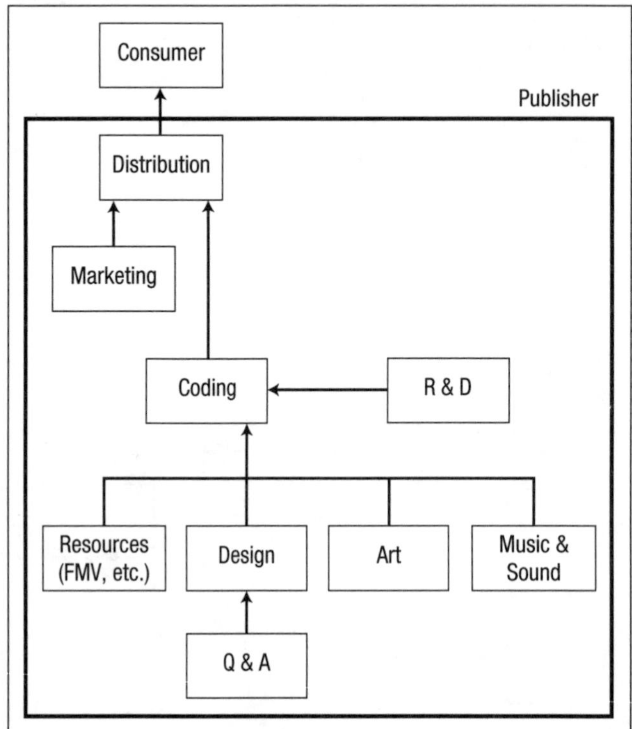

Figure 24.2
Old model of the game industry.

So, on the assumption that the future evolution of the industry is unequivocally progressing towards a single attractor point and is not perturbed by any sudden shocks, what structure might we expect for the development environment in 10 years' time? Figure 24.3 shows one possibility that currently enjoys widespread acceptance. In a keynote speech at the Develop 99 conference in London, Chris van der Kuyl, CEO of VIS Interactive, likened game development as "moving towards the Hollywood model, where creative talent joins together on a per-project basis. Contract work will then be the order of the day—for those who can get it, since such a system would undoubtedly benefit most the gold-standard developers who can unite decent projects."

Van der Kuyl is describing a variant of the "super developer" idea that we looked at in Chapter 15. However, whereas the future financial structure of the industry may well progress along the lines of the Hollywood model, there is another comparison from a development perspective that is perhaps even more accurate: book publishing. What is referred to as the *publisher* in Figure 24.3 is in the book industry known as the *distributor*. The *developer* in fact corresponds to a book *publisher*, who defines a goal and then draws together and manages the creative talent needed to achieve that goal. The creative talent—the designers, programmers, artists, and musicians—tend to remain freelance. Some will become star names and, like best-selling authors, will sign lucrative multiproject deals with the super developer. Others will work as independent contractors, probably in teams of 6 to 10 individuals as this is the theoretical ideal unit size for an efficient team. (It will be the task of the super developer's planning group to cohere several such teams into an effective staff for each project.)

Notice that research and development is shown in Figure 24.3 as existing on the overlap between the development company and the universities (academia). The super developers will be able to fund blue-sky departments that in many cases may produce the leading research in those subjects. An instance right now is the work being done at CyberLife (creators of *Creatures*) in the field of artificial life. This is made possible because CyberLife is able to leverage use of its A-Life technology into many business applications. The *Creatures* games themselves are in one sense merely a pretty showcase for that technology. Being based in Cambridge, England, may also assist CyberLife in forging links with academia.

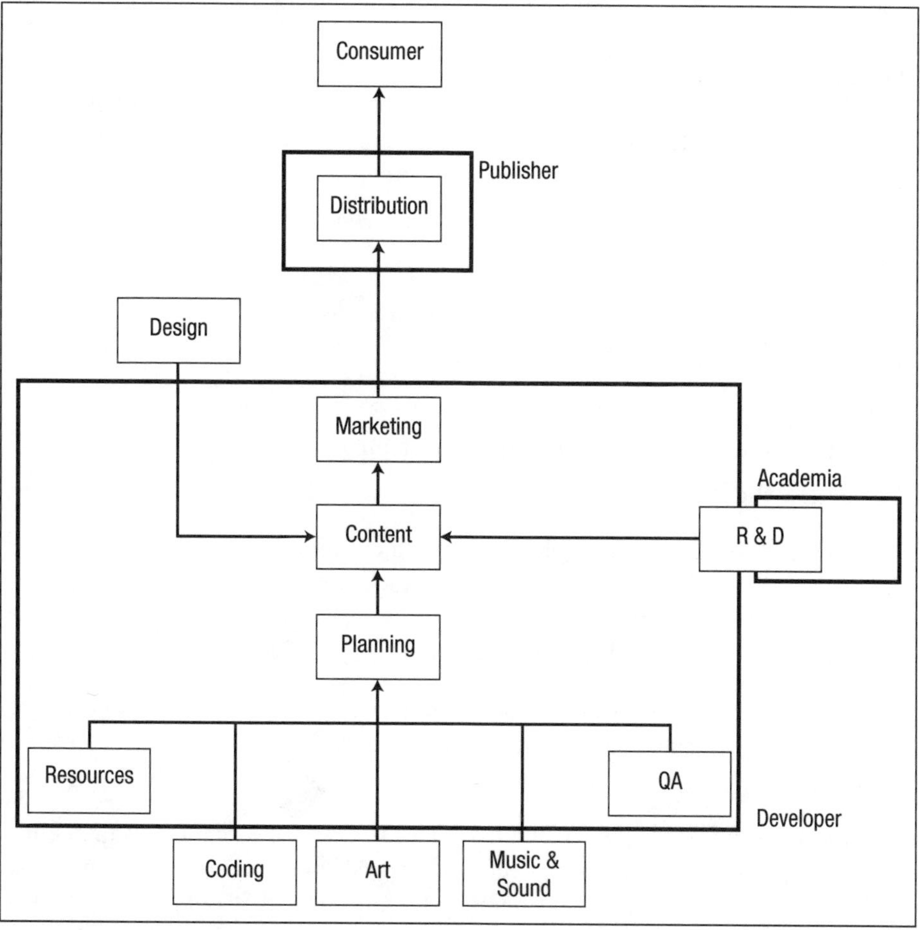

Figure 24.3
Future model of the game industry.

Future Development

We will now look at the constituent units of the super developer—first at the departments likely to be incorporated within the development company itself, then at the freelancers who constitute the creative part of the process.

Marketing

As Figure 24.2 shows, marketing was traditionally located off the main concept-to-market track. The role of the marketing department in old-style publishers was simply to arrange publicity for the game in the run-up to release, as this quotation indicates:

"Levels are falling into place and you're approaching that exhausting time, working eighteen hours a day, with the whole team pulling together to get this baby out of the door. It's time to show the game to the marketing people."

—Peter Molyneux, "The Essentials of Game Design", Develop *magazine, (May 1998)*

Marketing should not, however, be restricted merely to publicity. The marketing department in Figure 24.3 is shown as the direct supplier of the game to the publisher. A properly constituted marketing department would have ultimate responsibility for approving or disapproving all projects. The tasks of the marketing department are

- To decide which game concepts are likely to succeed,
- To foresee trends in the market,
- To target the platforms on which the game is to be delivered,
- To define the requirements of the project,
- To collect and make available whatever resources are needed,
- To facilitate the planning department in developing the game, and
- To publicize the game to the user.

This is not so far off the studio's role in the production of a movie, or the publisher of a book. It is rather broader than the capacity in which marketing has often operated in the past, but it is the logical framework to adopt as the industry consolidates. The effect on development is that projects should be much more efficiently targeted from the start.

"Oh," but some people will say, "that would mean we'd never get any original games. *Populous* and *Ultima* and *Lemmings* would never have seen the light of day if it'd been left to the marketing people."

Arrant nonsense. Evidently *somebody* filled what I'm describing as the new marketing role and gave the green light to those projects and others. The marketing departments of the super developer won't be staffed by publicists who have no idea about games. These people will be the development directors, managers, and gurus who truly understand the industry.

As long as there's evidence that innovative products can be successful, we shall see innovative products. (It's even possible that a marketing goal might simply be: "Hire John Carmack and let him do whatever he likes with a budget of $2 million.") Under the new model, what we should see less of are not successes but failures.

Case Study 24.1 illustrates how things went wrong in the past because publishers failed to place due emphasis on the strategic role of marketing. The names, of course, have been changed, but this is a true story.

Content

In a super developer, the Content Department will function as the creative filter that feeds product to the marketing department. Content managers will be responsible for assembling teams to develop products in line with the company's market strategy. In the book industry, these people would be the editorial directors. By the film industry analogy, they are equivalent to producers.

The good content manager is a jack-of-all-trades. He should understand a little bit about everybody else's job, from game design and programming to packaging and PR. He may have risen from a role elsewhere in development after discovering a flair for that special combination of flattery, guile, and effortless man-management that is required to oversee creative personnel. The functions of the Content Department are:

- To solicit designs and technology to fulfill the company's marketing goals
- To ensure projects remain consistent with the expressed goals
- To interface between creative personnel and the company structure
- To maintain a repository of resources for development to draw on
- To appoint key development personnel (designer, director, and planner)
- To facilitate the work of the developers

Look to Case Study 24.2 for an example of how development can go badly awry when content management is divorced from marketing, its true customer.

In assembling a team, the content manager will first look for a project director. This is the primary development role, as the project director takes ownership of the product and provides the unifying vision throughout. The importance of this role is well illustrated by this quote from a leading authority on software development:

No great software has ever been created by committee; ultimately it is always one person with a clear and unwavering vision of a product who delivers the next killer application. VisiCalc, Lotus 1-2-3, Word, and Notes—each was owned by a single visionary.

Case Study 24.1 Marketing Means Targeting

Josh was lead programmer on *Gravity*, a 3D simulation, in the days when lead programmers were often saddled with the role of project manager as well, whether they liked it or not.

Halfway through development, a very successful game in the same genre caused the publisher to focus more attention on *Gravity.* It soon became clear from the publisher's memos that they had very different expectations of the game than Josh and his team had supposed. In particular, no one seemed to have decided on the target technical specification.

Josh sought clarification from Ken, the publisher's head of marketing. "Obviously, we'd like it aimed to the lowest spec possible," said Ken in answer to Josh's questions. "P90 would be good."

"We've been working to a hardware-only version," pointed out Josh. "Are you saying that the people with P90s will have installed 3D accelerator cards? Wouldn't they upgrade their machines?"

"The lower the spec, the more we'll sell," countered Ken. "I'm not sure about the hardware-only version, either. Based on the sales that *Xeno's* been getting, we should be looking at gamers outside the core market, and they won't have cards."

"We need a software version, then," said Josh, thankful that he had an earlier engine to fit the bill. "But P90? We're talking about release in 14 months from now, and the current spec is P200."

"Little people don't upgrade as much as you and I do," said Ken. "Call it a P120, minimum."

Josh paused at the door. "Do you have any market research that would tell us for sure?"

Ken laughed. "Get outta here!"

Josh went back to his team. "They think they want a mass-market game for a minimum spec of P120," he said. "But if we try to push back to that, we'll undo the last six weeks' work and very probably they'll fail us at the next milestone because they won't like what they see."

"I don't like the comparison with *Xeno*, either," said Paul, the lead designer. "Haven't they read the spec? This is a gamer's game. They ought to realize that, because they decided against a PlayStation conversion of *Gravity*, and *Xeno* has one coming out next month."

Josh shook his head. "You can bet that they haven't read the spec, and they have no real idea of the target market. I have to tell you, I find this infuriating because we are professional craftsmen and we can deliver whatever the client wants, but the trouble is that the client doesn't know what they want. So we're going to have to wing it."

Terry, the technical designer, grinned. "P166 it is, then!"

In this instance, the publisher misunderstood how to direct creative talent. In effect, the development team had no choice but to take on the marketing role themselves. In fact, by the time of *Gravity's* release, the typical recommended spec for a comparable game was Pentium 200. So the team underestimated, but not as badly as the publisher's supposed marketing chief had.

Case Study 24.2 Development Without Strategy

This is a cautionary tale that illustrates what can go wrong when development is given no goals by marketing.

Carter was called in as a freelance designer on a new project. Larry, the development manager, told him that the company had recently hired a new programmer, Max, who had brought with him an AI editor of his own invention.

Larry got Max to demonstrate the AI editor's features. "It's still at an early stage, but the structure's there," explained Max. "You select a character and you get a menu of goals, attitudes, and temperaments, which you can set. So I might set a goal like 'find food', or I could be more specific—'go to tile 9872'."

"Attitudes and temperaments sound intriguing," said Carter. "What's the difference?"

"Attitudes are the way the character does something. So 'find food cautiously' means he won't risk damage to himself, 'find food recklessly' means he will. Temperament is the basis on which characters change goals or attitudes. An 'impatient' temperament causes the character to change his goal readily if the original goal isn't getting results."

Carter nodded. "I see. Though wouldn't it be better to build the attitudes as sliders, so you could set the attitude on a spectrum from caution to recklessness and so on? It might end up that players just prefer to select from a menu of preset attitudes, but that's an interface decision. We should aim for maximum versatility at this stage, then narrow it down later."

Max didn't answer but just kept looking at the screen, tight-lipped. After a moment, Larry said, "So, what we need is to decide the best game concept to go with this. I called you in, Carter, because of that Viking raiders idea we discussed. I see this as a strategy game where you raid civilized nations or other Viking settlements. Instead of lots of mouse-clicking, you set the AI of your men and then sit back and watch."

"Okay," agreed Carter. "Give me a week to write it up as a treatment."

A week later Carter and Larry met for lunch. Larry looked over the treatment. "What did you think of Max's AI editor?" he asked.

"Fine. It's not how I'd design an AI editor, but it works."

"Why isn't it how you'd design it?" asked Larry, frowning.

"It's top-down. Though it purports to be generic, there are hidden assumptions that at the moment you can't crack into through the editor. I'd prefer something where you'd define needs—'dies without food' and instincts—'doesn't want to die'. So then you'd get 'look for food' deriving from those as a goal, but you could change the settings lower down to change the goals. Also, you could decide how much the character didn't want to die and so on."

"The player wouldn't want to do all that!" said Larry.

"No, so you'd have an extra interface layer that presented the player only with the necessary choices. But the AI editor itself should be bottom-up and generic."

"We don't need that versatility," decided Larry. "If we like it with this game, Max can always tweak it for others. It hardly costs much. He's a one-man band."

Later that week, Larry phoned Carter. "Sorry, but we can't go ahead with the Vikings concept," he said. "Max is doing the game design himself. It's going to be warring cavemen and stone-age fishing tribes. Max wants the look of that old Raquel Welch film with the rubber dinosaurs."

"Sure," laughed Carter. "So call me when he's dug himself a deep enough hole!"

A year later, Carter bumped into Larry at E3. "So how's it going with Max and Raquel Welch?" he asked.

Larry gave him a blank look. "You mean the robot Vikings game? We had to can it. Max did a brilliant design—only it wasn't a game, it was a generic AI editor."

"Well, at the risk of being really annoying, I did say that's how it should've been from the start. But here's the good news: I just finished a game, so now you can hire me to do something cool to go with Max's editor!"

"No, I can't," sighed Larry. "He was so disgruntled at his project being cancelled that he's decided to quit."

No doubt all three were unhappy at the time they had wasted, but who was at fault? In fact, it was the company organization itself that caused the problem. Larry, a good development manager, had been given no direction by the senior management. He therefore had no basis but his own judgment for deciding between a Viking game, a dinosaur game, or a robot Viking game. Nor was he equipped to judge whether getting Max simply to design an AI editor rather than a game would fit in with the company's long-term goals.

"The visionary must participate in every meeting in the early days of the project. It is his sole job to keep his eyes on the vision, to hold an unwavering grip on the essence of what he wants to build. The software analyst may help him flesh out the vision and understand its ramifications, but if the customer cannot recognize the core of his vision in the final product, then the process has failed."

—Jesse Liberty, Beginning Object-Oriented Analysis and Design*, 1998*

Just as a film director needs his first assistant director to spare him from getting tied up in scheduling and administration, so the project director will need his own right-hand man or woman. The assistant director is what we nowadays call a project manager. He is apt to spend much of his time with Visio and Microsoft Project, creating the flowcharts and schedules around which development will be planned. As development proceeds, he may also have to function as the director's liaison with the Content Department.

The important point is that the assistant director is a middle-management role, and managers (although indispensable) are not by nature visionaries. Often in the past, game development has come unstuck because capable project planners have been appointed as the creative champion of a project, which is a role that does not suit them. The best that can be said of this system is that it is a small improvement on the bad old days when the lead programmer was often expected to serve as manager, team leader, and designer all rolled into one. However, as developers nowadays find a new zeal for formal planning and management, there is a real risk of forgetting that the central axis of the process must always remain creative.

Management is needed at the top level (marketing and content) to provide goals. Middle-level management is also needed within development, to provide structure. The visionary who directs the project, however, must not be a manager but a *leader*.

Planning

In the past, developers would sometimes say, "We don't bother with a design. We just let it all come together in development." It is not only amazing that an intelligent person can seriously make such a comment; it is still more amazing that they should make it with pride. There is always a design. The trouble is that, if it's left in people's heads, you may find that what you have are a dozen different designs. Why design at all? Because it's cost effective: an initial design is a run-through with a small team.

The message of this book is that development commences with design and that design does not stop until the product is ready to ship. The game begins with a concept, followed by a feature-based description. A software plan and technical architecture are then mapped out and *maintained* and *modified* throughout development.

Tip

The three things you need for trouble-free development are a plan, a plan, and a plan.

In a small team, planning helps to keep you on the critical path even when several tasks pile up and demand your attention. In a big team, planning is the oil that keeps the machine from jamming.

Despite the fatalistic warning of many developers, you can plan for the unexpected. You do this by experimentation, using paper-and-pencil prototypes and testbeds. This is part of the design phase. It lets you see what you will need to complete the game—that is, you can build an inventory. Additionally, the design forms the basis of your schedule, and without a schedule it is very unlikely you will be able to acquire a client who is willing to invest in your game.

Obviously, the design will change during development. As we saw in Chapter 4, there are too many interdependencies to be able to cast each design phase in stone before proceeding to the next, which is why we cannot expect a pure waterfall model to work. The important point is that, when you need to change something, *change the plan as well.*

For example, suppose you are building the ground floor of a cabin. Somebody else is assembling the upper story, which will be lifted into place later. When you get to the site, you discover an area of subsidence that means the foundations cannot be taken as far back as the architect intended. So you have to build the floor six feet short of where it was supposed to go. You make the change, but naturally you also mark that change on the master plan. Otherwise, the upper story will arrive to be fitted and would have a six-foot overhang. Most confusion about and resistance to comprehensive planning arises because developers fail to appreciate that planning is an ongoing process.

In the super developer of the future, the Planning Department has these responsibilities:

- Develop new reusable components,
- Maintain the reuse repository,
- Fit newly acquired technology to the company's standard format,
- Derive soft and hard architecture based on the gameplay specification,
- Produce and evolve the technical design of the game,
- Network with the project director and game designer to ensure development goals are maintained,
- Control changes to a design undergoing development, and
- Act as the nexus whereby separate resources (art, music, and so) interface with the company.

Developers

Since the Planning Department needs to directly cater to the goals outlined by Marketing and defined by Content, it is logical to maintain it within the company. The same is not true of the developers working at the code face. Just as a film crew's rank-and-file (I do not mean the term in a derogatory sense) are hired for specific projects—and the writers and artists who create the product of the book industry are for the most part independent contractors—we can expect a similar trend in game development.

To get work with a super developer, you will need to conform to their terminology and working practices. The very least they will require is that you work to a phased or tier-based development cycle. This permits the Planning Group of the super developer to control changes in the design; it also means that they can pull the plug without suffering severe sunk costs. In a worst-case scenario, they know they can salvage all work up to the last completed tier.

Wait a moment. Is that good? We're saying that developers should acquiesce to building the game in tiers so as to make it easy for the company to abort the project. Wouldn't it be better to make yourself indispensable by following a less tightly controlled procedure?

In fact, a development team that insists on using irregular procedures will, quite simply, not be offered work. Think of a mechanic who has devised his own idiosyncratic units of measurement and refuses to use standard terminology. Would you employ him as part of a team? So the super developers will define the universal methodology, and developers who want to run with the pack will have to conform to it. On the positive side, fitting your development practice to universal standards will make it far easier for you to incorporate extra team members at short notice. And the increased confidence you earn from the super developers in fact ensures that you will be sought after. Even if they cancel one project of yours (perhaps because of a change in marketing strategy), the fact that your reliability allowed them to salvage the completed modules for reuse means that they are more likely to employ you again.

Small Is Beautiful Too

Just in case you are horrified at the thought of becoming a lackey in a huge development corporation, it's not all bad news. Most developers in the future will be contractors whom super developers hire for specific projects, but there is still room for small developers to thrive between the cracks.

Small-scale development will be made possible by standardization of technology, maintained in libraries and available for license. Very possibly, the super developers themselves will maintain these libraries, which will comprise their own previous-generation software.

With modular technology and vastly improved Software Development Kits (SDKs), small-scale game development becomes simply a question of content creation, the same way that multimedia development works today. Proper design and planning remain essential to all development projects, but small teams are able to dispense with the extremes of formal process and may find that other models work better: for example, the "surgical team" model, in which each member has enough all-around capability and familiarity with his comrades that the team dynamic emerges spontaneously.

Small teams will not be able to create blockbuster products possessing the raw capacity to amaze that is made possible when you can afford leading-edge special effects. Nonetheless, they have a respectable template to follow in the low-budget movie (such as *The Blair Witch Project*) that takes everyone by surprise when it gives the likes of *Star Wars* a run for its money. If the original *Populous* could be created in a couple of man-years, as we saw in an earlier chapter, then a game with equally revolutionary concept and gameplay could be created now in much the same time. By slotting in modules for the physics or graphics, those little games can still compare reasonably to the blockbuster product of the super developers. They may not reap the same rewards but, on the upside, the risks and massive investments aren't needed either.

To summarize: in the future, we'll have very large-scale productions in which the contribution of each individual is restricted to his or her own specialization, like movies. But, there will also be very small-scale projects, built using off-the-shelf software, that will have the leeway to allow more-democratic input. Adopting a colorful analogy, we might liken these to huge infantry battles and commando raids, respectively. Everybody thinks it's most glamorous to be a commando, but wars are really won by the big battles, in which the demand is for raw manpower.

Building The Team Of The Future

Throughout this book, we have often cited financial and structural parallels with the film industry, but the fact is that computer game development requires the merging of many more disparate creative skills even than movies. To forge a new model that works efficiently requires more than an elegant methodology (although a methodology is essential); it also requires an understanding of character, morale, and motivation—in short, the human element.

Character

Most of the hundreds of the do-it-yourself team-psychology manuals are—to put it charitably—one step above astrology. However, I consider one of them to be accurate, scientific, and useful when building teams. The system was devised by Dr. R. Meredith Belbin. What follows is a summary, but for the full version and how to apply it in practice, look at **www.belbin.com**.

The Belbin theory identifies nine team roles. Only exceptional individuals correspond 100 percent with a single role. More usually you might be 30 percent Shaper, 50 percent Specialist, and 20 percent Finisher, for example.

An understanding of the roles is useful in planning the dynamics of the group, which is especially important if you intend to apply the formal process extolled in this book. Additionally, knowing the role(s) you are taking helps you to identify your weaknesses. (You may be surprised by what you learn. When I first took the Belbin Test myself, I assumed it would show me which roles I had no aptitude for. In fact, it had two more important benefits. Firstly, it showed me how best to communicate what I wanted to different personality types within the team. And, also, most interestingly, it revealed the potential downside of what I had considered my strengths.)

The nine roles are

- Catalyst
- Shaper
- Specialist
- Investigator
- Implementer
- Evaluator

- Coordinator
- Team Worker
- Finisher

A **Catalyst** is the source of innovative proposals and solutions. These individuals are interested in the big picture, not in the fine details. They are radically minded but can be defensive in the face of criticism and are frequently poor at integrating with the team. This gives them a reputation for being difficult. Nonetheless, Catalysts are the people who get things going.

Probable activities: any, but especially valuable in design, concept art, software planning, marketing

A **Shaper** is strongly motivated and focused. The Shaper enjoys a challenge and expects others to keep up. He or she is a scientist by inclination: always looking for patterns and using them to formulate theories and plans. Shapers are usually the first to seize on the raw material stirred up by Catalysts and start to turn it into a vision. However, they can be overemotional and impatient, even paranoid.

Probable activities: game design, software planning, senior management

A **Specialist** combines pragmatism and creativity. The Specialist's depth of knowledge provides a resource for the team to draw on. These are the people who have developed stunning 3D graphics, inverse kinematic systems, and so on. The negative aspect of this type is that capable Specialists are expensive!

Probable activities: R&D, technical architecture

An **Investigator** is inquisitive and enthusiastic, the "scout" of the group who makes new contacts and finds out what else is happening in the industry and elsewhere. The Investigator is useful for networking with the client as well as bringing outside developments and possibilities to the team's attention.

Probable activities: marketing, R&D, negotiation

An **Implementer** is the type who turns grand plans into practical procedures. The Implementer is characterized by efficiency, self-discipline, and good common sense. He or she sees to every task, not just the easy ones. Get a team of coders like this, and your game will ship three months early! On the downside, Implementers are inclined to be inflexible and resistant to new ideas.

Probable activities: art, coding, management, and technical architecture

An **Evaluator** keeps a check on progress, analyzes problems, and evaluates new suggestions. Typically, Evaluators have sound judgment and, although hard headed, are fair and easy going. However, a lack of inspiration makes the Evaluator poor at motivating others.

Probable activities: level design, QA testing, middle management

A **Coordinator** excels in assessing others and ensuring the team works to its strengths. Good character judgment means that they are mature and good at delegating tasks. A Coordinator is useful in marshalling all members of the team to focus on the shared goal. (But try to avoid having both Coordinators and Shapers at the same management level because their differing styles often lead to a clash.)

Probable activities: management, scheduling

A **Team Worker** is mild, easy going, and adaptable. The Team Worker provides the glue that cements disparate types together. Team Workers are good listeners who can get on with anybody. They defuse interpersonal difficulties but nonetheless can be indecisive in a crisis. (Perhaps surprisingly, Team Worker types are also useful as managers because they are one of the few types who can capably delegate. However, for a Team Worker to be effective at senior level, he or she will require a Shaper at middle management to provide innovation.)

Probable activities: art, coding, and management

A **Finisher** is the guy who likes to cross the *T*s and dot the *I*s—and he won't forget the *J*s either! The Finisher tends to be introverted and prone to work too much, although it is often difficult to notice this as he or she rarely complains. This type's major skills are the ability to concentrate accurately over long periods. They are very poor at delegating and can be intolerant of team members who seem uncommitted.

Probable activities: tools, level design, interface, art, testing

Motivation

A while back, we were called on to apply the methods espoused in this book to troubleshoot a project that was way behind schedule and seemed to have lost its way. After the initial evaluation, we saw that the problem was not going to lie in mapping out the new methodology, but rather in selling it to the team.

While many team members knew that the project was in trouble and were keen to embrace any likely solution, they were still skeptical as to whether this particular methodology would do the trick. More seriously, others adopted what they called a "healthy cynicism."

However, cynicism is never healthy. A skeptic is one who reasonably asserts that he will not believe anything without evidence to support it. A cynic is merely someone who sneers at any suggestion. Skeptics developed the scientific method and created all of the wonders of modern civilization. Cynics sat on the sidelines and said things like, "What's the point of a wheel? It can't possibly be as good as just carrying things on your back."

The difficulty of motivating people to adopt formal methodologies goes back to earliest history. In our first presentation to the team, therefore, we didn't start by discussing software development at all. Instead, I told the story of a young king of ancient Mesopotamia whose army had suffered a series of crushing defeats. The generals had responded by stepping up the pressure to attack quickly onto enemy defensive lines, but this only lead to worse setbacks. Then the king noticed that, when the warriors charged into battle, the fastest would arrive at the enemy first and many would fall before the slowest caught up with the action. "From now on we'll stand shoulder to shoulder and advance towards the enemy in an orderly line," he told his men. "So, instead of practicing swordplay today, we're going to practice marching up and down and turning in an orderly fashion."

"That's stupid," scoffed a veteran soldier. "How can we get to be better fighters by marching about in a line? Perhaps you'd rather train us to be dancers?"

"Good idea," said the king. He sent for some dancers from the temple. "These girls will show you how to move in unison to signals from the drum and trumpet."

Some old soldiers were proud of their cynicism. Those were chauvinistic times, and men didn't think they could be taught valuable lessons of warfare by dancing girls. When it came time for the next battle, those cynics broke from the line and charged lustily towards the enemy just as they had always done. Of course, they were cut down. Then the rest of the army advanced in formation into the unorganized ranks of the enemy. Now they had the advantage that the entire killing power of the formation was concentrated along a continuous line. The enemy fought as individuals, but the Mesopotamians fought as a team, and the new methodology of formation warfare won the day.

Over the four millennia that have passed since then, the same scenario has been played out many times. Countless barbarian armies thought the Romans were just engineers, not warriors—only to learn that the Romans had engineered an approach to warfare that swept them aside. Still today, armies use formal training procedures that would not be completely unrecognizable to Alexander or Hannibal. In other disciplines, too, formal process has led to supremacy, not stagnation.

"All very well," said one of the development team when I had finished the story, "but it doesn't prove that *this* methodology will work."

And he was quite right. However, although game development has many aspects that set it apart from typical software projects, it has many more in common. Nor is game development utterly unique in any way: there are always parallels that can be drawn. Consequently, it is reasonable to assume that the methodology that works for other projects will work, with modifications, for games as well. It merely stands to reason, and sweet reason, we have found, is the best way to motivate intelligent men and women.

A further concern that developers have when faced with the changeover to formal process is that it will burden them with too much management. In fact, the aim of formal process is to remove much of the need for management. Instead of having a manager who demands reports and continual ill-structured meetings, formal process builds that into the team dynamics. It aims to take a dozen (or more) talented individuals and turn them into a team.

"But we always did things that way," some developers will protest. "We're a democratic team. We don't need this formal process stuff."

But democracy itself requires a formal process (constitutional law). Without formal process, the amount of input you get into the team depends on how noisy you are. With formal process, you get exactly the input that is needed to ensure everybody can work at peak efficiency.

Development is a science that (like all sciences) draws heavily on inspiration and creativity. And the scientist knows above all that, sometimes, faith is the rational option. Communicate this to your development team and they will be motivated to adopt formal process because they will start to see that it is the best way to facilitate creativity and teamwork.

Morale

Morale differs from motivation because motivation determines whether a team *wants* to achieve a goal, while morale determines whether they think they will be *able* to achieve it.

Figure 24.4 shows how the efficiency of a team is affected when you introduce formal process. Initially, there is a downturn that can be as much as 25 percent. This is when team members are struggling with new ways of doing things that have yet to become second nature. If, for example, they are used to making changes on the fly without going through change control, then the need to refer the change up to the Architecture Group may seem a waste of time. You will often hear comments such as, "I'm expected to document everything when I ought to be writing code."

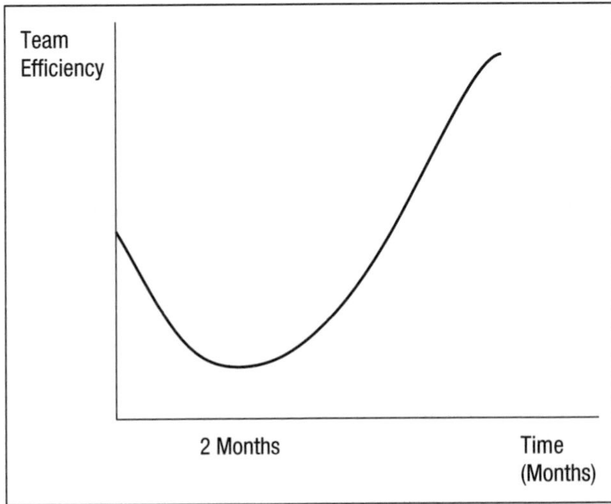

Figure 24.4
The effect of change on team efficiency.

That is how it is every time we try anything new. At first we feel awkward and foolish. We may even want to give up. Morale saps away. Yet, if we are to reach the point at which the new skills come together, somehow we have to overcome our trepidation and press on.

The best way I have found to help developers deal with the change to formal process is simply to show them the graph right at the start. Point out that efficiency will dip in the first couple of months. Having analytical minds, they will immediately see that it is the area under the curve that matters. After four months, they will have caught up with where they would have been without the new methods. After that, there's no looking back.

A couple of times, I've had developers fretting about what the upturn in the graph means. You need to allay their fear that it means they are going to have work twice as hard! In fact, the graph shows the efficiency of the team. Increased efficiency means that people don't have to work twice as hard: quite the opposite, it means they will achieve twice as much without extra effort. Furthermore, the improvement is not located in individual skill, but occurs instead because of an improvement in teamwork. Humans are social animals (yes, even programmers), and the buzz of working well as a team is a great tonic for keeping enthusiasm high. Telling your developers all this at the outset will ensure morale is maintained even during the difficult early days of the new process.

New Directions In Development

The size and improved organization of the super developer will enable (in fact, demand) a very different approach to how games are developed. A full examination of these trends is a subject for another book, so let's briefly sketch out some of the probable changes we might expect over the next ten years.

The Holistic Approach

Web-based businesses are mushrooming at the moment. All aim to deliver services and/or content via the new Web market. Take the case of a company supplying electronic components. Its Web site is the point of contact with the customer, and visitors to the Web site should be effortlessly guided to the equipment that they are interested in. If they need information to help make a choice, that too should be easily to hand. Visitors should *not* have to be familiar with the site—even the first-time user should find it child's play.

And, yet, I'm surprised at how many new Web companies are looking to technical staff to manage their Web sites. This is equivalent to starting a new magazine and recruiting one of the typesetters as managing editor. If we heard about that happening five hundred years ago, we might write it off as a legitimate mistake. Movable type printing was then a revolutionary new technology: people were so dazzled by it that we can understand they could confuse the medium with the content. If it happens today with Web companies, then it's a sorry instance of history repeating itself. The skills you need to put a good Web site together are concerned with the presentation and communication of information. The technology is a means, not an end.

Game development has always been about content, but this fact has been somewhat obscured by the extraordinarily impressive leaps and bounds made by the technology over the first couple of decades. Consequently, games have too often been technology led at the expense of gameplay, whereas the best have managed to unite gameplay and technology with no detriment to either.

Technological issues as we have known them in the past will evaporate. This is not to say that games will not continually need to draw on new technology, merely that R&D will move out of development towards being a separate supplier. In turn, we will see greater emphasis on game development as a question of content creation. I said before that this is how the small developers will fit into the industry—like multimedia authors and artists rather than coders—but I need to be very careful in making this point. I am not saying that technology will disappear from the scene. To say that a 3D engine of the future could come as standard on your video card is not the same thing as saying just anybody will be able to use it effectively. Anyone can buy a movie camera, but the role of the expert cinematographer is all-important in creating the look and feel needed for a great movie.

What we will see, therefore, is not the preeminence of gameplay over technology, but the rise of gameplay at last to a point of equal importance. The great developers are those who recognize the value of both, and whose games thus derive from a perfect marriage of technology and content, as this quotation from a respected colleague illustrates:

Atmosphere is just as important as technology. In fact, the two cannot be separated. Atmosphere plays directly on the emotions of the player. In many ways it is an extension of the emotions of the creators. To me it is integral to the creation of a good game.

Atmosphere can be defined visually, through sound, content, and game play. The best will include all of these.

In terms of visual atmosphere, when I started in 3D graphics back in the late eighties, I thought atmosphere was merely the fastest Bresenham's line algorithm, the best triangle rendering code, or an amazing screen fill algorithm. Back then we thought that all that mattered was how fast you could get your math code and polygon engines.

Maybe it was then, but now anyone can write fast polygon stuff. Just use D3D or OpenGL and some nice graphics hardware with some special rendering effects and some translucency here, fogging there, specular reflection, and maybe some bump mapping to go with. It will get you nowhere. You might as well get a random number generator to choose a combination of these effects and you probably will get the same results. (Although I hope not, or I'll be out of a job!)

It is not the number of effects your game contains that dictate the atmosphere. It is like matching color: some effects and techniques go together well and some don't. Give the same algorithms and effects to two different development teams with similar skills and the results will still be different. It is like having two different bands performing the same song. Each will sound different. Atmosphere is also personal. It tells you something about the developer.

A game with good atmosphere has to be consistent. Look at Quake *and* Doom. *Everything in the world, from texturing, texture sizes, complexity of the scene, lighting, etc., is very consistent. The true skill is to choose the right thing at the right time.*

As a starting point, it is vital to understand what story your game is trying to tell, what world you are trying to represent, and follow that closely. Okay, you may have to change a few things here and there later, but this is important as a hard-and-fast rule. Understand everything: the techniques at hand, the textures, and the models. A medieval world is dark (well-defined shadows maybe), misty (some cool localized fogging), cold (some nice tricks with lighting). These effects, applied to carefully created textures, will be a good start. Pictures and numbers are interdependent.

Also use tricks—anything that will help you to get to your goal, always with the proviso that you must first know what the goal is. In Plague, *for example, I wanted to achieve the effect of velvet on the landscape. I tried applying the math correctly and did not get the required results. What the eye perceives to be a correct representation may not be what the actual numbers truly reflect. I then tried placing the light sources underneath the terrain! And they were "wrong" but they worked very well. Similar combinations gave* Plague *the look of a model landscape. It was just what we originally wanted, but it required a combination of creativity, experience, and trial and error to get us there.*

Strive for consistency. This is the main guideline that will ensure that you are on the right track. The best games are created by the perfect marriage of technology and concept. Don't get tempted to change things for the sake of it, or you may lose the look and feel and, ultimately, risk jeopardizing the game you were originally striving for.

—Sam Kerbeck, lead programmer of Plague *(Eidos Interactive)*

"Jurassic Park" Software

In embryo development, a class of genes (called homeobox genes) controls the principal architecture of the organism. The remarkable thing is that these homeobox genes, by isolating specific features of the organism as modules, have allowed evolution to refine those features without disrupting a viable core architecture that has served most life forms on Earth since the Cambrian period.

For example, a specific gene tells the developing organism, "Build an eye here." This gene doesn't give any instructions about how to build an eye. That's a separate module. Instead, this gene functions as a call for the organism's specific eye-making genes to go into action. As evidence that the architectural genes have proved successful and unchanging for millions of years, it is possible to take the eye-initiating gene from a mouse and use it to replace the equivalent gene in a fruit fly embryo, for example. The fruit fly then develops eyes normally—fruit fly eyes, that is, not mouse eyes!

This system is analogous, of course, to what in object-oriented design is called *encapsulation*. The "wrapping architecture" isolates the modules and deals with the interaction between them so that it is possible to modify a module without setting off a cascading change throughout the entire structure.

The diversity of life that we see around us is all built on a root architecture that dates back around 550 million years. The *same* architecture (an evolutionary upgrade of that root architecture, not a wholly new version) is shared by all fish, birds, reptiles, and mammals. We might fancifully say that, before God could create Man, He had to create a genetic architecture of which Man was one possible end product.

By analogy, super developers creating the games of the future will look towards metadesign. Metadesign regards any product as a specialized case of a truly generic system. This approach will allow not only reuse of modules but of the architecture itself. The payoff will be software that is more robust, more readily profiled, and more certain to ship on time.

I believe that there are other lessons to be learned from genetics that can help us to build better game software. One is that genes do not store a blueprint of an organism; they contain rules (behaviors, in fact) that will build that organism. The exact comparison is between bitmaps, where graphical data is stored in memory, and vector graphics, where what is stored are the instructions for how to draw the image. As processing power increases exponentially, the leverage to be got from building at runtime rather than downloading from memory becomes ever more significant. Especially, the processing approach allows for scalability: if you get a machine that's twice as powerful, the game will run twice as well. One company, Criterion Technologies, has even gone so far as to trademark the phrase, "Compute, don't store." We may lament the small impoverishment of the language that this entails, but the validity of the statement is uncontestable.

I likened this before to "Jurassic Park" software. In the movie, *Jurassic Park*, dinosaurs are re-created from DNA found in blood-sucking insects trapped in amber. The DNA extracted is only fragmentary, but the scientists are able to reconstruct the missing segments because of the genetic predilection for polymorphism—the use of a module to achieve several different effects according to context:

"Whenever the time came to elaborate a new structure or a new function—for example, let's take the limbs, whenever the time came that an animal "wanted" to have limbs, so to speak—then, instead of designing a completely new system with new genes and new regulatory systems and so on, which is expensive, evolution just went back to some kind of stock of genes doing similar things somewhere else and used them to make a limb. So, the overall workload per gene increased and increased throughout evolution, because genes have been recruited to do additional things."

—Professor Denis Duboule, geneticist, quoted on Horizon *(BBC Television)*

Consider the advantages of game code written the same way. Instead of vast teams of artists toiling to create all of the character artwork needed for the photorealistic environments of future games, characters could be generated by altering "genes" controlling morphology, texturing, physical attributes, and so forth. If you are downloading a game—given a finite limit on how fast data can be transmitted on a land line—you obviously want the amount of data you are having to receive to be as small as possible. One way to achieve this is obviously through data compression, but there, too, is a limit. The "Jurassic Park" system yields another saving, in that you would download only the segments that make this game different from the last release by the same publisher. Thus, I could have the super developer's metadesigned architecture permanently resident on my machine. Everything from strategy to adventure games could come down the line as the code sequences that made each game unique.

Immanent And Transcendent Worlds

Immanence and *transcendence* are terms taken from theology. There, the argument is between those who believe the universe is moderated by a set of laws external to the system (the transcendent model) and those who believe that the innate behaviors of physical objects govern the process from within (the immanent model).

A rule that we never see violated in the universe, and which consequently forms a scientific article of faith, is the conservation of energy. When an atom goes from one state to another, a packet of energy—specifically, a photon—is released. This will travel on through space until it hits another atom and raises it to a higher energy state—a principle exploited when performing spectroscopic analysis of interstellar gas, for example. Energy can be changed in form (and one familiar form is, of course, matter), but it cannot be created or destroyed. I am incidentally ignoring quantum effects, such as the "fizzing" of virtual particles within the parameters of the Uncertainty Principle, because even there no energy is observably created or destroyed.

Now, the consequence of the energy-conservation rule is that there must logically be a total, constant amount of energy in the entire universe. Whatever energy the universe started out with is the same as it has now. Crucially, however, there is no such thing as a Universal Energy Count that is responsible for maintaining energy conservation. Instead, each object is responsible for yielding or receiving energy in its own interactions only. We can say that the universe from the scientist's viewpoint is immanent, not transcendent.

The purpose of this digression into physics is that an analogy exists in software architecture: the client/server model. There, responsibility for data is maintained in the server. This is a transcendent system. Over extremely extended networks (for example, the vast virtual world of an online CRPG), the rationality of attempting to centralize control of the data is open to question. Ideally, all interactions would be carried out instead according to the immanent model—agents, called *infotons* (fundamental particles of information, analogous to photons), would carry packages of information between objects without the need for a centralized server.

Under the infoton-based immanent system, there would be no such thing as a physics plug-in for use with your game architecture. The physics of your game world would not be an encapsulated module but an integral part of the architecture itself. In fact, the arguments of medieval theologians aside, we have no evidence that a truly reliable physics can exist unless it is an emergent property of the system.

Let's first look at the issues that the client/server system is designed to address. Each client is capable of running the game locally, and all supporting code for object behavior is present at the client end. A client informs the server of any changes locally, and the server updates its global database and updates all other clients with such changes, making each client session consistent. The server ensures that all clients are doing the same thing within the game world.

When a game is about to start (assuming short games here like a typical *Starcraft* or *Quake* session), the server waits for clients to join this game session. Each client registers its request to join the game with the server. The clients can locally configure some aspects of the game (player colors, which sides to take, and so on) and then send such data to the server, which in turn ensures that there are no clashes between all the clients' requests.

When the server receives enough clients, the game can start. The game's communication modules send the data to the server in predetermined packets. Packets are labeled in the header section describing what they are and what action they dictate or request. There are communications control packets, game control packets, and data packets.

During the game, each client sends its player's position to the server, which in turn updates the global database for the session. The client then requests information about other players from the server to update its own position for the local game. Or it might receive such updates automatically, depending on the implementation.

To take an example: the player uses a stick of dynamite. The client creates a new object (an explosion) and sends this command to the server:

```
CLIENT[CREATE]:
ObjectCreate(player,object_type,object_position,object_attributes)
```

Where **player** is the client's player ID

object_type is the class type, an explosion in this case

object_position is the position in the world

object_attributes are any exceptional data regarding the explosion

The server receives the command and updates server database accordingly.

```
SERVER[RECEIVE]:
```

```
Receive(OBJECT_CREATE,player,object_type,object_position,
object_attributes)
```

The server then informs other clients of the presence of the new object.

```
SERVER[NOTIFY_BROADCAST]:
ObjectCreate(player,object_type,object_position,object_attributes)
```

The clients are then able to update their local game with the new object accordingly.

In multiplayer games, the client/server is mainly used to address the following issues, so if an infoton-based model is to be viable it must be also be able to do so:

Synchronization

This is a perennial problem in multiplayer games. There are timing issues, depending on various user machine and connection speeds. Using client/server, the role of the server is to ensure that every player has their correct presence in the world relative to each other when interaction is required. Frame rate issues are also dealt with in the same manner. The clients receive the synchronized update data for the whole session from the server and update their local worlds accordingly.

The infoton system would require the infotons to establish a local interaction rate that is based on the slowest connection. This does mean that, if applied using current hardware, what seemed to be a brief fight in one corner of the game world could take the same time as half a dozen fights elsewhere. This is perhaps the biggest problem with an immanent model—the real universe does not maintain simultaneity (because of relativistic effects), but that is something we'd rather avoid on the small scale of our virtual worlds.

More easily, the immanent world could be maintained in its entirety on a central machine. This is close to, but not quite the same as, a traditional client/server relationship. Instructions from each player then are intentions rather than completed actions, and data sent back is what has already happened to you. If you have a slow machine, your reactions in the game world will be slow.

Data Storage

This is necessary for keeping track of a game at all times when clients are online or offline.

For an online session, the server stores data received from clients in its global database and updates clients throughout the session. Also, a permanent database can be used to carry forward games sessions between logins, so that a player can start where he left off. This is obviously essential for RPG games.

In a pure immanent model, you can no more vanish from the game world than you can from the real world. The system would in that case have to represent any player logging out as in stasis beyond an event horizon, meanwhile distributing responsibility for maintaining world data onto other players' machines. More probably, though, there would be a "passive" server ready to maintain each player's existence and locality in the world by stepping in with a virtual presence when the player logged out (which means that, if a tree falls in a virtual world, it does still make a noise even if there are no players in the world to hear it).

Global System Control

Code governing communication and game control protocols is installed at the server end to deal with various issues. For instance, a client suddenly logs out halfway through the game. What should happen? The server code can spring into action to rectify the problem—not to say that any of these techniques work properly, but it is vital to include mechanisms to deal with these types of events.

Also, starting and ending the global game is the responsibility of the server. As we have seen, an immanent world is pretty much constrained to be persistent: you cannot switch a universe off all that easily!

What are the advantages of immanence over transcendence? Why might we wish to adopt this model? Most obviously, there should be an increased processing speed: you can cast your spell in one corner of the game world without needing to wait while a battle is resolved on the far coast. Much more importantly, we could in theory attain a degree of robustness that could never be achieved in a client/server setup. The real universe operates reliably without crashing precisely *because* it makes no attempt to achieve any centralization of data. However, the hardware is still some years off from being able to deliver immanent processing. Right now, the risk of infoton evaporation is still too high, such that an immanently structured online world could suffer its own premature "heat death." But, this is a field worth investigating further, and indeed some companies using A-life technology have talked of using agents to be the carriers of information in such a system.

The Shape Of Things To Come?

To conclude, let's indulge a little imaginative license and try to envision what a development cycle might look like in the future.

It is a bright spring morning as Andy, a game designer, arrives at the offices of Imaginary Forces, Inc., one of the "big six" super developers of the year 2007. He has come to meet Tim, a content manager at the company.

Andy is not cold-calling. His agent put him in touch with Tim because he knew Imaginary Forces was looking for a murder-mystery game to use with their "Detective Lector" license. Andy explains his design concept, and they discuss how it could be adapted to incorporate new technology that the company has been funding. Tim commissions Andy to write a treatment document, and, a few weeks later, the project goes to the New Projects Committee (the senior management "marketing" arm), which agrees to fund the design stage.

Andy first completes a gameplay document. Tim then brings in David, from the company's Architecture Group, who turns the design into a software plan and prepares a testbed. Andy recommends Ben, a freelance artist, to draw the concept sketches that will feature in a full presentation to the New Projects Committee.

Twelve weeks after the initial meeting, Tim makes his report to the Committee, which is particularly interested in the opportunities to use new technology. "We have an agent-based artificial fiction system from Hadron Software that would really enhance this project," Tim tells them. "But that's still in evaluation, so we can either hold up the go-ahead on the Lector game for three months, or we can start now and plan to use the Crystal Clear AI editor if Hadron's system doesn't make the grade."

The Committee decides to approve the project to start right away. The next step is to appoint a Project Director. Tim first offers this role to Andy (not entirely unprecedented, just as there are writer-directors in Hollywood), but he is reluctant to commit to such a grueling schedule. Mindful of the continual updating of the design that will be necessary to get full value out of the new A-fiction system, he feels he'll have his hands full anyway. So, Tim brings in Jeff, a freelance director.

As director, Jeff has "ownership" of the project. He has creative responsibility and, in theory, makes all the decisions. (In practice, directors must put up with continual niggling interference from their content managers, who in turn have to please the senior management, but Jeff has worked with Tim before and finds him more flexible than most.)

Jeff is attached to the Architecture Department and now recruits his key staff: Andy, game designer; David, software planner and lead architect; Kerry, tools; and Nick, assistant director.

The first task is to prepare a full project plan. Working with Andy, the core team breaks down the design into modular form and assesses which modules will need to be created from scratch. The incremental development structure is mapped out in such a way as to leave time for adjusting the design when the artificial fiction system from Hadron Software is fitted in. Andy has meanwhile been looking at the evaluation version of the Hadron system and is impressed. "If I'd known about this, I'd have designed a whole different game," he tells Jeff.

"Save it 'till the next one," says Jeff, nonetheless copying his reply to Tim in case the company wants to wait for a redesign.

The predevelopment stage is completed after six weeks. Jeff has meanwhile been looking around for his development staff. He outsources the coding to a company in Bombay, Varuna Coders, which provides 12 programmers he has worked with before. He also gets Ben and a computer artist to create the art guidelines for the project. These guidelines will be followed exactly by 15 "session" artists whom he recruits from an agency. For the placeholder graphics and interface artwork, he brings in two people from Imaginary Forces' in-house art department.

Development proceeds in weekly increments, following the cycle:

- Plan—decide what this phase will achieve
- Build—add the features for this phase
- Test—evaluate the work to date
- Review—decide what changes are needed to the design before the next phase

After three months, the artificial fiction engine is plugged in but, after some soul searching, Andy and Jeff are forced to conclude that fully exploiting the new technology would require a radical rethink of the design from the ground up. The decision is referred up to Marketing, with Jeff's recommendation that they go with the old Crystal Clear system after all.

The decision is made: the A-fiction engine can wait for another project. Another four weeks brings the main build to a conclusion. The team now shrinks again to just Jeff, Andy, and the in-house staff. The game system is now complete, but the specific game scenarios ("levels," as they used to be called) remain to be written. Jeff and Andy hire on a couple of scenario writers to assist, and a month later the Detective Lector game is ready to go to QA. Scenario writing continues in parallel for another six weeks, and the project is then ready to ship. The timeline from first concept to conclusion has been 11 months, and the work invested (excluding testing) is around 150 man-months.

Is that how it's going to be? Well, almost certainly not! There are far too many variables to pretend that a prediction can be made with any accuracy. Maybe modular development will be so advanced that actual code writing ceases to be part of development altogether. Maybe teams will be *much* larger. Maybe procedural modeling will allow 1 artist to do the work of 10. Maybe the game designer will always be the one to direct the project, or maybe the company structure will be organized differently.

Regardless, it seems likely that this example contains the kernel of certain truth—which is that game development will become better targeted, designed, and organized. By dispelling the "fog of war" that descends when groups are working without process or plan, development in the future will be liberated to focus on the creative tasks themselves. There will be a signal improvement in the use of developers' time. We may reasonably hope that the games themselves will improve just as much.

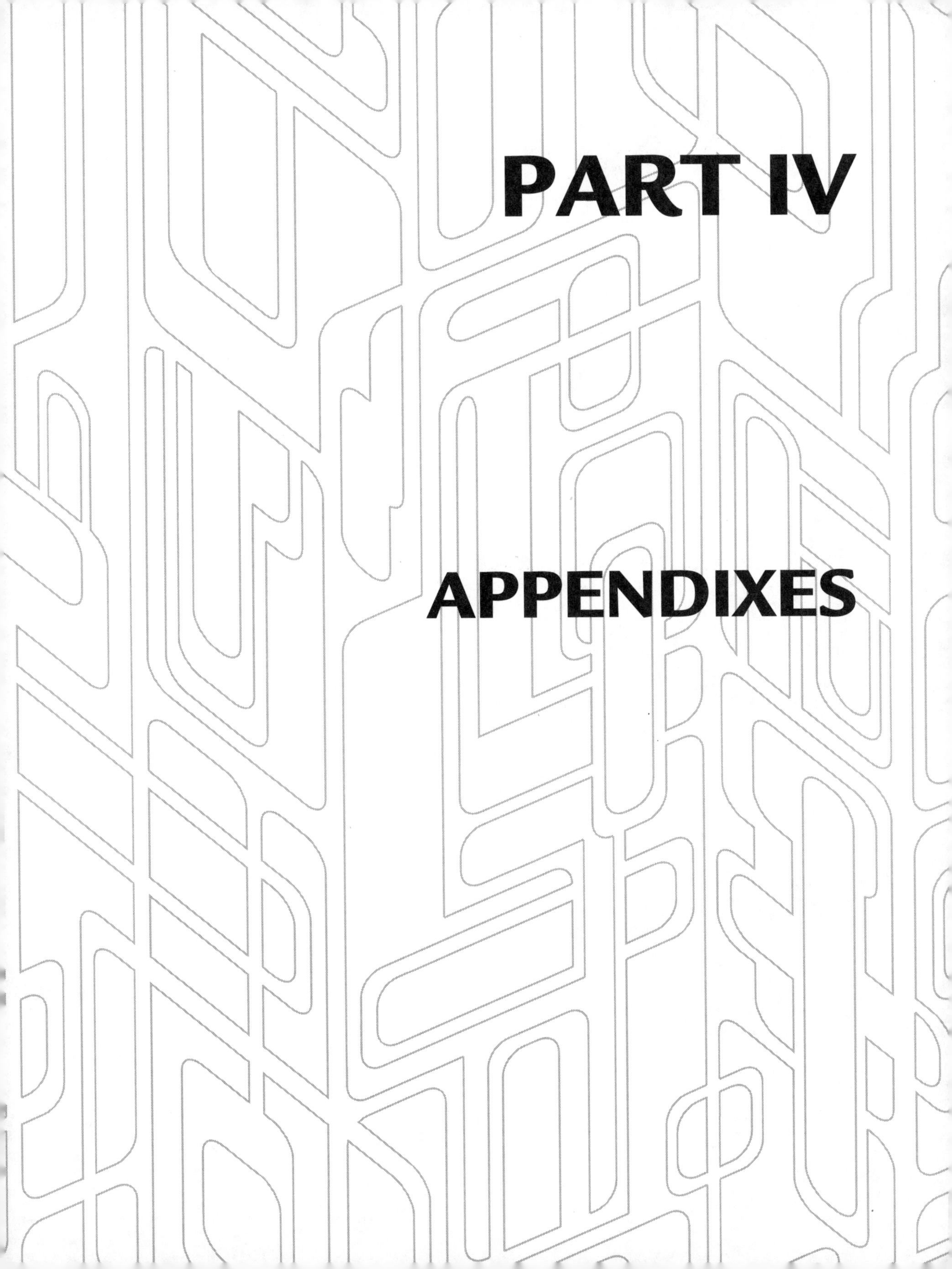

PART IV

APPENDIXES

Appendix A
Sample Game Design Documents

Key Topics:

- ***Detailed design discussions***
- ***Initial treatments and sample designs***
- ***Technical specifications***
- ***Code review forms***
- ***Test scripts***

Detailed Design Discussions

These documents describe the overall working architecture for a project. Our example for this section is the following design overview of *Balls!*

1. *Balls!* Introduction

Balls! is a level-based, quasi-isometric, 3D puzzle game, designed to be intuitive and addictive to play. It is based upon the interactions between balls of different capabilities on a block-based play area.

This design has been carefully thought out and refined by taking a reasoned comparison of other successful puzzle games. It is important to note that the game was not *designed* based on this premise, but that certain refinements were made and questions were asked based on the analysis. Where necessary, modifications were made. These design specifications are all subject to change pending further investigation.

2. Overview Of Gameplay

The two main modes of gameplay are *strategic* and *action*.

Level success conditions are the same for both types of game and usually involve getting a certain number of balls to the exit.

The strategic game is more thought based and requires traditional reasoning skills within a fixed time limit. In the strategic game, each level is split into two phases. A timer runs through both phases, although for some levels it may be restarted at the beginning of the second phase.

The first half of the first phase allows you to look at the level and the balls and blocks you are provided with to complete the level. The second half of this phase allows you to place the balls and blocks and tweak the starting parameters.

The second phase begins by clicking on the Go button and plays out the level as per your starting conditions. You will know in advance where and when a ball is going to fall, so you have time to arrange to receive it by arranging blocks. As the difficulty progresses, this warning time will be less, and it may contain less information (for example, you may not know exactly where and/or when the ball will appear).

If the level success conditions are reached within the time limit, the level is successful, and you are given the chance to replay or continue. If you fail, you are given the option of retrying the level.

Every now and then, both in the strategic game and the action game, you will get a special ball. Getting this ball to the exit will earn a huge bonus. This special ball will in most cases act like a normal ball, but it is possible that it will also have properties of one or more of the other types of ball (for example, a hot balloon).

It is possible that both types of action level will integrate well. Certainly, the latter design features are a subset of the former.

A third level-design concept for the action game is *continuous play*, which is closer to *Tetris* in concept.

This type of level starts in a similar fashion to the second type, but layers of blocks will be added or removed as you progress. Initially, things progress slowly, but, as you get further into the game, more-diverse ball types and blocks will be added to spice things up.

Block layers are added after a time interval (decreasing as you get further) or by losing a ball. There are no levels in this action mode. The game just gets progressively harder and faster, rather like *Tetris*.

Because players like to have a sense of achievement, the game will have conceptual level numbers, based upon the number of balls saved and the score. When a level is increased, the game becomes harder and faster. After some time, the floor size can also be decreased to make things more difficult.

Care will have to be taken to ensure that this progression is smooth, as it was in the Game Boy *Tetris*.

With the continuous game, there is a definite possibility of adding two- (or more?) player functionality via DirectPlay. The extent of network message traffic would be negligible, and the response would not need to be instant, so Internet latency would not appear to be a problem.

3. Platforms

Initial target platforms are Windows 95/98/NT, with the possibility of a no-frills (or few-frills) implementation on Windows CE. Two graphics engines are being developed. The initial prototype engine will be sprite based, and the advanced engine will be Direct3D based. The two engines will be developed in parallel to some extent, and will probably both be in the final game. The sprite-based system would be suitable for low-end machines or puzzle-game purists, and the Direct3D-based system would appeal to whizzy 3D card owners. It should be emphasized here that the focus of the game is not whizzy graphics. The graphics will be attractive and functional, but not over the top (like those, for example, in *Sentinel II*).

Due to its simplicity, this design has a lot of potential for other platforms such as the Sony PlayStation, Nintendo 64, and even the Color Game Boy, although I would rather wait for the next-generation handheld. The development for these alternative platforms would be outsourced as required. The design is such that all the platform-specific code is separated from the game logic, so conversion work would be easier than usual, because a large proportion of the code could be directly reused with only minimal modification. Doing so would help keep costs down.

The PC distribution will be on CD-ROM, and the others on whatever format they natively support.

Target Audience

The target audience for this game is effectively everybody. It is intended to have an appeal similar to *Tetris*. While I feel that this is a very difficult task (and near impossible to achieve to any great degree by design), the basic design concepts are pure enough to allow a fair attempt.

This game is abstract enough to appeal to a wider audience than something such as *Puzzle Bobble*, but may be perceived as too "computery" to be the next *Tetris*. The advantage that *Tetris* had was that it was simple enough to fit the design on one page and that you didn't feel as if it were a computer game you were playing. The interface to the hardware was forgotten and was irrelevant.

It is important to try to emulate this simplicity with *Balls!*. This will be made more difficult by the fact that it is a 3D game—which automatically labels it as a computer-oriented game, as opposed to *Tetris*, which was just a game that happened to be on a computer. It is interesting to note that the 3D versions of *Tetris* did not achieve anything like the same level of success as the original.

This may have been because a simple idea was overcomplicated before its time. However, this does not mean that *Balls!* is an inherently bad idea or that it is too complex. It just means that the emphasis of design needs to be on hiding the complexity behind a simple interface and presenting it in a completely natural feeling way. This, I think, has been achieved in the design.

4. Time Scales

Given sufficient free time, a basic, no-frills implementation could be put together in six months, although this implementation would possibly contain only one of the gameplay modes and no multiplayer mode. This would be a functional prototype.

If the structure of the application was carefully thought out, then additional effects could be plugged in. The majority of time will be spent on level design.

The full product could be completed in under one year, given one artist and two or three programmers, one of these with some art skills, though this may not include the full set of enhanced features.

Given 18 months, the product would be entirely complete on the PC platform.

If time were running short, the enhancements discussed later in this document could be pared down or omitted entirely. The enhancements add very little to the game itself, but they do give a slightly more polished appearance and enhance the sense of achievement when a player reaches a certain level.

A fair amount of groundwork has already been put in place in developing resource access and graphics and sound libraries that have been used successfully in other projects.

Basic Concepts

The fundamental idea behind *Balls!* is that it will be a simple and addictive game of the *Tetris* ilk.

Every element of gameplay has been examined and analyzed. There are no cases of "Wouldn't it be cool if …" or "This would be a neat feature—It would look amazing" that seem to be prevalent in most games today, which increasingly seem to be a triumph of style over content.

The graphics in *Balls!* are pleasant but functional, and any embellishments are provided as rewards for progress. Most of the effort has been spent on defining the gameplay.

5. Why Puzzle Games Aren't As Good As They Used To Be

The games industry has made several attempts to follow in the footsteps of *Tetris*; not many of them, however, have made the grade. Usually, they repeatedly fall into the same traps inadvertently set up by marketing men who have dollar signs in their eyes, and completely overlook playability.

A notable example of this was the release of a puzzle game on 14 or so different platforms with a huge and expensive marketing campaign and lots of magazine coverage.

The marketing man concerned was convinced that he had a sure-fire winner, which would match *Tetris* in sales. Unfortunately for him, the game concerned was too complicated. A game of that nature must be intuitive. Some aspects of the game were not suitable for the style of game that they wanted to achieve.

Without delving too deeply into the whys and wherefores of the failure of that particular game, the main point here is that the game failed because it started with a marketing concept and ended with a product. This is the wrong order. Start with a well-designed product, and then plan the marketing.

6. Puzzle Game Appeal

For puzzle games to have a wide appeal across the sexes, a few simple guidelines should be followed. These do not guarantee success, but it is possible that they could help. Of course, there are exceptions to every rule.

Don't Be Too Cute

Sickening cuteness doesn't work. Contrary to industry opinion, girls are not interested in sickly cuddly things, and neither are boys. However, an example of where this has worked well is *Lemmings* (the first release only—people got a bit fed up with them after a few releases), but this was offset by the humor within the game, which had an altogether darker edge to it.

The cuteness was not overdone, unlike—for an example of where this has failed—*Fury of the Furries*.

Avoid "Serious" Violence

This is quite an abstract rule. For example, *Zoop* fell foul of this rule by using shooting. The player shot colored shapes to remove their color. However, *Lemmings*, although violent in places, worked well because it was cartoon violence.

This worked to counterbalance *Lemmings*' cuteness, although players do not want to see their favorite cute pet die horribly. In *Lemmings*, players do not get the opportunity to become attached to individual characters, due to the fact that the lemmings themselves are anonymous, which also reduces their cuteness. In the later *Lemmings* games, the graphics for the lemmings were improved, which I believe actually reduced the appeal of the game.

In short, if you have to be violent, make it funny.

Keep It Abstract, But Not Too Abstract

Tetris is a good example. It is abstract, but it can be mentally related to sliding-block puzzles.

Some very successful games on the ZX Spectrum were enhanced sliding-block puzzles, an example being *Confuzion*, which involved sliding segments of fuse wire around to dispose of the sparks traveling along it. *Lemmings* is abstract to an extent: the individual lemmings are not very detailed, and character development is not attempted. *Zoop* was too abstract, as was *Endorfun*. They bore no relationship to any other experience. Players have to have something to mentally relate to. For the wide appeal, you have to suspend the players' belief that it is a computer game and allow them to imagine that the game could be actually happening for real.

Give Rewards For Progress

In *Pac-Man*, the main reward apart from gaining a high score is a set of animated sequences that occur every fifth level.

Similarly, in *Lemmings*, the reward is gained by reaching new and visually different levels. Past a certain level of Game Boy *Tetris*, a reward animation is played. This was a surprise, and the element of surprise is important. People appreciate rewards more if they do not expect them.

7. Why *Balls!* Would Be Good

The game involves positioning a set of balls and/or blocks with varying characteristics onto an array of blocks that affect them in different ways.

In the strategic game, the player positions the balls so that their eventual paths and interactions achieve some arbitrary level goal. The goal could be to get a certain number of balls into an exit location or into a certain pattern, with or without a time limit. There are some constraints on placing the balls, such as positioning, direction of initial travel, and a time limit.

Once the balls are placed, they are set in motion, and the player watches the results. This is very much a thinking puzzle game.

In both types of action game, the players are able to influence the behavior of the balls after release, by dropping blocks to affect their path.

The three games types can be used together to allow people who prefer whichever type of game to play it. The three types of game are actually aimed at three different types of player or player mood.

The first type, the *strategic* game, is designed to have long-term appeal to the deep-thinking puzzler. Think of it as the "crossword" mode. If they cannot figure out a level, they can come back to it later with fresh inspiration, or they can retry the level in *action* mode.

The second type of game, the *level-based action* game, is again designed for long-term appeal, but this time the emphasis is on quick reflexes and fast thinking. Think of this as the "speed chess" mode. Again, if the player cannot get past a level in this mode, they have the ability to retry it in the strategic mode. Of course, they get more points if they complete it in both modes. Note that the player gets points for completing a level only once per mode: you cannot repeatedly play the same level in the same mode to bump up your score.

The third type, the *continuous action* game, is designed for when the player fancies a quick blast of *Tetris*-type adrenaline. It is designed to allow the player to dip in for a quick game, and then hook them into that "just one more go until I get to level 13" feeling, before the player realizes that they have been playing for half the night. Think of this as the "*Ballstris*" mode. There are no separately designed levels here; the game just gets algorithmically more difficult as gameplay progresses.

This mode has no long-term goals. It is just a quick fix, hopefully with a killer addictive hook. This mode is the only one that provides a multiplayer game.

A fundamental point of the game is that the balls cannot gain in potential energy; that is, they cannot gain height to get a block higher than the one they are on. Individual balls will never change speed, only direction. The system is based on much-simplified "real" physics, with some liberties taken for the purposes of gameplay.

Balls! would appeal because it can be readily related to common phenomena such as rolling balls or marbles. Even though the laws of physics in the game are slightly different than in the real world, they are close enough to be readily accepted. This is a strong advantage.

The player is given a visual reward for completing some (or all) of the levels. The movement of the balls could be designed to trigger a sequence of actions that cause some event. Some of these could have two outcomes—nice and nasty—depending on how you completed the level. These outcomes could be integrated into the level. This is discussed in more detail later. (Note that the in-house level editor is being produced to release quality, so we can include it as part of the package and increase replay value.)

Look And Feel

The look and feel of the game is very important. It should be simple and not an obstacle to the game (that is, giving virtually instant access to the game itself).

A consistent theme should run throughout, and the interface should be simple and easy to understand. Although the standard windows interface is dull, a similar but more harmonious approach could be used to provide familiarity. The other approach is to base the interface on a familiar piece of everyday equipment. This approach has been used reasonably successfully in a number of games (usually driving games), but it has the disadvantage of having to find a bit of everyday equipment that everybody is familiar with and that fits the theme of the game.

The former approach is the most likely here, and it is possible that a design based on a game level and using the game engine may be a good idea. As well as acting as a good testbed for the dynamics, it will also add consistency. This will be fine, as long as it does not appear too contrived and get in the way of what the interface was trying to achieve in the first place. Figure A.1 shows an overview of the program structure.

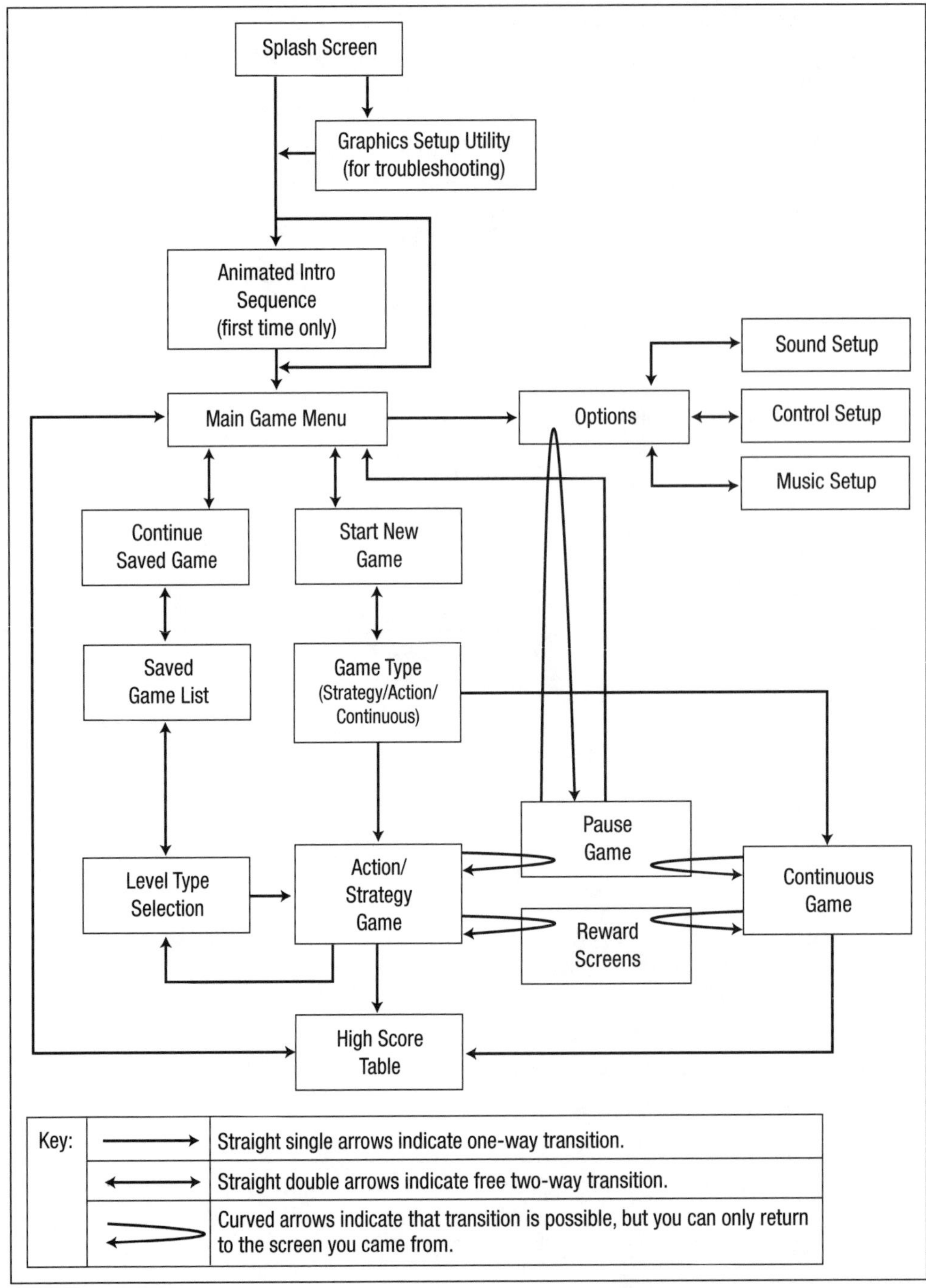

Figure A.1
Balls! program structure.

8. Game Design: User Interface Elements

The user interface is split into two parts: the "game configuration" interface, and the "in-game" interface. The idea is to make these as seamless as possible.

This does not include the Windows-based graphics troubleshooting application, which will use a standard Windows interface in case the in-game graphics are configured badly, so that the screen cannot be viewed.

Game Configuration Interface

The game configuration user interface will be based on elements of the game engine. For example, the configuration of blocks shown in Figure A.2 represent a slider bar.

The player operates the slider bar by clicking on either of the buttons.

Block A is a push-button switch. Blocks 1 and 3 are directional blocks, and block 2 is a sticky block that holds the ball.

Clicking on button A causes block 1 to become a sticky block, and block 2 to become a directional block of the same type as block 3. This will cause the ball to move towards block 1 because block 2 is now a directional block propelling it towards button A. The ball will then stop on block 1, which is the new sticky block.

Clicking on button B will have the reverse effect.

This particular slider bar has six settings, increasing from A to B.

Note that a slider bar could also be implemented using a magnetic block with a metal ball instead of the sticky block.

The two types of switch block are push-button and toggle switch. The push button is in the ON position only for as long as there is pressure on it. The toggle switch is toggled from the ON position to the OFF position and vice versa every time it is pressed (see Figure A.3).

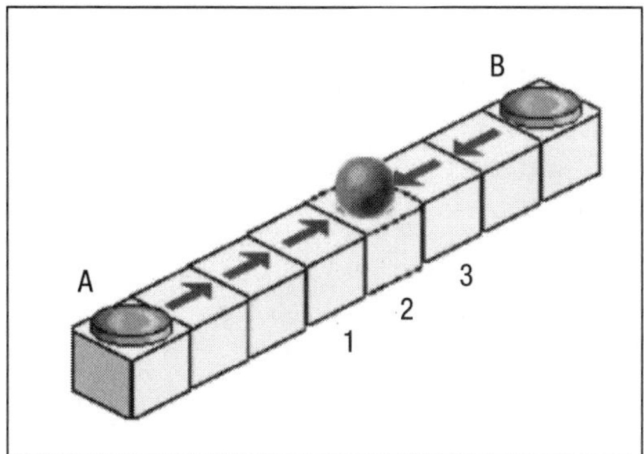

Figure A.2
Slider bar.

Level Design (For Level-Based Game Modes)

All level types derive from a base level template shown in Figure A.4.

The level template has two phases and a timer running through both. The timer object is quite flexible: it can run, as shown, through all phases, or it can be deactivated for any or all phases. The timer can also be reset at the beginning of phase II, if desired.

All levels must have at least one phase. This represents the general format of all levels, including the strategic type.

The designer is free to implement any level he or she likes, with the emphasis on action, strategy, or any combination of both. The *Balls!* system is flexible enough to accommodate both types.

Strategic Game

The strategic game is similar in mental approach to a chess problem. You are presented with a configuration of blocks and a set of balls to place on them. Some balls may already be in place. You may also be provided with a limited set of blocks, which can be used to modify the configuration already in place. Various other parameters such as release times of blocks and balls and initial direction of movement may also be configurable at the behest of the level designer.

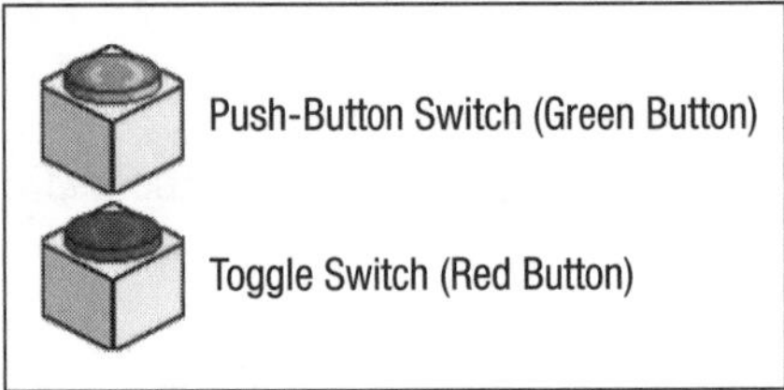

Figure A.3
Toggle and push switches.

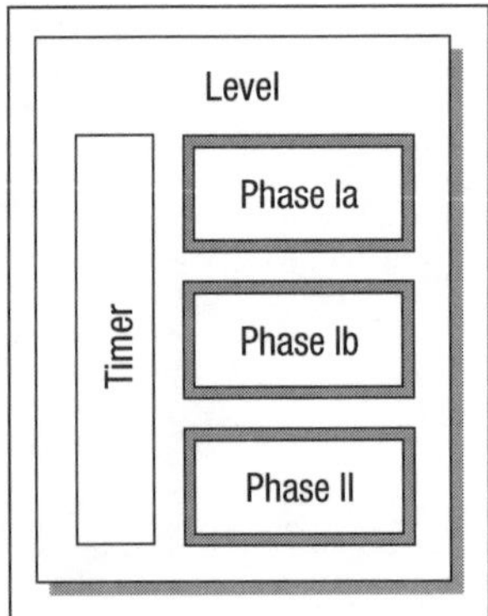

Figure A.4
Level template.

This configuration process may have a time limit, which is equivalent to phase "Ia" and "Ib" in the level template. This timer can either be allowed to run through both phases or restarted at the beginning of phase II. Phase II is initiated by clicking on a Go button.

The player then watches the results of the phase I setup. If the success conditions are met before the phase II time limit runs out, then the level is completed; otherwise, the player is allowed to retry the level.

Action Game (Level Based)

The action game will progress into a fast and frenetic mayhem zone. The action game could have two types of levels, but, until playtesting, I am unsure which sort of level type will be more suitable. It is possible they will both be fine. Fortunately, the issue is only one of level design and not of programming. If one level type isn't suitable, it can be redesigned.

The basic idea is that blocks fall from above and must be steered and rotated into positions to enable the balls to reach the target squares. The balls can either already be on the level or they can fall from above.

If balls fall from above, the player gets some form of warning that they are coming and where they will fall. The level designer decides the format of the information. The player cannot steer falling balls.

Level Type I

The first level type is similar to the thinking game, in which there is a complex configuration of blocks with some balls already stationed on them. This level can be split into two phases, the lengths of which is set by the designer using the timer.

In the first phase, the player gets the opportunity to examine the block-and-ball configuration. He does not know which blocks will be falling, but he may be informed if any other balls apart from those already on the level will be falling.

These levels usually have two phases, but the first phase is optional for the level designer.

Level Type II

The second type is closer to *Tetris*, in that you start with a simple floor of blocks and blocks and balls fall from above. As in the first level type, the balls cannot be steered and you get some sort of warning as to when and where they will arrive, but the emphasis here is on building your own structures to get the ball to the exit block, which may not appear immediately in the level and fall in only later.

Action Game (Continuous)

The continuous action game is closer to *Tetris* in concept, in that there is continuous action with no respite. It is derived from *action level type II*, in that you start with a flat, one-layer-thick floor of blocks. Blocks and balls fall from above, and, as before, only the blocks can be steered. You will still get a warning as to when and where balls will appear, although this will be algorithmically decreased as you progress.

The difficulty increases algorithmically as time progresses. For example, new layers will be added every so often. The time intervals between layer additions will decrease as the game progresses, probably bottoming out at around 10 seconds (subject to playtesting). Also, as the game progresses, the layers may get smaller—starting out at, say, 12×12 and ending at 6×6 (again subject to playtesting). With this, there may need to be some way to allow re-extension of the floorspace, in order to balance out the gameplay.

Losing a ball causes a layer to be added, and saving a ball causes a layer to be removed.

Also, the interval between the arrival of new balls steadily decreases, and the frequency of different ball types appearing increases.

In the continuous game, the target block appears at the beginning. Layers are added from below, so the target block always appears on the top layer. It is impossible for the lowest layer to be destroyed. Blocks may be discarded by dropping them over the edge of the level or through the target block, but doing this too many times will incur an added layer. It should be possible to get some sort of bonus multiplier to remove more than one layer at once.

For the two-player game, an additional block type is required, the wormhole block. This allows blocks and balls to be sent to the other player. The wormhole block is used in a similar fashion to the target block, but it sends the block or ball to the other player. Sending a ball through the wormhole block will not remove a layer, and there is no penalty for dropping blocks through it. It can be used only once before reverting to a normal block. If a layer that is destroyed contains any wormhole blocks, then one extra layer per wormhole block is added to the other player's game.

The two play modes are *cooperative* and *competitive*. The fundamental difference between the two is in the attitude of the players. The wormhole block behavior is the same, but the emphasis in the cooperative mode is in using them to help the other player, rather than hinder them as in the competitive mode. For the purposes of the high-score table, the scores of each player in cooperative mode are summed, and both names (and a team name) are entered into the high-score tables on both machines.

Level Progression

The level design will be implemented to gradually introduce the player to all the features of the game.

The first 10 or so levels will be tutorial levels to familiarize the player to game features and the basic ways they can be manipulated. In this set of levels, simple ball-and-block types will be introduced.

The difficulty of the continuous action game will be algorithmically increased, probably based on a logarithmic scale.

9. Physics Of *Balls!*

Figure A.6 shows the timing of ball movements. Note that all balls reach the center of the blocks simultaneously.

Ball types are shown in Table A.1.

Balls cannot change speed, except to stop. Empirically, their speed is either full speed or zero speed. Of course, some animations (for example, rolling halfway up a slope) may give the impression that the ball is slower, but—as far as the game engine is concerned—all balls will reach the center of a square simultaneously as shown in Figure A.5.

A comparable system also applies for ball-ball collisions and 90-degree ball deflections, as shown in Figure A.6.

The game is timed on the presumption that all balls reach the center of a block at the same time, no matter what action they are taking at the time. This presumption ensures that the simplified physics system deals only with the situations that are covered in this document.

Table A.1 Ball types.

Ball Types	Image	Properties
Normal Ball	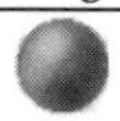	The default ball. The time that this ball takes to get from the center of one square to the next is one game 'turn.'
Metal Ball		This ball will stick to a magnetic block if it is adjacent to the magnet. If it collides with a hot block, it will become a hot ball.
Mimic Ball		A mimic ball takes on the characteristics of the ball that it last struck. Its uninitialized characteristics are that of a normal ball. It can also have a limit on the number of transitions it can make before it sticks in one form. It will always look slightly different to the ball type it is mimicking.
Balloon Ball		It will float across single gaps in blocks, and burst on contact with spikes. It can be blown off course by fan blocks, and does not affect switch blocks. It does not stop on sticky blocks.
Glass Ball		If it drops any distance it will break, unless it lands on a balloon ball or a soft block, and is resistant to pools of acid on top of acid blocks.
Snow Ball		It will melt after a short period of time or on coming in contact with a hot block. If it collides with an ice block, it will take longer to melt. (The melt timer will be reset to new.)
Explosive Ball		It will explode on dropping any distance, destroying the block it lands on, except the soft block.
Hot Ball		This ball is a hot metal ball. If it collides with a snow ball, the snow ball will melt, and the hot ball will cool to become a normal metal ball. The same applies for collision with an ice block. If it collides with a magnetic block, the magnetic block becomes a normal block.

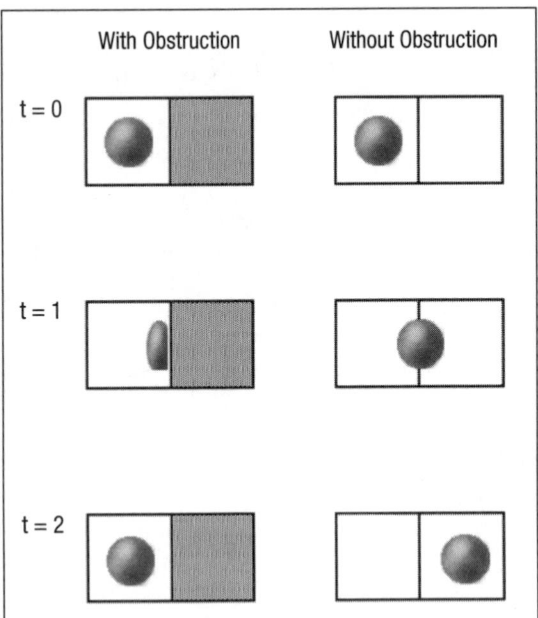

Figure A.5
Simple ball-block collisions.

When a ball collides with a block, it should take the same amount of time to travel from the center of the square, rebound, and return to the center of the square as it would to travel to the center of the next square if there had been no obstruction.

As far as the physics system is concerned, no matter what size the balls appear visually, a ball is large enough to be able to collide with a ball on an adjacent block when both balls are in the center of their blocks. This implies that the balls' diameter is the same as the length of the side of the block. This will be considered true for collisions. An exception to this rule is when the collision occurs from above (a ball dropping on another ball); otherwise, the described behavior wouldn't occur.

Another exception is required when balls are traveling through archways in blocks. For these purposes, the balls will be considered to have a diameter of approximately three-fourths of the length of a block's side. These minor inconsistencies will not be noticed.

Note that no one complained that in *Tetris* you could rotate pieces in gaps that would strictly be too small to allow such rotation. The game uses simplified baby physics. It is deterministic, meaning that there can be no randomness.

Note

The complex ball-block collisions above follow naturally from and can be derived from the simple ball-ball collisions in Figure A.6, and the ball-block collision in Figure A.5.

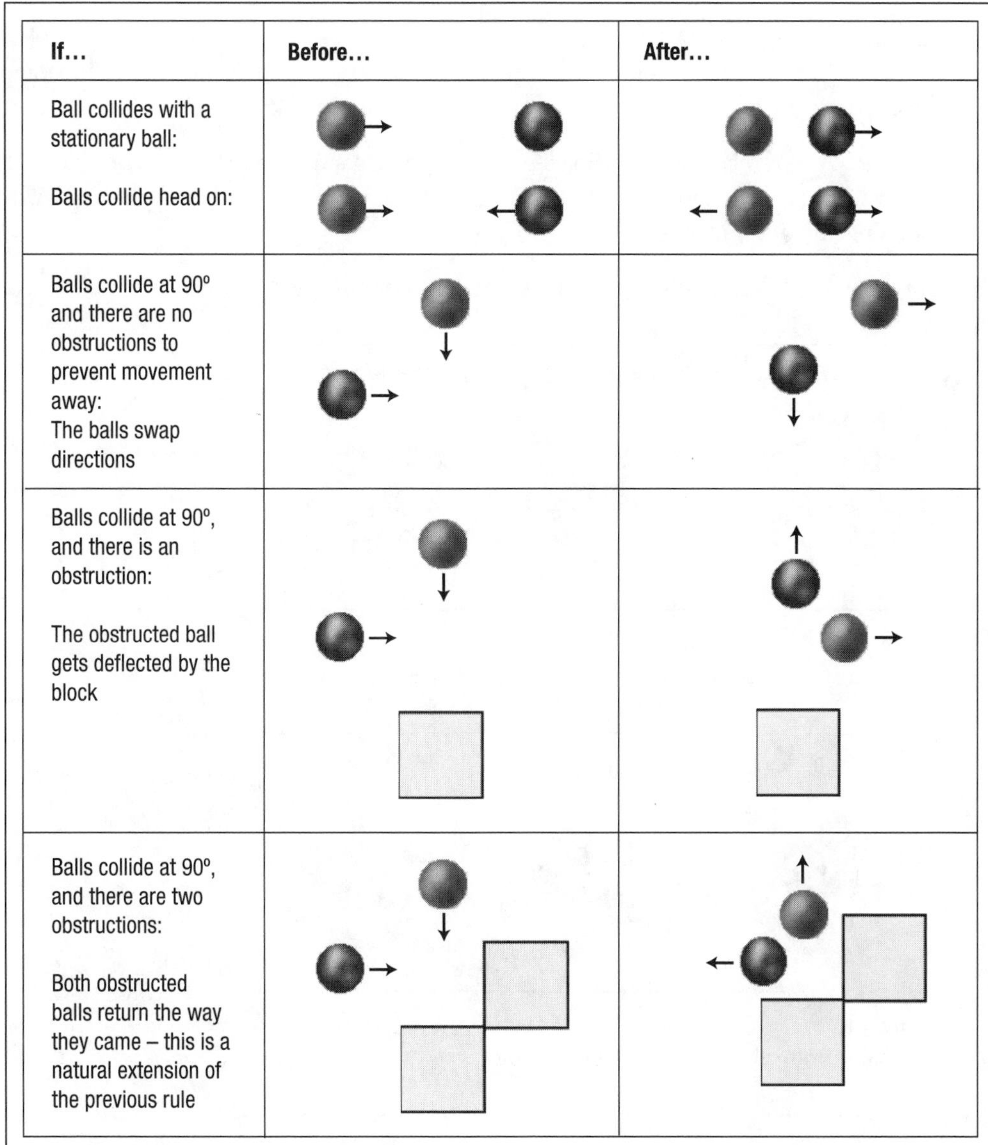

If...	Before...	After...
Ball collides with a stationary ball: Balls collide head on:		
Balls collide at 90° and there are no obstructions to prevent movement away: The balls swap directions		
Balls collide at 90°, and there is an obstruction: The obstructed ball gets deflected by the block		
Balls collide at 90°, and there are two obstructions: Both obstructed balls return the way they came – this is a natural extension of the previous rule		

Figure A.6
More-complex collisions.

Figure A.7 shows a ball falling from a block.

In Figure A.8, the ball falls into the redirection block, which deforms to give it room. It is then sprung out in the new direction by the redirection block.

In Figure A.9, the balloon ball floats over the single gap to land on the other block. Note that, with this block configuration, it will then fall off the edge and land on the X, without touching any other blocks.

In Figure A.10, a ball falls from a block and lands on another ball, then the balls carry on.

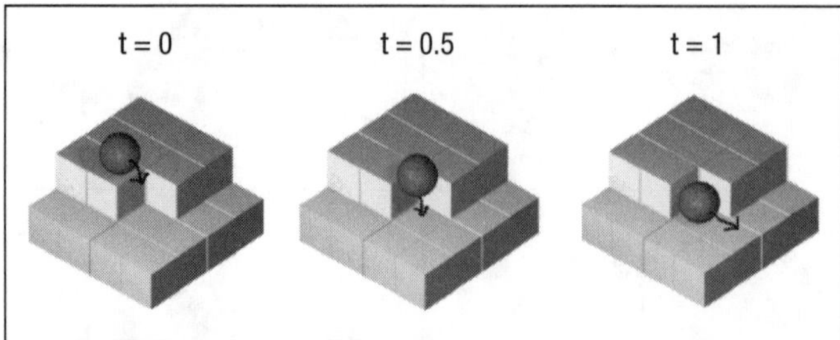

Figure A.7
Ball falling from a block.

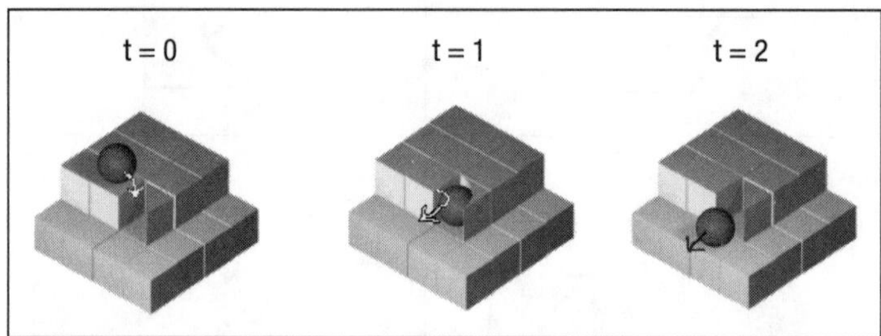

Figure A.8
Ball falling from a block into a redirection block.

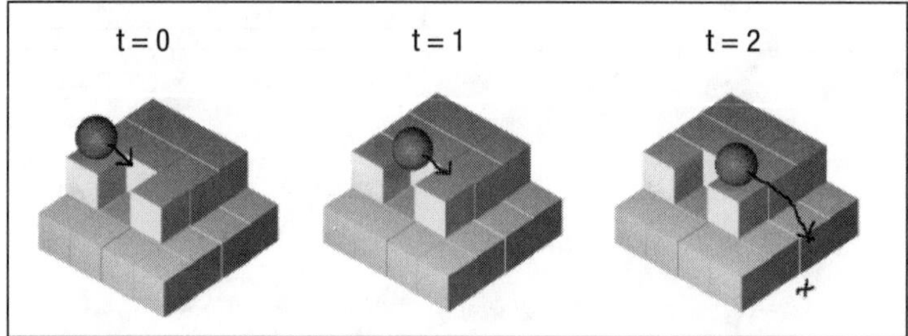

Figure A.9
Balloon ball floating over a gap.

Figure A.11 shows a similar situation as in A.10, except that the lower ball is a balloon ball. The ball is able to jump the gap by bouncing on the balloon ball. If the gap is two or more units wide, the ball is unable to jump it, unless the gap is completely bridged by balls.

In Figure A.12, the ball rolls halfway up the slope, stops, and rolls back down.

In Figure A.13, one ball approaches down a slope, one ball up a slope. The collision occurs on the slope; then the balls bounce back the way they came.

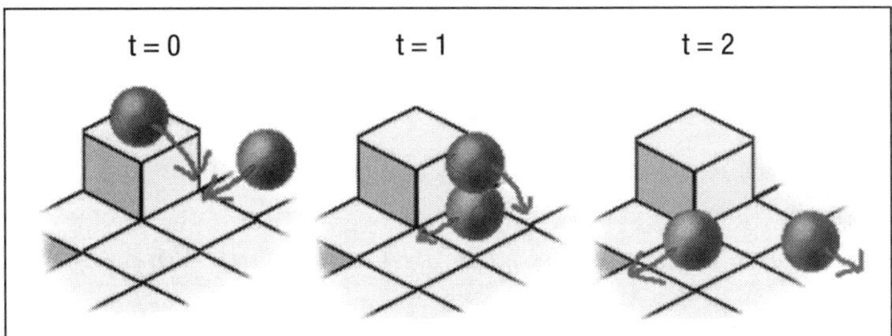

Figure A.10
Ball-ball collisions from above.

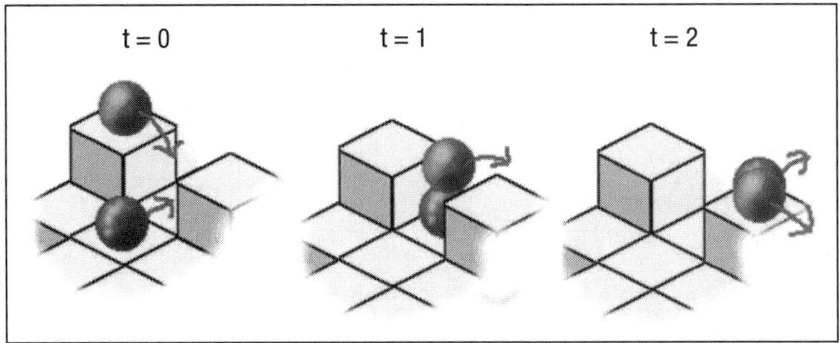

Figure A.11
A similar collision with a ball underneath.

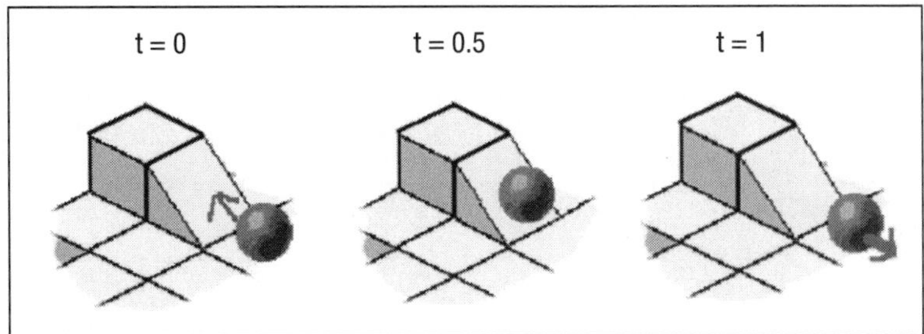

Figure A.12
Ball rolling up a slope.

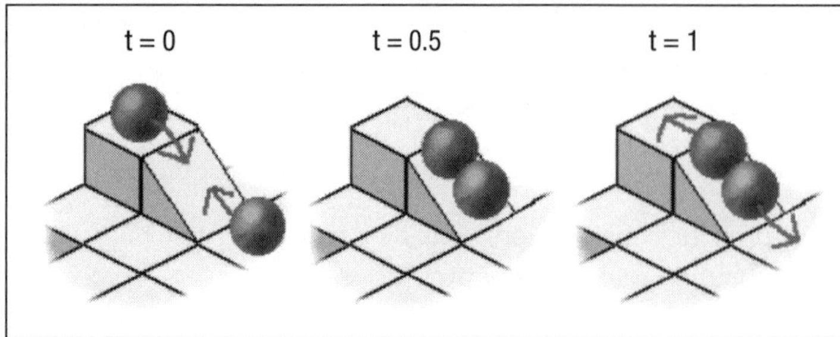

Figure A.13
A direct collision on a slope.

The situations shown in Figures A.12 and A.13 are the only exception to the rule that balls do not gain potential energy. It is resolved by defining only integral potential energy (PE). Hence, the ball does not lose any PE until it reaches the bottom of the slope (strictly past halfway), so it can legitimately roll back the way it came.

Many more-complicated situations could be defined, but they emerge naturally from these basic rules.

10. Blocks

Tables A.2, A.3, and A.4 describe the types of block present in the game.

Figure A.14 describes the ball-block interactions.

Table A.2 Types of blocks—part 1.

Block Types	Image	Properties
Normal Blocks		If a ball hits a flat side of a block, and no other rules prevail, then it rebounds back the way it came.
Redirection Blocks		Deflects a ball by 90 degrees. As the ball hits the block, it deforms to allow the ball to get to the center of the square, and give the impression of springing the ball away. Any block landing on top treats this as a solid block. How a ball falls depends on the direction of approach.
Archway Blocks		Allows a ball to go through a block. If balls go through at right angles, collision rules are followed as in Figure A.6.
Spiky Blocks		Will burst the balloon ball.

(continued)

Table A.2 Types of blocks—part 1 *(continued)*.

Block Types	Image	Properties
Ramp Blocks	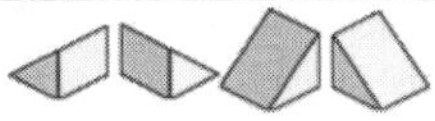	Balls go down but not *up* ramps. If they try they get halfway up and then roll back down. If a ball hits any other side of a ramp, it rebounds as if it had hit a solid block. If a cubic block is at the base of the ramp, preventing a ball from rolling, the ball will become stuck (unless any other rules apply). If any block falls onto a ramp, it will destroy the ramp, and replace it, unless the falling block is destroyed as well.
Magnetic Blocks		If the metal ball passes adjacent to the magnetic side, it will stick until another ball collides with it. The magnet will become a normal block on contact with the hot ball or hot block.
Starting Blocks		Starting blocks may have directional arrows indicating the allowed start directions. The starting position may appear on any flat-topped cubic block.

Table A.3 Types of blocks—part 2.

Block Types	Image	Properties
Switch Blocks		Switch blocks have a number of effects including removing blocks, opening archways, removing spikes, controlling directional blocks, etc. Illuminated is ON. Switches can either be toggled or push buttons. Any block falling here apart from the crumbling block, will keep the switch permanently on, or toggle it in the case of a toggle switch. The crumbling block releases the switch when it crumbles, if it is a push-button switch. Green switches are push-button switches, and red switches are toggle switches.
Soft Blocks		This pinker-than-pink block cushions the landing of the glass ball and the explosive ball, so that they are not destroyed.
Hot Blocks		This block is the same as a normal block except that it is hot. It will destroy any ball that comes in contact with it except the metal ball, which becomes the hot ball. If the ball is the explosive ball, it will destroy the block. If the ball is the snow ball, it will neutralize the block, causing it to become a normal block. If the ice block collides with this block, it will melt, and the hot block will become a normal block. If the magnetic block collides with this, the magnetic block will lose its magnetism.
Ice Blocks		This block is solid ice. If a hot ball comes into contact with it, the block will melt, any block on top of it will fall, and the hot ball will cool into a metal ball. If the snow ball comes into contact with it, it will be able to stay frozen longer. If a hot block collides with this, the hot block becomes a normal block, and the ice block will melt.

Table A.4 Types of blocks—part 3.

Block Types	Image	Properties
Fan Blocks		This will blow the balloon ball away from the fan if it passes. If its new path is blocked by an obstruction, the balloon ball will lodge in place until knocked out by another ball. The radius affected is one square.
Acid Blocks		This block will dissolve any ball that crosses it, except the glass ball. Any block landing here will dissolve in the same amount of time a crumbling block takes to crumble.
Target Blocks		The object of the game is to get the balls here. This block cannot be destroyed. If a block lands here, it will disappear after a few seconds, taking the same amount of time it takes for a crumbling block to crumble.
Directional Blocks		The directional block allows travel in only one direction, and will propel the ball in that direction, indicated by an arrow. A timer can allow cycling through the arrows. If a block falls here, it will remain there and not be propelled in the direction of the arrow.
Crumbling Blocks		Will disintegrate on contact with any ball. It allows one ball to travel over it before disintegrating after a short delay. If this block falls, it will disintegrate, even if it is falling in as part of the game. In this way it can be used to trigger switches without covering them.
Sticky Blocks		This block has a ball-shaped indentation. Any ball apart from the balloon ball will stop dead when it hits this block. It can only be dislodged by a collision with another ball.
Wormhole Blocks		This is a multiplayer-only block, which acts in a similar fashion to the target block, except that items sent through it will appear in the other player's level. Anything disposed of in this fashion is not counted as going through an exit block, or as being lost. It simply goes to the other player.

	Normal	Metal	Mimic	Balloon	Glass	Snow	Explosive	Hot
Normal					Ball breaks on fall		Destroy ball and block it falls on	
Reflector					Ball breaks on fall		Destroy ball and block it falls on	
Archway				Burst ball	Ball breaks on fall		Destroy ball and block it falls on	
Spikes					Ball breaks on fall		Destroy ball and block it falls on	
Ramp					Ball breaks on fall		Destroy ball and block it falls on	
Magnet		Ball sticks to block			Ball breaks on fall		Destroy ball and block it falls on	Normal block
Start					Ball breaks on fall		Destroy ball and block it falls on	
On/Off Switch	Press switch	Press switch	Press switch		Ball breaks on fall/presses switch	Press switch	Destroy ball and block it falls on else press switch	Press switch
Toggle Switch	Toggle switch	Toggle switch	Toggle switch		Ball breaks on fall/toggle switch	Toggle switch	Destroy ball block it falls on else ball moves	Toggle switch
Directional	Ball moves	Ball moves	Ball moves	Ball moves	Ball breaks on fall else ball moves	Ball moves	Destroy ball and block it falls on	Ball moves
Crumble	Destroy block	Destroy block	Destroy block		Ball breaks on fall and destroy block	Destroy block	Destroy ball and block it falls on	Destroy block
Target	Ball goes through exit	Ball goes through exit	Ball goes through exit	Ball goes through exit	Ball goes through exit	Ball goes through exit	Ball goes through exit	Ball goes through exit
Hot	Destroy ball		Destroy ball	Destroy ball	Destroy ball	Melts ball/ cools block	Destroy ball/ destroy block	Destroy ball
Ice					Breaks on fall	Resets ball melting timer	Destroy block it falls on	Melts block/ metal ball
Fan				Ball blown	Breaks on fall		Destroy ball and block it falls on	
Acid	Destroy ball	Destroy ball	Destroy ball	Destroy ball	Breaks on fall	Destroy ball	Destroy ball and block it falls on	Destroy ball
Sticky	Stops ball	Stops ball	Stops ball		Stops ball	Stops ball	Stops ball	Stops ball
Soft								
Wormhole	Ball goes to other player	Ball goes to other player	Ball goes to other player	Ball goes to other player	Ball goes to other player	Ball goes to other player	Ball goes to other player	Ball goes to other player

Figure A.14

Ball/block interaction table.

11. Special Case Block-Block Collisions

Note that all block destruction takes one game turn.

Figure A.15 shows that the hot block cools to a normal block. The ice block is destroyed.

Figure A.16 shows that the hot block remains hot. The magnetic block cools to a normal block.

Figure A.17 shows that the target block remains the same. Any other block will vanish through the exit.

Figure A.18 shows that the wormhole block becomes a normal block. Any other block will vanish through to the other player.

Figure A.19 shows that the acid block remains the same. The other block dissolves in the same amount of time that it takes the crumbling block to crumble.

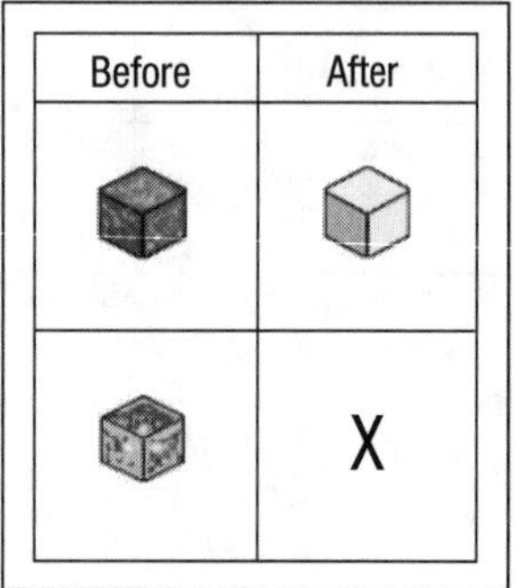

Figure A.15
Hot block and ice block.

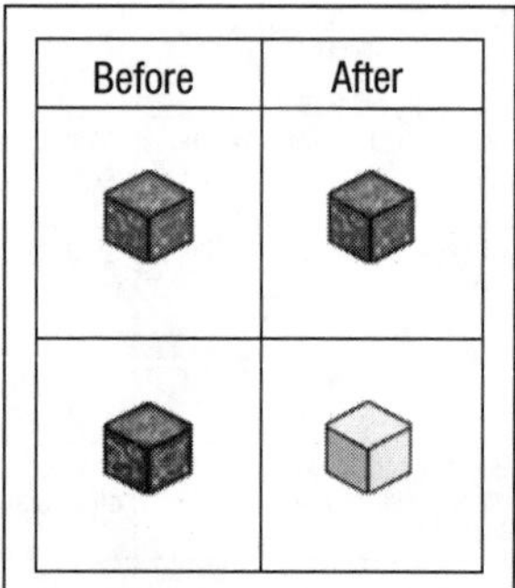

Figure A.16
Hot block and magnetic block.

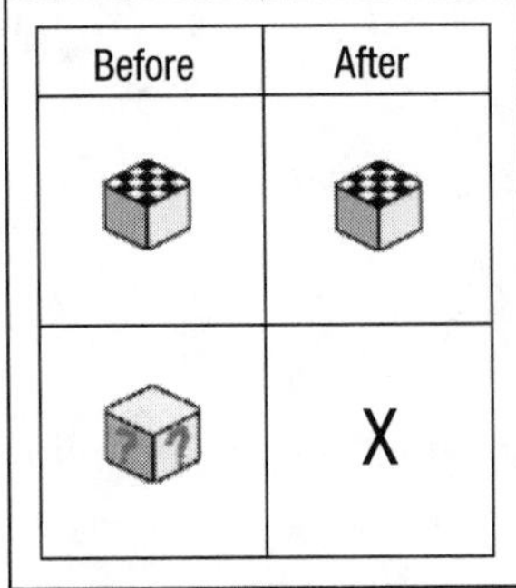

Figure A.17
Any block falling on target block.

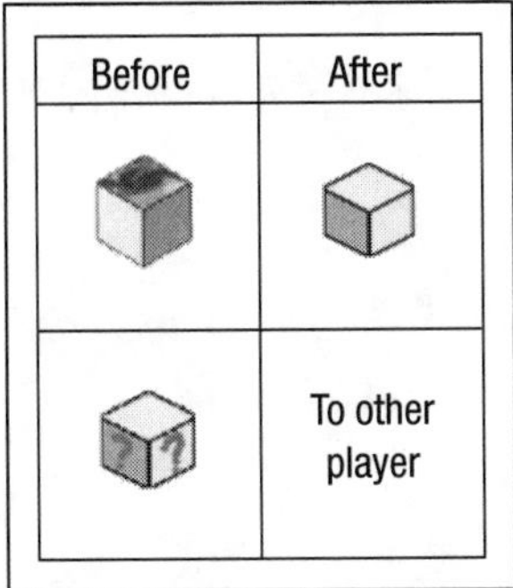

Figure A.18
Any block falling on wormhole block.

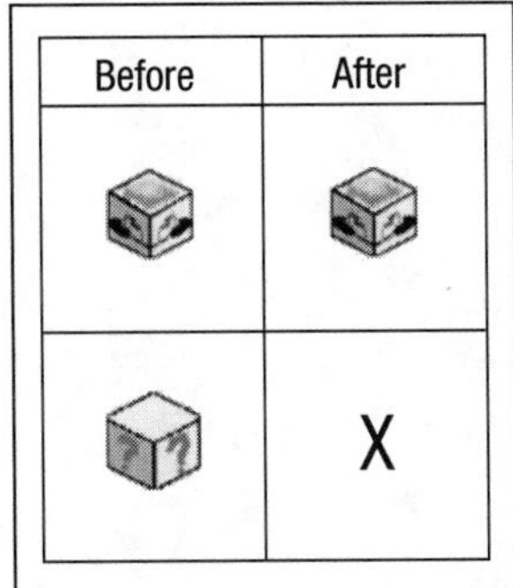

Figure A.19
Any block falling on acid block.

Figure A.20 shows that any block that isn't destroyed by the fall activates the push-button switch and leaves it activated.

Figure A.21 shows that the crumbling block keeps the push-button switch pressed until it disintegrates.

Figure A.22 shows that the ramp is destroyed by the falling block.

If any block falls on a ball, then the ball is destroyed in that game tick. In the following game tick, the block/block interaction is resolved.

12. Playing The Game

This section discusses the gameplay of both the strategic and the action gameplay modes.

Strategic Game

In the 5×5×5 level shown in Figure A.23, the player has three balls to play: a normal ball, a balloon ball, and a glass ball.

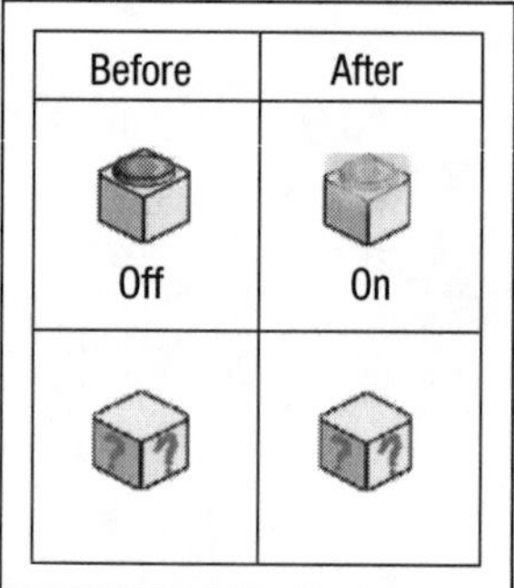

Figure A.20
Any block (except crumbling block) falling on push-button block.

Before	During	After
Off	On	Off
		X

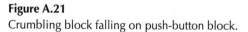

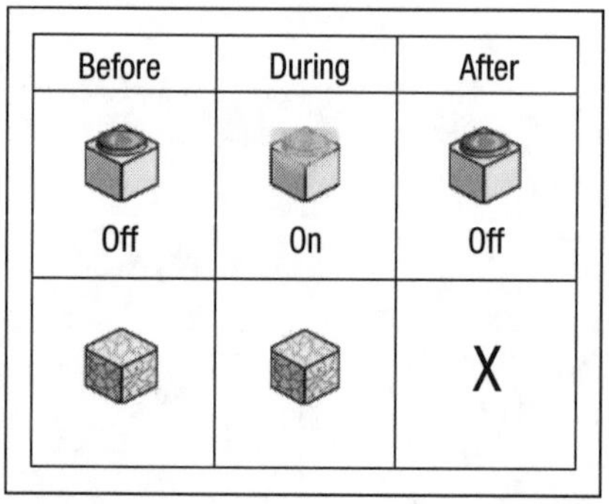

Figure A.21
Crumbling block falling on push-button block.

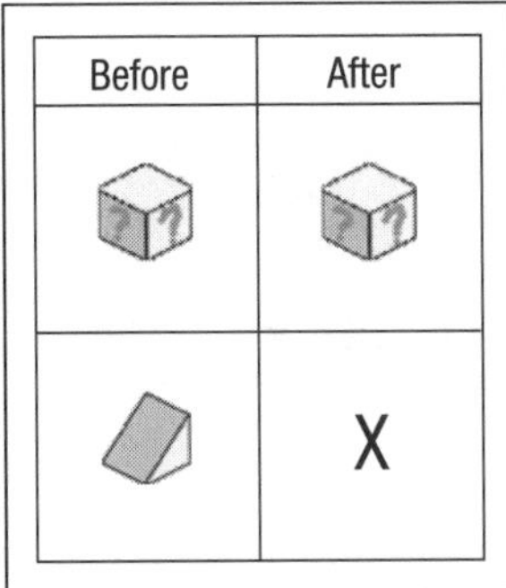

Figure A.22
Any block falling on ramp block.

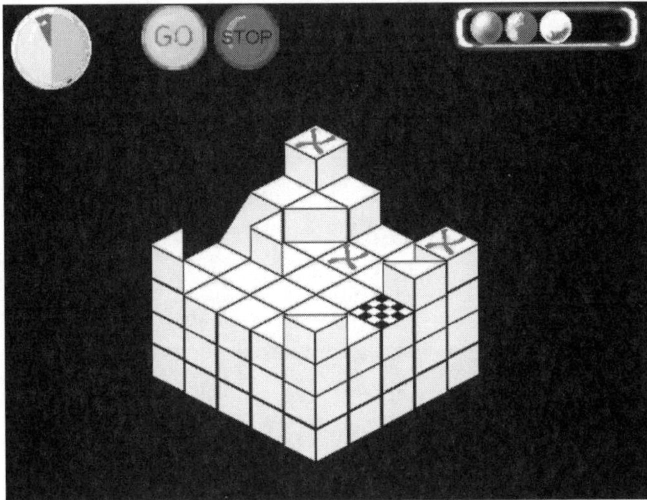

Figure A.23
A conceptual screen shot.

The objective of the level is to get all three balls in the exit. This screenshot shows only the format of the levels; it is not representative of in-game graphics. This is similar to one of the views in the level editor.

While you think about the ball placement, a timer ticks down, limiting your thinking time. Clicking on a ball will take it, and you can then place it on a starting cross. Arrows will appear for the starting directions available (if any). Choose one with the mouse. You can change your mind about the placement of any ball by clicking on it again. You can also delay the release of a ball using a timer attached to the starting square.

Once you have placed all the balls, click on the Go button to start the balls rolling.

The level finishes when the level objectives are complete, or, in the case of fuzzy objectives, when the last ball has gone, the Stop button is pressed, or a timer runs out.

When the level has finished, you get the option to retry or go onto the next one if you completed the level objectives.

Examples of objectives are:

- Get all the balls to the exit.
- Get at least six balls to the exit. This could be timed.
- Get the balloon ball to the exit.
- Get the balls to the exit in a certain order.

Level-Based Action Game

The incoming balls in the level shown in Figure A.24 are a hot ball and a snow ball.

The incoming blocks are a redirection block, an ice block, and another redirection block.

The objective for this level is to get both balls to the exit. Any other result is a failure condition.

The level starts when a hot ball falls in at arrow A.

The hot ball is propelled around by the arrows and strikes the ice block, B, which melts.

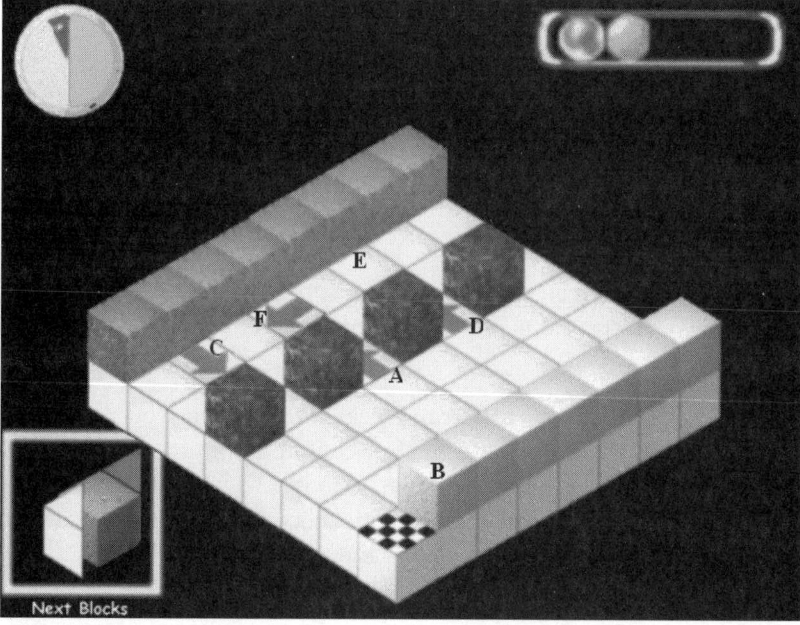

Figure A.24
A conceptual screen shot.

The ball bounces back from the melted block and is reflected back the same way by the arrow block C. If this is allowed to continue, it will fall off the edge.

While this is happening, a redirection block falls in, which must be placed where block B used to be and oriented so as to deflect the incoming hot ball into the target zone.

Next, a snow ball drops at arrow D, and an ice block falls in. The ice block must be used to quickly neutralize hot block E before the snow ball reaches it.

Finally, a redirection block falls, which must be used to redirect the snow ball towards arrow F.

This is a fairly simple level that would appear quite early on, after the introduction and tutorial levels. Each ball uses only one of the incoming blocks, and each is used only once.

13. Further Embellishments

Although *Balls!* is designed to have a straightforward implementation on as many platforms as possible, various ideas could be applied to the game to spruce up the appearance.

The decision whether to do this depends on the sort of impression the game is meant to give. The design, as described so far, is aimed at producing a *Tetris*-style game—that is, abstract but recognizable. This perfectly valid approach has advantages as well as drawbacks. The key advantage is that there is nothing getting in the way of the gameplay, but it means that the gameplay has to be perfect. The key disadvantage is that it may be considered too spartan for magazine reviewers. (Most game players probably wouldn't care, but, unfortunately, the state of the industry is that reviewers mainly ignore gameplay if the product isn't graphically and sonically showy, and good reviews mean good sales no matter how well it plays.) Increasingly, however, graphics also have to be damn good, especially with the advent of 3D cards. There really is no excuse anymore.

Lemmings is an example of a game in which embellishments worked well. I think that a similar style of approach should be taken here.

Every fifth level could be a special level that will provide light relief.

I have two ideas for this. The first is that additional tasks have to be completed in order to get a graphical reward. This is the more complicated option. A simpler option would be to replace the balls with special objects, such as small furry animals, cars, sports balls, and so on.

As an example for the first option, some embellishments could be:

- Growing some flowers
- Turning an Archimedian screw
- Boots kicking something
- Hammers hitting something

- Sending a message to aliens
- Building space rockets and launching them
- Rescuing a kitten from a tree
- Setting off a flock of birds
- Disturbing a hive of bees
- Making a sandwich
- Building a dog kennel for a puppy
- Causing or preventing nuclear holocaust
- Baking a cake
- Choosing between Heaven and Hell for a departed soul
- Milking a cow
- Ringing a bell
- Opening or closing a book
- Lighting a candle
- Exorcising a ghost
- Rescuing a test beagle
- Squashing a goose-stepping dictator
- Releasing some balloons
- Hatching an egg
- Setting off fireworks

If an event requires more than one action to trigger it, then the previous levels should give the player a warmup for what is expected.

For example, the case of an exorcism requires a bell, a book, and a candle, and the levels could progressively build up to this exorcism in the following manner:

- Level **(*n*-3)** Ring a bell.
- Level **(*n*-2)** Open a book.
- Level **(*n*-1)** Light a candle.
- Level **(*n*)** Exorcise a ghost.

I'll briefly explain how some of these ideas could be implemented.

The First Option

This is the more detailed option, with special bonus functionality built into the levels. Here are some examples.

- *Contacting aliens*—There would be five Tannoy-style loudspeakers arrayed around the screen, with switches linked to them. The object of the level is to get the balls to activate the switches in the correct order to play the five-note alien contact message from *Close Encounters*, and get them all into the exit. If the message is correct, a UFO flies down and buzzes around the screen before landing. The occupant (a gray) will get out, wave at you, and then get back in and fly off.
- *Baking a cake*—This level presents a system of delivering ingredients (custard, sugar, chocolate, butter, and cream) down a ramp into a cooking bowl. The ingredients are placed on top of crumbling blocks, and, when the blocks are destroyed, the ingredients fall onto directional blocks that propel them into the bowl. The catch is to avoid losing balls in the same way. If you succeed in baking a cake without losing any balls then you get to see the cake rise.
- *Rescuing a kitten*—A kitten crawls around the level chasing after the balls. Avoid crushing the kitten and keep it safe. If possible, lead it to a cushion so it can fall asleep.

The Second Option

For the second option, replacement graphics for the balls could be rewards for every tenth level. This would require much less work than the first option and would be more suitable for multiplatform release.

Some examples could be:

- Sports balls
- Small furry animals
- Alcohol (bottles and cans)
- Cars
- Cakes
- Vegetables
- Insects
- Planets
- Ghosts and monsters
- Fruit
- Lemmings
- Wild West
- Robots

- 1950s Sci-Fi
- Fish
- Types of cheese
- Livestock
- Rodents in "hamster-balls"

Initial Treatments And Sample Designs

Two design documents are presented here in some detail as examples.

Racketeers is a treatment, not a full game design. The purpose of the document is to present the concept in broad outline so that a decision can be made to put it into development. Consequently, you will see that not all aspects of the game are covered in rigorous detail: instead, the aim is to convey the feel of what the game will be like. The next step after this is to produce a full gameplay specification to the template shown in Chapter 2.

Liberator illustrates the point at which the design gives rise to the software plan. With the gameplay spec written, the development is mapped out in terms of the soft architecture. This is an example of an initial treatment document for a simple game. This shows that the initial treatment is just a very simple document, almost a brochure that sums up the basic idea behind the game. A good way of picturing what to write in an initial treatment is to imagine that it is the introductory section of the game manual—the part that explains how the game is played, but with a bit more detail thrown in for good measure.

After these are complete, it is possible to prepare initial versions of the tier documents that will guide phased development. And then the coding starts.

Racketeers: Gang Warfare In The Roaring Twenties

High-contrast monochrome evokes the classic images of film noir.

Rain-soaked streets reflect streetlamps in blurred pools of light, breaking up as car tires skid across them with the damp hiss of rubber on wet asphalt. The sultry, smoky sounds of a sax playing jazz somewhere in a bar down the street is interrupted by the blare of a Duesenberg horn. There is the squeal of brakes and the staccato rattle of Tommy-gun fire…

Once again, the mobs are at each others' throats, and honest citizens had better run for cover.

1. Overview

In this networkable realtime game set in Chicago during the Prohibition, players are gang bosses who must build up their district of the city while fighting off rival gangs. There is more than one route to victory, as players can either attempt to rub out the opposition or else manage their part of the city so well that they can buy police protection and go legit.

Everything takes place on a scrolling isometric view of the city. The city is divided into districts of a few blocks each. Some districts contain recognizable landmarks and are worth extra respect or confer other benefits. For example, if you control the district containing City Hall, you can bribe the mayor.

Slum districts that contain no useful resources or locations are not entirely without value. Gangs can meet there to parlay or trade.

You begin with just a small group of "foot soldiers" whom you have to assign to various tasks: collecting protection money, running numbers, transporting hooch, standing watch, and so on. These characters are given a name and get better at their jobs over time. Sources of income are smuggling, speakeasies, gambling, protection money, and blackmail. As you get more money, you can equip your men with Tommy guns, bulletproof vests, cars, and so on.

The more-experienced fighters in your gang are the "wise guys." They can patrol your district, or launch attacks on rivals: drive-by shootings through barbershop windows, robbing banks, and so forth.

Civilians populate the city, with the number in each district representing the number of people living there (though obviously not on a 1:1 scale). You enlarge your gang by recruiting from the pool of civilians. It's also possible to send one of your gangsters into another district where he will pose as a civilian. He might then be recruited by the rival player and can rise in his gang until the time when it suits you to reactivate him as your own man.

The game runs in realtime. And, because it takes place within one city, the time scale and rate of incidents is much more credible than in, say, *Warcraft* where a farm can be built in the same time it takes a knight to kill an ogre. Given the scale of *Racketeers*, it's perfectly reasonable that I might drive across town to join in a gun battle that's raging between two other players. (Note, however, that although I can scroll my view right across the city at any time, I get a view of people who are there only if I have one of my own men in my line of sight. This means you need to keep spies out on the streets or you might end up driving straight into an ambush.)

Success in *Racketeers* calls for subtlety. This is because the districts you are fighting to control are also the source of your revenue. It's no use wresting a district away from another gang boss if it gets so shot up in the process that people move out and the place becomes a slum.

This factor imposes a pace on the game that allows for a more considered strategy than in most sudden-death, realtime games. Information and communication with other players is handled via your desk icons, which include a telephone, newspapers, and in-and-out trays to raise matters requiring your attention. You can also call up dossier files on key city figures whom you may have bribed or blackmailed, to remind you of your influence over them.

Building up your district's economy and dealing ruthlessly with your foes increases your respect until you get the chance to bribe major city figures like the mayor and the chief of police. This in turn allows you to further expand your economy (for instance by disregarding planning laws) and to commit crimes with greater impunity.

The game thus comprises constant action and decision making as you launch attacks on rival districts (both to inflict damage and steal money), fight off enemy attacks, build up your own district's buildings and economy, hire and train new gang members, and deal with "crisis management" matters—fires, police raids, petty crime, and petitions from residents who look to you as their Godfather.

2. Game Objectives

As gang boss, your aim will be to expand your territory and strengthen your gang. Your ultimate objective is to take over all the districts of the city, either by forcing rival gangs to submit to your authority or by destroying them and moving in to take over their territory. Whether this calls for violence or a gradual choking off of their economy is up to you. But remember that a cornered boss is a dangerous boss.

The City Mode view (see 3: Graphics) shows the gradual spread (or otherwise) of your territory. As you gain more districts, you will be able to increase your stock of the three primary resources: money, respect, and influence.

Money

Money is needed to recruit and equip new gang members and to acquire upgrades in weaponry, and so forth. Money also enables you to set up service locations (such as bars and diners) that will draw in more revenue. Just as importantly, it can be used for bribes.

Money can be used to buy respect by various means, ranging from buying fine works of art, dressing your gang in sharp suits, or throwing big parties. In all cases, the transaction is quite costly: this isn't an efficient way to gain respect, but it may be useful in a crisis.

Money is generated by civilians, whom you can get to part with it in two ways. The best long-term option is to set up shopkeepers, bar owners, and the like who will draw civilians into your territory to spend their wages. Alternatively, if you need money in a hurry, you can always get your gang members to mug passing civilians, the downside being that this lowers respect.

Money is collected from shops by numbers runners and stored at your townhouse.

Respect

Respect is all-important to a gang boss. Respect is gained by:

- Acquiring districts
- Ruthlessly wiping out rivals
- Negotiating successfully
- Fighting or bribing the cops

- Hiring special freelancers
- Improving the quality of your own districts

Respect is vital because it entitles you to more-experienced gang members (the wise guys). If your respect drops, wise guys whom you're no longer eligible to command will start to drift away.

Computer players respond to respect—as do the cops, to a lesser extent. A gang that has been weakened in battle is instant prey to its neighbors if the boss's respect is low; if his respect is high, they might be more wary. Respect can sometimes be all the defense you need. At the very least, it will buy you time.

Influence

By bribery and blackmail, you can get a grip on key city figures, extending your influence, which in turn helps when exerting respect or spending money.

Influence is made possible by seizing control of key districts. Money must then be set aside for bribes, which are akin to an investment that can be called in later. For example, if some of your gang are arrested, it is possible to get them released from custody. Alternatively, you can get a similar effect using blackmail, which costs respect instead of money.

The downside of bribes is that, when things are going badly, city officials will tend to forget all those favors you did them, whereas blackmail never loses its effectiveness.

3. Graphics

The view is isometric and peopled with 3D figures. Display is 640×480 or 320×200.

Visually, *Racketeers* will be very close to black-and-white. Sepia tints are used to identify different gangs, but, other than that, the game will derive its look primarily from old black-and-white gangster movies like *Little Caesar*. A few scenes will make use of color, but even then only in the form of monochrome—hot yellow for a mob leader's desk lamp, cold blue tints for impending violence, a momentary wash of red when a gangster is killed.

The game is controlled through three screens: City, District and Block views.

City View

This is used between levels, comprising a 2D plan view of Chicago (not to scale). Districts are shown as distinct regions, the color of each district indicating which gang controls it. Districts known to be neutral are shown as gray, and districts the player has no knowledge of are shown as white.

In this view, the player can scroll across the city examining available intelligence regarding each district. The player can always see the resources in a neighboring district or one that he has previously controlled. Details as to which gang inhabits a district—and how strong they may be—is a function of distance from the player's own territory.

Special information about other districts can sometimes be acquired during a level (either by sending out torpedo characters or by interrogating captured enemies) and this updates the city view map.

City view gives access to the following actions:

- Load/save
- Game settings
- Send a message
- Trade resources and prisoners
- Change standing orders in your controlled districts
- Make a bribe
- Zoom to localized view (District view)

The City view is equivalent to the global maps shown between levels in games such as *Warcraft* and *Command & Conquer*, with the difference being that the map changes as a result of the player's success or failure in successive missions. This means that the full campaign version of *Racketeers* has a long-term strategic element.

District View

This view is used to examine a district in detail. It is an isometric view that is derived from the engine used for tactical encounters in Block view, but sufficiently zoomed out so that you can see the entire district.

In this view, you can distinguish your own gangsters from the enemy (by their color) but not individual gang member types. District view is for strategic organization: getting your gang members to the right place, either to intercept or ambush enemy gangsters, to establish a good defensive layout, or launch a raid into a neighboring district.

Specific locations, resources, and traps (when known to the player) will be visible in District view. As in City view, the player can adjust the game settings from here. Additionally, he can do any of the following:

- Move grouped characters
- Observe freelancers and intruders
- Issue standing orders
- Assign resources
- Pay for repairs
- Activate locations

Again drawing an analogy with *Command & Conquer*-type games, District view is like the top-down view of an entire level. However, instead of being visible at the side of the screen like a radar map as in C&C, the player flips between District and Block views as required.

Block View

This is the close-up, overhead, isometric view used for combat and other detailed orders. Distinct character types can be identified. It is possible to scroll across the whole district in Block view, or you can move more quickly by switching to District view and clicking where you want to see. Remember that you cannot see enemy characters, even on your own territory, unless you have one of your own characters in line of sight.

Commands possible in Block view include:

- Recruit a civilian into your gang
- Group a number of gangsters
- Assign a lieutenant to oversee a group
- Give orders to individual gangsters

In Block view, the player can take direct control of individual gangsters. Control is via a point-and-click interface. This enables you to order hits, raids, patrols, ambushes, bribes, and so on.

Only a group of gangsters led by a smart lieutenant (see 6: Personality) or the boss himself can get from street to street by going through a building. Fights never take place inside a building (the rival gangsters move outside first), so the player does not need to be able to see inside buildings.

A single keystroke zooms between District and Block views so that players can keep an eye on the big picture even in the thick of battle. Note that what is shown on both views is only what the player's gang members and controlled civilians are able to see.

4. Playing A Game

In each level, you must establish a new operation in a district. Your opponents will typically be rival gang bosses who also want control of the district. You must capture the enemy boss to win the level. In some cases, you may have special objectives such as:

- Gain a set amount of respect
- Assassinate a key character
- Establish a set number of businesses
- Find a character
- Bribe or otherwise deal with the cops

When a level is complete, you gain undisputed control of the district, which now appears in your color on the City view. You can assign standing orders for the district (whether to maximize economy, defense, or whatever) before proceeding to the next level.

Each level is played out in realtime. However, the campaign game that links the levels is effectively a turn-based one because you receive income for all your districts at the completion of a level, no matter how long you had taken to play through that level.

The campaign structure is very freeform. You have the whole of Chicago gangland to rule—and no time limit. Events are not highly structured and predetermined (the way levels are in a C&C campaign, for instance). Instead, the outcome of every district battle really does change the face of the city map.

To keep things unpredictable, special events such as interference by cops will be triggered by specific milestones in the development of your gang. A tycoon might hire the gang to launch a raid on a rival. A federal agent might enter the district and infiltrate your gang. A series of arrests might decimate the top gangs, leaving a power vacuum that must be swiftly exploited.

A nonlinear, semirandom system will be in place to govern these events. This ensures no two campaign games are ever the same.

5. Character Types

The population of the city is represented by civilians controlled by simple rule-based routines. For example, civilians spend money at joints you control, so it's useful when they stick around. But they avoid streets where there are signs of blood (left after a fight) so even successfully resisting a raid on your district could still result in the civilians being scared off.

Characters are of two types: those under a player's direct control (collectively termed gangsters) and those controlled by the game AI (for example, civilians and cops).

Gangsters are further divided into fighters, whom the player controls most of the time, and nonfighters, who are usually assigned a task and then left to carry on with it until the player has a different use for them.

The gangsters who will occupy most of your attention are the fighters. However, support-function gang members are also important. These are the guys whom you assign to a garage to keep your car tuned up or to a lab to concoct drugs. More about them later.

Recruitment

You recruit gangsters from the civilian population by clicking on a location and choosing from the recruiting options available. Different character types are recruited at different locations. The cost (in money and sometimes also respect) depends on the character type. Then click on the civilian you want to convert. Usually the civilian must be in your district to qualify for conversion; an exception is provided by grifters. (See below.)

Experience Levels

Newly recruited combatant gangsters are called *foot soldiers*. After a few successful fights, they progress to *wise guys*. Wise guys are tougher than foot soldiers, so it's generally true that a wise guy of any type will beat a foot soldier of any type in a straight fight.

Gangsters

The fighters in your gang fall into three subtypes: *goons*, *vamps*, and *torpedoes*. In general, goons will beat vamps in a straight fight but are easily picked off by torpedoes, whereas vamps can generally finish off torpedoes before the latter can do much damage. There is no single "best" gangster type, although different missions may call for different specializations.

Goon (Fighter)

Goons are very tough. Newly recruited goons fight with fists, and the wise guys wield iron pipes. Goons are slow moving. They are the strongest character type in close combat, with plenty of hit points and the ability to inflict serious damage with each blow.

Appearance: Goons are big lugs who barely seem to fit inside their suits.

Vamp (Fighter)

Vamps are swift and vicious, but not as strong as goons. They are equipped with flick knives when first recruited, but acquire long stilettos when experienced. Vamps are fast on their feet, but their hit points and close-combat ability are average. They are the most vicious gangster type and can be ordered to kill an incapacitated opponent. (Other character types will ignore a foe once he's down.)

Appearance: Vamps are long-legged dames in sweeping coats and fedoras.

Torpedo (Fighter)

Torpedoes are stealthy and can climb walls, travel underground, and vanish into the shadows. They are able to use ranged weapons: newly recruited torpedoes are armed with handguns, later acquiring heaters (Tommy guns). They can move over light obstacles, like fences, that block other characters. Normally they appear as civilians to other players, but, if the torpedo attacks, then the disguise is lost and not regained until the torpedo moves out of sight range of all rival gang members.

Appearance: Torpedoes are thin, slinking characters dressed entirely in black and wearing shades.

Worker (Nonfighter)

Workers are the guys who drive your trucks or perform other menial tasks that would offend a gangster's sense of personal honor. Assign a worker to a distillery to have him deliver hooch to your speakeasies, for example.

Boss (Fighter)

Each player begins a level with a single boss character. If he is killed, you've lost!

Grifters (Nonfighter)

Grifters are useful for bringing in new gang members. You can recruit any civilian that the grifter is adjacent to, whereas normally you can only recruit a civilian if he's in your own district. This means that a single grifter on enemy territory can suddenly recruit a gang. For this reason, grifters are not openly tolerated, and, by common consent, they can be killed without any comeback if caught off their home territory. Grifters' other function is a vector for in-level bribes. (See Cops, below.)

Mechanic (Nonfighter)

Mechanics are useless in a fight but are nonetheless valued members of the gang because of their ability to build weapons and traps, repair vehicles, and operate radios. Like fighters, mechanics also have experience levels that are gained over time. Mechanics can be assigned to a location (workshop, distillery, townhouse, or garage). This enhances the standard functions of that location and gives the player access to additional special functions if the geek is of a high-enough level. They can also be sent out to do repairs in the field and to place traps.

Numbers Runner (Fighter)

Numbers runners are street kids who collect the money generated at your locations and bring it to your headquarters. So it is worth robbing rival numbers runners, but this isn't easy because they are fast on their feet. You don't have to give orders to numbers runners, because they automatically collect your earnings if given no other instructions. Numbers runners are restricted to the use of catapults and thrown bottles in a fight. Thus, they are of nuisance value only.

Freelancer (Fighter)

Freelancers appear from time to time when you've "made your bones," that is, earned enough respect. These are guys who are expensive to hire but are very fast and tough—and so useful for hitting other players' gangs. They operate alone: you pay them, send them into a rival district, and there they will sabotage and murder on your behalf until eliminated or bribed to switch sides.

Freelancers are personalities who (if they survive) will soon build up a history and reputation. For example: Pedro Los Alamos, who uses dynamite; Harry Kiri, a ninja whom enemy players will find hard to spot; Big Ben Blighty, an English gent who fights with a sword cane; and Flavia Van Flamme, a lady arsonist who'll burn down buildings in a rival's district.

A big advantage of the freelancer is that, unlike most regular gang members, they will still attack an enemy who is down. (This makes a kill much more likely.) The downside is that freelancers have zero loyalty and are greedy. Make sure you're offering more than the opposition, or you might find the freelancer turning on you when the going gets tough.

Undertaker (Nonfighter)

Undertakers are the lowliest of gangsters—wretched individuals who work constantly to clean away bloodstains and cart off dead bodies that would otherwise upset your civilians.

Non-Gang Members

Civilian (Nonfighter)

Civilians form the recruitment pool for your gang as well as generating wealth for your districts. Violence and overly squalid conditions will drive them out of a district; amenities and a sense of security will bring them in. You do not issue orders to civilians. They are autonomous characters that behave according to simple AI rules.

Beware of enemy torpedoes in your district who appear as civilians until they attack.

Associate (Nonfighter)

A civilian can be temporarily converted into an associate by spending money. The associate continues to act like any other civilian and still isn't under your control, but now you get to see what is going on around him in the "fog of war," just as you can with your controlled characters. This represents the fact that the associate is constantly passing gossip on to your gang. The range of vision that you get from the associate is a function of your respect score.

An enemy torpedo will happily accept payment to work as your associate. The difference being that his reports will be calculated to mislead, so you won't see any characters from his own gang unless one of your other units can also see them.

Shopkeeper (Nonfighter)

Shopkeeper is a generic term for the individuals who manage service locations (like bars, casinos, and flophouses). (See also the section on Economy.)

Shopkeepers are spawned when a new business is set up. Usually this happens when a gang boss pays to get the business started, but sometimes businesses spring up of their own accord. Either way, the shopkeeper is not a gangster and is not under any player's direct control. He is there to attract business—and hence cash—and the gang boss is then free to take as much or as little of that cash as he wants.

Shopkeepers are therefore very important characters. They are the medium by which you extract cash from the civilians on your streets.

Cop (Fighter)

The cops are autonomous characters under the control of a computer player. Their aim is to locate and close down illegal operations. Cops remember specific grudges against gangs who have defied them, and they will deal more harshly with those gangs in future. Attacking cops earns a player hefty respect, but it is rarely worthwhile because it lessens the effectiveness of bribes and blackmail.

After a fight, cops pick up fallen gangsters and carry them off for a spell in prison. If the gangster survives, he will eventually be released and can rejoin your gang.

Bribing the chief of police is expensive but means you will get a lot less interference from cops at all times. Additionally, if you have a bribe in place, you can:

- Get the lowdown on other districts.
- Buy "insurance." (The cops step in if you're attacked.)
- Ask the cops to put pressure on a rival gang.

It is also possible to bribe individual cops on the spot by moving a grifter up to them and spending money on a short-term bribe. The cop will then turn a blind eye to your activities for a while. This requires a little more management to get right, because you have to keep an eye out for cops, but it can be more cost effective than a blanket bribe.

Petty Criminals (Nonfighters)

Petty criminals are spawned as a small proportion of the population of a district and will prey on civilians and shopkeepers. If left unchecked, they can drive businesses out of the district and lower people's respect for you. Petty criminals look just like ordinary civilians most of the time. If you can catch them, a threat from a goon is usually enough to revert them to obedient civilian status. Alternatively, they can be recruited into your gang as grifters.

6. Personality

(The personality rules are the least certain aspect of the design. Although innovative, it is not certain that they will enhance the gameplay experience. Therefore, take care to treat this as a particularly speculative area of the design that will need to be subjected to playtesting.)

Personalities are defined by one aspect of behavior in which the gangster performs well. In other ways, that gangster will have some randomness to his behavior. So a fearless gangster will march right through a hail of gunfire but might not always do exactly what you told him.

Personality traits are:

- **Fearless** The gangster has no regard for danger. (Other gangsters sometimes panic.)
- **Reliable** The gangster sticks closely to the last orders you gave him. (Other gangsters gradually forget or "improvise" orders over time.)
- **Smart** The gangster can get from street to street by going through buildings. (Other gangsters have to take the long way around.)

You can easily tell a gangster's personality because different attitudes are animated differently. Fearless gangsters walk with a reckless swagger; reliable gangsters walk unhurriedly; smart gangsters stop and look around now and again as if alert to trouble.

Personality traits show up only when a gangster progresses beyond the foot-soldier stage, so you have to make the best of what you get. The personality types are important because much of the time you won't be able to directly control all your gangsters (your attention can't be everywhere at once). They also act continually in realtime based on the last orders you gave them as interpreted by their personality traits. (Of course, if you see a gangster going wrong you can always step in and give him a direct order.)

Delegating Authority

Personality is a big factor in running an efficient gang. You need reliable guys in the key positions. Becoming the "Capo di tutti i Capi" will take more than ruthlessness and cunning; you need to be a good organizer, too. As your gang gets bigger, you have to break it down into manageable units. You might become immersed in running one of these groups and you want to be sure that the others won't get themselves into trouble in the meantime. This is where delegation comes in.

The gangster you put in charge of each group is the lieutenant for that group. He will impose his personal stamp on the men under him there. Appointing a fearless lieutenant means you can expect to see that mob being led into frequent hair-raising situations. A smart lieutenant can lead his whole mob through buildings, and so on.

Because the lieutenants have their own personalities, you can (if you wish) just decide overall strategy and then sit back and watch what they do. But don't be surprised if you find you constantly have to intervene to salvage a situation. That's why you're the boss, after all.

For instance, Lefty Field gets bored and, craving excitement, decides to go and get his own back on Tony Baloni who knifed him in a street fight a year ago. This puts Lefty on a murder rap, and you have to pay hefty bribes and lawyer's fees to get him off. Or do you choose to let him rot in jail? He's a good gunman, but maybe your gang can't afford such an unreliable member.

Players who are adept at coping with multiple tasks will optimize manpower resources at high levels, assigning appropriate standing orders to fit each gangster's capabilities. More-focused players will have to restrict themselves to smaller gangs of highly trained and reliable men.

Loyalty

Look after your men. Patch them up after a gun battle, keep them in fighting trim, and buy them a drink now and then. They'll remember favors and good treatment—as well as just punishment—and loyalty will affect how much risk they'll take on your behalf. The longer you leave a gangster unsupervised, the more likely he is to act on his own initiative. This can be a serious problem: he could go over to a rival gang or (worse) become that loose cannon that sparks off a gang war.

You can click on your gang members to get a remark that will give a clue to their loyalty. You can keep loyalty high by rubbing out gang members who run away from a fight or otherwise fail to do their duty. Although this improves overall reliability if applied occasionally, it mustn't be done too often or it has the reverse effect (although it always increases respect).

7. Orders

You can always select a gangster and give him a direct order, but the most efficient way to run your gang is to give standing orders to your lieutenants and allow their individual AI to decide how to implement those orders. Bear in mind that, in the later stages of the game, you will often be fighting on multiple fronts. You will not be able to take hands-on control of all your men all of the time. This is why gang organization, planning, and delegation are critical.

For example, you tell a lieutenant to threaten shopkeepers who have been holding out on you—a simple task requiring only one character (a goon). The lieutenant won't do it in person but will choose the most suitable guy for the job from the people under his command.

Organizational commands are issued by means of your desktop icons, which you can access at your townhouse. These include orders to set up businesses, calls (bribes) to the mayor and chief of police, strategic objectives for your lieutenants to interpret, and so on.

Full details of all the possible commands can wait for the finished spec. Essentially, there are personal commands (such as "go to this point" and "kill this person") and operational commands (such as "collect income" and "clear up dead bodies"). Note that certain character types (numbers runners, undertakers) have default operational commands that apply automatically.

Some examples of personal (direct) commands are:

Torpedo

Move

Attack

Sneak: High stealth, but moves slower

Follow: Trails designated character

Goon

Move

Attack

Guard: Guards character or place; will not move more than fixed distance from them.

Threaten: Extracts money from a civilian or shopkeeper; converts petty criminal to civilian.

Vamp

Move

Attack

Patrol: Moves in a circuit between designated waypoints.

Kill: Takes extra time to finish off a character.

8. Combat

The aim of conflict between the gangs is to establish supremacy. However, the gangster's code of honor means there is a tendency not to pursue violence beyond necessary limits. As with struggles in the animal kingdom, fatalities are rare.

The game purpose of this is to allow gang members a long-enough lifespan that the player sees them as individual personalities as opposed to mere cannon-fodder.

Normally a gangster reduced to zero hit points is just incapacitated. After a time, he or she will recover enough to stagger back to the nearest surgery to get patched up. Only vamps and freelancers will take the time to slit the throat of a fallen foe, and even then you have to tell them to do so.

Deadlier weapons can be obtained if you have enough money and influence. These include grenades, machine guns, armored cars, and Molotov cocktails. The use of any these will very definitely not be ignored by the cops. These weapons do inflict killing damage. Therefore, as the game progresses and the stakes get higher, gang warfare becomes increasingly lethal.

Battles for control of a district will typically involve a dozen or so gangsters on each side. Combat thus become a question of "body-hopping"—you can always maintain complete control of one gangster at a time, but the trick is to keep an eye on what the others are doing, too. As discussed under Section 7: Orders, gangsters don't have to just stand around when you aren't controlling them. You can give standing orders that they'll continue to follow to the best of their AI ability.

A detailed combat system will be included in the full spec. The essence of the system is the paper-scissors-stone relation embodied by the three standard combatant types (goon, vamp, and torpedo). This is the same combined-arms relation that can be traced back to the earliest days of warfare. It can be summed up as: ranged weapons beat slow opponents; fast opponents can catch those with ranged weapons; and stronger opponents are usually slower.

To give some idea of the attributes that might be used in the game:

- **Strength** determines how much damage the gangster inflicts in close combat. Goons have very high strength.

- **Melee skill** is the character's chance of scoring a hit in close combat. Equal for goons and vamps, and lower for torpedoes. Increases with experience.
- **Missile skill** is the character's chance of scoring a hit with a ranged weapon. Modified by target moving, in cover, poor light, and so on. Increases with experience. Goons and vamps lack this ability.
- **Movement** is the character's speed. Vamps are the fastest characters, with the exception of some freelancers.
- **Hits** are the measure of how much damage a character can take. Goons have high hits scores; torpedoes have low hits. Damage reduces a character's hits. The character falls unconscious when his or her hits reach zero. Additionally, taking enough hits in one blow/attack can cause other penalties.

9. The Game World

The city is populated by civilians who form the basis of the economy of a district. Although ruled over by gang bosses, they are not full members of the gang and are not directly controlled by the player. Instead, their behavior is governed by simple AI rules.

The number of civilians in each district represents the number of people living there. You enlarge your gang by recruiting from the civilians. Of course, this means there won't be as many civilians fueling the local economy, so there is a direct tradeoff between manpower and income.

It's also possible to send one of your torpedoes into another district where he will pose as a civilian. He might then be recruited by the rival player and can rise in his gang until the time when it suits you to reactivate him as your own man.

The Economy

Occasionally, shops and other service locations will spring up spontaneously in a district. However, the main impetus to new business comes from the players. Shops attract civilians with money to spend, so that financing a shop is an investment for the controlling player: the shop feeds back into the wealth of the district.

Numerous vacant properties indicate a rundown district, but such a district can still be developed if the gang boss who controls it is prepared to spend the money needed.

The economic subsystem of the game is based on the behavior of the resident civilians. To visualize this system in its simplest form, imagine a number of blocks with (initially) 10 civilians on each. At intervals of maybe five minutes, each civilian acquires his wages and decides what he's going to spend it on by randomly selecting an activity. Having chosen an activity, he looks for a location catering to that activity:

Activity	Location
Drinking	Speakeasy
Gambling	Casino
Eating	Diner
Entertainment	Theatre
Sleeping	Hotel
Pool	Pool Hall
Pray	Church

The attractiveness of a location is a function of:

- **Proximity** Nearby locations are favored over distant ones.
- **Quality** All services are given a random quality level when first established. This tends to increase over time, so a long-established bar is favored over one that hasn't yet built up a reputation.
- **Price** The controlling player sets the price charged at each location. More-expensive services tend to be less attractive to customers than cheaper ones (although, of course, you'll get more cash out of the customers who do go there). (Civilians will reselect an activity and location if their first choice would cost more than they have on them.)

The district in which a service is located also makes a difference:

- **Dilapidation** A locality that is rundown and dirty has less appeal than a prosperous-looking one.
- **Danger** Violence deters honest customers. Bullet holes on the brickwork and blood on the sidewalk act as negative modifiers when a civilian is working out his route. (These gradually fade with time.)
- **Stiffs** Civilians will not enter a street where there's a dead body. If they do come across one, they stop and decide on a new destination. This is why it's worth having undertakers. If there's a dead body on the street, the undertaker will go and collect it. Dealing with a body takes time, however, so there's a limit to how much carnage one undertaker can deal with in a given time.

On arriving at his destination, the civilian spends the cash required for his chosen activity and takes a preset time to complete the activity. Then, if he has any cash left, he chooses another activity, and so on. If a civilian runs out of cash, he will wander the streets, following a random walk with equal choice at each intersection, until the next payday.

Cash spent at the location remains there until collected by your numbers runners or stolen by rival gangsters.

The idea behind the economic system is that the more service locations you can provide, the more certain you are that civilians will spend their wages at those locations.

Prices

The price charged by a service location can be low, standard, or high. You decide this for any service location you control. (Naturally, the standard price varies according to the type of service on offer. A shot of whisky is more expensive than a game of pool, and so on.) As well as setting prices, you also set the proportion that you skim off the top. This is the cash that goes into your reserves. Be careful: if you're too greedy, you may drive out the shopkeepers.

New Businesses

The game starts with some businesses already in place. As a boss, you can spend money to set a shopkeeper up in business, the idea being that you'll eventually make that back by your cut of the profits. Also, shopkeepers will sometimes move into your district and set up on their own initiative (more on that below).

You cannot place a new business just anywhere. Only certain locations (two or three on each block, say) are eligible to be turned into service locations.

Migration Of Business

Each week a shopkeeper compares his takings with the average for the same business on neighboring blocks. He'll move (leaving a boarded-up vacant site behind) if he sees an advantage, that is, if the average in all adjacent districts is higher. However, if a shopkeeper in the wealthier district is also deciding to move, the first shopkeeper closes down altogether. In theory, a cascade of this type can lead to economic depression.

One way to deter migration of businesses out of your districts is to shoot shopkeepers as soon as they try to pack up and move out. You still lose the shop, but other shopkeepers will get the message that it's not a good idea to move. Their memory of this decays over time.

New Civilians

If a civilian is killed, a new one is spawned after a random interval. The chance of the new civilian appearing on any given block is a function of its population relative to other blocks.

10. Joints

Each district contains a number of vacant locations that can be used to start a shop or other business. The generic term for an active location is a *joint*. To set up a new joint, move your boss to a vacant location, choose the Start Business option, and spend the money required.

Joints can be suppliers, outlets, or both. Suppliers enable other locations to function. For example, a distillery is needed in order for a speakeasy to operate. Some suppliers provide direct support for your gang rather than enabling outlets. For instance, a garage supplies and maintains automobiles for your gang.

Outlets generate money when civilians visit them, and your numbers runners will collect it and bring it to your townhouse. However, it is also possible for rival gangs to lean on your shopkeepers and force them to pay protection money—or they might burn the joint down. Consequently, you should assign some of your gangsters to patrol areas in which you have joints.

Illegal joints often generate more money than legitimate shops and services. However, do not place too many illegal operations too close together as this tends to drive out honest citizens.

The key to generating money first lies in maintaining a steady flow of goods between your suppliers and your outlets without interruption by police, rival gangs, or treacherous employees. Secondly, you must make sure the money generated at the outlets is returned to your townhouse.

Graphically, it's likely that joints will just be shown as exteriors, so as to avoid having to switch views to look inside a location. Anyone at the joint would then be shown standing outside. An alternative is to cut away the wall of a joint when the player selects it, allowing him to see inside. This would be better from a stylistic point of view, but it has the drawback that the player can't see inside without specifically selecting the joint.

Joints include:

Clinic

Advantages: Injured gang members can be patched up here, getting them back into action faster. A worker assigned to the clinic will go out and carry back any of your gangsters who are lying wounded on the streets.

Disadvantages: A good doctor costs money.

Accountant

Advantages: Increases your income; gives useful advice.

Disadvantages: An obvious target for rivals.

Garage

Advantages: Allows you to buy and repair automobiles (one per garage).

Disadvantages: You need a mechanic, and repairs cost money.

Chemist

Advantages: Helps when distilling hooch; can manufacture incendiaries; increases the efficiency of the clinic.

Disadvantages: Expensive to maintain; frequently raided by cops.

Pizza Parlor

Advantages: Keeps gang members happy and loyal; provides some income.

Disadvantages: A common target for rival gangs.

Gambling Den

Advantages: A source of income.

Disadvantages: Gambling debts act as a spur to petty crime.

Speakeasy

Advantages: Prohibition means that there's no shortage of customers. Also, send your gangsters here to make them fearless for a limited period.

Disadvantages: With so much strong liquor being consumed, you need reliable enforcers to keep the peace.

Distillery

Advantages: More convenient than smuggling in hooch from out of town.

Disadvantages: A prime target for police raids; disloyal gang members may "skim off the top" by diverting supplies to your rivals.

Tailor

Advantages: Maintains respect. (A boss and his men must always be smartly dressed.)

Disadvantages: A tailor gets to know many of his patrons' secrets. (All players can see whatever is in a tailor's line of sight.)

Townhouse

This is where the boss lives.

Advantages: You have to have a base to coordinate your entire operation. The boss character has to be at this location before you can access your desk screen. Send your gangsters here to make them reliable for a time.

Disadvantages: It's a fine line between being accessible and being vulnerable.

Barbershop

Advantages Maintains respect; provides some income.

Disadvantages: The most common target for drive-by shootings.

Gym

Advantages: Helps keep gang members in shape; boxing matches provide entertainment.

Disadvantages: Grudges can form between your gang members while sparring. (Sometimes a gang member will have to go to clinic.)

Cinema

Advantages: Provides entertainment when gangsters are bored, thus maintaining loyalty.

Disadvantages: Watching too many gangster flicks will give your boys a taste for the high life.

Hotel

Advantages: A good place to get blackmail info on a public figure.

Disadvantages: Hotels in a district can lose a lot of money if you don't make sure the district is a place worth visiting.

Church

Players have no control over the placement of churches, of course, and no way of closing them down. They represent an authority that the intelligent player will learn to coexist with. Churches provide neutral territory where you can go to meet other players and make alliances (or issue threats, or exact tribute).

Advantages: A priest is vital to keep the citizens of your district happy.

Disadvantages: Time spent in church is time that the civilian isn't spending in your joints.

Nightclub

Advantages: Generates a good income.

Disadvantages: Club singers are often police informers.

Shops

Small shops of various types.

Advantages: Provide income; also some special advantages. (For example, a laundry cleans telltale bloodstains off gangsters' clothes.)

Disadvantages: Shopkeepers will leave the district if it becomes rundown or they perceive it to be unsafe.

Offices

Ordinary businesses of various types.

Advantages: Legitimate businesses allow the laundering of money from other sources, decreasing the chance of criminal charges against you.

Disadvantages: Businessmen must make a profit or they will leave the area.

11. Messages

Messages can be sent to other gangs while in City view. You can also send text messages to other human players. For interaction with computer players, and when interplayer communication needs to be swift, several message templates are available.

Offer Tribute

You send money to the other gang. Both sender and recipient gain respect. Computer players will remember tribute sent to them and will react to you accordingly.

Help

You can request or send help in the form of combatants to fight alongside the other gang. After the battle, the surviving combatants are returned to their original gang. The sender of help gains respect; the one who requests help loses respect (whether the help is sent or not).

Threat

You tell an attacking gang what you will do to them, expressed in casualties and damage to their joints. A deadline must be issued with the threat. There is a chance (based on your respect) that computer players will then back down from the attack. If they go ahead, you must make sure to carry through with your threat: doing so earns you respect, but failure means you lose respect.

Insult

Insulting another boss causes him to lose respect, the amount depending on the relative strength of your gangs. (A weak gang insulting a strong gang causes high loss of respect.) You in turn will gain a proportion of the respect that the insulted boss loses. Be warned that insults are highly likely to bring violent retribution, this being the only way for the other boss to regain face. An insult can be withdrawn at any time: the boss you insulted gets back all the respect he had lost, and you lose twice that much for backing down.

12. Tutorial Campaign

In the solo game, the player starts out as lieutenant to Al "Scarcheek" Capulet, one of the minor crime lords of Chicago. This is a highly structured campaign designed to guide a new player through the game system step by step.

Mission One: Make 'Em An Offer

The McCluskey Gang are small-time operators in the dockside area. Since the Prohibition, they have gotten richer by controlling illicit whisky shipments. They're a thorn in Don Capulet's side. Deal with them.

Objectives: Wipe out Mad-Dog McCluskey's gang or force him to accept your boss as overlord.

Mission Two: Drink And Be Merry

The police have been clamping down on illicit drinking places. Don Capulet gives you the chance to show what you can do.

Objective: Open a speakeasy and keep it going without a raid until it's made $10,000.

Mission Three: The Bonnie Situation

Don Capulet's daughter has run off with Johnny Syracuse from the East Side. If she's not back by midnight, there'll be mob war!

Objective: Keep the peace between the gangs while finding Bonnie and bringing her back.

Mission Four (A): A St. Valentine's Greeting

Applies if Johnny Syracuse was killed in the last scenario: your boss wants an end to the war with the Syracuse family. In fact, he wants an end to the Syracuse family.

Objective: Lead the men in wiping out Don Capulet's rival.

Mission Four (B): Set Up A Meeting

Your boss wants to have a word with Don Syracuse, but they aren't on speaking terms. It's up to you to invite him to a meeting. Don't take "no" for an answer.

Objective: Take a small team and kidnap Don Syracuse. Secondary objective: Get information on which city figures Don Syracuse is bribing so your boss can blackmail them.

Mission Five: Consolidation

The gangs in neighboring districts are cramping the Capulet family's style. It's time to expand.

Objective: Extend the Capulet family influence into all neighboring districts. Secondary objective: Encourage gang members to switch loyalty to you personally.

Mission Six: To Be The Don

Don Capulet is warned by the heads of the five families not to get too ambitious. Maybe it's time for him to slow down?

Objective: Maybe it's time he retired altogether. Take control of the gang. Secondary objective: Make sure Don Capulet sleeps with the fishes.

Mission Seven (Conditional): Payback Time

If Don Capulet escaped, he comes gunning for you when you're alone in your townhouse. Where are your men? If you survive this, then heads will roll.

Objective: Kill Don Capulet without getting mortally wounded in the process. Secondary objective: Find the evidence that will show which of your men betrayed you.

Mission Eight: King Of Chicago

Things have gotten too confused. It's time to put things in order. One city, one boss: you.

Objective: Take control of the Chicago underworld by any means possible.

Mission Nine: Mark Of The Beast

A serial killer is terrorizing Chicago. The mayor is indecisive, the chief of police is corrupt, the cops are powerless. The citizens look to you for justice.

Objective: Rub out the serial killer. Secondary objective: Legitimize your operation in time for the end of Prohibition while keeping the Revenue men off your back.

Mission Ten (Conditional): Taking Care Of Business

A crime lord's work is never done. If the player chooses not to go legit, the game continues indefinitely with random events and new gangs to contend with.

13. Target Platform

Hardware and operating-system specifications anticipated for *Racketeers* are as follows:

- Pentium 90
- Dual speed CD-ROM
- 24-bit graphics card
- Windows 95

With regard to further platform support, hardware requirements and the game's strategic complexity mean that a console version at this time can be ruled out. A conversion to Power PC-based Mac would be worthwhile.

Postscript

We originally wrote this treatment back in 1996, but for various reasons never took it on to development. It is interesting now to see how it anticipated elements of games such as *Dungeon Keeper*, which at that time was still to be released.

In the light of our experience of *Dungeon Keeper*, we would now probably play down the autonomy of the gangsters. The original intention was to give the player lots of things to take care of (some of his gang wandering off into trouble of their own accord, and so forth). In retrospect, this may have become a case of making the player's main problem the game itself instead of the other players. (Evidently, we had some concern about that at the time—hence, the introductory note in the Personality section.)

Liberator

1. Introduction

Why Liberator?

Liberator is a simple game and is designed to be simple to implement. This is literally a test project for us, and as such is a deliberately uncomplicated one. The game mechanics are simple, as is the game model.

What's The Story?

Prisoners of the evil Xarg Empire are trapped in prison compounds in vast underground complexes, awaiting the brave and valiant rescuers (read "bounty hunters"). That's you.

You have piloted your mothership to the outer planet of the solar system, Wolf 359, and are even now preparing your ThrustDevil drop-ship to make planet-fall. The underground compounds are hidden in an intricate network of well-defended tunnels drilled deep into the crust of the planet. Deactivate the defenses and rescue the prisoners, returning them to your mothership, which is hovering on autopilot above the planet surface. As you release the locks and feel the surge of acceleration, your drop-ship plunges through the atmosphere. Out of eyes half-closed through *g* forces, you notice another mothership...and another.

It seems as if you have some competition for the bounty. Lucky you have those frag mines to even up the odds a little. *Let the carnage begin!*

What Is Liberator?

Liberator is a multiplayer, two-dimensional, space combat rescue game, although it is important that the single-player game is also very strong. The simplest contemporary way to describe it would be a cross between *Thrust* and *Defender* in a multiplayer environment. It is set in an underground tunnel complex where you control a ship by rotating and thrusting in a constant gravitational force. Prisoners are hidden in prison compounds within the tunnels, and you must rescue them and return them to your mothership. When you return, ship supplies are also replenished.

Your mothership has a capacity of 200 prisoners, and, once full, there is a brief hyperdrive trip to a safe world, before proceeding to the next level.

In the multiplayer game, each player has a ship and a mothership. By attacking the other players' motherships (and running the gauntlet of their defenses), you can panic the prisoners into launching lifepods. These can then be scooped up to boost your bounty at the expense of the other player.

2. Game Elements

The following sections (Figures A.25 through Figure A.33) describe the game elements of *Liberator*.

```
ThrustDevil Operational Specs:
Propulsion:          10g Thrust Engine
Turning rate:        180°/s
Cargo capacity:      6 passengers
Weapons:             Single-shot 10MW pulse cannon
                     5 Frag-mine bays
                     1 Smart bomb bay
Fuel capacity:       90-second sustained thrust
Shield:              Absorbs 6 direct collisions
```

```
+++ ThrustDevil craft +++ designed for atmosphere use +++ dockable with
mothership +++ space for 6 passengers +++ limited range craft +++ close quar-
ters combat capability +++ builtin shield generator +++
```

The player pilots the ThrustDevil craft and has a single-shot gun that can be fired rapidly to form a stream of bullets. Frag mines are proximity mines that fragment into explosive pieces on approach. Smart bombs destroy all enemies on screen.

The craft operates according to the usual thrust controls: Thrust, Rotate Left, Rotate Right, Fire, and Engage Shield. The player has to pilot the craft through the caverns, gently alighting on landing pads, and docking with the mothership, while engaging in combat with other players and enemy drones.

Flying

Use combinations of rotation and thrust to keep the ship under control in spite of gravity.

Landing

Land very gently with the nose vertical (as above). You need virtually zero speed on landing and no drift.

When landed, your shield will lose no excess energy, even though it is in contact with the ground.

Docking

Align with the center of the mothership, and thrust vertically upwards into the docking bay. (Lights will flash red to indicate entry point.)

Note

Solid boxes represent states. Arrows represent allowable transitions, and dotted boxes represent actions that may be taken in that state.

Actions in square brackets are automatic actions that occur when in that state.

Figure A.25
The ThrustDevil craft.

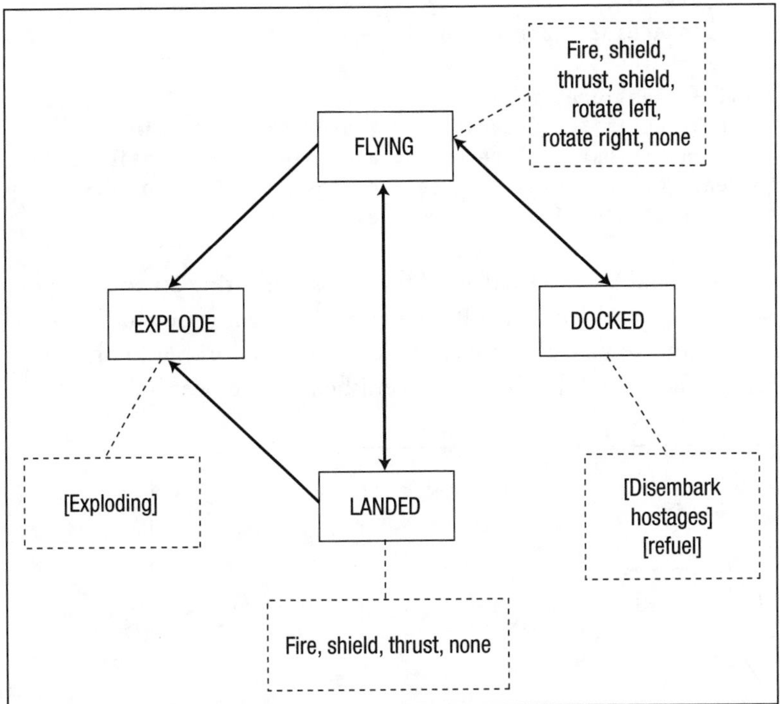

Figure A.26
State diagram for ThrustDevil.

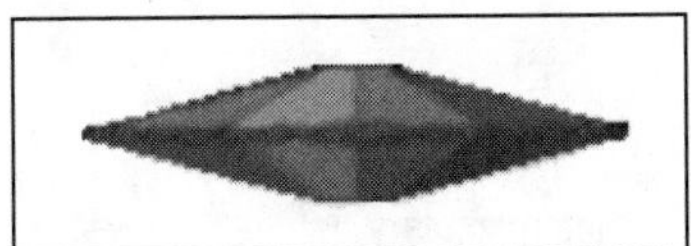

Figure A.27
The mothership.

```
Mothership Operational Specs:

Propulsion:         HyperDrive
Cargo capacity:     200 people, 1 Active ThrustDevil, 4 Reserve ThrustDevils
Weapons:            Tri shot 20MW pulse scatter cannon
Fuel capacity:      1200 second fuel reserves for ThrustDevil
                    HyperDrive draws energy from Artificial Quantum Singularity
Refuel rate:        5 seconds from ThrustDevil empty
Shield:             Absorbs 240 direct collisions

+++ mothership unit +++ designed to accept one ThrustDevil craft +++ space for
200 prisoners +++ near unlimited interstellar travel range +++ limited atmo-
sphere capabilities +++ ThrustDevil refueling and shield regeneration capabili-
ties +++ light offense capabilities +++ heavy defense capabilities +++ equipped
with escape pods +++ space for 4 spare ThrustDevils +++
```

The mothership drifts around over the surface of the landscape, firing on enemy craft only when attacked, and raising its shield when it collides with anything or is under attack. It acts as a refueling post for the player's ThrustDevil craft. Upon docking (with or without prisoners), the ship is refueled and the shield is replenished. This process takes five seconds

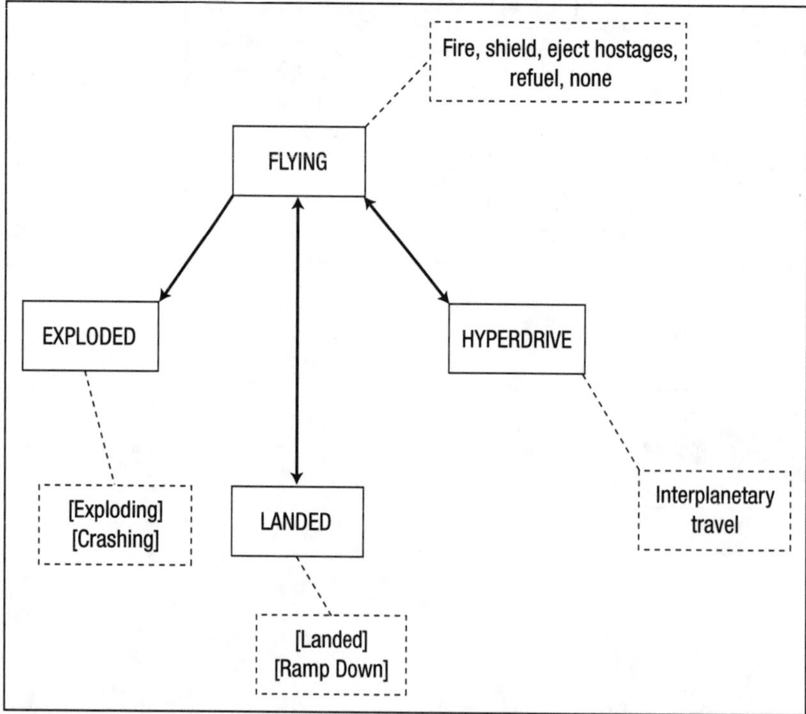

Figure A.28
State diagram for mothership.

from empty. The player is allowed to dock only with his own mothership. Attempting to dock with an enemy player's mothership will result in that player being attacked by the mothership (shields up and cannon spray), and the enemy player is notified that his mothership is under attack.

If the player has (up to six) prisoners in his hold, then these are transferred to the mothership on docking.

Attacking an enemy mothership will cause prisoners to panic, and they will abandon ship in single-man lifepods. These can be scooped up and returned to your own mothership.

Once the level is complete (either there are no prisoners remaining or the time limit is expired), then a klaxon alarm sounds from the mothership signaling that the player has 60 seconds to return to the mothership before it breaks atmosphere.

Once a set of levels is complete, the mothership will be nearly full of prisoners, and will need to return to a safe haven. At this stage, there will be a graphical interlude of the mothership landing in a small town and the prisoners unloading from the craft, to the joy of the other inhabitants.

```
Prisoner Data

+++ bipedal humanoid +++ cybernetic enhancements to allow labor in hostile
atmosphere +++ imprisoned in deep crust installations +++ offer bounty for
release and return to safe haven +++
```

Prisoners are held captive in compounds below the crust. Once freed, a prisoner will attempt to run towards your craft if you are landed. If you are airborne, the prisoner runs around the surface stopping to wave its arms periodically. It will not climb a gradient of greater than 80 degrees, and will return the way it came. If it reaches your craft and there is room aboard, it will enter. If there is no room, it will continue milling around the surface. If you are sick enough to engage your shield as they run towards your craft, they will hit it and melt. A prisoner is sensible enough to try not to let this happen, so will run towards your

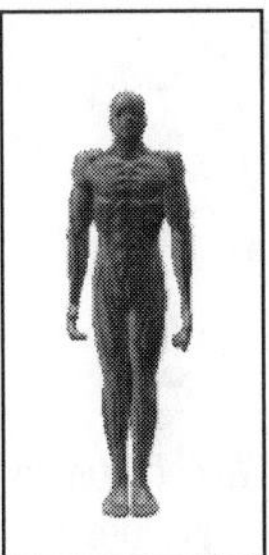

Figure A.29
A prisoner.

ship only when you have the shield off. If the shield is on, they will run away from your ship. Some aliens attempt to capture and kill prisoners, but prisoners are too stupid to intelligently avoid the aliens, and will just mill around the landscape until they are rescued or killed.

```
Prison Complex

+++ up to 15 prisoners housed in one complex +++ deactivate security system by
shooting +++ when doors open prisoners are released +++ doors close and lights
go out when all prisoners released +++ land adjacent to prison complex and
prisoners will enter your ship +++

Refueling Complex

+++ land adjacent to this to refuel your ship and replenish your shields +++
shooting will cause a large explosion +++
```

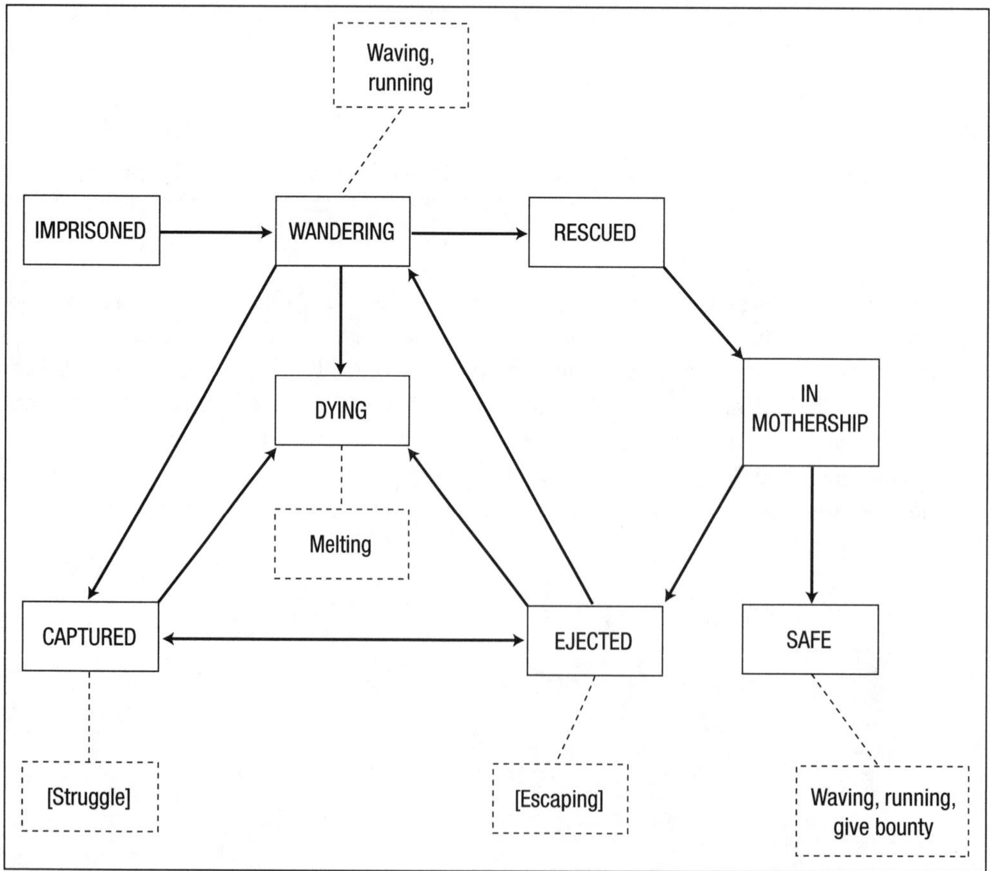

Figure A.30
State diagram for prisoner.

Figure A.31
Prison complex.

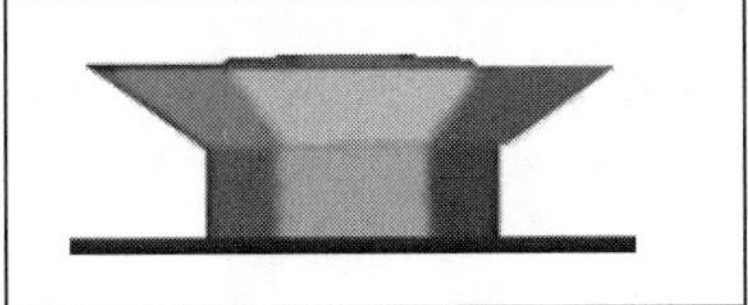

Figure A.32
Prison complex.

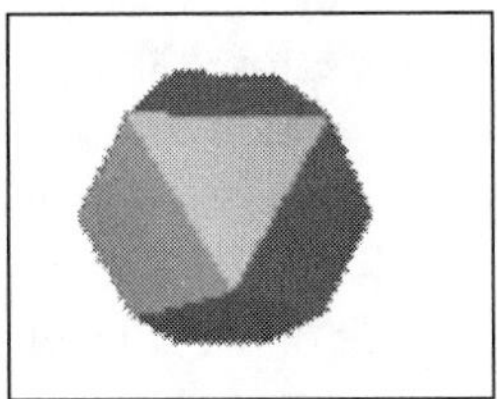

Figure A.33
Enemy generator.

```
Enemy Generator

+++ generates enemies +++ destroys all in cave network to stop influx of enemies
+++ can be mobile or fixed installation +++ drifts around caverns if mobile
heading for trouble spots +++ takes many shots to destroy +++ may generate many
different kinds of enemies +++ artificially intelligent +++ will generate
enemies most needed to defend prison complexes against your incursion +++
```

3. How Does It Play?

This section describes the gameplay as it is currently defined. The important point is that the single-player game must be as close to the multiplayer game in terms of fun and excitement as possible.

To give an idea of scale, the player's ship is about 10 meters long.

Single-Player Game

The single-player game plays very much like an up-to-date version of an old 16-bit classic, *Oids*. Starting the level, the player's mothership descends to approximately 200 meters above the planet surface.

The player's ship is released from inside the mothership and begins to drop towards the landscape below.

At this point, the player has control of the ship.

The prisoners are in compounds below the surface that are hidden in a network of caverns. The player must fight his way through the automated defenses and land the ship on the landing pad next to the compounds. To land, your ship must be pointing vertically upwards, and you must be descending gently with no sideways drift.

Once landed, the prisoners will run out of the compound and try to board your ship. Only six prisoners may board your ship at any one time. When your ship is full, you must return to the mothership and dock with it to unload the prisoners. Any prisoners not on your ship will have to fend for themselves until you return to collect them.

To dock, your ship must be vertical and you must thrust gently upwards while below the center of your mothership. When you are close enough, a tractor beam will lock on and you will be drawn into the ship. Docking refuels your ship, replenishes your shield, and unloads the prisoners into the mothership. The mothership has enough space for 200 prisoners. When the mothership is full, the player is treated to a graphical interlude in which the mothership lands on a moon among a small town. The rescued prisoners get out, greet their families, and wave at the player. This will occur every eighth level. (The mothership's 200-prisoner capacity is reached by rescuing the approximately 25 hostages on each level.)

Each prisoner you rescue gives you a bounty, which will vary depending on the prisoner.

If you are too far away from your mothership and require fuel, you may be able to find a refueling post. Landing next to one of these will refuel you and replenish your shields, as well.

While this is going on, you will be under constant attack from a vast number of enemy defense drones. These fall into three categories: threat to you, threat to prisoners, and threat to both you and prisoners.

To defend yourself, you have a rapid-fire plasma gun and a limited shield, as well as proximity mines and a smart bomb.

The level ends when all prisoners are either on board the mothership or destroyed. Once this happens, you have a 60-second time limit to return to your mothership before it departs without you. Failure to reach the mothership or crashing en route results in the loss of a ship. The mothership starts off with two spare ships, but more can be purchased with the bounty received from rescuing prisoners.

While the mothership is breaking atmosphere, a graphical display will show you how many prisoners you rescued and increment your bounty accordingly.

Multiplayer Game

The multiplayer game is fundamentally similar to the single-player game, with the added interaction of other players competing for the prisoners' bounty by fair means or foul.

You can dock only with your own mothership. Attempting to dock with another player's mothership will result in it attacking you. However, by attacking another player's mothership, you may panic some rescued prisoners into bailing out in life pods, where you can scoop them up to augment your own etotal. Each player will have a color-coded ship and mothership. However, the player's ship will always appear with red lights on it to allow easy identification.

Technical Specifications

This is an example technical specification taken from the *Balls!* documentation. This specification gives detailed instructions for a developer to create a graphics engine for the game, without having to refer to the code to see how to do it (because the interface and expected behavior is fully described).

This doesn't mean the developer is not allowed to look at the code (he or she may need clarification of some points), but it shouldn't be needed for the most part.

Technical Specification: Fully 3D Plug-In Graphics Module For *Balls*!

The modifications necessary to completely isolate the graphics engine have been made.

The developer needs to check the registry on startup to configure certain aspects such as lighting, texture detail, Globally Unique IDentifier (GUID) of the device to use, and other such salient details.

The graphics engine is configured from a separate graphics troubleshooter application. This application sets the registry entries to be read by the graphics engine.

Figure A.34 is a picture of the dialog box I expect to use to configure the graphics engine.

Notes For Developer

All the configuration data will be written into the registry, and the graphics DLL should read it on startup. Don't worry about it for now, but insert dummy hook functions, and make sure that that the graphics can be initialized with different parameters. Only things that are direct attributes of the 3D engine will be needed for this module (for example High-LOD (level of detail) models, dynamic lights, lower-detail texture mapping, alpha blending (for the glass ball), and RGB lighting as opposed to monochromatic lighting).

Ignore double buffering (as the generic graphics module will handle that): there will be just one render target to deal with, and this will be provided to you once per frame as a standard

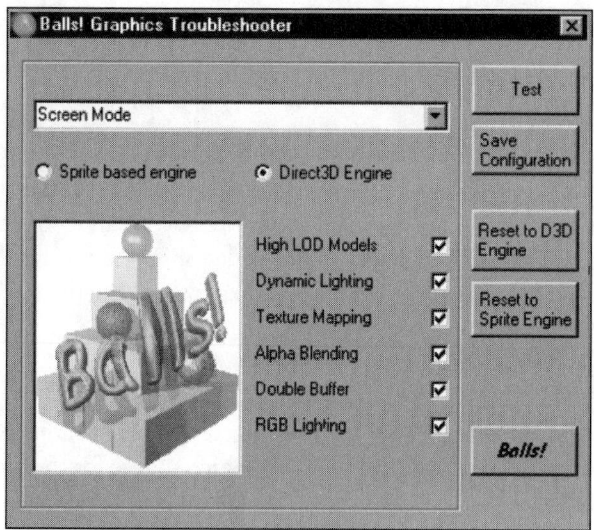

Figure A.34
Graphics troubleshooter screen.

pointer to a DirectDraw surface. Note that a z-buffer shouldn't be necessary. No objects overlap to any great degree. This will save on graphics memory and hopefully improve the render speed.

Listing A.1 shows the header file to be used for the graphics interface.

Listing A.1 The header file for the graphics interface.

```
/*
 * $Log: $
 */
// external include file for graphics DLLS
#ifndef _GRAPHICS_INTERFACE
#define _GRAPHICS_INTERFACE

// You should include a source line : #define BG_EXPORT __declspec(
// dllimport ) before you include this file.

#ifndef BG_EXPORT
#define BG_EXPORT __declspec( dllimport )
#endif

#include "Balls\BallsSharedStructs.h"
///////////////////////////////////////////////////////////////////////////////
// CGraphicBase class - interface returned by class factory
///////////////////////////////////////////////////////////////////////////////
class CGraphicBase
```

```
{
public:
    BG_EXPORT virtual bool PrepareFrame(SObjectState& objState_) = 0;
};

//////////////////////////////////////////////////////////////////////////////
// class responsible for drawing the level
//////////////////////////////////////////////////////////////////////////////
class CLevelGraphics
{
public:
    BG_EXPORT CLevelGraphics(CVector3D& vecCentreScreen_,
                             bool bDisplayLoadingScreen_ = true)
        {
        }
        BG_EXPORT virtual bool Draw(int iTick_) = 0; // current level tick
        BG_EXPORT virtual bool SetCamera(CVector3D& vecCameraPosition_) = 0;
        BG_EXPORT virtual CVector3D& GetCamera() = 0;

        // the following two functions are going to be moved to a graphics
        // controller class. Implement them for now, but don't bother
        // doing anything special.
        BG_EXPORT virtual bool IsWindowed() = 0;  // if in doubt, false
        // useful to display debug info!
        BG_EXPORT virtual void DrawLoadProgressScreen(double dProgress_) = 0;
};

//////////////////////////////////////////////////////////////////////////////
// create a new level graphic object
//////////////////////////////////////////////////////////////////////////////
BG_EXPORT CLevelGraphics *GetNewLevelGraphics(CVector3D& vecCentreScreen_, bool
bDisplayLoadingScreen_ = true);

//////////////////////////////////////////////////////////////////////////////
// CGraphicBase class - interface returned by class factory
//////////////////////////////////////////////////////////////////////////////
BG_EXPORT CGraphicBase *GetNewGraphicObject(eObjectType objType_);

#endif      // #ifndef _GRAPHICS_INTERFACE
```

This is not completely finalized, but I think that I won't be changing what is there (apart from the removal of the **IsWindowed** and **DrawLoadProgressScreen** members from the **CLevelGraphics** object).

On the other hand, there will be a member passing a pointer to an **IDirectDrawSurface2** interface to the back buffer. (Don't release it!)

I think you can get everything you need from that. I'll discuss each of the objects and functions in turn:

```
BG_EXPORT CLevelGraphics *GetNewLevelGraphics(CVector3D& vecCentreScreen_, bool
                                               bDisplayLoadingScreen_ = true);
```

This function returns a pointer to an instantiation of a graphics engine.

The parameter **vecCentreScreen_** contains a 3D vector that should be at the center of the screen. As an example, if I wanted the origin to be at the center of the screen, the vector (0,0,0) would be passed. By implication, the camera always points at this vector.

The second parameter, **bDisplayLoadingScreen_**, is a simple Boolean value that specifies whether a loading/progress screen is to be displayed or not. These two parameters are in any case passed directly to the constructor of your level object.

```
BG_EXPORT CGraphicBase *GetNewGraphicObject(eObjectType objType_);
```

This returns a pointer to the object specified in the passed parameter, **objType_**. This can be one of the following enumerations:

Balls:

NORMAL_BALL_TYPE,

METAL_BALL_TYPE,

MIMIC_BALL_TYPE,

BALLOON_BALL_TYPE,

GLASS_BALL_TYPE,

SNOW_BALL_TYPE,

EXPLOSIVE_BALL_TYPE,

HOT_BALL_TYPE,

SMILEY_BALL_TYPE

Blocks:

NORMAL_BLOCK_TYPE,

ARCHWAY_BLOCK_DL_TYPE, ARCHWAY_BLOCK_DR_TYPE, DOUBLE_ARCHWAY_BLOCK_TYPE,

ARROW_BLOCK_DL_TYPE, ARROW_BLOCK_DR_TYPE,

ARROW_BLOCK_UL_TYPE, ARROW_BLOCK_UR_TYPE,

CRUMBLE_BLOCK_TYPE,

TARGET_BLOCK_TYPE,

HOT_BLOCK_TYPE,

ICE_BLOCK_TYPE,

MAGNET_BLOCK_TYPE,

PUSHSWITCH_BLOCK_TYPE,

TOGGLESWITCH_BLOCK_TYPE,

SOFT_BLOCK_TYPE,

DEFLECTOR_BLOCK_D_TYPE, DEFLECTOR_BLOCK_L_TYPE,
DEFLECTOR_BLOCK_R_TYPE, DEFLECTOR_BLOCK_U_TYPE,

SPIKY_BLOCK_TYPE,

RAMP_BLOCK_DL_TYPE, RAMP_BLOCK_DR_TYPE,
RAMP_BLOCK_UL_TYPE, RAMP_BLOCK_UR_TYPE,

FAN_BLOCK_TYPE,

ACID_BLOCK_TYPE,

STICKY_BLOCK_TYPE,

START_BLOCK_UR_TYPE, START_BLOCK_DR_TYPE,
START_BLOCK_DL_TYPE,START_BLOCK_UL_TYPE,
START_BLOCK_URDL_TYPE, START_BLOCK_ULDR_TYPE,
START_BLOCK_URDR_TYPE, START_BLOCK_DLDR_TYPE,
START_BLOCK_ULDL_TYPE, START_BLOCK_ULUR_TYPE,
START_BLOCK_NOT_DR_TYPE, START_BLOCK_NOT_DL_TYPE,
START_BLOCK_NOT_UL_TYPE, START_BLOCK_NOT_UR_TYPE,
START_BLOCK_NONE_TYPE, START_BLOCK_ALL_TYPE,

SUPERTARGET_BLOCK_TYPE,

WORMHOLE_BLOCK_TYPE, BASE_BLOCK_TYPE

Other:

SCORE_OBJECT_TYPE

Note that there may be more special object types added.

I wouldn't worry about how scary this looks. (It looks a lot worse than it is.) The geometry files (*.x) files to load will be provided, and most of the graphics work is already done. There are some special cases, but I will discuss each of these in turn. In most cases, there will be only two .x files: a ball and a block with different textures. I'll go into this—and the exceptions—in more detail later.

Next is the **CGraphicBase** class, which is nice and simple as there is only one function to support.

```
BG_EXPORT virtual bool CGraphicBase::PrepareFrame(SObjectState& objState);
```

This is a pure virtual function that each object you create must define.

The **SObjectState** struct is quite big, and contains all the information you need to position and orient the object in 3D space and display it in the correct state. Shadow information is also included. This function must set the internal state of the graphic object so that it can be drawn correctly on request. (See **CLevelGraphics::Draw()**.)

This function is called for each active object **TURNTICKS** times a second, where **TURNTICKS** is an application-defined value.

The SObjectState Structure

Here is a description of the **SObjectState** structure:

```
typedef struct _statestruct
{
        eObjectType         Type;
        CVector3D           vecPosition;
        CVector3D           vecVelocity;
        EObjectProperty     Property;
        EObjectEvent        Event;
        eOrientation        Orientation;
        SShadowInfo         Shadows;
        int                 Score;
} SObjectState;
```

This structure consists of a number of members that give all the info you need to be able to draw the requested object.

```
eObjectType SObjectState::Type;
```

This contains the type of the object to be drawn (currently unused).

```
CVector3D SObjectState::vecPosition;
```

This contains the position of the object.

```
CVector3D SObjectState::vecVelocity;
```

This contains the velocity. I don't think it's needed for the true 3D engine. (In the sprite-based engine, I use it in combination with the turn ticks to figure out which rotation sprite to display.)

```
eObjectProperty SObjectState::Property;
```

This contains the object's intrinsic properties. This can take the following combination of values (Boolean ORed together):

PROP_NORMAL,

PROP_HOT,

PROP_COLD,

PROP_METAL,

PROP_SHARP,

PROP_ACID,

PROP_STICKY,

PROP_SOFT,

PROP_LIGHT,

PROP_WARM,

PROP_COOL.

They are mainly used in the game engine, but you may want to make use of them to make a hot or warm object emit light or some other visual cue. I don't use them (yet).

```
eObjectEvent SObjectState::Event;
```

This one is important. It tells you what the object is currently doing.

It can take one of the following values:

EVT_NONE,

EVT_MOVE,

EVT_COLLISION,

EVT_CHANGECOURSE,

EVT_GRAVITY,

EVT_WORMHOLE,

EVT_FINISH,

EVT_DESTROY.

For most of these events, the object appears normally. The only ones that directly affect the appearance are *destroy*, *finish*, and *wormhole*. Textures and animations will be provided. All others use the standard mesh for that object type.

```
eOrientation SObjectState::Orientation;
```

This can take the following values:

OO_UL,

OO_UR,

OO_DL,

OO_DR,

OO_UNIMPORTANT.

This is used with the following blocks:

- arrow block
- single-archway block
- double-archway block
- deflector block
- one-way start block
- two-way start block
- three-way start block
- four-way start block
- ramp block

Rather than having multiple models of these at different orientations, the orientation is passed in as part of the state.

The SShadowInfo Structure

I'll describe this, but I'm not sure how you could use it in the same way as I do without dynamically modifying textures on the top of blocks. (It might be nice though—a 50-percent alpha circle for balls, and just a 50-percent darken on the top of the block for other block shadows.)

```
SShadowInfo SObjectState::Shadows;
```

Shadows are assumed to be cast vertically downwards. The game logic engine calculates which shadows will be cast in a fairly efficient manner.

This is the structure used:

```
typedef struct _shadowstruct
{
    bool bBlockShadow;
    CVector3D vecBlockOffset;
    unsigned int uiNumberOfBallShadows;
    CVector3D vecBallOffset[5];

} SShadowInfo;
```

These fields are discussed here:

```
bool bBlockShadow;
```

If this is set to TRUE, just darken the entire top surface of the block.

```
CVector3D vecBlockOffset;
```

This is not used.

```
unsigned int uiNumberOfBallShadows;
```

This is the number of ball shadows (always less than or equal to six).

```
CVector3D vecBallOffset[5];
```

This is the vector offsets of balls casting shadows. These can be used to offset the shadow casting onto the top of the block.

```
int SObjectState::Score;
```

This is only used by the score object. (Yes, this is a hack, and is discussed later.)

The Level Graphics Object

```
CLevelGraphics::CLevelGraphics(CVector3D& vecCentreScreen_,
                               bool bDisplayLoadingScreen_ = true)
```

This initializes the graphics object. The camera always looks at **vecCentreScreen_**, which is the geometric center of the level. This knowledge may allow some optimizations (one of these is that the underneath of blocks will never be visible, so we only need to texture the tops and sides of blocks).

The parameter, **bDisplayLoadingScreen_**, controls the behavior of the **DrawLoadProcessScreen** function. If this parameter is set to FALSE, no loading screen will be displayed. **DrawLoadProcessScreen** should just immediately return in this case.

```
virtual bool CLevelGraphics::Draw(int iTick_) = 0; // current level tick
```

This draws all the objects in the level. To handle this in the sprite code, I keep a stack of objects. Each time **ProcessFrame** is called for a graphics object, I insert a pointer to that object onto a stack.

When **CLevelGraphics_2D::Draw** is called, I pop the entire stack, calling an internal **Draw** member for each graphic object on the stack, which draws each in its current state. I would suggest a similar approach here. I have to use a more complicated stack than you will, because I need to sort the stack to get objects to display in the correct order. Direct3D handles all this for you, so I would suggest using the STL stack class. Of course, you may come up with an entirely better approach.

The **iTick_** parameter contained the current level tick. It is a number such that

0 <= iTick_ < TURNTICKS

It is not guaranteed to increment by one for every call, because the internal logic engine is decoupled from the screen update. In the sprite-based engine, I use it to control animation and which frames to display.

For example, because all the ball rotations are synchronized, I know that, if **iTick_** is equal to **TURNTICKS/2**, then every ball is rotated by 180 degrees around an axis perpendicular to their direction of motion, because we are halfway through the turn. It is also used for tracking which frame of an animation (for example, the destroy animation) to play.

```
virtual bool CLevelGraphics::SetCamera(CVector3D& vecCameraPosition_) = 0;
```

This sets the camera position. It's not called much at the moment. In fact, I need to check where and how it is called. It's possible I set it too far out for a full 3D engine, If so, I'll modify it. You may need to tell me a set of parameters that are suitable (that is, minimum useful distance/maximum distance from the center of the level). The current default value is (100, 100, 100.)

Anyway, it can be set anywhere in a hemisphere above **z = 0**, so that's how I know we won't need to texture the underside of blocks!

```
virtual CLevelGraphics::CVector3D& GetCamera() = 0;
```

This returns the camera position set with the **SetCamera** function.

The following two functions will be implemented in a generic graphics controller class. At the moment, this class isn't written.

```
virtual bool CLevelGraphics::IsWindowed() = 0;   // if in doubt, false
```

I'm not sure if you can tell if you are windowed or not. The general rule is that debug mode is windowed, while release mode is not.

The developer will be provided with several executables: DEBUG windowed, RELEASE windowed, and RELEASE full screen. That way you can tailor this function to your needs. Whatever you do, don't return TRUE for this function in full-screen mode. It will crash, and you'll have to reboot the machine!

```
virtual void CLevelGraphics::DrawLoadProgressScreen(double dProgress_) = 0;
```

where **dProgress_** is the percentage of the level loaded.

Here you can put anything you want. At the moment, I use it to display progress and debug info during loading. It's going to be moved to the graphics controller class, but it's useful for you here for the time being. If the object constructor was called with **bDisplayLoadingScreen_** as FALSE, then just return without displaying anything.

Discussion Of Each Of The Drawable Objects In Turn

I'm not sure of the best approach to use for the majority of the objects.

They all have the same meshes with different textures, so it may be worth just wrapping the textures when they are needed. (That way, only the textures needed for a level need to be kept in memory.)

Block Events

This section covers block events. In general, blocks are always drawn exactly the same. However, two events cause either the meshes or the textures to change.

EVT_FINISH (and **EVT_WORMHOLE**)

Odd level ticks : State 1

Even level ticks: State 2

EVT_DESTROY

Eight state changes over the course of **TURNTICK** ticks.

Types Of Block

NORMAL_BLOCK_TYPE

This is a cube with the texture **NormalBlockTexture.bmp** on all sides.

EVT_FINISH

STATE 1: Textured with **NormalBlockTexture.bmp**

STATE 2: Textured with **NormalBlockTextureFinish.bmp**

Note: This makes the block flicker its illumination level. It is possible that this could be done instead by changing the light level of this object.

EVT_DESTROY

The cube changes for each state: **NormalBlockDestroyTexture<*x*>.bmp**, where **<x>** takes the values 0 to 7.

ARCHWAY_BLOCK_DL_TYPE, ARCHWAY_BLOCK_DR_TYPE, DOUBLE_ARCHWAY_BLOCK_TYPE

This is a mesh **ArchwayBlockMesh.x** (or **DoubleArchwayBlockMesh.x**) with the texture **NormalBlockTexture.bmp** on all sides.

EVT_FINISH

STATE 1: Textured with **NormalBlockTexture.bmp**

STATE 2: Textured with **NormalBlockTextureFinish.bmp**

EVT_DESTROY

The texturing changes for each state: **NormalBlockDestroyTexture<*x*>.bmp**, where **<*x*>** takes the values 0 to 7.

ARROW_BLOCK_DL_TYPE, ARROW_BLOCK_DR_TYPE, ARROW_BLOCK_UL_TYPE, ARROW_BLOCK_UR_TYPE

This is a cube, the same as the normal block, except it has **ArrowBlockTexture.bmp** as the top surface. One model, rotated, is used for all four block types.

EVT_FINISH

STATE 1: As normal block, except for the top where **ArrowBlockTexture.bmp** is used.

STATE 2: As normal block, except for the top where **ArrowBlockTextureFinish.bmp** is used.

EVT_DESTROY

As normal block.

CRUMBLE_BLOCK_TYPE

This is a cube with the texture **CrumbleBlockTexture.bmp** on all sides.

EVT_FINISH

STATE 1: Textured with **CrumbleBlockTexture.bmp**

STATE 2: Textured with **CrumbleBlockTextureFinish.bmp**

EVT_DESTROY

As normal block.

TARGET_BLOCK_TYPE

As normal, **TargetBlockTexture.bmp** on top.

EVT_FINISH

STATE 1: Textured with **TargetBlockTexture.bmp**

STATE 2: Textured with **TargetBlockTextureFinish.bmp**

EVT_DESTROY

Never received.

SUPERTARGET_BLOCK_TYPE

As normal, **SuperTargetBlockTexture.bmp** on top.

EVT_FINISH

STATE 1: Textured with **SuperTargetBlockTexture.bmp**

STATE 2: Textured with **SuperTargetBlockTextureFinish.bmp**

EVT_DESTROY

Never received.

HOT_BLOCK_TYPE

This is a cube with the texture **HotBlockTexture.bmp** on all sides.

I would like it if it also acted as a light source of the same color as the texture. (This could be achieved by creating a dummy light inside.)

EVT_FINISH

STATE 1: Textured with **HotBlockTexture.bmp**

STATE 2: Textured with **HotBlockTextureFinish.bmp**

EVT_DESTROY

The cube changes for each state: **HotBlockDestroyTexture<*x*>.bmp**, where **<*x*>** takes the values 0 to 7.

ICE_BLOCK_TYPE

This is a cube with the texture **IceBlockTexture.bmp** on all sides.

EVT_FINISH

STATE 1: Textured with **IceBlockTexture.bmp**

STATE 2: Textured with **IceBlockTextureFinish.bmp**

EVT_DESTROY

The cube changes for each state: **IceBlockDestroyMesh<y>.x**, where **<y>** takes the values 0 to 7. (The texture remains unchanged.)

MAGNET_BLOCK_TYPE

This is a cube with the texture **MagnetBlockTexture.bmp** on all sides.

EVT_FINISH

STATE 1: Textured with **MagnetBlockTexture.bmp**

STATE 2: Textured with **MagnetBlockTextureFinish.bmp**

EVT_DESTROY

As normal block.

SOFT_BLOCK_TYPE

This is a cube with the texture **SoftBlockTexture.bmp** on all sides.

EVT_FINISH

STATE 1: Textured with **SoftBlockTexture.bmp**

STATE 2: Textured with **SoftBlockTextureFinish.bmp**

EVT_DESTROY

The cube changes for each state: **SoftBlockDestroyMesh<y>.x**, where **<y>** takes the values 0 to 7. (The texture remains unchanged.)

BASE_BLOCK_TYPE

Uses **BaseBlockMesh.x**, **BaseBlockTexture.bmp**—does not respond to any events.

SPIKY_BLOCK_TYPE

This uses **SpikyBlockMesh.x**. It will probably contain all necessary references to the textures, so will not need to be done at runtime. For reference, it is a normal block with spikes on top. The spikes will use **MetalBallTexture.bmp**.

EVT_FINISH

STATE 1: Cube textured with **NormalBlockTexture.bmp**. Spike texture with same texture as metal ball (**MetalBallTexture.bmp**).

STATE 2: Textured with **NormalBlockTextureFinish.bmp**. Spike texture with same texture as metal ball (**MetalBallTextureFinish.bmp**).

EVT_DESTROY

For the sprite-based engine, I use the normal block destroy animation. Unless the developer feels particularly creative, the 3D engine should do the same.

RAMP_BLOCK_DL_TYPE, RAMP_BLOCK_DR_TYPE, RAMP_BLOCK_UL_TYPE, RAMP_BLOCK_UR_TYPE

This block uses **RampBlockMesh.x**, and is textured with **NormalBlockTexture.bmp**.

EVT_FINISH

STATE 1: Cube textured with **NormalBlockTexture.bmp**

STATE 2: Textured with **NormalBlockTextureFinish.bmp**

EVT_DESTROY

Textured as for the normal block destroy sequence, but still using the **RampBlockMesh.x**. I think that it may be nice if we smoothly scale the z height down to zero during the destroy animation, so that it looks like it is collapsing. This last step is optional. The 2D sprite engine doesn't do that.

FAN_BLOCK_TYPE

This block is different from the others, in that it is constantly animated with a rotating fan on each of its four vertical sides. I think the best way to handle this will be to provide you with a cube mesh with circular holes in the side, a fan mesh, and let you place them and rotate them according to the turn tick. This is not trivial and needs discussion.

EVT_FINISH

STATE 1: Cube textured with **NormalBlockTexture.bmp**. Fan textured with same texture as metal ball (**MetalBallTexture.bmp**).

STATE 2: Textured with **NormalBlockTextureFinish.bmp**. Fan textured with same texture as metal ball (**MetalBallTextureFinish.bmp**).

EVT_DESTROY

For the sprite-based engine, I use the normal block destroy animation.

Unless you feel particularly creative, you should do the same!

ACID_BLOCK_TYPE

This is a cube, the same as the normal block, except it has **AcidBlockTexture.bmp** as the top surface. One model, rotated, is used for all four block types.

EVT_FINISH

STATE 1: As normal block, except for the top where **AcidBlockTexture.bmp** is used.

STATE 2: As normal block, except for the top where **AcidBlockTextureFinish.bmp** is used.

EVT_DESTROY

As normal block.

STICKY_BLOCK_TYPE

This block will use **StickyBlockMesh.x** and be textured with N**ormalBlockTexture.bmp**.

EVT_FINISH

As normal block.

EVT_DESTROY

As normal block.

WORMHOLE_BLOCK_TYPE

This block will use **WormHoleBlockMesh.x** and be textured with **NormalBlock Texture.bmp**, except for the top, which will be textured with **WormHoleBlockTexture.bmp**.

EVT_FINISH

As normal block, except for the top (**WormHoleBlockTextureFinish.bmp**).

EVT_DESTROY

Not received.

DEFLECTOR_BLOCK_D_TYPE, DEFLECTOR_BLOCK_L_TYPE, DEFLECTOR_BLOCK_R_TYPE, DEFLECTOR_BLOCK_U_TYPE

This block will use **DeflectorBlockMesh.x** and be textured with **NormalBlockTexture.bmp**

EVT_FINISH

Textured as normal block, but with **DeflectorBlockMesh.x**.

EVT_DESTROY

Textured as normal block, but with **DeflectorBlockMesh.x**.

START_BLOCK_ALL_TYPE

START_BLOCK_DR_TYPE, START_BLOCK_UR_TYPE, START_BLOCK_UL_TYPE, START_BLOCK_DL_TYPE

START_BLOCK_URDL_TYPE, START_BLOCK_ULDR_TYPE, START_BLOCK_URDR_TYPE, START_BLOCK_DLDR_TYPE, START_BLOCK_ULDL_TYPE, START_BLOCK_ULUR_TYPE

START_BLOCK_NOT_DR_TYPE, START_BLOCK_NOT_DL_TYPE, START_BLOCK_NOT_UL_TYPE, START_BLOCK_NOT_UR_TYPE

START_BLOCK_NONE_TYPE

This is complex. Basically, it's the same as most other blocks, but there is a wide choice of textures to put on the top, depending on the type.

PUSHSWITCH_BLOCK_TYPE

TOGGLESWITCH_BLOCK_TYPE

Note: **PUSHSWITCH_BLOCK_TYPE** and **TOGGLESWITCH_BLOCK_TYPE** state transitions are not handled yet.

These blocks will use **ButtonBlockMesh.x** and be textured with **NormalBlockTexture.bmp**, except for the button that is colored green for a push switch and red for a toggle switch (with no texturing).

When the button is depressed (state ON), it should emit a suitably colored light. I may split this into two meshes—the normal block mesh, and a button mesh—and then you can manually move the button mesh up and down relative to the block, depending on the state.

EVT_FINISH

As normal block.

EVT_DESTROY

As normal block.

Ball Events

In general, balls are always drawn exactly the same, except for rotation.

As with blocks, two events cause either the meshes or the textures to change.

EVT_FINISH (and EVT_WORMHOLE)

Odd ticks : State 1

Even ticks: State 2

EVT_DESTROY

Eight state changes over the course of **TURNTICK** ticks.

Optional:

EVT_COLLISION

You may want to cause mesh deformation with collisions.

Types Of Ball

There are eight types of ball to deal with.

NORMAL_BALL_TYPE

Uses standard ball mesh, **Ball.x**.

Textured with **NormalBallTexture.bmp**.

EVT_FINISH

STATE 1: Textured with **NormalBallTexture.bmp**

STATE 2: Textured with **NormalBallTextureFinish.bmp**

See normal block notes for more details.

EVT_DESTROY

The ball changes texture for each state: **NormalBallDestroyTexture<x>.bmp**, where ***<x>*** takes the values 0 to 7.

METAL_BALL_TYPE

Uses standard ball mesh, **Ball.x**.

Textured with **MetalBallTexture.bmp**.

EVT_FINISH

STATE 1: Textured with **MetalBallTexture.bmp**

STATE 2: Textured with **MetalBallTextureFinish.bmp**

EVT_DESTROY

The ball changes texture for each state: **MetalBallDestroyTexture<*x*>.bmp**, where **<*x*>** takes the values 0 to 7.

MIMIC_BALL_TYPE

Uses standard ball mesh, **Ball.x**.

Textured with **MimicBallTexture.bmp**.

Note that the transition of the mimic ball is handled in the game logic. When the mimic ball wants to draw itself as a different ball, it calls the **ProcessFrame** member for that object. There is no need to handle it in the graphics engine.

EVT_FINISH

STATE 1: Textured with **MimicBallTexture.bmp**

STATE 2: Textured with **MimicBallTextureFinish.bmp**

EVT_DESTROY

The ball changes texture for each state: **MimicBallDestroyTexture<*x*>.bmp**, where **<*x*>** takes the values 0 to 7.

Optionally, the developer can also randomly perturb the vertices of the ball, so that it seems to shimmer out of existence.

BALLOON_BALL_TYPE

Uses standard ball mesh, **Ball.x**.

Textured with **BalloonBallTexture.bmp**. (with an alpha value of 25 percent if possible—option set in registry).

Maybe the mesh could oscillate slightly to show it was a balloon.

EVT_FINISH

STATE 1: Textured with **BalloonBallTexture.bmp**

STATE 2: Textured with **BalloonBallTextureFinish.bmp**

EVT_DESTROY

The ball changes texture for each state: **BalloonBallDestroyTexture<*x*>.bmp**, where **<*x*>** takes the values 0 to 7.

Set the color key of these texture surfaces to black. That way, the texture will be displayed as transparent in black areas, giving the balloon the appearance of bursting.

GLASS_BALL_TYPE

Uses standard ball mesh, **Ball.x**.

Textured with **GlassBallTexture.x** (with an alpha value of 75 percent if possible—option set in registry).

EVT_FINISH

STATE 1: Textured with **GlassBallTexture.bmp**

STATE 2: Textured with **GlassBallTextureFinish.bmp**

EVT_DESTROY

The ball changes texture for each state: **GlassBallDestroyTexture<*x*>.bmp**, where **<*x*>** takes the values 0 to 7.

Set the color key of these texture surfaces to black. That way, the texture will be displayed as transparent in black areas, giving the appearance of shattering glass. Alternatively, the developer can explode the glass ball into component polygons.

SNOW_BALL_TYPE

Uses standard ball mesh, **Ball.x**.

Textured with **SnowBallTexture.bmp**.

EVT_FINISH

STATE 1: Textured with **SnowBallTexture.bmp**

STATE 2:Textured with **SnowBallTextureFinish.bmp**

EVT_DESTROY

The ball changes mesh for each state:

SnowBallDestroyMesh<y>.bmp, where **<y>** takes the values 0 to 7.

EXPLOSIVE_BALL_TYPE

Uses standard Ball mesh, **Ball.x**.

Textured with **ExplosiveBallTexture.bmp**.

EVT_FINISH

STATE 1: Textured with **ExplosiveBallTexture.bmp**

STATE 2: Textured with **ExplosiveBallTextureFinish.bmp**

EVT_DESTROY

Display a scaled explosion sprite (decal) over the ball with color key 0 and 10-25 percent transparency (depending on what looks good.)

ExplosiveBallDestroyDecal<y>.bmp, where **<y>** takes the values 0 to 7.

HOT_BALL_TYPE

Uses standard ball mesh, **Ball.x**. (Red/orange light source if possible—option set in registry.)

Textured with **HotBallTexture.bmp**.

EVT_FINISH

STATE 1: Textured with **HotBallTexture.bmp**

STATE 2: Textured with **HotBallTextureFinish.bmp**

EVT_DESTROY

The ball changes texture for each state: **HotBallDestroyTexture<*x*>.bmp**, where **<*x*>** takes the values 0 to 7.

SMILEY_BALL_TYPE

Uses standard ball mesh, **Ball.x**.

Textured with **SmileyBallTexture.bmp**.

EVT_FINISH

STATE 1: Textured with **SmileyBallTexture.bmp**

STATE 2: Textured with **SmileyBallTextureFinish.bmp**

EVT_DESTROY

The ball changes texture for each state (uses hot ball sequence): **HotBallDestroy Texture<*x*>.bmp**, where **<*x*>** takes the values 0 to 7.

More information can be found in Table A.5. (Note that there were also entries in the original document for blocks as well as balls, but these were cut in the interests of brevity.)

Table A.5 Table of possible values in ObjProperty structure for each ball type.

Type Balls	Position	Velocity	Property	Event	Orientation	Shadows	Score
Normal Ball	Position in 3D space	Current velocity	Normal	Any	N/A	N/A	N/A
Metal Ball	Position in 3D space	Current velocity	Metal	Any	N/A	N/A	N/A
Mimic Ball	Position in 3D space	Current velocity	Normal	Any	N/A	N/A	N/A
Glass Ball	Position in 3D space	Current velocity	Normal	Any	N/A	N/A	N/A
Snow Ball	Position in 3D space	Current velocity	Cool	Any	N/A	N/A	N/A
Explosive Ball	Position in 3D space	Current velocity	Normal	Any	N/A	N/A	N/A
Hot Ball	Position in 3D space	Current velocity	Warm	Any	N/A	N/A	N/A
Smiley Ball	Position in 3D space	Current velocity	Normal	Any	N/A	N/A	N/A

Code Review Form

Figure A.35 shows a sample blank code review form.

This is a very simple form. The fields are filled in as follows:

The *Problem* field is filled in with a description of the problem found by the reviewer.

The *Comment* field is filled with any comments or recommended actions decided upon as an outcome of any discussions in the review meeting.

The *OK?* field contains the initials of the code author to show that he agrees with the comments that have been made.

The *S/O* field contains the initials of the reviewer, once he believes that all review points have been fixed satisfactorily.

The rest of the fields on the form are labeled in the diagram. Once the review meeting has taken place, the code author is responsible for combining all the comments into a single amalgamated review form that contains all the review points. This is then stored electronically for metrics gathering.

Test Scripts

Figure A.36 shows a simple test script form.

This form can be used electronically or in paper format to define scripts for testing. The form is fairly straightforward and is explained in the diagram. For each test, the steps

CODE REVIEW FORM

Module: <<module name and location in source control system>>
Version: <<version in source control system>>
Date: <<date of review>>
Author: <<the author being reviewed>>
Reviewer: <<name of reviewer>>

	Problem Description	Comment	OK?	S/O
1				
2				
3				
4				
5				
6				
7				
8				
9				
10				
11				
12				

Further Notes: <<any special instructions>>
Completed: <<date of completion>>
Final Sign Off: <<signature of review chairman>>

Figure A.35
A code review form.

required to perform the test and the expected results of the tests are described. There is a field that allows the tester to enter whether the test has passed or failed.

If the test has failed (as can be seen in the diagram), then there is a reference to a bug report document, describing the results of the test, and how they differed from the expected results.

TEST SCRIPT

Module: <<module name here>>
Version: <<module source control version here>>
Test Version: <<test version here>>
Date: <<date test performed here>>

Test No.	Test Description	Test Steps	Expected Result	Result
1	Testing general string printing capabilities.	1.1 Type "Hello World" into test harness application, and select coordinates (0,0)	Text should appear in top left corner of screen.	OK
		1.2 As 1.1, but selecting coordinates (0, center)	Text should appear on left side of the screen, vertically centered.	OK
		1.3 As 1.1, but selecting coordinates (center, 0)	Text should appear at top of screen, horizontally centered	OK
		1.4 As 1.1, but selecting coordinates (center, center)	Text should appear both horizontally and physically centered on screen.	Failed. BR416
2	Testing font handling capabilities.	2.1 Blah-blah!	Blah!	
		2.2 Blah-blah!	...	
		2.3 Blah-blah!	...	
3	Testing exact text positioning.	3.1 Blah-blah!	...	
		3.2 ...	...	
		3.3 ...	...	

Figure A.36
A test script form.

Appendix B
Bibliography And References

In writing this book, we used a wide variety of different references in order to crystallize our random thoughts and ideas into a form more palatable for the reader.

The following references proved invaluable to us when we needed to clarify an idea and get some of our more nebulous concepts down on paper, as well as to provide further verification and hard evidence as to the effectiveness of the methods that this book has presented.

Binmore, Ken; *Fun and Games,* 1992

Despite the title, this is a serious, in-depth text on game theory. A good level of mathematics is assumed.

Campbell, Joseph; *The Hero with a Thousand Faces,* 1949

Often cited as the definitive analysis of heroic myth, this allegedly served as George Lucas' template when creating the *Star Wars* saga.

Herz, J C; *Joystick Nation,* 1997

An interesting, if patchy, history of the video game industry. It has been subject to some criticism for bias, judging by the reviews on **www.amazon.com**, but it is still a worthwhile read.

LeGuin, Ursula; *The Language of the Night,* 1979

Superlative essays on fantasy and science fiction. If you are working in these genres, this is the book you must read.

Liberty, Jesse; *Beginning Object-Oriented Analysis and Design with C++*, 1998

One of the best introductions to OOD we've seen, made particularly interesting to game developers because of the extensive example of *Phish*, a software toy, which is analysed from concept to delivery.

Maguire, Steve; *Debugging the Development Process*, 1994

Still the best overview for team leaders, project champions, and managers.

Maguire, Steve; *Code Complete*, 1993

A great book for rock solid coding advice and detailed information on solving common coding difficulties. We could do with a new edition focusing more on object oriented techniques and the latest methodologies.

McConnell, Steve; *Software Project Survival Guide,* 1997

Essential reading for developers and managers alike. Covers the A to Z of surviving through the ups and down of projects, and reveals secrets of how to maintain your social life while doing so.

McConnell, Steve; *Rapid Development,* 1996

A comprehensive guide to building software rapidly and efficiently. Covers all aspects of the development process from team dynamics to coding. This is most assuredly not a recommendation to rush projects—the message, in fact, is 'More haste, less speed.'

Moorcock, Michael; *Wizardry and Wild Romance*, 1987

An inspirational survey of what makes fantasy stories powerful—combined with scathing attacks on the works that don't measure up. Moorcock is a brilliant, passionate writer whose criticism is an education in itself.

Nalebuff, Barry J., and Brandenburger, Adam M.; *Co-opetition*, 1996

Illuminating game theoretical analysis of business strategies.

Sheff, David; *Game Over*, 1999

A fascinating history of the rise to dominance of Nintendo. It has recently been updated to cover the new ascendancy of Sony.

Tolkien, J.R.R; *Tree and Leaf,* 1964

The father of modern fantasy literature explains why fairy stories are not kids' stuff.

Vogler, Christopher; *The Writer's Journey,* 1992

A storytelling toolkit containing many useful tips, though the insistence on a "unified narrative" theory is not always convincing.

Periodicals

The following is a list of periodicals.

CTW (U.K.)

Trade weekly covering latest news and future trends. Like MCV, a must-read for senior management.

Develop (U.K.)

Regular industry news and articles of interest to developers.

Edge (U.K.)

The coolest and best of all computer game magazines (despite the sometimes obfuscatory graphic design). Articles preview works-in progress as well as covering new releases and a wide range of development issues. If you want a job in the industry, then you could do worse than look here.

Gamasutra (U.S.A.)

The definitive game development Web based magazine, closely linked with *Game Developer Magazine*. This site contains the latest industry news and opinions, as well as public discussion forums for the current hot development topics. The "Geek of the Week" feature is questionable, however. (**www.gamasutra.com**)

Game Developer Magazine (USA)

Real nuts-and-bolts material for the working developer. This is where you will find the meaty stuff on fuzzy logic, game physics, route finding, and much more. This magazine is the monthly bible of game development, and is available free within the U.S.A. Even if you are not in the U.S.A., it's more than worth the subscription. (**www.gdmag.com**)

MCV (U.K.)

Trade news for professionals. Essential reading if you want to stay informed.

Newsgroups

There are many Internet newsgroups containing game design and development issues, denoted **comp.games.***, or **rec.games.*** that you can find.

The game design groups are usually filled with thoughtful and considered discussions. Make sure you don't confuse game design with game technology when you are taking part in a discussion. It's a sure fire route to getting flamed!

Glossary

Application Programming Interface (API)—A set of low level commands that enable a developer to program to a particular collection of hardware (such as the Windows API, which allows Windows programming.)

Architecture Mine—An investigation of an unknown body of source code to discern the structure of the program.

Artificial life (A-life)—A "bottom-up" simulation of a system using objects and agents with fundamental behaviors.

Artificial intelligence (AI)—A method of simulating intelligent behavior for computer opponents in games. This can be implemented using a number of techniques including script based programs.

Automagically—A complex process that is hidden from the user is said to occur automagically.

Avatar—A player's alter-ego in a virtual world (e.g., an online CRPG).

Big/Little-Endian—Indicates the order of bytes native to a processor. (See CPU.)

Bit—The smallest unit of information that a computer can handle. This can take two values—1 and 0.

Byte—The standard unit of information. A byte is eight bits. It can hold 256 distinct values.

Central Processing Unit (CPU)—The core of a computer. The CPU executes all the instruction in a program. Usually includes a built-in FPU.

Compact Disc Read-Only Memory (CD-ROM)—A storage device used for most computer games capable of holding about 600 megabytes of data.

Computer role-playing game (CRPG)—A game in which the player controls only a single character or a small team. The emphasis is on storytelling, often with an element of skill-advancement.

Cut scene—A segment between two levels of a game. (See Full Motion Video (FMV).)

Digital Versatile Disc (DVD)—A new technology that contains a higher storage capacity than a standard CD-ROM.

DirectX—Games and multimedia API developed by Microsoft.

Dynamic Lighting—A game feature where the lighting of objects is calculated in realtime.

Floating Point Unit (FPU)—A dedicated piece of hardware that performs floating point operations for a CPU. The speed is measured in GFLOPS.

Full motion video (FMV)—Computer-generated, non-interactive "movie" sequences used in games as scene-setting or plot exposition.

GameSprockets—Macintosh equivalent to *DirectX*.

Gedanken-experiment—A hypothetical experiment used at the initial planning stage to predict probable results. Used most famously by Einstein to derive the entire Special and General Theory of Relativity in the absence of experimental data.

GFLOPS—Giga floating point operations-per-second

Megabyte—Contains 1,048,576 bytes and is the standard unit of storage.

Non-player character (NPC)—A computer-player character in a role-playing game.

PC—(1) Player-character; in a role-playing game, a character controlled by a player. (2) An abbreviation of Personal Computer (usually taken to mean the IBM-PC.)

Pixel—An abbreviation of picture element. A rectangular region on a 2D surface that is assigned a property (usually color.) See Voxel.

Realtime Strategy game (RTS)—A game such as *Starcraft*, *Warcraft II* or *Command And Conquer*, that simulates simplified warfare in realtime.

Stone-Paper-Scissors (SPS)—A generic term for a non-transitive conflict mechanic, whether three-way or higher.

Tier—(1) A single iteration in the incremental development of a game. (2) A term from client-server architecture denoting the division of the network into segment types.

Voxel—An abbreviation of volume element. A 3D analogy to a pixel. A volume is split up into cubic regions, and each region is assigned a property (usually color.)

Index

C

D

E

F

G

H

I

M

N

Q

R

S

T

U

V

W

X

Z

What's On The CD-ROM

Game Architecture and Design Book's companion CD-ROM contains elements specifically selected to enhance the usefulness of this book, including:

- *Balls Level Viewer Demo BETA*—This is a piece of beta software that allows viewing of *Balls!* levels.
- *NeMo Player 1.9*—Including "Space Race" and "Lavaworld" demo projects.
- *Python 1.5*—Python is an interpreted, interactive, object-oriented programming language.
- *Universal Save SDK and GameExplorer Software*—The Universal Save technology improves the game playing experience by providing a universal framework to manage the storage and manipulation of data generated during game play.
- *WebVise Totality*—Everything you need for working with Web graphics and animations.
- *Universal Animator*—Allows you to create and preview GIF animations in any application you own.
- *Cool Edit 96*—Digital audio software, that packs enough top-quality digital effects modules to fill a room of rack mounts, and can mix up to 64 tracks together, using just about any sound card.
- And many more!

System Requirements

Below are the system requirements for PCs and Macs.

Software For (Windows PC)

- Your operating system must be Windows 95, 98, NT4 or higher, unless otherwise stated.
- *WinZip* (or other decompression utility) is needed to decompress some of the files on the CD-ROM. (The software is not provided on this CD-ROM.)
- *Adobe Acrobat Reader* is required to view some of the documents on the CD-ROM. (The software is not provided on this CD-ROM.)

Hardware (Windows PC)

- An Intel (or equivalent) Pentium 100MHz processor is the minimum platform required; an Intel (or equivalent) Pentium 200MHz processor is recommended.
- 32MB of RAM is the minimum requirement.
- A high color monitor and video card combinations (65,536 colors or more) is recommended.

Software (Macintosh)

- Your operating system must be System 7 or higher, unless otherwise stated.
- *Adobe Acrobat Reader* is required to view some of the documents on the CD-ROM. (The software is not provided on this CD-ROM.)

Hardware (Macintosh)

- 32MB of RAM is the minimum requirement.
- The applications on this CD-ROM require varying amounts of disk storage: 50MB-250MB.
- A high color monitor and video card combinations (65,536 colors or more) is recommended.